DATE DUE			

Television
Production
Handbook

Third
Edition

Television Production Handbook

Third Edition

Herbert Zettl

San Francisco State University

Wadsworth Publishing Company, Inc.
Belmont, California

To Erika

791.450232
zest
105753
July 1978

Communications Editor: Rebecca Hayden

Designer: Gary Head

Production Editor: Rebecca Hayden

Illustrator: Steve Renick

ISBN 0–534–00414–8

L. C. Cat. Card No. 75–35421

Printed in the United States of America

3 4 5 6 7 8 9 10—80 79 78 77

Photo Credits

Akai America, Ltd.: pages 29, 224, 490

Albion Optical Co., Inc.: pages 52, 53

Ampex Corporation: pages 222, 223, 225, 228, 230, 284, 471, 473

Audio Designs and Manufacturing, Inc.: page 178

Berkey Colortran, Inc.: pages 100, 102, 105, 109, 115

CBS: page 320

Central Dynamics: page 207

EECO: page 287

Electro-Voice, Inc.: pages 158, 181, 182, 183, 184, 185

Jawad Esmaili: page 350

General Electric: page 17

Gotham Audio Corporation: page 182

Grass Valley Group, Inc.: pages 265, 305, 307

Houston-Fearless Corporation: pages 60, 62, 65

Stuart Hyde: page 49

International Video Corporation (IVC): pages 29, 225

Keep America Beautiful, Inc.: page 425

Kliegl Bros.: pages 101, 136

Stuart Lefkowitz: pages 45, 72, 73, 74, 75, 76, 192, 198, 270, 275, 308, 314, 331, 350, 493

Mole-Richardson Co.: pages 100, 102, 103, 104, 108, 112, 113

NBC: page 63

Orrox Co.: page 290

Philips Audio Video Systems Corp.: pages 11, 22, 28

Q-TV of Q-Co. Industries: page 368

RCA: pages 14, 17, 28, 29, 64, 178, 181, 184, 223, 228, 240, 241

Steve Renick: pages 12, 17, 20, 26, 38, 45, 51, 52, 53, 54, 59, 60, 61, 65, 77, 79, 82, 83, 91, 94, 95, 96, 98, 99, 105, 107, 108, 109, 110, 111, 112, 113, 114, 115, 116, 130, 138, 139, 172, 174, 175, 176, 177, 190, 196, 197, 199, 200, 201, 202, 203, 204, 205, 208, 246, 247, 264, 303, 304, 306, 307, 322, 323, 329, 337, 339, 363, 364, 365, 366, 369, 406, 490, 491

Sennheiser Electronic Corporation: page 181

Shure Brothers, Inc.: pages 156, 158, 182, 183, 184

Sony Corporation of America: pages 183, 224, 226, 229, 495

Swintek: pages 161, 185

Vega Electronics Corporation: pages 182, 185

Alexander Zettl: color plate IX

Herbert Zettl: pages 4, 5, 41, 45, 46, 47, 49, 73, 76, 78, 80, 81, 82, 83, 94, 95, 97, 101, 118, 124, 125, 126, 127, 128, 129, 135, 137, 152, 153, 157, 158, 159, 167, 168, 169, 170, 194, 195, 205, 229, 233, 242, 243, 271, 272, 273, 274, 280, 298, 301, 309, 324, 325, 327, 338, 342, 345, 346, 347, 407, 408, 414, 415, 422, 423, 450, 485, 486, 492, 494, 495, 497, 498

Preface

The third edition of *Television Production Handbook* is not a simple revision of the second edition; it is a new book. The dramatic new developments in television equipment and subsequent production techniques have made such a step necessary.

Bringing the earlier edition up to date called for thorough reorganization. In order to incorporate the new developments of production equipment and techniques, and the changes they triggered on each other, I have not only revamped the original chapters but added several new ones. Subjects that seemed to require an entire new chapter included: the machinery and the principles of postproduction; the production process and the possible application of a production systems design; directing; and small-format television operation, usually called "video." Scenery, properties, and graphics are now combined in a single chapter on design. The chapter on television talent covers not only the elementary performance and acting techniques but, briefly, the basic makeup and dress requirements as well.

Basically, this book discusses the major tools of present-day color television production and their use under normal circumstances. However, since black-and-white television is still widely used in broadcast education, I have retained discussion of some of the prominent monochrome equipment and its operation.

Three special features of this text are designed to help the reader cope with a large amount of detailed information without being overwhelmed by it. First, major emphasis is put on *equipment categories and production principles* rather than on specific name brands or equipment codes as used by the various manufacturers. Thus, a minor change of name or equipment number by a particular manufacturer will not render the information contained in this book invalid. I have, nevertheless, provided tables and illustrations that contain brand names and equipment numbers, so that certain equipment items currently used can be clearly identified by production and engineering personnel. Second, the *key terms* used in a given chapter are collated and defined at the beginning of that chapter. This device offers the reader the opportunity to preview the new terminology, to see the words again in the context of the actual equipment or production situation as discussed in the chapter, and then to reinforce his or her learning by checking the meanings once again in the glossary. Third, some of the important, yet peripheral, aspects of television equipment and production techniques appear as *information in reduced type,* usually in the outside columns.

I have used photographs rather than drawings whenever appropriate in order to reduce the jump from print to the real thing.

Fortunately, even the most sophisticated machine cannot replace human judgment entirely in television production. Therefore, in this edition, I give attention to some of the basic aesthetic principles, such as picture composition, picture continuity, and sound mixing. I enjoin the reader to realize that the dos and don'ts of television production techniques as expressed in this book are intended as a guide, not as a credo. And, after all, I understand that we need to learn the conventional approach before we can go beyond it, or abandon it with some degree of authority.

Once again, Wadsworth Publishing Company proved to be a knowledgeable, cooperative, and entirely delightful partner in this venture. For special, well-deserved praise I should like to single out Becky Hayden, Gary Head, Bill Ralph, Steve Renick, Bob Sass, and Olga Stacevich, all of Wadsworth. I am also greatly indebted to a number of people who have willingly and repeatedly extended their expert help: Darryl Compton, San Francisco State University; Peter Dart, University of Kansas; Lynda Egener and Tim Hazen of San Francisco State University; Kathie Head; Jerry Higgins, Stuart Hyde, and Stuart Lefkowitz, all of San Francisco State University; Donald E. Lincoln, Group W Station KPIX; Houshang Moaddeli, KXTV; Walter C. Nichol, Group W Station KPIX; Grace O'Connell; Paul Courtland Smith and Jack Schaeffer of San Francisco State University; Jean Schuyler; Alex Toogood, Temple University; Victor M. Webb, KNXT; and the many television production instructors who offered suggestions on a questionnaire sent to them by the publisher.

Many more people and organizations deserve much credit for assisting me with specific information or materials, among them: ABC; Akai America, Ltd.; Ampex Corporation; Angenieux Corporation, Los Angeles; Audio Designs and Manufacturing, Inc.; Berkey Colortran, Inc.; Broadcast Communication Arts, BCA 595(2), Fall Semester 75/76; CBS; CMX Systems; Commercial Electronics, Inc.; Ed Cosci, KTVU; Cunningham and Walsh, Inc., Los Angeles; Electro-Voice, Inc.; Gotham Audio Corporation; Grass Valley Group, Inc.; Ray Holtz, Group W Station KPIX; International Video Corporation; Keep America Beautiful, Inc.; KGO; Marshall King, CBS; Kliegl Bros.; KRON; KTVU; Hal McIntyre, KPIX; Mole-Richardson Co.; NBC; Dick Newmann, RCA; Bill Noethens, KNXT; Orrox Co.; Philips Audio Video Corp.; Jim Provence, San Francisco State University; Q-TV of Q-Co Industries; RCA; Michael Sales, San Francisco State University; Frederick J. Schuhmann, ABC New York; Sennheiser Electronic Corporation; Shure Brothers, Inc.; Walt Stewart, KPIX; Swintek; Robert Tat, Fireman's Fund; Vega Electronics Corporation; Vital Industries, Inc.; Ken Wilson, KGO; Howard Yuen, KPIX; Ian Zellick, KTVU.

I also extend a special word of thanks to Ben Duban for his excellent prints of many of the photographs.

Many thanks to my wife, Erika, and to my children, Renee and Alex, who not only tolerate my writing but make sure that I do the best work I can.

H. Z.

Contents

Television Production Handbook

Third Edition

1 Learning Television Production

This chapter presents an overview of what is involved in learning television production. It describes briefly what the essential tools are, and how we should go about using them for optimally effective communication. In general, the presentation of these tools and their use in this chapter follows the same sequence as the subsequent chapters.

Television production is a process that involves the use of a rather complex machine and the coordination of a team of production specialists. The general, and so deceptively simple, division of television production into hardware and software, and hardware and software people, is both misleading and counterproductive. Regardless of whether you will eventually spend most of your time operating a videotape machine or writing television scripts, you will need to know rather intimately the basic elements and workings of the machine that translates the communication idea into a television program. Television is not just a pipeline through which the software is pushed by the hardware people; rather it is a creative process in which people and machines interact to provide the viewer with significant experiences. Television production therefore requires an intimate knowledge of the creative process—of how machines and people interact.

To learn television production is not an easy task. The major problem is that you should know everything at once, since the various production elements and activities interact and depend on one another. Since nobody can learn everything at once, we are more or less forced to take up the production elements step by step. As in any other craft or art, we need to know what tools there are before we can hope to use them effectively. The following chapters will, therefore, describe the major elements of the television machine, such as the cameras, lighting instruments, and microphones, what they can and cannot do, and how they can best be used for the most common production tasks. The coordination and integration of these elements and production activities are described in the chapters on television directing and producing.

In order to provide you with an overview of television production, we will briefly outline (1) what the tools are, and (2) how they are used.

What the Tools Are

The most obvious production element, the *camera,* comes in all sizes and configurations. Some are so small that they can be easily carried and operated by one person, while others are so large and heavy that they need at least two people just to lift them onto the camera mount. There are cameras that reproduce a scene in black and white, others in color. There are certain technical requirements that permit some cameras to be used for on-the-air broadcasting, and restrict others to closed-circuit, or nonbroadcast, use.

Regardless of size and relative sophistication, all television cameras work on the basic principle of converting whatever the camera lens "sees" (the optical image) into electrical signals that can be reconverted by a television set into screen images, the television pictures.

Knowledge of this conversion is essential for understanding several other production elements and procedures—lighting, for example—which facilitate this process.

Television (meaning "far-seeing") is a type of photography (meaning "writing with light"). As such, the *lens* is as important a part of the camera as it is of the still or film camera. In all photography, the lens selects part of the visible environment and produces a small optical image of it. This image is then transferred either onto a film or, in the case of television, onto a special camera pickup tube. Lenses that can take in a large vista are said to have a wide angle of view. Others are said to have a narrow angle of view. They permit you to see less of the vista but bring far objects to close range, very much as good binoculars do. Other lenses (zoom lenses) permit you to move continually from a wide vista to a closeup view without moving the camera. The lens, therefore, is important because it determines to a large extent not only *what* the camera sees but also *how* it sees.

The *mounting equipment* is important especially for the heavy studio cameras. By being able to move the camera about the studio floor, turning it into any direction, and raising and lowering it, you can not only follow a moving object reasonably well but also change the point of view in order to dramatize a particular shot or scene.

Like the human eye, the camera cannot see without a certain amount of light. Indeed, since it is not objects we see but merely the light that is reflected off them, it stands to reason that a manipulation of the light that falls on the object will influence the way in which we finally perceive it on the screen. Such manipulation is called *lighting.* A thorough knowledge of the various *lighting instruments,* what they can and cannot do, is of course a prerequisite for effective television production. Without good lighting, the best of cameras will not be able to produce effective screen images. At the same time, all the lighting in the world will not help you to achieve the desired television picture if the camera cannot "see" well, because it is either badly designed, badly adjusted, or badly used. The *lighting techniques* must be adjusted to the demands of the scene and also to the technical demands of the camera.

Although the term television does not include *audio,* the sound portion of a television show is nevertheless one of its most important elements. Television audio not only communicates precise information, but also contributes greatly to the mood of the scene, that is, how we feel about what we see. In order to realize the value of the information function of sound, simply turn off the audio during a newscast. Even the best actor would have a hard time communicating news stories through only facial expression and an occasional film clip. The aesthetic function of sound (to make us perceive, or feel, an event in a particular way) becomes quite obvious when you listen to the background sounds during a police story, for example. The squealing of tires during a high-speed chase is real enough; but the rhythmically fast, exciting background music that accompanies the scene is definitely artificial. After all, the police car and the getaway car are hardly ever followed in real life by a third vehicle with the orchestra playing the background music. But we have grown so accustomed to such aesthetic intensification devices that we certainly do not consider them strange bedfellows for the actual event. In fact, we would probably feel dissatisfied if they were missing from the scene.

The relative complexity of the *video* portion (the pictures) of television production (camera, lighting, scenery, editing, and so forth) has seduced many a production person into neglecting the audio portion. Thus, you will find that television audio is often inferior in quality. In order to remedy this all-too-frequent discrepancy, you should pay special attention to the audio production elements.

First, the microphones. You have to know not only the various types of microphones available, but also which ones will perform optimally in various contexts. One type that performs extremely well for the pickup of a symphony orchestra may be almost useless for the outdoor pickup of a marching band. A small microphone that works quite well for the voice pickup of a newscaster may be less than desirable when used on the drums of a rock band.

Second, the audio console. It permits the mixing of several sound signals, whereby each sound input can be separately controlled in loudness and tone quality.

Third, the various audio recording and playback devices are as important to a successful television production as are the cameras and

1·1 Television production requires the coordination of a team of specialists and a variety of complex equipment. Performers, and production and engineering personnel, must all work in harmony in order to achieve the desired effect.

lenses. The more you know about the sound equipment and its use, the easier it will be for you to operate the equipment and to achieve the desired communication effect relative to the video.

Although television production can occur practically anywhere, the *studio* still provides maximum *control.* Together with its *control room* and *master control,* the studio is equipped in such ways that the various production elements and activities can be used and coordinated effectively and efficiently. When shooting outdoors, for example, you are generally dependent upon the available light, even if there is additional lighting, such as the large stadium lights during a football game. In the studio, the amount of light, as well as the way in which the lights are used, can be carefully controlled. The camera movement and picture control, the audio setup and audio control, and the sequence of the pictures and sounds—all are afforded maximum flexibility and control. The

various audio and video recording and playback devices are readily available. No wonder, then, that a great deal of television production still originates in the studio, or at least from control centers that are built into large vehicles, the so-called remote trucks. *(See 1.1 and 1.2.)*

Most shows you see on television have been prerecorded on *videotape* or *film.* Although the most unique feature of television is its aliveness—that is, its ability to capture and distribute an event to millions of viewers while it is actually taking place—the control over production (the creation of a show) and programming (when and over which channel the show is to be telecast) has made videotape and film two indispensable production elements.

With videotape, you can record a program (pictures and sound) and play it back immediately afterwards, or at any later time. No processing is necessary. Sophisticated computer-assisted elec-

1·2 The actual coordination of production persons and equipment takes place in the control room. Here decisions are made about what kinds of pictures and sounds are to be stored on videotape or sent directly over the air.

tronic editing makes videotape even more flexible than film in postproduction activities. *Postproduction* generally refers to the assembly of a continuous show from prerecorded video and audio segments, or, more specifically, videotape and film editing. Videotaped programs can also be easily duplicated for distribution to the various television stations.

Videotape recorders vary in size and sophistication as much as television cameras. Some of them use 2-inch videotape for high-quality recording; some of the small, portable machines, which are no larger than an oversized handbag, use ¼-inch tape (similar to reel-to-reel audio tape) for non-broadcast productions. The video cassette machine has simplified the recording and playback of videotape to such an extent that it is seriously threatening the dominance of 16mm film in broadcasting as well as in education and industry.

Nevertheless, 16mm film still comprises a major television programming source. Most feature films (generally distributed in the 35mm format for theater projection and network use) are reduced to the 16mm format for local television, and many television news departments still find it easier to use film instead of videotape for their local news stories. But even here the improved quality and ease of operation of the portable television camera and videotape recorder, the immediate videotape playback capability, and the relative ease of videotape editing have made videotape a serious competitor for film. Already, many stations transfer commercial or news film to videotape cassettes for more convenient on-the-air operation. Nevertheless, the *film island,* which contains at least one film projector, a slide projector, and a mirror system that reflects the film or slide image into its stationary television camera, is still very much a part of standard television equipment.

Successful *picturization,* which includes all aspects of controlling a shot sequence so that the sequence becomes a structural whole, depends on two further production items: the switcher and electronic videotape editing equipment. The switcher permits instantaneous editing; the electronic editor, the postproduction assembly of videotaped program portions.

The *switcher,* which consists of several rows of buttons, allows you to select pictures from a number of video inputs (from such picture sources as camera, film, slide, or videotape) and assemble them sequentially through transition devices, or simultaneously, as in the superimposition of two pictures. The most common transition devices are the cut, an instantaneous change from one image to another; the dissolve, the temporary overlapping of two images; and the fade, whereby the picture either goes gradually to black or appears gradually from black. The most common simultaneous combinations of two pictures are the superimposition, whereby one picture is electronically laid over another, and the key, whereby one picture is electronically cut into another.

If your material has already been prerecorded on videotape, you can achieve the proper picture sequence through *postproduction* editing (in contrast to the production, or instantaneous, editing with the switcher). This involves a more or less sophisticated *electronic editor,* which is part of the videotape machine. With the electronic editor, you can assemble a great variety of videotaped program portions onto another videotape without having to splice them together physically, as is customary in film or audiotape editing.

Other important production elements are *scenery* and *properties,* which are both used for creating a suitable physical environment (for example, a living room with furniture, pictures, ashtrays, flowers, lamps), and *television graphics,* which includes title cards, charts, and graphs.

How the Tools Work

The mere knowledge of what tools are available or necessary for television production is not enough; you should also learn how to use them for a variety of production tasks. A book can serve only as a guide in this endeavor. After all, the most practical way of learning how to use a tool is by working with it, not merely by reading about it. You should, therefore, consider the portions of this book that describe the use of the equipment as a basic grammar of television production, a road map, and not as a substitute for actual production experience. We would certainly experience intense discomfort if everybody were content with reading cookbooks without ever engaging in the process of cooking.

However, it would be equally wrong to assume that we dispense entirely with the theory of production and merely rush into the studio to learn everything "from the bottom up." Reinventing the wheel through discovery may be a pleasant enough experience, but it is also a wasteful one and, in the end, utterly inconsequential. What we need to do is to learn quickly that there is such a thing as the wheel, and then find out how it can be used in order to contribute positively to individual and social growth. The same goes for television production. Why should you not benefit from the countless trials and errors of previous productions and from the principles and practices that have proved successful? Indeed, once you have learned these principles, you can go beyond them, or ignore them altogether if your communication purpose requires such extreme steps. In any case, don't be afraid of using the conventional approaches. They have become conventional because they work most of the time. Triteness and clichés in production are more frequently caused by the lack of a clearly defined communication purpose, by the lack of having something important to say, than by the conventional use of the medium. Achieving eloquence and style in production does not mean necessarily that you have to invent entirely new techniques, but rather that you use the production tools in such a way that the viewer perceives a significant communication experience. You don't have to put the speaker upside down in order to entice the viewer to stay tuned to your message; simply give her something significant to say, and then let the viewer see and hear her as clearly as possible.

The chapters on *producing* and *directing* offer some of the principles that contribute to the choice of television production elements for a certain communication task, and to the coordination of these elements in order to produce the desired effect.

And yet, in a time where effective mass communication has become essential for personal and social growth, we should not and cannot remain content with either the available tools or their conventional use. It does not really matter whether the need for nonbroadcast television communication or the search for new art forms has led to the development of self-contained, *portable,* easy-to-use *television equipment,* or whether the development of the small equipment has led to new communication approaches. In either case, the small equipment (such as portapaks and other relatively inexpensive video cameras, and recording and playback devices) provoked a change in the use of television that is aptly called the *video revolution.* Free from the pressures of large commercial concerns, or equally institutionalized noncommercial television stations, the *video artist* went about his or her experiments in a refreshingly new, though often naïve, way. While the commercial video engineer tried desperately to produce a picture free from electronic interference, the video artist often purposely produced such interference in order to intensify the expression of his ideas. As in any other development of new techniques, the line between when the ideas were intensified by electronic distortion or other unusual production techniques and when they actually suffered from such treatment was not always as clear-cut as one would have wished.

But the real worth of such video experiments was to show to the producer and consumer alike that the television medium was anything but neutral, that it was not merely a pipeline of ready-made messages, a mere distribution device, but that it could be used effectively in the *formulation,* in the building, *of the message itself.* Thus, the so-called program content was only part of the message; the other, and equally important, part was the use of the medium—specifically, the television production techniques.

With this in mind, you are certainly encouraged to experiment with the medium, occasionally to break the rules and conventions of production, and to try out new ways of using the tools, if the communication so requires. But such experimentation will remain satisfying and effective only after you have learned the *basic* use of the production tools—the basic techniques of television production.

Summary

Whatever part you play, you should realize that television production is *team work.* Even with a portapak, you will find that you need somebody else to help you with the cable, or to hold the microphone. The more complicated the equipment gets, the more people it takes. In fact, the major task of television production is working with *people,* the ones in front of the television camera (talent) and those behind (production and engineering crews, directors, and other station personnel). *(See tables 14.8 and 14.10.)*

Even the most sophisticated television production equipment cannot make ethical and aesthetic judgments for you; it cannot tell you exactly what part of the event to select and how to frame it for optimal communication. *You* have to make such decisions, within the context of the general communication intent and through communication with the other members of your production team. In television production, then, you are expected to know how to work with other persons, in order to generate creative ideas and solve problems.

Television production is a process that involves the use of complex equipment and the coordination of a team of production specialists. A knowledge of the elements, or tools, of the process and how they work is the other essential task. These tools include the camera, lenses, mounting equipment, lighting instruments and the techniques of television lighting, audio, the studio and its control centers, master control, videotape and film, picturization (which means the controlling of a shot sequence through instantaneous or postproduction editing), scenery, properties, television graphics, costuming, and makeup. In essence, knowing the tools and how a production team manipulates them for a specific communication purpose is what television production is all about. To this end, the following chapters are designated.

2 The Camera

This chapter contains some basic information about the single most important part of television production equipment, the camera. Specifically, we will discuss these major points:

1. The parts of the camera, including the lens, the actual camera head with the major pickup tubes and the viewfinder, and the major units of the CCU, the camera control unit.

2. How the camera works, or the conversion of light into electrical signals.

3. The black-and-white, or monochrome, camera; in particular, its major camera pickup tubes and its operational and electronic characteristics.

4. The color camera, with a discussion of chrominance and luminance channels, internal optical system, color separation, and operational and electronic characteristics.

5. The major types of cameras and the principal use of each.

Almost everything you can see on your television set has been preseen by a television camera. The pictures that appear on your screen are determined by what the television camera can see and how it sees it. For example, when you are out for a walk, a typical night scene will look perfectly acceptable to your eyes. You may be able to see quite distinctly parts of buildings, doorways, lighted windows, some people walking along the sidewalk, the cars going by. The illumination by streetlamps, car headlights, and lighted shop windows, which seems adequate for your eyes, may, however, prove utterly inadequate for the television camera. The scene will then appear muddy and unclear on the screen, if it reproduces at all.

In fact, most other television production equipment and production techniques are either directly determined by what the camera can and cannot do, or at least greatly influenced by it. The use of microphones and lighting instruments, the way the performers move and talk, even the art of writing and directing—are all greatly influenced by, if not dictated by, the camera's capability and versatility.

In this chapter, we will cover these major points: (1) parts of the monochrome (black-and-white) and the color camera, (2) the operational and electronic characteristics of the camera, and (3) the various types of television cameras.

Parts of the Camera

The standard television camera consists of three main parts *(see 2.1):* (1) the lens, which selects a certain field of view and produces a small optical image of this view. The lens and certain attachments to it are called the *external optical system;* (2) the camera itself with its camera pickup tubes and internal optical system, which converts the optical image produced by the lens into electrical signals; and (3) the viewfinder, which converts these electronic signals back into a visible screen image.

The camera, which combines the lens, the pickup tubes and internal optical system, and the viewfinder, is called the *camera head,* since it is at the head of a chain of other essential electronic camera control equipment *(see 2.4).* The camera head itself has a series of attachments and controls that helps the operator use the camera efficiently and creatively *(see 2.2 and 2.3).*

How the Camera Works

Most cameras have remotely controlled, or even automatic, features that make them relatively easy to operate in the studio or on remote location without much understanding of their intricate electronics. However, since almost all production equipment and production procedures are dependent to a large extent on what the camera can and cannot do, a thorough knowledge of at least the basic workings and electronic characteristics seems a desirable prerequisite to effective television production.

Additive Primary Colors Red, blue, and green. Ordinary white light (sunlight) can be separated into the three primary light colors, red, green, and blue. When these three colored lights are combined in various proportions, all other colors can be reproduced.

Burn-in, or Sticking Image retention by the camera pickup tube. If the camera is focused too long on an object with strong contrast, the picture tube may retain a negative image of the contrasting scene, although another object is being photographed. Occurs especially in I-O (image-orthicon) tubes, or occasionally in vidicons, that have been in use for a relatively long time.

Camera Chain The television camera (head) and associated electronic equipment, consisting of the CCU (the camera control unit), the power supply, the sync generator, and the encoder (for color cameras only).

Camera Control Unit Equipment, separate from the camera head, that contains various video controls, including color balance and contrast and brightness. It is operated by the video engineer before camera operation (camera setup) and during camera operation (camera shading).

Camera Head The actual television camera, which is at the head of a chain of essential electronic accessories. In small, portable cameras, the camera head contains all the elements of a camera chain.

Chrominance Channel The color (chroma) channels within the color camera. A separate chrominance channel is responsible for each primary color signal—that is, one for the red, one for the blue, and one for the green.

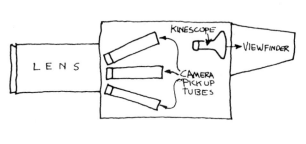

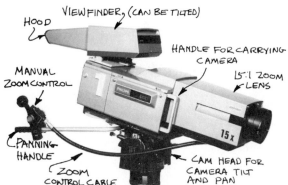

2·1   Basic Parts of the Television Camera.

2·2   Philips LDK-25 Color Camera.

All television cameras, whether they are color or monochrome, big studio models or small portable ones, work on the same basic principle: the conversion of an optical image into electrical signals that are reconverted by a television set into visible screen images. *(See 2.5.)* Specifically, the light that is reflected off an object (a) is gathered by the camera lens (b) and focused on the front surface of the camera pickup tube (c). The pickup tube is the principal camera element that transforms the light into electrical energy, called the video (picture) signal. The very weak video signal

---

Contrast Ratio   The difference between the brightest spot and the darkest spot in a scene (often measured by reflected light in foot-candles), expressed in a ratio, such as 20:1.

Dichroic Mirror   A mirror-like color filter that singles out, of the white light, the red light (red dichroic filter) and the blue light (blue dichroic filter), with the green light left over.

External Optical System   The zoom lens, or the various lenses on a lens turret.

Falloff   The "speed" (degree) with which a light picture portion turns into its shadow areas. Fast falloff means that the light areas turn abruptly into shadow areas. Slow falloff indicates a very gradual change from light to dark, or little contrast between light and shadow areas.

Foot-Candle   The measure of light intensity, or unit of illumination. The amount of light produced by a single candle on a portion of a sphere one foot away; one foot-candle per square foot is called one lumen. (Foot-candles times the surface area in square feet = lumens.)

Grayscale   A scale indicating intermediate steps from TV black to TV white. Maximum range: 10 grayscale steps; good: seven steps; poor: five steps.

Image-Orthicon, or I-O   A specific type of pickup tube used in some monochrome cameras.

Internal Optical System   The dichroic mirrors, reflecting mirrors, relay lenses, and color filters inside the color camera.

Lag, or Comet-Tailing   A cometlike smear that follows a moving object or motion of the camera across a stationary object. Occurs especially with vidicon cameras under low light levels.

a

b

2·3 RCA TK-60 Monochrome Turret Camera: (a)
side view; (b) rear view.

from the pickup tube is then strengthened by the
preamplifiers (d) and sent through a cable to the
camera control unit (CCU). From there, the properly adjusted picture is distributed to the monitors (television sets) in the studio and control
rooms, and ultimately to the transmitter. Also,

Luminance Channel A
signal that is matrixed
(combined) from the
chrominance channels and
provides the black-and-
white signal. The lumi-
nance channel gives the
color picture the necessary
brightness contrast and allows a color camera to
produce a signal that is receivable on a black-and-
white television set.

Monochrome Literally
"one color." In television,
it means black-and-white
(in contrast to color).

**Pickup Tube, or Camera
Tube** The main camera
tube that converts light
energy into electrical
energy, the video signal.

Plumbicon A registered
trademark of N. V. Philips
for a vidicon-type pickup
tube. Used almost exclu-
sively in good- to high-
quality color cameras. Because the Plumbicon has a
lead-oxide-coated photo-
conductive (light-sensitive)
front surface, variations of
it are sometimes called
lead-oxide tubes.

Prism Block A compact
internal optical system that
combines the dichroic
(color-separating) elements
(filters) and light-diverting
elements (prisms) all in
one small blocklike unit.

Relay Lens Part of the
internal optical system of a
camera that helps to transport (relay) the separated
colored light into a pickup
tube.

Resolution The fine picture detail as reproduced
on the video monitor. A
high-resolution picture is
desirable, since fine detail
can be read on the screen.

the video signal is sent back to the camera viewfinder (e) so that you can see exactly what your camera is photographing.

The Monochrome (Black-and-White) Camera

Although the color camera is used exclusively in professional broadcast operations, and frequently in nonbroadcast television productions, you should still know about the major types of monochrome cameras and their basic differences. First, large studio-type monochrome cameras are still used in many colleges and universities. Second, most of the popular and inexpensive portable cameras are black-and-white. Third, the color camera, though more complicated than the black-and-white, nevertheless works in quite similar ways.

In the monochrome camera, white light (which is a combination of all colors) enters the camera.

Since the picture is monochrome, of one color only (shades of gray ranging from black to white), we need only one camera pickup tube for the transformation of monochrome light to the single monochrome video signal *(see 2.5)*. Depending on the quality and basic construction of the pickup tube and its electronic accessories, the camera will deliver high-definition, broadcast-quality pictures, or fairly low-quality television pictures that are below the accepted broadcast standard. Let us now briefly indicate the major types of pickup tubes and the corresponding quality of the cameras in which they are used.

Pickup Tubes

There are two major types of pickup tubes used in monochrome television: (1) the image-orthicon, or I-O, tube and (2) the vidicon tube. The I-O tubes are further classified into the 4½-inch I-O and the 3-inch I-O, indicating the size of the light-sensitive front surface of the tube. The vidi-

---

Signal-to-Noise Ratio The relation of the strength of the desired video (picture) signal to the accompanying electronic interference, the noise. A high signal-to-noise ratio is desirable (strong video signal and weak noise).

Stability The degree to which a camera (or camera chain) maintains its initial electronic setup.

Star Filter A lens attachment that changes high-intensity light sources into starlike light images.

Subtractive Primary Colors Magenta (bluish red), cyan (greenish blue), and yellow. When mixed, they act as filters, subtracting certain colors.

Video Noise A spurious electronic signal that interferes with the desired video signal. Generated unavoidably within the system, it shows up as "snow," white (or colored) spots in the picture.

Video Signal Electrical impulses (voltage) generated by the camera pickup tube. The amplified video signal provides the necessary information for generating a picture.

Vidicon A type of pickup tube, used extensively in small, portable, monochrome cameras as well as in color cameras.

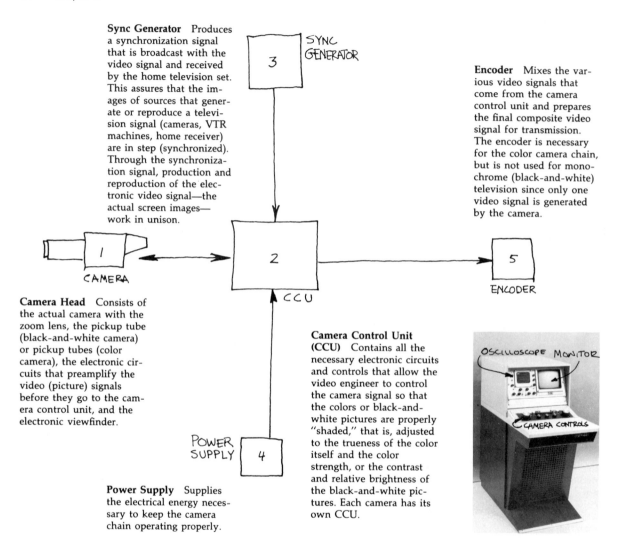

Sync Generator Produces a synchronization signal that is broadcast with the video signal and received by the home television set. This assures that the images of sources that generate or reproduce a television signal (cameras, VTR machines, home receiver) are in step (synchronized). Through the synchronization signal, production and reproduction of the electronic video signal—the actual screen images—work in unison.

Encoder Mixes the various video signals that come from the camera control unit and prepares the final composite video signal for transmission. The encoder is necessary for the color camera chain, but is not used for monochrome (black-and-white) television since only one video signal is generated by the camera.

Camera Head Consists of the actual camera with the zoom lens, the pickup tube (black-and-white camera) or pickup tubes (color camera), the electronic circuits that preamplify the video (picture) signals before they go to the camera control unit, and the electronic viewfinder.

Camera Control Unit (CCU) Contains all the necessary electronic circuits and controls that allow the video engineer to control the camera signal so that the colors or black-and-white pictures are properly "shaded," that is, adjusted to the trueness of the color itself and the color strength, or the contrast and relative brightness of the black-and-white pictures. Each camera has its own CCU.

Power Supply Supplies the electrical energy necessary to keep the camera chain operating properly.

2·4   Camera Chain: The camera chain consists of (1) the camera head, which is what we ordinarily call the television camera; (2) the camera control unit, or the CCU; (3) the sync generator; and (4) the power supply. The color camera has an additional part, (5) the encoder.

The camera control unit (see photo at right) contains the electronic equipment necessary to achieve optimal quality.

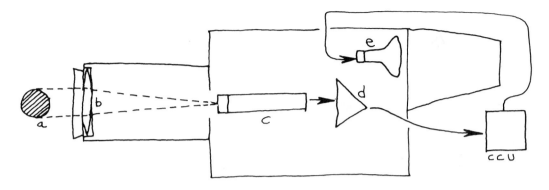

2·5   Basic Principle of Television Camera: (a) light reflected off object; (b) lens gathers light and focuses image of object onto front surface of pickup tube; (c) camera pickup tube with photosensitive surface that converts light into electrical energy, the video signal; (d) preamplifier, which strengthens signal; (e) electronic viewfinder, a small television set that shows what the camera is photographing. In most color cameras, the viewfinder produces only a black-and-white picture.

con tubes come in a ⅔-inch, 1-inch (25mm), or 1¼-inch (30mm) front surface size. *(See 2.6.)*

Similarly, we speak of 4½-inch I-O, 3-inch I-O, and vidicon cameras. Generally, the I-O cameras deliver higher-quality pictures than the vidicon. Although technically not quite correct, we may compare the different camera pickup tubes with the picture quality of differently sized film. If you make a print from a small negative, such as a 16mm film, you will not achieve the quality you would get from a 35mm or 70mm negative. The vidicon tube surface corresponds approximately to the frame size of a 16mm film—therefore vidicon cameras take 16mm-format film lenses—and the 3-inch image-orthicon tube corresponds to the area of a 35mm film frame—hence, image-orthicon cameras take 35mm-format lenses. The 4½-inch image-orthicon tube corresponds to an even larger negative and produces, therefore, clearer and better pictures, al-

though 35mm-format lenses are also used for this camera since the image enlargement occurs within the I-O tube.

But the I-O cameras are not without serious disadvantages over the vidicon cameras. In order to show you the basic differences between I-O and vidicon cameras, we will briefly compare their operational and electronic characteristics. Keep in mind that there are, of course, great quality differences among the various models of both types. Thus it can happen that a high-quality vidicon camera outperforms quite easily a low-quality I-O.

Operational Characteristics

There are two operational characteristics that are especially pertinent to a comparison of image-orthicon and vidicon cameras: (1) size and weight and (2) ruggedness.

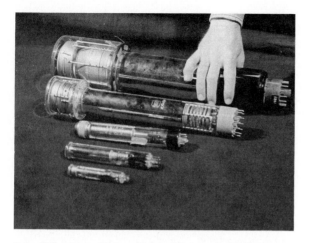

2·6 Television Pickup Tubes (from top to bottom): 4½-inch image orthicon; 3-inch image orthicon; 25mm Plumbicon; 1-inch vidicon; ⅔-inch vidicon.

Size and Weight   Because of the large tubes, the I-O cameras are relatively large and heavy. The 4½-inch cameras, for example, are so heavy that even two strong men have to struggle to mount the camera on a pedestal. Even the smallest of the I-O cameras is difficult to use in the field, and none of them can be carried in the field by one person.

The small vidicon tube and its relatively uncomplicated electronic accessories permit the construction of a variety of vidicon cameras, ranging from the extremely small, low-quality industrial cameras without viewfinders (see page 17) to the rather large viewfinder studio cameras that approach the I-O camera in size and weight *(see 2.7)*. But most viewfinder vidicon cameras that are used for nonbroadcast production are small and light enough for one person to handle quite easily.

The vidicon tube, however, has made it possi-

ble to produce small viewfinder cameras that can be handled almost like an 8mm film camera. These highly portable, low-cost cameras and recording equipment have revolutionized television production by liberating it from the exclusive hold of the professional production companies and opening it up to individuals and small groups of interested people. The small, portable camera has democratized television. Community television has developed apace with its advent, and video artists have found it a viable tool for their craft. Unfortunately, the picture quality of these vidicon cameras does not yet meet broadcasting standards (an agreed-upon electronic standard of picture resolution and strength). However, under ideal circumstances, they can produce pictures that are good enough to be broadcast, especially when dubbed up to 2-inch videotape and electronically corrected—with a device called a time-base corrector (see pages 221–222)—during the dubbing.

Ruggedness   The I-O tube, as well as the whole I-O camera, is much more temperamental electronically and sensitive to shock and rough handling than the vidicon camera. When the I-O camera is warm, moving it over rough terrain or taking it off the pedestal is inadvisable. The vidicon, on the other hand, will withstand a reasonable amount of jolting while in operation. Of course, you should always treat any camera as gently as possible, especially when you are working with it away from the studio.

Electronic Characteristics

The basic electronic characteristics of I-O and vidicon cameras particularly important in the context of production are: (1) picture quality and stability, (2) operating light level, (3) burn-in, and (4) contrast range.

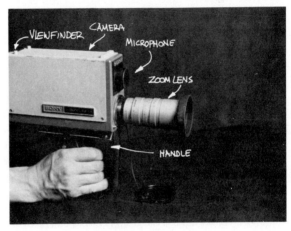

2·7 Vidicon Cameras: (a) RCA-TK 15 vidicon camera, a viewfinder studio camera; (b) General Electric industrial camera, a type used for closed-circuit observation; (c) Sony "portapak" camera, a highly portable camera used in conjunction with a small ½-inch videotape recorder.

Picture Quality and Stability The popularity of the I-O camera in on-the-air telecasting stems from its superior picture quality. And since picture quality is the single most important criterion in the performance of a camera, the I-O camera kept its supremacy until the advent of color.

Picture quality means basically that we can see fine detail in the television image and that there are strong blacks and whites with a sufficient number of easily distinguishable grays between them. Technically, the television picture should have high *resolution,* which means that the television system is capable of reproducing extremely fine object detail. The picture should also display high *contrast,* that is, deep blacks and brilliant whites, and a good *grayscale*—a good number (up to 8, see page 335) of easily distinguishable brightness gradations of grays that lie between the television black (darkest screen area) and television white (brightest screen area).

Furthermore, the picture should be as "quiet" as possible, which means that it should be as free from *video noise* as possible. A "noisy" picture has a great amount of *snow,* white vibrating spots in the picture that occur when the video signal as produced by the pickup tube is not strong enough to override the electronic interference, which the system usually and unfortunately generates. Video noise works very much like audio noise. Even the best high-fidelity system has some inherent electronic noise. You can hear the speakers hum a little as soon as you turn on the amplifier. Or, when the music is very low (which is equivalent to a weak audio signal), you may become aware of the rumble of the turntable. As soon as the music gets louder again (equivalent to a stronger audio signal), you are no longer aware of the noise. The relation of the strength of the picture signal to the accompanying interference, the noise, is generally expressed in a *signal-to-noise ratio.* A high signal-to-noise ratio is desirable. It means that the signal is high (strong) relative to the noise under normal operating conditions.

Finally, the picture should generally not display any *lag,* or *comet-tailing,* also called "smear" and "following image." A lag shows up as a cometlike smear that follows a moving object, or motion of the camera across stationary objects. Lag occurs especially in vidicon cameras under low lighting conditions, and when the object is very bright against a dark background.

As pointed out before, the I-O camera does well in most respects. Most importantly, it produces a higher resolution image than the vidicon.

The contrast is adequate in the I-O, although more limited than the vidicon. We will take up contrast and grayscale response of the I-O and vidicon cameras in a separate paragraph. Although the vidicon tube is basically quieter than the I-O tube, the superior resolution of the I-O tube and its ability to produce a fairly strong signal even under low light levels make up for this deficiency. The vidicon tube is highly susceptible to comet-tailing, while the I-O tube is virtually free of it.

Picture stability means that once the camera has been properly adjusted it should need little or no further adjustment for some time (up to the whole day of telecasting). Before a camera becomes fully operational, it has to be "set up," or aligned. Any camera, except for the rather uncomplicated vidicon cameras, including the portable ones, needs to *warm up* before the video engineer can begin with alignment procedures. The longer the warmup period, the better the alignment will be, and the less the camera will get out of adjustment later on. Unfortunately, many production people do not realize the importance of the warmup period and call for pictures before the camera is warm enough to operate. Especially in the beginning of the broadcast day, the schedule should take this warm-up time into consideration—half an hour is considered minimum for I-O cameras, and one hour is generally sufficient. Color cameras, however, take even longer to warm up. Depending on the sophistication of the vidicon camera, it may need as little as five minutes (for the portable models) to one hour for the studio models.

After the warmup time, the video engineer will check various aspects of picture quality, such as resolution, contrast, and grayscale response with a test chart and a waveform monitor, also called an oscilloscope. Vidicon cameras will keep such an alignment for several days, even after they have been turned off and on several times. I-O cameras, however, are more temperamental. Often they need to be realigned even after a relatively short telecast. I-O cameras have a tendency to "drift" and therefore need constant attention.

Operating Light Level To perform at peak efficiency, every television camera needs a certain amount of light. Picture quality will suffer if the camera is used under lighting conditions that are below a certain operating level. When the tube is not receiving enough light energy, it will turn out a video signal that is too weak to drown out the video noise. What, then, is the proper operating light level? For most I-O cameras, the operating light levels generally range from 75 to 100 foot-candles. Vidicon cameras need approximately twice the amount of light as I-O cameras, from 150 to 250 foot-candles. (We will discuss light levels more thoroughly in Chapter 5).

Burn-in Like light bulbs, television pickup tubes have a limited service life. I-O tubes have a shorter service life (usually 1,000 hours) than vidicon tubes (well over 2,000 hours). The older an I-O tube gets, the more sensitive it becomes to "burn-ins" or "sticking." A burn-in means that the tube remembers the picture it has taken and carries a gray negative image of that particular picture over the following shots. This rather annoying picture retention is caused especially when you focus the camera on a scene for an extended period with no movement of either the camera or object, or by focusing on a scene with strong black-and-white contrast, such as a black studio card with white lettering on it. With an old I-O tube in your camera, you can burn in the opening title of the show and carry the burn-in over several of the shots following.

Vidicon tubes are comparatively insensitive to burns and can be focused on high-contrast stationary objects for a relatively long time. But once a burn-in has occurred in a vidicon tube, it is more difficult to remove its traces than from an I-O tube. If a burn-in has occurred in an I-O tube, you can remove it in most cases by panning your camera back and forth on a well-lighted, neutral surface, such as the studio floor or the cyclorama.

Contrast Ratio The image-orthicon tube is highly sensitive to extreme black-and-white contrast. A somewhat limited contrast range will greatly enhance picture quality. Generally, I-O tubes cannot tolerate a contrast ratio that exceeds 20:1, that is, the brightest spot in your scene should be only twenty times brighter than the darkest spot. If the scene exceeds this limit, the video operator will have to adjust the picture either to reduce the bright spots, thereby rendering the darker areas uniformly black, or to lighten the dark areas, thereby overexposing and washing out the light areas. However, if you show nothing but a variety of medium grays in your scene, your picture will, indeed, look "medium." There is nothing wrong with using dark colors in your set, so long as you don't put something extremely bright and highly reflecting directly in front of or adjacent to them. As a matter of fact, your video operator will probably appreciate having something white and something black in the set so that he has a reference for his shading adjustment. Reflections off extremely bright objects, such as jewelry or brass instruments, that exceed the tolerance of the tube will cause "blooming" or "halo" effects. Blooming shows up as a black rim or halo around the reflecting object. Besides looking bad, it is quite harmful to the I-O tube. Because of this light sensitivity, you should never point the I-O camera into bright lights and obviously not into the sun. Even a few seconds of focusing on a bright light may cause the I-O tube to burn out or to be damaged beyond repair.

Vidicon tubes generally tolerate a higher contrast (up to a 30:1 ratio) and are less subject to

2·8   30mm (1¼ inch) Plumbicon Tube.

blooming. But they, too, will burn out if the camera is focused for any length of time into a bright light. But even with the vidicon's greater tolerance to brightness contrast, it is easier to get better picture quality if you maintain a 20:1 limit in your scene. An extreme brightness contrast will additionally emphasize the *falloff* characteristic of the vidicon tube. While in the light areas, the vidicon camera can produce beautifully subtle and distinct shades of gray, in the shadow areas it has a tendency to see everything uniformly dark. The vidicon tube has a fast falloff and therefore does not differentiate well between light and very dark shadow areas. The I-O tube has a more evenly spaced falloff and shows, within the specified contrast range, equally spaced grayscale steps even in the darker end of the scale.

The Color Camera

The color camera works on the same fundamental principle as the monochrome camera: the conversion of light into electrical energy. But color television is technically much more complex than monochrome television. A knowledge of some of the basic workings of the color camera will help you greatly in understanding the specific production techniques for color television. We will, therefore, briefly discuss these basic points: (1) Plumbicon pickup tube, (2) chrominance and luminance channels, (3) internal optical system, (4) operational characteristics of the color camera, and (5) electronic characteristics of the color camera.

Plumbicon Pickup Tube

All newer model broadcast quality television cameras use Plumbicon[1] tubes. Manufactured under various trade names, the Plumbicon tube is basically an improved vidicon tube. Contrary to the vidicon, it has a lead-oxide-coated photoconductive (light-sensitive) front surface, and otherwise improved light-converting elements. Sometimes the Plumbicon tubes are simply called "lead-oxide" tubes. Plumbicon tubes come in a 1-inch (or 25mm) format, or the more widely used 1¼-inch (or 30mm) format *(see 2.8)*. Many lower quality color cameras use the standard vidicon tubes or smaller format Plumbicon tubes (such as ⅔ inch). In most cases, the vidicon and Plumbicon tubes are interchangeable with only minor electronic adjustments in the camera.

Chrominance and Luminance Channels

While in the monochrome camera the light, as caught by the camera lens, is focused directly into the single camera pickup tube, the color camera first splits the entering light into the three primary colors: red, green, and blue *(see color plate II)*. Each one of these is then focused individually on

---

[1] Plumbicon is a registered trademark of N. V. Philips.

a separate pickup tube: one for the red light, one for the green light, and one for the blue light. In effect, we have three cameras, or channels, in the color camera in order to produce and process three individual video signals, a "red" signal, a "green" signal, and a "blue" signal. Since these channels process the primary colors, they are called *chrominance channels* (from the Greek *chroma* = color).

In the older color camera, there used to be a fourth tube and channel that produced the necessary brightness differentiations (from black through various shades of gray to white—see grayscale in Chapter 12). This channel, which provides the color picture with the necessary brightness differences, is called the *luminance channel* (from the Latin *lumen* = light). In the present cameras, the luminance signal does not require a special pickup tube but is produced by matrixing (combining) the red, green, and blue signals again into a monochrome (black-and-white) luminance signal.

The green signal, which carries a great amount of image detail, is often used for an electrically generated effect that gives the appearance of increased picture resolution and therefore of a sharpened image. This effect, called "contours-out-of-green," gives the color picture crispness and snap.

Internal Optical System and Color Separation

The light as gathered by the lens is separated by a series of *dichroic* (color-separating) *mirrors* into the three primary colors of light *(see color plate III)*. The dichroic mirror D_1 splits off the red color from the incoming light, letting the green and blue light pass. Dichroic mirror D_2 splits off the blue color, letting the remaining green color pass. Regular high-quality *mirrors* (M_1 and M_2) reflect the separated colored lights into their respective pickup tubes.

The *relay lenses* (R_1, R_2, R_3) help to transport, relay, the three separate colored light images to the pickup tubes. The lenses help to keep the images sharp and clear until they reach the pickup tubes.

The *filters* (F_1, F_2, F_3) keep out all unwanted light that might interfere with each of the primary colors, red, green, and blue.

The camera *pickup tubes* (P_1, P_2, P_3) may be Plumbicon or vidicon or any combination thereof. High-quality cameras usually have an "extended red" Plumbicon tube, which is designed especially to convert the red light into the video signal of the red channel with a minimum of distortion, and "separate mesh" Plumbicon tubes for the green and blue channels. The separate mesh tubes virtually eliminate comet-tailing, or lag.

Because the mirrors and relay lenses take up a considerable amount of light before the colors reach the pickup tubes, and because the alignment of the mirrors and the lenses is obviously quite critical, another, more efficient, internal optical system is used in many color cameras. This system combines the dichroic, color-separating elements (filters) and the light-diverting elements (prisms) all in one small beam-split *prism block (2.9; see also color plate II)*. Since the pickup tubes can be attached directly to the prism block, relay lenses are no longer necessary.

Operational Characteristics

The major operational characteristics of the color camera are (1) size and weight, (2) ruggedness, and (3) type of cable.

Size and Weight   Because the color camera is actually three cameras in one, it is obviously quite heavy and bulky. A high-quality studio camera

2·9 Prism Block.

cannot be carried by one person, and it takes at least two persons to move one onto or off of a studio pedestal or tripod.

Some portable color cameras can be carried and operated by one person, but even these stripped-down models are bulky and tiresome when carried for any length of time.

There are small portable color cameras on the market that have only two pickup tubes, and in some instances only one. In the two-tube cameras, chrominance channels for only two of the primary colors are provided, the third color being electronically derived from the leftover signal, which by necessity must represent the third primary color. In the one-tube color camera, the front surface of the special pickup tube is covered with vertically striped filters that separate the incoming light into the primary colors. However,

what is gained in portability and ease of operation is often—but not always—lost in picture quality and stability. Constant efforts are being made to develop a portable color camera that is extremely light and easy to operate and that will produce high-quality pictures. *(See 2.11.)*

Ruggedness   In general, its intricate internal optical system makes the color camera quite vulnerable to physical shock. Although the portable cameras are a little more rugged than studio cameras, they too can be easily jolted out of adjustment, especially those that use the dichroic mirror system instead of the prism block. Since the three channels make the color camera particularly sensitive to alignment, be extremely careful in moving the camera at the end of the warmup period and while it is in operation.

Type of Cable   Depending on the electronic design of the camera chain, various types of cable must be used from camera head to the CCU. The continual quest for lighter and more compact television makes the weight of the camera cable an important operational consideration. Obviously, the lighter the cable, the easier it is to handle. The standard television cable for monochrome cameras and some color cameras (called the TV-81 cable) is quite heavy. Through computer-type digital control circuits and multiplexing techniques (putting more than one signal through the same wire), a very light *triaxial* cable (which has only three concentrically arranged wires) can be used. Philips Broadcast Equipment Corporation, which makes such digitally controlled color cameras, gives an interesting weight comparison between the standard and triax cables: 5,000 feet of the standard TV-81 cable weighs 4,370 pounds, while the same length of triaxial cable weighs only 333 pounds. Of course, the increased complexity of the circuit design

Plate I When mixing colored light, the additive primaries are red, green, and blue. All other colors can be achieved by mixing certain quantities of red, green, and blue light. For example, the additive mixture of red and green light produces yellow.

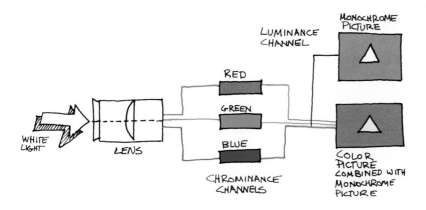

WHITE LIGHT

LENS

RED

GREEN

BLUE

CHROMINANCE CHANNELS

LUMINANCE CHANNEL

MONOCHROME PICTURE

COLOR PICTURE COMBINED WITH MONOCHROME PICTURE

Plate II The light that enters the camera is divided into the three additive primaries and treated separately as red, green, and blue signals. In a three-tube camera, each tube creates a separate video signal for each primary color. The chrominance channels (color signals) produce the color picture, and the luminance channel (a combination of the color signals) the black-and-white picture.

Plate III   White light enters the camera through the lens and is split by dichroic mirrors into red, green, and blue light. These three light beams are directed through regular mirrors and relay lenses into three camera pickup tubes: one each for the red, green, and blue light. Special filters correct minor color distortions before the light beams enter the tubes.

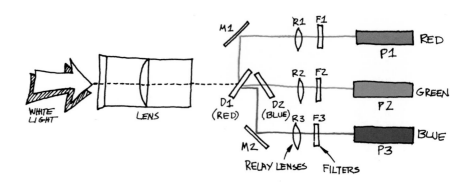

Plate IV   Most color cameras use a beam-split prism block instead of dichroic mirrors for their internal optical system. The incoming white light is split and relayed into the three pickup tubes through dichroic layers and color filters.

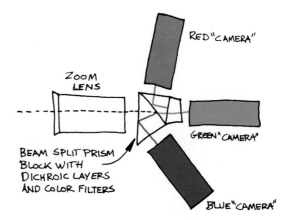

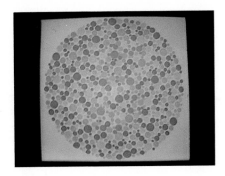
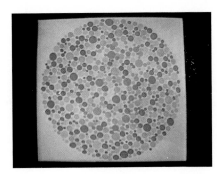

Plate V Since the black-and-white camera responds primarily to the brightness attribute in color (and not to hue and saturation), the black-and-white camera is color blind. It cannot detect differences in hue when the brightness remains the same.

Plate VI Although the hue is sufficiently different for this letter to show up on color television, it is barely readable on a black-and-white monitor. The brightness contrast is insufficient for good monochrome reproduction.

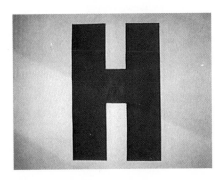

Plate VII The lettering on this card has enough hue and brightness contrast to show up equally well on a color and black-and-white television receiver.

Plate VIII The colors on the left appear on the monochrome monitor as shown on the right. Note which colors appear as the same gray (same brightness) and which are distinctly different. It is the brightness variation, not hues, that makes colors appear as different grays on monochrome television.

Plate IX Because of brightness contrast, this slide reproduces equally well on color and black-and-white television.

makes such cameras, once again, more of a liability electronically than the standard cameras.

Electronic Characteristics

The electronic characteristics of the monochrome camera are equally relevant for the color camera. We will, therefore, look briefly at (1) picture quality and stability, (2) operating light level, (3) burn-in, and (4) contrast range.

Picture Quality and Stability   The Plumbicon tube lacks the resolution power of the I-O tube. Fortunately, the color differentiation helps to dis-

tinguish between smaller picture portions and to define object contour. Like the vidicon, the Plumbicon tube is fairly quiet, which means that it has a favorable signal-to-noise ratio. However, the picture quality deteriorates drastically if the tubes do not receive a sufficient amount of light.

If you have to worry about aligning three tubes instead of one, you will obviously have more potential alignment drifts (the camera drifting out of setup values), than you would with a one-tube camera. However, when given enough warmup time, the color camera is no more critical in alignment than an I-O camera, for example.

The one rather serious drawback of the Plum-

2·10   Ordinary white light, like sunlight or the light from a light bulb, can be separated into three basic, or primary, colors: red, green, and blue. Obviously, when we mix the three primaries together again, we get white light. But we can also mix these three primary colored lights in various proportions, that is, various light intensities, and achieve almost all the colors we ordinarily perceive. For example, take three slide projectors and put a clear red slide (filter) in one, a clear green one in the second projector, and a clear blue one in the third projector. Then hook each of the slide projectors to a separate dimmer. When you have the dimmers up full (assuming equal light transmission by all three filters) and shine all three light beams together on the screen, you get white light, as we mentioned before. Full-strength red and full-strength green will give you yellow. But if you now dim the green projector a little, the yellow will turn orange. If you dim the red instead of the green projector, you will get a brownish color. The blue and red together will yield a reddish purple, called magenta. This mixing process of colored light is called *additive color mixing*. When we mix paints of two colors together, however, they filter each other out and form a new color. They subtract each other's wavelength. This process is, therefore, called *subtractive color mixing*. The subtractive

primary colors are magenta (a bluish red), cyan (a greenish blue), and yellow. Since it is light, not paint, that enters the camera, color television operates with the additive color-mixing process.

In color television, the light entering the lens is split into the three additive primaries, red, green, and blue, and processed by three separate channels, the chrominance (color) channels, which act very much like the three slide projectors. In the receiver, the screen is lined with many dots arranged in groups of red, green, and blue. These are activated by three "slide projectors," called electron guns, each one hitting with its beam all the dots representing one particular color—all the red dots, all the green dots, or all the blue dots. By changing the intensity of one, or all, of the beams, you can create a variety of colors. If all three beams activate the dots fully, you get white; if the guns are turned off, you get black. If only the guns that activate the red and the green dots fire, but not the one that activates the blue, you get yellow. Since the color dots lie very close together, you perceive them as various color mixtures.*

---

* Herbert Zettl, *Sight-Sound-Motion* (Belmont, Calif.: Wadsworth Publishing Co. 1973), pp. 58–83.

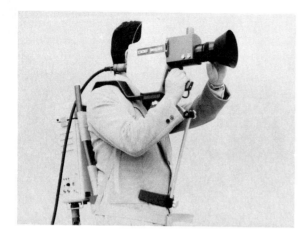

2·11 High-Quality Portable Color Camera (Philips LDK-11).

bicon tube has been its problem of faithfully reproducing highly saturated (strong) reds. The cooler reds (bluish reds) and the strong, dark reds are notably susceptible to distortion. The rather expensive "extended red" Plumbicon is more capable of reproducing reds without distortion than the regular Plumbicon tube, but even the more costly one has some problems with reproducing highly saturated dark reds without distortion.

When vidicon tubes are used in the color camera, the electronic characteristics are much the same as for the black-and-white camera.

Operating Light Level Most color cameras need from 200 to 400 foot-candles of illumination to produce optimal pictures. You will hear and read that a camera can produce a good color picture (called "full video," which means that the video signal has a certain prescribed intensity) with as little as 5 foot-candles of illumination through "bias lighting" (an electronic intensity booster). This is true as long as your video operator has the time, skill, and energy to go through

a precarious color-balancing act, and as long as you don't have a high-contrast, fast-moving scene. An average illumination of 250 foot-candles will make the camera and everyone who works with it considerably more effective.

The normal Plumbicon tube, like the vidicon, produces comet-tailing, or lag, under low lighting conditions. You may have seen this effect during the televising of a football game: the player who runs from a brightly lighted area of the field to a shadow area and suddenly seems to be trailing a ball of fire. Although in this case such an effect may accurately symbolize the player's power and emotion, comet-tailing is not always so appropriate. As indicated before, the "separate mesh" Plumbicon tube reduces this sort of lag to a large extent. The best assurance against comet-tailing is still a sufficient amount of light.

Burn-in The Plumbicon tube is virtually free of burn-in and can tolerate a high-contrast scene for a fairly long period without any trace of image retention.

Contrast Ratio The contrast range of the Plumbicon tube is quite close to that of the vidicon tube. Generally, the Plumbicon tube can handle a contrast up to 30:1 without danger to the tube itself. However, if you want clear, undistorted colors, the color camera, too, should not be exposed to a contrast that exceeds the 20:1 ratio. The primary reason for this narrow range is that one of the most important colors requiring true reproduction is the skin tone. When using color chips, you may be able to balance your colors against one another even within a contrast range of more than 30:1, that is, where the brightest color is more than thirty times brighter than the darkest color. However, within such a high-contrast range, you may have to shade the lighter colors down a little (make them darker than they really are) in order to differentiate among the darker colors; or you may have to bring the darker and mid-range colors up a little in order to compensate for the brighter ones. But you can't do this with a face. You can't shade skin tones lighter or darker simply to adjust for the surrounding colors. Skin tones have, after all, a fixed color standard that suffers noticeably from the slightest distortion.

Besides electronic shading devices, the color camera, like the broadcast-quality black-and-white camera, has a filter wheel that can hold a variety of neutral density filters, color filters, or special effects devices, such as star filters. The *neutral density filters* act like sunglasses of varying density. They simply reduce the amount of light that falls on the pickup tubes without distorting the actual colors of the scene. The color filters also help to correct color distortion. *(See 2.12.)*

Contrary to the I-O and vidicon tubes, the Plumbicon tube is virtually free of the halo effect, or blooming, when subjected to highly reflecting objects. In fact, dazzling jewelry or brass instruments lend the picture energy and sparkle. You can even point the Plumbicon color camera directly into the studio lights without damaging the tubes themselves. What used to be an annoying problem with the I-O cameras has now been made into a virtue in color production. Most color cameras come equipped with a variety of star filters, which transform any bright light source into starlike light beams with four, six, eight, or however many points the star filter is made to produce. *(See 2.13.)*

Types of Cameras

There is a bewildering array of television cameras on the market. Their names and the way they are classified seem equally confusing. Some are

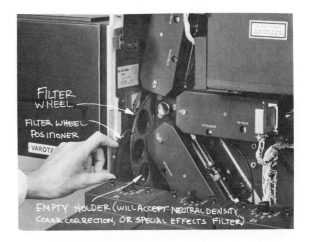

2·12 Filter Wheel: The filter wheel can hold a variety of neutral density or color correction filters. In some cameras, the filter wheel can be turned by remote control.

classified by what they are primarily able to do, their function; others by how good they are, their quality. Still others are named for the type of pickup tube, or whether they have a lens turret or a zoom lens.

The simplest way to keep them straight is to classify them according to their function—what they are supposed to do or how they are principally used.

We will, therefore, distinguish among three broad types of cameras: (1) broadcasting and nonbroadcasting, (2) monochrome and color, and (3) studio and portable.

Broadcasting and Nonbroadcasting Cameras

What we ordinarily call "broadcast quality" refers to cameras that are intended for open-circuit, on-the-air telecasting. Nonbroadcast cameras are used for closed-circuit transmission, which means

2·13 Star Filter Effect: The star filter changes extremely bright light sources into four-, six-, or eight-point starlike light beams.

that the transmission process does not use public airwaves. Closed-circuit television includes any type of surveillance by television, self-contained distribution of television material in educational institutions, medical centers, or business establishments, or even the CATV (Community Antenna Television; in short, cable television) productions, which are distributed via cable from the CATV studio directly to the wired homes.

Broadcast quality means that the camera chain must deliver a picture that fulfills certain established engineering standards—as written by the EIA (Electrical Industries Association) and the FCC (Federal Communications Commission). But there is still a great difference between the top-priced broadcast television camera and the medium-priced broadcast camera. The top camera has several automatic correction circuits built in that make the camera function at peak efficiency even under adverse conditions. The medium-priced camera, on the other hand, works quite well under ideal production conditions, such as

the availability of a great amount of even lighting and simple colors. But as soon as a production becomes a little more demanding—in the way of high-contrast lighting, subtle differences in colors, precise rendering of skin tones, and so forth— the medium-priced camera can no longer keep pace. With all but the top broadcast cameras, even a fast zoom in or out may cause noticeable color distortions.

Nonbroadcast cameras have no regulated performance standards. They are judged merely by how well they do the job for which they are designed. For example, there is no need to worry about a high-quality picture if the only requirement for the camera is to watch cars in a parking lot. But if the closed-circuit camera is used for instruction in a broadcasting course, or for showing a delicate operation to a number of medical students, top picture quality and true color renditions are essential.

Monochrome and Color Cameras

One of the most obvious differences in function is whether the camera should deliver a black-and-white picture or color, or both. Color cameras must, by law, be able to produce compatible color; that is, the color signal must be convertible into black-and-white images on a monochrome television set.

Almost all broadcast cameras used in television stations throughout the developed countries are color. Of course, many black-and-white television cameras are still used in closed-circuit operations, such as educational systems in schools and industry; and open-circuit broadcasting is occasionally done in black and white. (Unfortunately, color is used rather indiscriminately regardless of aesthetic appropriateness. In many instances, it is not only unnecessary but often detrimental to

communicating emotional intensity and depth.[2])
Monochrome cameras are, therefore, far from obsolete. For the student of television production,
the monochrome television camera is obviously
the first logical step. For the television artist,
monochrome television represents a means of expression whose graphic potential we have
scarcely recognized, let alone tapped. *(See 2.16.)*

While all color cameras (with the exception of
some small industrial color cameras used for observation only) have zoom lenses, the monochrome camera has either a zoom lens *(zoom camera)*
or one or more fixed-focal-length lenses that are
attached to a lens turret *(turret camera)*. (*See 2.3*, page
12).

As indicated earlier, monochrome cameras are
generally classified by the pickup tube they use.
Thus, we have image-orthicon, or I-O, cameras
and vidicon cameras, the latter commonly used
for closed-circuit operations.

Studio and Portable Cameras

The name "studio camera" is somewhat
misleading since the studio camera can also be
used in the field. However, the term is used to
describe a high-quality camera that is so heavy
it cannot be maneuvered properly without the aid
of a pedestal, or some other type of camera mount
(see pages 61–63). A more appropriate name
would be pedestal camera, since we could distinguish it more readily from the portable camera,
which can be carried around by its operator.

The portable camera has obviously many operational advantages over the studio camera. It can
be carried and operated by one person, needs no
camera mount (you are the mount), and is highly

2.14 New products in the television equipment
market reflect the continual striving for broadcast-
quality cameras that are extremely light and compact
and that perform well under a great variety of production conditions. One innovation is the use of an
extremely light camera cable for computer-type digital circuitry and signal-multiplexing. Attempts are
also being made to automate the camera as much as
possible. This means incorporating in the camera
mechanism many functions that were previously
performed by either the camera operator or the
video operator at the CCU.

You can compare the automated television camera
with an automated 8mm movie camera, which will
do practically anything for you except the looking.

All you do is pop the film cassette into the camera, point it in the desired direction, and press a
button. The camera will look at the scene you are
filming, read the reflected light, and adjust the lens
iris for correct exposure; and while you do your dramatic zooming in and out, it will keep in focus. If
the scene is too dark for the film you are using, the
camera will tell you. The professional film maker
might scoff at such automation; but the person using
such a camera will nevertheless enjoy properly exposed, clear, technically professional-looking movies.

The same goes for automated television color cameras. The more the technical functions, such as color
and brightness controls, are taken over by the camera, the more attention you can devote to the event
itself and to the aesthetics of your interpretation of
it. While technical adjustments can very well be
done by the machine (the camera chain), the aesthetics of communication is truly a human function.
Of course, if aesthetically you decide to go against
the technical standard as programmed into the camera, you must then have an opportunity to override
the automation. If, for example, you want color distortion to emphasize a particular mood, you must be
able to tell the camera not to worry and not to self-
adjust for standard color balance. Otherwise, both
the camera and you will have lost an important
creative potential.

---

[2] Herbert Zettl, *Sight-Sound-Motion* (Belmont, Calif.: Wadsworth Publishing Co. 1973), pp. 92–93.

a

2·15 Color Cameras: (a) Philips LDK-5 (top quality); (b) RCA TK-45A (top quality); (c) IVC 7000P (broadcast-quality portable); (d) CEI–280 (good quality); (e) Akai VC-150 (nonbroadcast color portapak).

b

2·16 Monochrome (Black-and-White) Cameras: (a) RCA TK-60 4½-inch image-orthicon camera (top quality); (b) RCA TK-11 3-inch image-orthicon camera (good quality), industry standard for a long time; (c) Akai VC-115 portable vidicon camera, used in conjunction with a ¼-inch videotape deck.

a

c

d

e

VIEWFINDER HOOD

FOCUSING KNOB

CAMERA

INTERCOM OUTLET

CAMERA CABLE

VIEWFINDER

LENS TURRET (DETACHABLE)

LENS

Telerston

TALLY LIGHTS

b

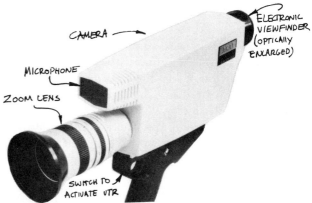

CAMERA

ELECTRONIC VIEWFINDER (OPTICALLY ENLARGED)

MICROPHONE

ZOOM LENS

SWITCH TO ACTIVATE VTR

c

maneuverable. Wherever you can walk, the camera can go. The studio camera, once fairly portable, has unfortunately become so laden down with production accessories, such as the bulky teleprompter (see pages 368–369), camera lights, and the like, that it can hardly be moved at all. Such bulk, and the convenience of the zoom lens, entices many a camera operator to let the camera sit as though it were bolted to the ground, thereby drastically reducing its production potential.

On the other hand, as mentioned earlier in this chapter, the portable camera has liberalized television as to production technique and, in conjunction with refined videotape editing techniques, has become a formidable competitor to film.

Summary

The television camera is one of the most important single production elements. Most other elements in the process are greatly influenced by what the camera can and cannot do.

The *camera head,* which we ordinarily refer to as the camera, consists of (1) the lens and attachments, sometimes called the external optical system, (2) the camera itself with the pickup tubes, or tube, and attachments called the internal optical system, and (3) the viewfinder.

The *camera chain* consists of (1) the camera head, (2) the camera control unit, or CCU, (3) the sync generator, (4) the power supply, and, for color cameras, (5) the encoder.

All television cameras work on the same basic *principle:* the conversion of an optical image into electrical signals, which are reconverted by a television set into visible screen images—the television pictures.

There are black-and-white, or monochrome, television cameras, and color cameras. Monochrome cameras use two major types of *pickup tubes:* the image-orthicon, or I-O, and the vidicon. Color cameras have as their main pickup tubes either Plumbicon tubes (a modified vidicon tube with a lead-oxide front surface), or vidicon tubes. The pickup tube used in the camera head, and the electronic accessories determine the basic *electronic characteristics* of the camera: (1) picture quality and stability, (2) operating light level, (3) burn-in, and (4) contrast range.

The *operational characteristics* of the camera include (1) size and weight, (2) ruggedness, and (3) type of cable.

Color cameras contain two major channels: (1) the chrominance channel, which deals with the three primary light colors, red, green, and blue, and (2) the luminance channel, which deals with the dark and light areas, the brightness, of the picture.

In three-tube color cameras, a complex *internal optical system* splits the incoming white light into the three primary colors. The main parts of the system are (1) dichroic mirrors or a prism system with dichroic filters, which split the incoming light into the primary colors; (2) regular mirrors, which deflect the separate colored light into the respective pickup tubes; (3) relay lenses, which help to keep the image sharp and clear until it reaches the pickup tubes; (4) color filters, which correct the color for the pickup tubes; and (5) the vidicon or Plumbicon pickup tubes themselves.

In large, professional cameras, three tubes are used, one for each primary color. There are also two-tube cameras, in which only two primary colors are used, with the third one being reproduced electronically. In the one-tube color camera, the surface of the pickup tube is striped vertically with a series of extremely narrow filters that divide the light into the primary colors.

Television cameras are *grouped* by various criteria, such as broadcast or nonbroadcast cameras, color or monochrome cameras, studio or portable cameras.

3 *Lenses*

In the preceding chapter, we talked about the television camera. An important production element of the camera is its lens. The lens produces the light image that the pickup tube of the camera converts into video signals, and affects greatly how we perceive an environment as shown on the television screen.

This chapter is, therefore, devoted to two main aspects of lenses: (1) their optical characteristics, including focal length, focus, f-stop, and depth of field, and (2) their performance characteristics, including the field of view, lens settings in respect to particular production effects, and how to work lenses, and the manual and automatic units that control their operation.

Lenses are used in all fields of photographic art. Their function is mainly to produce a small, clear image of the viewed scene on the film or, in the case of television, on the camera pickup tube. The particular lens used determines how close or how far away an object will appear, assuming a fixed distance from camera to object. One lens will make an object or action look far away although the camera is relatively close to it; another will show the object or action at close range, even though the camera is some distance from it.

A *zoom lens* can duplicate the characteristics of several lenses; in effect, it is many lenses in one. It can show an object far away or at close range, and make far objects appear to move continuously closer, or close objects continuously farther away.

As mentioned earlier, all broadcast-type color cameras and many black-and-white cameras use zoom lenses, or, as they are called in technical language, *variable-focal-length* lenses. Other studio cameras have up to four *fixed-focal-length* lenses attached to a turret. Although zoom lenses are much more prevalent in television than fixed-focal-length lenses, we will use the latter as frequent reference in our discussion of *optical* and *performance characteristics* of lenses because the basic optical principles are more easily explained and understood this way. We will transfer the basic principles from the fixed lens to the zoom lens whenever necessary.

Optical Characteristics of Lenses

To determine when and why you should use a particular lens, or zoom-lens setting, you will need at least a basic knowledge of (1) focal length, (2) focus, (3) f-stop, (4) depth of field, and their interrelations.

Back Focus   The distance between zoom lens and camera pickup tube at which the picture is in focus at the extreme wide-angle zoom position. In monochrome cameras, the back focus can be adjusted by moving the pickup tube through the camera focus control.

Depth of Field   The area in which all objects, located at different distances from the camera, appear in focus. Depth of field is dependent upon focal length of the lens, f-stop, and distance between object and camera.

Fast Lens   A lens that permits a relatively great amount of light to pass through (low f-stop number). Can be used in low lighting conditions.

Field of View   The extent of a scene that is visible through a particular lens; its vista.

Focal Length   The distance from the optical center of the lens to the front surface of the camera pickup tube with the lens set at infinity. Focal lengths are measured in millimeters or inches. Short-focal-length lenses have a wide angle of view (wide vista); long-focal-length (telephoto) lenses have a narrow angle of view (closeup). In a variable-focal-length lens (zoom lens) the focal length can be changed continuously from wide angle to narrow angle or vice versa. A fixed-focal-length lens has a single designated focal length only.

Focus   A picture is in focus when it appears sharp and clear on the screen (technically, the point where the light rays refracted by the lens converge).

Front Focus   The proper relationship of the front elements of the zoom lens to ensure focus during the entire zoom range. Front focus is set at the extreme closeup position with the zoom focus control. Color cameras have a front-focus adjustment only because the pickup tubes cannot be moved.

Focal Length

In general, we can group lenses into (1) short, or wide-angle, lenses, (2) long, or narrow-angle, lenses, and (3) zoom, or variable-focal-length, lenses. The long lenses are sometimes called telephoto, or (quite ambiguously) closeup lenses.

The "short" and the "long" in this connection refer to the focal length of a lens; that is, the distance from the optical center of the lens (often the midpoint between the front and back lens elements) to the point where the image as seen by the lens is in focus *(see 3.1)*.

A thorough knowledge of how to measure focal length is not too important for proper usage of camera lenses. Fortunately, since short lenses usually look short and long lenses look long, it is easy to tell whether the camera operator is using a short- or a long-focal-length lens.

With a short, or wide-angle, lens you can see

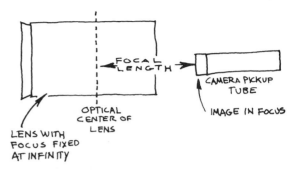

3·1   Focal Length.

more; you have a wider vista. What you see looks comparatively small. With a long, or narrow-angle, lens you see less; you have a narrower vista. But what you see is greatly magnified. A short lens creates an effect similar to looking through binoculars the wrong way. A long lens is similar to binoculars used correctly.

---

f-Stop   The calibration on the lens indicating the aperture, or diaphragm opening (and therefore the amount of light transmitted through the lens). The larger the *f*-stop number, the smaller the aperture; the smaller the *f*-stop number, the larger the aperture.

Lens Format   A somewhat loose term for the grouping of lenses that have focal lengths appropriate to a particular size of film or camera pickup tube. There is a lens format for 35mm film, another for 16mm film; one for 3-inch I-O pickup tubes, another for 1-inch Plumbicons.

Normal Lens   A lens with a focal length that will approximate the spatial relationships of normal vision when used with a particular film or pickup tube format.

Range Extender   An optical attachment to the zoom lens that will extend its narrow-angle focal length.

Selective Focus   Emphasizing an object in a shallow depth of field through focus, while keeping its foreground and background out of focus.

Servo Controls   Zoom and focus controls that activate motor-driven mechanisms.

Slow Lens   A lens that permits a relatively small amount of light to pass through (high *f*-stop number). Can be used only in well-lighted areas.

Telephoto Lens   Same as long-focal-length lens. Gives a closeup view of an event relatively far away from the camera.

Turret Lens   A lens that is mounted on the turret of a camera. Usually in contrast to a zoom lens.

Zoom Lens   Variable-focal-length lens. It can change from a wide shot to a closeup in one continuous move.

Zoom Ratio   The zoom range, from the widest angle position to the narrowest angle position, expressed in a ratio, such as 10:1 (wide angle 17mm to a narrow angle 170mm).

3·2   In the discussion of focal length, it is important for you to realize that there are lenses of various *formats,* which, although they may be identical in focal length, nevertheless will give you different angles of view.

In order to project a clear image of its view upon the photoconductive (light-sensitive) front surface of the camera pickup tube, the basic lens format must match the size of the pickup tube. The large front surface of the image-orthicon tube, for example, requires lenses of a larger format than for the small vidicon tube. I-O cameras use lenses that fit a 35mm film format, and the 1-inch (25mm) vidicon or Plumbicon tubes generally use lenses that fit the 16mm film format.

Most color cameras use either the 1-inch (25mm) or the slightly larger 1¼-inch (30mm) vidicon or Plumbicon pickup tubes. Even this slight variation in tube size requires different formats of zoom lenses.

For lenses of a larger pickup tube format (such as the 35mm film format), a focal length of 50mm constitutes a short, wide-angle lens. For the smaller format lenses (such as the 16mm film format), a focal length of 50mm is considered a rather long, narrow-angle lens.

When using zoom lenses, you really don't have to worry too much about this lens format difference. Hopefully, the attached zoom lens has been purchased to match the pickup tubes inside the cameras. However, if you have to work with cameras that have pickup tubes of various sizes—such as an I-O and a vidicon monochrome camera with turret lenses, and a 1¼-inch Plumbicon color camera with a zoom lens—you may want to remember this simple formula: *the larger the lens format is, the wider the angle of view (the larger the vista) of a lens with a given focal length (or focal-length setting on a zoom) will be.*

Turret lenses have a fixed focal length—you cannot change the angle of view—and therefore you need several lenses on a turret. Turret lenses are usually marked according to their focal length, which is given either in millimeters (mm) or in inches (in). There are 25mm to one inch. The smaller the focal-length number, the wider the angle of view.

Contrary to the turret lenses, the *zoom lens* with its variable focal length allows you to change the focal length of the lens from long to short or from short to long in one continuous operation. A complicated series of interacting lenses keeps the object in focus at all times during the zooming operation, assuming that the zoom lens focus has been preset for this particular zoom. To "zoom in" means to change the lens gradually from a wide-angle lens (faraway view) to a narrow-angle lens (close view). On the television screen, a zoom appears as though the object is gradually getting larger and, therefore, coming toward the viewer. Through a zoom-in, the scene is brought closer to you. To "zoom out" or "zoom back" means to change the lens from a closeup to a distant shot. The scene seems to move away from you.

The degree to which we can change the focal length (and thereby the angle of view, or vista) of a zoom lens is its *zoom range.* This is often given in a ratio, such as 10:1. A 10:1 zoom range indicates that you can increase your focal length ten times, from 17mm to 170mm for example. When you are zoomed all the way out, your lens has a focal length of 17mm, which represents a rather wide angle of view for most television pickup tubes. When you are zoomed all the way in to 170mm, you have narrowed your angle of view to a tenth of the original one. You will now have a rather big closeup of the scene. Of course, you can stop anywhere within this zoom range and operate your lens at any focal length between 17mm and 170mm.

Focus

A picture is "in focus" when the projected image is sharp and clear. The focus depends on the distance from lens to film (in a still or movie camera) or from lens to camera pickup tube or tubes (in a television camera). Simply changing the distance from lens to film, or pickup tube, brings a picture into focus or takes it out of focus.

In television photography, the pickup tube takes the place of the film. To keep in focus, you must adjust the distance between the lens and the single pickup tube (for monochrome cameras) or pickup tubes (for color cameras). You can change this distance in two principal ways: (1) When using turret lenses on monochrome cameras, you can move the camera pickup tube toward and away from the lens by turning a special focusing knob on the side of the camera. (2) When using a zoom lens, you can focus anywhere within the zoom range by moving certain lens elements within the lens through mechanical or electrical focus devices attached to it and to the camera.

Because the basic principle of focusing the television camera can be explained more readily through the operation of a monochrome camera with a turret lens (fixed focal length), we will first take up the focus procedure of moving the pickup tube, and then progress to the more common television practice of focusing a zoom lens.

Moving the Pickup Tube You focus monochrome turret cameras by moving the pickup tube toward or away from the lens, a procedure accomplished simply by turning the focus knob or crank on the side of the camera. When you "dolly in" (move the camera toward the object), you generally crank the focusing knob counterclockwise, toward you. This pulls the pickup tube back in the camera toward you, and thereby increases the distance between the lens and the pickup tube.

3·3 When using fixed-focal-length lenses in still photography or in motion pictures, you adjust the focus by turning the ring on the lens barrel with the distance scale imprinted on it. By turning the ring, you can move the lens either closer to the film or farther away from it. The closer you hold the camera to the object, the farther the lens must be from the film. The farther away the object is, the closer the lens can be to the film. A typical 35mm film format lens on a still camera might show two distance scales on the distance ring: one in feet, ranging from 1.5 feet to infinity, and the other in meters (m), ranging from 0.45m to infinity. At the infinity setting, the lens is turned all the way in, closest to the film. Since most television cameras have a device that moves the pickup tube rather than the lens, the lenses—except those for small industrial-type cameras—do not have a distance calibration on them but have their distance setting fixed at infinity.

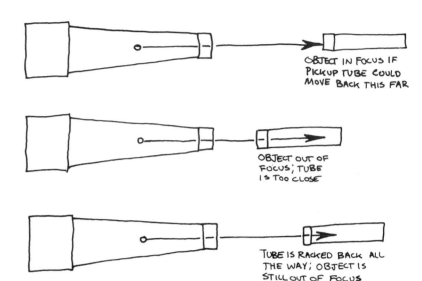

3·4 Focusing the Turret Lens Camera.

The closer the camera gets to the object, the farther back the tube has to travel in order to stay in focus. When you "dolly back" (move the camera away from the object), you crank the focusing knob clockwise, or away from you, pushing the pickup tube toward the lens and thereby decreasing the distance between the tube and the lens.

Because the travel of the pickup tube is obviously restricted within the camera, there are limitations to focusing, especially when long lenses are used. For example, you cannot take an extreme closeup of a postage stamp with a long lens, because you cannot rack into focus when you are close enough to the object to fill the screen with it. The reason for this dilemma is that long lenses have a long focal length; that is, the picture comes into focus relatively far behind the optical center of the lens. Operationally, you must rack the pickup tube back a considerable distance to align the sharp image from the lens with the front surface of the pickup tube. The closer the camera

gets to the object, the farther back the tube has to travel in order to stay in focus. If the pickup tube cannot go back any farther, the picture will be out of focus until either the object or the camera backs up *(see 3.4)*. So an extreme closeup of a very small object requires a wide-angle lens, which has a shorter focal length and for which the tube travel within the camera is sufficient. Of course, extreme closeups with wide-angle lenses cause lighting problems, because the camera blocks out the light when it is close to the object. Closeups of this nature must be carefully planned before the show.

Zoom-Lens Focusing A zoom lens has several internal lens elements that move in relation to one another when you zoom as well as when you focus. One set of these sliding elements, normally located at the front part of the lens, takes care of the focusing. The focus controls, which come in various configurations, are usually mounted on one of the panning handles, or attached close to the actual zoom control (see page 53).

Assuming that neither the object nor the camera moves very much, you won't have to focus while zooming in or out provided that you have properly *preset your zoom.* This procedure is slightly different for monochrome than for color cameras. Since it is explained more readily on monochrome cameras than on color cameras, we will discuss prefocusing in order of camera complexity.

When you are *zoom prefocusing for a monochrome camera*—let us assume that you will have to zoom in and out on the newscaster and the map behind him—these are the steps you must take:

1. *Zoom all the way out* to a long shot (widest angle lens setting on your zoom lens). Now focus up on the scene with the *camera focus control.* In effect, you are moving the pickup tube relative to the lens, very much like focusing a turret lens.

2. As soon as you are in focus, zoom all the way in *to the map,* the object farthest away from the camera that needs to be included in your shot. Most likely the map will look out of focus. Do *not* correct focus now with the camera focus control. Rather, focus up on the map with the *zoom control.* Make sure that you are zoomed in all the way, to your narrowest angle lens setting.

3. Now zoom back again slowly, without touching any focus control. You should remain in focus throughout the zoom. Sometimes, when you are zoomed out all the way again, you may have to touch up the focus just a little with your *camera focus control.* Then zoom in again, and check whether you are still in focus on the closeup of the map. If not, correct the focus again very slightly with the zoom control. By now, you should have a fairly even focus throughout your zoom range.

Because the adjustment with the camera focus concerns the "back matter" of the camera—the pickup tube—this focus is called *back focus.* The closeup adjustment with the zoom focus concerns "front matter" of the camera—the lens elements

in the zoom lens. This focus is, therefore, called *front focus.*

As soon as you move your camera into a different position, you must obviously go through another presetting procedure. Otherwise, your zoom will most likely not remain in focus from the new location.

Zoom prefocusing for color cameras is a very different process. Since the internal optical system of the color camera is extremely critical in its alignment, the pickup tubes cannot be moved for focusing. Therefore, there is no easy way of back-focusing, and indeed, the internal optical system is set in such a way that the camera is more or less permanently backfocused. The color camera has no camera focus (which you would need for back-focusing) but only a front focus, the zoom-lens focus controls.

Here is what you should do to preset your zoom on a color camera:

1. Zoom *all the way in* on the farthest object in your zoom range, like the map behind the newscaster. Focus on the map with the zoom focus control. In effect, you are adjusting the front focus.

2. Zoom all the way back to your widest angle lens setting. Since the back focus is already adjusted for this lens setting, your scene—the whole news set—should be reasonably in focus. If not, once again make a slight adjustment with the zoom focus control.

3. Now zoom in again. You should maintain focus pretty much throughout the entire zoom range.

Because of the preset back focus in a color camera, you may find that the wide-angle shots are slightly out of focus, at least not quite as crisp as you may like them to be. But if you have to compromise with your focus, it is better to have a crisper, sharper closeup picture of an object and a slightly softer long shot (wide-angle view) of the scene than the other way around. Also, the

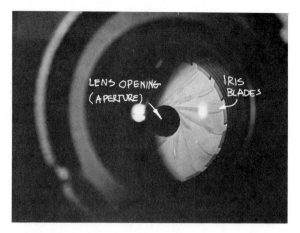

3·5 Lens Iris: The lens iris, or diaphragm, consists of a series of thin metal blades that form, through partial overlapping, a lens opening of variable size.

3·6 *f*-Stop: The *f*-stop is a calibration that indicates how large or small the iris, or lens opening, is.

colors themselves help to define the overall scene sufficiently so that a slightly softer focus is generally unnoticeable on the home receiver.[1]

Like long-focal-length lenses, the zoom lens sets some limitations on how close the camera can get to an object and still remain in focus. Without special attachments, the closest focusing distance for most zoom lenses lies between two and four feet with the lens zoomed in all the way to its maximum focal length, or, as it is frequently called, maximum *telephoto position*. In wider-angle positions, you can, of course, move the camera or object somewhat closer without losing focus.

f-Stop

Similar to photographic film, the camera pickup tube will operate properly only within a certain range of light intensity. If too little light falls on

the pickup tube, or tubes, the picture quality will suffer as much as if it receives too much light. Since you will probably use the camera not only indoors but also outdoors on remote telecasts, you will have to adjust for the extreme difference in light. There are several ways of controlling the light level. First, in the studio you can regulate the lighting itself. Second, if you are outdoors, you have recourse to a variety of *neutral density filters* that admit a certain amount of light. Third, and most importantly, the lens itself has a *diaphragm,* or *iris,* that can be "opened up" to permit more light to pass through the lens, or "stopped down," made smaller, to permit less light to enter. The opening in the diaphragm is called *aperture (see 3.5).*

On a fixed-focal-length lens, there is a ring around the lens barrel (similar to the distance calibration) that, when turned clockwise or counterclockwise, will either increase (open) or reduce (close down) the iris opening. The different positions of lens (iris or diaphragm) openings are calibrated in *f*-stops. The *smaller the f-stop number,* such

---

[1] Herbert Zettl, *Sight-Sound-Motion* (Belmont, Calif.: Wadsworth Publishing Co., 1973), pp. 187–188.

as *f*/1.4, the *larger* the iris *opening.* The *larger the f-stop number,* such as *f*/22, the *smaller* the iris *opening. (See 3.6.)*

The quality of a lens is measured not by how little light it allows to enter the camera (small aperture with large *f*-stop number) but by how much light it lets in (large aperture with small *f*-stop number). A *fast lens,* which permits a large amount of light to enter, can be used in low-light-level conditions. A *slow lens,* through which relatively little light can pass, requires relatively high-level lighting conditions. In general, short-focal-length (wide-angle) lenses are faster than long-focal-length (narrow-angle or telephoto) lenses.

Zoom lenses for color cameras (for the 1-inch or 1¼ -inch Plumbicon pickup tube formats) have a maximum aperture (iris opening) of *f*/1.8 or *f*/2.0. The zoom lenses for the I-O pickup tube format are generally slower.

Since the iris opening is one of the most important video control elements, it is usually remotely controlled by the video operator. In fact, it is changed continually during a telecast in order to control and balance the light striking the camera tube, or tubes. The more sophisticated color cameras have an automatic iris control: the camera senses the light entering the lens and adjusts the lens opening in such a way as to produce an optimal picture.

Depth of Field

If you place objects at different distances from the camera, some of them will be in focus and some of them out. The area in which objects are seen in focus, called "depth of field," can be shallow or great. When it is shallow, only objects in the middleground will be in focus; the foreground and background will be out of focus. When the depth of field is great, all objects (in the fore-, middle-, and backgrounds) will be in focus.

If the depth of field is great, you will find it rather easy to keep the performer in focus, although he or she may move rapidly toward or away from your camera. If the depth of field is shallow, he or she will have to move very slowly toward or away from your camera in order to stay in focus.

The same rules apply, of course, when the camera moves. A great depth of field makes it easy for you to stay in focus while dollying. A shallow depth of field makes it extremely difficult to dolly without getting out of focus *(see 3.7).*

It seems as though a very great depth of field would be the most desirable condition in television studio operation. But a medium depth is often preferred because then the in-focus objects are set off against a slightly out-of-focus background. Thus, the object will be emphasized, and busy background designs or the inevitable smudges on the television scenery will receive little attention. Foreground, middleground, and background will be better defined.[2]

You can control the depth of field by coordinating three factors:

1. The focal length of the lens used. Given a fixed camera-to-object distance, short-focal-length lenses, or wide-angle zoom positions, have a great depth of field. Long lenses, or narrow-angle zoom positions, have a shallow depth of field.

2. The lens opening (*f*-stop). Large lens openings (small *f*-stop numbers) cause a shallow depth of field. Small lens openings cause a great depth of field. A low light level will necessitate the opening of the lens diaphragms and a subsequent decrease in the depth of field. More light will permit you to stop down your lens (decrease the lens opening) and thereby increase the depth of field.

3. The distance between camera and object. The farther away the object is from the camera, the greater the depth of field. The closer the object is to the camera, the shallower the depth of field.

---

[2] Zettl, *Sight-Sound-Motion,* pp. 188–191.

3·7   Depth of Field.

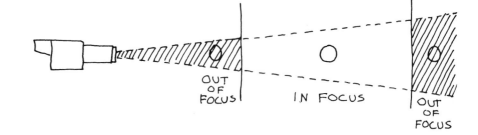

OUT OF FOCUS   IN FOCUS   OUT OF FOCUS

In a closeup with a wide-angle lens, or a zoom lens zoomed out (wide-angle position), for instance, your distance from camera to object will be small; the initially large depth of field (wide-angle lens) will become quite shallow (distance from camera to object is small). If a similar closeup is taken with a long lens, or a zoom lens zoomed in (narrow-angle or telephoto position), the distance from object to camera may be comparatively great (great depth of field); the long focal length of the lens, however, will reduce the depth of field considerably.

When you are zoomed in, you have a shallow depth of field; when zoomed out, you have a larger depth of field. *In general, we can say that closeups have a shallow depth of field, long shots a great depth of field.* Quite frequently, a shallow depth of field can work to your advantage. Let us assume that you are about to take a quick closeup of a medium-sized object, such as a can of dog food. You don't have to bother to put up a special background for it. All you need to do is to move your camera back and zoom in on the display (or use a narrow-angle lens). Your zoom lens will now be in a telephoto (narrow-angle) position, decreasing the depth of field to a large extent. Your background will now be sufficiently out of focus to prevent undesirable distractions. This technique is called *selective focus,* meaning that you can focus either on the foreground, with the middleground and background out of focus; or on the middleground, with the

foreground and background out of focus; or on the background, with the foreground and middleground out of focus.

You can also shift emphasis from one object to another quite easily with the help of selective focus. For example, you can zoom in on a foreground camera, thus reducing the depth of field, and focus (with your zoom lens at the telephoto position) on it. Then, by simply "racking focus"—that is, by refocusing—on the person behind it, you can quickly shift the emphasis from the camera (foreground) to the person about to take a picture (middleground). *(See 3.8.)*

The advantage of a shallow depth of field also applies to unwanted foreground objects. In a baseball pickup, for example, the camera behind home plate may have to shoot through the fence wire. But since your camera will most likely be zoomed in on the pitcher, or other players performing at a considerable distance from the camera, you will work with a relatively short depth of field. Consequently, everything fairly close to the camera, such as the fence wire, will be so much out of focus that for all practical purposes it becomes invisible. The same principle works for shooting through bird cages, prison bars, or similar foreground objects.

A large depth of field is necessary when there is considerable movement of camera and/or subjects. Also, when two objects are located at widely different distances from the camera, a great depth

a

b

3·8 Selective Focus: (a) In this shot, the camera (foreground object) is out of focus, drawing attention to the woman (middleground); (b) here, the focus is shifted from the woman (middleground) to the camera (foreground).

of field will enable you to keep them both in focus simultaneously. Most outdoor telecasts, such as sports events and other remotes, require a large depth of field, the principal objective being to help the viewer see as much and as well as possible. Fortunately, during daytime remotes, there is usually enough light to stop down the lenses considerably, an arrangement which, as we have seen, will help to increase the depth of field. In night telecasts, make sure that there is enough light so that you can work within a reasonably great depth of field.

Performance Characteristics

The performance characteristic of a lens refers to what it can and cannot do, and how it generally behaves in common production practice. Since the camera will process only the information the lens can see, a knowledge of the performance characteristics of lenses will aid you greatly in many production tasks. As a director or associate director, for example, you must know which lens or zoom-lens position to use in order to let the viewer see the important parts of an event. Or you may want to use a specific zoom position or lens in order to achieve an important aesthetic effect. As a microphone boom operator, you must know how lenses function so that you can keep your microphone out of the picture yet as close to the sound source as possible. As talent, your knowledge of lenses will aid you in where to look, how to move, or how to hold an object so that the camera can see it as well as possible.

Three topics especially pertinent to the discussion of performance characteristics of television lenses are: (1) field of view, including focal length and zoom range, (2) relationship of focal length to performance, and (3) operational controls.

3·9   10:1 Zoom Range: (a) Zoomed out: at 20 feet (or approximately 6m) away from the camera, the field of view is 15 feet (or approximately 4.5m) wide. (b) Zoomed in: at 20 feet from the camera, the field of view is now only 1.5 feet wide (1/10 of the wide-angle field of view).

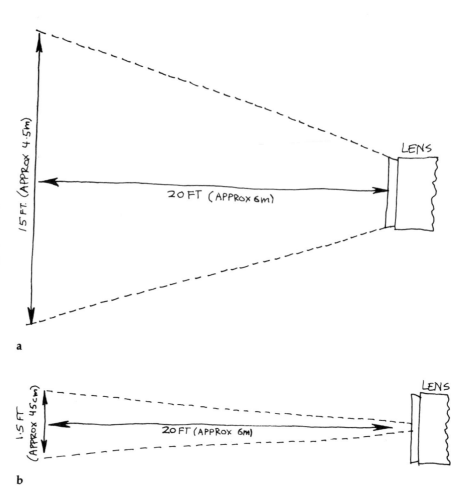

Field of View

Field of view refers to how much of a scene you can see through a particular lens. The wide-angle, or short, lens—through which you can see more—gives you a wider field of view than the narrow-angle, or long, lens. The same is true for a zoom lens. At the widest zoom setting, or widest focal-length position, you have the widest field of view, or the greatest vista. At the narrowest zoom set-ting, or narrowest focal-length or telephoto posi-tion, you have the narrowest field of view. But what you see is greatly enlarged, especially the middleground and background objects. Between the widest zoom position (all the way out) and the extreme telephoto position (all the way in) —the *zoom range*—there are innumerable grada-tions. Since most zoom lenses have a 10:1 or 15:1 zoom range, the field of view increases or decreases approximately tenfold or fifteenfold. To visualize a 10:1 zoom range, imagine that you are standing twenty feet, or approximately six meters, away from the camera. Assuming that your zoom lens (for 1-inch Plumbicon) has a range of 17mm to 170mm, it will cover a field of view approximately 15 feet (or roughly 4.5 meters) wide when zoomed all the way out *(see 3.9a)*. You will be able to move a good seven feet to either side of the stationary camera and still remain in the camera's field of view. When zoomed all the way in, however, you had better stand in one place, without moving at all *(see 3.9b)*. The camera's field of view has appropriately enough shrunk to one-tenth of the wide-angle zoom position, to 1.5 feet (roughly 45 cm).

When the camera is used outdoors, or in large indoor spaces, the normal 10:1, or even 15:1, zoom range no longer suffices. Most likely, you will find that your widest angle zoom position is too wide to be useful, and that your most extreme telephoto position does not get close enough to the event. Zoom lenses come, therefore, with a variety of *range extenders,* which are either attached to the front of the lens or activated automatically by a simple switch. Three range extenders usually fulfill most production requirements: one that extends the maximum focal length by 1.5 times, another that doubles the maximum focal length (2.0 times), and still another that extends the maximum focal length by 2.5 times. But as soon as you put on a range extender, you automatically lose your original widest angle, or shortest focal length, position of the lens. The lens retains its 10:1 zoom ratio. You simply start a little closer to the object with a range extender, and therefore get a little closer to the object in your extreme telephoto position. Let's use our 10:1 zoom lens, which has a range from 17mm to 170mm and see how the 1.5x, the 2x, and the 2.5x range extenders influence the focal-length range.

3·10 The different-sized Plumbicon tubes require slightly different lens formats. Zoom lenses that fit the 1-inch (25mm) Plumbicon pickup tubes exclusively vary in size slightly from those that are made for the 1¼-inch (30mm) pickup tube format. Since the optical and performance characteristics of the lenses are quite similar, we will largely ignore this difference.

3·11

The most common wide-angle zoom positions are:

For color cameras: 17mm (or wider)–30mm

For I-O cameras: 35mm–60mm

The most common wide-angle turret lenses are:

For I-O cameras: 35mm (extreme wide-angle lens)

                       50mm (or 2-in, wide-angle lens on normal turret)

For vidicon cameras: 10mm (extreme wide-angle)

                       12½mm (½-in, wide-angle lens on normal turret)

Normal zoom range without
extenders: 17mm–170mm

With 1.5x range extender: 25.5mm–255mm

With 2.0x range extender: 34mm–340mm

With 2.5x range extender: 42.5mm–425mm

Unfortunately, range extenders are not without disadvantages. The rule that says, the longer the maximum focal length, the slower the lens, applies also to the range extenders. The $f/2$ of the above zoom lens is reduced with the range extenders to $f/3$, $f/4$, and $f/5$, respectively; so obviously the 2.5x range extender requires a large amount of light. If used outdoors in daylight, the range extenders work quite well; indoors, with limited lighting, they can present a serious production problem. The added lens elements of the range extenders, which act in effect as a magnifying glass, sometimes impair the overall crispness of the picture. Try, therefore, to move your camera as close to the event as possible, so that you can do without range extenders. If you have to use them, make sure that enough light is available for the reduced aperture.

The tables on pages 43, 44, and 48 will give you information on the most common zoom ranges and the focal lengths of turret lenses.

Focal Length and Performance

In order to discuss the relationship of focal length to the performance characteristics of the lens, we will group the focal lengths of the turret lenses, as well as the focal-length positions of the zoom lens within its range, into (1) wide-angle (short-focal-length) lenses, or wide zoom-lens position; (2) the normal lens, or midrange zoom-lens position; and (3) the narrow-angle (long-focal-length, or telephoto) lens, or telephoto zoom-lens position.

The Wide-Angle Lens, or Wide Zoom-Lens Position   When speaking of the relationship between focal length of a lens and its performance characteristics, these factors should be considered: (1) field of view and object proportion, (2) dolly capability and object speed, (3) maximum aperture (iris opening), and (4) focus capability and depth of field.

The wide-angle lens gives you a *wide vista.* You can have a relatively wide field of view with the scene rather close to the camera. With a wide-angle lens, you can make a small room or studio look quite large, or stretch normal hallways into seemingly endless tunnels. Objects relatively close to the camera look large, and objects only a short distance away look relatively small. The *proportions* of the object are therefore *exaggerated* by the wide-angle lens. This distortion—large foreground objects, and small middleground and background objects—helps to increase the illusion of depth. Since parallel lines seem to converge faster than we ordinarily perceive with this kind of lens, you can create a forced perspective that makes objects—desks, automobiles, houses—look longer than they actually are. *(See 3.12 through 3.15.)*

This distortion, however, can also work against you. If you take a closeup of a face with a wide-angle lens, the nose, which is closest to the lens, is unusually large compared to the more distant parts of the face *(see 3.16).* In an extreme wide-angle position, or with an extreme wide-angle lens, you may notice that the vertical lines of the background appear to be somewhat curved. This is called "barrel distortion," because the vertical lines look like the curved sides of a barrel.

Looking down on an object can also create undesirable distortions. A closeup of a washing machine, for instance, shows an obvious distortion when the camera dollies in and observes it from above *(see 3.17).* You can reduce such distor-

a

b

3·12 Wide-Angle Distortion: (a) Here, the dock building appears to be much longer than it is. Note that the mooring line is larger in the foreground than the entire ship. (b) Even a small car, like a VW, can be made to look like a rather powerful racer.

3·13 The length of this hallway is greatly exaggerated by the wide-angle lens.

3·14 Ordinary gestures can become quite commanding through wide-angle lens distortion. Note how the hand, which is relatively close to the lens, is larger than the woman's head just a short distance behind.

3·15   Shooting through a prominent foreground piece with the wide-angle lens creates a spatially articulated, forceful picture.[3]

3·16   Wide-angle lens distortion of a face is generally undesirable, unless you want to imply in the shot some psychological distortion.

tions by placing the objects on a level approximate with the lens height *(see 3.18)*.

Another negative aspect of the wide-angle lens is overshooting. The wide-angle view of the lens does not stop where the scenery ends. If you overshoot the set on top or at the sides, the great depth of field will point up the overshot areas clearly and embarrassingly.

The wide-angle lens is a good *dolly lens,* because its wide field of view de-emphasizes camera wobbles and bumps. The great depth of field of the lens helps you to keep in focus while dollying. Unless you have to move the camera in quite close to the subject, you probably will have to adjust the focus only minimally, if at all.

Unfortunately, the zoom lens makes it so convenient to move from a long shot to a closeup or vice versa that dollying with a color camera has almost become a lost art. But there is a significant aesthetic difference between a zoom and a dolly.

While the zoom seems to bring the scene toward the viewer, a dolly seems to take the viewer into the scene.[4] Since the camera does not move during a zoom, the spatial relationships between objects remain constant. The objects appear to be glued into position; they simply get bigger (zoom in) or smaller (zoom out). In a dolly, however, the relationships between objects change constantly. You seem to be moving past and around them; you are enticed to participate more in the action than during a zoom. But it is just as easy to dolly with a zoom in a wide-angle position as with a wide-angle lens. There is only one problem. At the end of your dolly, you can't all of a sudden zoom in from the new position without first presetting your zoom again. Otherwise, you will surely get out of focus, or at best have a difficult time adjusting focus while zooming.

The wider the lens or the zoom position, the more rapidly the objects increase or decrease in

---

[3] Zettl, *Sight-Sound-Motion,* pp. 211–213.

[4] Zettl, *Sight-Sound-Motion,* pp. 194–197, 288.

3·17 The wide-angle lens distortion in this shot makes the washing machine appear much too dynamic and unstable.

3·18 When shot more from eye level (either by lowering the camera or by placing the object closer to lens height), or by using a longer lens, the undesirable effect of distortion is greatly reduced.

size during a dolly, and the more exaggerated the dolly speed becomes. Similarly, the movement of objects toward and away from the camera seems greatly accelerated by the wide-angle lens.

The *f-stop rating* of a zoom lens applies over the entire zoom range. A maximum iris opening of $f/2$, for example, does not decrease (to $f/2.8$ or $f/3$) during the zoom in. It will remain at $f/2$ even in its telephoto position because the diaphragm is adjusted automatically as the lens changes focal length.

Fixed-focal-length lenses, on the other hand, become slower the longer they get. This means that wide-angle lenses have generally a wider maximum iris opening (lower *f*-stop) than long, or narrow-angle, lenses. Under unfavorable lighting conditions, you may still get acceptable pictures with the fast wide-angle lens, but you may not be able to use the slower narrow-angle (long-focal-length) lenses.

As you remember, wide-angle lenses have a *large depth of field.* You can therefore get very close

to the object with a wide-angle lens and still rack the pickup tube back far enough (in monochrome cameras) to keep in focus. Even with a zoom lens you can sometimes produce a larger screen image by zooming out to a fairly wide-angle position and moving the camera close to the subject than by simply zooming in to a narrow-angle lens position at some distance from the subject.

Be sure to check carefully, however, on whether the camera can get physically close enough to the object. Sometimes a large dolly, the zoom lens itself, or even the sunshade on a long lens mounted on the turret with the wide-angle lens, may prevent you from pushing the camera close enough to obtain the desired closeup.

The Normal Lens, or Midrange of the Zoom Lens While the wide-angle lens makes objects seem farther apart and rooms larger than they actually are, *normal lenses,* or midrange zoom positions, make objects and their spatial relationships appear close to our normal vision.

3·19   The most common midrange zoom positions are:

For color cameras: 35mm–45mm

For I-O cameras: 75mm–90mm

The most common normal lens on a turret is:

For I-O cameras: 75mm or 90mm

For vidicon cameras: 25mm, or 1-in lens

3·20   The most common narrow-angle, or telephoto, zoom range positions for studio use are:

For color cameras: 50mm–200mm without range extenders

For I-O cameras: 135mm–400mm (16 in) without range extenders

The most common narrow-angle turret lenses are:

For I-O cameras: 135mm, 8-in (200mm), and 12-in (300mm)

For vidicon cameras: 75mm (3-in), 100mm (4-in)

For field use, range extenders are used with zoom lenses (see table on page 44). There are also fixed-focal-length lenses available:

For I-O cameras: 15-in, 17-in, and 25-in field lenses

For vidicon cameras: 6-in (152mm) and 12-in (300mm)

The normal lens is a reasonably *good dolly lens* although camera wobbles become a little more noticeable than with the wide-angle lens. Also, you will find that it is harder to keep in focus while dollying with the normal lens than with the wide-angle lens.

The normal lens is still a *fast lens* (large maximum iris opening) and permits good closeups without your having to bring the camera too close to the object.

When shooting graphics, especially title cards, you should use the normal lens or put the zoom into the midrange position. This method has several advantages: (1) You can quickly correct the framing on the card by zooming in or out slightly, or by dollying just a little in or out without undue focus changes. (2) You will be far enough away from the easel to avoid camera shadows, yet close enough so that the danger of someone's walking in front of your camera is minimal. (3) The floor-person, by placing the easel at a standard distance from the camera, can help you frame up and focus on the easel card with a minimum of effort and time.

The most common mistake is to zoom in on an easel card from a fairly great distance. There are three major disadvantages to this method: (1) Your focus at the telephoto zoom position is quite critical. (2) If the director requires a closer shot when you are zoomed in most of the way already, you will have to move the whole camera closer to the easel and preset your focus again—a maneuver that can be quite time- and energy-consuming. (3) As already mentioned, if you are too far from the easel, studio personnel unaware that you are focused on the easel card may walk right in front of your camera.

With the normal lens, you can get fairly close to the object and still be able to focus up.

The Narrow-Angle Lens, or Telephoto Zoom Lens Position   The narrow-angle, or long, lens

3·21 By using a telephoto lens, the background is greatly enlarged compared to the foreground. The distance between the cars seems, therefore, reduced and the impression of a traffic jam is heightened.

3·22 This shot was taken with a zoom lens in an extremely long focal length position. Note how the runner, the pitcher, the batter, the catcher, and the umpire all seem to stand only a few feet apart from one another. As you know, the actual distance between the pitcher and the batter is 60½ feet.

has a *narrow field of view,* and it magnifies objects in the lens's field of view. Because the enlarged background objects look rather big in comparison to the foreground objects, an illusion is created that the distance between foreground, middle-ground, and background has decreased. The long lens seems to shrink the space between the objects, in direct contrast to the effect created by the wide-angle lens, which exaggerates object proportions and therefore seems to increase relative distance between objects. A narrow-angle lens, or a zoom lens in its telephoto position, crowds objects on the screen.

This crowding effect can be positive or negative. If you want to show how crowded the freeways are during rush hour, for example, use a long lens, or use your zoom lens in the telephoto position. The long focal length will reduce the distance between the cars and make them appear to be driving bumper to bumper *(see 3.21).*

But such depth distortions by the narrow-angle lens also work to disadvantage. You are certainly familiar with the deceptive closeness of the pitcher to home plate on your television screen. This depth distortion occurs because the zoom lens is used in a fairly extreme telephoto position, since the camera is placed far to the rear of the pitcher, on the other side of the field from home plate. Since in most sports events, television cameras must remain at a considerable distance from the action, the zoom lenses usually operate at their extreme telephoto positions or with powerful range extenders. The resulting telephoto effect of shrinking space makes it difficult for the viewer to judge actual distances and to tell with accuracy who is ahead of whom *(see 3.22).*

You *cannot dolly* with a *long lens,* or with a zoom lens in its telephoto range. Its magnifying power makes any movement of the camera impossible. If you work outdoors, even wind can become a

3·23   Among the many manufacturers of optical equipment and lenses, there are four whose top-quality television lenses have found wide acceptance here in the United States and elsewhere. Their products are the Japanese *Canon* lenses, the French *Angenieux* lenses, the British *Rank-Taylor-Hobson Varotal* lenses, and the German *Schneider Variogon* lenses. The more expensive Angenieux and Schneider lenses are considered the best in the field.

3·24   Most *lens turrets* are equipped to hold four different lenses. The most common studio lens complement consists of a wide-angle lens, a medium lens, and a narrow-angle lens. It is good practice to put the widest-angle lens on your turret opposite the longest lens because then you will avoid having the long lens show in your wide-angle picture. The problem of a lens visible in the picture is sometimes called "cropping." If you use a standard lens complement, cropping is no problem, whatever the position of the lenses on the turret may be.

The *standard lens complement* for an I-O camera turret is (1) the 50mm lens—a wide-angle lens; (2) the 75mm or 90mm lens—the normal lens; and (3) the 127mm or 135mm lens. The standard lens turret is often referred to as the 2–3–5-inch turret (corresponding to the 50mm or 2-inch lens, the 75mm or 3-inch lens, and the 127mm or 5-inch lens).

Some television stations include in their standard lens complement the 8-inch or 8½-inch lens, which enables you to get fast closeups of objects located at a considerable distance from the camera.

The standard lens complement for vidicon turret cameras is a 12.5mm (½-inch) for the wide-angle lens, a 25mm (1-inch) for the normal lens, and a 75mm (3-inch), or a 100mm (4-inch) for the narrow-angle lens.

problem. A stiff breeze may shake the camera to such a degree that the greatly magnified vibrations become clearly visible on the television screen.

In the studio, the telephoto position of the zoom lens may present another problem for you. The director may have you zoom in on part of an event, such as the lead guitar in a band concert, and then, after you have zoomed in, ask you to truck (move the camera sideways) past the other members of the band. But this movement is extremely difficult to do in the telephoto zoom position. Rather you should dolly in with a *wide-angle zoom position* and then truck, with the lens still in the wide-angle position.

Another important performance characteristic of the long lens, or the zoom lens in a telephoto position, is the illusion of reduced speed of an object moving toward or away from the camera. Since the narrow-angle lens changes the size of an object moving toward or away from the camera much more gradually than the wide-angle lens, the object seems to move more slowly than it actually does; in fact, an extreme narrow-angle lens virtually eliminates such movement. The object does not seem to change its size perceptibly even when it is traveling a considerably large distance relative to the camera. Such a slowdown is especially effective if you want to emphasize the frustration of someone running but not getting anywhere.

As pointed out before, the relatively slow, narrow-angle lenses usually have a *smaller maximum aperture* than wide-angle lenses and, as a result, need more light. Zoom lenses maintain their maximum aperture throughout the entire zoom range, but range extenders reduce the aperture rating of the lens considerably.

Since narrow-angle lenses have a rather *shallow depth of field*, any object that is moving fairly close to the camera is difficult to keep in focus. If someone walks toward the camera past the minimum

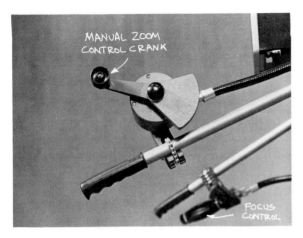

3·25 Zoom Control: With most zoom controls, you turn the handle clockwise to zoom in and counterclockwise to zoom out. The faster you turn the handle, the faster the zoom will be.

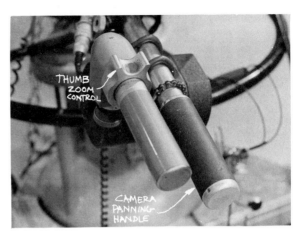

3·26 Servo Zoom Control: This zoom control is simply mounted next to the camera panning handle.

distance you need to keep in focus, the person will go out of focus. No amount of screaming from the control room personnel will help to correct this problem. If, however, the action happens quite a distance from the camera, the lens acts more like a wide-angle lens again (since the field of view increases) and therefore your depth of field increases accordingly.

Operational Controls

You need two basic controls to operate a zoom lens: (1) the *zoom control unit,* which activates the variable focal length of the lens (the zooming mechanism), and (2) the *focus control unit,* which activates the intricate focus mechanism in a zoom lens. Both zoom controls can be operated either *manually* or by automatic "servo" control.

Zoom Control Unit The *manual zoom* control usually consists of a small crank mounted on the right panning handle or on a special extender at the right of the camera. A small lever next to the crank enables you to select at least two turning ratios, slow or fast. The slow ratio is for normal zooming, the fast for exceptionally fast zooms. Some manual controls have two levers that allow four adjustable zooming speeds. When you turn the crank, a special zoom drive cable mechanically activates the zoom mechanism in the lens. Obviously, the faster you turn the crank, the faster the zoom will be. *(See 3.25.)*

The *servo zoom control* unit does not activate the lens mechanism directly; rather, it signals a complex motor system that in turn drives the zoom mechanism in the lens. In actual operation, the servo control unit is quite similar to the mechanical zoom controls. It is normally mounted on the right panning handle, and you zoom in and out by moving the thumb lever either right or left. The farther you move the lever from its original central position, the faster the zoom will be. A

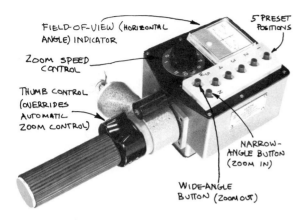

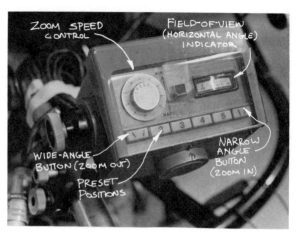

3·27 Shot Box: The shot box comes in a variety of configurations, but with similar components, such as the field-of-view meter, zoom speed control, wide-angle and narrow-angle zoom buttons, and buttons for preset positions.

two-speed switch permits you to select a zoom speed four times as fast as the normal zoom rate. With the servo system, the zoom speed is automatically reduced as the zoom approaches either of the extreme zoom positions. This reduction prevents jerks and abrupt stops when you reach the end of the zoom range. *(See 3.26.)*

There are several advantages to the servo system: (1) Your zoom will be steady and smooth, especially during extremely slow zooms. (2) The zoom control is easy to operate and allows you to concentrate more on other camera functions, such as panning, tilting, and focusing. (3) With the automatic zoom slowdown, you will never get caught reaching the end of the zoom range at full speed.

To make the zoom even more precise, a zoom preset system has been developed, called a *shot box.* Generally mounted on the right panning handle, it allows you to preset any of a number of zoom speeds (up to twelve in some models) and several (four or five) zoom positions. By activating wide-

and narrow-angle buttons or switches, your lens will zoom either out or in. A special meter indicates the angle of view of the lens. The shot box is usually combined with a servo zoom control unit that lets you override the shot box at any time. *(See 3.27.)*

Focus Control Unit   The *manual focus control* unit ordinarily consists of a twist grip, very similar to a motorcycle handle. It is generally mounted on the left panning handle. Two or three turns are usually sufficient to achieve focus over the full zoom range.

As with the zoom, the focus operations are transferred by drive cable from the panning handle control to the lens. *(See 3.28.)* The most common servo focus control unit is a three-spoked capstan wheel. *(See 3.29.)* It is generally mounted in the left panning handle or attached directly to the side of the shot box.

There are provisions for fast and slow focusing

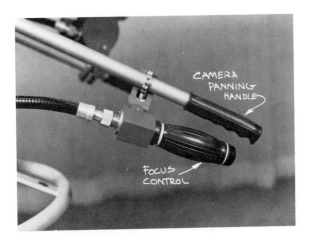

3·28 Manual Focus Control: The twist grip of the manual focus control turns clockwise and counter-clockwise for focusing.

speeds and for compensating the turning of the focus control when the lens reaches long focal lengths. Remember, the tighter the shot, the smaller the depth of field. Consequently, when you zoom in for a tight shot, the focus becomes more critical as you get tighter, and you therefore have to increase the turns of the focus control. The servo system can compensate for this change and keep the turning rate constant. Because of their experience with mechanical focus devices, however, most camera operators are already so used to the different turning ratios at close range that even with the servo system they prefer to compensate for the different close-range focus requirements themselves. The switch is, therefore, frequently left in the "uncompensated" position.

For similar reasons, the servo focus control unit is not very popular. The preselected focus is useful only when the positions of the camera and subject are exactly the same in the show as in the rehearsal.

3·29 Servo Focus Control: The servo focus control does not transfer your movement of the focus wheel mechanically; instead, it activates a motor that drives the focus mechanism in the zoom lens extremely smoothly.

3·30 Some of the portable broadcast cameras, and a number of nonbroadcast cameras, have rather simple zoom devices. Some zoom lenses are activated by a *small lever* that turns part of the lens clockwise or counterclockwise, thereby making the lens zoom in or out, respectively; or the front part of the lens is turned directly by hand.

Some of the simpler zoom lenses on nonbroadcast cameras are operated with a *control rod* that extends through the camera to the back. By pushing the rod in or pulling it out, you can zoom in or out. Some zoom lenses work in reverse. By pushing the rod in, you zoom out; and by pulling the rod back, you zoom in. By turning the focus wheel at the end of the rod, you can adjust focus while zooming. *(See a.)*

You *change turret lenses* by rotating the lens turret with the turret control handle in the back of the camera. By pressing the inside part of the turret handle back, you will release the turret so that it can be rotated either clockwise or counterclockwise. Once the desired lens is in the "on-the-air" position, which is marked by a dot on the camera, you should release the grip gently until it engages in a catch, thereby locking the turret solidly in its new position. Since the turret control is spring-loaded, be sure to depress and engage the turret handle slowly and easily; otherwise the loud clicks of the engaging springs will be picked up quite noticeably by the microphone. *(See b.)*

The focus control for turret cameras is a knob on the right side of the camera. The number of turns of the knob necessary to keep the picture in focus depends on the speed of the camera or object, the focal length of the lens used, and the iris opening of the lens. Some focusing knobs have an additional little crank that permits fast focusing *(see 2.3, page 12)*.

a   Zoom Rod

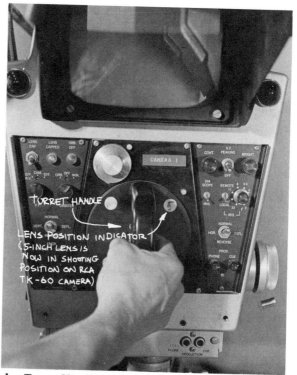

b   Turret Handle

Summary

The function of a lens on the television camera is to produce a small, clear optical image of the viewed scene on the front surface of the camera pickup tube. There are basically two types of lenses: (1) the variable-focal-length, or zoom, lens, and (2) the fixed-focal-length, or turret, lens.

The *zoom lens* can change its focal length continuously, which means that it can make an object appear to look far away or at close range, or make the "far" object move continuously closer, or the "close" object continuously farther away—all with the camera remaining in a fixed position. The fixed-focal-length lens shows only one particular angle of view. In order to make an object appear at close range, or farther away than with the lens used, we need to use lenses with different focal lengths, assuming that the camera does not move.

Important *optical characteristics* of lenses are (1) focal length, (2) focus, (3) *f*-stop, and (4) depth of field.

The *performance characteristics* of lenses are (1) field of view, including focal length and zoom range, (2) relationship of focal length to the performance of the lens, and (3) operational control units of the lens, such as zoom and focus controls.

Turret as well as zoom lenses are dependent upon the format (size of the target area) of the camera pickup tube or tubes.

All studio color cameras use zoom lenses.

4 Mounting Equipment and Camera Operations

Now that you have learned the major aspects of television cameras and their lenses, you need to know how to operate a camera. In this chapter we will take up four main topics, all of which relate to camera operation: (1) camera mounting equipment, (2) the most common camera movements, (3) how to work a camera in a production situation, and (4) some aspects of picture composition.

You will find that, although high-quality cameras may become considerably smaller and lighter than they presently are, you will still need a camera mount for smooth and efficient studio operation.

Camera Mounting Equipment

Ease and fluidity of camera movement are essential in television production. Three basic units have been developed that enable us to move the camera freely and smoothly about the studio: (1) the tripod dolly, (2) the studio pedestal, and (3) the studio crane.

The Tripod Dolly

The tripod dolly consists of a metal tripod usually fastened to a three-caster dolly base. The three casters can be used either in a freewheeling posi-tion, which ensures quick and easy repositioning of the camera in all directions, or locked into one position for straight-line dollying. If you don't want the dolly to move, you can lock each caster into a different direction so that each one works against the others. In effect, you have "put the brakes" on your tripod dolly. *(See 4.1.)*

Various cable guards in front of the casters help to prevent their rolling over or hitting the camera cable. Make sure that you screw the cable guards close to the studio floor, especially when using a small-diameter minicable on your camera.

That the tripod and the dolly base are collapsi-ble makes them the ideal camera mount for most remote operations. The tripod can also be adjusted to the height of the camera operator, but this manipulation takes time and energy. Quick and easy elevation of the camera is, therefore, not possible. *(See 4.2.)*

Arc To move the camera in a slightly curved dolly or truck.

Balance Relative structural stability of picture elements (objects or events). Balance can be stable (little pictorial tension), neutral (some tension), or unstable (high pictorial tension).

Bust Shot Framing of a person from the upper torso to the top of the head.

Cam Head A special camera mounting head that permits extremely smooth tilts and pans.

Closeup Object or any part of it seen at close range and framed tightly. The closeup can be extreme (extreme or big closeup) or rather loose (medium closeup).

Closure Short for psychological closure. Mentally filling in spaces of an incomplete picture.

Crab Sideways motion of the camera crane dolly base.

Cradle Head Cradle-shaped camera mounting head. Permits smooth up-and-down tilts and horizontal pans.

Crane 1. Camera dolly that resembles an actual crane in both appearance and operation. The crane can lift the camera from close to the studio floor to over ten feet above it. 2. To move the boom of the camera crane up or down. Also called boom.

Depth Staging Arrangement of objects on the television screen so that foreground, middleground, and background are clearly defined.

The Studio Pedestal

With the studio pedestal, you can dolly very smoothly, and elevate and lower the camera easily while on the air. The more portable field-studio pedestals still allow easy up-and-down movement, but not when the camera is on the air. This up-and-down movement adds an important dimension to the art of television photography. Not only can you adjust the camera to comfortable working height, but you can also look up at an event or down on it. We have known for centuries that looking up at a thing or an event makes it appear more powerful; looking down on it makes it less powerful than it would appear from eye level. With the studio pedestal you can, at least to some degree, bring about these points of view.

Of the great variety of available studio pedestals, we will consider only the most commonly

4·1 Locking Position of Tripod Dolly Wheels.

used: (1) the lightweight field-studio pedestal, (2) the counterweighted studio pedestal, and (3) the pneumatic studio pedestal.

Dolly 1. Camera support that enables the camera to move in all directions. 2. To move the camera toward (dolly in) or away from (dolly out or back) the object.

Headroom The space left between the top of the head and the upper screen edge.

Knee Shot Framing of a person from the knees up.

Long Shot Object seen from far away or framed very loosely. The extreme long shot shows the object from a great distance.

Medium Shot Object seen from a medium distance. Covers any framing between long shot and closeup.

Nose Room The space left in front of a person looking toward the edge of the screen.

Over-the-Shoulder Shot Camera looks over a person's shoulder (shoulder and back of head included in shot) at another person.

Pan Horizontal turning of the camera.

Pedestal 1. Heavy camera dolly that permits a raising and lowering of the camera while on the air. 2. To move the camera up and down via studio pedestal.

Tilt To point the camera up and down.

Tongue To move the boom with the camera from left to right or from right to left.

Truck To move the camera laterally by means of mobile camera mount.

Two-Shot Framing of two people.

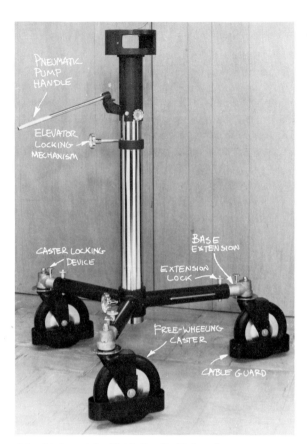

4·3   Lightweight Field-Studio Pedestal.

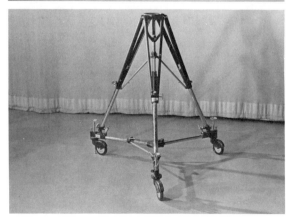

4·2   Tripod Dolly Collapsed and Assembled.

The Lightweight Field-Studio Pedestal   This pedestal is a cross between a tripod and a studio pedestal. The dolly with its sturdy, oversized casters can be easily separated from the pedestal. As with the tripod dolly, the casters can be either independently freewheeling or locked into up to six specific index positions, including the braking position. Most field-studio pedestals have adjustable cable guards.

The pedestal itself can be raised and lowered, either by a hand crank or pneumatically through

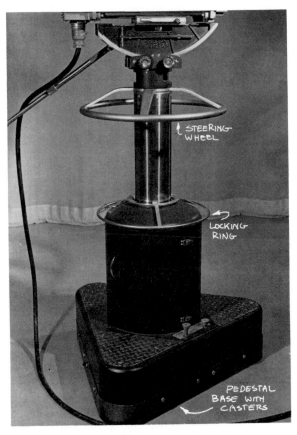

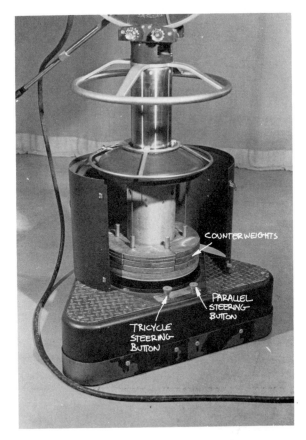

4·4 Counterweight Studio Pedestal.

compressed air. Neither method is smooth enough to allow the camera to be raised or lowered while on the air.

Whenever you use a tripod dolly or a field-studio pedestal on a remote, be especially careful with the assembly and operation of the camera mount. Since everybody is in a hurry during remote operations, the usual safety precautions are unfortunately not always upheld. Although field-studio pedestals are designed for heavy color cameras, the terrain on which you have to

dolly is never quite as smooth as your studio floor. A sudden stop may cause the camera to tip over, or at least receive a heavy jolt. *(See 4.3.).*

The Counterweighted Studio Pedestal This pedestal has proved to be one of the most reliable and workable pieces of studio production equipment. You can lower and raise the camera while on the air, and you can steer the pedestal smoothly in any direction with one control, the

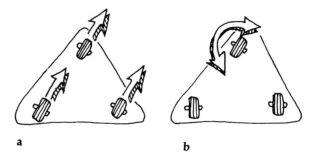

a   b

4·5   Pedestal Steering: (a) parallel; (b) tricycle.

STEERING WHEEL

AIR TANK
(COMPRESSED AIR
BALANCES WEIGHT
OF CAMERA)

CABLE
GUARD

4·6   Pneumatic Studio Pedestal.

large steering wheel. The pedestal column, which raises and lowers the camera, can be locked at any vertical position by a special device, usually a locking ring at the top of the counterweight base *(see 4.4)*. Generally, you work the pedestal in the parallel synchronized, or crab, steering position. This means that all three casters point in the same direction. If, however, you want to rotate the pedestal itself in order to get the whole piece of equipment closer to the easel, you must switch to the tricycle steering position in which only one wheel is steerable *(see 4.5)*.

The counterweight dolly is, however, not without disadvantages. It is very heavy to move about, especially when loaded down with a color camera, big zoom lens, and perhaps a teleprompter to boot. Because it is so heavy, it cannot be taken readily on remote location. While the camera can be elevated to about 6½ feet (approximately 2m) above the studio floor, it can be lowered to only about 4 feet (approximately 1.20m). This is low enough for most normal productions, but it can become a serious handicap if you want to use the camera creatively—in a drama, for example. From this height, you cannot tilt up the camera enough to look at somebody who is standing on the studio floor.

The Pneumatic Studio Pedestal   This pedestal operates quite similarly to the counterweighted studio pedestal. In fact, some models look so much alike that it is hard to tell at first glance which kind it is. They both have a large steering wheel that activates the synchronized or tricycle steering mechanism, and a smaller ring for locking the elevator column. But, because the pneumatic pedestal uses a column of compressed air to counterbalance the weight of the camera instead of actual weights, it is much lighter than the counterweighted pedestal. The advantage of the pneumatic pedestal is that you can maneuver it around much more easily. The disadvantage is that you need an air compressor to replenish the air that inevitably escapes even when you don't operate the dolly for some time.

Some pneumatic pedestals have an air tank for additional air and an electric brake that locks the pedestal into place at a particular camera height *(see 4.6)*.

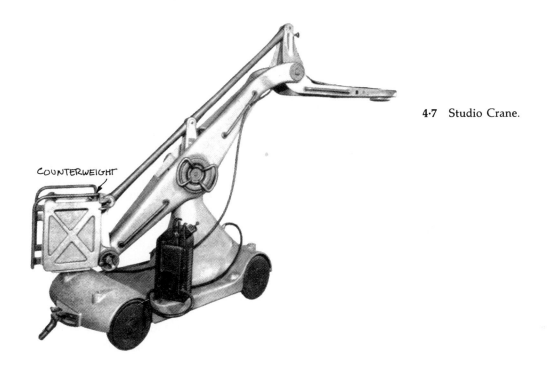

COUNTERWEIGHT

4·7   Studio Crane.

The Studio Crane

There are several types of studio cranes in use. All of them work on similar principles. Although a crane is desirable for creative camera work, it is of little use in small studio operation. In most cases, limited floor space and ceiling height prohibit the use of a big one (3 x 13 feet, approximately 1 x 4 meters, base). Also, a crane needs at least one dolly operator in addition to the camera operator; if motor-driven, then it needs two extra—the driver and the boom operator. These are sound reasons for its unpopularity in small stations. In colleges and universities, however, where studio facilities and manpower may very well accommodate the presence of a crane, important research in production techniques may necessitate its use.

A studio crane permits fast and multiple camera repositioning. The camera can be lowered to approximately two feet (61cm) off the studio floor and raised to about ten feet (approximately 3m). The crane boom can be panned a full 360 degrees, still allowing the camera a panning radius of 180 degrees. All movements can be carried out simultaneously, allowing excellent opportunities for creative camera work. *(See 4.7.)*

When a studio crane is used, it is desirable to install a monitor directly on the crane for the dolly operator to watch. The coordination of camera operator and dolly operator is essential for smooth and effective camera handling, and the latter will be greatly aided in his job if, in addition to listening to the director's signals, he can actually see the pictures the camera is taking.

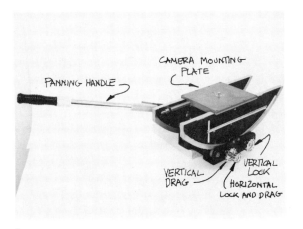

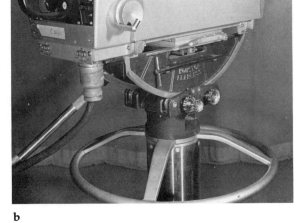

a   **b**

4·8   (a) Cradle Head. (b) Cradle Head with Camera
Mounted.

Camera Mounting Heads

The camera mounting heads connect the camera
to the tripod or camera pedestal. The mounting
head allows the camera to be tilted vertically and
panned horizontally. Two types of mounting
heads have proved to be most useful: (1) the cradle head, and (2) the cam head.

The *cradle head* assures fairly good camera balance, since the center of gravity of the camera is
evenly distributed for most tilting angles. If the
heavy camera tilts or pans too freely on the cradle
head, you can control the vertical tilting by adjusting the tilt drag, and the horizontal pan by
adjusting the pan brake. You can (and should)
lock the head for the tilt and the pan whenever
you leave the camera unattended.

The disadvantages of the cradle head include
a somewhat limited tilt range, and a certain difficulty in keeping the drag properly adjusted during heavy use *(see 4.8)*.

The *cam head* uses two cams, one on either side

of the mounting head, for balancing even the
heaviest of cameras during tilting and panning.
The cam head is better than the cradle in that it
keeps the camera perfectly balanced during the
entire tilt and allows for a greater tilt angle. Like
the cradle head, the cam head has individual tilt
and pan drag and locking controls. *(See 4.9.)*

Some cradle and cam heads use the *wedge mount,*
which simplifies the job of attaching the heavy
camera to the camera mounting head. A plate
with the male wedge is attached to the underside
of the camera, and then slid into the female wedge
plate, which has been bolted onto the cradle or
cam mounting head. Once you have adjusted the
wedge for proper camera balance, all you have to
do is slide it into the mounting-head wedge plate
and the camera will arrive at the properly balanced position. You will find that the wedge plate
is especially helpful during remotes, where you
constantly mount and dismount cameras. *(See
4.11.)*

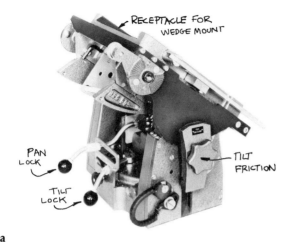

a   **b**

4·9 (a) Vinten Cam Head. (b) ITE Cam Head.

The Most Common Camera Movements

Before learning to operate a camera, you should become familiar with the most common camera movements. "Left" and "right" always refer to the camera's point of view. *(See 4.12.)*

Pan: Turning the camera horizontally, from left to right or from right to left. To "pan right," which means that you swivel the camera to the right (clockwise), you must push the panning handles to the left. To "pan left," which means to swivel the camera to the left (counterclockwise), you push the panning handles to the right.

Tilt: Making the camera point down or up. A "tilt up" means that the camera is made to point up gradually. A "tilt down" means that the camera is made to point down gradually.

Pedestal: Elevating or lowering the camera on a studio pedestal. To "pedestal up," you raise the pedestal; to "pedestal down," you lower the pedestal.

4·10 The most popular cam heads are the Houston Fearless and the slightly more sophisticated and flexible Vinten.

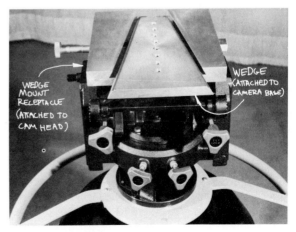

4·11 Wedge Mount.

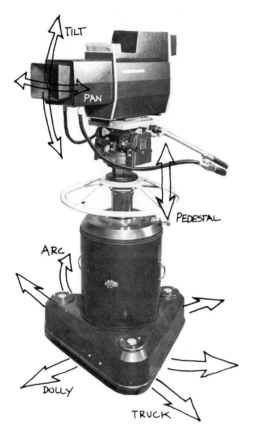 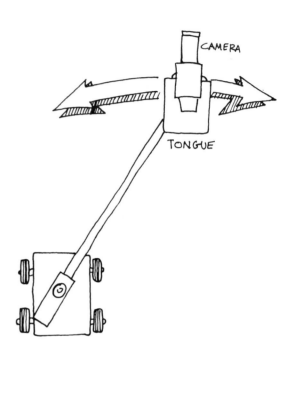

4·12 Principal Camera Movements.

Tongue: Moving the whole camera from left to right or from right to left with the boom of a camera crane. When you tongue left or right, the camera usually points into the same general direction, with only the boom moving left (counterclockwise) or right (clockwise).

Crane or Boom: Moving the whole camera up or down on a camera crane. The effect is somewhat similar to pedestaling up or down, except that the camera swoops over a much greater vertical distance. You either "crane, or boom, up" or "crane, or boom, down."

Dolly: Moving the camera toward or away from an object in more or less a straight line by means of a mobile camera mount. When you "dolly in," you move the camera closer to the object; when you "dolly out, or dolly back," you move the camera farther away from the object.

Truck: Moving the camera laterally by means of a mobile camera mount. To "truck left" means to move the camera mount to the left with the camera pointing at a right angle to the direction of the travel. To "truck right" means to move the camera mount to the right with the camera pointing at a right angle to the direction of the travel.

Crab: Any sideways motion of the crane dolly base or its smaller cousin, the crab dolly. A crab is similar to a truck, except that the camera mount does not have to stay lateral to the action all the time; it can move toward or away from the action at the same time. "Crabbing" is used more in film than in television.

Arc: Moving the camera in a slightly curved dolly or truck movement with a mobile camera mount. To "arc left" means to dolly in or out in a camera-left curve or to truck left in a curve around the object; to "arc right" means to dolly in or out in a camera-right curve or to truck right in a curve around the object.

Zoom: Changing the focal length of the lens through the use of a zoom control while the camera remains stationary. To "zoom in" means to change the lens gradually to a narrow-angle position, thereby making the scene appear to move closer to the viewer; to "zoom out" means to change the lens gradually to a wide-angle lens position, thereby making the scene appear to move farther away from the viewer.

How to Work a Camera

In this section, we will concentrate on some of the basic steps of how to work (1) a studio camera and (2) a portable camera. Like bicycling, you learn how to work a camera by doing it. There is no substitute for practice. The following guidelines are intended only to facilitate the learning process.

Working the Studio Camera

When operating a camera, you must go through some basic steps *before, during,* and *after* the show or the rehearsal.

Before

1. Put on your earphones and check whether the intercommunication system is functioning.

2. Unlock the pan and tilt mechanism on your camera mounting head and adjust the drag, if necessary. Check whether the camera is balanced on the mounting head. Unlock your pedestal, and pedestal up and down. Check whether the pedestal is correctly counterweighted. A properly balanced camera remains put in any given vertical position. If it drops down or moves up by itself, the pedestal is not sufficiently counterweighted.

3. See how much camera cable you have, and whether it is tightly plugged in at the wall outlet and the camera head. Is the cable coiled so that it will uncoil easily when you move the camera? If not, recoil it.

4. If your camera is already warmed up and correctly aligned by the video engineer, ask to have your camera uncapped, or whether you can uncap it. You will now see in your viewfinder the pictures your camera actually takes. Is the viewfinder properly adjusted?

5. Check your zoom lens. Zoom in and out. Does your zoom lens "stick," that is, does it have problems moving smoothly throughout the zoom range? What exactly is your range? Get a feel of how close you can get to the set from a certain position. Does the shot box work? Preset for a few zoom positions and see whether the zoom lens actually moves to the preset position. Is the lens clean? If it is unusually dusty, use a fine camel's hair brush and carefully clean off the larger dust particles. With a small rubber syringe or a can of compressed air, blow off the finer dust. Don't just blow on it with your mouth. You will fog up the lens and get it dirtier than it was.

6. Rack through your focus. Can you move easily and smoothly into and out of focus?

7. If you have a teleprompter attached to your camera, check all the connections. Since this mechanism is usually operated by a member of the floor crew, ask him or her to check it out.

8. Lock your camera again (pedestal, and panning and tilt mechanism) before leaving it. Don't ever leave a camera unlocked even if it is for only a short while.

During

1. Put on earphones and establish contact with the director, technical director, and video control. Unlock your camera and recheck tilt and pan drag, and the pedestal movement.

2. Preset your zoom at each new camera position. Make sure that you can focus over the entire zoom range.

3. Preset your zoom positions if operating with a shot box. Preset your focus if working with automatic focus control. Don't move your camera after you have preset your shot box; if you must move, preset your zoom positions again.

4. When checking your focus between shots, rack through your focus a few times so that you can determine at which position the picture is the sharpest.

5. If you anticipate a dolly with your zoom lens, make sure that the lens is set at a wide-angle position. With a turret camera, use a wide-angle lens for your dolly. When dollying with a zoom lens, preset your focus approximately at the midpoint of the dolly distance. With the zoom lens at the wide-angle position, your depth of field should be large enough so that you need to adjust focus only when you get close to the object or event.

6. You will find that a heavy camera pedestal allows you to dolly extremely smoothly. However, you may have some difficulty getting it to move, or stopping it without jerking the camera. Start slowly to overcome the inertia, and try to slow down just before the end of your dolly or truck. If you have a difficult truck or arc to perform, have a floorperson help you steer the camera. You can then concentrate on the camera operation. In a straight dolly, you can keep both hands on the panning handles. If you have to steer the camera, steer with your right hand. Keep your left hand on the focus device. With a turret camera, keep your left hand on the panning handle and steer the camera with the right hand. If the focus gets critical (when the camera begins to move close to the object or event), put your right hand back to the focus knob and move the camera with the panning handle.

7. If you pedestal up or down, make sure that you brake the camera before it hits the stops at the extreme pedestal positions.

8. When you operate a freewheel dolly, always have the wheels preset in the direction of the intended camera movement. This will prevent the camera dolly from starting off in the wrong direction. Make sure that the cable guards are down far enough so that you don't hit the camera cable with the casters.

9. Be sure you know the approximate reach of your camera cable. Know how much you have before you start a dolly in or a truck. Cable drag on the camera can be irritating when it prevents you from achieving a smooth dolly. Although the minicables (such as the triaxial cables) have reduced drag to a minimum, you may still find that in a long dolly the cable tugs annoyingly at the camera. Don't try to pull the cable along with your hand. To ease the tension, you may want to carry it over your shoulder, or tie it to the pedestal base, leaving enough slack so that you can freely pan, tilt, and pedestal. On complicated camera movements, have a floorperson help you with the cable; otherwise, the dragging sound may be picked up quite clearly by the microphone. If your cable gets twisted during a dolly, don't just drag the whole mess along. Have a floorperson untangle it for you.

10. At all times during the show, be aware of all other activities around you. Where are the other cameras? The microphone boom? The floor monitor? It is your responsibility to keep out of the view of the other cameras, and not to hit anything (including floor personnel or talent) during your moves. Watch especially for obstacles in your dolly path, such as scenery, properties, floor lights. Be particularly careful when dollying back. A good floor manager will help to clear the way and will also tap you on the shoulder to prevent you from backing into something.

11. In general, keep your eyes on your viewfinder. If the format allows, you can look around for something interesting to shoot between shots. Your director will appreciate good visuals in an ad lib show (in which the shots have not been previously rehearsed). But don't try to outdirect the director from your position. He is

the only one who knows at any given point what the other cameras are doing.

12.   Watch for your tally light to go out before moving your camera into a new shooting position, presetting your zoom, or racking lenses.

13.   During rehearsal, inform the floor manager or the director of unusual production problems. If you simply can't prevent a camera shadow, the lighting must be changed. Your camera may be too close to the object to keep it in focus. Or the director may not give you enough time to preset your zoom again after your move into a new shooting position. Alert him if your zoom is in a narrow-angle position (zoomed in fairly close) and he has you move the camera while on the air. Sometimes it is hard for the director to tell from his preview monitor at exactly what zoom position your lens is.

14.   If you work without shot sheets, which give you the exact sequence of shots for your camera, try to remember the type and sequence of shots during the rehearsal. A good camera operator has the next shot lined up before the director calls for it. If you work from a shot sheet, go to the next shot immediately after your previous one. Don't wait until the last minute. The director may have to come to your camera ("punch it up" on the air) much sooner than you remember from rehearsal.

15.   Mark the critical camera positions on the studio floor with some masking tape. If you don't have a shot sheet, make one up on your own. Mark particularly your camera movements (dollies, trucks) so that you can set your zoom in a wide-angle position. Be sure to line up exactly on these marks during the actual show.

16.   Try to avoid unnecessary chatter on the intercom. Use your talkback system only in emergencies.

17.   Listen carefully to what the director tells all the camera operators, not just you. This way, you will be able to coordinate your shots with the shots of the other cameras. Also, you can avoid wasteful duplication of shots by knowing approximately what the other cameras are doing.

4·13   If you work with a turret camera, make sure that your tally light is out before changing lenses. Change your lenses as quickly as possible, and as quietly. Careless lens racking can be very noisy, especially when your camera is close to a hot (switched-on) microphone. Be very careful with your racking if you have long lenses on your turret because abrupt lens changes can easily damage the mechanism. Be sure to have the lens positions clearly marked on your turret so that you can rack to the required lens without having to go through the whole rotation.

After

1.   At the end of the show, wait for the "all clear" signal before you lock your camera.

2.   Ask the video engineer whether your camera may be capped.

3.   Now lock your camera mounting head and your pedestal and push the camera into a safe place in the studio. Don't leave it in the middle of the studio; a camera can be easily damaged by a piece of scenery being moved or by other kinds of studio traffic.

4.   Coil your cable again as neatly as possible in the customary figure-eight loops.

Working the Portable Camera

In all major phases, the operation of the portable camera is quite similar to that of the studio camera. There are a few steps, however, that need special attention. Again, we will discuss the principal operational steps before, during, and after the telecast or rehearsal.

Before

1.   Before you pick up the portable camera head and the camera control backpack, check all cable connections.

2.   Check the main camera cable that leads from your backpack to the remote truck. How much cable do you have? Is this length within the permissible limit? If not, your picture quality will suffer. Some cameras have built-in compensators for a variety of cable lengths. Are you compensating for the correct cable length?

3.   Make sure that you know the action radius of your camera cable. If your camera isn't wireless (some backpacks have a transmitter built in, or contain a videotape recorder), where exactly can you walk with it? In the heat of the show, you may forget just where you can go until you are jerked to a stop by the camera cable. Familiarize yourself with the action of the event and your own action radius.

4.   If a microphone is plugged into the mike outlet on your camera, are the connections secure? Check whether the announcer has enough cable to perform his duties relatively independent of your position.

5.   If you operate a backpack videotape recorder, make sure that it is working satisfactorily. Test-record some scenes.

6.   If your camera is battery-powered, make sure that the battery is fully charged before the show. Double-check the battery just before you go on the air.

7.   As always, make sure that your intercommunication system is working. Good intercommunications are essential to successful remote operations.

8.   Now, check your zoom lens. Does it zoom smoothly and keep focus over the entire zoom range? Familiarize yourself with the zoom range relative to the event. (Since your viewfinder is relatively small on your portable camera, make sure that it is in perfect working condition. Adjust the viewfinder controls for optimal picture quality.)

During

1.   At all times, try to keep the camera as steady as possible. Try to zoom as smoothly as possible. Unless told otherwise, zoom slowly; after all, it is the event you want to show the viewer, not your zooming technique. Try to keep in focus at all times. If you get out of focus, try to focus up again smoothly. It is better to take a little more time to get into focus than to rack right through the focus into another out-of-focus position.

2.   If you walk while the camera is on the air, try to keep the camera as steady as possible. Aim your camera with the whole upper body; have your legs absorb all the wiggles and bumps.

3.   Make sure you have enough cable for your move, and that the cable does not get tangled up along the way.

4.   Walk only in a wide-angle lens position. If you are asked to move to another location while your camera is on the air and in a narrow-angle lens position

zoomed in fairly close), you must zoom out to a fairly wide-angle lens position before you can move. Otherwise, the wobbles of your camera will be so exaggerated that the picture will be unusable.

5. Preset your zoom again from every new camera position.

6. Don't panic if you lose your subject temporarily in the viewfinder. Keep your camera steady, look up out of the viewfinder and see where the subject is, and aim your camera smoothly into the new direction. Or, simply zoom out to a wide shot until you have reoriented yourself to the new situation. With your zoom lens in the extreme wide-angle position, you are often closer to the object than your viewfinder image indicates. Watch, therefore, that you don't bump into something or somebody with your zoom lens, especially if you walk your camera into a crowd or other tightly spaced group of people.

7. If the microphone of the announcer is plugged into your camera, make sure that you don't outrun the announcer.

8. Watch the tally light inside your viewfinder hood at all times. Even when you are off the air, don't go through unnecessary wild maneuvers. It is very hard to predict when the director will need to have your camera punched up. With a portable camera, consider yourself at all times in a "ready" position.

9. Some portable cameras have several warning signals built into the viewfinder hood, such as battery charge, amount of videotape left, and so forth. Try not to ignore them, even if the event you are covering happens to be very exciting.

10. When shooting under low light level conditions, watch your focus carefully. The low light level necessitates a wide lens opening, which in turn reduces the depth of field. Also, you will find that keeping in focus while walking the camera is more difficult in dim light than in bright light. Avoid any fast camera movement. Under low light conditions, even the best Plumbicon tubes are not entirely lag free. Any fast object or camera motion will therefore produce the undesirable comet-tailing.

11. If you have a videotape recorder connected with the portable camera, frequently check the amount of tape left. Even the most beautiful camera work doesn't do any good if your tape has run out.

12. Finally, keep on top of the event. On a remote, the director does not always know what is going on. He has to rely on an alert crew. If you witness an action that seems like a significant development, show it to the director. He still has the choice of taking or not taking the shot, depending on his view of the overall event context.

After

1. Don't just drop the camera and backpack on the ground because you heard the "all clear" over the intercom. Walk back to the camera control position and *carefully* put the camera down and take off the backpack. Don't unplug anything unless you are specifically told by the technical director or video engineer to do so. Since a warm camera is especially sensitive to shock, be very gentle in moving it around.

2. Roll up or coil your camera cable. Don't pull the camera connectors through the dirt. Carry them, or wrap them in a plastic bag for extra protection.

3. Don't forget to have the camera batteries recharged as soon as possible.

Picture Composition

Your basic purpose in framing a shot is to show things as clearly as possible, and present them so that they convey meaning and thought. What you do essentially is to clarify and intensify the event before you. Although it is the director who is concerned with the overall clarification and intensification of an event for the viewer, the camera operator should nevertheless know how to provide the director with optimally effective shots.

Television pictures are, like any other pictures, subject to the conventional aesthetic rules of pic-

Step	Symbol	Framing
Extreme Long Shot	XLS OR ELS	
Long Shot	LS	
Medium Shot	MS	
Closeup	CU	
Extreme Closeup	XCU OR ECU	

4·14 Field-of-View Steps: Note that these shot designations are relative and that several steps lie between each designation. If you start with a rather tight medium shot, which may be similar to our closeup framing, your extreme closeup may end up considerably tighter than the one shown here.

ture composition. But there are factors peculiar to the television medium that influence your framing process to a certain extent.

1.   The size of the television screen is small. To show things clearly, you must show them relatively large within the frame of the screen. In other words, you have to operate more with closeups (CU) and medium shots (MS) than with long shots (LS) and extreme long shots (XLS). Since the home viewer cannot see the whole event in its overall context, you must try to pick those details that tell at least an important part of the story. Shots that do not obviously relate to the event context are usually meaningless to the viewer.

2.   You must always work within a fixed frame, the television aspect ratio of 3:4. If you want to show something extremely tall, you cannot change the aspect ratio into a vertical framing.

3.   The pictures on the television screen are two-dimensional. You must create the impression of a third dimension through special arrangement of objects within the frame and the demonstration of relative size: objects closer to you are bigger, objects farther away seem smaller. Overlapping planes, a limited depth of field, and special lighting effects can also contribute to the illusion of a third dimension. A good three-dimensional effect always needs a clear picture division into foreground, middleground, and background.

4.   The object in front of the camera (which is a substitute for the viewer's eyes) generally moves about. This means that you must consider motion as well as static arrangement of objects within the frame. About 10 percent of the picture area gets lost through the television transmission and reception process (see discussion on essential area in Chapter 12). You must compensate for this loss by framing somewhat more loosely than what you have visualized. Some camera operators draw black lines on their monitors to indicate the essential framing area.

Most likely you are already familiar with the basic principles of picture composition. You can probably tell, for example, whether a color photograph is well or badly composed, whether it is properly balanced, whether it contains aesthetic tension, or whether it is dull. Learn to look at pictures from a design point of view.

In the following discussion of television framing, no attempt is made to give you an exhaustive treatment of media aesthetics;[1] nevertheless, understanding the few compositional principles and conventions should aid you in framing optimally effective shots with sureness and ease.

These principles include (1) field of view, (2) organizing the screen area, (3) organizing screen depth, and (4) organizing screen motion.

Field of View

The field of view of the camera is basically organized into five steps (*see 4.14*). There are five other customary shot designations *(see 4.15).*

Organizing the Screen Area

When shooting objects or people that do not move, you organize your screen area very much as the still photographer does with his camera, or the painter with his canvas. What you are basically doing is *structuring,* composing, the *two-dimensional field* of the television screen.[2]

The most important organizing principle is *balance.* Balance implies that the objects within the screen are arranged not in a completely stable way but in such a way that we perceive their relationship to one another and the borders of the screen as stable (stable composition), neutral (neutral composition), or unstable (labile composition). *(See 4.16 through 4.19).*

Step	Symbol	Framing
Bust Shot	*Bust Shot*	
Knee Shot	*Knee Shot*	
Two-Shot (two persons in frame)	*2-Shot*	
Three-Shot (three persons in frame)	*3-Shot*	
Over-the-Shoulder Shot	*O-S*	

4·15 Other Shot Designations.

---

[1] For such a treatment, see Herbert Zettl, *Sight-Sound-Motion* (Belmont, Calif.: Wadsworth Publishing Co., 1973).
[2] Zettl, *Sight-Sound-Motion,* pp. 99–172.

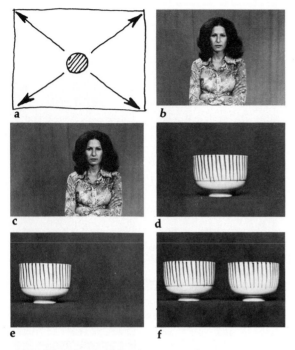

a

4·16 The most stable picture area is screen-center
(a). If you want to convey stability, or show or emphasize a single object as directly as possible, put
the object into screen-center. Through this position,
the screen area is symmetrically balanced. Put a
speaker who is talking directly into the camera into
screen-center (b). To place her slightly off-center (c)
will not make her or her message any more interesting than it is already; it will merely detract from
what she has to say.

If you show a commercial product, such as a single object, place it screen-center (d). The message
about the product is direct; there is no need for
visual gimmickry.

Framing the product off-center (e) does not improve the message; all it does is communicate an
aesthetic error.

Or, (f) you may want to stabilize your picture by
symmetrically balancing an object on one side of the
screen with a duplicate, or a similarly prominent object, on the other side.

4·17 (a) When other forces enter the picture—
such as the force of someone's looking into a particular direction (other than straight into the camera)
—you must compensate for them by placing the
person somewhat off-center. Your balance now
achieves a neutral state.

(b) The more profile the performer turns, the more
space you must leave in front of her. This space is
generally called "nose room."

(c) If you keep the performer centered while she is
looking to the side, your picture will become annoyingly unbalanced.

b

c

a

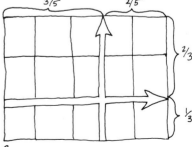

b

4·18 When framing landscapes or other large vistas with distinct vertical objects—people, trees, telephone poles, spires—you will find that by letting the prominent horizontal and vertical lines divide the picture nonsymmetrically (or asymmetrically), your picture will look more interesting than with a symmetrical arrangement (a, b).

Division ratios of roughly ⅖ to ⅗ or ⅓ to ⅔ are the most common asymmetrical neutral states of balance (c).

4·19   Any camera angle that is drastically different from our ordinary visual experience will render an otherwise balanced picture unstable. Tilting the usu-ally level horizon line will create this effect. An un-stable balance usually conveys heightened event energy.

Another important organizing principle is *closure* (or psychological closure, as it is technically called). In closure our mind fills in spaces that we cannot actually see on the screen *(see 4.20 through 4.27.)* We constantly apply psychological closure in our perceptual process. Take a look around you. You actually see only parts of the objects that lie in the field of your vision. There is no way you can ever see an object in its entirety from a single stationary position. Through experience we have learned to supply in our minds the missing parts. This procedure we call psychological clo-sure, or closure for short. Since the television screen is relatively small, we often show objects and people in closeups, leaving many parts of the scene to the imagination of the viewer. Thus, the television viewer frequently is forced to apply psychological closure.

4·20   In this shot, we certainly perceive the whole figure of a person although we actually *see* only a relatively small part of him. But the shot is framed in such a way that we can easily apply closure, that is, fill in the missing parts with our imagination.

a

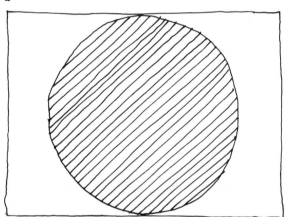

b

c

4·21 (a) This shot is badly framed because we can apply closure within the frame—that is, perceive the detail as a complete picture. (b) We can see a complete thing within the frame, and this prevents us from continuing the figure beyond the frame. (c) This tight closeup is more properly framed. We can easily extend the parts of the head beyond the screen.

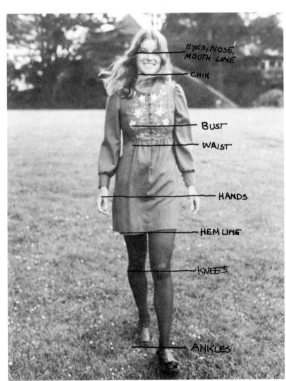

EYES, NOSE, MOUTH LINE
CHIN
BUST
WAIST
HANDS
HEM LINE
KNEES
ANKLES

4·22 In general, try not to have *natural cutoff lines,* such as neck, shoulders, hemline, or feet, coincide with the screen edge. Rather, try to have these cutoff lines fall within or without the screen.

4·23 Try to compensate for awkward differences in height, even though you are applying the cutoff principle. If, for example, you have a tall woman talk to a small child, either the woman should stoop down to the child or the child should be put on a riser. Don't just frame the child, chopping off the woman's head and feet.

4·24 Because we usually have space above us, indoors as well as out, you should leave space above people's heads in normal closeup, medium, and long shots. Don't have the top of a person's head glued to the top part of the screen. You must leave some *headroom.*

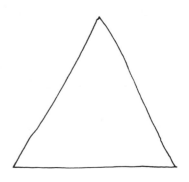

4·25 We tend to see similar things together and to put them into simple geometrical shapes. You can use this organizing tendency to group similar objects into easily recognizable patterns. This group of cups forms an easily perceivable pattern: a triangle.

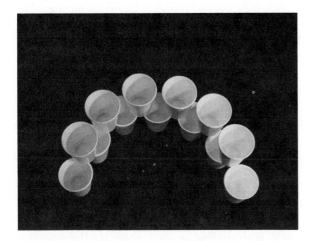

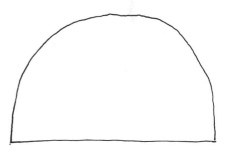

4·26 These objects organize the screen space into a prominent semicircle.

4·27   This tendency for closure into simple patterns, however, is not always positive. The desire to see screen space organized into simple patterns frequently works even against reason. Try to avoid odd juxtapositions of performers with background objects, such as giving the appearance of plants growing out of people's heads.

How about this for a balancing act? A good camera operator would have avoided such a distracting juxtaposition simply by trucking a slight distance to one side or the other, or by dollying in or out.

Organizing Screen Depth

Since the standard television screen is a flat, two-dimensional piece of glass upon which the images appear, we must create the *illusion* of a *third dimension*. Fortunately, the principles for its creation have been amply explored and established by painters and photographers for a long time.[3] Also, we have already talked about the various lens angles (wide, normal, narrow) and the depth of field, and how they affect the illusion of a third dimension on the television screen. We know that a strong foreground, and distinctive middle- and backgrounds contribute greatly to screen depth. Here are a few examples of how to frame objects so that the three grounds—foreground, middleground, background—are especially clear and intense. (*See 4.28.*)

Organizing Screen Motion

Contrary to the painter or still photographer, who deals with the organization of static images within the picture frame, the television camera operator must almost always cope with framing *images in motion* on the television screen. Composing moving images requires your quick reaction and your full attention throughout the telecast. Although the study of the moving image is an important part of learning the fine art of television and film production, we will at this point merely point out some of its most basic principles.[4] (*See also 4.29 through 4.32.*)

Movements *toward or away from the camera* (downstage or upstage) are *stronger* than any type of lateral motion. Fortunately, they are the easiest to

---

[3] Zettl, *Sight–Sound–Motion,* pp. 173–220.

[4] For further information on the aesthetics of the moving image, see Zettl, *Sight-Sound-Motion,* pp. 243–326.

a

b

c

4·28 If you include a prominent foreground piece in your shot, you will immediately distinguish more clearly between foreground and middle- and backgrounds than without the foreground piece (a, b, c).

With wide-angle lens distortion, you can exaggerate this type of depth staging to an extreme. Be careful, however; don't just depth stage for the sake of depth staging. You should have proper motivation, whether it is for clarifying an event, or for intensifying it. Compose your shots in such a way that they tell most about the selected event detail, and that they tell it in line with the overall event context.

frame. You simply keep your camera as steady as possible and watch so that the moving object will not go out of focus as it approaches your camera. Remember that a wide-angle zoom lens position (or a wide-angle lens) gives the impression of accelerated motion toward or away from the camera, while the narrow-angle zoom lens position (or the narrow-angle lens) slows the motion for the viewer.

If you frame lateral movement—that is, motion to screen left or screen right—you should *lead* the person or the moving object with your camera. The viewer wants to know where the object is going, not where it has been. Also, the forces of an object moving toward the screen edge must be absorbed by leaving some space ahead of the moving object.

If you are on a closeup and the object moves back and forth, don't try to follow each minor wiggle. You might run the risk of making the viewer seasick; at least he will not be able to concentrate on this sort of motion for very long. Keep your camera pointed at the major action area, and let the subject move in and out of your frame. Or, zoom out (or pull back) to a slightly wider shot.

4·29   In following lateral movement, lead the moving object or subject. Don't trail it.

4·30   If you have a two-shot and one of the persons moves out of the frame, stay with just *one* of them. By zooming back in order to catch them both, you may overshoot the set, or reveal the boom microphone.

4·31 If two persons block each other in a two-shot, correct the situation through a slight arc or truck to the right or the left.

4·32 If you are to animate a static scene through camera movement, such as a photo of a seagull in flight, pan *against* the direction in which the object is expected to move (and was actually moving when the photo was taken). Otherwise, the object seems to travel backwards.

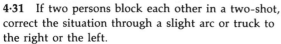

Whatever you have to do in organizing screen motion, do it smoothly. Even when you move your camera fairly fast, the viewer should not become aware of its motion but simply perceive the object motion within the intended context. Most often, you are simply to report the object motion as clearly as possible. Don't create unnecessary (and therefore distracting) motion with your camera, unless you intend to achieve a special effect.

Summary

Camera mounting equipment is necessary for ease and fluidity of camera movement in the studio. There are three *basic mounting units:* (1) the tripod dolly, (2) the studio pedestal, and (3) the studio crane.

The camera is attached to the camera mount through a *mounting head.* The most useful and widely used types are (1) the cradle head and (2) the cam head.

The camera mounting device and the mounting head enable the camera to pan, tilt, pedestal, tongue, crane or boom, dolly, truck, arc, and, with the aid of the zoom lens, zoom (although the camera does not need to move during the zooming).

When *working the camera,* the operator should follow certain steps before, during, and after the show or rehearsal.

Besides understanding the mechanical operation of the camera, the camera operator must be familiar with the basic *principles of picture composition* so that he or she can frame a scene or portions thereof with sureness, and produce pictures that have visual clarity and impact.

Some major points of picture composition are (1) field of view, from XLS to XCU, (2) organizing the screen area, which includes the structuring of the two-dimensional field of the television screen, (3) organizing screen depth, the creation of the illusion of a third dimension on the two-dimensional screen, and (4) organizing screen motion, the way to make screen motion convincing and continuous.

5   *Lighting*

We have two broad purposes for lighting: (1) to provide the television camera with adequate illumination so that it can see well—that is, produce technically acceptable pictures—and (2) to convey to the viewer the space, time, and mood of the event. Lighting helps to tell us what the objects shown on the screen actually look like, where they are in relation to one another and to their immediate environment, and when the event is taking place in respect to time of day, season, or weather conditions. Lighting also serves to establish illusion and/or the general mood of the event.

In this chapter, we will therefore consider:

1. The technical lighting objectives, which include baselight levels and techniques, contrast, shadow densities, falloff, contrast ratios, and skin tones.

2. The nontechnical objectives, which include form and dimension through lighting, illusion of reality and nonreality, and mood.

3. The two basic types of illumination, directional and diffused light.

4. The tools with which we can accomplish our objectives—the lighting instruments and control equipment.

How to light, the actual lighting techniques, will be the subject of Chapter 6.

Like the human eye, the television camera needs light in order to see and function properly. Unlike the human eye, the television camera is much more demanding as to the amount of light, the color of the light, and its relative harshness and direction.

While, for example, we may see quite well with only a flashlight as the illuminating source or under extremely bright sunlight, the camera may be allergic to both these types of light. The flashlight may not radiate enough light for the pickup tube to give off sufficient electricity. The resulting television picture will lack signal strength and consequently suffer from an excess of video noise, called picture snow. Bright sunlight, on the other hand, may be too much for the camera to handle. At best, the picture will look washed out; at worst, the superabundance of light will destroy the camera pickup tube.

A lamp, which appears to the eye to give off a perfectly white light, may look so red to the camera that the resulting picture will have a reddish tint on the color monitor. Another lamp may produce light that looks to the camera quite bluish, although our eyes again perceive it as normal white light.

A harsh light, or a light coming from an unusual direction, may produce shadows that conceal rather than reveal the actual shape of an object.

The television camera demands, therefore, that we control carefully the illumination of an object or a scene. This control we achieve through *lighting*.

Technical Lighting Objectives

The technical lighting objectives are to provide enough light so that the camera can see well; to

---

Barn Doors Metal flaps in front of lighting instruments that control the spread of the light beam.

Baselight Even, nondirectional (diffused) level of studio lighting. Customary baselight levels: for standard three-tube Plumbicon color cameras, 200 ft-c (foot-candles)–400 ft-c; for image-orthicon monochrome cameras, 75 ft-c–100 ft-c; for portable monochrome vidicon cameras, 100 ft-c–300 ft-c, with 200 ft-c–250 ft-c the norm.

Bias Lighting An electronic boosting of low light levels that enter the camera so that the pickup tubes can operate relatively noise-free.

Broad A floodlight with a broadside, panlike reflector.

C-Clamp A metal clamp with which lighting instruments are attached to the lighting battens.

Color Temperature Relative reddishness or bluishness of light, as measured in degrees of Kelvin; television lighting instruments have a range of 3,000°K–3,400°K, with 3,200°K the norm. Color temperature can be measured with a color-temperature meter.

Cookie (A short form of *cucalorus,* Greek for breaking up light, also spelled *kukaloris*.) Any cutout pattern that, when placed in front of a spotlight, produces a shadow pattern. The cookie, usually made from a thin, cutout metal sheet, is inserted into a pattern projector.

limit the contrast between highlight and shadow areas, or light and dark colors; and to produce white light that will not discolor the scene when it is lighted.

Hence, we will take a closer look at (1) operating light level: baselight; (2) contrast; and (3) color temperature.

Operating Light Level: Baselight

To make the camera "see well" means to provide enough overall light, called *baselight,* so that the camera chain can produce pictures that are relatively free of video noise and color distortion.

As mentioned in an earlier chapter, every television picture has a certain amount of picture noise, generated by the mere movement of electrons. Most likely, you have seen the snowlike effect on the screen when the set is not properly tuned in on a particular station. When tuned carefully, the strong signal will virtually drown out the video noise and the picture will appear clear.

The same problem occurs in television lighting. If the operating light level falls below the light requirements of the pickup tubes and their associated electronic equipment, the noise will outweigh the picture signal; the picture will have an abundance of snow. When the picture noise outweighs the picture signal, we speak of a low (poor) *signal-to-noise ratio.* In a high (good) signal-to-noise ratio, the operating light level is sufficiently high so that the camera chain can produce a signal strong enough to make the picture noise no longer apparent. We measure the operating light level by the amount of baselight.

Baselight Levels   Many an argument has been raised concerning adequate minimum *baselight levels* for various cameras. The problem is that baselight levels do not represent absolute values but

---

Diffused Light   Light that illuminates a relatively large area with an indistinct light beam. Diffused light, created by floodlights, produces soft shadows.

Dimmer   A device that controls the intensity of the light by throttling the electric current flowing to the lamp.

Directional Light   Light that illuminates a relatively small area with a distinct light beam. Directional light, produced by spotlights, creates harsh, clearly defined shadows.

Ellipsoidal Spotlight   Spotlight producing a very defined beam, which can be shaped further by metal shutters.

Floodlight   Lighting instrument that produces diffused light.

Fluorescent Light   Cold light produced by large, gas-filled glass tubes.

Fresnel Spotlight   One of the most common spotlights, named after the inventor of its lens, which has steplike concentric rings.

Gaffer Grip   A strong clamp used to attach small lighting instruments to pieces of scenery, furniture, doors, and other set pieces. Sometimes called *gator clip.*

Gel   Short form for gelatine, a colored material that acts as color filter for lighting instruments. A red gel in front of a spotlight will color its beam red. Since gels are sensitive to moisture and extreme heat, plastic gels, such as cinemoid, are generally used in television lighting.

Incandescent Light   The light produced by the hot filament of ordinary glass-globe light bulbs. (In contrast to fluorescent or quartz light.)

are dependent on other production factors, such as lighting contrast, iris opening of the lens, and the general reflectance of the scenery. Also, such electronic developments as *bias lighting* boost low light levels electronically so that the camera can function in operating light levels that would ordinarily be too low for the pickup tubes.

Nevertheless, through experience, general baselight levels have been established that prove satisfactory for most ordinary television productions. These are:

For the standard three-tube Plumbicon color camera:	200 ft-c–400 ft-c (foot-candles), with 250 ft-c the norm
For the I-O monochrome camera:	75 ft-c–100 ft-c
For portable monochrome vidicon cameras:	100 ft-c–300 ft-c, with 250 ft-c the norm

Generally, the video engineer will have less trouble producing high-quality, crisp pictures when the baselight level is fairly high and the contrast somewhat limited than under a very low baselight level with high contrast lighting.

Also, if the baselight levels are too low, the lens iris must be wide open in order to allow as much light as possible to strike the camera pickup tubes. But, since the depth of field decreases as the lens opening increases, a lens whose iris is set at its maximum opening will give you a fairly shallow depth of field. Consequently, focusing becomes a noticeable problem when baselight levels are low.

If you need a large depth of field, high baselight levels are prerequisite.

A set whose colors and texture absorb a great amount of light obviously needs more illumination (higher baselight level) than one whose brightly painted surface reflects a moderate amount of light.

Incident Light Light that strikes the object directly from its source. Incident light reading is the measure of light (in foot-candles) from the object to the light source. The foot-candle meter is pointed directly into the light source.

Pantograph Expandable hanging device for lighting instruments.

Patchboard Also called patchbay. A device whereby light cables can be routed to specific light controls.

Pattern Projector An ellipsoidal spotlight with a cookie (cucalorus) insert, which projects the cookie's pattern as shadow.

Pin To sharpen (focus) the light beam of a spotlight, either by pulling the light-bulb reflector unit away from the lens or by moving the lens away from the light bulb. The opposite of spread.

Preset Board A program device into which several lighting setups (scenes) can be stored, and from which they can be retrieved, when needed.

Quartz Light A high-intensity light whose lamp consists of a quartz or silica housing (instead of the customary glass) and a tungsten-halogen filament. Produces a very bright light of stable color temperature.

Baselight Techniques   You can achieve a sufficient baselight level in two quite different ways. First, you can establish a basic, highly diffused illumination through floodlights, upon which you then superimpose the spotlights for the specific lighting of people and set areas.

Second, and this is generally done more often, you light the people and specific set areas as carefully as you can with spotlights, and then add fill light to reduce harsh shadows, without initially worrying about the baselight level. Once you have completed your lighting, you take a general baselight reading of the set, hoping that the light spill and reflection off the scenery and the studio floor will have established quite incidentally a sufficient baselight level. If not, you can then add some floodlights in specific areas in order to raise the operating light level. This technique seems to create the most plastic, exciting, and expressive television lighting so far achieved. Unfortunately,

it demands a little more skill and time than the baselight-first method. On remote locations, where time and lighting facilities are limited, establishing the baselight first is definitely the more practical method.

Contrast

The control of contrast is closely tied to (1) shadow density, (2) falloff, (3) contrast ratio, and (4) skin tones.

Shadow Density   The color camera has some trouble reproducing shadow areas. If the shadows are dense, the camera may fail to reproduce all the shadow detail, and the colors in these areas will often look unnatural and distorted, especially on color sets with high color intensity.

Contrary to lighting for monochrome television, where deep shadows can be accommodated

---

Reflected Light   Light that is bounced off the illuminated object. Reflected-light reading is done with a light meter (most of them are calibrated for reflected light) that is held close to the illuminated object from the direction of the camera.

Scoop   A scooplike television floodlight.

Scrim   A spun-glass material that is put in front of a scoop as an additional light diffuser.

Softlight   A television floodlight that produces extremely diffused light. It has a panlike reflector and a light-diffusing material over its opening.

Spotlight   A light instrument that produces directional, relatively undiffused light.

Spread   To enlarge (diffuse) the light beam of a spotlight by pushing the light-bulb reflector unit toward the lens, or the lens closer to the light bulb; the opposite of pin.

Tungsten-Halogen   The kind of lamp filament used in quartz lights. The tungsten is the filament itself; the halogen is a gaslike substance surrounding the filament.

by the camera, lighting for color calls for less dense (dark) shadows, especially if the viewer is expected to make out reasonable detail within the shadow area. You should, therefore, pay special attention to making overly dense shadow areas somewhat translucent through a generous amount of diffused fill light. Such lighting is especially important on performer's faces. Be careful, however, not to eliminate the shadows altogether; otherwise you may end up with a picture that looks much too flat, especially on a black-and-white receiver.

Falloff   As defined earlier, falloff describes the speed with which a light area changes into the darkest shadow area. In *fast falloff,* the change from light to dark shadow is very *abrupt;* in *slow falloff,* the change is more *gradual.* Sharp corners have a fast falloff; a rounded surface has a slow falloff. In color television, a slower falloff is desirable. A lightening of the shadow areas results inevitably in a slowing down of falloff.[1] Again, this does not mean eliminating shadow areas. A good television picture needs shadows, even fairly dark ones. Slowing down simply means to lighten up the very dense shadows to such an extent that detail can still be seen in them, and that the colors in the shadow area can be identified.

---

[1] Herbert Zettl, *Sight-Sound-Motion* (Belmont, Calif.: Wadsworth Publishing Co., 1973), pp. 23–26.

5·1   The strict adherence to the 20:1 contrast ratio, however, still does not guarantee a balanced color picture. If you start out with a "black" (any color of your darkest area) that is fairly bright, your "white" (the brightest area in your picture) may be much too bright for the system to handle adequately, although this light color is only 20 times brighter than your black. Or, conversely, you might have as your brightest spot a rather dark color, which would make any other color that is 20 times darker much too "black." When this happens, an inattentive or insensitive video control operator might electronically "pull the whites" down to a manageable level, thereby destroying the middle and lower brightness ranges in your picture, or "stretch the blacks," thereby causing the lighter colors and picture areas to lose detail and to bloom.

To achieve a balanced color picture, you need to establish *reference points* for the *darkest and lightest* areas in your scene. These are called *reference black* and *reference white.* You can establish them simply by finding the colors that reflect the least light and the most light. Theoretically, absolute black would reflect nothing; you would have a reflectance of zero percent. Pure white would reflect all the light; you would have a reflectance of 100 percent. In practice, of course, there is no color material that absorbs or reflects all the light falling on it, nor is there any camera system that would accurately respond to these extreme values. The actual light reflectance lies somewhere near them.

For color television, the reference black should not go below 3 percent reflectance and the reference white should not go beyond 60 percent (which is in accordance with the contrast ratio: the white is 20 times lighter than the black).

An example may help to relate these concepts for you. Let us assume that you are asked to establish reference white and reference black in a scene in which a performer wearing a yellow shirt and a medium-gray suit stands in front of a dark blue background. For convenience' sake, let us also assume that the key and fill lights falling on the performer total 400 ft-c. You measure this light intensity by pointing a foot-candle meter into the lights from the performer's position. This way you are reading the *incident* light, which in our example is at a level of 400 ft-c. Most foot-candle meters are *incident* light meters *(see a).*

In order to measure the *reflected* light, you must use

Contrast Ratio   Although the Plumbicon pickup tube can tolerate a great contrast (you can shine your camera into the studio lights on a long shot, for example, without doing harm to the tube), a somewhat limited contrast will nevertheless enhance your color pictures to a great extent. Apart from a few sparkling highlights, such as the light reflected off jewelry, the brightest area in your picture should not exceed a *contrast ratio* of 20:1 (the brightest area in the picture is twenty times lighter than the darkest area). Some video engineers like to stretch the acceptable contrast ratio to 30:1. If you exceed this brightness spread, you run the risk of severe color distortion.

There are two ways of achieving contrast ratio:

(1) You adjust your picture in such a way that you can discern the dark colors (or the darker portion of the grayscale), thereby making the whites, or light colors, uniformly bright. The light, washed-out colors will then tend to lose detail. In extreme cases, or especially in black-and-white television, the light areas will begin to "bloom," to glow as though they were actually emitting the light themselves. (2) You adjust the picture for the light areas, but then the dark colors tend to look uniformly dark, if not muddy. But don't be too much of a slave to all these contrast ratios. If you light sensibly for color, which means that you lighten up somewhat the very deep shadows with fill light, and if your overall baselight level is not

a reflected-light meter (most common photographic light meters can measure reflected light) and point it close to the lighted object, such as the performer's yellow shirt *(see b)*. If you have lighted the subject properly, your meter might read 240 ft-c, the ideal 60 percent reflection of your original 400 ft-c falling on the subject. You have now established your

white reference point. You then measure the darkest spot in your picture, probably the dark blue background. If this background happens to reflect 12 ft-c, which is the lower 3 percent limit of the 400 ft-c of main illumination, you have established your black reference.

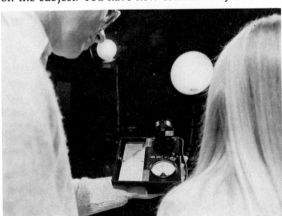

a   Incident Light Reading: Light meter is pointed into the lights.

b   Reflected Light Reading: Light meter is pointed close to the lighted object, thereby measuring the light reflected by the object.

5·2 The color camera reacts somewhat like color film. If you use outdoor color film (daylight) and shoot indoors with it (assuming that corrective devices, such as filters or blue flash or blue indoor lights, are not used), you will end up with extremely reddish pictures. The reverse is true when using indoor film (tungsten) for shooting outdoors; everything will have a bluish tinge. This color distortion occurs because outdoor film counteracts the very high color temperature of outdoor light (quite bluish) with slightly reddish colors. When used indoors, where the light is reddish anyway, everything turns orange. Indoor lights, on the other hand, are made to counteract the reddish indoor lights with slightly bluish colors. When used in the blue light outdoors, everything takes on a slightly greenish-blue tinge.

too low, you should not have too much of a problem with contrast. In any case, check your monitor.

Some people get so involved with contrast ratios, color temperatures, and all sorts of numbers that they forget entirely the most important final criteria for television lighting—criteria that are aesthetic rather than technical. A critical look at the color and monochrome monitors often tells more about the quality of your lighting than readings of a variety of meters and scopes do. If the picture looks good—that is, if it looks as you intended it to look—your lighting is correct. As in all artistic endeavors, the technical aspects should become an aid rather than a master to your creative expression. In television lighting, as in all other aspects of television production, your major guide is still your aesthetic sensitivity and, above all, common sense.

Skin Tones The only standard reference we have for adjusting the color scheme on the home receiver is the performer's skin tones, inaccurate as it may be. Obviously, the skin tones should be reproduced as faithfully and as naturally as possible. One of the chief ways of preserving the natural skin tone throughout a scene is to light all performers as evenly as possible. Even if the performer is to walk from a bright scene to a dark one, such as from a brightly illuminated living room to a moonlit balcony, her or his face should not change drastically from light to dark. Indeed, to achieve the difference between living room and balcony lighting, you wouldn't have to touch the lighting on the face at all. All you would have to do is to change the background lighting from light to dark. Also, in maintaining skin tones, try to avoid color reflections on the face from clothing and scenery. In a normal scene, don't use colored lights (lights that have color gels, or cinemoid filters) on a performer, as helpful as they may be for special effects of background lighting, or you will certainly destroy the very much needed color reference for the viewer.

Color Temperature

Color temperature is a standard by which we measure the relative reddishness or bluishness of white light. You have certainly noticed that a fluorescent tube gives off a "colder" light than a candle. The fluorescent tube gives off a bluish light; the candle a more reddish light. This difference can be precisely expressed in degrees of *color temperature.* You can also observe the change of color temperature by carefully watching a light being dimmed. When the lamp is on full, you see a bright white light that looks something like the sun at high noon. But when the lamp is greatly dimmed down, the light begins to take on a reddish tinge, similar to the red sun at sunset.

Whereas the monochrome camera is relatively insensitive to color temperature, the color camera is greatly affected by it. What exactly is color temperature? What does it have to do with temperature if it is a measure of the relative reddishness or bluishness of light?

Color temperature is measured in degrees Kelvin (K), which stand for actual temperatures. As you know, the hotter a flame gets, the bluer it becomes. The same is true of light. The hotter the filament of a lamp (such as a quartz lamp) gets, the whiter, and even bluer, the emitted light becomes. The Kelvin scale has been devised by heating a theoretically totally light-absorbing filament, called "black body," from absolute zero to various degrees centigrade. If the black body is heated to 3,200°K (3,200 degrees from absolute zero), it radiates a fairly white light, with just a little reddish (warm) tinge. If you now take a quartz lamp and adjust it in such a way that its light approximates as closely as possible that of the black body with a color temperature of

3,200°K, you can rate the quartz lamp as having a color temperature of 3,200°K—assuming that it receives its full voltage (not dimmed in any way). As soon as you begin to dim this quartz lamp, however, its color temperature begins to decrease, causing the color of the light to get redder. If you boost the voltage beyond the one for which the instrument is rated, the lamp will get hotter, the color temperature will increase, and the light will get bluer.

While this change of color can hardly be noticed in direct observation, the color camera reports it quite readily by producing a distinct color tint (reddish or bluish) over the entire picture. Especially in the lower ranges of light intensity (when the light is dimmed down extensively), the orange glow of the lower color temperature shows up quite prominently. This suffusion is especially distracting when it occurs on performers' faces.

Generally, the illumination for color television is kept within a 3,000°K to 3,400°K range; with 3,000°K and 3,200°K the preferred color temperatures. Almost all quartz lighting instruments are rated at 3,200°K.

Some lighting experts warn against any dimming on performers and performing areas, since the lowering of the color temperature will discolor the skin tones. However, practice has shown that you can dim these lights by a good 200°K, especially in the upper intensity ranges, before the color change becomes too noticeable on the monitor. Even so, dim the performing area lights only when you have to balance your overall lighting, and refrain from dimming the lights on performers while the show is in progress.

Nontechnical Lighting Objectives

The nontechnical, or aesthetic, lighting objectives are (1) to indicate form and dimension, (2) to cre-

a

b

5·3 Indication of Form and Dimension through Shadows: (a) It is often the shadow that reveals the true shape of the object. In this picture it is difficult to tell whether the object is a flat figure or a cube. (b) Darkening of the shadow area makes it immediately apparent that the object is a cube.

ate an illusion of reality or nonreality, and (3) to indicate mood.

Form and Dimension

Since the television screen has only two dimensions, height and width, the third dimension, depth, must be created by illusion. A proper control of light and shadow is essential for the clear revelation of the actual shape and form of three-dimensional objects, their position in space and time, and their relation to one another and to their environment. In fact, it is often the *shadows that indicate the form and dimension* of an object rather than the light. You will find, therefore, that the purpose of lighting is more frequently the control of the placement and the relative density of the shadow than the creation of bright picture areas. *(See 5.3 and 5.4.)*

The emphasis or de-emphasis of shadows on a surface of an object will also help to sharpen, or reduce, the textural characteristics of the object. Lighting that emphasizes shadows can make a relatively smooth surface look richly textured, or a relatively rough surface rather smooth.

Reality and Nonreality

Lighting helps to achieve an illusion of reality or nonreality. It aids in setting a *specific* time and place. For example, long shadows suggest late afternoon or early morning; harsh, bright light helps to establish a sun-flooded outdoor scene. The periodically flashing light as seen through the closed Venetian blinds from the inside of a motel room will give us a quick clue as the the kind of establishment, if not the whole neighborhood. A windowless interior rather brightly lighted can

a

b

5·4 Spatial Articulation through Shadows: (a) How far is this person away from the background? Without a separation of her shadow from the dark background (background shadow), it is difficult to judge her position accurately in relation to her environ- ment. (b) With a special light separating the shadows, and another light giving some definition to the background, we have now a clearer idea as to her spatial position.

give the impression that it is still daylight outside. But the same interior with rather low-key lighting (high-contrast and low overall light level) suggests nighttime.

Special lighting techniques can also help to create the illusion of a specific source of illumination. For example, many lighting instruments may be needed to give the impression that a scene is lit by a single candle.

Illogical or special effects lighting can create the illusion of nonreality. For example, an extremely low-contrast scene that is purposely washed out may provide us with an environment as unreal as one in which the contrast is purposely pushed beyond the acceptable limits. We are greatly aided in special effects lighting by electronic manipulation, such as polarity reversal, for example, where all the dark areas turn light and the light areas turn dark. You will find more information on special effects in Chapter 11.

Mood

Next to sound, lighting is one of the chief means of creating a desired mood. Various psychological effects, such as gaiety, mystery, or gloom, can be achieved through lighting techniques. *(See 5.5.)*

The long shadows looming in the deserted street suggest danger; the reflection of water and the shadows of leaves dancing on a face or a wall suggest happiness and calm. Intense lighting from the back tends to glamorize the fashion model.

Lighting from below eye level can create a mysterious mood. Since under normal conditions we experience the principal illumination as coming from above, we expect the shadows to fall below the object. A reversal of the shadows immediately suggests something unusual. If all the other production elements—set design, color, sound, actions—are in harmony with the special lighting effect, the mysterious mood is firmly established.

a

b

5·5 Mood through Shadows: (a) Lighting from above, whereby the shadows fall in the customary below-the-object position, gives the scene a normal appearance. (b) Lighting from below creates an unreal, mysterious mood. We perceive the shadows in what seems to be an unnatural position.

Note that one production technique, such as lighting, is usually not strong enough alone to establish a feeling of nonreality or mystery, for example. We usually need to have *all other production elements work in unison* to achieve the desired effect.

Types of Illumination

In all photographic lighting, including television, we use two types of illumination, (1) directional and (2) diffused.

Directional light illuminates only a relatively small area with a distinct light beam. It produces well-defined shadows and causes *fast falloff*, which means that the light area changes rather abruptly into the dense shadow areas. Thus we use *spotlights*, which emit a directional beam.[2]

Diffused light illuminates a relatively large area with a wide, indistinct light beam. It produces soft, rather undefined, shadows and causes *slow falloff*, which means that there is a low contrast between light and dark, and that the light changes gradually into soft, transparent shadow areas. Thus, we use *floodlights*, which emit a diffused beam.

Before you can immerse yourself in lighting for form and dimension, reality and nonreality, or mood, you should acquaint yourself first with the necessary tools of lighting. They include (1) studio lighting instruments, (2) portable lighting instruments, and (3) lighting control equipment. As with any other piece of equipment, your learning of the lighting tools will be facilitated greatly if you use them right away in simple lighting exercises.

Studio Lighting Instruments

All studio lighting is accomplished with a variety of spotlights and floodlights. These instruments (sometimes called luminaires) are designed to op-

[2] Zettl, *Sight-Sound-Motion*, pp. 23–24.

5·6   Most lighting instruments used in television studios have *quartz,* or *tungsten-halogen,* lamps. The more common, though less accurate, name "quartz" refers to the lamp itself, which is made out of quartz or a silica, glasslike material. Tungsten-halogen refers to the lamp filament. But you will also find instruments with the older, familiar *incandescent* light bulbs, very much like the bulb you use in your home.

There are, however, some distinct advantages in using quartz lights in television production over the traditional incandescent lights.

The illumination efficiency of quartz lamps is extremely high. Under ideal conditions, a quartz lamp may produce twice the illumination of an incandescent bulb of the same wattage. You need, therefore, fewer quartz instruments, or instruments of a lower wattage, than you would incandescent lights for the same amount of illumination. Also, because of the superior light output of the quartz instruments, their size and weight are less than those of equivalent incandescent instruments. Since the quartz lamp itself is quite small, the housing for the lamp is smaller than that of incandescent instruments of equal wattage.

The light output of the quartz lamp does not decrease with age. Incandescent bulbs, however, gradually blacken with carbon and thus decrease in light efficiency. Also, the color temperature of the quartz lamp remains unchanged during the entire life of the bulb, while the incandescent bulbs, because of carbon blackening, may change color temperature considerably during their life.

Unfortunately, the quartz instrument is not without disadvantages: (1) The life of the quartz lamp is about half that of the incandescent bulb. It is rated for a maximum of 150 to 500 hours, depending on the size and type of instrument used. (2) The quartz instruments get extremely hot and also radiate more heat than incandescent lights. This characteristic can become rather annoying to studio crews and performers, and it is fairly destructive to such standard light attachments as barn doors, scrims, and color gels. Often a scrim, which lasts for months on an

Comparison of Incandescent and Quartz Lamps: Quartz lamps are smaller and more efficient than incandescent lamps.

incandescent instrument, will be burned up by a quartz lamp within weeks.

In some of the older quartz instruments, especially the ones that do not use the relatively large quartz globe, the light beam is still rather difficult to control. Although the narrowing and spreading of the beam is possible, it cannot be shaped as precisely as the incandescent light beam. When the spotlight with a horizontal lamp is pinned to a narrow beam, the light tends to concentrate on the rim of the beam, leaving a "blind" or dark spot in the middle of whatever happens to be lighted. Also, it produces an abundance of spill. The blind spot is especially noticeable and vexing when the light is concentrated on a face, for example, and the spill makes precise light control difficult.

You will probably find that quite a few stations still use both types of lights, quartz and incandescent, in some combination. The reason for using both lights is most often economical; as long as the old incandescent lights still do the job, nobody is going to throw them away. Some lighting experts, however, combine the two lights for aesthetic reasons. They like to use the incandescent instruments in areas where high control is imperative and where a slightly less brilliant light is desirable, and the quartz instruments in areas that need more general, but intense, illumination.

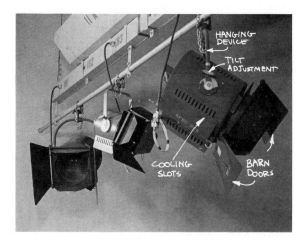

5·7   Fresnel Spotlight.

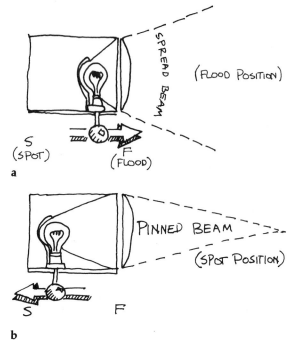

erate from the studio ceiling. Although they are seldom moved from one studio location to another, their size and weight are still important production factors. The lighter and smaller *quartz instruments* are, therefore, preferred in most studio productions to the rather bulky incandescent lighting instruments.

Since the types, application, and basic operation of the quartz lights are quite similar to those of the incandescent, we will not make any differentiation in our discussion of the instruments themselves. Just realize that in general the incandescent instruments are heavier, larger, and bulkier than the quartz instruments of equal wattage, and that the mechanisms for adjusting the light beams differ slightly.

Spotlights

You will find that most studio lighting can be accomplished with two basic types of spotlights (1) the Fresnel spotlight and (2) the ellipsoidal spotlight.

The Fresnel Spotlight   Named for Augustin Fresnel, who invented the lens used in it, the Fres-

5·8   Beam Control of Fresnel Spotlight: (a) In order to spread the beam, turn the focus spindle or focusing loop so that the bulb-reflector unit moves toward the lens. If the lighting instrument has an outside indicator, the indicator should move toward F (for "flood" position). (b) In order to pin, or focus, the beam, turn the focus spindle or focusing loop so that the bulb-reflector unit moves away from the lens. The focus indicator should move toward S (for "spot" position).

nel spotlight is the most widely used in television studio production *(See 5.7).* The Fresnel spotlight is relatively light and flexible. It has a high light output, and its light beam can be made narrow or wide by a spot-focusing device. The spotlight can be adjusted to a "spread" beam position, which then gives off a rather wide, flooded beam;

or it can be "pinned" to a sharp, clearly defined light beam. There are several ways of *spreading* (adjust to a wide, flooded beam), or *pinning,* or *focusing* (adjust to a narrow, clearly defined beam) a Fresnel spotlight.

The most common method is to push or pull the bulb-reflector unit inside the light instrument toward or away from the lens. To *spread* a spotlight beam, turn the focusing spindle or focusing loop in such a way that the bulb-reflector unit *moves toward* the lens. To *pin,* or *focus,* the beam, turn the spindle or focusing loop so that the bulb-reflector unit *moves away from* the lens. *(See 5.8.)*

Whenever you adjust the beam, do it gently. You can't very well adjust a light beam with the instrument turned off. But when the bulb is turned on, it is highly sensitive to shock. In order to protect the hot lamp as much as possible from any damaging jolt, two further focusing devices have been developed.

On the back of some smaller quartz fixtures, you will find a lever that can be moved horizontally—or, in other models, turned clockwise or counterclockwise—for quick spreading or pinning of the beam. This device is called a *sweep focus* (see 5.9).

In order not to move the hot lamp at all, some lighting instruments focus by having the *lens* move toward or away from the fixed (and spring-mounted) lamp. In this way, called the "ring-focus" method, you can adjust the drag of the focus ring so that you can focus the instrument with a lighting pole from the studio floor, even after the lamp has been on for several hours. *(See 5.11.)*

Fresnel spotlights come in different sizes, depending on how much light they are to produce. Obviously, the larger instruments produce more light than the smaller ones. The *size* of Fresnel spotlights is given in the *wattage of the lamp,* or the *diameter of the lens.*

What size of lighting instruments you should

5·9   Sweep Focus: The beam can be spread or pinned by moving the sweep knob horizontally to flood (spreading) or spot (pinning) position.

5·10   The most prominent manufacturers of professional television lighting equipment are Berkey ColorTran, Century Strand, Kliegl, and the Mole-Richardson Company. Their various instruments all have trade names. A 1,000-watt Molequartz Baby-Baby Solarspot may be quite similar to the Color-Tran Quartz King dual 1000, for example. It makes more sense, therefore, to label lighting tools according to their function rather than name of manufacturer. Each manufacturer issues periodically a rather complete catalog of its latest lighting equipment.

RING FOCUS

5·11   Ring-Focus Mechanism: By turning the ring (often with a lighting pole from the floor), you can either spread or pin the light beam.

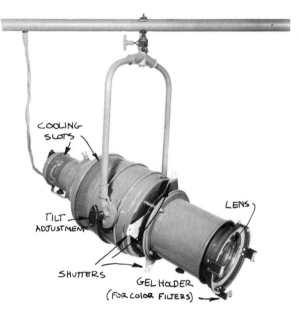

COOLING SLOTS

TILT ADJUSTMENT

LENS

SHUTTERS

GEL HOLDER (FOR COLOR FILTERS)

5·13   Ellipsoidal Spotlight.

5·12   The range of spotlights is from 150 watts to 10,000 watts (10 kilowatts). In motion pictures, where you might have to boost even the superpower of the sun with artificial light sources, even larger instruments, such as the high-intensity "brutes" are used. These brutes generate light by an intensely hot carbon arc.

When classified by lens diameter, you will find 3-inch Fresnels (150 to 250 watts), 6-inch Fresnels (500 to 1,000 watts), 8-inch Fresnels (1,000 to 2,000 watts), 10-inch Fresnels (2,000 to 2,500 watts), and 12-inch Fresnels (2,500 to 5,000 watts).

use depends on several factors: (1) the type of camera used and the sensitivity of the pickup tubes, (2) the height at which the instruments are suspended, and (3) the reflectance of the scenery, costumes, and studio floor.

Color cameras generally need more light than monochrome I-O cameras. The lower the lights are relative to the scenery and action areas, the less light you need. And highly reflecting scenery, costumes, and studio floor need less light than if they were dark and absorbent.

In most television studios, the largest Fresnel spotlights rarely exceed 5,000 watts. Generally, the most commonly used Fresnels are of the 1,000-watt and 2,000-watt variety. For maximum lighting control, most lighting technicians prefer to operate with as few as possible, yet adequately powerful, lighting instruments.

5·14 "Cookie" Pattern on Cyclorama.

The Ellipsoidal Spotlight This kind of spotlight can produce an intense, sharply defined light beam. For example, if you want to create pools of light reflecting off the studio floor, the ellipsoidal spot is the instrument to use. Even in their pinned, or focused, position, the Fresnels would not give you that sharp an outline.

As with the Fresnel, you can pin and spread the light beam of the ellipsoidal. Similar to the ring-focus Fresnel, you push or pull the lens away from the lamp, rather than moving the lamp. Because of the peculiarity of the ellipsoidal reflector (which has two focal points), you can even *shape* the light beam into a triangle or a rectangle, for example, by adjusting four metal *shutters* that stick out of the instrument *(see 5.13)*.

Some ellipsoidal spotlights can also be used as *pattern projectors*. In this case, the lighting instrument has a special slot right next to the beam-shaping shutters, which can hold a metal pattern called a cucalorus or, for short, *cookie.* The ellipsoidal spot projects the cookie as a clear shadow pattern on any surface. Most often, it is used to break up flat surfaces, such as the cyclorama or the studio floor. *(See 5.14.)*

5·15 Sometimes you may find that a television show requires the use of a *follow spot,* a powerful special effects spotlight that is used primarily to simulate theater stage effects. The follow spot generally follows action, such as dancers, ice skaters, or single performers moving about in front of a stage curtain.

The follow spot has controls through which you can simultaneously pan and tilt the instrument, spread or pin, and shape the light beam, all while following the action.

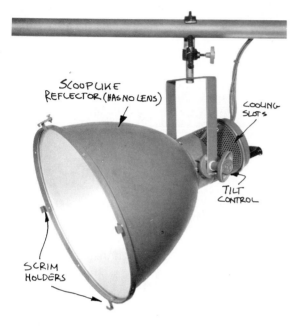

5·16 Scoop.

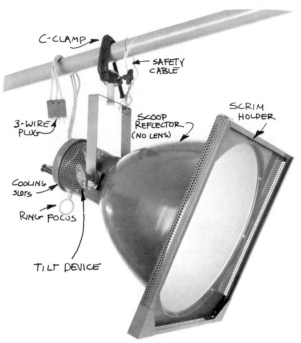

5·17 Ring-Focus Quartz Scoop.

Ellipsoidal spotlights come in sizes from 500 watts to 2,000 watts, but the most commonly used is the 1,000-watt. The ellipsoidal spot is generally used, not for the standard television lighting, but only when specific, precise lighting tasks have to be performed.

Floodlights

Floodlights are designed to produce a great amount of highly diffused light. They are principally used to slow down falloff (reduce contrast between light and shadow areas) and to provide baselight.

Since even in floodlights the spread of the beam should be somewhat controllable so that undue spill into other set areas can be minimized, some floodlights, like spotlights, have adjustable beams.

There are four basic types of floodlights: (1) the scoop, (2) the broad and softlight, (3) the floodlight bank, and (4) the strip, or cyc, light.

The Scoop   Named for its peculiar scooplike reflector, this floodlight is one of the most versatile and popular. Like most other floodlights, the scoop has no lens.

There are *fixed-focus* and *adjustable-focus* scoops. The fixed-focus scoop permits no simple adjust-

---

5·18   Most scoops range from 1,000 watts to 2,000 watts. Scoops are also classified by the diameter of the scoop reflector. Thus, we have 14-inch, 16-inch, and 18-inch scoops. The 14-inch and 16-inch scoops with 1,000-watt lamps are most often used in television lighting.

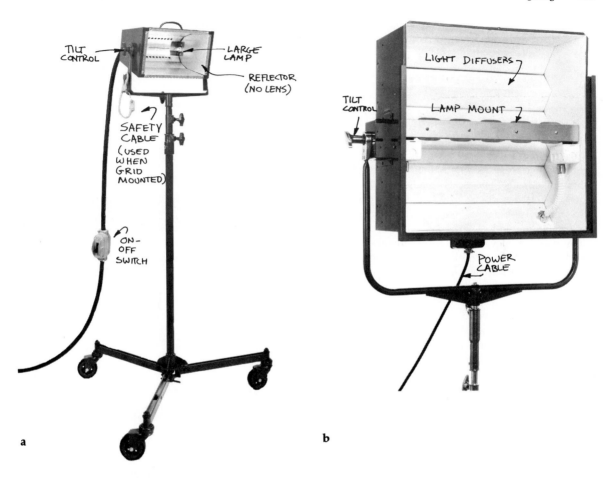

a

b

5·19 (a) Small Broad. (b) Large Broad.

ment of its light beam. Pinning the beam is not possible at all. You can, however, increase the diffusion of the light beam by attaching a *scrim* in front of the scoop. A scrim is a spun-glass material held in a metal frame. Although the light output is considerably reduced through their use, some lighting people put scrims on all scoops, not only to produce highly diffused light but to protect the studio personnel in case the hot lamp inside the scoop shatters. *(See 5.16.)*

Some of the quartz scoops have adjustable beams, from medium-spread positions to full flood. The adjustable scoops are especially handy for filling in shadows in precisely defined areas. *(See 5.17.)*

The Broad and the Softlight The *broad* (from broadside) and *softlight* instruments are used to provide extremely diffused, even lighting.

5·20   The most widely used broads in television lighting range from 600 watts to 1,000 watts. Soft-lights range from 1,000 watts to large 8,000-watt units; the 1,000-watt–2,000-watt units are generally used in television lighting and the larger ones for motion picture work.

The high-efficiency quartz lamps are, of course, the ideal light source for all floodlights, especially the broads and softlights. All softlights have a per-manently attached scrim, sometimes called "silk-dif-fuser."

Some softlights have fluorescent tubes instead of quartz lamps. However, these can be used only in location shooting, where the general lighting comes from overhead fluorescent tubes. Thus, the softlights match the overall lighting in color temperature.

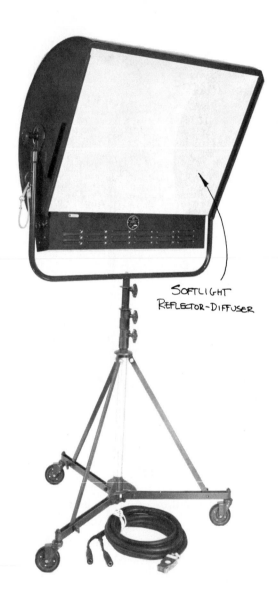

SOFTLIGHT
REFLECTOR-DIFFUSER

5·21   Softlight.

Broads act like a series of scoops. They illuminate evenly a rather large area with diffused light, with some provision for beam control. *(See 5.19.)*

Some broads have barn doors (see page 115) to block gross light spill into other set areas; others have even an adjustable beam, similar to the adjustable scoops. They are sometimes called "multiple broads."

Softlights, on the other hand, are used for extremely diffused, even lighting. If, for example, you want to increase the baselight level without in the least affecting your specific lighting (highlights and shadow areas carefully controlled), you can turn on a few softlights. They act like fluorescent tubes, except that they burn with a lower (3,200°K) color temperature. *(See 5.21.)*

The Floodlight Bank This consists of a series of high-intensity internal reflector bulbs arranged in banks of six, nine, twelve, or more spots. The floodlight bank is mostly used on remotes as *daylight booster.* Because they are large and awkward to handle, you will not often find them in studios. For studio lighting, the softlight outperforms the floodlight bank, at least in operational ease. *(See 5.22.)*

The Strip, or Cyc, Light This is commonly used to achieve even illumination of large set areas, such as the cyc (cyclorama) or some other uninterrupted background area. Very similar to the border or cyc lights of the theater, television strip lights consist of rows of from three to twelve incandescent or quartz lamps mounted in long, boxlike reflectors. The more sophisticated strip lights have, like theater border lights, glass color frames for each of the reflector units, so that the cyc can be illuminated in different colors. *(See 5.23.)*

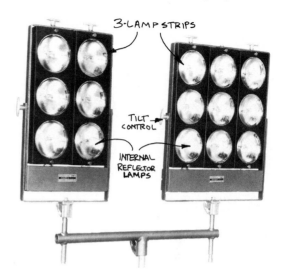

5·22 Floodlight Bank: The floodlight bank consists of at least six individual internal reflector lamps, stacked as two three-lamp strips. Larger banks stack three, four, or even five three-lamp strips for a total of nine, twelve, or fifteen internal reflector bulbs.

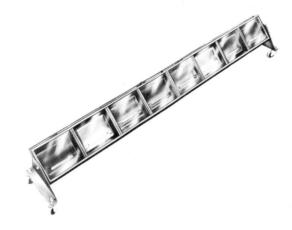

5·23 Strip, or Cyc, Light.

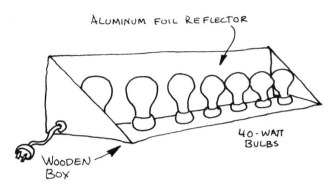

5·24 Simple Striplight.

Homemade versions of the strip light are often quite adequate for routine cyc lighting. The reflector is a simple wooden box (made of 1 X 8 boards), and illumination is provided by a series of simple (40-watt or 60-watt) frosted household bulbs. *(See 5.24.)*

You can use strip lights also as general floodlights by suspending them from the studio ceiling, or you can place them on the studio floor to separate ground rows from the cyclorama, or pillar and other set pieces from the lighted background. Strip lights are ideal instruments for silhouette lighting (where the background must be evenly illuminated, with the foreground pieces remaining unlit).

Portable Lighting Instruments

Obviously, you can use studio lighting instruments on remote location. However, you may find that they are too bulky to move around easily, that their large three-pronged plugs or twist-lock plugs do not fit the household receptacles, and that, once in place and operating, they do not provide the amount or type of illumination you need for good remote lighting. Besides, most studio lights are suspended on the overhead lighting grid. To take them down each time you have

to light a remote telecast not only wastes valuable production time, but more important, robs the studio of valuable lighting instruments.

Special *portable lighting packages* have, therefore, been developed that can fulfill the basic lighting requirements for simple productions away from the studio. You will find that the basic requirements for remote lighting are (1) a great amount of illumination with as few instruments as possible; (2) compact instruments that take up very little room, and that can be set up and struck (taken down) with minimal time and effort; and (3) instruments that can be operated with household current without danger of overloading circuits.

Even in studio lighting, such portable units can prove extremely helpful, especially if your studio is rather small or if your studio ceiling is too low for overhead suspension of lighting instruments —as in a converted classroom, for example. As with the studio lighting package, the portable lights are grouped into (1) spotlights and (2) floodlights.

Spotlights

Portable spotlights are designed to be light, rugged, efficient (which means that the light output is great relative to the size of the instrument), easy to set up and transport, and small enough so that they can be hidden rather effectively even in cramped interiors.

The two most frequently used are (1) the external reflector spotlight and (2) the internal reflector spotlight.

The External Reflector Spotlight Mainly because of weight consideration and light efficiency, this spotlight has no lens. We use the term "external reflector" so as to distinguish it from the small Fresnel studio spot (which, of course, can also be

5·25   External Reflector Spots.

used on remote location) and the internal reflector spotlight, which we will discuss below.

The lack of a good lens makes the beam of the external reflector spot less precise than that of the Fresnel spot. But in most remote lighting tasks, a highly defined beam would offer no particular advantage. Since you will usually have to work with a minimum of lighting instruments on remote location, a fairly flat, yet *even*, illumination is often better than a dramatic, yet extremely spotty, one. Still, even on remote location, you should try to light as precisely as possible without sacrificing a sufficient operating light level.

The external reflector spot makes fairly precise lighting possible. You can pin or spread the beam of the high-efficiency quartz lamp through a sweep-focus control lever or knob in the back of the instrument. *(See 5.25.)*

Unfortunately, the pinned beam is not always even. When you have to place the lighting instrument rather close to the object, you may notice (and the camera will surely notice) that the rim of the beam is quite intense and "hot," while the center of the beam has a hole, a low-intensity dark spot. In extreme cases, especially when lighting a face, this uneven beam may look as

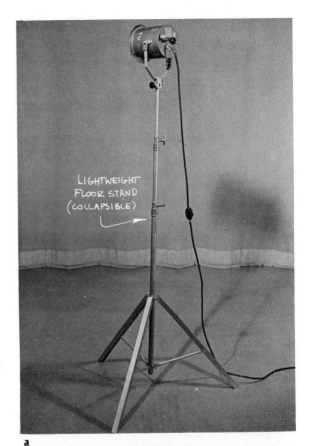

a

b

5·26   (a) External Reflector Spot on Stand. (b) External Reflector Spot with Gaffer Grip.

5·27 Clip Light.

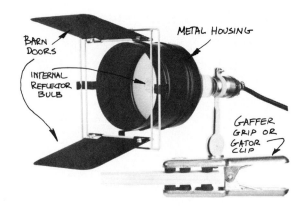

5·28 Clip Light with Metal Housing and Barn Doors.

though you had forgotten to turn on one of the instruments. By spreading the beam a little, however, you can correct this problem rather easily.

All external reflector spotlights have a special bracket for floor mounting on a lightweight stand *(see 5.26a)* or on a heavy clip, called a gaffer grip, or gator clip *(see 5.26b)*.

Most external reflector spotlights can be plugged into a regular household receptacle. Be careful, however, not to overload the circuit; that is, don't exceed the circuit's amperage.

The smaller Fresnel spotlights are, of course, also used in remote lighting. Make sure in such instances that they are equipped with special mounting devices for fastening them onto lightweight mounting stands, and that you have light-plug adapters for plugging the instruments into the household receptacles.

Internal Reflector Spotlight This spotlight looks like an overgrown, slightly squashed household bulb. You have probably used it already in your still photography. The reflector for the bulb is inside the lamp. All you need for using this kind of spot is a light socket and a clamp with

which to fasten the bulb onto a chair, a door, a windowsill, or a small pole. Because internal reflector spotlights are usually clipped onto things, they are often called *clip lights.*

You can use clip lights to light small areas easily and also to fill in areas that cannot be illuminated with the other portable instruments. The clip light is an excellent device to provide additional highlights and accents in areas whose lighting looks too flat. *(See 5.27.)*

Internal reflector spots come in a *variety of beam spreads,* from a soft, diffused beam to a hard, rather precisely shaped beam. For even better beam control, as well as for the protection of the internal reflector bulb, the lamp can be used in a metal housing with barn doors attached *(see 5.28).*

While most internal reflector spotlights are incandescent lights, there are also a number of high-intensity quartz lamps on the market, one of the most popular being the "sun gun" *(see 5.29).*

Floodlights

Since the principal objective in most remote lighting is adequate, even illumination, floodlights are

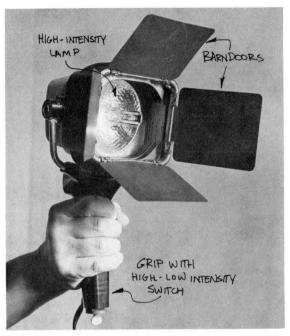

5·29 Sun Gun with Barn Doors.

5·30 Nook Light.

often the more efficient, though not necessarily the more versatile, of the portable lighting instruments.

Unless you work in a large room, such as a gymnasium or the town hall, the studio scoops usually prove too heavy and bulky for remote use. The relatively light and highly efficient broads and softlights are, therefore, preferred for this kind of work (see page 103). Most of these instruments have a two-way switch for low and high intensity, and can be mounted easily on lightweight, collapsible tripods. If you need to light a very small area, you can use a *nook light,* which is a very small floodlight. Like the internal reflector spot, the nook light can be attached to a piece of scenery or furniture. However, since it gives off a relatively great amount of diffused light, it is an ideal instrument for filling in small shadow areas. *(See 5.30.)*

Portable floodlights, like spotlights, usually come with three-wire extension cables that fit ordinary household receptacles. Some of the extension cables have on-off switches next to the instruments, making it unnecessary to unplug the instrument each time you want to turn it off. By the way, there are three good reasons why you should keep portable lighting instruments turned off as much as possible: (1) You will prolong the life of the bulb. (2) You will keep the performance areas as cool as possible; the excessive heat radiation of the quartz instruments makes working in cramped quarters especially uncomfortable. (3) You will conserve energy. (*Note:* Wear gloves when handling instruments that are turned on.)

Lighting Control Equipment

Television operation, especially in small stations, necessitates extremely flexible lighting equipment for several reasons: (1) Constantly moving television cameras and microphone booms make any permanent lighting setup on the studio floor impossible. (2) When only a small amount of lighting equipment is available, what there is must be flexible enough to provide adequate light for every corner of the studio. (3) There is rarely enough time or manpower to design and execute a proper lighting plan for each television production. The lighting setup must be flexible enough to allow one person to change the studio lighting with speed and the least effort.

The necessary control and flexibility of light is achieved primarily by three methods: (1) directional control, (2) intensity control, and (3) color control.

Directional Controls

Directional controls for lighting instruments help you to mount the instrument in a given position, point the lighting beam in a given direction, and keep the beam from spilling into unwanted areas.

Thus, we have four basic directional controls: (1) basic mounting devices, (2) basic hanging devices, (3) mounting devices for floor or portable lights, and (4) barn doors.

Basic Mounting Devices   Studio lights are hung from either fixed *pipe grids* or *counterweight battens,* which can be lowered and raised to a specific vertical position. *(See 5.31 and 5.32.)*

Basic Hanging Devices   The lighting instruments are either directly attached to the light batten by a *C-clamp,* or hung from the batten by hanging devices that enable you to *vary* the *vertical posi-*

5·31   Pipe Grid: The pipe grid consists of rather heavy pipe strung either crosswise or parallel and mounted from 12 to 18 feet above the studio floor. The height of the grid is, of course, determined by the studio ceiling height, but even in rooms with low ceilings, the pipe should be mounted approximately two feet below the ceiling so that the lighting instruments or the hanging devices can be easily mounted onto the pipe.

tion of the instrument without raising or lowering the battens. If you have a fixed pipe grid rather than the movable counterweight system, these hanging devices are especially important. The most common are the *pantograph,* the *sliding rod,* and the *telescope hanger. (See 5.34 through 5.39.)*

Mounting of Floor Lights   While in motion picture production a large part of the lighting is done from the studio floor, television resorts to such lighting only occasionally. As pointed out before, the moving television cameras require that the studio floor be kept uncluttered. Also, the danger of having the lights picked up by one of the cameras is much too great to make lighting from the floor a viable production technique. But

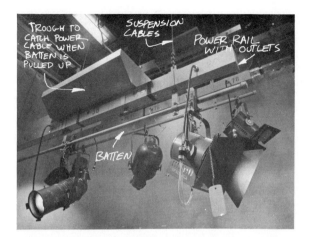

5·32 Counterweight Battens: The *counterweight battens* can be lowered and raised to any desired position and locked firmly into place. The battens and the instruments are counterweighted by heavy steel weights and moved by means of a rope-and-pulley system or individual motors. The advantage of counterweight battens over the pipe grid system is that the instruments can be hung, maintained, and adjusted to a rough operating position directly from the studio floor. However, even this arrangement does not altogether eliminate the use of a ladder. Especially in small studios, the studio floor is rarely sufficiently clear of cameras, microphone booms, or scenery for the battens to be lowered all the way to comfortable working height. You will find that after having adjusted the lighting instruments as to direction and beam focus, you will still need a ladder or the lighting pole for the accurate final trimming once the battens have been raised to the proper position.

you may find that you will need to supplement the overhead lighting with some floor lights.

Floor lights are usually mounted on vertical *roller-caster stands* that can be vertically adjusted up to eight feet. Such stands can hold any type of lighting instrument—scoops, broads, spots, and even strip lights. The more elaborate ones have a light switch attached to them so that you can regulate the floor instrument without having to go through the dimmer control. *(See 5.40 and 5.41.)*

Barn Doors These are movable metal flaps that can be inserted into a special slot in front of any spotlight. They are intended to *block the light* very much the same way as you shield your eyes from the sun with your hand.

5·33 There are further rail-type mounting devices for lighting instruments, which are highly specific in their application. Generally, a sliding track (which can even carry the electric current) is attached directly to the ceiling, and the lighting fixtures slide along the rail into limited horizontal positions. The principle of the rail-type mounting is quite similar to the traverse rod on which household curtains are hung and moved along. The double disadvantages of such mountings are the high installation cost and limited positions of the lighting instruments. However, in the conversion of low-ceilinged classrooms into small television studios, rail-type mountings sometimes prove to be the most effective lighting arrangement.

5·34 C-Clamp: With the C-clamp, you can securely attach even the heaviest lighting instrument to the mounting pipe. A bolt at the bottom of the C-clamp enables you to swivel the instrument into the desired position. For increased safety, secure each instrument directly to the grid by a small chain or cable.

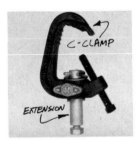

5·35 C-Clamp with Extension: Some C-clamps have a small extension hanger attached, which makes the turning of the lighting instruments a little easier than with the standard C-clamp.

5·36 Pantograph: The most versatile and most frequently used hanging device is the *pantograph.* This is a spring-counterbalanced hanger that can be adjusted quickly and easily from the studio floor to any height within its more than sufficient 12-foot range. Depending on the lighting instrument attached to it, you need one or two sets of springs for counterbalancing. Heavier springs permit the mounting and counterbalancing of other equipment, such as a studio monitor. In most studios, where the grid height rarely exceeds 18 feet, you can pull the lighting instrument down to almost floor level, make the necessary lighting adjustment, and push the instrument back into the desired position, all in a matter of seconds. Even if you have counterweight battens, you can still use pantographs to make some of your lighting instruments even more flexible.

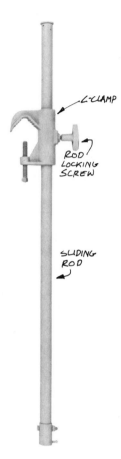

5·37 Sliding Rod: The *sliding rod* is another hanging device that allows vertical positioning of lighting instruments. However, in the up-position, the sliding rod needs a considerable clearance between grid and ceiling; otherwise it cannot be pushed up high enough. An additional problem is that any adjustment has to be made from the grid, which requires a bulky ladder and much time.

5·38 Telescope Hanger: The *telescope hanger* is similar to the sliding rod, except that the rod telescopes into itself when the hanger is pushed up. Thus the telescope hanger needs little clearance between grid and ceiling.

5·39 The ideal hanging devices are, of course, motorized telescope hangers or winches for each instrument. Occasionally you will find such an extravagant hanging system in large television production centers. For small station operation, such devices are much too costly and really not necessary.

5·40 Floorstand: The floorstand can support any type of lighting instrument, and can even be adapted for an easel stand.

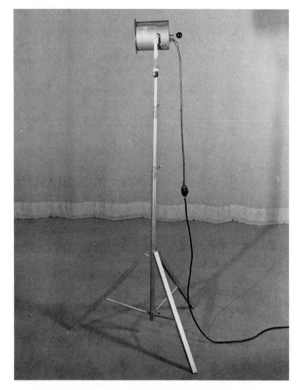

5·41 Collapsible Floorstand: Portable lights do not require as heavy a floorstand as studio lights. For all portable lighting instruments, special collapsible stands have been developed that telescope from a 2-foot minimum to an over 8-foot maximum height. On some models the legs can be extended individually so that the light remains level even if standing on steps or uneven ground.

This admittedly crude beam control method is extremely effective if you want to block certain set areas partially or totally from illumination. For example, if you want to keep the upper part of some scenery dark, without sacrificing illumination of the lower part, you simply "barn-door" off the upper part of the beam. Or, if you want

to eliminate a boom shadow, you may be able to do so by partially closing a barn door. *(See 5.42 and 5.43.)*

Since the barn doors slide into their holders rather easily, they have a tendency to slide out of them just as readily. Make sure, therefore, that they are chained to the instrument so that they can't drop on you, especially when you are adjusting them from the studio floor with a light pole. Also, barn doors get very hot. Wear asbestos gloves if you handle them while the instrument is turned on.

We have already mentioned the *spun-glass diffusers,* or scrims, which you may put in front of the floodlights in order to diffuse the beam even more than in its extreme flood (spread) position.

Intensity Controls

The simplest way of controlling light intensity is obviously to turn on only a certain number of lighting instruments of a specific size (wattage). Unfortunately, since television lighting techniques and the delicate control of shadows call for light to come from very specific directions, it is not always possible to turn a light either on or off simply because the camera receives too little or too much light. With a *dimmer,* you can easily manipulate each lighting instrument, or groups of instruments, to burn at any given intensity, from zero (off position) to full strength.

Although dimmers are technically quite complex, their basic operational principle is simple: *by allowing more or less current to flow to the lamp, the lamp burns with a higher or lower intensity.* If you want the lighting instrument to burn at full intensity, the dimmer lets all the current flow to the lamp. If you want it to burn at a lesser intensity, the dimmer reduces somewhat the voltage that flows to the lamp. If you want to dim the light completely, called a *blackout,* no current—or at least an inadequate current—reaches the lamp.

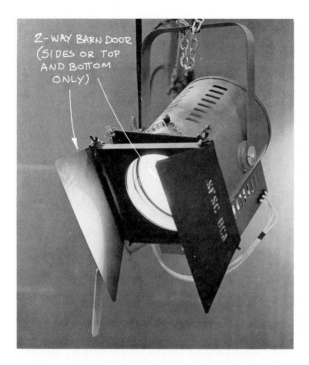

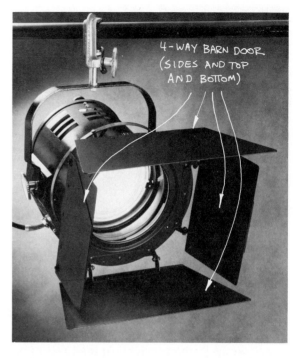

5·42 Two-Way Barn Door: The two-way barn door has two movable metal flaps. They can be attached to the lighting instrument so that they block either the top and bottom part of the light beam or its right and left spread.

5·43 Four-Way Barn Door: With the four-way barn door, all four sides—top and bottom, and left and right sides—of the beam spread can be blocked simultaneously.

All dimmers, regardless of make and relative complexity, are designed to fulfill these principal functions: (1) *Contrast control:* Through dimmers, we can control even the most subtle differences between light and shadow areas. The subtle manipulation of falloff requires their use. (2) *Light changes:* Dimmers enable you to change quickly and easily from one type of lighting in a particular area to another. Also, with the use of a *dimmer board* and its related equipment, you can light several studio areas at once, store the lighting setup in the preset board, and activate any part or all of the stored lighting information whenever

necessary. (3) *Special effects lighting:* With the help of the dimmer board, you can achieve a variety of special effects lighting (such as silhouette, or a series of pools of light) without affecting the standard lighting setup in any way.

Three features of a good dimmer system are especially important in the context of the major functions just mentioned: (1) the calibration of the individual dimmer, (2) the patchboard, and (3) the preset board.

Calibration Each individual dimmer has a calibration from 0 to 10. At the zero position, the

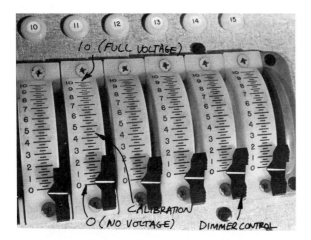

5·44 Dimmer Calibration: At a dimmer setting of 0, no current flows to the lamp; at a setting of 10, the full current flows to the lamp, and the lamp burns at full intensity.

lighting instrument is dimmed down completely; consequently, it emits no light. At the 10 position, the lighting instrument receives its full current and burns with maximum intensity. The dimming steps between 0 and 10 are generally large enough to be detected readily by the camera. *(See 5.44.)*

This calibration is particularly useful in the initial setting of light intensities, and in recording and repeating the rehearsal lighting intensities for the final telecast.

The Patchboard Sometimes called a patchbay, this device connects lighting instruments to dimmer control. Regardless of make and design, all patchboards work on the same principle: *to connect widely scattered instruments to a specific dimmer,* or separate dimmers, on the dimmer control board. Most of the important lighting instruments in the studio terminate at the patchboard. Let's assume that you have fifty overhead lighting instruments in

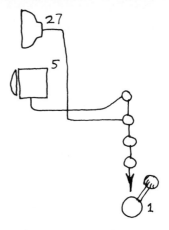

5·45 Patching: As you can see, the patches for the lighting instruments No. 5 (spot) and No. 27 (scoop) are both patched into dimmer No. 1. Consequently, both lighting instruments respond identically to any No. 1 dimmer setting.

your studio. Let's further assume that each one of these has its corresponding patch. Each of the fifty outlets on the light battens is numbered, and the patchcords for each light have corresponding numbers. (Don't number the instrument itself, since, if you were to shift the instrument into a different position, your patchcord number would no longer correspond with the lighting instrument.)

Now, for example, if you want to patch instru-

5·46 Let's try to patch some instruments so that you can effect a simple lighting change for a specific studio area. First, you light the designated studio area A with three spotlights. These happen to be plugged into the batten outlets Nos. 5, 12, and 18. Since all the spotlights should turn on and off at the same time and burn at the same intensity, you can patch them into the same dimmer, dimmer No. 1. Now, let's assume that you want to change from this rather harsh spotlighting to a softer floodlighting of the same area. You will now pick three scoops that will illuminate area A from the direction of the spotlights. These scoops happen to be plugged into the batten outlets Nos. 6, 13, and 19. You look for the patchcords Nos. 6, 13, and 19 at the patchboard and plug all three patches into the dimmer No. 2 receptacles.

If you bring up dimmer No. 1, area A is illuminated with three spotlights. If you now want to change to the diffused lighting of the scoops, you simply bring down dimmer No. 1 (which turns off the spotlights) and bring up dimmer No. 2 (which turns on the scoops). If you bring up dimmer No. 2 while bringing down dimmer No. 1, your light change will be very gradual, very much like a picture dissolve.

If you want to control each light separately, so that you can balance the intensity of each of the six lighting instruments (the three spots and the three scoops), you will have to assign a separate dimmer to each instrument. Therefore, spot No. 5 will be patched into dimmer No. 1; spot No. 12 into dimmer No. 2; spot No. 18 into dimmer No. 3; scoop No. 6 into dimmer No. 4; scoop No. 13. into dimmer No. 5; and scoop No. 19 into dimmer No. 6. *(See a.)* Unless you have further sophisticated grouping or preset facilities, you will now have to work all six dim-

mers simultaneously to effect the simple lighting change in area A. As you can see, without a preset board, it is often more practical to patch several lighting instruments into a single dimmer than to use a separate dimmer for each one. *(See b.)*

a Single Patching.

b Multiple Patching.

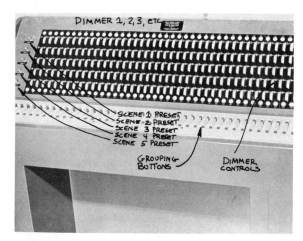

5·47 Five-Scene Preset Board.

ment No. 5 (a spotlight plugged into the No. 5 batten outlet) and instrument No. 27 (a scoop plugged into the No. 27 batten outlet at the other end of the studio) into dimmer No. 1, you simply take the patchcords No. 5 and No. 27 and plug them into the receptacles for dimmer No. 1. Depending on the rated power of the dimmer, you may plug several lighting instruments into a single dimmer. If you now bring up dimmer No. 1 at your dimmer board, both instruments, spotlight No. 5 and scoop No. 27, will light up simultaneously *(see 5.45).*

The patchboard thus allows many combinations of specific lighting instruments from different studio areas so that they can be controlled individually or in groups as to their intensity.

The Preset Board This is a storage device for several different lighting setups. Whether mechanical or computer assisted, the preset board can memorize the lighting setups for several scenes. You can, for example, use one instrument, such as our spotlight No. 5, and preset it so that it will operate at full intensity in scene 1, at one-

half intensity in scene 2, at three-quarters intensity in scene 3, and at full intensity again in scene 4, even though it is patched into only one dimmer. The preset board stores the different settings of dimmer No. 1 (full, ½, ¾, full) and relates this information to the lighting instrument according to whichever scene (1, 2, 3, or 4) is activated.

Most sophisticated preset boards have further *grouping devices,* which make your light combinations even more flexible. For example, the grouping buttons allow you to preset within each scene special lighting effects, such as silhouette lighting. All you do in this case is group all the floodlights together that illuminate the background while keeping the other lights completely dimmed down. *(See 5.47.)*

Highly sophisticated dimmer systems are computer assisted. Special punch cards (similar to the familiar IBM cards) contain the necessary dimmer information (as gained during rehearsal) and activate even the most complicated dimmer operations with ease and reliability.

Color Controls

Color control in lighting includes (1) color temperature control, and (2) actual production and manipulation of colored light.

Color Temperature Control We have already discussed how different lamps may burn at various color temperatures, and how dimming affects color temperature. To repeat: the most common methods of controlling color temperature are (1) to use lamps in your lighting instruments with a uniform Kelvin rating, such as 3,200°K; (2) to dim not at all, or only slightly, the lights that are used for the principal performance areas; (3) to use color correction filters, and color temperature correction circuits in your camera chain, if available.

An additional color control, which is frequently

used in motion picture lighting but only occasionally in television, is to put a variety of color temperature correction filters directly in front of the lighting instruments. If the color temperature is too high (light too bluish), you use an orange filter in front of the lighting instrument to lower the color temperature. If the color temperature has to be boosted (to bring indoor light sources to match the cool outdoor light, for example), you need a blue filter.[3]

Colored Light Control   You can produce a great variety of colored lights simply by putting a *colored filter*—colored gelatin or the more durable plastic, such as *cinemoid*—in front of the lighting instrument. Again, do not use colored light in performance areas, at least not if you intend the scene to look normal. Limit it to background lighting, or use it for special effects.

As you remember from our discussion of how the camera works, *colored light mixes additively,* not subtractively as paints do. In a colored light mixture, red and green gives off a rich yellow, not a muddy brown as paints would produce.[4]

Summary

Like the human eye, the television camera needs light in order to function effectively. The *control* of light is called *lighting.*

Objectives for lighting may be either technical or nontechnical.

The *technical lighting objectives* are (1) to achieve the proper baselight level, which means to provide enough light so that the pickup tube or tubes and the electronic accessories can function with some degree of efficiency, (2) contrast, which refers to a basic limit between highlight and shadow areas, or light and dark colors, and (3) color temperature, which refers to the relative reddishness or bluishness of white light as produced by the lighting instruments.

The *nontechnical lighting objectives* are (1) to indicate form and dimension, (2) to create the illusion of reality or nonreality, and (3) to indicate mood. These three objectives require the careful control of shadows.

There are two types of *studio lighting instruments:* (1) spotlights and (2) floodlights. Both can have either quartz (tungsten-halogen) or incandescent lamps. The most prevalent *spotlights* are (1) the Fresnel spot, and (2) the ellipsoidal spot. The most common *floodlights* are (1) the scoop, (2) the broad or softlight, (3) the floodlight bank, and (4) the strip, or cyc, light.

Portable lighting instruments include small external and internal reflector spotlights, and floodlights.

Lighting *control equipment* consists of directional controls, intensity controls, and color controls. The *directional controls* include (1) basic mounting devices, (2) basic hanging devices, (3) mounting devices for floor or portable lights, and (4) barn doors. The most common *intensity control* is the dimmer. *Color control* includes the control of the color temperature through the use of variously rated (in degrees Kelvin) lamps and correctional filters, and the actual production and manipulation of colored light through color filters.

---

[3] For precise color temperature filter values, see Eli L. Levitan, *An Alphabetical Guide to Motion Picture, Television, and Videotape Production* (New York: McGraw-Hill Book Co., 1970), p. 131.
[4] You will find more information on how to use color "gels" in any good book on theater lighting.

6 *Techniques of Television Lighting*

The techniques of television lighting tell you what instrument to use in what particular position and with what intensity to achieve a desired lighting effect. Since light impressions (in the form of brightness and color) are primarily what the viewer perceives on the television screen, the technique of lighting—or the art of controlling light—is obviously an essential and powerful aspect of production.

A knowledge of these five areas is especially important for mastering the techniques of television lighting: (1) definitions of lighting terms, (2) the photographic, or triangle, lighting principle, (3) additional light sources, (4) special lighting techniques, and (5) operation of lights.

The section on key terms will contain only such definitions that are not already included in the first part of this chapter.

Since you now know the most important aspects of the lighting tools, let's put them to work.

In small stations, lack of proper equipment, space, time, and manpower influences lighting techniques and usually limits lighting possibilities to a considerable extent. These limitations, however, do not mean that good and creative television lighting is impossible; they simply call for greater ingenuity on the part of the lighting technician.

There are usually many solutions to one problem; therefore, a universal lighting recipe that works for every possible lighting situation cannot and should not be given here. An attempt is made, however, to list some basic lighting principles, which can be easily adapted to specific television lighting problems. You can then adapt these principles to your specific requirements, but do not start with the anticipated limitations. Start with how you would like the lighting to look and then adapt to the existing technical facilities.

Definition of Lighting Terms

You can apply the techniques of television lighting only if you are, first of all, thoroughly familiar with the basic terminology. In lighting for television (as well as for film and still photography) the instruments are labeled according to *function*, that is, their particular role in the lighting process.

Baselight is an extremely diffused, overall illumination in the studio, coming from no one particular source. A certain amount of baselight is necessary for the technical acceptability of a television picture.

Key light is the apparent principal source of directional illumination falling upon a subject or an area.

Back light is directional illumination coming substantially from behind the subject.

Fill light is a generally diffused light to reduce shadow or contrast range. It can be directional if the area to be "filled in" is rather limited.

Cameo Lighting Foreground figures are lighted with highly directional light, with the background remaining dark.

Light Angle The vertical angle of the suspended lighting instrument. A 45-degree angle is considered normal.

Light Ratio The relative intensities of key, back, and fill. A 1:1 ratio between key and back lights means that both light sources burn with equal intensities. A 1:½ ratio between key and fill lights means that the fill light burns with half the intensity of the key light. Because light ratios depend on many other production variables, they cannot be fixed. A key:back:fill ratio of 1:1:½ is often used for normal triangle lighting.

Lighting Triangle Same as Photographic Principle: the triangular arrangement of key, back, and fill lights.

Photographic Principle The triangular arrangement of key, back, and fill lights, with the back light opposite the camera and directly behind the object, and the key and fill lights opposite each other to the front and side of the object. Also called triangle lighting.

Vertical Key Light Position The relative distance of the key light from the studio floor, specifically with respect to whether it is above or below the eye level of the performer. Not to be confused with high- and low-key lighting, which refers to the relative brightness and contrast of the overall scene.

Background light or *set light* is an illumination of the background or set separate from the lights provided for the performers or performing areas.

Side light is a directional light that illuminates the front side of a subject, usually opposite the key light.

Kicker light is a directional illumination from the back, off to one side of the subject, usually from a low angle.

Camera light is a small spotlight mounted on top of the television camera. It is used for additional fill or eye sparkle, as principal light source for objects located in dark corners of the studio, or to provide illumination when another instrument causes the camera to cast an unwanted shadow.

You should realize that there are several variations for these terms; however, most television operations use this terminology as their standard.

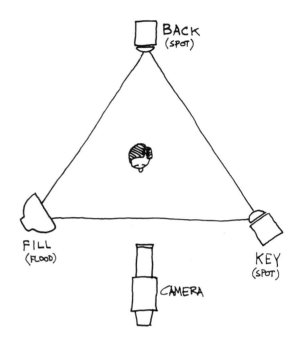

6·1 Basic Photographic Principle: As you can readily see, the three principal lights, key (spot), back (spot), and fill (flood), form a triangle, with the back light as its apex, opposite the camera.

The Photographic Principle, or Basic Triangle Lighting

As one of the photographic arts, television is subject to photographic lighting principles.

The most basic photographic lighting principle —or, as it is frequently called, basic triangle lighting—consists of three main light sources: (1) key light, (2) back light, and (3) fill light.

Each of the three main instruments is positioned in such a way that it can optimally fulfill its assigned function. This arrangement is the *lighting triangle (see 6.1 and 6.2)*. But what exactly are the functions each instrument is to fulfill? Let's find out.

Functions of Main Light Sources

Each of the three main light sources, key, back, and fill, has to fulfill a very specific function so that the major objective can be reached: the revelation of form and dimension—or, in lighting terms, the manipulation of light and shadow in order to produce the impression of a three-dimensional object on the two-dimensional television screen.

Key Light   As the principal source of illumination, the major function of the key light is to reveal the *basic shape* of the object *(see 6.3)*. In order to reveal the basic shape, the key light must produce distinct shadows. Fresnel *spotlights,* medium spread, are normally used for key illumination.

In order to reveal as much of the object as possible, and to conform with our expectancy for the

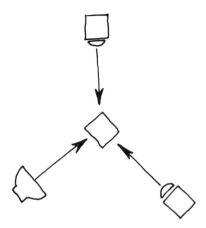

6·2 Basic Triangle Lighting: This is how the photographic principle lighting appears on the television screen. All three main light sources contribute to the revelation of the three-dimensional object on a two-dimensional screen.

principal light source to come from above, the key light is placed above and to the right or left front side of the object, from the camera's point of view.

If you look at figure 6.3a, which shows the cube illuminated with the key light only, you will notice that the falloff is very fast and that the shadows of the cube blend in with the background, making its true dimension rather ambiguous. To help make the object appear more distinct, we obviously need light sources other than the single key light.

Back Light   The back light has several important functions. As you see in figure 6.4a, it helps to distinguish between the shadow of the cube and the dark background; it emphasizes the outline, the *contour* of the object, separating it from its background. We can now perceive not only what the object itself looks like but also where it is

situated in relation to its environment, at least relative to its background. The back light has added a new spatial dimension. It also adds life and sparkle to the scene.

Generally, try to position the back light as directly behind the object (opposite the camera) as possible; there is no inherent virtue in placing it somewhat to one side or the other. A more critical problem is controlling the angle at which the back light strikes the object. If it is too close, or if the object moves too much under the back light, you will get undesirable top light instead of good back light. Top light is less effective since, instead of revealing the contour of the object, it simply overbrightens its top.

In general, lighting angles of 45 degrees are considered ideal for normal lighting situations.

In order to get good back lighting in a set, make sure that the *performance areas* (the areas in which performers will move) are *not too close* to the sce-

a

b

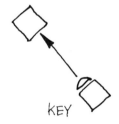

KEY

6·3 The key light represents the principal light source and reveals the basic shape of the object.

nery. Furniture used by the performers, such as chairs, tables, sofas, beds, should always be moved away from the walls as far into the center of the set as possible. Otherwise you will have to place the back lights at so steep an angle that undesirable top light will result. From a purely technical standpoint, it is better not to tilt the lighting instrument down too steeply, since in some instruments an extreme downward position prevents the heat from ventilating properly and causes the lamp to explode.

Fill Light   Now take another look at figures 6.3a and 6.4a. The falloff from light to dark is extremely fast, and the shadow side of the cube is so dense that the camera sees no object detail. If the cube were rendered in color, the color would be either lost entirely in the dense shadow area or, at best, grossly distorted. We must now try to slow down this falloff and lighten up the dark side of the cube without erasing the shadow effect altogether, which would eliminate the modeling effect of the key light.

a

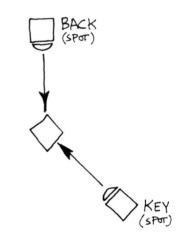

b

6·4 The back light helps to separate the object from its background and to reveal more of the object's true form and dimension.

You can *fill in* some of the shadows by placing a floodlight, generally a scoop, in front and a little to the side of the cube, *on the opposite side of the camera from the key light.* If you have a dimmer, put the fill light on a dimmer and see how you can render the shadow progressively translucent by supplying an increasing amount of fill light. *(See 6.5 through 6.7.)*

Since you simply want to lighten up a shadow area rather than produce new, harsh shadows on the other side of the cube, your fill light should be reasonably diffused.

Sometimes you may find that the fill light spills into other set areas. If your scoops have a focus control, focus the beam to its narrowest spread. Or, if you want even more beam control, you can use a Fresnel spotlight as fill light by spreading the beam as much as possible. With barn doors, you can then prevent part of the spread beam from hitting the other set areas.

For very soft fill, use softlights or broads with a light-diffusing scrim attached to them.

With the three main light sources in the triangle position, you have now established the basic

BACK
(SPOT)

FILL
(FLOOD)

KEY
(SPOT)

6·5 The fill light is placed opposite the key light to slow down falloff and to make the shadow areas more translucent.

photographic principle of television lighting. But you are not through just yet. You should now take a good hard look at the lighted object or, if possible, the studio monitor, to see whether or not the scene (in our case, the cube) needs some further adjustment for optimal lighting. Are there any undesirable shadows, or shadows that distort, rather than reveal, the object? How is the light balance? Does the fill light wash out all the necessary shadows? Or are the shadows still too dense? Is the key-fill combination too strong for the back light?

We are obviously still concerned with the finer points of directional and intensity controls.

Let's replace the cube with a person, or, if you can't find anybody who wants to sit still for that long, with a plaster bust, and see what final adjustments might have to be made to the direction and intensity of the light beams.

Directional Adjustments

Assuming that you have hung all three light instruments—the key, the back, and the fill lights

6·6 With too little fill, the shadow detail remains ambiguous.

—into approximately the right triangular position and that you have pointed them reasonably well toward the subject, there are usually two major areas that need further attention: (1) vertical key light position and eye shadows, and (2) boom shadows.

Key Light and Eye Shadows A fairly *high* key-light *position,* which means that the key light strikes the object from a *steep angle,* will cause large dark shadows under any protrusion or in any indentation, such as in the eye sockets, under the nose, and under the chin. If the subject wears glasses, you may find that the shadow of the upper rim of the glasses falls right across her or his eyes, thus preventing the camera (and the viewer) from seeing them clearly. *(See 6.8a)*

There are several ways of reducing these undesirable shadows. First, try to widen the angle of the key light by either lowering the light itself or using a key light farther away from the subject *(see 6.8b).*

If you lower it (with a movable batten or a pantograph), you will notice that the eye shadows seem to move farther up on the face, or at least get smaller, the lower the key light moves and the nearer it approaches the subject's eye level. When the key light reaches eye level, the eye shadows will have disappeared altogether. If you move it *below the eye level* of the subject, however, the shadows will now reverse themselves, producing a *ghostly* and *mysterious effect.* You have seen these "lighting from below" effects many times in mystery movies *(see 5.5b).*

Unfortunately, in television, where the cameras must move freely about the studio floor, lighting instruments that hang so low are a definite production hazard. Not only will they create a serious traffic problem, but they will also make it almost impossible for the other cameras to get a clear view of the scene, or for the boom to move about.

But since the vertical positioning of the key light is so important to lighting aesthetics (illusion of reality and nonreality, and mood), you should nevertheless try to make the Fresnel spots, which are used mostly for key lighting, as verti-

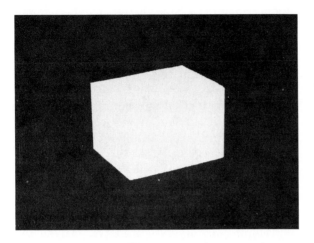

6·7 With too much fill, important form-revealing shadows are eliminated.

a

b

6·8 (a) The angle of the key light causes the upper rim of this woman's glasses to fall right across her eyes. (b) By lowering the key light instrument somewhat, you can eliminate the shadows.

cally flexible as possible. Perhaps you might try to suspend them on pantographs, although such practice hasn't found much acceptance so far.

If you can't move the key light down closer to the eye level of the subject, try to use a Fresnel spot that is farther away. The light beam coming from a greater distance will necessarily strike the subject from a flatter angle and cause less prominent eye shadows.

The second method is to use a fill light that

500-W SPOTLIGHT

6·9 Camera Light: A small spotlight is sometimes mounted on the camera to provide additional fill light, highlights (to add sparkle to eyes, for example), or general illumination for easel cards.

strikes the subject from a low angle. This is the preferred method of filling in eye shadows, since the fill lights will at the same time produce the necessary illumination for the baselight. Most scoops are, therefore, mounted on pantographs, or telescope poles, so that they can be pulled down into the desired low-angle fill position. Some lighting experts prefer to point some of the scoops toward the light-reflecting studio floor. This reflected, highly diffused, light will strike the subject from below eye level, filling in shadows without causing the ghostly from-below key light effect.

The third solution is to use a *camera light,* sometimes called inky-dinky, which is a small 150-watt baby spotlight mounted on the camera *(see 6.9).* This can be controlled by the camera operator through a small dimmer. Be careful not to dim the camera light too severely, especially on a closeup, or you will lower the color temperature of the lamp so much that the reddish light will cause color distortion.

Boom Shadows Now if we move a boom microphone in front of the lighted scene—in this case a single person—and move the boom around a little, you may notice boom shadows whenever your microphone or the boom passes through a spotlight beam. (You can easily substitute a broomstick or the lighting pole for the boom.) The more diffused light of the scoop will cast a soft, less-defined shadow. One obvious solution to this problem is to light everything with diffused light, so that the shadows are barely noticeable. Or, you may want to "wash out" the boom shadow with additional fill light. Both of these methods are unacceptable, since they cause also the elimination of *needed* shadows, making the lighting too flat.

What we must do instead is to light in such a way that the boom shadows are cast into places where the camera will not see them. Whenever a boom is used, try to position the boom or the key light in such a way that the boom will *not* have to *travel through the key light.* Or, you may have to light *steeper* than usual (use a spotlight that hangs overhead, yet fairly close to the subject, so that it has to be pointed down at a steep angle) in order to throw the boom shadows onto floor areas that are hidden from the camera's view.

Barn-dooring off part of the key light is another useful method of avoiding some of the boom shadows.

The easy way out, of course, is not to use the boom microphone but to rely on hand, desk, or lavaliere microphones (see Chapter 7). The nature of the show, however, may make their use not always possible or desirable.

Intensity Adjustments

Even if you have carefully adjusted the position and beam of the key, back, and fill lights, you will still need to *balance* their relative *intensities.* In fact, it is not only the direction of the lights that will orient the viewer in time, for example, but also their relative intensities. A strong key and back, and a low-intensity fill light can create the illusion of sunlight, while a strong back light, extremely low key, and medium-intensity fill can suggest moonlight.[1]

There is some argument about whether to balance the key and back lights first, or the key and fill lights. Actually, it matters little what you do first, as long as the end effect is a well-balanced picture.

We will, therefore, briefly talk about *relative intensities,* rather than priority. Again, you should realize that the proper balance depends on so many other production factors that it is impossible to give universally valid ratios. All we can do here is give you some basic clues.

Key-to-Back-Light Ratio   Generally, in normal conditions, back lights have approximately the same intensity as key lights. An unusually intense back light tends to glamorize the subject; a back light with an intensity much lower than that of the key will tend to get lost on the monitor. Without a strong back light, hair will look lifeless. A television performer with blond hair and a light dress or suit will need less back light than a dark-haired performer in a dark dress or suit.

The 1:1 key-to-back-light ratio (key and back lights have equal intensities) can go as high as 1:1½ (the back light has 1½ times the intensity of the key) if you need a fair amount of sparkle.

Key-to-Fill-Light Ratio   The fill-light intensity depends on how dense the shadows are that need to be filled and on the desired speed of falloff. If you want *fast falloff, little fill* will be needed. If you want very *slow falloff, higher-intensity fill* will be needed. It is, therefore, futile to state a standard

key-to-fill-light ratio. Just for starters, you may want to try a fill-light intensity that is one-half that of the key light, and go from there. Just remember that the more fill light you use, the less modeling the key light is doing, since the form-revealing shadows are all but eliminated. If you use almost no fill light, the dense shadows reveal no picture detail, and you run the risk of serious color distortion in the shadow areas. If, for example, the detective refers to the small scar on the left side of a woman's face, and your closeup of her face shows nothing but a dense shadow where the scar should be, your key-to-fill-light ratio is obviously wrong.

Again, as helpful as light meters are to establish rough lighting ratios, don't rely solely on them. Your *final criterion* is *how the picture looks on the monitor.*

Since you are now aware of the range of lighting ratios, you can try to light a person with the following intensities: key light, 200 ft-c; back light, 200 ft-c or slightly more; fill light, 100 ft-c, and background illumination of approximately 100 ft-c. *(See 6.10.)*

Your ratios in this setup are: key to back 1:1, and key to fill 1:½. The combination of these light intensities should give you a baselight illumination of approximately 200 ft-c to 230 ft-c. If this level is too high for you, simply dim the whole setup down a little. Be careful not to dim too heavily; otherwise the color-temperature change will become noticeable on the monitor.

The Photographic Principle and Continuous Action

One added problem in television lighting is movement—movement of the performer or performers, and movement of the camera or cameras. Fortunately, the basic photographic principle of key, back, and fill lights can be multiplied and used for each performing or set area. Even if you

---

[1] Herbert Zettl, *Sight-Sound-Motion* (Belmont, Calif.: Wadsworth Publishing Co., 1973), pp. 44–45.

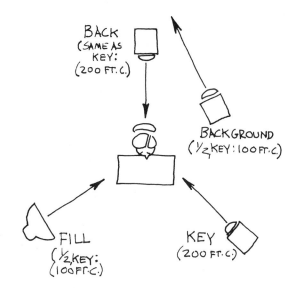

BACK
(SAME AS
KEY:
(200 FT.C.)

BACKGROUND
($\frac{1}{2}$KEY: 100 FT.C.)

FILL
($\frac{1}{2}$KEY:
(100 FT.C.)

KEY
(200 FT.C.)

6·10 Lighting Ratios.

have only two people sitting at a table *(see 6.11),* you will have to use a multiple application of the photographic principle.

In order to compensate for the movement of the performers, you should illuminate all adjacent performance areas in such a way that the basic triangle-lighted *areas overlap.* The basic purpose of overlapping is to give the performer continuous lighting as she moves from one area to another. It is all too easy to concentrate only on the major performance areas and to neglect the small, seemingly insignificant, areas in between. You may not even notice the unevenness of such lighting until ·the performer moves across the set. All of a sudden she seems to be playing a "now you see me, now you don't" game, popping alternately from a well-lighted area into dense shadow. This is the time when a light meter might come in handy. To spot such lighting "holes" before the cameras are

on, take a foot-candle meter and pan it smoothly along the set area, as the camera would in following the performer. Watch the needle. If it doesn't fluctuate too much during the pan, your lighting is fairly even. If, however, your intensities change from 200 ft-c to 10 ft-c, and back to 185 ft-c, you will have to add more lights to even out the overall illumination.

In lighting several set areas at once for continuous action, you may find that you don't have enough instruments to apply the overlapping triangle lighting. You may then have to place the lighting instruments in such a way that each one can serve two or even more *different functions (see 6.12).*

In reverse-angle shooting, for instance, the key light for one performer may become the back light for another, and vice versa. Or, you may have to use a key light to serve as directional fill in another area. Because of their diffused light beam, fill lights are often used to serve more than one area simultaneously.

Of course, the application of lighting instruments for multiple functions requires *exact position* of set pieces, such as tables and chairs, and *clearly defined* performing areas and blocking (movements of performers). Directors who decide to change blocking or move set pieces after the set has been lighted are not very popular with the lighting technicians.

Accurate lighting is always done with a basic *camera position* and viewpoint in mind. It helps greatly, therefore, if the lighting technician knows at least the basic parameters of the camera movement. For example, an object that appears perfectly well lighted from a six o'clock camera position may look woefully unlit from a ten o'clock camera position. Sometimes, as in variety shows, for example, "unlighted" shots from shooting angles that lie outside the lighted parameters may look quite dramatic; in most other

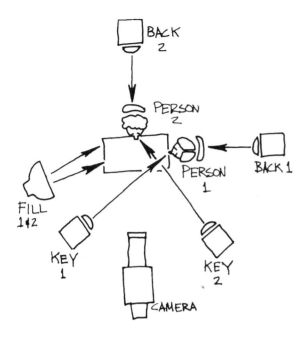

6·11   Multiple Application of Lighting Triangle: In the multiple application of the basic photographic principle, separate key and back lights are used for each person (performance area). Note, however, that the same fill light is used for both areas. Make sure that if person No. 1 is keyed from his left, person No. 2 must be keyed from the left also. A key-light reversal (person No.1 from left, person No. 2 from right) and the resulting shadow reversal would be very confusing to the viewer, especially when persons No. 1 and No. 2 are separated by closeups.

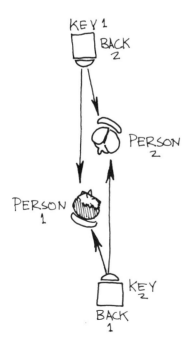

6·12   Multiple Function Lighting: In this multiple-function lighting, key light No. 1 also functions as back light No. 2, and key light No. 2 as back light No. 1.

6·13 Large Area Lighting: Large area lighting usually employs cross-keying, whereby the Fresnel spotlights assume multiple functions. From one side they serve as key lights; from the other, as directional fill; and from a side camera position, they may even act as back lights. The regular back lights are strung out behind the main action area, opposite the major camera positions. If any fill is necessary, it usually comes directly from the front. In effect, we have simply partially overlapped the triangles of the basic photographic principle.

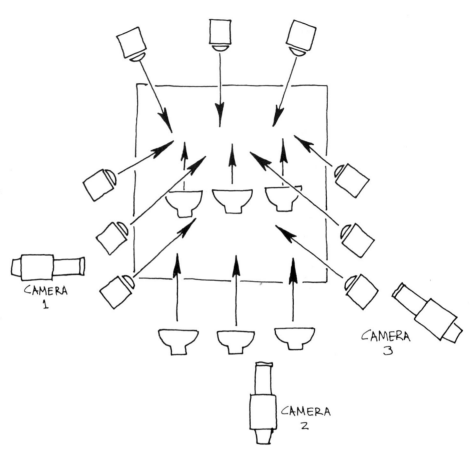

shows of less flexible lighting formats—news shows, interviews—these shots simply look bad.

For lighting a large area, such as an audience area or an orchestra, the basic photographic principle still holds. All you do is partially overlap one triangle over another, until you have adequately covered the entire area. However, instead of key-lighting just from one side of the camera and fill lighting from the other, you key-light from both sides of the camera. This method is generally called *cross-keying* (see 6.13). The key lights from one side act as fill for the key lights from the other side. The back lights are strung out in a row or a semicircle opposite the main camera position. The fill lights, if necessary, come directly from the front. If the cameras move to the side, some of the key lights also function as back lights.

Additional Light Sources

Several additional light sources are often used in connection with the basic photographic lighting setup. They include (1) the background or set light, (2) the side light, (3) the kicker light, and (4) the camera light (described on page 130).

6·14 Background Lighting: Through a change in background lighting, you can easily effect a change in locale, with no rearrangement of the actual lighting of the performance area. As you can see here, we can transform a scene from a prison to a church by a mere change of cookies (background projection). Together with appropriate music, such a change is entirely convincing to the viewer.

The basic functions of the additional light sources are to sharpen the viewer's orientation in space and time, to add sparkle and snap to the picture, and to help establish a general mood. In short, they help in clarifying and intensifying the screen event for the viewer.

Background or Set Light

The most important additional light source is the background light or, as it is frequently called, the set light. Its function is to *illuminate the background* (walls, cyclorama) of the set, or portions of the set that are not a direct part of the principal performing areas *(see 6.14)*. This light frequently goes beyond its mere supporting role to become a major production element. Besides accentuating an otherwise dull, monotonous background with a slice of light or an interesting cookie, the background light can be a *major indicator* of the show's *locale, time of day,* and *mood.* For example, a cookie projection of prison bars on the cyc, in connection with the clanging sounds of cell doors closing, will immediately set the scene. Simply by replacing the prison bar cookie with that of a cathedral window or silhouette of a cross, and the clanging

6·15 Don't confuse low-key and high-key with low and high vertical positions of the key light. They refer to the general mood of the lighting. Low-key means dark background, low overall light level, and fast falloff lighting, usually with strong back lights. High-key means generally a light background, bright overall illumination. The falloff may be fast (for sunshine) or slow (for bright, overcast outdoor scenes, or evenly lighted indoor scenes).

sounds with organ music, we will have transferred the prisoner instantaneously into a different environment, without ever touching the lighting on the actor himself.

A long slice of light, or long shadows, falling across the the back wall of an interior set will suggest, in connection with other congruent production clues, late afternoon or evening.

Dark backgrounds suggest, of course, a downward, low-key mood; light backgrounds an upbeat, happy mood. *(See 6.15.)*

Colored background lighting plays an especially prominent role in the production of musical shows and dance performances. You can achieve a variety of moods, or pure visual excitement, through certain combinations and changes of background colors. In certain instances, where you light more for the expressive intensification than for the clarification of the event, such as a rock concert, you may even use colored lights in the performance areas. Be very judicious here, however, as the undistorted skin tones are the principal color reference for the viewer, who has no way of knowing just what colors you are broadcasting. Colored lights in performance areas obviously render this common reference worthless.

In normal background lighting of an interior setting, for example, try to keep the *upper portions* of the set rather *dark,* with only the middle and lower portions (such as the walls) illuminated. The reasons for this common lighting practice are quite apparent: First, most indoor lighting is designed to illuminate low working areas rather than the upper portions of the walls. Second, the performer's head will be more pleasingly contrasted against a sightly darker background. Too much light at that height might cause a silhouette effect, rendering the face unusually dark. On the other hand, furniture and medium- and dark-colored clothing are nicely set off from the lighter lower portions of the set. Third, the dark upper

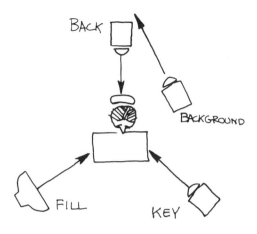

6·16 Direction of Background Light: When using a background light, make sure that the background light and the key light come from the same direc-

tion. Otherwise, the viewer experiences a shadow reversal in the same shot.

portions hide the lack of a ceiling and help to eliminate undesirable boom shadows.

You can darken the upper portions of the set rather easily by barn-dooring off any spotlight (including the background lights) that would hit those areas.

Make sure that the background lights strike the background from the same side as the key strikes the subject. Otherwise we may assume that there are two separate light sources illuminating the scene or, worse, that there are two suns in our solar system. *(See 6.16.)*

The Side Light

Generally placed directly to the *side of the subject,* the side light is used in place of or, more frequently, in addition to the fill light. It helps to reduce dense shadows that are not reached by the front fill light, and accentuates the contour of the subject. It becomes an essential light source if the camera's shooting parameter is exceptionally

wide. If, for instance, the camera arcs around the subject from a six o'clock position to a ten o'clock position, the side light will take on the function of the key light and provide essential modeling (lighting for three-dimensional effect). *(See 6.17.)*

Fresnel spotlights, with a wide beam, are generally used for side lighting.

For brilliant high-key lighting, you may find it helpful to support the key light with side fill light. This gives the "key" side of the subject basic illumination, with the key light providing the necessary sparkle and accent. For such side lighting you use, of course, a floodlight rather than a spotlight. *(See 6.18.)*

The Kicker Light

The kicker light, generally a sharply pinned Fresnel spot, strikes the subject *from behind and off to one side.* Its main purpose is to *highlight the contour* of the subject at a place where key-light falloff is the densest, where the dense shadow of the subject

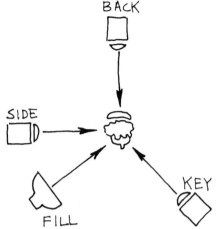

6·17   Side Light: The side light, striking the subject from the side, acts as additional fill light and pro-

vides contour accents. It can also act as a key light for extreme camera position.

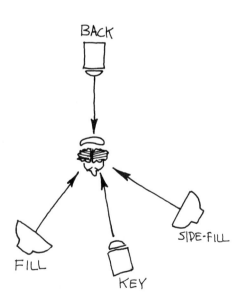

6·18   Side Fill Light.

opposite the key-lighted side tends to merge with the dark background. The function of the kicker is quite similar to that of the back light, except that the kicker light "rims" the subject not at the top-back, but at the lower side-back. It usually strikes the subject from below eye level. *(See 6.19.)*

Kicker lights are especially useful for creating the illusion of moonlight.[2]

Special Lighting Techniques

Four special lighting techniques deserve our further attention: (1) cameo lighting, (2) rear screen lighting, (3) chroma key lighting, and (4) remote lighting.

Cameos

Certain television shows, especially those of a dramatic nature, are staged in the middle of an empty studio against an unlighted background.

---

[2] Zettl, *Sight-Sound-Motion*, p. 43.

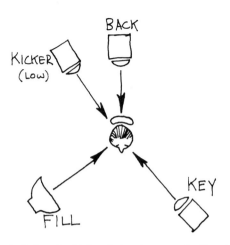

6·19 Kicker Light: The kicker light rims the object opposite the key and thus emphasizes contour. Like the back light, the kicker helps to separate the object from the background.

This technique, where only the performers are highlighted against a dark background, is commonly known as *cameo lighting* (from the cameo stone in which a light relief figure is set against a darker background stone).

All cameo lighting is *highly directional* and is achieved entirely with spotlights. In small studios, the background areas are carefully shielded with black, light-absorbing draperies from any kind of distracting spill light.

While cameo lighting is a highly effective technique in monochrome television, it is rather difficult to handle in color. The major problems are the high contrast, dense shadows, and the low baselight levels, all adverse factors to good color lighting. However, in certain circumstances, cameo lighting can, even in color, be highly effective.

Rear Screen Performance Area

For some kinds of shows, a picture of a scene is thrown onto the rear screen from the reverse side. The translucent screen allows the camera to pick up the projected image from the front.

The intensity of such a rear screen projection depends, like any ordinary slide projector, on the power of the projector. But even the most powerful home slide projector will produce pictures of poor quality if you turn on the lights or open the curtains and allow sunlight to flood the room. Similarly, any light that falls on the rear screen projection damages the picture partially or fully. Lighting in its close vicinity, therefore, must be highly directional. You can use only spotlights with barn doors carefully adjusted so that no spill light will hit the screen. You must also move performers and lighted set pieces at least six feet away from it. Since the lighting area in front of the rear screen is confined, the performers are restricted in their movements. In general, only stationary action is possible. Should the performer walk back to the rear screen, he or she would move beyond the performance area lights and would change immediately into a dark silhouette against the bright rear screen.

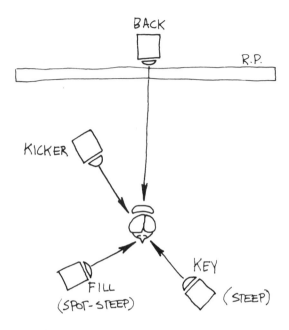

6·20 Lighting for the Rear Screen: Lighting for the rear screen requires highly directional light sources that do not produce any light spill on the projection. The performer must be some distance away from the screen in order to avoid spill and silhouette effects.

When the rear screen slide is exceptionally bright, you may get a silhouette effect, since your performance area lighting may not be enough to offset the brightness of the slide. You may try to use additional lights (directional fill) to brighten up the performer's face. But each additional light source, in turn, increases the light spill on the rear screen. As you can see, rear screen lighting is anything but easy. *(See 6.20.)*

When you have to light several sets besides the rear screen area, the inevitable spill light and the high amount of baselight may cloud the rear screen projection. This cloudiness occurs most often in small studios, where the sets are necessarily close together. The only solution is to separate the performing areas as much as possible and

to keep them on opposite sides of the studio so that the lighting is directed away from the rear screen. If the spill-light problem becomes too great, a photo mural may have to be substituted for the light-sensitive rear projection.

Careful pinning of the Fresnel spots, and equally careful barn-dooring, will help you to achieve the necessary directional control for rear screen lighting. Also, you may have to key-light and fill-light from steeper than normal lighting angles in order to avoid hitting portions of the rear screen with the light beam.

Chroma Key Set Area

The chroma key set area consists of a blue background and the foreground area, such as a newscaster's desk or interview chairs and table. The blue background is used for chroma key matting (see page 303).

The most important aspect of lighting the chroma key set area is *even background illumination.* In order to achieve an optimally effective chroma key matte, the blue background must be lighted with highly diffused instruments, such as softlights or scoops with scrim attachments. If there are hotspots on the blue background, or unusually dark areas, the matte (electronically supplied background image) will look discolored, or, worse, will have a tendency to break up. When lighting the foreground set, make sure that there are no spotlight beams hitting the background area so that you can preserve the evenness of the chroma key background illumination.

Sometimes you may have noticed that the outline of the newscaster vibrates with a variety of colors, or that the contour is not sharp during a chroma key matte. One of the major reasons for such moiré effects (vibrating color patterns) is that especially dark colors or shadows at the contour line take on a blue tinge, similar to the blue of the background. During the chroma key process, these blue spots become transparent and let the background picture show through. In order to counteract the bluishness of the shadows, you might try putting yellow or light orange gels (color filters) in all of the back lights or kicker lights. Thus, the back lights not only separate the foreground subject from the background picture through contour illumination, but also neutralize the blue shadows through the complementary yellow color. Be careful, however, not to let any of the yellow light hit the face, arms, or hands of the newscaster.

Remote Telecasts

Because of severe limitations in time, space, manpower, and facilities, precise studio lighting can rarely be duplicated on remote locations. Fortunately, remote telecasts rarely demand subtle aesthetic lighting effects; they need mostly a basic functional light level so that the camera can see well, or at least adequately. Therefore, the major objective in remote lighting is, as already mentioned, to provide a fairly even, *operational light level* with a *minimum* of lighting instruments.

Almost more than in the studio, the lighting technician should consult with the director as to where the performance areas are, what the cameras are supposed to see, and what the nature of the event is.

Low ceiling heights are generally the most serious problem, especially for setting back lights. Try to suspend the back lights from small wooden battens that you have positioned close to the ceiling by lightweight stands or polecats (springloaded aluminum poles that can be wedged between floor and ceiling). If you find that all you can do is hide one back light in one corner of the room, spread the light beam so that it covers as large a back light area as possible. In some instances, you may have to work only with top light, or without back lights altogether. Yet, try to get some back

lights into the location, even if it takes an extra effort. Hurried remote lighting looks characteristically flat and dull, not because of the diffused light used for key and fill lighting, but because of a *lack of back lighting.*

As mentioned before, floodlights, or combination lights, such as focusing broads, are more effective in remote lighting than highly directional spotlights.

You will find that on most remote telecasts the cameras will inevitably have to look through a door toward one or several windows. Don't try to use the outdoor light for your indoor shooting. In order to avoid a silhouette effect, you must block, at least partially, the excessive window light by drawing curtains or shutters. There are also large sheets of plastic filters available which, when placed over the windows, reduce the incoming light and lower the color temperature to that of the indoor lights (3,200° K).

Operation of Lights

When initially hanging the lights, divide the studio into major performance areas and hang the appropriate instruments (spotlights and floodlights) in the triangular arrangements of the basic photographic principle. Try to position the instruments so that they can serve *multiple functions.* This procedure will help you to illuminate all major performance areas adequately with the least number of instruments and effort.

In the actual operation of lighting instruments and the associated control equipment, you should heed the rule for all production activities: *safety first.* Secure the lighting instruments to the battens by *safety chains.* If you have pantographs, make sure that they are securely fastened to the battens, and the light instruments safety-chained to the pantographs. Chain all barn doors to the instruments. If you have diffusers in front of the scoops,

6·21 Table of Lighting Instruments.

Light Source	Type	Size (Watts)		Position	Effect
		Monochrome	**Color**		
Key	Fresnel spot	1,000–1,500	2,000	(45 degrees)	Principal source
	Quartz Fresnel	1,000	1,000–2,000	Side and above	Reveals basic form
				Below eye level	Creates a mood of mystery
				Far above eye level	Emphasizes eye shadows and features
Back	Fresnel spot	750–1,000	1,000–2,000	(45 degrees) behind and above	Separates figure from background, highlights hair and shoulders
	Quartz Fresnel	400–1,000	1,000–2,000		
Fill	18-inch scoop	1,500	1,500	Low front or front side	Softens shadows
	Quartz scoop	500	1,000		
	Quartz broad	500	1,000		
	Fresnel spot	1,000	1,000–2,000	Low front or side (spread)	Softens shadows in a specific area
	Quartz Fresnel	500	1,000		
Background or set	Fresnel spot	1,000	1,000–2,000	Varies with scenery	Livens background, sets mood, indicates locale and time
	Quartz Fresnel	500	1,000	Along cyclorama	Even illumination of cyclorama
	Cyc lights incandescent or quartz with glass color frames	300	500		
Side	Fresnel spot	1,000	1,000	Side of subject opposite key	Supplies directional fill, additional modeling
	Quartz Fresnel	500	1,000		
Kicker	Fresnel spot	1,000	1,000–2,000	Side back	Supplies modeling highlights
	Quartz Fresnel	500	1,000		
Camera	Fresnel spot or R-40	150	150	On camera	Serves as additional fill and modeling; principal source for easel cards, etc.

make sure that they are securely fastened in place. Check all C-clamps periodically, especially the bolts that connect the lighting instruments to the hanging device.

When the lights are on, be very careful when moving the instrument. Since the *hot lamps* are especially *vulnerable* to physical shock, try not to jolt the lighting instrument. Move it gently.

Whenever you adjust the beam, such as the focus device or the barn doors, without the use of a light pole, make sure that you *wear gloves.* The quartz lights especially get extremely hot.

When moving ladders for fine trimming (fine beam adjustment), watch for obstacles below and above. Don't take any chances by leaning way out to reach an instrument. Move the ladder.

When adjusting a light, try *not* to *look directly* into it. Rather, look at the object to be lighted and see how the beam strikes it. If you have to look into the light, wear dark glasses.

When patching lights at the patchboard, have all dimmers in the "off" position. *Do not* "hot-patch"; otherwise, the patches themselves will become so pitted that they no longer make the proper connection.

Try to "warm up" large instruments through reduced power. You will not only prolong the lamp life but also prevent the Fresnel lenses from cracking.

Don't overload a circuit. It may hold during rehearsal but then go out just at the wrong time during the actual show.

Don't waste energy. Bring the lights up full only when necessary. Dry runs (without cameras) can be done just as efficiently when illuminated by work lights as with full studio lighting.

6·22 A word about checking your lighting on the studio monitor. As we have said before, your lighting is correct if the studio monitor shows what you want the viewer to perceive. In order to get to this point, you should use the monitor as a guide to your lighting, rather than the less direct light meter. But you may run into difficulties. Your video engineer will tell you that he cannot align the cameras before you have finished the lighting. And your argument may be that you cannot finish the lighting without checking it on the monitor.

Let's approach this argument with a readiness for compromise, since both parties have a valid point.

You can do the basic lighting without the camera. A foot-candle meter will help you in detecting gross inadequacies, such as insufficient baselight levels, or extremely uneven illumination. With some experience, you will also be able to tell whether or not a shadow is too dense for adequate reproduction of color and detail. But then, for the fine trimming, you will need at least one camera. Ask the video engineer to work *with* you. After all, it is his or her responsibility, too, to deliver technically acceptable pictures. This single camera can be roughly aligned to the existing illumination and pointed into the set. With the direct feedback of the picture on the studio monitor, you can now proceed to correct glaring discrepancies, or simply touch up some of the lighting as to beam direction and intensity.

After this fine trimming, *all* cameras can then be aligned and balanced for optimal performance.

Summary

In all television lighting, the *basic photographic,* or triangle, *lighting principle* of key, back, and fill light is used. The *key light* is the principal source of illumination, which reveals the basic shape of the object. The *back light* distinguishes the shadow of the object from the dark background and emphasizes its outline. The *fill light* makes the shadows less dense.

In lighting for *continuous action,* we can use multiple lighting triangles (each one consisting of key, back, and fill) that overlap.

Additional light sources are often used in connection with the basic photographic lighting setup. These are (1) the background, or set, light, which illuminates the background of the scene; (2) the side light, which acts as a directional fill, generally opposite the key light; (3) the kicker light, which is used to highlight the contour of an object that would otherwise blend in with the background; and (4) the camera light, which acts as an occasional additional fill light.

Special lighting techniques include (1) cameo lighting, (2) rear screen lighting, (3) chroma key lighting, and (4) remote lighting.

In the *operation* of lights, safety is the first principle, as it should be in any other television operation.

The table of lighting instruments (page 142) applies to a small- to medium-size studio in which monochrome or color cameras are used.

7   *Audio*

In the preceding chapters, we have been concerned primarily with the video, the picture portion of television. In this chapter we will discuss another essential part of production —audio, the sound portion of television.

To keep this vast topic within manageable limits, three major factors will be emphasized. They are:

1. Sound pickup, including the kinds of microphones and their electronic and operational characteristics,

2. Recorded sound, covering the various types of sound-recording and playback equipment for television, and the techniques for using them.

3. Sound control, dealing with the principal equipment and the techniques of creative sound mixing.

You should realize that sound control is an important production field in its own right, and that it requires specific and unique skills. If you are especially interested in television audio, you should make a concerted effort to learn as much as possible about radio techniques, sound recording techniques, and the finer points of television and film audio production.

Audio (from the Latin verb *audire,* to hear) stands for the sound portion of television and its production. Although the term *tele-vision* (far-seeing) ignores audio entirely, the sound part of television plays a vital part in the television communication process. Frequently, it is the sound that gives us more precise *information* than the pictures. At one time or another, you have surely experienced a temporary interruption of the picture transmission right in the middle of a fascinating program. As long as you could hear the audio portion, you were probably still able to follow the story more or less accurately. But have you noticed how difficult it is to keep up when the sound portion fails? Besides giving information, audio can help to establish a specific *locale,* such as a downtown location through traffic noises, or a specific *time,* through typical day or night sounds. Sound is essential for the establishing of *mood,* or for the *intensification* of action. There

is hardly a good chase sequence that does not have a whole barrage of intensified sounds accompanying the natural ones. Sound also helps us to *connect* the visual pieces and fragments of the relatively small, low-definition television image into a meaningful whole.

If sound is, indeed, such an important production element, why do we have such a preponderance of bad sound on television? Even when you produce a short little scene as an exercise in your studio, you will probably notice that, while the pictures may look acceptable, the sound portion certainly could stand some improvement.

Unless you show a film on television, where a large part of the audio portion is produced independently of the action and then carefully matched at a later time with the picture portion, good television sound is difficult to achieve. In most television productions, even when videotaped, the sound is picked up, mixed (balanced),

---

Audio The sound portion of television and its production. Technically, the electronic reproduction of audible sound.

Blast, or Pop Filter A bulblike attachment (either permanent or detachable) to the front of the microphone that filters out sudden air blasts, such as plosive consonants (*p*'s, *t*'s, *k*'s) delivered directly into the mike.

Cardioid The heart-shaped (cardioid) pickup pattern of a unidirectional microphone.

Cart See Cartridge.

Cartridge, or Tape Cartridge Also called "cart" for short. A video- or audiotape recording or playback device that uses tape cartridges. A cartridge is a plastic case containing an endless tape loop that rewinds as it is played back, and cues itself automatically.

Cassette A video- or audiotape recording or playback device that uses tape cassettes. A cassette is a plastic case containing two reels, a supply reel and a takeup reel. Many cassettes cue and rewind themselves automatically.

Condenser Microphone A microphone whose diaphragm consists of a condenser plate that vibrates with the sound pressure against another fixed condenser plate, called the backplate.

Diaphragm The vibrating element inside a microphone that moves with the air pressure from the sound.

and telecast or recorded on videotape simultaneously with the actual event. Because of the demanding complexity of good video, the sound portion, unfortunately, takes a back seat in most television productions. It is frequently assumed that by sticking a microphone into the scene in the last minute we have taken care of the audio requirements. Television audio, like any other production element, should not be "added"; it should be *integrated* into the production planning from the very beginning.

Sound Pickup

The pickup of live sounds is done through a variety of microphones. How good or how bad a particular microphone is depends not only on how it is built, its electronic characteristics, but especially on how it is used. We will, therefore, talk briefly about the basic electronic characteristics of microphones, and then concentrate on their use, or operational characteristics.

Electronic Characteristics

All microphones *convert sound* waves into *electrical energy*, which is amplified and reconverted into sound waves by the loudspeaker. Microphones are often classified primarily according to how they convert sound into electrical energy, or by their *sound-generating element*. Another way of classifying them is by their *pickup pattern*.

Generating Element Microphones classified according to their generating element are (1) dynamic, (2) ribbon, and (3) condenser. Generally, *dynamic* mikes are the most *rugged*. They can tolerate reasonably well the rough handling television microphones frequently (though unintentionally)

Dual Redundancy The use of two identical microphones for the pickup of a sound source, whereby only one of them is turned on at any given time. A safety device that permits switching over to the second microphone in case the active one becomes defective.

Dynamic Microphone A microphone whose sound-pickup device consists of a diaphragm that is attached to a movable coil. As the diaphragm vibrates with the air pressure from the sound, the coil moves within a magnetic field, generating an electric current.

E.T. Electrical Transcriptions; a somewhat outdated designation for phonograph records used exclusively for on-the-air broadcasts.

Fader A sound-volume control that works by means of a button sliding vertically or horizontally along a specific scale. Similar to pot.

Fishpole A suspension device for a microphone; the microphone is attached to a pole and held over the scene for brief periods.

FM Microphone A wireless microphone that contains not only the sound pickup and generating elements but also a tiny FM transmitter.

Full Track An audiotape recorder, or recording, that uses the full width of the tape for recording an audio signal.

Generating Element The major part of a microphone. It converts sound waves into electrical energy.

Giraffe A medium-sized microphone boom that can be operated by one person.

Half-Track An audiotape recorder, or recording, that uses half the width of the tape for an audio signal. The other half can then be used for additional recorded material.

7·1   All microphones have (1) a *diaphragm,* which vibrates with the sound pressures, and (2) a *generating element,* which changes the physical vibrations of the diaphragm into electrical energy.

In the *dynamic* microphone, the diaphragm is attached to a coil, the voice coil. When somebody speaks into the mike, the diaphragm vibrates with the air pressure from the sound and makes the voice coil move back and forth within a magnetic field. This produces a fluctuating electric current, which, when amplified, transmits these vibrations to the cone of a speaker, making the sound audible again.

Because the diaphragm–voice coil element is physically quite rugged, the microphone can withstand and accurately translate high sound levels or other air blasts close to the microphone.

In the *ribbon* or *velocity* mike, a very thin metal ribbon vibrates within a magnetic field serving the function of the diaphragm and the voice coil. The ribbon is so fragile, however, that even moderate physical shocks to the microphone, or sharp air blasts close to it, can damage and even destroy the instrument. When it is used outdoors, even the wind will move the ribbon and thus introduce a great amount of noise. You should, therefore, not use this kind of microphone outdoors, or in production situa-

receive. They can be worked very close to the sound source and can withstand extremely high sound levels without damage to the microphone or even excessive distortion of the incoming sound. Ribbon and condenser mikes are much more sensitive to physical shock or input over-load than the dynamic mikes, and are therefore used primarily for stable, highly controlled recording tasks. Although the dynamic mike does not respond as well to extreme frequencies and subtle tone characteristics (such as timbre and presence) as the others, it is nevertheless pre-

Input Overload Distortion   A distortion caused by a microphone when subjected to an exceptionally high-volume incoming sound. Condenser microphones are especially prone to this kind of distortion.

ips   An abbreviation for inches-per-second, indicating tape speed.

Key-In   To switch to a sound source via an on-off (or channel) key.

Lavaliere   An extremely small microphone that can be clipped onto the revers of a jacket, a tie, a blouse, or other piece of clothing. A larger variety is suspended from a neckcord and worn in front of the chest. Also called neck or chest mike.

Microphone   Also called mike. A small, portable assembly for the pickup and conversion of sound into electrical energy.

Mixing   The combining of two or more sounds in specific proportions (volume variations) as determined by the event (show) context.

Multiple-Microphone Interference   The canceling out of certain sound frequencies when two identical microphones in close proximity are used for the same sound source.

Omnidirectional   A type of pickup pattern in which the microphone can pick up sounds equally well from all directions.

Pickup Pattern   The territory around the microphone within which the microphone can "hear well," that is, has optimal sound pickup.

Polar Pattern   The two-dimensional representation of a microphone pickup pattern.

Post-Dubbing   The adding of a sound track to an already recorded (and usually fully edited) picture portion.

tions that require its frequent movement. A good ribbon mike, such as the classic RCA 77-DX, is nevertheless an excellent recording mike, even in television productions. Although it has a low tolerance to high sound levels, the delicate ribbon responds well to a wide frequency range and reproduces with great fidelity the subtle nuances of tone color, especially in the bass range.

In the *condenser* microphone, the diaphragm constitutes one of the two plates necessary for a condenser to function. The other, called the backplate, is fixed. Since the diaphragm moves with the air vibrations against the fixed backplate, the capacitance of this

condenser is continuously changed, thus modulating the electrical current. The major advantage of the condenser microphone over the other types is its extremely wide frequency response and pickup sensitivity. But this sensitivity is also one of its disadvantages. If placed close to high-intensity sound sources, such as the high-output speakers of a rock band, it will overload and distort the incoming sound—a condition known as *input overload distortion.* However, if properly placed, the condenser mike is a superior recording mike, especially when used under highly controlled conditions of studio recording.

ferred in television production because of its stable performance characteristics even in adverse conditions (such as extreme temperature change or high humidity) and its general ruggedness. Best of all, its relatively simple electronics permits the construction of extremely small instruments.

Microphone Pickup Patterns Like our ears, any type of microphone can hear sounds from all directions as long as the sounds are within its hearing range. But while some microphones hear sounds from all directions equally well, others hear better in a specific direction. The pickup pat-

Pot Abbreviation for potentiometer, a sound-volume control.

Pot-In To fade in a sound source gradually with a pot or fader.

Quarter-Track An audiotape recorder, or recording, that uses one-fourth of the width of the tape for recording an audio signal. Generally used by stereo recorders. The first and third tracks are taken up by the first pass of the tape through the recording heads; the second and fourth tracks by the second pass, when the tape has been "reversed" (that is, the full takeup reel becomes the supply reel for the second recording).

Reel-to-Reel A tape recorder that transports the tape past the heads from one reel, the supply reel, to the other reel, the takeup reel. Used in contrast to cassettes or cartridge recorders.

Ribbon Microphone A microphone whose sound-pickup device consists of a ribbon that vibrates with the sound pressures within a magnetic field. Also called velocity mike.

Shotgun Microphone A highly directional microphone with a shotgun-like barrel for picking up sounds over a great distance.

Sound Effects Special sounds—such as wind, thunder, car traffic, jet airplanes—recorded in advance for multiple use in a variety of productions.

Unidirectional A type of pickup pattern in which the microphone can pick up sounds better from one direction, the front, than from the sides or back.

Volume The relative intensity of the sound, its relative loudness.

VU Meter A volume-unit meter; measures volume units, the relative loudness of amplified sound.

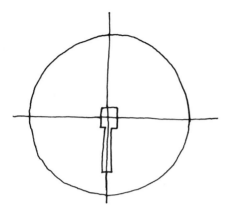

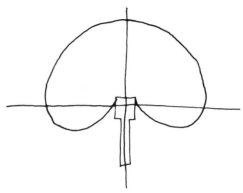

7·2 Omnidirectional Pickup Pattern: You can think of the omnidirectional pickup pattern as a large rubber ball with the mike in its center. All sounds that originate within the confines of the rubber ball (the pickup pattern) will be picked up by the microphone without any marked quality difference.

The two-dimensional representation of its pickup pattern is called the *polar pattern,* which for an omnidirectional mike is roughly circular.

7·3 Cardioid Pickup Pattern: The most common unidirectional pickup pattern is called *cardioid,* heart-shaped. If you think of an apple with the mike sticking into it where the stem should be, you will have an idea of the three-dimensional pickup pattern of most unidirectional television microphones.[1]

As you can see, the pickup at the side of the microphone is considerably reduced with the cardioid microphone, and almost eliminated at its rear. The polar pattern of the cardioid microphone clearly shows the heart-shaped pickup area.

tern shows the territory within which the microphone can hear well.

Generally, in television production, we have *omnidirectional,* or *nondirectional,* microphones and *unidirectional* microphones.

The *omnidirectional* microphone hears sounds from *all* (*omnis* in Latin) *directions* equally well. The *unidirectional* microphone hears better in *one* (*unus* in Latin) *direction,* the front of the microphone, than from its sides or back. *(See 7.2 and 7.3.)*

Operational Characteristics

When classifying microphones according to their use, we have those that are designed for picking up moving sound sources, and others that are designed for picking up stationary sound sources.

The former we simply call *mobile microphones,* the latter *stationary microphones.* (See 7.48.)

Mobile Microphones The *mobile* microphones include (1) boom microphones, (2) hand microphones, (3) lavaliere microphones, and (4) wireless, or FM, microphones.

If the scene requires that you keep the microphone out of the picture, the most practical instrument you can use is a *boom microphone*—that is, one that is suspended from a microphone boom. The choice is usually a high-quality *dynamic, cardioid* mike (dynamic, because it is relatively insensitive to the inevitable shocks and wind noises generated by the moving boom; cardioid, because it

---

[1] Electro-Voice, *Microphone Primer* (Buchanan, Mich.: Electro-Voice, Inc., n.d.).

must pick up sounds that originate a considerable distance from the microphone without undue loss of presence) or a *condenser, cardioid* microphone (because of its superior quality). The boom facilitates rapid and smooth movement of the microphone above and in front of the sound sources from one spot to another anywhere in the studio within its extended range. In order to keep the microphone out of the picture while following a moving sound source, you can extend or retract the microphone with the boom, simultaneously pan the boom horizontally, move it up and down vertically, and rotate the mike at the end of it to allow for directional sound pickup. During all these operations, you can have the whole boom assembly moved to various locations, in case it cannot reach them when fully extended. *(See 7.5.)*

But there are some major disadvantages in using the "big boom" in a small studio or in small station operations: (1) For proper manipulation it needs two operators: the boom operator, who works the microphone boom, and the boom dolly operator, who helps to reposition the whole assembly whenever necessary. (2) The floor space that the boom takes up may, in a small studio, cut down the maneuverability of the cameras considerably. (3) The boom requires special lighting so that its shadow falls outside camera range. Even in larger studios, the lighting problems often preclude the use of a boom, available manpower and space notwithstanding. Often, when the use of the boom has not been carefully preplanned in conjunction with lighting and camera movements, you will find that the boom operator "rides" the boom much too high for good sound pickup, merely to keep the mike and the boom, or their shadows, out of the camera shots.

The smaller boom, called a *giraffe,* is often preferred in small studios. It can do almost anything the big boom can do with the exception of exten-

7·4 Microphones with both omnidirectional and cardioid pickup patterns are used extensively in television production. Why both types? Whenever a mike can, or must, be worked close to the sound source, such as the performer's hand mike on a windy outdoor location, the omnidirectional mike is to be preferred. It is less subject to breath pops—the loud popping noises that might occur when held close to the mouth—than the cardioid mike.

If, however, you must use the microphone relatively far away from the sound source, such as a boom mike, the cardioid pattern is far superior. It will be able to pick up the sound over a relatively large distance without loss of presence or quality. Also, random noise, which is always present in a busy television studio, will be largely ignored by the cardioid mike, while the omnidirectional mike would pick up sounds from all directions.

7·5 Big Boom: The big microphone boom is mounted on a special dolly, called a perambulator, that permits rapid relocation anywhere in the studio. The operator's platform can be cranked up or down to the necessary operating height. Usually, a line monitor is mounted on the boom for the operator. The counterweighted boom can be extended, tilted up and down, and the microphone itself can be rotated by about 300 degrees.

sion and retraction of the boom itself. However, since the giraffe is on casters, the boom operator alone can move the whole boom assembly quite easily toward or away from the sound source. There are some more advantages of the giraffe over the big boom: (1) it takes up much less studio space; (2) because of its low height and narrow wheelbase, it can be easily moved from one studio to another through narrow doorways or hallways; and (3) it can be disassembled quickly and taken to remote locations if necessary.

Unfortunately, even the giraffe is not without serious operational disadvantages: (1) The lighting is at least as critical for the giraffe as for the big boom and, in fact, becomes more of a problem since the giraffe usually works at a lower height and closer to the sound source. (2) Because of the considerable weight of a good dynamic, cardioid boom microphone, the extension of the relatively light giraffe boom is limited. This requires the boom operator to stand closer to the sound source, a position that not only tends to increase the general noise level but may also prevent the camera from getting wide cover shots of the scene. (3) Even with vertical extensions for the rotating device and the mike suspension, the boom has to remain relatively low, another danger of getting the microphone into the picture or causing unwanted mike shadows. (4) Because of its lightness, the boom is subject to shock and vibrations. Therefore, the microphone attached to the giraffe *(figure 7.6)* is more exposed to physical shock than that on the smoothly operating big boom.

In certain production situations, even the small giraffe boom is not flexible enough for a quick and accurate audio pickup. What you can use then is an extremely simple yet very effective device: a hand-held aluminum or bamboo pole to which a microphone is attached. As "boom opera-

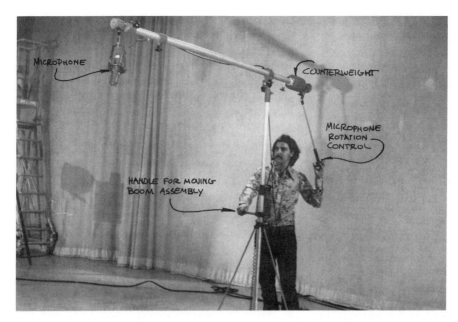

MICROPHONE

COUNTERWEIGHT

MICROPHONE
ROTATION
CONTROL

HANDLE FOR MOVING
BOOM ASSEMBLY

7·6   Giraffe, or
Medium Boom.

tor," you hold this *fishpole* device into the scene for brief periods of audio pickup. One of the best ways to hold it is to anchor it in your belt. Then you can drop the microphone close to the audio source, as though you were "fishing" for the appropriate sound. When you work a fishpole, you usually stand behind some piece of scenery or you walk into the scene alongside the camera.

The advantages of the fishpole technique are obvious: (1) the microphone is extremely flexible; it can swing easily up and down and sideways; (2) the fishpole is easy to operate and needs only one person per microphone; (3) it takes up very little space; and (4) it can be worked around the existing lighting so that the mike shadow falls outside the picture.

The various disadvantages of using a boom microphone have proved serious enough in small station operation that, especially since the dramatic development of high-quality, extremely

small lavaliere microphones (see pages 158–159), it is used only for special productions, such as dramas, certain commercials, or in scenes with many rapidly changing sound sources that do not allow the microphone to be seen.

Nevertheless, the combination of a high-quality boom mike and a good boom operator produces a high-quality sound that is hard to beat with other mobile microphone techniques. You should, therefore, acquaint yourself with the *basic operational techniques* of boom microphones.

As a television boom operator, you are responsible for keeping the microphone as close as possible to the sound source without getting it or the boom into the picture, or causing undesirable shadows in the scene. Doing this involves a great amount of coordination and anticipation. Simultaneously you must (1) keep the microphone above and in front of the sound source, (2) watch the audio balance in case there is more than one sound source, (3) listen to the director's signals, (4) watch the movements of cameras and their relative zoom positions, or lenses used, (5) watch for undesirable boom shadows, and (6) anticipate as much as possible the movements of the performers.

Here are some of the major *operational techniques* you should remember when working a boom microphone:

1. Try to keep the microphone as *low* as possible without getting it into the picture, and *in front* of the sound source. Don't ride the mike directly above the performer's head; after all, he speaks with his mouth, not with the top of his head.

2. If you have a line monitor (which shows the picture that goes on the air or is videotaped) on your boom dolly, try to ascertain during rehearsal how far you can dip the microphone toward the sound source without getting the mike or the boom into the picture. The closer you are with the mike, the better the sound will be. (In boom-mike operation, you will never get close enough to violate the minimum distance required of cardioid mikes in order to avoid breath pops or similar sound distortions.)

3. If the boom gets into the picture, it is better for you to *retract* it than to raise it. By retracting, you will pull the microphone out of the camera's view and at the same time keep the mike in front rather than on top of the sound source.

4. Watch shadows. Even the best lighting engineer cannot avoid shadows but can only redirect them into areas that are hopefully not picked up by the camera. If your boom positions are known before the show, work with the lighting engineer so he can light around the major moves of your boom. Sometimes you may have to sacrifice audio quality in order to avoid boom shadows.

If you discover a boom shadow when the camera is already on the air, do not try to move the microphone too quickly. Everybody will then be sure to see the shadow travel across the screen. Rather, try to sneak it out of the picture very slowly, or, better, just keep the mike and the shadow *as steady as possible* until a relief shot permits you to move the mike into a more advantageous position.

5. Anticipate the movements of performers so that you can *lead* them, rather than frantically follow them, with your microphone. Unless the show is very well rehearsed, don't lock the pan and tilt devices on your boom. If the performer rises unexpectedly, she may bump her head on the locked microphone. Not even dynamic mikes are that shockproof.

6. Watch for good audio balance. If you have to cover more than one sound source, place the microphone between the two. In general, favor the weaker source by pointing the microphone more toward it than the stronger source. Once you have found an acceptable balance, try to keep the microphone as steady as possible. Unless you are very experienced, rotating the mike rapidly between the two sources will rarely produce good balance, especially if both sound sources are within the mike's pickup pattern anyway.

7. When moving the perambulator, make sure that you warn the boom operator of this move, and that you do it extremely smoothly. Watch for cables on the floor and especially for low lighting instruments.

A slight movement of the performer can mean a complicated boom operation. Even though the performer merely turns her head from left to right while talking, for instance, you will have to pan the boom horizontally several feet and rotate the microphone in order to keep it in front of the sound source. If the performer simply stoops down while talking, a great vertical drop of the boom is required. Vertical movements are usually difficult to manipulate quickly, especially when the boom is racked out as far as it will go.

If the performer turns to a blackboard while talking, you will have to rack the boom out in front of her and rotate the microphone around so that its live side is pointing toward the sound source. This procedure requires smooth, fast coordination. Usually, by the time you have racked the boom into its correct position, the performer will have turned around again to speak to the camera, and the same fast boom movement becomes necessary in reverse. In the above-mentioned example, it would be more practical to place the microphone to the side and compromise pickup quality. Much better results can, of course, be achieved if the performer talks only when she faces the camera and not while her back is turned.

As the name implies, the *hand microphone* is handled by the performer. It is used in all production situations in which it is most practical, if not imperative, for the performer to control the sound pickup.

Such production situations include, most obviously, remotes, where you often work in the midst of much surrounding commotion and noise. With the hand mike, you can still achieve good audio by holding the instrument close to the mouth of the speaker. Since hand mikes are always seen on camera and need no special precautions for concealment, you can hold the mike as close to the sound source as necessary. On a windy day, or in the middle of a cheering crowd, that will probably be very close in order to shut out as much of the surrounding noise as possible. If you interview someone under such adverse conditions, you will have to hold the microphone close to yourself when asking the questions, and close to the other person whenever he or she answers.

In the studio, the hand microphone is used extensively by singers and in audience participation shows. In the latter case, the performer can talk at random to anyone in the audience simply by walking up to a person with the hand mike and picking up his or her comments. Such random interviews would be extremely difficult to cover with boom mikes. You would probably need at least three booms to cover a good-sized audience, and you would still not get as precise an audio as when you walk up to the various people with the hand mike.

7·7 When there are three or more sound sources, you may have to move the microphone to the person who is talking; this is not an easy job, especially if the sequence of the persons speaking has not been predetermined. Again the talent can help by cooperating closely. A practical example might help to explain this problem.

Situation: There are two major audio areas: (1) a group of seven high school students covered by a mobile big-boom microphone and (2) a political personality who wears a lavaliere mike. The students direct random questions at the politician.

Problem: You must anticipate which student will ask the next question so that you can place the boom microphone before the question is asked.

Two Possible Solutions: The *sequence* of students asking questions is predetermined, or the students asking questions *identify* themselves by raising their arms. The person being interviewed can then point out the particular student he wishes to hear. This gives you a little time to position the boom before the student speaks.

7·8   Shure SM61 Hand
Microphone.

Although technically the use of a boom would be quite feasible for the performance of singers, most of them prefer to work with a hand microphone. One of the reasons for this preference is that with a hand mike the singer retains some control over the production of the sound. You may have noticed how a singer may hold the mike extremely close to her mouth in order to emphasize a soft, intimate passage of a song. The closeness of the mike increases the sound presence, which, especially when coupled with a closeup picture, lets the audience perceive a psychological and physical closeness to the singer. In louder, more external passages, the skilled singer will hold the microphone farther away, thus helping the engineer keep the volume within tolerable limits, but she also does it so as to externalize the sound, to pull back a little from the viewer. Another reason is that, through the hand mike, the sound of the singer and the sound of the band or orchestra can be fairly well separated. This distinctness is essential for the audio engineer to balance a small or very soft voice with a rather loud instrumental group.

The wide variety of usage makes heavy demands on the performance characteristics of a hand mike. Since it is handled so much, it must be rugged and rather insensitive to physical shock. Since it is often used extremely close to the sound source, it must be insensitive to plosive breath pops and input overload distortion. Since it is often used outdoors on remote locations, it must be able to withstand rain, snow, humidity, summer heat, and extreme temperature changes. And yet, it must be sensitive enough to pick up the full range and subtle tone qualities of a singer's voice. Finally, it must be small and slim enough to look unobtrusive and to be handled comfortably by the performer.

Most *hand mikes* are, therefore, *dynamic* and *omnidirectional.* The dynamic generating element gives them the necessary ruggedness without undue loss of quality, and the omnidirectional pickup pattern allows the close working range that is essential for reducing interference from surrounding noise. *(See 7.8.)*

Again, hand mikes are not without some serious disadvantages: (1) The quality of a hand microphone is simply not as good as that of a good boom mike. (2) When using a hand microphone, the performer is tied to a limited operation radius by the microphone cable. Outside and inside the studio, these cables become a menace to the freely traveling cameras. (3) In addition to everything else, the performer will have to learn how to handle the microphone—that is, to hold it in the optimal pickup area, so as not to impair the audio portion, and to refrain from using it as a prop, swinging it widely through the air in order to make a point or twirling it by its cord like a propellor. Neither the mike nor the audio engineer can stand such rough treatment for very long.

Operation of the hand microphone requires dexterity and foresight. Here are some considerations for working with it.

1.   Although the hand mike is fairly rugged, treat it gently. If you need both hands during your performance, don't just drop the mike; put it down gently, or wedge it under your arm.

2. Before the telecast, check your action radius and see whether the mike cable is long enough for your actions, and laid out for maximum mike mobility.

3. If you happen to run out of mike cable, don't yank on it. Stop and try to get the attention of the floor manager.

4. When walking a considerable distance, don't pull the cable with the mike. Tug the cable gently with one hand, while holding the microphone with the other.

5. Under normal, controlled sound conditions, such as the studio or a quiet outdoor location, hold the hand mike about a foot below and slightly in front of your mouth and *speak across* the screen (which acts as a wind screen and breath pop filter). Don't speak into the mike. In very noisy surroundings, put the mike closer to your mouth, but still try to speak across, rather than into, it. *(See 7.9.)*

6. In interviewing someone, hold the microphone to your mouth whenever you are speaking and to the guest's whenever he or she is answering. This obvious procedure has been unfortunately reversed by many a beginning performer.

7. Check out the microphone before the show by speaking into it. But do not blow into it.

The development of extremely small, high-quality *lavaliere microphones* has helped to improve television audio considerably, while at the same time simplifying production procedures.

The larger lavaliere microphones (about as big as your little finger) are hung on a neckcord close to the chest of the performer; the small ones (about the size of a small thimble) are clipped to the dress or the tie. *(See 7.12 through 7.14.)*

The omnidirectional lavaliere microphone, with a dynamic or condenser generating element, is designed primarily for voice pickup. The *quality* of even the smallest one is amazingly *good.* It reproduces equally well the high-frequency overtones that give each voice its distinct character, and the deep bass resonance that some voices possess. The small lavaliere is quite immune to

7·9 Correct Hand-Microphone Position: As you can see, the reporter holds the mike in the correct position: fairly close to her mouth in order to avoid picking up the surrounding noise, yet low enough so that she can *speak across* rather than into it. Note the blast filter on top.

7·10 If you want to impress on the performer the sensitivity of a microphone, especially that of the hand mike, turn it on to a high volume level and feed the clanks and bangs back out into the studio for the performer to hear. Even a gentle handling of the microphone will produce awesome noises.

7·11 Some of the more commonly used hand microphones are: the Electro-Voice 635A, the Shure SM61, the Shure SM57 (Unidyne), the Shure SM58 (same as the SM57, plus a blast filter) the Shure SM82, the Electro-Voice RE-55, the Shure SM53.

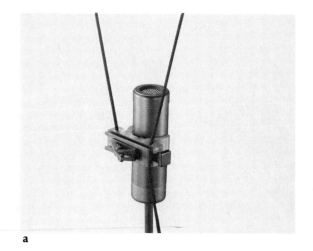

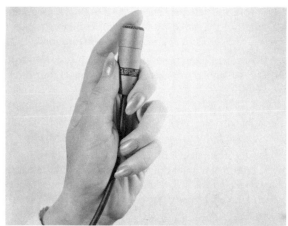

a

b

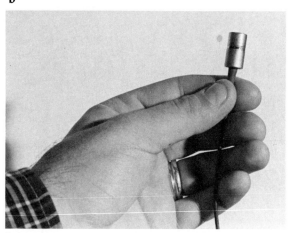

c

7·12   Lavaliere Microphones: (a) Shure SM51 lavaliere with neckcord; (b) Electro-Voice 649B; (c) Sony ECM-50.

physical shock and to other noise-generating factors, such as the rubbing of clothes.

Once the lavaliere microphone is properly attached to the performer (approximately six inches below the chin, *on top* of the clothes, and away from anything that could rub or bang against it), he or she needs no longer worry about the sound pickup. The audio engineer, too, has less difficulty "riding the gain" (adjusting the volume) of the lavaliere than the boom or hand

mike. Since the distance between it and the sound source does not change during the performance, an even sound level can be achieved more easily than with other mobile microphones.

The use of lavaliere microphones frees the lighting people from "lighting around the boom" in order to avoid shadows; they can now concentrate more on the aesthetic subtleties of lighting as required by the scene.

Although the action radius of the performer is

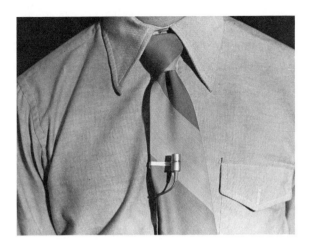

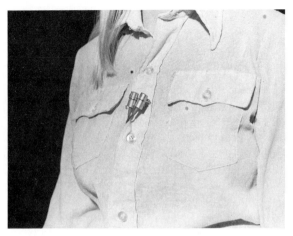

7·13 Correct Lavaliere-Microphone Position: This lavaliere mike is properly attached for maximum sound pickup. It is securely fastened *on top* of the clothing, minimizing the danger of causing highly distracting rubbing noises. The mike cord is concealed. In spite of its small size and its distance from the sound source, the quality of sound pickup in this small microphone is excellent.

7·14 Dual-Redundancy System: A special clip permits the use of two lavalieres for dual-redundancy pickup. In case one microphone goes out, the audio engineer simply switches over to the other without losing audio. Two single clips will work in an emergency.

still limited by the lavaliere microphone cable, the cable nevertheless is so light and flexible that she can move quickly and quite unrestrictedly in a limited studio area without having to hold a microphone in her hand, or worry about being followed by the boom mike. The attached mike permits the performer to work even in cramped quarters without the need for special operators or special booms or stands.

Again, there are some disadvantages to the lavaliere microphone: (1) The wearer cannot move the mike any closer to his or her mouth; consequently, if there is extraneous noise, it will be easily picked up by this omnidirectional mike. (2) The lavaliere can be used for only one sound source at a time, that of the particular wearer. Even for a simple interview, the interviewer and the guest will each have to wear his or her own

microphone. For a small discussion group you will need several. (3) Although the lavaliere mike allows considerable mobility, it limits the performer's activity to some extent. When two or more performers are "wired" in this fashion, their movements are even more restricted. (4) Unless you can hide the lavaliere completely while maintaining its sound quality, you cannot use it for dramatic scenes in which the visible mike would be inappropriate.

Operation of the lavaliere microphone is fairly simple once it is properly installed.

1.   Make sure to put it on. You wouldn't be the first performer to be discovered sitting on, rather than wearing, his microphone by air time.

2.   Clip the mike firmly to a piece of clothing so that it will not rub on anything, such as a jacket or jewelry.

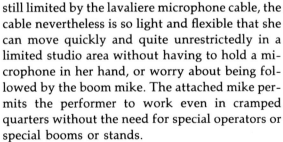

7·15 The high quality of the lavaliere microphone has extended its production use considerably. Here are come examples:

Panel shows: Rather than using desk mikes, which are apt to pick up the unavoidable banging on the table, you can achieve excellent audio by using individual lavaliere microphones.

Interview: As long as the interview takes place in one location, the wearing of lavaliere microphones by the interviewer and each of the guests assures excellent audio.

News: The lavaliere mike is the most efficacious sound pickup device for all types of news shows.

Instructional Shows (with a principal performer, or television teacher): The lavaliere works beautifully as long as the instructor moves within a limited performance area (from desk to blackboard, for example).

Music: The lavaliere mike has been successfully used on singers (even when accompanying themselves with a guitar, for example), and for the pickup of certain instruments, such as a string bass, where it is taped below the fingering board. In this area, there is still room for experimentation. Don't be too awed by convention. If the lavaliere sounds as good as or better than a larger, more expensive mike, stick to the lavaliere.

The most commonly used lavaliere microphones are: the Sony ECM-50, the E-V 649B, the E-V RE-85, the Shure SM51, the E-V CO-85.

Do not cover it with anything. Make sure to fasten the microphone cable to your belt or clothing so that it cannot pull the microphone sideways.

3. If you use the dual-redundancy microphone system (which uses two microphones for each sound source in case one of the mikes becomes inoperative), have both mikes fastened securely so that they don't touch each other. There is a special clip that holds two lavaliere microphones. *(See 7.14.)*

4. Avoid hitting the microphone with any object you may be demonstrating on camera.

5. After the show, put the microphone down gently.

Wireless, or FM, microphones would be ideal for television, such as a lavaliere microphone without its cable. Some efforts have been made to produce such an instrument with varying degrees of success. Some wireless microphones are rather large lavaliere mikes with the transmitter built directly into the microphone. A small sending antenna either sticks out of the mike or is part of the neckcord. Other wireless microphones use a very small lavaliere, with a cord leading to a small pocket transmitter. A special receiving station can pick up the microphone signal from as far away as 1,000 feet (approximately 350 meters), amplify the signal, and send it to the master audio mixer. Since the signal transmission from the microphone to the receiving station represents, in fact, a miniature FM broadcast, you will *need an FCC license* for operating *wireless microphone.*

Despite the obvious advantages of wireless microphones, such as the great mobility of the wearer, their operation has been restricted to some highly specific production tasks. Most often, they are used in remote locations where microphone cables cannot be strung for one reason or another. They are less frequently seen in the studio, though they have been tried successfully for dramatic shows, and are occasionally used by singers. The major problems of using wireless mikes in small station operation are (1)

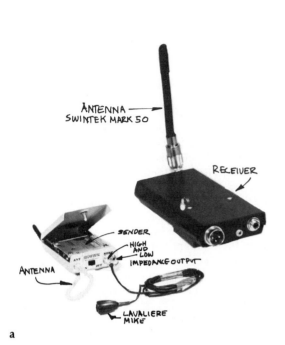

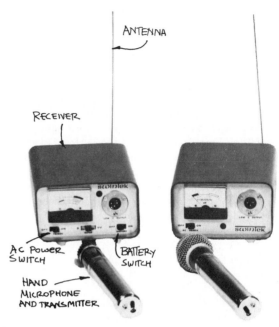

a

b

7·16 Wireless Microphones: (a) The wireless microphone has as its sound-pickup device a small lavaliere mike which is attached to a transmitter. A special receiving station receives the signal and sends it on to the master mixer. (b) Wireless hand mikes and some large lavalieres comprise a single unit, with the transmitter built into the microphone itself.

the relative expense of their operation requiring one mike per sound source, and engineers who operate the receiving station; (2) the rather high probability of transmission interference; and (3) the slight inferiority of sound quality compared to the regular lavaliere or, especially, the boom microphones. *(See. 7.16.)*

Stationary Microphones The *stationary* microphones include (1) desk, (2) stand, (3) hanging, and (4) hidden microphones.

Desk microphones, as the name implies, are usually put on tables or desks. They are widely used in panel shows, public hearings, news shows, and all other programs where the performer is working from behind a desk, table, or lectern. These microphones are used for *voice pickup* only. Since the performer behind the desk is usually doing something—shuffling papers, putting things on the desk, accidentally bumping the desk with feet or knees—desk microphones must be rugged and quite insensitive to physical shock. *Dynamic, omnidirectional* microphones are generally used. If, however, the mike is employed primarily for off-camera announcements—as in a television announcement booth, for example—higher quality, cardioid microphones such as ribbon or even condenser mikes may well be preferred.

Generally, most hand mikes can be put into a desk stand and used as desk microphones.

As with the hand mike, no attempt is made to conceal the instrument from the viewer. Nevertheless, when placing it on the desk or table, you should consider the camera picture as well as op-

7·17   The basic problem in television audio is to pick up sound adequately over a comparatively great distance. This becomes especially apparent in televising remote events. In sports telecasts, for example, it is fairly easy to get a close look at faraway action through long lenses, but it is quite difficult to accompany such pictures with adequate sound.

Two basic *long-distance* microphone techniques have, therefore, been developed: (1) the strategic placement of microphones in the field and (2) the operation of ultradirectional microphones.

Whenever the sound occurs in stable and fairly predictable areas, rugged dynamic microphones are placed directly in the field and aimed in the general direction of the anticipated sound source. We call these microphones *field microphones.* The cables for them are strung back to the remote-control center, which is usually located in the remote truck some distance away.

This method sounds simple, but it is difficult to execute. First, you need several microphones to cover even a fairly restricted area. Second, the many cables that have to be strung over a wide area and long distances not only cause traffic problems, but

increase the vulnerability of the whole audio system. Third, people in the field might accidentally hit the microphones or use embarrassing expletives near the live mikes.

In large network news conferences, you may have noticed the use of long, machine-gun-like microphones that are aimed at whoever is speaking. These ultradirectional, *shotgun* or *machine-gun microphones* are so heavy that they have to be operated with a special pedestal that permits simultaneous tilting and panning. Despite its ultradirectional pickup pattern (created by a series of long tubes in front of an omnidirectional microphone), the shotgun mike picks up much extraneous noise, and should therefore be used only when sound quality is the least important factor in the sound pickup and transmission.

Sometimes, if the camera is not too far away from the sound source, you may achieve similar results by attaching a cardioid unidirectional boom mike directly to the camera. The microphone will thus be aimed with the camera at the person speaking, or whatever the sound source may be.

Generally, long-distance microphones are not used in small station operation.

---

timal sound pickup. The camera-conscious performer will appreciate it if the camera shows more of him than of the microphone. If possible, you should therefore place the desk mike somewhat to the side of the performer, and point it toward his collarbone so that he can speak across rather than into it. A good *working distance* for desk mikes is 10 inches to one foot for omnidirectional, and approximately 17 inches to two feet for cardioid microphones. *(See 7.18.)*

If you employ the *dual-redundancy* system, use identical desk mikes and put them side by side *(see 7.19).* But do not activate them both at the same time. Keep one turned off or you may get what is called *multiple-microphone interference.* When the mikes are close to each other and fed the same

audio material, they sometimes cancel out certain frequencies, occasionally giving the voice a very odd sound quality. Multiple-microphone interference does not occur, however, when you feed each microphone into a separate channel for stereo sound pickup. You can, therefore, have many mikes close together as long as each microphone is feeding a separate receiving channel. You have probably seen microphones bunched together like grapes at the lectern of a famous politician. Since each one of these feeds a separate source, such as various radio and television stations, or film cameras, multiple-microphone interference does not occur.

When desk mikes are used in a panel discussion, you don't need to give each panel member

7·18 Desk Microphone for Single Performer: When using a desk mike, put it to the side of the performer (if he uses a floor monitor, put it to the monitor side, since a person will be more apt to speak toward the monitor than the opposite side) so as to maximize the camera view, and pointed up toward his collarbone so that he will speak across the mike rather than directly into it. If the talent uses his desk a great deal, put the microphone on a soft pad to absorb at least some of the shocks.

7·19 Dual-Redundancy Microphones: Two identical microphones can be used side by side, as long as only one is turned on; otherwise, multiple microphone interference will cancel out certain frequencies. The dual-redundancy system is used as a backup system, in case one of the two microphones fails during the telecast.

a separate microphone. If you use one for each two members, you will not only save on microphones, setup time, and control activity at the audio board, but you will also avoid multiple-microphone interference. When you use a multiple-microphone setup, try to keep the desk mikes at least three times as far apart as any microphone is away from its user. When two people are sitting opposite each other, mike each one separately. *(See 7.20.)*

Another problem—not too serious but nevertheless demanding attention—is the proper *concealment* of *microphone cables.* Don't just drop them in front of the desk; rather, try to string them as neatly as possible along the side of the desk to their respective microphone plugs. You can use

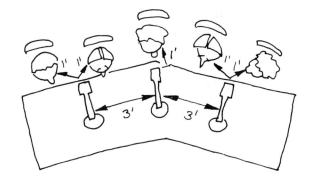

7·20 Multiple Desk Microphone Setup: When using a multiple-microphone setup, you should keep the individual microphones at least three times as far apart as any microphone is away from its user.

masking tape to cover exposed microphone cables on the studio floor. Special news or panel desks sometimes have holes through which the cables can be dropped and concealed from the cameras.

Stand microphones are used whenever the sound source is fixed and the type of programming permits them to be seen. For example, there is no need to conceal the microphones in a rock group. On the contrary, they are an important show element. Since no attempt is made to conceal stand microphones, high-quality instruments are generally used.

The sound pickup of an *instrumental group,* such as a rock group, is normally accomplished with *several* stand microphones. These are placed in front of each speaker that emits the amplified sound of a particular instrument, or in front of the unamplified sound source, such as the drums. The use of multiple microphones is essential when multiple track recordings are made (each microphone, or group of microphones, is recorded on a separate tape track), and extremely helpful even in single-track recordings (as in television) for maximum audio control during the sound mixing.

The type of microphone used depends on such a variety of factors that specific suggestions would probably be more confusing than helpful at this stage. For example, studio acoustics, the type and combination of instruments used, and the aesthetic quality of the "sound" finally desired—all play an important part in the choice and placement of microphones. Quite generally, rugged, dynamic, omnidirectional or cardioid mikes are used for the singers and in front of extremely high-volume sound sources, such as drums and electric guitar speakers, while ribbon or condenser mikes are used for the "more gentle" sound sources, such as strings and acoustical guitars.

Realizing that there are many factors that influence the type of microphone used and its placement, figures 7.21, 7.22, and 7.23 may give you

7·21 Microphone Setup for Singer and Acoustic Guitar: The customary way to mike a singer who is accompanying himself or herself on an acoustic guitar is to have two microphones on a single mike-stand, such as an Electro-Voice RE-15 pointing at the guitar and a Shure SM61 pointing at just below the singer's mouth.

some idea of how three different, yet typical, musical groups might be "miked."

Hanging microphones are used whenever any other concealed-microphone method (boom or fish-pole) is impractical.

You can hang the microphones (high-quality cardioid) by their cables over any fairly stationary sound source. Most often, hanging mikes are used in dramatic presentations, where the action is fully blocked so that the actors are in a precise location for each delivery of lines. The actor will have to make sure to speak only within the "audio pool" of the hanging microphone. Similar to the spotlight pool, where he is visible only as long as he moves within the limited area of the light, the actor is heard only when he speaks within the limited range of the audio pool. *(See 7.24.)*

In general, the audio quality of the hanging microphone is not the best. The sound source is always relatively far away from the microphone

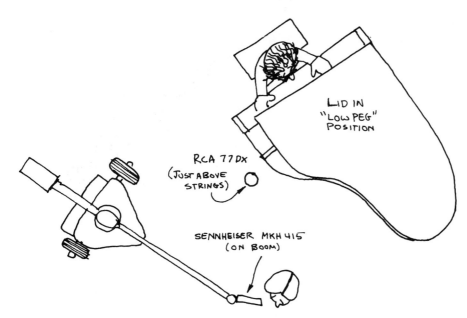

7·22 Microphone Setup for Singer and Piano: A singer who is accompanied by a piano might be miked with a Sennheiser MKH-415 (or even an 815) suspended from a boom. There could be an RCA 77-DX for the piano, placed just above the strings on the high-string side, with the lid in the low-peg position (half open). The formality of the recital probably forbids the use of a hand microphone.

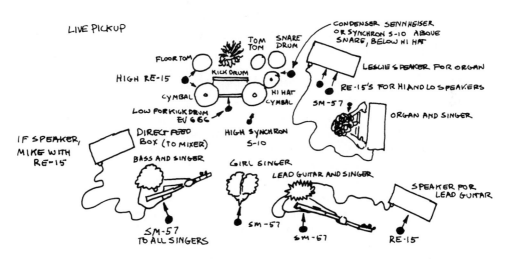

7·23 Microphone Setup for a Small Rock Group: When miking a rock group, you need microphones for the singers, drums, and other direct sound-emitting instruments, such as flutes and pianos, as well as for the speakers that carry the sound of the amplified instruments, such as electric guitars and organs. The microphones must be placed so that they do not cause audio feedback or multiple audio interference.

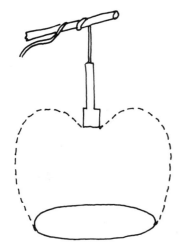

7·24 Hanging Microphone: A high-quality microphone is suspended from the lighting grid to the lowest position that the camera's view can tolerate over the designated performance area. The maximum audio pickup limits are within the "audio pool," a pickup configuration very much like a wide pool of light. Be sure to separate the microphone cables from the AC cables of the lighting instruments; otherwise you may experience electronic interference.

and the sound never quite reaches it directly; most of the time the sound is picked up as reverberations. Hang the microphone as low as possible and, if necessary, mark the studio floor for the actor at the spot of the best sound pickup.

Try to stay away from *hidden microphones,* if at all possible. If, however, you must use them, don't place them too close to hardwall scenery. The set may act as an echo chamber and distort the sound considerably.

In well-blocked dramatic scenes, however, where the position of the actors can be precisely predetermined, hidden microphones can relieve the boom operator from precarious and difficult boom swings. As with all other methods of sound

pickup, if it sounds right and if you have the time, use the hidden microphone by all means. However, the sound achieved rarely justifies the effort of setting it up. *(See 7.25 and 7.26.)*

Recorded Sound

Recorded sound includes the *recording* of sound and the *playback* of the recorded sound with the television video. You will find that during a normal production day in a small or medium-sized station, you will use your audio facilities more for the playback of recorded sound than the production of it. Nevertheless, most audio facilities are used for both.

Sound Recording

In television, the sound is most often recorded on videotape concurrently with the video. Sometimes you may be engaged in *post-dubbing,* which means that the sound is added later to the independently edited videotape (see Chapter 9). In news and documentary film production, too, the sound portion is often recorded simultaneously with the picture either directly on the optical or magnetic sound track of the film (see Chapter 9), or on a ¼-inch audiotape recorder that runs synchronously with the film. Except for news footage, most sound tracks for films are produced through post-dubbing.

Sometimes you may be engaged in recording station breaks or short promotional and public service announcements on audiotape for later playback over slides, short videotape inserts, or film clips. In the absence of a video feed, you may have to record news stories, which are telephoned in by the field reporter, on audiotape.

Most stations do not have the resources to video record each of their newscasts or news commentaries for archival purposes. In this case, you

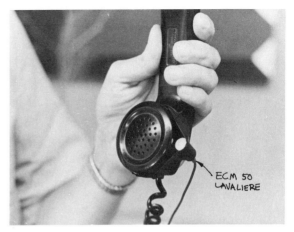

7·25 Hidden Microphone: Sometimes a small lavaliere microphone can be concealed rather easily. For this telephone conversation, a Sony ECM-50 was simply taped to the lower (transmitter) part of the phone.

may do well to audiotape the sound portion so that you have a record of what has been said. If the newscaster does not tell the day and the year of the newscast as a regular feature of the show, make sure the date is recorded at the beginning or end of the newscast. Telephone talk shows, even when on television, are audio-recorded as a matter of routine.

We will talk more about the recording techniques on videotape and film in Chapter 9.

Playback

Recorded sound can be played back from four major sources: (1) videotape, (2) film, (3) records, and (4) audiotape. With the playback of videotape and films, their respective sound tracks are mechanically synchronized with the video. Records and audiotape, however, are only indirectly coupled with the picture portion. They are independent of the video and can be played back either synchronously or nonsynchronously with it.

7·26 In the early days of television, it was quite popular to conceal microphones in such ingenious places as tufts of flowers, telephone dials, desk drawers, behind name plates, curtains, or commercial props. But with the increasing demand for better audio quality, and the development of high-quality microphones, this practice is no longer feasible. The major difficulty with the hidden microphone is, as with the hanging microphone, that the sound source is rarely in a position for optimal sound pickup. Also, the close proximity of the microphone to sound-reflecting or sound-absorbing objects (hard-wall scenery, props, or curtains) makes clear sound pickup extremely difficult, if not impossible. Microphone cables always present a problem. You will have to hide not only the microphone but its cable as well.

7·27 Although microphone cables are shielded against electronic interference from outside sources, try not to string them along light cables or any other AC-power cables. If you have to cross a power cable with a mike cable, do so at right angles in order to minimize electronic interference.

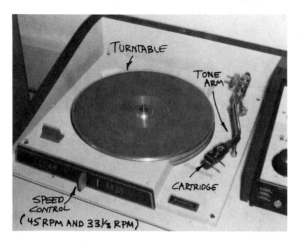

TURNTABLE

TONE ARM

CARTRIDGE

SPEED CONTROL
(45 RPM AND 33⅓ RPM)

7·28 Turntable.

The most basic audio recording and/or playback equipment includes (1) records, (2) audiotape recorders, and (3) audiotape cartridge systems.

Records Records—or electrical transcriptions (E.T.'s), as they are sometimes called if they have been made exclusively for broadcasting—are used most frequently as background music and sound effects. On occasion, rather than singing a number live in the studio, a singer may prefer to "mouth the song" on camera, meaning that he or she pretends to sing while in reality the sound portion is supplied by a record. The advantages of this method are obvious: (1) The audio quality is always excellent. (2) The singer can be accompanied by a full, well-rehearsed orchestra, a luxury that most small stations can hardly afford for a two- or three-minute song. (3) It allows the singer great flexibility. She can dance and twirl through the set with breathtaking speed and go right into the next portion of the song, seemingly unaffected by all the physical strain. Or, she can walk outdoors through a noisy city street or along

a windy lake without any outside sound interference, and with the orchestra always right behind in perfect balance. (4) Neither the set designer, the lighting technician, the camera operators, nor the director have to worry about complex microphone setups and complicated boom movements. While the singer will probably want to carry a microphone in order to make her act look real, the mike is strictly a prop and serves no audio function.

This "mouthing" technique is, however, not without drawbacks. Technically, lip-and-action synchronization with the record must be flawless for the overall effect of the presentation to have authenticity. Aesthetically, prerecording removes the viewer just one more step from the actual event. Hence, the energy and apparent spontaneity of the event are impaired. Psychologically, the viewer will feel let down, if not tricked and cheated, once he becomes aware of this presentation technique.

In order to play back records, you need two *turntables.* Professional turntables are very much like the one you probably use at home, except that the drive mechanism and the cartridge and needle are probably of somewhat higher quality than the home models. You need two turntables in order to switch smoothly (by segue or crossfade) from one record to the next.

Turntables have provisions to play all speeds, 78 rpm (revolutions per minute), 45 rpm, and 33⅓ rpm, and all record sizes. You will need a special attachment to play the wide-hole 45 rpm records. Most cartridges come with a stereo stylus, which allows you to play all records except the utterly outdated 78's. Some turntables play only two speeds, 45 rpm and 33⅓ rpm.[2] *(See 7.28.)*

[2] For further information on how to operate turntables, see Stuart W. Hyde, *Television and Radio Announcing,* 2nd ed. (Boston: Houghton Mifflin Co., 1971), or any of the books dealing specifically with audio control.

Audiotape Recorders (Reel-to-Reel) As mentioned before, the audiotape recorder in television is used frequently to record material that must or should be saved for reference or archives. The audiotape recorder is also a convenient device for playing back longer pieces of audio material. For example, background music for a long scene in a television play, or any other background sound effect, such as traffic noise, is generally premixed (prerecorded) on audiotape and then played back during the actual production. You will find that premixing background sound effects from various records or live sounds to a continuous audiotape will make the actual production much smoother than if you try to handle all the different audio sources at the time of the show. You will be busy enough with controlling the live studio mikes for optimal sound pickup.

Although there is a great variety of audiotape recorders used in television production, they all operate on similar principles. All use ¼-inch magnetic tape, and record and play back at various speeds. The most popular recording speeds are 3¾ ips (inches of tape travel per second), 7½ ips, and 15 ips. The higher the speed, the better the fidelity of the recorded material. The most *common speed* used in television operation is 7½ ips. Some of the professional audiotape recorders do not play at 3¾ ips. If someone hands you a tape recording to play on the air, make sure that your tape recorder can play back the tape at the speed it was recorded. Except for critical music programs, the 15 ips speed is rarely used. *(See 7.29.)*

The tape moves from a *supply reel* to a *takeup* reel over at least three "heads": (1) the erase head, (2) the record head, and (3) the playback head. *(See 7.30.)* This arrangement is standard for all tape recorders. When the audiotape recorder is being used for recording, the *erase head* clears the portions of the tape that receive the recording (tracks) of all audio material that might have been

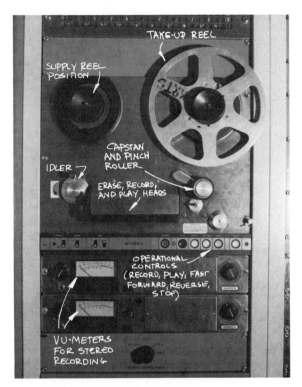

7·29 Reel-to-Reel Tape Recorder.

left on the tape from a previous recording; the *record head* then puts the new audio material on the tape. When playing back, the *playback head* reproduces the audio material previously recorded on the tape. The erase and recording heads are not activated during playback.

When threading the tape, make sure that the magnetic (usually dull) side of the tape moves over the heads. The base (usually shiny) side does not carry any sound.

Usually, the ¼-inch tape is divided into various *tracks,* each of which can receive separate audio information. Some machines use up half of the tape for a single track; other machines use up only a quarter of the tape for a single track.

7·30 Head Assembly of the Reel-to-Reel Tape Recorder.

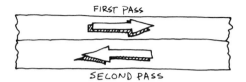

7·31 Half-Track Monophonic, or Monaural System: In monophonic, or monaural (one-channel) recording, the recording head puts audio information on half the tape. When the tape is reversed—that is, if after the first complete pass of the tape you use the full takeup reel as supply reel and thread the tape again for another pass—the other half of the tape receives new audio information.

Hence, we have half-track and quarter-track, or four-track, machines. While the quarter-track machine can play tapes that are recorded on a half-track machine, quarter-track tapes with separate audio information on all four tracks cannot be reproduced on a half-track machine.

When you play back audiotape, quickly check the following items: (1) Tape speed. What was the recording speed? Can you play back at the recording speed (some home recorders may record at speeds that are too slow for your machine). (2) Tracks. Is it a half-track or quarter-track recording? Is it mono or stereo? Do all tracks contain audio information? (3) Length of recording. For example, is the recording of sound effects long enough for the scene?

Audiotape Cartridge Systems You will find that a great proportion of your audio playback consists of short announcements, musical bridges, news inserts, and other types of brief informational material that accompanies slides or brief film clips and videotape inserts. The most efficient

method for playing such short audio material is the *tape cartridge system.* Tape cartridge playback units can hold and play back several (often ten or more) cartridges individually or simultaneously. All you do is plug in a cartridge (which contains an endless tape loop that rewinds itself as it is played back) and press the button of the cartridge you want to play back. The cartridge, which cues itself automatically, plays back the tape immediately without annoying *wows* (initial sound distortion before the record or tape is up to speed) or pauses. *(See 7.35.)*

There are special audio recorders that record the audio information directly onto cartridges. You can, of course, transfer information onto cartridges from any other audio recording.

Audio cartridge systems are extremely reliable and easy to operate. The only thing to watch in using an audio cartridge is to let it recue itself before you punch the button again for a possible replay or before ejecting it from the playback machine.

The only disadvantage of the cartridge system

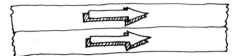

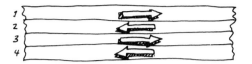

7·32 Half-Track Stereo System: In a tape recorder equipped for stereophonic recording, both tracks will receive audio information on the first pass. One half will carry the audio information of the first channel (left), the other half will carry the audio information of the second channel (right). Since both halves of the tape are already taken up, the tape cannot be reversed for a second pass. Otherwise, you will erase the first recording.

7·33 Quarter-Track, or Four-Track, Stereo: Most stereophonic audiotape recorders record and play back on quarter-tracks, or four-tracks. Two tracks (1 and 3) are used for the two channels on one pass, and two further tracks (2 and 4) on the reverse pass.

is that the playing time of the individual cartridge is rather brief—a maximum of four minutes.

Because of their reliability and almost instant cuing, tape cartridges are the ideal device for playing *sound effects.* You can transfer needed sound effects from the disc library to cartridges.

There are some sounds, however, that are more easily and precisely done *live.* Unless you do post-dubbing, the sound of gunshots is almost impossible to match exactly with the live action, even if you use a tape cartridge. Unless off-camera, gunshot sound effects are always done live. A word of caution to the gunslingers, however: Try not to shoot off your gun close to the microphone. Even the rugged dynamic mikes might falter under the extreme shock wave.

Telephone rings are frequently done live. There would be no problem with using a cartridge for the ring as long as the audio engineer has a good view of the action so that he can stop the ringing as soon as the phone is picked up. Unfortunately, the audio man is "working blind" most of the time. A floorperson, working a simple bell battery

7·34 All professional audiotape recorders have five control buttons that regulate the tape motion, besides the switch for the various recording speeds. These buttons are (1) *play,* which moves the tape at the designated recording speed; (2) *fast forward,* which advances the tape at high speed; (3) *stop,* which brakes the reels to a stop; (4) *reverse,* which rewinds the tape at high speed; and (5) *record,* which activates both the erase and record heads.

In operating these buttons, you usually go from play to stop, from fast forward to *reverse* (to slow down the tape) to stop; from reverse to *fast forward* to stop (again to slow down the tape). When you record, press *both* the *play and record* buttons. When you play back, press the *play* button *only.*

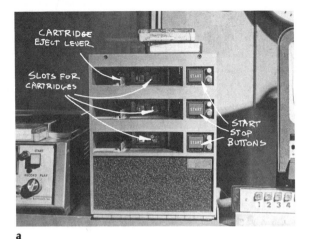

a

b

7·35   (a) Three-Unit Cartridge Machine. (b) Cartridge.

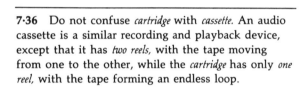

7·36   Do not confuse *cartridge* with *cassette.* An audio cassette is a similar recording and playback device, except that it has *two reels,* with the tape moving from one to the other, while the *cartridge* has only *one reel,* with the tape forming an endless loop.

unit close to the live mike in full view of the action, can do a much more precise matching job of sound effect and action than the audio engineer who is isolated in the control booth.

Sound Control

At the beginning of this chapter we have briefly talked about two important aspects of sound control: the choice of microphone and the handling of it. There are two more important aspects of sound control that originate in the audio control booth: (1) patching and mixing of various sound sources, and (2) volume control. A third area, the quality control of sound including sound perspective, equalization, and reverberation, would go beyond the scope of this handbook. For more information, you should consult books and articles on advanced audio control.

In order not to divorce the equipment from the functions it is to fulfill, we will take up (1) the patch panel and (2) the audio console.

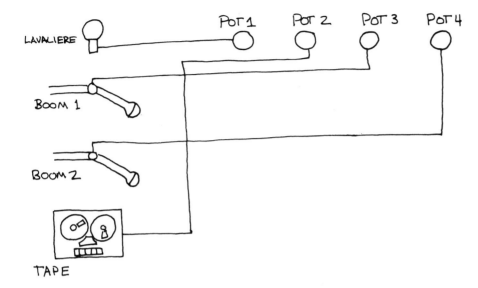

7·37 Patching: Lavaliere microphone patched into pot 1; boom microphone no. 1 into pot 3; boom microphone no. 2 into pot 4; and the tape recorder into pot 2.

The Patch Panel

The primary function of the patch panel is the connecting and routing of various pieces of equipment. Let us assume that you want to have three microphones and a tape recorder operating during a dramatic scene. Mike No. 1 is the announcer's lavaliere; mikes No. 2 and No. 3 are boom mikes. The tape recorder is for playback of background music. Just as the individual lighting instruments can be patched to any one of the dimmers, you can now patch any one of these audio "inputs" to individual volume controls (pots) in any order desirable. Let's assume that you would like to operate the volume controls in the following order: lavaliere, audiotape, boom mike No. 1, boom mike No. 2, from left to right. All you have to do is patch these inputs to the control board in this order. If you want to reverse the order, you don't have to unplug the microphones physically on the studio floor. All you do

is pull the patches and repatch the inputs in the new order. *(See 7.37 and 7.38.)*

The Audio Console

Regardless of the individual designs, all audio consoles, or audio control boards, are designed and built to perform three major functions: (1) to *select and amplify* the incoming sound signals, the inputs; (2) to *control the volume* of the various inputs; and (3) to *mix* (combine) and balance two or more incoming sound signals.

When working the board, you will find that the major operating controls can be grouped together according to (1) controls for source selection, (2) volume (loudness) controls, and (3) mixing.

Source Selection During most productions, you have more signals from sound sources coming in than you will ever need at one time. In order to keep the audio console as simple and manageable

a

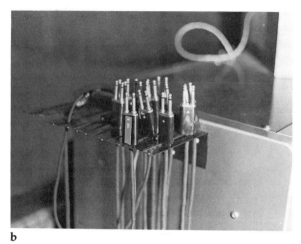

b

7·38 (a) Patch Panel: All major audio inputs terminate in the patch panel, or patchbay. Each piece of equipment that can be patched has an "in" and an "out" designation. (b) Patches: Several patches are usually kept near the patch panel for convenience.

as possible, there are fewer controls than inputs. This means that you have to select the particular input, or inputs, with which you will work at a given time. The *input selector switches,* or buttons, will make it possible for you to select the sound sources with which you have to work. *(See 7.39.)*

Once you have selected the incoming signal, you can turn it on or off, like controlling the light with a light switch. On simple consoles, you can turn this switch to P for program, which sends the selected sound source to final amplification to the *line-out.* The line-out feeds the transmitter, in case of a live telecast, or the audio track on the videotape, or the audiotape recorder, for example. If you flip the switch to A for audition, you will be able to hear the particular sound in the monitor speaker.

The on-off switch in more complex audio consoles is the *channel selector switch.* If you operate on channel 1, for example, you will send the sound signal to the line-out by turning the chan-

nel selector switch to channel 1. The center position of the switch is generally the "off" position. *(See 7.42.)*

Additional selector switches, which come in various configurations, enable you to switch from studio to network and remote inputs, to monitor various program and intercommunication sources, and to assign different functions (network, remote, studio) to the VU (volume unit) meter.

Volume Control   During the actual operation of the audio console, you will be most continually concerned with the *balance of sound,* which technically means the volume control of the various preamplified sound signals. Each selected and preamplified sound signal is sent to its own volume control, called *pot* (from potentiometer) or *fader.*

The pots are either knobs or sliding faders, called slide-faders. To increase the volume, which

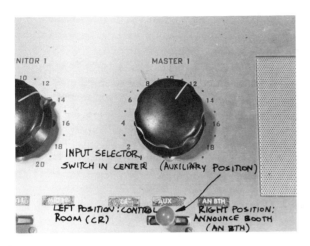

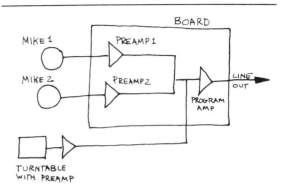

7·39 Input Selector Switch: Most input selector switches are of the three-position type, which means that you can choose among three different audio inputs. In this case, you have a choice among control room (CR), auxiliary (AUX), and announce booth microphone (AN BTH).

makes the sound louder, you turn the knob clockwise, or push the slide-fader up, away from you. To decrease the volume, which makes the sound softer, turn the knob counterclockwise, or pull the slide-fader down, toward you. *(See 7.44 and 7.45.)*

The advantages of slide-faders over volume-control knobs are: (1) you can work several faders simultaneously more easily than the equal number of knobs (for example, you can rather deftly work four faders at one time, while with rotary knobs this action would constitute quite a feat); and (2) you can readily *see* a "mixing pattern" with faders, while such a visual impression of the volume setting of each individual knob is very difficult to achieve, if at all possible.

In spite of the calibration on the pots and the visual impression of relative volumes you can glimpse from their respective settings, the accurate volume indicator is the *VU (volume unit) meter.*

7·40 The weak sound signals that originate from a microphone or a turntable cartridge need to be boosted by a *preamplifier,* or preamp, before they can be controlled (as to volume, which is just like the loudness control on your hi-fi set) and distributed throughout the audio console. The preamplified signals are then amplified again by the *program amplifier* to make them strong enough for the line-out.

The audio console has preamplifiers for microphones only. Turntables, tape cartridge machines, and tape recorders usually have their own preamplifiers; the signals from these inputs go, therefore, directly to the program amplifier.

7·41 More complex audio consoles have more than one output channel. Each channel has its own line-out, which means that you can have the audio console mix and feed two completely separate programs at the same time. For example, you may have part of the board tied up in videotaping a short on-camera announcement on channel 1 (with the line-out No. 1 feeding the videotape recorder) while the other part of the board, on channel 2, is processing a telephone call from a field reporter and sending it on line-out No. 2 to an audiotape recorder. Stereo boards must always have two output channels. Do not confuse output channel with mixing channel. The number of mixing channels is determined by the number of mixing controls, the pots or faders.

7·42   Channel Selector Switch.

7·44   Rotating Potentiometer.

7·43   Other names for volume control are *mixer, gain control,* and *attenuator.*

The needle of your VU meter will oscillate back and forth along a calibrated scale with the volume variations *(see 7.46).* If the volume is so low that the needle barely moves from the extreme left, you are riding (the gain or volume) "in the mud." If the needle oscillates around the middle of the scale and peaks at, or occasionally over, the red line on the right, you are riding correct gain. If the needle swings almost exclusively in the red, right part of the scale, and even hits the right edge of the meter, your volume is too high; you are "bending the needle," or "spilling over." Aside from distorting the sound, bending the needle can actually "bend" a few more parts in the audio console and thus effectively destroy the equipment.

Once you have set the volume levels for each individual input, you can make adjustments to the overall volume of the mixed signals by yet another volume control, the *master pot.* Usually, however, you set the master pot at a given level and work the individual pots for proper sound balance.

Your *monitor speaker,* which reproduces the mixed audio before the line-out, has its in-

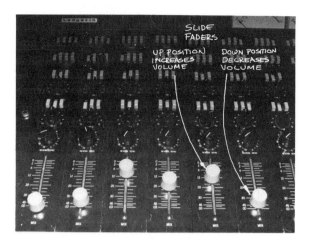

7·45 Vertical or Horizontal Faders.

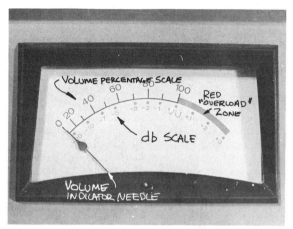

7·46 VU Meter: The VU (volume unit) meter indicates the relative sound volume, the loudness of sound that has been picked up by a microphone and amplified. The lower figures ranging from -20 to +3 are the volume units (decibels). The upper figures represent a percentage scale, ranging from 0 to 100. If the needle swings within the left section (thin line—it is black on the VU meter) from 0 to 100, the sound volume is kept within tolerable limits. If the needle "peaks" primarily in the red line section (the thick black line in this figure on the right side of the meter), the sound is amplified too much; it is too loud and subject to distortion.

dividual volume control. Note that this control does not affect the volume of the program sound you are monitoring. It simply helps you to adjust the monitor speaker to a level that feels most comfortable to you.

Mixing The audio console allows you to *mix* together *two or more sounds* or, more accurately, the signals from two or more sound sources. *(See 7.47.)* Let's take a simple scene from a television drama. Two people, a man and a woman, are sitting on the porch of their small country home. It is late evening. The telephone rings just as a car drives up. Since this scene happens in the studio, many of the actions are suggested by sound effects only. Assuming that you have not premixed any of the necessary sound effects, you will be quite busy mixing and balancing the various sounds so that, in combination with the video, the sound will help to convey the intended message.

What audio inputs do you need? First, the two people on the porch. Since it is a realistic scene, the microphones must be out of camera range. For the porch, we use a boom mike. Second, for the

woman answering the phone off camera inside, we can use a stand mike, or a small boom. We use the same mike for the mechanical ring. We don't want to use a sound effect for the ring, since you as the audio console operator can't see just when she is picking up the phone. Third, we need sound effects to help (with the lighting, of course) establish the time, late evening, and the locale (country). Most likely you will use cricket sounds (night and country), and an occasional dog barking in the distance. Perhaps you can think of more original sound effects for the establishing of time and place, but don't be afraid to use the conven-

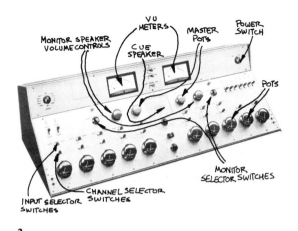

7·47 Audio Console: (a) A traditional audio console (RCA BC-7 Audio Consolette). (b) A four-channel television audio console with slide-faders (Audio Designs BC-5).

tional. After all, these sounds do exist and they are easily recognized by the viewer. They have become conventional because they work.

Then you need the sound effect of a car driving up. Since the driveway of the old country home is probably not paved, the sound of the car approaching should include some tires-on-gravel effects.

So you have two microphone inputs, the boom and the stand mike near the off-camera telephone. The crickets chirp throughout the outdoor part of the scene, which means that you need a reel-to-reel tape recorder for the playback of this sound effect. Since the dogs bark only occasionally, you can put the bark on a cartridge. If possible at all, you should prerecord the continuous background sounds of the crickets and the occasional dog barks on a single quarter-inch tape. Since the car driving up is a relatively short affair, you can put this sound effect on a second tape cartridge. Don't forget that we should hear the car

off in the distance for some time before it gets to the driveway, especially since we tend to hear better at night than in daytime, mainly because of the absence of the usual ambient daytime noises. So, don't record on your cartridge just the sounds of the car driving into the driveway, but include also the sounds of a gradually approaching car.

For dramatic emphasis, the director wants background music throughout the scene up to the ring of the telephone.

Let's try to mix these sounds within the context of the scene. Since each of the various sounds is to fulfill a slightly different function (informational function in what they say; orientation function as to time and place of the scene; function of establishing feeling and mood through music), mixing now no longer simply means combining a number of sound signals from various inputs, but it especially implies the *balancing* of the various sounds so that each one serves its assigned function with optimal effectiveness. Thus, some sounds should be perceived as foreground sounds and others as background sounds.

The *foreground* sounds need to be heard "closer," that is, they must primarily have a higher volume (and, of course, more presence if possible) than the *background* sounds. Obviously, you should ride the conversation (the boom microphone) at a higher level than the audiotape with the crickets on it. In fact, the crickets should be kept so low that they can be heard but not necessarily consciously perceived by the television viewer. The dog barking overrides the crickets, but it is still much lower than the conversation on the porch. When the distant car sounds are heard, the occasional dog bark may become louder (indicating that the watchful dog has spotted the approaching car). Now the telephone rings. The balance of this ring depends on its dramatic importance. If it is clearly to interrupt the tranquil scene, the ring must be very loud, even overpowering the conversation. If the call was expected and is merely routine in the context of the dramatic structure, the ring should be kept realistically low (since the phone is inside) and brought up briefly when the woman opens the door. We have now zoomed in on a closeup of the man listening. He is trying to hear the woman talking on the telephone. Close the boom mike, since the man has no lines, and bring up the stand mike to a level where the woman's voice sounds low, but where it is easily perceivable. The car approaches the house. This event is done entirely with sound effects and an ellipsoidal spotlight moving briefly across the man's face (simulating the car's headlights). Again, if the car is dramatically significant, its sounds will have to drown out the woman's voice. The closer the car gets to the man, the more you have to bring up the cartridge pot with the car sounds. And until the telephone call, you have had background music on a turntable at a fairly low level.

Let's recall the various sound sources you are required to mix for this relatively simple scene. You have five or six separate inputs into five or six separate pots, depending on whether or not you have premixed the crickets and the dogs barking. If you have premixed the two background sounds, you will have to control simultaneously two microphones (boom and stand mikes), the audiotape with the cricket and dog barking sounds, the cartridge with the car approaching, and the record with the background music. If you have not premixed the dogs barking —so that you can make the barking louder when the car approaches the house—you will need another, separate cartridge channel for the bark.

A mere look at the single VU meter will no longer suffice to indicate proper volume for this complex mixing job. What you now need most of all is *good ears*. The VU meter may indicate a perfectly acceptable overall level, but it will *not tell* you anything about *how well you balanced* the various sound sources. Another important point should become quite apparent. You need to know very intimately the total play, the director's concept of it, its development, climaxes, dramatic structure, and progression. You are now no longer a "board operator," you have become an *artist*.

Be sure to *label* with masking tape each pot clearly as to its input, or, if you prefer, its function. Mike pot 1 would read: boom, or porch talk; mike pot 2: stand mike, or phone; turntable pot 1: BG (background) music; audiotape pot 1: tape, or crickets; audiotape pot 2: cartridge car, or simply car; audiotape pot 3, or auxiliary input (if needed): cartridge dogs, or simply dogs. With clear labeling, you won't have to try several pots before finally discovering the one that actually needs the volume adjustment; nor do you have to burden your brain with remembering which pot does what. You can pay full attention to the job required: good, creative mixing.

Operation   Here are a few more simple guide-lines for operating the audio console:

1.   Make sure that the line-out switch is on if you are feeding either the transmitter, the videotape, or any other facility. Otherwise, the sound will go nowhere except into the control-room monitor speakers.

2.   During a television show that requires your control of inputs from several different sources (such as live mikes, videotapes, audiotapes, cartridges), as in a news show, *pot in* the various sources, do not *key* them in. To *pot in* a source means to have the *on-off switch on program* (on-position) already, or on the channel you are using, with the pot in the zero position (where it does not let any sound signal through). On cue, quickly bring the pot up to the position of the desired sound level. This position you determine by "taking a level" during re-hearsal or—if you can't take a level, as with some news film or videotape sound tracks—by experience. To *key in* a source means that you have the *level preset on the pot,* flipping the on-off switch to the "on" (program or channel) position on cue. The advantage of potting in over keying in is that, if you miss the cue slightly, you don't suddenly cut in a source in midsentence (called upcutting) but fade the sound in more gradually. A mistake isn't quite so noticeable this way. Also, if your announcer runs over with his introduction to a video-tape insert, you can pot in the videotape sound track, while the introduction is still taking place. There is one exception to this practice, however. If the announcer runs long in his introduction to a film or tape commer-cial, the commercial audio takes precedence.

3.   Check out all pots and see whether they really control the sources as labeled. In case you want to test several mikes that are in close proximity to one an-other, have the floor manager gently scratch the surface of the mike. The scratch is picked up by the "on" mike only. In any case, don't blow into the mikes.

4.   Make sure that your input-selector switches, in-cluding the monitor-selector switch, are all properly positioned.

5.   Watch the script and the monitor. Anticipate the director's cues. Your anticipation can help make for a smoother show by cutting to a minimum the delay time between cue and your reaction.

6.   If you have remote inputs, double- and triple-check your patching and your selector switches. Make sure that you have got a signal through before you actually need to use the remote sound source.

Summary

Television audio, the sound accompanying the pictures, is a major part of production. Generally, television sound is hard to achieve, owing to the varying distances from moving sound sources to microphones, the use of microphones in outdoor locations, and the inevitable studio noises during a production.

The *electronic characteristics* of television micro-phones include (1) the generating element, which can be dynamic, ribbon, or condenser, and (2) the microphone pickup patterns, which can be om-nidirectional or unidirectional.

The *operational characteristics* help to classify mi-crophones into mobile and stationary varieties. *Mobile microphones* include (1) the boom micro-phone, (2) the hand microphone, (3) the lavaliere microphone, and (4) the wireless, or FM, micro-phone. The operational techniques differ greatly according to the type. *Stationary microphones* include (1) the desk microphone, (2) the stand micro-phone, and (3) the hanging microphone. Again, the setup for any one of these depends on the specific production, and the sound pickup re-quirements.

Recorded sound includes the recording and the playback of sound. Most television sound is re-corded on audio tape (reel-to-reel or cassette) or videotape, and played back primarily from (1) videotape, (2) film, (3) records, or (4) audiotape.

Sound control includes the patch panel and the audio control console. The audio console is ex-tremely important for the control of the volume and for the mixing of two or more sounds.

7·48   Table of Microphones.

Type		Pickup Pattern	Characteristics	Use
Sennheiser MKH-815		Super cardioid, extremely directional	Condenser, sensitive, excellent presence	Boom, long-distance pickup; good for orchestra pickup
Sennheiser MKH-435		Cardioid, very directional	Condenser, sensitive, excellent presence	Fishpole, small boom, long-distance pickup; also good stand mike
Electro-Voice DL-42		Cardioid, very directional	Dynamic, fairly rugged, especially with screen	Boom, fishpole, or handheld for long-distance pickup
RCA BK 5-A		Cardioid, directional	Ribbon, fairly rugged, good quality	Boom, stand

7·48   Table of Microphones (cont.).

Neumann U-87		Cardioid, fairly wide pattern	Condenser, very good quality, rather sensitive	Stationary boom principally for music pickup in recording studio
Electro-Voice RE-15		Super cardioid, extremely directional	Dynamic, very good quality, fairly sensitive	Desk, hanging, stand; good for music recording
Vega Synchron S-10		Cardioid, directional	Condenser, very good quality	Stationary boom, stand; for pickup of high-frequency sounds (strings)
Shure SM53		Cardioid, directional	Dynamic, fairly rugged	High-quality all-purpose mike; desk, stand, hand; good for music pickup

Shure SM57 (Unidyne)	Cardioid, directional	Dynamic, quite rugged	All-purpose mike; desk, stand, hand; good for close audio pickup
Electro-Voice 635A	Omnidirectional	Dynamic, very rugged	Old, yet good work-horse; hand, desk, stand; excellent outdoor use
Shure SM61	Omnidirectional	Dynamic, rugged, good blast filter	Excellent hand mike; also good on stand for singers or music pickup
Shure SM58	Cardioid, directional	Dynamic, fairly rugged	Good hand, desk, stand mike; good for close audio, such as singers

7·48   Table of Microphones (cont.).

Shure SM82		Cardioid, directional	Condenser high-quality; can be used with extremely long cable runs	Hand, stand, desk—on remote locations
RCA 77-DX		Cardioid, multiple settings	Ribbon, sensitive, quite large, excellent quality	Classic mike used for voice and music pickup; stand mike
Electro-Voice 666		Cardioid, fairly directional	Dynamic, extremely rugged	Stand mike; good for high-volume sound sources, such as bass drum
Sony ECM-50		Omnidirectional	Condenser, excellent quality, very small and lightweight	Excellent lavaliere

Electro-Voice 649B		Omnidirectional	Dynamic, fairly rugged, relatively large	Lavaliere
Vega 5L		Omnidirectional	Dynamic, good quality; rather large range: 750 feet	Wireless lavaliere
Swintek Mark V		Cardioid (uses Shure SM56 Unidyne mike)	Dynamic, good quality; no wire; range: 500 feet	Wireless hand mike; good for singers
Swintek Mark 50		Omnidirectional (uses Sony ECM-50 mike)	Condenser, good quality; range: 500 feet	Wireless lavaliere; good even for singers

8 *The Television Studio and Control Centers*

The television studio and control centers are built so that they afford maximum control of all production elements. In this chapter, we will highlight three major production facilities:

1. The studio itself, including its physical requirements and its major installations.

2. The control room, with its systems and devices for controlling the studio activities, switching, audio, and lighting.

3. Master control and its principal functions of program input, program storage, and program retrieval.

4. The studio support areas, including property and scene storage, and makeup and dressing rooms.

You should realize that the studio should not become an involuntary prison for television production, simply because it is available. The highly mobile cameras and recording facilities make it less and less the only, or even the major, place for production. Why bring the City Hall into the studio when you can go to City Hall? Nevertheless, the studio does, and will for some time to come, represent an essential television production environment for many types of production.

Telecasts can originate anywhere, indoors and outdoors, as long as there is enough room for one camera and its associated equipment, power facilities to drive the camera chain and audio equipment, and enough light so that the camera can see. With the development of highly portable cameras and recording facilities, television is no longer bound by the traditional confines of the studio. In tandem with satellite transmission, it now has literally the whole world as its stage.

Television's newfound and important freedom from the studio, however, does not render the studio obsolete by any means. The major reason for the continued existence of television studios is that, if properly designed, they can afford *maximum control* of every production element with the least effort. Since the two basic functions of the television studio and its associated facilities are optimal use of the television equipment and maximum control of the various production elements, we must be concerned with three major production centers: (1) the origination center, the television studio, (2) the control center, the studio control room and master control room, and (3) studio support areas.

The Television Studio

The television studio should be designed in such a way that it provides for the proper coordination of all major production elements—cameras, lighting, sound, scenery, action of performers.

Most decisively, however, the studio is designed around the *workings of the camera,* that is, to give the cameras great maneuverability with little or no interference from other production equipment. We will briefly look at (1) the physical layout of the typical studio, and (2) the major studio installations.

Physical Layout

Most studios are rectangular with varying amounts of *floor space.* Although the zoom lens has

Acoustic Treatment Application of sound-deadening material to the walls of a television (or sound) studio to create an environment for optimal sound pickup (usually by rendering the studio less "live").

Audio-Follows-Video An appliance that automatically switches the accompanying audio along with the video source.

Control Room A room adjacent to the studio in which the director, the T.D. (technical director), the audio engineer, and sometimes the lighting technician perform their various production functions.

Double Headset A telephone headset (earphones) that carries program sound in one earphone and the P.L. information in the other. Also called split-intercom.

House Number The in-house system of identification; each piece of recorded program must be identified by a certain code number. This is called the house number, since the numbers differ from station to station (house to house).

Intercom Abbreviation for intercommunication system. The system uses telephone headsets to facilitate voice communication among all production and engineering personnel involved in the production of a show.

Interruptible Feedback Also called the I.F.B. system. Same as Program Interrupt.

Line Monitor Also called master monitor. The monitor that shows only the line-out pictures, the pictures that go on the air, or on videotape.

drastically reduced the actual movement of the cameras, the size of the room still affects production complexity and flexibility to a great extent.

Size   The larger the studio, the more complex the productions can become, and the more flexible the productions will be. If, for example, you use a studio for a traditional news program only, you can get by with an amazingly small space. The sets, the cameras, and even the newscasters will have their assigned positions and rarely, if ever, move from them. Lighting and audio facilities, once set up, will remain unchanged from show to show. Simple interviews and panel shows need not much more space.

More complex productions, however, such as musical groups or orchestras, dramas, dance, or audience-participation shows need larger studios. A symphony orchestra, multiple sets, or a room-filling audience obviously does not fit into a tiny studio. It is always easier to produce a simple show in a large studio than a complex show in a

small one. Generally, a 40 X 60 foot studio will be sufficient for most production requirements of a medium-sized station. *(See 8.1.)*

Floor   The floor itself should be level and even so that cameras can travel on it smoothly and freely. Also, it should be hard enough to withstand the moving about of heavy equipment, scenery, and heavy set properties.

Most studios have concrete floors that are polished, or covered with linoleum, tile, or a hard plastic spray.

Ceiling Height   Adequate ceiling height is one of the most important design factors in a television studio. If the ceiling is too low, the cameras will overshoot the scenery, revealing the overhead lights and boom microphones. Since the average television scenery is 10 feet high, a minimum ceiling height of 12 feet is essential for normal, professional operation. A higher ceiling (25 to 30 feet) is much better, since it allows some

---

Log   The major operational document. Issued daily, the log carries such information as program source or origin, scheduled program time, program duration, video and audio information, code identification (house number, for example), the title of the program, the program type, and additional special information.

Master Control   Nerve center for all telecasts. Controls the program input, storage, and retrieval for on-the-air telecasts. Also oversees technical quality of all program material.

Monitor   1. Television receiver used in the studio and control rooms. 2. Loudspeaker that carries the program sound.

P.A.   Public address loudspeaker system. Same as Studio Talkback.

P.L.   Abbreviation for Private Line, or Phone Line. Same as Intercom.

Preview Monitor   1. A monitor that shows the director the picture he intends to use as the next shot. 2. Any monitor that shows a video source, except for the line (master) and off-the-air monitors.

Program Interrupt   Also called the P.I. system. A system that feeds program sound to a tiny earphone worn by the performer. It can be interrupted with P.L. information at any time.

8·1 Large Production Studio (Studio 1, San Francisco State University).

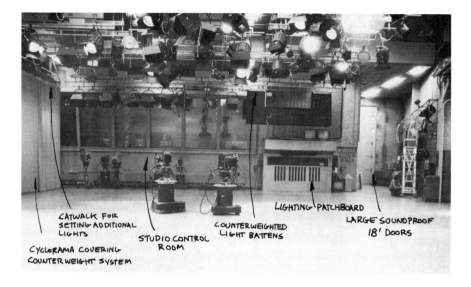

CATWALK FOR SETTING ADDITIONAL LIGHTS

CYCLORAMA COVERING COUNTER WEIGHT SYSTEM

STUDIO CONTROL ROOM

COUNTERWEIGHTED LIGHT BATTENS

LIGHTING PATCHBOARD

LARGE SOUNDPROOF 18' DOORS

working and cooling space above the lighting grid or movable battens. You will find that a low ceiling is the most serious problem in a room that is to be converted into a television studio. In a high-ceilinged studio, you can always drop in a false ceiling, if it is to be seen on camera as part of the set. But there is no way of pushing up one that is too low. If you work in a low-ceilinged studio,

Program Monitor Speaker, or Program Speaker A loudspeaker in the control room that carries the program sound. Its volume can be controlled without affecting the actual line-out program feed.

Program Storage The physical storage of recorded program material (film or videotape).

Studio Monitor A monitor located in the studio showing the program in progress.

Studio Talkback A public address loudspeaker system from the control room to the studio. Also called S.A. (studio address) or P.A. system.

Switcher 1. Engineer or production person who is doing the video switching (usually the T.D., the technical director). 2. A panel with rows of buttons that allows the selection and assembly of various video sources through a variety of transition devices.

Telecine The place from which the film islands operate. The word comes from *tele*vision and *cine*matography. Occasionally, the telecine room is used for film storage and some minor film-editing jobs.

Videotape Room The place where all large videotape recorders are kept. Often serves also as videotape storage and editing room.

try to mount the lighting instruments as close to the ceiling as possible. Make sure that you then have enough vents in it to divert the intense heat of the lights.

Acoustic treatment All walls and the ceiling are usually acoustically treated. Generous layers of rock wool, held in place by wire mesh, have proved to be the most practical sound-deadening material. In a classroom conversion, however, you might try using empty egg cartons for acoustical wall treatment. If snugly arranged, they not only prove highly effective as sound deadeners but are also quite attractive to look at.

There should be *no windows* in the studio, since the outside light would make controlled lighting difficult, if not impossible. Also, the windows would admit unwanted sounds from the outside.

Air Conditioning The lack of windows, however, makes it necessary to install an efficient air conditioning system. Besides keeping the studio at a tolerable temperature, the air conditioning must operate as quietly as possible. If it produces even the slightest hissing and rumbling or excessive air movement when it is operating, you will find yourself shutting it off every time you do an important show. And since all shows are important during production, your air conditioning will be turned off more than it is turned on, much to the detriment of man and machine.

Doors Another important point in the design and use of a television studio is the size and construction of its doors. You need heavy, soundproof doors that are large enough to accommodate large pieces of scenery, furniture, and set or commercial properties, such as grand pianos, appliances, and automobiles. There is nothing more frustrating for production personnel than to have to squeeze scenery and props, and people, through undersized studio doors, or to have the

doors transmit outside sounds, like somebody coughing or laughing, in the middle of the show.

All access doors to the studio should have some warning mechanism that alerts people about to enter the studio that rehearsals or on-the-air shows are in progress. These devices may range from "Stand-by" and "On the Air" signs above the studio doors to revolving and flashing red lights similar to those on police cars.

Major Installations

While any fairly large room with a high enough ceiling can serve as a studio in case of need, there are certain basic installations that are essential for effective studio operations. These are (1) the intercommunication system, (2) studio monitors, (3) program speakers, (4) wall outlets, and (5) the lighting patchboard. In some studios, the dimmer control board is also located in the studio, although you will find that many stations prefer to have it in the control room.

Intercommunication System The intercommunication system, or for short "intercom," is one of the most important, though often neglected, studio installations. It allows all production and engineering personnel actively engaged in the production of a show to be in constant voice contact with one another. For example, without the intercom system, the director would have no way of telling the floor manager in the studio what cues to give to which performers, or the camera operators what shots to take. Other production personnel—the audio engineer, boom operators, technical directors, videotape operator—rely equally on the intercom for the split-second coordination of their tasks.

In most small stations, the *telephone intercommunication,* or P.L. (private or phone line) system is used. All production and engineering personnel that need to be in voice contact with one another

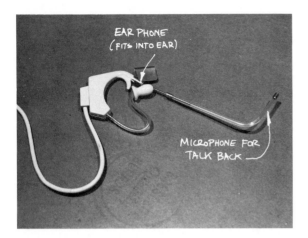

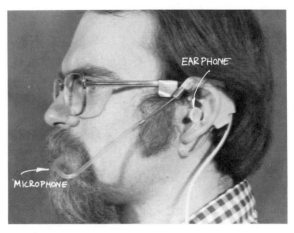

8·2 Intercom Headset: The most vital link in television production is the intercommunication system. All production and engineering personnel that need to be in voice contact wear telephone headsets with a small earphone and a microphone for talkback.

wear standard telephone headsets with one small earphone and a small microphone for talkback. *(See 8.2.)* Each major production area has one or several intercom outlets for plugging in the headsets. For example, each camera generally has two intercom outlets: one for the camera operator, and the other for the floor manager or another member of the floor crew. If possible, though, the members of the floor crew should avoid connecting their earphones to the camera; it not only limits their operation radius but also interferes with the camera's flexibility. Usually, the floor personnel connect their earphones to separate intercom wall outlets through long, flexible, lightweight cables. But difficulties can arise with this arrangement, too, if the cable gets in the way of moving cameras and microphone booms or becomes tangled up in one of the many pieces of scenery on the studio floor.

Larger studios employ, therefore, a *wireless intercom system* for the floor personnel. They wear a small earplug, instead of the cumbersome headset, and carry a small pocket receiver that picks up signals sent into the studio by a transmitter. Unfortunately, the floor personnel cannot talk back to the control room with this system. At least the floor manager, who definitely needs two-way communication, should wear a talkback telephone headset.

Sometimes it is necessary to supply program sound and control-room signals simultaneously to such production personnel as the microphone boom operator or studio musicians (usually the band or orchestra leader) who have to gear their actions to both the program sound and the director's cues. In this case, a *double headset* is used in which one of the two earphones carries the intercommunication signals and the other the program sound. Although you may not need this split-intercom system very often, it should nevertheless be available to you.

In most television operations, production and engineering crews use the same intercommunication channel, which means that everybody can be heard by everybody else. Most intercom systems, however, have provisions for separating the lines for different functions. For example, while the technical director confers with the video engineer on one intercom channel, the director may, at the same time, give instructions to his floor crew. More often, the separate channels are used to switch into or out of the intercom systems of other studios or remote production centers.

In shows with highly flexible formats, or where important program changes are likely to occur, such as in newscasts or special events telecasts, a special intercommunication system is used to connect the control room (director, producer) directly with the performers. This system is called the P.I., *program interrupt system,* or the I.F.B, *interruptible feedback system.* Here the performer wears a small earpiece that carries the program sound unless the director, or any other member of the production team connected with the system, interrupts the program sound with special instructions. For example, the field reporter in Washington who is describing on camera the details of the arrival of foreign dignitaries hears himself until the director cuts in and tells him to "throw it back to New York"—that is, to tell the viewers that he is returning the program to the origination center in New York. But while the director is giving these instructions, the viewer still hears the field reporter's description of the event. Relaying such messages through an off-camera floor manager would be much too slow and inaccurate in as tight a show as a live special events telecast. Needless to say, such a system works only with a highly experienced announcer. There are numerous occasions when the program interrupt system has unfortunately acted also as a performer interrupt device because the inexperienced performer could no longer maintain his commentary while listening to the director's instructions.

The *studio talkback,* or S.A. (for studio address),

system is used by the control-room personnel, principally the director, to give special instructions to people in the studio not connected with the telephone intercom system. The talkback system is a great aid to the director, who, especially in the beginning stages of a rehearsal, needs to talk to everybody in the studio at once. Also, if most of the personnel happen to be off the intercom system, as is frequently the case during a short break, the director can use the talkback system to call them back to work.

Some directors use the talkback almost exclusively rather than calling on the floor manager to relay their instructions to the performers. If you have to work with a large cast, this is an effective way of giving directions. A floor manager would have to yell, or repeat the instructions several times in order to reach everybody. However, if you work with a fairly small cast, total dependence on the talkback system is not always desirable. If you happen to be impatient to get things moving in the studio, the talkback system communicates your nervousness directly to the performers, along with your instructions, and in an amplified way at that. A sensitive floor manager, on the other hand, can relay your messages more calmly and provide the human contact so badly needed in tense rehearsal situations. Also, the floor manager can often correct minor blocking difficulties much more easily from the floor than you can from the isolated control room. On the other hand, an occasional firm and direct instruction through the talkback can work wonders with a slightly tired or inattentive floor crew or group of performers.

Considering the importance of the intercommunication system, you should include it in your routine program facilities checks. If you discover faulty earphones or an imperfect intercom line, report it to the maintenance crew and have it fixed. A faulty intercom can be more detrimental to a production than a defective camera.

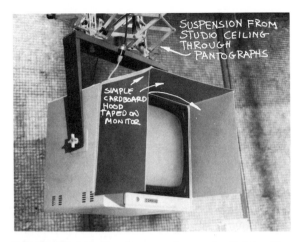

SUSPENSION FROM STUDIO CEILING THROUGH PANTOGRAPHS

SIMPLE CARDBOARD HOOD TAPED ON MONITOR

8·3 Studio Monitor: In case of excessive light spill in the studio, you can build a simple cardboard hood for the monitor that will shield the screen from the light and make the picture more visible.

Studio Monitors   If camera and floor personnel, and occasionally the performers, can see the shots the director has selected, they will be greatly helped in anticipating their future tasks. You need, therefore, at least two mobile studio monitors in the average-sized television studio. For example, if the director has selected camera 1's closeup of a book cover, camera 2, after seeing this on the studio monitor, can go to a two-shot of the interviewer and the guest, or to another shot that does not needlessly duplicate camera 1's closeup. The floor personnel will see on the monitor how to position themselves relative to the performer without getting into the camera's shots. And, if the boom operator does not have a monitor on the boom dolly, he or she can see by the studio monitor where to position the mike so that it will not be in the shot. Sometimes the performer must see the monitor, especially if he has to narrate over a short film clip or videotape, or gear his narration in any other way to the video. But be careful about letting an inexperienced per-

former, or especially an eager guest, see the studio monitor unnecessarily. Some of these people, members of the studio audience in particular, may become so fascinated by their screen image that they forget all about the actual show. If you include the studio audience in your show, try to turn off the audience monitors whenever someone in the audience is on camera, unless you feel that the embarrassed smiles, gestures of mock horror, or waves to mom at home are essential to the program, or indicative of the true nature of human beings.

Since the studio and audience monitors are generally at a considerable distance from the persons who are supposed to watch them, they should have a fairly large screen. The coaxial cable and the power cable should be long enough so that the monitor can be pushed into every performance area in the studio.

Sometimes the bright studio lighting will wash out, or at least reduce the visibility of, the monitor picture. A simple cardboard hood, or better a permanently attached metal shield, will help to reduce the light spilling onto the screen. *(See 8.3.)*

In small studios, you can suspend a single monitor from the lighting grid with a pantograph, which enables you to lower and raise the monitor according to need.

Program Monitor Speakers   The program speakers (for short) fulfill a function for audio similar to what the studio monitors do for video. Whenever necessary, they can feed into the studio the program sound, or any other necessary sound—dance music, telephone rings, or other sound effects that call for synchronization with the studio action. When the program speakers are on, the studio microphones are generally cut off, unless you put the studio speaker controls on the audio board in the override position. In that case, the studio speakers operate at low volume without cutting off the studio microphones. When using override, make sure to test out the volume limits of the program speakers in order to avoid feedback.

If your studio has a special audience area, the program speakers are fed by the line-out only, and are usually left on during the entire show, provided that they do not present a feedback problem.

Wall Outlets   As insignificant as they may seem at first, the number and position of wall outlets are important factors in studio production. Separate camera and microphone outlets in at least two opposite corners of the studio can, for example, immensely aid in setup and on-the-air production operations. If you have all camera and microphone outlets concentrated in one studio location, you will be forced to string exceedingly long and cumbersome cables around the various sets in order to get the equipment into the desired shooting and pickup positions. A second and even a third outlet box in a different studio location can eliminate such time-consuming and awkward cable routing. *(See 8.4.)*

Besides outlets for cameras and microphone cables, you will need several distribution boxes for studio monitor video lines as well as many standard A.C. utility outlets staggered along all four walls for easy accessibility. You will need a few high-amperage utility outlets for rear screen projectors or high-power lighting equipment.

The intercom outlets should, of course, also be distributed along all studio walls and perhaps from the lighting grid in order to avoid overly long cables.

All wall outlets should be *clearly marked,* especially since most of them are apt to be hidden behind the cyclorama or pieces of scenery placed against the studio walls.

Lighting Patchboard   If you have a dimmer control for your lighting, the lighting patchboard

8·4   Camera Wall Outlets.

is generally located in the studio, where you can spot the various lighting instruments and patch them into their respective dimmers without having to run in and out of the room. The usual way of patching is for one member of the lighting crew to call out the numbers of the lighting instruments needed, and for another member to patch them into the designated dimmers. With both people in the studio, this job becomes relatively fast and easy.

If the dimmer board is also in the studio, it is usually located in the corner that has the least studio traffic. The advantage of having it there is that it situates the dimmer-board operator right where the production takes place and where he can see at least some of the lighting instruments used. The disadvantages, however, make its location in the studio less desirable. They are (1) most of the time, the scenery and set properties prevent you from seeing most of the lighting instruments anyway; (2) wherever you may put the dimmer board, it will surely be in the way of someone at any given time; (3) unless the dimmer board is very well shielded, its electronics are liable to interfere severely with the cameras or audio pickup.

The Television Control Room

The control room is generally located in a separate room adjacent to the studio. You will find some control rooms that have visual access to the studio through soundproof, double-glass windows, and

8·5 Control-Room Monitors: The many monitors in the control room represent the video choices for the director. He or she cannot choose an image for on-the-air use that does not first appear on any one of the monitors in front of him. The monitors show images as supplied by live studio cameras, telecine cameras, the various VTR machines, special effects and character generators, remote inputs. Then, there are the preview, line, and off-the-air monitors that show the on-the-air choices.

others that are completely windowless. For strictly professional operation, the window is not essential. Most of the older control rooms with windows have so many monitors or other equipment blocking the window from the control-room side, and cycloramas or scenery from the studio side, that the window is, for all practical purposes, useless anyway.

Still, some case can be made for the retention of the window, especially in places where television production is taught. First, unless you are an experienced director, the control monitors alone will not always be able to show you the complete studio traffic pattern. The picture the camera

takes and relays to the control-room monitors cannot always tell you how far the camera is from the studio wall or a piece of scenery, for example. Or you may call for a dolly-back of a camera whose dolly path is blocked by the boom or another camera. A look through the control-room window will alert you to such studio traffic problems at a glance. Second, while you are learning television production, the control-room window allows you to see how the various production elements in the studio *work together*. The coordination of the various production elements is an extremely important aspect of television production that is difficult to comprehend when the control-

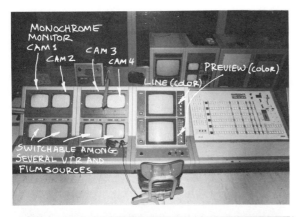

room activities and the studio activities have to be watched separately. Third, assuming that the window affords a good view of the studio, the audio engineer and the lighting control board operator will be greatly aided in anticipating the director's cues if they can see what is going on in the studio.

We will now take a look at the control room itself. Most of them have four distinct controlling areas: (1) the program control, (2) the switcher, (3) the audio control, and (4) the light control. Sometimes, the audio and light controls are located elsewhere, but the video controls are placed in the control room.

Program Control

The television director and his associates are in charge of the program control. The director must be able to preview all video sources, such as pictures from all studio cameras, telecine cameras, videotape machines, and remote sources; listen to the program sound; converse with all members of the production and engineering crews; watch the time for various specific purposes; and see what pictures finally get on the air. Accordingly, the program control area is equipped with (1) video monitors, (2) speaker for program sound, (3) intercom system, and (4) clock and stopwatches.

Video Monitors   Even a simple control room holds an amazingly large number of video monitors. There is a monitor for each of the studio cameras; if you can work four cameras at once in your studio, you will need four preview monitors in the control room. There is a monitor for each film island (consisting of two film projectors, and one slide projector). If you have two film islands, you will have two additional monitors. Ideally, there should be a separate monitor for each videotape machine (although sometimes one switchable monitor will serve several machines). So, if you have three VTR machines, you will have three additional monitors. If you have a videotape cassette machine for short commercials or videotape inserts, you will need another monitor. And there is usually a separate monitor for the character generator (the machine that generates titles electronically), or other electronic effects. Now you need a special preview monitor that displays the upcoming picture (or special effects, if no separate monitor is used) before it is punched up (put on the air), and the line or master monitor that shows you the picture that is fed to the line-out and that appears finally on the television set of the home viewer or on the videotape, if the program is recorded. Finally, there is the off-the-air monitor, a regular television set that receives off the air what you are telecasting. If you do a remote, or if you are connected with a network, you need at least one more monitor so that you can preview what the remote source or the network is feeding. Now, let's tally them up.

Camera preview	4
Film island	2
VTR	3
Videotape cassette	1
Character generator	1
Preview	1
Line	1
Air	1
Remote	1
Total	**15 monitors**

These monitors are stacked up in a variety of configurations in front of the director. Usually, the line monitor (or master, or program monitor, as it is also called) and the preview monitor are large-sized, while the other preview monitors are relatively small. Except for the preview, line, and off-the-air monitors, which are in color, all other monitors are black-and-white. (If at all possible, you should have color monitors for at least the camera preview monitors, since color certainly plays an important part in picture composition.)

Speaker for Program Sound As a director you usually have your own speaker for program sound. A volume control permits you to turn the sound up or down without influencing the audio engineer's monitor speaker.

Intercommunication System We have already described the various intercom systems. The program control area contains outlets for several earphones and a selector switch, or switches, for the various intercommunication channels. There is

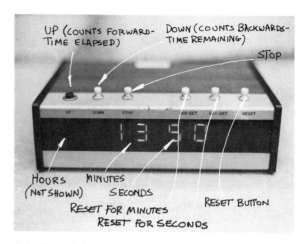

8·6 Digital Stopwatch: The digital stopwatch is an extremely helpful production tool. In the up, or forward position, it indicates the elapsed running time in hours, minutes, and seconds. You can set the watch for any given time, stop and start it at any given point, and reset it to zero. In the down, or reverse position, the watch shows time remaining. If you have three minutes left in your show, the stopwatch will show 3:00 on the dial. When it shows 0:-00:00, you should be off the air.

also a microphone for the director's talkback and the appropriate on-off switch. Also, the program control area has at least one regular telephone.

Clock and Stopwatches Time is the essential organizing element in television production. Programs are aired according to a second-by-second time schedule, the log. In commercial television, time is sold for large sums of money. The two essential timing tools for the television director are the clock and the stopwatch. The *clock* will indicate the spot when a certain program should start or finish. All television clocks in the country, and in the world, are precisely synchronized with one another as to minutes and seconds. The hour hands show local time. The *stopwatch* is used for

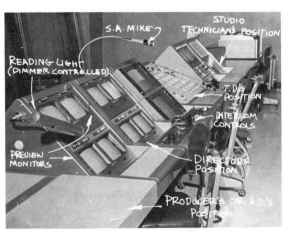

8·7 Program Control Area (Studio 1, San Francisco State University): The total program control area contains the various preview monitors, with line (master) and off-the-air monitors, intercommunication controls, audio monitor speaker controls, and an assortment of clocks and stopwatches.

timing the many inserts, such as 20-second commercial spots within a news program, and for timing programs that are videotaped. Most program controls have a digital stopwatch that can run forward and backward. For example, if you want to know how much time you have left in a given program, you set your digital stopwatch for reverse and start it at the beginning of the program, at 27:30 min., for example. The clock will run backwards until it reaches 00:00 min., at which point your program must have ended. Or, if you want to run the stopwatch forward, you start at 00:00 min. and end at 27:30 min. *(See 8.6.)* Although the ordinary television stopwatch is more limited in its accomplishments, it is still an indispensable timing tool.

The Switcher

The switcher, a large panel with many buttons, is located right next to the director so that he can manipulate the buttons himself or communicate his decisions directly to a technician sitting beside him. *(See 8.8 and 10.8.)* The switcher can perform three major tasks: (1) selection of an appropriate video source from several inputs, (2) transition between two video sources, and (3) creation of special effects. Most switchers have further provisions for remote start and stop of videotape recorders and cassettes, film and slide projectors.

All switchers have four basic areas of operational control: (1) preview, (2) mix, (3) effects, and (4) program.

The *preview* controls make it possible to display on the director's preview (or preset) monitor a particular picture or some special effect, such as a program title over the opening shot of a football field, without having it go on the air.

Through the *mixing* controls, you can select any one of the video inputs, such as live camera pictures, film, slides, videotape, and remote, and route it to the preview controls, or to the program line, where it is sent through master control directly to the transmitter, or recorded on video-

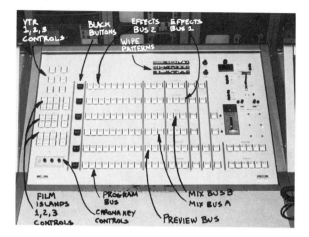

8·8 Program Switcher (Studio 1, San Francisco State University): The switcher selects on-the-air images according to the director's choices. It consists of four operational controls: (1) the preview controls, (2) the mix controls, (3) the effects controls, and (4) the program controls.

tape. But whenever a video source is "punched up" and sent to program line-out, we say the source is "on the air." The mixing controls also permit a variety of transitions, such as the cut, the instantaneous change from one image to another; the dissolve, a going from one image to the next with the two images temporarily overlapping, sometimes called "mix"; or a fade, with one picture fading out and the other fading in.

With the *effects* controls (which may consist of separate rows of buttons, or of the same as the mixing controls, providing the switcher has a "mode" selector between mix and effects), you can create special electronic effects, such as wipes, keys, or mattes. We will talk more extensively about the switcher and its operation in Chapter 10.

The *program controls* bypass all preview controls and put the selected video source directly on the air.

The switching is usually done by the T.D., the technical director, who is responsible for all technical aspects of production and who customarily assigns himself to the switching position. Sometimes the switching is done by another production engineer, who is simply called "switcher."

In some stations, the director is doing his own switching, although this arrangement has more disadvantages than advantages. The advantages are that the director, when switching an exceptionally fast show, can cut at the precise instant, without having to relay his messages to a second party. Also, and this is an important consideration in small stations, the elimination of the switching position will save manpower and, ultimately, money.

However, even the simpler shows employ electronic effects that require complex switching operations. If the director—who has to watch all the monitors, listen to the audio, give cues to production and engineering personnel, read the script, and keep track of at least two different times—is additionally burdened with operating the switcher, you are inviting trouble. The make-good on missed commercials and frequent retakes in videotaping may turn out to be much more expensive than the employment of a separate person who operates the switcher.

The Audio Control

The audio-control facilities can be considered a small radio station attached to the television control room. Sometimes a sliding glass door connects the audio control area with the rest of the control room. The reason for this separation is that the audio engineer must be able to work undisturbed from the seeming confusion and inevitable noise of the control room, which handles primarily video functions. The audio engineer listens to the director's cues either through

8·9 Audio Control: The audio control area contains the audio control board, through which the various sound inputs are selected, amplified, mixed, and distributed to the line-out, reel-to-reel tape machines, or at least the controls for them, tape cartridge machines, turntables, speakers and intercom controls, and patching facilities. In essence, the audio control area in the television control room represents a small radio station.

8·10 Lighting Control: The lighting control board consists of the dimmers and their preset controls, through which a variety of lights can be adjusted for their intensity either individually or in unison, depending on how they are patched.

his intercom telephone headset or a small intercom speaker in his booth. Often, you will find that the audio engineer has the door to the control room open, so that he is in physical contact with the rest of the operation. Many audio controls have, therefore, done away with this separation. The audio control booth houses the audio control board and the patch panel, two turntables, audiotape recorders and cartridge machines, cue and program speakers, a clock, and of course a line, or master, monitor. *(See 8.9.)*

One audio engineer usually takes care of all audio control operations during a show.

The Lighting Control

As pointed out previously, the actual lighting control board, the *dimmer board,* is placed in the control room to great advantage: (1) it puts the lighting control operator near the rest of the control activities, which makes for efficient communications; (2) it removes the lighting control board from the always crowded studio floor; (3) it establishes lighting control as one of the essential control activities not only before, but also during, the telecast.

The lighting control section contains the actual dimmer control board, the preset board, and, if the operator has no clear view of the director's monitors, at least a line monitor. The lighting control operator is tied into the general intercom system by telephone headset. *(See 8.10.)*

Some control rooms also house the *CCU's* (camera control units) and serve as the working station of the video control engineer, or shader. In some black-and-white operations, the T.D. occasionally takes care of the shading as well as the switching, but with color, shading has become a more complex and critical job. Many stations have, therefore, separated camera shading from the control room and put the CCU's into another room, most frequently master control.

Master Control

Master control is the *nerve center* of a television station. Every second of programming you see on your home television screen has gone through the master control room of the station to which you are tuned. Master control acts as a clearinghouse for all program material. It receives program feeds from various sources—productions from its own studios, network feeds, remote lines, and videotapes and films that are mailed to the station—and telecasts them at a specified time. The major responsibility of master control is to see that the *right programming material* (including commercials and public service announcements) is put on the air at the *right time.* Additionally, master control is responsible for the *technical quality* of the programs. This means that it has to check all program material that goes on the air as to technical

a

b

8·11 Master Control: (a) Broadcast Communication Arts Department, San Francisco State University; (b) KPIX, San Francisco. Master control is the nerve center of a television station. It oversees program input, since every bit of incoming material is eventually routed to master control; it stores it if necessary (except for live telecasts), and retrieves the appropriate program material for every second of the station's telecasting day. Additionally, master control is responsible for the technical quality of all program material being aired.

standards as set by the FCC (Federal Communications Commission).

All production activities of a station are greatly influenced by what master control can and cannot do. We will, therefore, briefly describe (1) program input, (2) program storage, and (3) program retrieval.

Program Input

As mentioned before, the program material may come into master control directly from its own studios, from remote lines (network, remote origination by own station, or someone else), or by mail in the form of videotape and film.

Except for the station-originated live programming (newscasts, special events), or network feeds sent through master control directly to the transmitter for immediate broadcasting, all pro-

gramming is reproduced via videotape, film, or slides. The videotapes are reproduced from high-quality videotape recorders and videotape cassette machines, which are all housed in the *videotape room (figure 8.12),* or located directly in master control. The films and slides are reproduced by various *film islands,* each of which consists of one or two projectors, one or two slide projectors, a multiplexer, and a television film, or telecine, camera. We will describe the film island in more detail in Chapter 9. The film reproduction equipment is housed in a room, or master control room area, called *telecine (figure 8.13).*

If the CCU's are located in master control, the *shading* is an additional master control activity. The location of the CCU's in or near master control is quite advantageous, since a single video control engineer, or shader, can shade (adjust electronically) cameras from different studios si-

8·12 VTR Room: The VTR room contains the VTR machines. All videotape editing is done in the VTR room, unless you work with a complex computer-assisted off-line system (see Chapter 10). Often, the videotape is also stored here.

multaneously. Also, with all CCU's in one location, the test equipment does not have to be moved from one studio control room to another. *(See 8.14.)*

Program Storage

All program material that is recorded on videotape, film, or slides is stored in storage bins located in the videotape room or in master control itself. Each tape, film, or slide is given a station code, or *house number,* for fast identification and retrieval. Although computer retrieval has introduced some commonality in terms, there is still no agreement among stations as to identification procedures and codes. Just use a code that works well for your operation. In designing a code, however, make sure that your symbols are unambiguous and easily identifiable. To use the letter *C* for "color" at one time, and for "commercial" at another is a sure way of creating confusion, if not

serious programming mistakes. Once programs are stored in a central program data bank, perhaps far away from the station, identification codes will have to be standardized to assure fast and accurate program retrieval.

Program Retrieval

Program retrieval means the *selection, ordering,* and *putting on the air* of any program material. Although the term "retrieval" implies the finding and putting on the air of recorded material, we will include live programming as well. In the context of master control operations, there is actually little difference between retrieving a show occurring live in a studio, a network feed, or a program that has been stored on videotape.

In discussing program retrieval, we will focus on (1) the log, (2) the master control switcher, and (3) computer-controlled automation system.

8·13 Telecine Room: Telecine contains the film islands, consisting of film projectors, slide projectors,
multiplexers, and television film, or telecine, cameras
(see Chapter 9). Often, the film is also stored here.
Film editing, however, is usually done in special
editing rooms.

8·14 Camera Control
Units (CCU's for twelve
monochrome cameras in
master control, San
Francisco State Univer-
sity): The CCU's con-
trol the picture quality
for each camera. The
CCU operator, called
video operator or
shader, can operate sev-
eral CCU's at the same
time. Keeping all CCU's
in a central location
makes it possible to
patch various cameras
in a specific order into
or from other studios,
without interfering with
their respective control-
room activity.

AIRTIME		I N T	SCHEDULED TIME			V	LINE NUMBER	PROGRAMS - SPONSORS 08/11 PACIFIC DAYLIGHT TIME PG# 10	SOURCE	TYPE	LENGTH	VIDEO	AUDIO	MONDAY REMARKS / CODE IDENTITY
START	FINISH		H	M	S									
			11	28	48			6 CROWN ZELLERBAC P	CM		30	VT	VT	V 314 (BZZB-1843-3)(NICE & SOFT)
			11	29	18			5 JAMES ALLAN & C MEATS	CM		30	VTS	VTC	V 207 (QL-1)(#6)
			11	29	48			S.F.P.D KIDS FISHING PROGRAM.	PS		10	VT	VT	1875-11
			11	29	58			THE BRIDGE WEDNESDAY 10:30P	S1		2	S	C	P-K678
			11	30	00			** SEARCH FOR TOMORROW	CN	E		CN	CN	
			11	59	28			5 KAL KAN (0609) DOG FOOD	CM		30	VT	VT	V 413 (KKDF-0010-3F)
			11	59	58			5 ABBEY CARPETS ONGOING	CM		30	VT	VT	V 627 (1975-28)
			12	00	28			7 KENT FRIED CHI 74-75 DAY	CM		10	VT	VT	V 613 (3-10)
			12	00	38			BRIDGE	S1		2	S	C	PK-678
			12	00	40			** EYEWITNESS NEWS AT NOON	L	N		B	B	
								** NEWS OPEN (10") 1549-11	L	N		VT	VT	

8·15 Program Log: As you can see, the log shows (1) the program origin, or source, (2) the scheduled event time, (3) the duration of the program, (4) specific video information, (5) specific audio information, (6) identification codes, (7) the title of the program, (8) the type of the program, or class, and (9) any pertinent special information. The log, issued daily, is the most important production and programming document; its actual format and arrangement varies from station to station. The major criteria for log format are easy readability and consistency.

The Log   The television log is the most important program and production document. It tells everybody concerned what program material is supposed to be on the air at every second of the program day. The television log is issued daily, usually one or two days in advance. It is distributed either in printed form, or displayed on CRT (cathode ray tube) screens, monitors that display written information. *(See 8.15 and 8.16.)*

The log will give you, in general, this information:

1. *Program source, or origin:* Network, local, which studio, or, if coded, the event number.

2. *Scheduled time:* What clock time is the program scheduled to start? When does the next program start?

3. *Duration, or length:* How long does the program run? 10 seconds? 57:30 minutes?

4. *Video:* How does the video portion originate? Live, film, videotape, slide? Which videotape recorder? Which videotape cassette?

5. *Audio:* Where does the audio originate? Studio, remote, network, announce booth, videotape, film?

6. *Code:* What is the house identification number? What other codes are needed for identification? Some commercials have product codes of their own, which must be included in the log.

7. *Title:* What is the name of the program or commercial?

8. *Program type:* Is the commercial a local spot? Public service announcement? Does it fall under news, entertainment, religious? (The FCC has specific program categories, which you should use for type and source identification; see Chapter 14 for more complete information.)

9. *Special information:* This log category can contain any information that is necessary for the accurate program retrieval and airing.

8·16 CRT Display of Log Information: If you have the assistance of a computer, the log, besides being available in a hard-copy printout, can be displayed on any of the CRT computer terminals at the push of a button. You can feed the computer last-minute log corrections and it will change, remember, and initiate the new roll cues for the various machines at the new times, and immediately produce an updated hard copy.

Master Control Switcher The master control switching area looks like the combined program control and switching area of the studio control room. Master control has preview monitors for all live studio cameras and for all videotape machines, videotape cassette machines, film islands, network and other remote feeds, plus at least one off-the-air monitor. The switcher itself looks similar to the studio switcher, except that it fulfills different functions. While one of the main purposes of the studio switcher is to switch among cameras and between cameras and recorded sources, the master control switcher facilitates the switching *between various program sources,* such as studio, VTR reel-to-reel machines, videotape cassettes, film islands, and network or other remote inputs. An essential feature of the master control switcher is the remote start and stop of the program reproduction equipment, such as videotape recorders, film and slide projectors, and

videotape cassette machines. The master control switcher also handles the *program distribution,* whether it is a simple house distribution to the client's booth or various offices, to the network if you originate a network feed, or to the transmitter. In educational institutions, master control also handles the *closed-circuit distribution* of programming to the several viewing stations on campus.

Most master control switchers have an *audio-follow-video,* or AFV, system, which means that each video input has its corresponding audio input. When the video is switched from one source to another, the audio changes with the video automatically. Large production switchers have a similar facility. *(See 8.17b.)*

a

b

8·17 (a) Master Control Monitor Bank; (b) Master Control Switcher; (c) Master Control Audio Section: The heart of master control is the switching station. From here, the various program inputs are distributed to the various points of destination. A live newscast, for example, is distributed directly to the transmitter for the on-the-air telecast. A discussion show might be fed into one of the videotape recorders. A network feed may be recorded on another videotape recorder for a delayed playback. The monitors display the major video inputs. The audio is usually switched with the video, but there is an audio control section for special audio needs. If the master control operation is computer-assisted, the various command stations are also located here at the switcher.

c

Computer-Controlled Automation System The daily programming tasks have become so complicated that sometimes even the most skilled master control engineers can no longer retrieve and switch the multitude of program material without error. Just watch a station break and try to figure out how many pieces of equipment had to be activated and how many changeovers between sources accomplished by the master control crew within the short period of a few minutes. No wonder that computer-assisted master control systems find more and more acceptance even in small station operations.

Depending on the given sophistication of the system used, the computer can (1) facilitate all data entries for the daily log; (2) facilitate any last-minute log changes; (3) display the daily updated log at the CRT terminals (looks like a typewriter–television set combination) throughout the station; (4) activate the machine assignment system, which will match the videotapes or films loaded into the machines with the ones specified in the log, "flashing" possible errors; (5) automatically preroll and stop the machines assigned, or activate the slide projector; (6) automatically switch video and audio of entire program sequences; (7) preroll and record incoming feeds from network or other remote sources; and (8) print a log of the programming that actually occurred during the broadcast day (which is a requirement of the FCC).

Besides the traffic department, which compiles and issues the log with the aid of the computer, the accounting department can use the computer at the same time for accurate accounting and billing.

And, since even the computer does not entirely trust itself, there is an override button that can be pushed to return the whole system to manual operation in case of emergency.

Studio Support Areas

The studio support areas include space for *property storage, scene storage,* and possibly scene construction, and *makeup* and *dressing rooms.* If you produce a large number of vastly different programs, from daily newscasts to highly complex television dramas, you need large prop and scenery storage areas. If your production is fairly limited, your support areas can be relatively simple. University and college television operations can make use of the usually extensive theater prop and scenery facilities, assuming that the two departments get along well with each other.

In any case, the most important part of any storage area is its *retrieval efficiency.* If you have to search for hours in order to find a few props with which to decorate your office set, even the most extensive prop collection is worth very little. A small, well-organized property collection that allows easy retrieval of props is obviously more valuable to you than a large, disorganized one.

If possible, makeup rooms, or a makeup room, should be close to the studio. Each makeup room should have good mirrors and even lighting that is of approximately the same color temperature as the studio lighting (incandescent, rather than fluorescent, lights).

The *film editing room* is sometimes included in the general production support areas. At other times, the news department considers all film editing as part of their exclusive production domain. Many stations process their own films. The film-processing lab, then, becomes part of the general production support area. However, neither film editing nor film processing has a direct relation to studio production activities.

Summary

While a telecast can originate indoors or out, the television studio affords maximum control to the production. It has three major areas: (1) the production origination center, the studio itself, (2) the production control center, situated in both the studio and master control rooms, and (3) the studio support areas.

The important aspects of the physical layout of the studio are the available floor space, the smoothness of the floor, adequate ceiling height for the lighting instruments, acoustic treatment of the walls, air-conditioning system, and large access doors.

The major studio installations include the intercommunication systems with the P.L. (phone line) and the S.A. (studio talkback) systems, studio video monitors, program monitor speakers, various utility, video, and audio wall outlets, and the lighting patchboard.

The television control room generally has four distinct controlling areas: (1) the program control, (2) the switcher, (3) the audio control, and (4) the light control. Sometimes, the light control is located elsewhere, but the video controls are placed in the control room.

The program control area contains a number of video monitors, speakers for program sound, intercom systems, and a clock and stopwatches.

The switcher is a large panel with buttons that can perform three major tasks: (1) select an appropriate video source from several inputs, (2) accomplish transitions between two video sources, and (3) create special effects. Some switchers (audio-follow-video) also switch the audio portion simultaneously with the appropriate picture.

The audio control area is a small radio station attached to the television control room. It controls all aspects of television sound.

The lighting control area contains the dimmer board and the preset facilities.

Master control is the nerve center of a television station. Its major responsibility is to see that the right programming material is put on the air at the right time, and that the video and sound signals come up to an agreed-upon technical standard. In general, master control takes care of program input, program storage, and program retrieval. These functions are all prescribed by a daily television log, which indicates the essential input, storage, and retrieval information.

The studio support areas include property storage, scene storage and possibly scene construction, makeup and dressing rooms, and film editing and processing rooms. All of these areas should be built so that they will permit you maximum control of all production elements.

9 *Videotape and Film*

A basic knowledge of the production requirements and potentials of videotape and film is important for mastering the techniques of television production.

This chapter will give you information on (1) the use of videotape in television production, (2) videotape recording systems, (3) types of videotape recorders, (4) operation of videotape recording, (5) the use of film in television production, (6) film specifications, (7) the television film chain, or film island, and (8) operation of film.

The process of editing videotape or film will be the subject of Chapter 10.

Videotape and film are the two major television program sources. Most of the programs you see on television have been prerecorded on one or the other.

While film is produced by its traditional film techniques and simply played back on television, videotape constitutes a major production element of television itself. Indeed, videotape has influenced television production techniques to a great extent.

Videotape in Television Production

Videotape is used principally for (1) time delay, (2) building of a whole show by assembling parts that have been recorded at different times and/or locations, (3) duplication and distribution of programs, and (4) records for reference and study.

Time Delay

Through videotape, an event can be recorded and played back immediately or hours, days, or even years after its occurrence. In sports, where it is known as "instant replay," this technique uses a video disc rather than videotape for recording and playback.

The *immediate playback* capability of videotape has several benefits. Instant replay, for example, can give the viewer another look at an important play right after it has happened. Or the playback of a videotape can give the athlete, or any other performer, the opportunity to see himself or herself in action right after the performance and correct possible mistakes. In television production, the immediate playback is an important learning device. As an announcer, you can observe yourself right after the performance, while your delivery and the problems connected with it are still

---

Academy Leader   Also called the SMPTE Universal Leader. A piece of film marked with numbers ranging from 8 to 3, each one second apart. It is attached to the head of a film for the purposes of cuing up and aligning the film.

Alpha Wrap   An indication of how the videotape is wound around the head drum of a helical scan VTR. In this case, the tape is wound completely around the head in an alphalike configuration.

Audio Track   The area of the videotape that is used for recording audio information.

Beeper   A series of eight low-frequency audio beeps, exactly one second apart, put at the beginning of each take for videotape cuing.

Color Bars   A color standard used by the television industry for the alignment of cameras and videotape recordings.

Control Track   The area of the videotape that is used for recording the synchronization information (sync spikes), which is essential for videotape editing.

Cue Track   The area of the videotape that is used for such audio information as in-house identification or the SMPTE address code. Can also be used for a second audio track.

Double-System   The simultaneous recording of pictures and sound on two separate recording devices: the pictures on film, and the sound on audiotape recorder, synchronized with the film camera.

fresh in your mind. As director, during the show you probably lacked the time and the state of mind to absorb the feel and relative quality of the total performance. You may remember one camera not framing correctly, the dissolve being too slow, or another camera's shaky zoom. But you may not even have been aware of the announcer giving the wrong address and telephone number over the last slide for his commercial tag. A playback immediately after your directing exercise, when you are more relaxed, will make it possible for you to perceive the camera handling, the general blocking, the cutting rhythm, and the announcer's delivery all together.

Time delay through videotape also means that the production can be scheduled at a time *most convenient* to the station personnel and the performers, and the program played back at a time most convenient to the viewer. Late night talk shows, for example, are recorded in late after-

9·1   *Immediate playback* and *instant replay* are actually two different production activities that require different equipment. Immediate playback means that, as soon as the event is recorded on videotape, the tape is rewound and played back within a matter of a few minutes. Instant replay refers to the recording and playback of event sections, mostly key sports actions, within seconds, or even a fraction of a second.

Since it would take too long to rewind and recue the particular event section of a videotape, a *video disc* is used, which allows extremely fast cuing, slow motion, and even arrested motion in its playback. (See page 230.)

Dubbing Down   The dubbing (transfer) of picture and sound information from a larger videotape format to a smaller one.

Dubbing Up   The dubbing (transfer) of picture and sound information from a smaller videotape format to a larger one.

Film Chain   Also called film island, or telecine. Consists of one or two film projectors, a slide projector, a multiplexer, and a television film, or telecine, camera.

Freeze Frame   Arrested motion, which is perceived as a still shot.

Helical Scan, or Helical VTR   A videotape recording of one- and two-head videotape recorders, whereby the video signal is put on the tape in a slanted, diagonal way (contrary to transverse scanning, which goes across the tape). Also called slant-track.

High-Band   Refers to the frequency of the video information. High-band videotape recorders operate on a high-frequency range (10 megacycles), which provides operationally higher quality pictures with less video noise and better resolution than low-band recordings. Most high-quality color machines are high-band.

Instant Replay   The recording of short event sections (such as key plays in sports) and immediate playback, sometimes in slow motion. Usually done with a video disc-recording device.

noon, mainly for the convenience of the guests who appear on them. But the whole production approach is geared to the late-night playback time.

Newscasts, which are telecast live in one time zone of the country, are videotaped in their entirety and played back at the same clock time in another time zone. Network news can, therefore, be seen at six o'clock local time regardless of time zone.

Building of a Show

Videotape is used to build a show from various prerecorded tape segments. Similar to film production, the various scenes of a television play, for example, are videotaped at different times and often at different locations for later assembly through editing. Thus, the use of videotape permits more complex and especially more polished

productions than live television. Major and minor production errors can be corrected by reshooting a particular scene. Contrary to film, which has to be processed before it can be viewed, the videotape recording of a scene can be replayed immediately after each take for close scrutiny. With time code editing (see Chapter 10), videotape can be assembled even more easily than film.

Program Distribution

Videotape can be easily duplicated and distributed to a variety of television outlets. Many production centers have syndicated their videotaped shows for distribution in major and minor markets. Because of improved playback facilities, videotape is used more and more instead of 16mm film for duplication and distribution of a variety of program materials, including commercials and public spot announcements.

Kinescope Recording Television program filmed directly off a kinescope (television picture) tube.

Low-Band Refers to the frequency of the video information. Low-band recorders operate in a relatively low-frequency range, which suffices for monochrome pictures but introduces excessive video noise in color.

Magnetic Sound, or **MAG, Track** Consists of a narrow magnetic tape that runs down one side of the film. It operates exactly like a normal audiotape.

Multiplexer A system of mirrors or prisms that directs images from several projection sources (film, slides) into one stationary television film, or telecine, camera.

Omega Wrap An indication of how the videotape is wound around the head drum of a helical scan VTR. In this case, the tape is wound halfway around the head drum, in an omegalike configuration.

Optical Sound Track Variations of black and white patterns, photographed on the film and converted into electrical impulses by an exciter lamp and a photoelectric cell. There are two kinds of optical tracks: variable area and variable density.

Records for Reference and Study

Videotape is an excellent device for preserving a television event for reference or study, especially one-time happenings—sports, political gatherings, a difficult operation in a medical center, examples of supreme human achievement and failure. Such videotaped records can be stored, retrieved, and distributed via television with relative ease. The events are thus available for careful study by scholars all over the world. For extremely important projects, the recorded event can be translated into a television signal and transmitted via satellite to the new destination. Usually, though, videotape records are dubbed onto a videotape cassette and mailed to the interested party.

Technically, the quality of the playback of a broadcast-type videotape is superior to that of the best film (even the 35mm format). On a home receiver, it is practically impossible to tell whether the program originates live or as a videotape playback, assuming that the videotape recording reflects the quality of the live event.

Videotape Recording Systems

Videotaping is quite similar to the audiotape recording process. The electronic impulses of television pictures (the video signal) and sound (audio signal) are recorded on the plastic videotape through magnetizing its iron oxide coating (dull side). During playback, the recorded video and audio signals are converted again into television pictures and sounds.

There are two basic systems of videotape recording: (1) the transverse scanning process, or the quadruplex video recording system, and (2) the helical, or slant-track, recording system.

Quadruplex, or **Quad** A scanning system of videotape recorders that uses four rotating heads for recording and playing back of video information. All quad recorders use 2-inch-wide videotape.

Runout Signal The recording of a few seconds of black at the end of each videotape recording in order to keep the screen in black for the video changeover.

Silent Film Film without a sound track, or film run silent.

Single-System The simultaneous recording of pictures and sound on the same film.

Slant-Track Same as Helical Scan.

Slate A little blackboard, or whiteboard, upon which essential production information is written, such as title of the show, date, scene and take numbers. It is recorded at the beginning of each videotaped take.

Slow Motion A scene in which the objects appear to be moving more slowly than normal. In film, slow motion is achieved through high-speed photography (exposing many frames that differ only minutely from each other) and normal (24 frames per second, for example) playback. In television, slow motion is achieved by a multiple scanning of each television frame.

SMPTE Society of Motion Picture and Television Engineers.

SMPTE Universal Leader See Academy Leader.

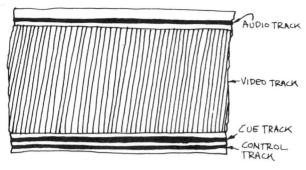

9·2 The 2-inch videotape for quadruplex videotape recorders normally has four tracks: the video track (television pictures), the audio track (television sound), the cue track (various code information or a second audio track), and the control track (essential for synchronization).

Transverse, or Quadruplex, Scanning

In the transverse, or quadruplex, scanning process, four tiny rotating (14,400 rpm) recording heads put the video signal on a 2-inch-wide tape that moves past the rotating recording heads at speeds of $7\frac{1}{2}$ inches per second (ips) or 15 ips. In this process, 15 ips is the speed normally used for high-quality broadcast recordings.

The quadruplex videotape recorder (VTR) normally puts four different tracks on the 2-inch videotape: (1) the video track (the signal representing the television picture information), (2) the audio track (the signal representing the television sound), (3) the cue or address track, and (4) the control track (see 9.2). Some quadruplex recorders put on an additional sound track (five tracks total).

The cue or address track is in effect a second audio track. You can use it, for example, to record

---

SOF Sound on film.

SOT Sound on tape. The videotape is played back with pictures and sound.

Stand-by A button on a videotape recorder that activates the rotation of the video heads or head drum independently of the actual tape motion. In the stand-by position, the video heads can come up to speed before the videotape is actually started.

Stop-Motion A slow-motion effect in which one frame jumps to the next, showing the object in a different position.

Time Base Corrector An electronic accessory to a videotape recorder that helps to make playbacks or transfers electronically stable. A time base corrector helps to maintain picture quality even in dubbing-up operations.

Tracking An electronic adjustment of the video heads so that in the playback phase they match the recording phase of the tape. It prevents picture breakup and misalignment especially in tapes that have been recorded on a machine other than the one used for playback.

Transverse Scanning The direction of the video signal scanning in quadruplex recorders. Transverse scanning puts the signal across (transverse) the videotape rather than in a helical (diagonal) or a lengthwise pattern.

the director's P.L. (phone, or private, line) for future reference, or in-house information, such as the identification number of the tape, or special product number. Most often, the cue track is used to carry an address code, an electronic signal that enables you to pick extremely quickly any spot in the videotape (address) for editing purposes. We will take up the address code more thoroughly in Chapter 10. But you can also put regular audio information on the cue track, such as the second channel of a stereo pickup, or special sound effects.

The control track consists of evenly spaced blips or spikes, called the sync pulse, which work like electronic sprocket holes.[1] The control track is essential for editing videotape, and we will discuss it in more detail in Chapter 10.

---

[1] Irving E. Fang, *Television News,* rev. ed. (New York: Hastings House, 1972), p. 305.

The audio track can be recorded simultaneously with the video track, or separately. You can have parts or all of the video or audio tracks erased independently from each other. Sometimes you may find that it is easier to record the video information first and the audio track later. This technique is especially advantageous if the audio track does not have to be tightly synchronized with the video, as in a running commentary over the video event, for example. When, in the playback of a videotape segment, the audio information is played with the video, we speak of SOT, sound on tape.

The majority of professional VTR's use the quadruplex, or transverse, scanning process.

Helical, or Slant-Track, Scanning

In the helical or slant-track scanning process, one or two recording heads that are mounted on a

---

Variable Area Track   An optical sound track on film. It modulates the light of the exciter lamp through various shapes of translucent areas so that, when received by the photoelectric cell, the light variations produce identical variations in the electric current (audio signal).

Variable Density Track   An optical sound track on film. It modulates the light of the exciter lamp through various shades of gray so that, when received by the photoelectric cell, the light variations produce identical variations in the electric current (audio signal).

Video Disc   A phonograph record-like disc that can store video (picture) information of short event segments. Used for instant playbacks, slow motion, and freeze frames.

Video Leader   Visual (and auditory) material that precedes any color videotape recording. The SMPTE prescribes for the standard video-portion blank tape for threading; 10 sec. of color bars; 15 sec. of slate information; 8 sec. of numbers or black; 2 sec. of black ahead of the program information.

Videotape   A plastic, iron-oxide-coated tape of various widths (from ¼-inch to 2-inch) for recording of video and audio signals.

Video Track   The area of the videotape that is used for recording the video information.

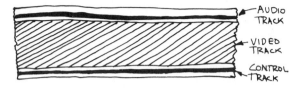

9·3 Helical Scan Videotape: The small-format helical scan videotape (1-inch width and smaller) typically has three different tracks: the audio track on the top edge of the tape, the slanted video track, and the control track at the bottom. Some helical recorders put an additional audio track on the tape, which then functions as a cue track.

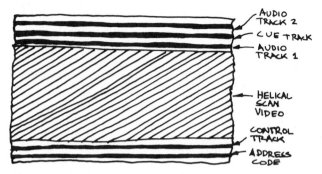

9·4 Two-Inch Helical Scan Videotape: The highly sophisticated 2-inch helical scan videotape has a total of six tracks: the slanted video track, two audio tracks, a cue track, an additional address code track, and a control track.

rotating drum, called "head drum," put the video information onto the tape in a slanted, diagonal, rather than transverse (up and down) manner. The audio track is usually at the top edge of the tape, with the control track running along the bottom edge.

More sophisticated helical VTR's have additional cue or audio tracks. Some of the top-quality helical videotape recorders (such as the 2-inch IVC-9000) have up to five tracks in addition to the video: two audio tracks, a cue track, a control track, and a separate address code track.

The second audio track, in addition to the cue and separate address code tracks, has definite production advantages: (1) Along with the regular program sound, you can record a second language, a very important extra in the broadcaster's quest to serve ethnic minorities. Until the television system operates in stereo-audio, you can broadcast the second audio channel, which now contains the program audio in a language other than English, over an FM channel that can be tuned in by the viewer on a standard FM radio.

(2) Even if you need only one audio track, you can edit the audio material on audio track No. 2, and then transfer the edited track to audio track No. 1 for the program audio, without ever running the risk of getting out of sync between audio and video. You can even edit complex lip-sync audio portions independently of the video. (3) With the pressures for multilanguage telecasts and aesthetic requirements for better audio quality, stereophonic telecasts will become common practice in television production very soon. The second audio track will then become a necessity.

Since the diagonal scan of the video signal occupies a relatively long section of tape, the *tape width* as well as the *tape speed* can be reduced.

Tape Width Most good helical VTR's use 1-inch tape, but there are also models that take ½-inch, or even ¼-inch. Helical scan videotape cassettes generally use ¾-inch tape. The top-quality helical broadcast VTR's, like the quadruplex machines, use a 2-inch tape.

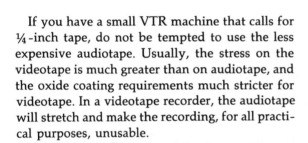

9·5 Helical, or Slant-Track, Scanning: In the helical, or slant-track, scanning process, the tape moves past the rotating heads (head drum) at an angle. Because the scanning occurs diagonally, it covers a longer area of the tape than its width.

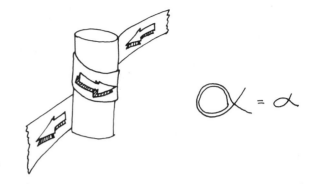

9·6 Alpha Wrap: If the tape has to be wound completely around the head drum, we speak of an alpha wrap, because the wind suggests the configuration of the Greek letter α.

If you have a small VTR machine that calls for ¼-inch tape, do not be tempted to use the less expensive audiotape. Usually, the stress on the videotape is much greater than on audiotape, and the oxide coating requirements much stricter for videotape. In a videotape recorder, the audiotape will stretch and make the recording, for all practical purposes, unusable.

Tape Speed The tape speeds of helical machines vary greatly, depending on the manufacturer or VTR model. Usually, they are all under the 15 ips customary for quality color recording with the quad machines. Some of the higher quality helical VTR's have tape speeds of 8 ips or 7 ips (6.91, to be exact); others go as low as 5 ips. Most helical VTR's have variable tape speeds; you can slow them down from full speed to a freeze-frame effect (zero tape speed).

Tape Wrap While in the quad machines, the tape passes past the four rotating heads in a straight line, the helical machines require a more complicated "wrap" in order to produce the necessary slant of the video track; the tape moves past the rotating head drum at an angle. *(See 9.5.)*

Some machines require an *alpha wrap*, others an *omega wrap*. In the former, the tape is wound once completely around the head drum, forming a 360-degree wrap that resembles the Greek letter alpha (α). In the omega wrap, the tape covers only half the drum (180-degree wrap), and resembles the Greek letter omega (Ω). *(See 9.6 and 9.7.)*

Operating Performance There are several production advantages of the helical machines over the quadruplex VTR's: (1) Because of simplified electronic design, they are generally less expensive; the one- or two-head drum assembly is less expensive than the four-head. (2) The simplified electronic design, and the small tape width make the helical VTR's much smaller. Some models are so small that they can be easily carried by one person like a medium-sized handbag (see Chapter 17). (3) The low tape speed permits more program material on a single reel. (4) Storage space is considerably reduced. And (5) the narrow-format tapes cost much less.

9·7 Omega Wrap: If the tape wind covers only half the head drum, we speak of an omega wrap, because it suggests the configuration of the Greek letter Ω.

9·8 The word helical in "helical scan" comes from the Greek word *helix,* meaning spiral, or a spiral wrap. The videotape wrap on the head drum resembles a partial spiral and is, therefore, called helical.

9·9 Some progress has been made toward standardization, and therefore interchangeability, of VTR equipment by the Electronics Industries Association of Japan (EIAJ), especially in the ½-inch-format helical scan VTR's.

Unfortunately, there are also serious drawbacks, which make the helical videotape system less than ideal: (1) Except for some high-quality and high-cost 2-inch and 1-inch VTR's, the helical scan VTR's do not fulfill broadcast-quality requirements. (2) Because of the variety in head-drum configuration, tape speeds, and tape widths, the tapes made by various machines are not always interchangeable or compatible. That is, a tape that was recorded on one type of 1-inch helical scan VTR often cannot be played back on another type of 1-inch machine. (3) Some less sophisticated helical scan videotape recordings cannot be "dubbed up" (transferred) to the larger 2-inch quad machines. (4) The less sophisticated helical scan VTR's do not have the electronic stability that is necessary for clean electronic editing. (5) All quadruplex-recorded tapes must first be dubbed onto the helical tape before they can be reproduced on a helical VTR, even if it is the high-quality 2-inch model.

Videotape Recorders

There are three basic types of video recording devices: (1) reel-to-reel videotape recorders, (2) video cassettes and cartridge machines, and (3) video discs. Depending on their electronic sophistication and primary use, there are high-quality broadcast videotape recorders (reel-to-reel and video cassettes) and lower quality recorders that are primarily used for nonbroadcast, closed-circuit television.

Reel-to-Reel VTR's

In reel-to-reel recorders, the videotape is fed from a supply reel past the video heads to a separate takeup reel. These machines are used to record and play back program material of considerable duration. With a maximum reel size of 14 inches for most quad (2-inch tape) recorders, you can record or play back uninterruptedly up to 96 minutes of program material at a tape speed of 15 ips, and 192 minutes at 7½ ips. With a broadcast-quality helical-scan 1-inch recorder, you can record 3½ hours when using the largest (12½-inch) reels. Some closed-circuit helical scan models, which run at slower tape speeds, can record even longer programs without a reel change.

Most broadcast quadruplex machines are too large to be moved very easily. They are usually mounted in the VTR room or in a large mobile van. *(See 8.12.)*

With the exception of the 2-inch helical scan broadcast videotape recorder, most other helical scan machines are portable. They range in size from a studio console down to a large shoulder bag. *(See 9.12.)*

Most advanced videotape recorders have certain electronic accessories that improve the picture stability during recording and playback, and permit electronic editing. Because the basic functions of all videotape recorders are the same, namely, to record and play back television pictures and sound, the operational controls are similar on all machines, regardless of relative quality and make.

Electronic Accessories The two most common electronic accessories are the *time base corrector* and *electronic editing*—or electronic splicing, as it is sometimes called.

The *time base corrector* helps to make the pictures from a videotape recording electronically as stable as possible. Tiny jitters and drifts in picture reproduction are automatically eliminated through time base correction. Operationally, a time base corrector helps to speed up the lockup time (the period from starting the tape recorder to the moment when the picture appears totally stable or when the tape machine is ready to record perfectly stable video images); it permits dubbing-up

9·10 Videotape recorders can also be classified according to their capability of recording color or monochrome. We have, therefore, color or monochrome videotape recorders. Whether or not a videotape recorder can record color has nothing to do with its size. There are some large, broadcast-quality machines that can record and play monochrome only, while some of the small portable models with a ½-inch tape format can record and play back in color.

Among the color recorders, you may come across the distinction between *high-band* and *low-band*. High-band machines operate in a high frequency range, which means operationally higher quality pictures with less video noise and better resolution than low-band color. Monochrome machines are usually low-band.

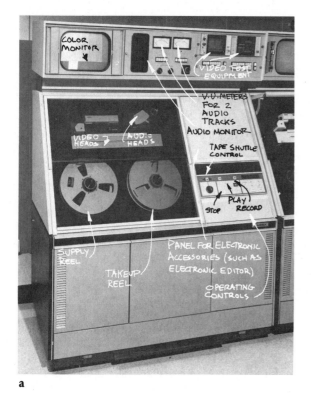

a

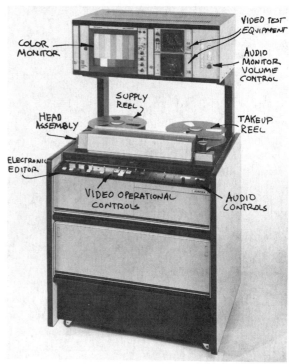

b

small-format helical scan tapes to quadruplex tapes without picture breakup or much deterioration, and the mixing of the recorded video signal with other video sources (camera, another VTR) without undue synchronization problems.

Electronic editing, or electronic splicing, makes it possible to build a program by adding segment to segment, or to insert certain program material, such as a commercial in the middle of a longer program, all without physically cutting the tape. You can have electronic editors in various degrees of sophistication, depending on your production needs and size of pocketbook. The most advanced system is computer-assisted time code editing. It can be used with quad and advanced helical scan

equipment. We will discuss electronic editing more thoroughly in Chapter 10.

Operational Controls The basic operational controls are similar for all videotape recorders, regardless of make. Like audiotape recorders, they have a button each for *play,* or *forward* (moves the tape past the recording heads for playback and record), *fast forward* (advances the tape at a high rate of speed without producing a recognizable video image), *rewind* (rewinds the tape at high speeds without producing a visible image), *record* (puts the machine in the record rather than playback mode [caution: the record mode will automatically erase all previously recorded material

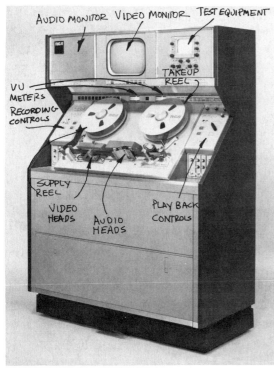

c

d

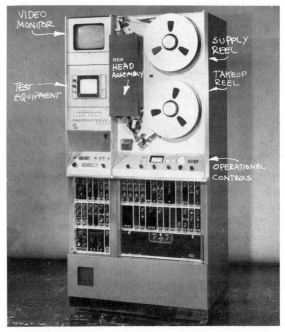

e

9·11 Quadruplex Videotape Recorders: (a) Ampex AVR-1 (top line); (b) Ampex AVR-2 (high quality); (c) RCA TR70-C (top line); (d) Ampex 1200-B (older, less sophisticated model; (e) RCA TR-61 (less sophisticated model). The large quadruplex VTR's are usually located in the VTR room, master control, or large remote vans. The electronic editor and essential test equipment are both part of the VTR unit.

a

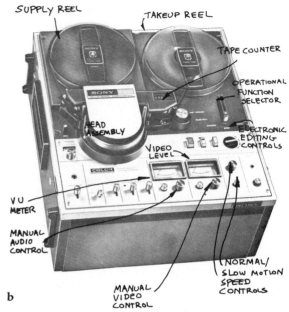

b

9·12   Helical Scan Videotape Recorders: (a) AKAI
VT-150 (¼-inch portable color VTR; shoulder bag);
(b) Sony AV-8650 (½-inch color recorder); (c) IVC-
960 (broadcast-quality 1-inch helical scan color recorder); (d) IVC-9000 (top quality 2-inch helical scan
high-band color recorder).

from the tape]), and *stop* (stops the reels almost
instantly, depending on the quality of the reel
brakes). Most machines have an additional *stand-
by,* or *ready,* button, which makes the video heads
rotate (getting them up to speed) before moving
the tape. *(See 9.13.)*

Most small-format (smaller than 2-inch tape
format) helical scan VTR's have additional controls for variable tape speeds and for viewing a
still frame or stop-motion (continuous viewing of
recorded video fields; looks like jerky slow motion). *(See 9.14.)*

The audio controls contain provisions for input
(recording) and output (playback) audio levels for

each audio track and cue track. High-quality recorders have VU meters for each audio and cue
channel.

There are additional selector switches for tape
speed, audio channels, and video and audio monitoring.

Machines that are equipped with electronic
editing have additional editing controls. We will
describe some of these in Chapter 10.

Video Cassettes and Cartridges

Video cassette and cartridge machines come, like
the reel-to-reel tape recorders, in either quadru-

c

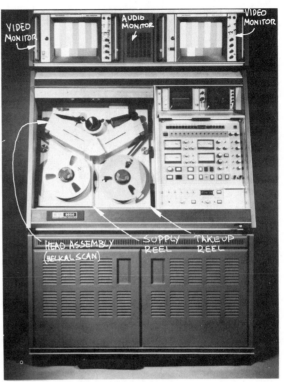

d

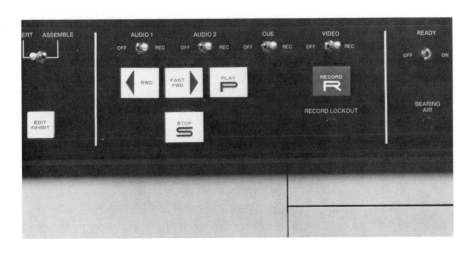

9·13 Operational Controls (Ampex AVR-2).

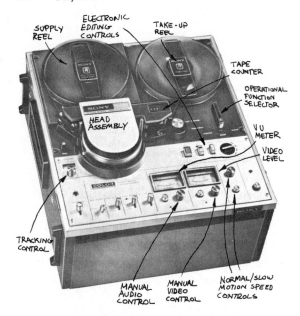

9·14 Controls for most helical scan VTR's include features, such as forward, fast forward, record, and stop. Some of the more advanced models have separate controls for slow motion and stop-motion, and stand-by (which starts rotating the video heads without moving the tape). The arrangement of the controls differs from model to model, but they fulfill identical functions. (Sony AV-8650.)

9·15 If you use small-format helical scan machines for playback, you might need to operate the *tracking control.* This helps you to adjust the video heads electronically so that tapes that have been recorded on another, similar VTR will play back with a minimum of picture jitter and misalignment.

plex or helical scan systems and in a variety of tape formats, such as ½-inch, ¾-inch, 1-inch, and 2-inch.

The videotape in the video cartridge or cassette is enclosed in a plastic box, which can be inserted either manually or automatically into the recorder for extremely efficient cuing, playing (in the play or record mode), and rewinding. The advantage of the cartridge or cassette over the reel-to-reel machine is the operational ease with which it can be played. All you have to do is push it into the slot of the recorder and press the record or play button. The machine will automatically cue the tape and put it on the air within an extremely short time. When the program is over, the tape will rewind itself and cue itself up again for another playback. In the automatic cartridge or cassette system, even the loading is done automatically.

The quadruplex video cartridge or cassette is used for all production situations where sequences of very short program material, such as a series of 10-second commercials, must be played back-to-back *(see 9.17a).* A simple back-to-back series of two 10-second commercials and a 20-second public service announcement would tie up three big VTR machines; a single video cassette machine takes care of this sequence automatically and with great precision.

The quad video cassette or cartridge recorders are used primarily for short program material during station breaks. You can program a sequence of short spots with the help of a small computer that is part of the more sophisticated 2-inch video cassette machines *(see 9.17b).* Once you have started the first cassette, the other cassettes (up to an additional twenty-three) will play continually in the programmed sequence. The computer also displays the house numbers and the exact lengths of the individual cassette programs. You can check the upcoming program to see whether or not it is in the right sequence without actually having to preroll off the air the upcoming spot.

The lockup time of the cassette tape is so short that the start of the tape and the playback or record mode is almost simultaneous. You therefore need no preroll time for the cassette. All you do is push the start button on the "take" cue and the program is on the air. The 2-inch video cassette machines have proved so reliable that almost all film commercials are immediately dubbed over to the 2-inch cassette. The cartridges or cassettes have a maximum playing time of up to six minutes. Some of the 1-inch helical scan cartridge machines, however, handle program items as short as 10 seconds, and up to a maximum of 60 minutes.

On some machines, you can record on one cartridge while another is playing back some other program material. All automated cartridge or cassette systems permit sequential or random selection of the program items.

The most popular, manually operated helical scan cassette system uses the ¾-inch tape format. You can record the signal from the television camera, or directly off the home television receiver. Most ¾-inch cassette units accept cassettes of 10, 15, 30, and 60 minutes. *(See 9.18.)*

There is also a ½-inch video cartridge machine on which you can either record or play cartridge recordings. Depending on the machine,[2] you can wind onto the cartridge reel any recording produced on a reel-to-reel machine.

Video Discs

The video disc is actually not a video *tape* recorder, since it uses a recording disc instead of the tape. This device is used for the recording and instant replay of very short event sequences (up to 35

9·16 As pointed out in Chapter 7, there is a difference between a cassette and a cartridge. A cassette has two reels, a supply reel and a takeup reel, encased in a plastic box. A cartridge has only one reel, which rewinds the endless tape loop at the same time it comes off the reel for playback or record. Unfortunately, the manufacturers of video equipment do not always make such a distinction. The quadruplex videotape "cartridge" recorder by RCA, for example, uses two reels for its tape transport and is, therefore, by definition a cassette recorder. In either case, the videotape is encased in a plastic box, called cart (for cartridge) or cassette, which facilitates cuing, play, and rewind operations.

[2] Only if the ½-inch reel-to-reel recorder operates on the EIAJ standard.

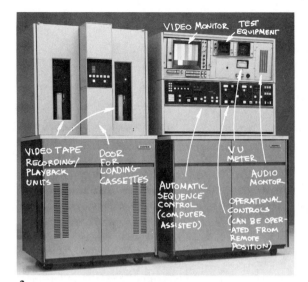

a

b

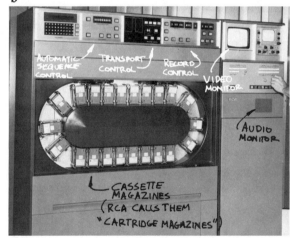

c

d

9·17 Videotape Cassette Machines: (a) Ampex ACR-25; (b) automatic sequence control for ACR-25; (c) 2-inch videotape cassette and tape; (d) RCA TCR 100-A. The 2-inch videotape cassette allows the back-to-back use of short videotaped program material, such as a series of consecutive 10-second spots. What would have been an impossible feat with two regular VTR's (loading, threading the tape, and starting the tape within five seconds, assuming a 5-second roll) is now done by the cassette machine automatically, with ease and reliability. The cassette recorder selects the tape cassette, threads the tape, and cues it, within seconds. (The start button starts the tape roll and puts the picture "on the air" in one operation. No preroll is necessary for the cassette. The cassette recorder can record off any VTR, or another of its cassettes.

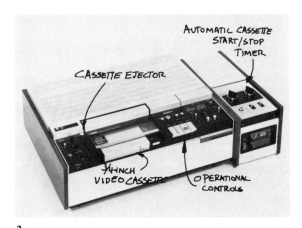

CASSETTE EJECTOR

AUTOMATIC CASSETTE START/STOP TIMER

¾-INCH VIDEO CASSETTE

OPERATIONAL CONTROLS

a

b

9·18 (a) Sony U-matic VO-1800 ¾-Inch Video Cassette and Timer: The ¾-inch helical scan cassette machine can hold cassettes with up to one hour of program material. It has automatic cuing and preroll, and can record material from a direct source, such as cameras, the television set, or from any standard playback device of recorded material (film chain, VTR). The ¾-inch cassette is the slant-track cassette standard. (b) A typical ¾-inch cassette.

seconds). The 20- or 35-second segment, which has been recorded in real time, can be played back at any rate, from *real time* through *slow-motion* speeds, to *stop-motion* (similar to a fast series of slides), to a *freeze frame* (stop-action). You can also play it backwards at any of the above modes; or you can record in time-lapse, which is very similar to frame-by-frame filming in animation. The time-lapse recording can then be played back at any of the speeds, from real time, to slow motion, to stop-motion. Thus, you can use the disc for *video animation.*

The most important feature of the video disc is the speed with which it can search out up to twenty different parts of the recorded segment within seconds (maximum of five) for instant replay. All you have to do is press a "cue" button at the spot you want the replay to begin. The disc will then automatically search out the cue and display a freeze frame of the cued action.

The versatility of the video disc makes it a valuable tool for experimental work. *(See 9.19.)*

Operation of Videotape Recording

Since videotape recording has become such a major factor in television production, even as the director you should have at least some knowledge of its principal technical and production aspects. Such knowledge will expedite not only the actual operation of a small-format, or even larger, VTR, but also, if not especially, your communication with the videotape operator.

Technical Factors

1.   Use only high-quality videotape. Low-quality tape will not only impair the recording, and therefore the playback of program material, but also "gum up" the

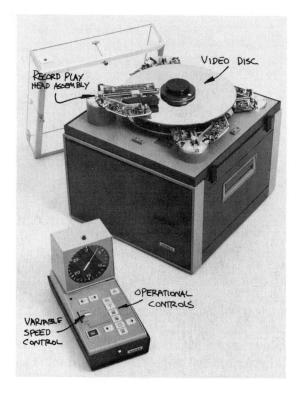

9·19 Ampex Video Disc: The video disc facilitates the recording and instant replay of short (up to 35 seconds) show segments. It can search out any part of the recorded action within seconds, and play it back at real time (normal speed), or any variety of slow-motion speeds down to a freeze frame.

video heads (by depositing large amounts of oxide coating).

2.   Before using a new videotape for recording, you should furbish it by running it once through the recorder without recording anything on it. This will "polish" it by removing any undue collection of oxide coating. The video heads must be cleaned immediately afterwards.

3.   When threading the tape (different machines have slightly different threading procedures), make sure that the head motor is turned off. The *stand-by* button must be in the *off* position. Otherwise, you run the risk of getting the tape tangled up in the rotating heads.

4.   After threading the tape, turn the takeup reel gently clockwise to see whether the tape moves freely from the supply reel to the takeup reel.

5.   After each tape stop, turn the takeup reel gently to eliminate any possible tape slack and to restore its necessary tension.

6.   Make sure that all recording and erase heads are clean. Clean them frequently.

7.   Make sure that you have enough tape on the supply reel to last for the entire segment you plan to record.

8.   Record only after the machine has "locked up," that is, fully stabilized for recording. With the help of a time base corrector, even the large quad machines lock up within a few seconds.

9.   Before recording the actual program, test-record a small section of it. Play it back and check whether the recording is satisfactory. Pay attention to audio and video levels.

10.   When the recording is finished, *spot-check* the recording before you release the production crew and performers. If you discover some recording problems, you can repeat part of the program much more easily with everybody still at his post than trying to recall crew and performers at another time.

Production Factors

There are certain operational steps in videotape recording that are especially important for preproduction, the production itself, and postproduction activities. Since we will discuss postproduction more thoroughly in Chapter 10, we will limit ourselves here to the major preproduction and production factors of videotaping.

Preproduction   If you simply record an entire event for time delay, all you really have to worry about is that you have sufficient tape to cover the whole event. If the event might run longer than the tape capacity of your largest reel, you need two recorders, or you will have to live with losing a few minutes of the event during reel change.

If, however, you plan to videotape in sections, preproduction planning becomes very important. Here are some of the major points to consider:

1.   Divide your script into the various scenes (organic small parts) you will need for later assembly. Mark your script carefully, exactly where you want a taping session to start and stop. Number the scenes.

2.   Indicate the approximate times for each scene so that you can tell the videotape operator how much tape you need for each scene.

3.   If possible, try to pick scenes that are organic. This means that you should choose your starting and stopping points not arbitrarily but rather where the action or the mood undergoes marked shifts. The *longer* and less interrupted the scene, the *better*. Television, by its very nature, requires a more lifelike rhythm than film. The shooting of a show in too many segments jeopardizes the natural flow and build not only of the show but also of the performer, who might lack the necessary continuity for his pacing and emotional buildup. Ill-matched and chopped-up show segments and performances are very noticeable on the concentrated television screen space.[3]

4.   Triple-check on the availability of a videotape recorder, or recorders, for the period of your scheduled taping sessions.

[3] Herbert Zettl, *Sight-Sound-Motion* (Belmont, Calif.: Wadsworth Publishing Co., 1973), pp. 244–269.

Production   If you have spent adequate time on the taping preparations during the preproduction activities, your taping sessions should go quite smoothly, barring major equipment disasters. Just before the taping, check about the anticipated duration of the scene or scenes you intend to videotape. Insist on a few short recording tests, if the operator has not done this on his own.

Videotape Cuing Procedure   For each videotape you need some initial technical and program identification, so-called tape leader information. You also need to know how to predict accurately the end of a tape, especially if you are replaying one that was recorded somewhere else.

Each videotape must carry program information that identifies the program, and production and technical information that helps the videotape operator adjust the machine to the electronic requirements of the tape for accurate playback. Furthermore, you need a device that allows you to roll the tape and put it on the air at the precise second. The SMPTE (Society of Motion Picture and Television Engineers) has issued a standard for the initial videotape information, sometimes called the *video leader* (a term borrowed from film). There is a video leader for monochrome videotapes, and another for color. *(See 9.20 and 9.21.)*

Contrary to the film leader, which you can buy in bulk and splice onto any film you intend to televise, the entire videotape leader must be recorded *continuously* with the same equipment with which the program is recorded. If you adjust your videotape recorder according to the technical information given in the videotape leader, you can be reasonably assured of a proper program playback. If, however, you were to edit in color bars from another tape, or stop the machine between each leader segment, the technical information of the leader would no longer reflect that of the program, and the leader information would be worthless for the program playback.

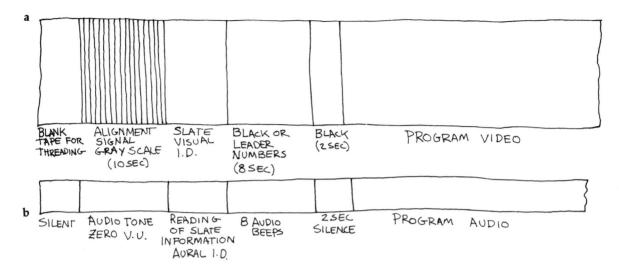

9·20   Monochrome Video Leader: (a) video; (b) audio.

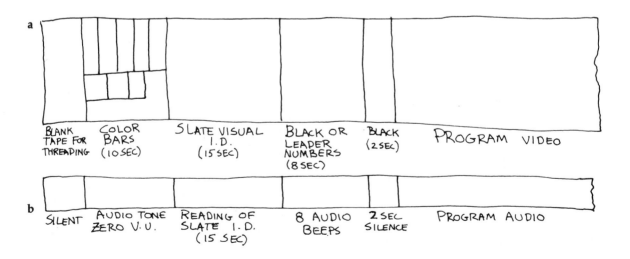

9·21   Color Video Leader: (a) video; (b) audio.

For the visual program identification, you record on tape an identification *slate,* a small black- or whiteboard in aspect ratio, which shows the title of the show, the scene and take number, the date of the recording, the anticipated duration of the recording, and such other optional information as anticipated playback, location of recording, and in-house identification numbers. *(See 9.22.)*

Make sure that all four corners of the slate are visible when you record it; this will help the videotape operator in further alignment of his machine, especially during playback.

During the recording of the slate, the information on it is *read aloud* for recording on the audio track either by the floor manager, who holds the slate in front of the camera, or by the audio board operator, who reads the information off the line monitor.

After the slate has been recorded for a minimum of ten seconds (you need to wait longer if it contains an unusual amount of program information), you take it to black and start the beeper cuing system.

The *beeper* normally consists of a series of eight low-frequency audio beeps, exactly one second apart, that are recorded on the audio track of the videotape. The last two seconds before the program recording are left silent, as a safety cushion for the following program audio. Make sure that your program video and audio start *exactly two seconds* after the last beep, otherwise you will not be able to use the beepers as an accurate playback cue.

Assuming that the beeper is correctly executed, it will enable the videotape operator to locate any recorded program segment quickly regardless of where it occurs on the tape. All the operator must do is listen to the beeps during the fast forward mode of the tape recorder. Because of the highly accelerated tape speed during fast forward, the beeps will appear in the audio monitor as a fast

9·22   The slate, which is recorded at the beginning of each take, shows vital production information, such as the title of the show, the scene and cut (take) numbers, the playback, and so forth.

9·23   The scene refers to the program portion you have selected and numbered in your script for one continuous taping; the take number refers to the number of times you repeat the same scene.

series of high-pitched tones. The operator can stop the recorder and recue the tape on any one of the eight beeps (depending on the cuing system) for playback.

Sometimes a *video cue* is used in addition to the beeper. Unless you have time-code facilities (see Chapter 10), you can record flashing numbers—similar to those on public buildings that show the time and temperature—from a "leader box." The *leader box* projects numbers from 10 to 3 in 1-second intervals onto its frosted glass surface. The box, which is synchronized with the audio beeps, goes automatically to black (as does the audio) for the last two seconds before the beginning of the program portion. When the tape is played back, you can see the numbers flash by on your VTR preview monitor, similar to the academy film leader.

The putting on of this type of video leader has proved quite cumbersome, however, and the video cue leader has never gained wide acceptance in television production. With the availability of a time code, the leader box is no longer useful.

In the absence of a time code display, the most accurate cuing device is the *tape timer*, which displays seconds, minutes, and hours of elapsed time. The tape timer permits fairly accurate pre-rolls and program end cues. If, for example, your station operates on a 7-second preroll for color and a 5- or 4-second preroll for monochrome (to allow the tape to get up to the operating speed where the pictures have maximum electronic stability), the videotape operator will locate the first picture (frame) of the recorded program and then wind the tape back seven seconds for color. (Incidentally, this spot should coincide with the fifth beep from the end, the last two seconds being silent.)

The preroll standards are especially important if you use a short videotape as an insert in a live newscast, for example. You must preroll the color

tape seven seconds before you actually need it on the air. (Anywhere from one and one-half to two lines of news copy.)

The tape timer is also helpful to tell you when the recorded program is coming to an end. Although you should time all videotape playbacks with your stopwatch, the tape timer is often a welcome safety backup. Some stations put an *audio end cue* on the videotape. This may, for example, be a 5-second continuous tone emanating from the cue track. As soon as you hear the end cue tone on the cue track audio monitor, you can alert everybody for the program changeover.

Let's go through a typical tape roll for recording. The exact calls may vary from station to station; however, the basic procedure for starting the tape, recording the leader material, and ending the recording should agree at least on major points. Here is an example:

Ready VTR one (if you have more than one VTR, you must call the number of the machine), *ready bars, ready slate on two* (camera 2), *ready beeper.*

Ready to roll VTR one. (At this point you should wait for some confirmation of the "ready" status from the VTR operator or the T.D. before you actually call for the roll.)

Roll VTR one. (Before giving any more cues, you must now wait until the videotape machine has reached the necessary speed for the signal to lock in, that is, to stabilize so that the recorded video signals will not produce flutter and tears in the pictures. Normally, the videotape operator will give you the "in record" or "speed" confirmation.)

Bars. (You should look at your stopwatch to make sure that you record a minimum of ten seconds. Generally, the video operator will record the ten seconds of bars automatically without a cue from the director. If a reference tone is recorded with the bars, the audio operator will feed a zero-level tone—one that peaks consistently at zero VU—to the VTR.)

Ready two, take two. (Assuming that the slate is on camera 2. You cut to camera 2 after a minimum of ten seconds of color bars.) *Read slate.* (Either the floor manager or the audio console operator reads the slate information over a hot mike onto the main audio track of the videotape recording.)

Ready black, ready beeper.

Black. Beeper. (The audio console operator now activates the beeper. There are only eight beeps on the tape. The last two seconds are silent. Either the A.D. [associate director] or the audio console operator will count backwards with the beeps, from ten to zero.)

Fade in one, or *Up on one.* (Camera 1 is now on the air and you have begun your videotaping session. Have you started your stopwatch?)

At the end of the videotape recording, you *go to black* and stay there for another ten seconds or so, in order to record the *runout signal.* This signal indicates that the tape is producing black rather than video noise at the end of the recording. Such a safety cushion is especially important if you do not switch to another video source immediately after the end of the recorded program, or if you want to edit on additional program material.

Don't forget to call for the *stopping* of the tape at the end of the recording. Some videotape operators will let the tape run until the director, or the T.D., tells them to stop it.

Spot-check the recording before you dismiss the crew and the performers.

Film Use

There are five major ways in which film is used in television: (1) as motion picture features, (2) as television film features, (3) as news films, (4) as local features, and (5) as commercials.

Motion Picture Features

Motion picture features include all film originally produced for theater presentation—all full-length feature films, the shorter travel films, educational features, and industrial features that have not been manufactured for television consumption.

Television Film Features

Television film features include motion pictures specifically produced and shot for television. Most popular westerns, police stories, and some situation comedy series are filmed for television.

News Films

News films include all films produced by national, international, or local news services or departments for daily television news shows.

Locally produced news film is very important in small station operation. The newscaster himself might on occasion double as film camera operator during "off hours" and shoot local news events. News departments of larger stations usually employ several full-time camera operators and up to twenty or more part-time camera operators—so-called stringers—who are located at strategic spots within the coverage area of the station. The stringers shoot everything newsworthy at their locations, with the hope that their television station will use the films on the air. More and more, however, news film is replaced by portable video equipment.

Local Features

Local features include all films produced locally outside of news films, such as interviews, documentaries, or special material for editorial telecasts. Local news photographers usually take care of the local film productions. Sometimes, freelance photographers are hired for especially ambitious local productions.

An additional, formerly very prominent use of film is the (almost extinct) *kinescope recording.* Here

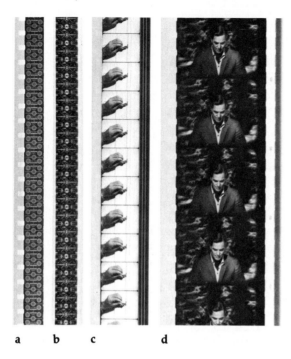

a   b   c   d

9·24   (a) 8mm; (b) Super-8mm; (c) 16mm; (d) 35mm.

9·25   The especially wide 70mm film is never used in television. All 70mm prints are reduced to either 35mm or 16mm before telecasting.

a specially designed film camera shoots film images that appear on a kinescope tube (small, high-resolution television screen). A kinescope recording is similar to a videotape recording, except that the video and audio signals are fed into the kinescope recorder rather than the videotape recorder. The end product is a 16mm *film.* However, compared to a film that has been shot directly, the kinescope recording shows a lower picture quality.

On occasion, videotape is changed into film via kinescope recording. This process, called "electronic transfer," is employed to make television material more accessible to film-oriented operations, such as schools, or to aid in frame-by-frame study or unusually careful editing. Kinescope recordings are of little use in today's small station operation.

Commercials

Many commercial spots are produced and distributed on film. However, since the videotape cassette machines make the playback of even short commercial inserts relatively easy, more and more commercials are produced and distributed on videotape.

Film Specifications

Major specifications include the *width* of the film and whether or not the film includes *sound.*

Film Width

Film is labeled according to its width: 8mm and Super-8mm, 16mm, and 35mm. Most television stations use 16mm film, although the improved quality of Super-8mm has become a serious contender. Some stations work with Super-8mm for their entire news film operation. *(See 9.24.)*

Major network origination and some "O and O" stations (Owned and Operated by one of the major networks) have 35mm film facilities, which permit the use of high-quality theater prints for broadcasting. But the film standard for most television film operation is 16mm. The slightly better picture quality of 35mm film simply cannot outweigh the many advantages of using 16mm film. For example, 16mm film is much easier to ship, store, and handle than 35mm film; it is cheaper than 35mm; almost all locally produced film is either 16mm or Super-8mm and, therefore, could not be played back on 35mm equipment. Since 16mm is still the most widely used film format in television, we will use 16mm film as the standard in our further discussions. If your television operation requires you to work with another film format, you can easily apply the principles of 16mm film to it.

Silent and Sound Film

Film can be "silent," with no accompanying sound printed on it, or it can be SOF (sound on film) whereby, along with the pictures, the film carries an audio track.

Many locally produced films are shot silent. The production advantages over SOF are numerous: (1) Silent film is easier to shoot. You can walk with your camera anywhere and shoot practically anything without having to worry about sound requirements, additional cables, microphones, and tape recorders. (2) You can shoot silent film entirely out of sequence with little consideration for a matching sound track. (3) Editing and splicing silent film is easier than SOF (see Chapter 10). (4) Live narration, background music, and sound effects are more flexible when played over silent film from a different source.

Of course, if the sound is as important as the pictures in the coverage of an event, you need to shoot SOF. For example, silent film would be of little use if you were to do a remote film interview

9·26 Super-8mm film has a picture area that is 50 percent larger than the normal 8mm frame, and therefore produces a sharper and brighter picture. The larger picture area is gained by a change in size and arrangement of sprocket holes.

of an important government official for the evening news. To have the newscaster summarize voice over what the official is saying, while we actually see the official talking, makes no sense at all. In this case, SOF coverage is a must, unless you have good-quality portable videotape available. Often used to capture the actual sounds surrounding an event, SOF gives the story a high degree of authenticity, even if the event could be shot silent. Regardless of how skillful an audio engineer you might have for the re-creation of sound effects of a four-alarm-fire story, for example, the actual sounds still carry more impact.

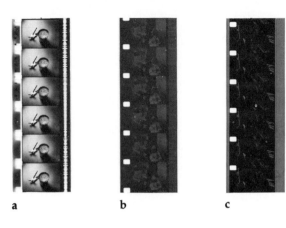

a   b   c

9·27 (a) Variable Area: The variable area sound track is an optical track whose light-transmitting areas differ, thus modulating (changing) the light of the exciter lamp. When received by the photoelectric cell, the light modulations are converted into electrical energy, the sound signal. (b) Variable Density: The variable density sound track operates similarly to the variable area sound track, except that the light variations of the exciter lamp are caused by varying degrees of film density (opaqueness) rather than areas. (c) Magnetic: The magnetic sound track consists of a tiny magnetic tape that runs down one side of the film, often called "mag stripe." A second magnetic stripe runs parallel to the actual sound stripe on the opposite side of the film. This "balance stripe" is merely to compensate for the extra thickness so that the film runs evenly through the projector.

9·28 To obtain sound from an optical sound track, a constant light source shines through the track into a photoelectric cell, which converts the light variations (caused by the area variations, the wiggles, of the variable area, or the density variations, the various degrees of gray, of the variable density track) into electrical impulses. These are amplified and sent to the loudspeaker.

Sound on Film (SOF)

SOF, sound on film, is an accurate definition: the sound is on the film with the pictures. In film, the audio track is called the *sound track.*

There are two major types of sound tracks: (1) optical and (2) magnetic. Good television film projectors can play back either one. Some of the more sophisticated models can even switch automatically from optical to magnetic, or vice versa.

The *optical* sound track can be a *variable area,* or a *variable density,* track. The *magnetic* sound track consists of a small strip of iron oxide, similar to a small audiotape, that runs down one side of the film. *(See 9.27.)*

The sound track can be put on the film in two different ways. One is to record pictures and sound simultaneously on the same length of film; this method is called *single-system* sound recording. Another is to record pictures and sound at the same time but on separate recording devices. The pictures are recorded on film (very much like silent film), while the sound is recorded on a magnetic audiotape recorder that runs in sync with the film camera. Because this method uses two separate recording devices (one for pictures and one for sound), it is called *double-system* sound recording. Picture and sound are later combined on the same film in the printing (developing) process.

The single system is more economical, since it needs only one recording element (the film). But it has several drawbacks: (1) Its sound is inferior to double-system. (2) Because the microphone is attached to the camera system (which includes the audio amplifier), the camera mobility is severely restricted. (3) Since the audio track is already attached to the film, editing is more difficult than with the double system, which permits separate editing for sound and picture. And (4) it allows less shooting and editing flexibility than double-system sound recording.

The Film Chain, or Film Island

The basic film chain or film island consists of at least one film projector, a slide projector, a multiplexer, and a television film camera, or, as it is frequently called, a telecine camera (from *tele*vision and *cine*matography). Occasionally the film island with its components is called the telecine system. Most film chains contain a second film projector. Let's take a brief look at each of these components: (1) the film projector, (2) the slide projector, (3) the multiplexer, and (4) the film camera.

Film Projector

The television film projector is especially designed so that the (16mm) film speed of 24 frames per second will correspond to the 30 frames of the television picture (see page 240). This synchronization is accomplished by the television film camera scanning the first film frame twice, the second three times, the third twice again, and so on. If a film projector is not synchronized with the television system, you will detect a slight flutter in the television picture and, sometimes, black shutter bars moving up and down the screen. When using Super-8mm film, you can usually vary the speed of the projector until you get a clear, flutter-free picture.

Most film projectors can accommodate large 20-inch (4,000-foot) reels (some even 5,000-foot reels) that allow a continuous projection of almost two hours of film programs, and very tiny ones (50-foot reels) for the commercial spots. Although the film projectors have automatic film tension compensators, it is a good idea to use a *takeup reel* of the *same size as the supply reel.* This way, you maintain uniform film tension and drastically reduce the danger of film breakage. *(See 9.29.)*

Film projectors usually have a number of devices that facilitate operations: (1) The threading mechanism is usually kept as simple as possible so that, with some experience, you can thread the film within seconds. Of course, film cartridge machines make loading even faster. (2) The projectors can bring the film with its sound up to full speed within a fraction of a second. This "zero preroll" eliminates a preroll countdown. But longer preroll starts are still prevalent. (See the section on operational factors, page 244.) (3) All film projectors have a remote start-and-stop mechanism, which can be activated manually, or triggered by computer control. Some of the more complex projectors have automatic cuing systems, whereby the film can be programmed in advance to stop and cue itself for the next segment in as many places as desired. This automatic cuing is accomplished by attaching small pieces of special tape to the film at the specific cuing points. The film projector senses these tapes and performs the necessary functions automatically. (4) Most film projectors have a pickup device for both optical and magnetic sound. Some projectors can switch automatically from one type to the other. (5) Most projectors can show a single film frame for extended periods without danger of burning the film. (6) The film can be run in reverse direction. (7) The projection lamp and the sound-exciter lamp exchange themselves automatically if they happen to fail during the film projection.

As mentioned above, most film islands have two film projectors to ensure maximum continuity of programming. As soon as the film of the first projector has run out, the second projector can be started and switched on the air. Sometimes you may find it convenient to have all the program film (such as a motion picture feature) on one projector and all the commercial film spots on the other. In case your program runs late for some reason, you can always switch to the commercials at the scheduled time, while letting some of the feature film run through off the air in order to

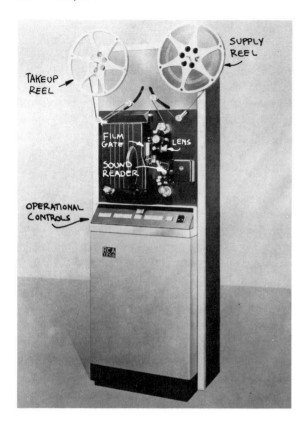

9·29   RCA TP-66 Film Projector: The professional television film projector adjusts the 24-frames-per-second 16mm sound speed to the 30-frames-per-second electronic scanning of television. It can be remotely started and stopped, backed up in reverse, and stopped for still-frame projection without burning up the film. The largest reels can accommodate almost two hours of continuous film programming.

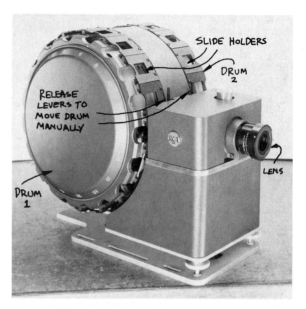

9·30   RCA TP-7 Slide Projector: The dual-drum slide projector holds a total of 36 slides, which can be rapidly advanced or, with special additional equipment, randomly selected. In case the lamp burns out, you can pull the lamp assembly quickly into the spare-lamp position. The slide projector accepts regular 2 x 2 slides, even in the traditional paper mountings. However, because the cardboard tends to buckle under severe heat and thereby go out of focus, all slides used should be mounted in a more heat-resisting frame.

make up for lost time (by the way, not a good substitute for accurate timing).

Slide Projector

Transparency slide projectors have slides arranged on two vertically or horizontally ar-ranged dual drums. The latter are called carousel drums. The more popular, vertically arranged dual drums have a slide capacity of 36 slides (18 each) *(see 9.30)*. Dual-drum slide projectors permit reloading or changing slides while the machine is in operation. Most new drum slide projectors are designed for forward and reverse action. Some are equipped with a random selection device, through which you can punch up any slide without waiting for the drums to rotate until the desired slide finally appears in the gate. In case

9·31 Multiplexer: The multiplexer consists of a series of mirrors or prisms that direct the light of the various program sources, such as film projectors or slide projectors, into the television film (also called telecine) camera.

the projector lamp burns out, you can pull a large handle and put the spare lamp into operation. Sometimes, standard 35mm single-drum carousel slide projectors, the kind you use at home, are used on the film chain.

Slides are generally easier to use than studio cards. First, keeping them in order is much simpler than handling loose cards on various easels. Second, they can be changed on the air more cleanly and rapidly than studio cards. And third, the use of slides will not tie up a studio camera.

The disadvantage of using slides rather than studio cards is that the fixed television film camera cannot move on the slides.

Multiplexer

The multiplexer is a series of mirrors or prisms that direct the images from several projection sources, such as slides and film projectors, into a single fixed television film, or telecine, camera

(9.31). Without the multiplexer, each film projector and each slide projector would need its own film camera. The mirrors, which direct the various video sources into the single camera, and the projectors themselves must be carefully aligned so that nothing of the picture information gets lost in this image-bending process . Most multiplexers are therefore heavy and sturdy and are mounted on a heavy concrete slab in order to withstand the inevitable vibrations caused by moving machinery and people.

Some multiplexers have provisions for two telecine cameras. You can then either increase the number of input sources (by adding a Super-8mm film projector to the two 16mm film projectors, or an additional dual-drum slide projector) or use the *second camera* for *previewing* the image from the upcoming projector while the signal from the other projector is still on the air. The openings for the projectors leading to the multiplexer mirrors are called "ports."

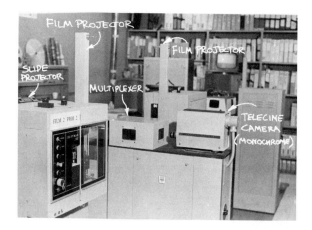

9·32   Monochrome Telecine Camera.

The Telecine, or Television Film, Camera

The telecine, or television film, camera can be monochrome or color. As with studio cameras, most are color. The monochrome telecine camera is a simple vidicon camera *(9.32)*.

The color telecine camera usually works on the three-tube principle, similar to the studio cameras *(9.33)*. The tubes are either vidicon or Plumbicon. Most telecine cameras have automatic brightness and color correction features, which adjust to the various degrees of color temperature, saturation, contrast range, or general density of the films or slides projected.

Since a complete film island takes up a considerable amount of space, constant efforts are made by manufacturers to reduce the size of the projection and multiplexing equipment and to combine the instruments in one unit. Whatever the arrangements may be, the basic principle of multiplexing the various video sources into one or two telecine cameras remains unchanged.

If your film island has only one telecine camera, you cannot preview or use a second video source while another one is on the air. For example, you cannot super a slide over a film if both are on the same island. In order to do so, you would need to put the film on the film projector of one film island, and the slide in the slide project of another (assuming that each island has one camera only).

Operation of Film

Film is such a widely known and widely discussed subject that we will limit ourselves in this section to its major operational factors only as they relate to television production.

Specifically, we will look at (1) film quality check and storage, (2) film projection, and (3) film cuing and timing. Film editing will be taken up in Chapter 10.

Quality Check and Storage

When you receive a film from outside, check it before putting it on a projector. There are machines on the market that check the film in one operation for *bad splices, torn sprocket holes,* and other injuries. If you don't have such a machine, run the film through your action viewer and check for the above-mentioned defects. Locally produced film will (hopefully) have undergone such scrutiny by the people in charge of film in the news department. In any case, if you are in charge of telecine operations, it might be wise to check every piece of film that is to be projected, time and circumstances allowing. Be sure to *clean* the film (by running it through a film cleaner) before projecting it.

Film quality check also includes a cursory screening as to *color consistency.* If you notice a marked change in color quality (from a warm, reddish overall hue, to a cold, bluish hue, or from intensely saturated colors to washed-out colors, for example), warn the video engineer. Although the automatic color correction will compensate as much as possible for such changes, the video engineer may have to correct drastic color changes manually.

Lastly, check for *content.* Although television has become somewhat liberated as to what is considered proper for home viewing, some unsuitable material may, nevertheless, have escaped the scrutiny of the traffic department, which usually takes care of such matters. But *don't play censor.* Alert the program manager or the traffic department if you perceive a piece of film as too offensive for broadcasting.

Like videotape, store the film in a dry, cool, dust-free place. Place it in tightly closed cans in order to keep it from drying out, since a very dry film becomes brittle and breaks easily in the projector. Label each film carefully with the title, category (feature, commercial), and house number.

Film Projection

When threading the film, follow the threading diagram that is usually supplied by the manufacturer. It is often attached to the projector. Here are a few items that deserve attention:

1. Before threading the film, make sure that the television film projector is on local control, rather than remote control. If you leave it on remote control, it may be accidentally started by someone from a control room, and you may get your fingers caught in the projector mechanism.

2. Be sure to thread the film *firmly* over the sound drum, and to adhere to the prescribed loops. Otherwise your film will be out of lip-sync.

3. Even if you are in a hurry, thread the film carefully. A careless threading job may result in severe film damage.

4. Once you have threaded the film, start the projector and run the film for a little while to make sure that you have loaded the projector correctly. Back up the

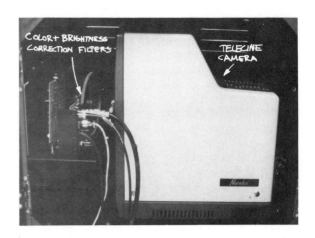

9·33   Color Telecine Camera.

film again to the number 4 (or whatever cue you have designated) of the academy leader.

5. Just in case your film should break, have the splicing equipment close at hand. Usually, a simple splicer and high-speed rewind equipment are located right next to the film islands.

6. If your projector does not have an automatic switchover from optical to magnetic sound, make sure that the sound pickup device on the projector corresponds to the film sound track.

7. Treat all film gently.

Film Cuing and Timing

With film, as with videotape, you need to employ some cuing and timing procedures in order to start and stop the film as programmed. Precise cues and timing are especially important if the films are integrated in a longer program, such as short news films within a newscast, or short commercial spots at a station break. We will briefly look at (1) some of the customary cuing procedures for film starts, (2) the academy leader, (3) end cues and timing.

9·34   Academy Leader: The Academy leader, or SMPTE universal leader, assists in the accurate cuing and picture alignment before the film is actually projected. The numbers, from 8 to 3, indicate 1-second intervals. The last two seconds of the leader are black in order to avoid showing numbers on the air if the film is punched up early. A clocklike dial at each number frame shows how close you are to the completion of each countdown second.

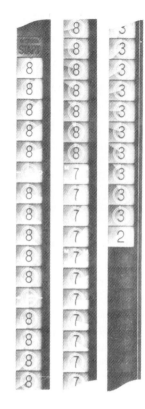

Cuing.   Although most television film projectors gain full picture and sound speed within a fraction of a second, television films are often started as much as four seconds ahead of the first film frame. The reason for the traditional "4-start" (4-second film start) is partially habit, partially a technical guarantee for the video to stabilize before the film is shown on the air. Another reason is the high degree of control during transitions from another video source to film, as, for example, the transition from a live introduction by an on-camera announcer to the film. A 4-start gives the performer the needed time to wind up his commentary just before the film appears on the screen. Also, the 4-start will tell you (the di-

rector) that the film is indeed rolling before you switch it on the air.

In order to make the 4-start (or any other type of prerolling) possible, you need to splice a special leader at the head of each film to be specially cued. This leader is traditionally called the *academy leader* or, more accurately, the *SMPTE universal leader.*

Academy Leader.   The academy leader consists of a strip of film showing numbers from 8 to 3 at equal 1-second intervals and a dial rotating around the academy leader numbers at each second *(see 9.34).*

The leader contains additional information that aids in synchronizing several film strips during the editing process. The leader (which is available commercially) is spliced at the head of any film that needs cuing. You splice the leader at the film to be shown with the "picture start" frame and the highest number farthest away, and the lowest number (number 3) and the two seconds of black closest to the beginning of the film to be cued.

If two films follow each other without interruption, you need the academy leader only at the head of the first film. The second film can be spliced directly to the "tail" (end) of the first one. But if you plan to switch to another video source between the two films, such as the newscaster between two news films, you will need to put an academy leader at the head of the first film, and between the preceding and following films. The second leader makes it now possible to stop the projector for any length of time and to cue up the second film so that it can be prerolled at a precise cue.

It is a good idea to place a 3-foot opaque leader in front of the first academy leader and a 2-foot opaque leader at the end of the last film on the reel. The front leader (sometimes called "head leader") will help in threading the film into the projector without using up the academy leader

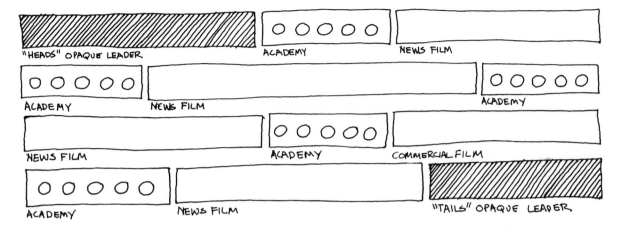

9·35 This schematic shows how various leaders must be used in the final "makeup" (editing) of a newsreel containing several news films and a commercial insert.

The head of the reel consists of an opaque and an academy leader for easy threading of the projector and accurate cuing. Then comes the first news film. Since you are cutting back to the newscaster, you need another academy leader for cuing the second news film (assuming that you work with an academy pre-roll). After the second news film, you cut back again to the newscaster; another academy leader is therefore required for cuing the third news film. Since the newscaster introduces the film commercial on camera, you need another academy leader (you must cut back to the newscaster for the live introduction to the film commercial). After the commercial, you come back to the newscaster for on-camera copy, which means that the fourth and last news film must be cued by an academy leader once again. At the end of the reel you need an opaque leader, to keep the television screen in black just in case you are slightly late in cutting back to the newscaster for the final story.

(which you need for cuing); the end leader (sometimes called "tail leader") will keep the television picture in black for a few seconds, giving everybody a chance for a smooth changeover to the next video source in case the end cue (usually a time cue or a word cue if SOF is used) has been missed. The head and tail leaders are usually marked with an inking pen as to program title, house code or number, date and time of airing, and whether the leader is "heads" or "tails"

(wound so that the beginning [heads] or the end [tails] of the film is on the outside of the reel).

If you use instantaneous starts, you do not need an academy leader, except perhaps at the very beginning of a film reel in order to help the video engineer with the alignment. All you then do is put a short piece of black leader (opaque leader) between the films that are interrupted by another video source. You simply roll the black leader down to the first frame of the next film and start

9·36   Roll Film.

the projector directly on cue (eliminating the preroll altogether). The advantage of the "black leader method" is that you do not have to calculate any preroll time into your cuing. You start the projector directly on cue. The disadvantages of this method are: (1) You don't have any verification in your preview monitor of whether or not the film has been accurately cued. With the academy leader, your preview monitor will show a big "4" on the screen (or at whatever number you want your preroll to occur). (2) Without the academy leader, you have no warning if the film projector does not work. If, due to equipment malfunction, the film does not roll, the academy leader (which does not move) will give you enough warning not to switch to the film and to stay with the live camera picture. (3) The black leader does not allow any preparation time for the changeover. As soon as the T.D. starts the projector through remote control, the image is (or is not) on the air. (4) The instantaneous start does not always give the video and audio enough time to stabilize fully.

Let's do a film roll with a 4-start and a live

introduction from the studio by the performer. Here is a workable sequence:

1.   The telecine operator or T.D. (through remote control) cues up the film on academy leader number 4. Make sure that the actual number appears on the preview monitor each time.

2.   The director signals to the T.D.: *Ready film. Roll film.*

3.   The T.D. starts the film projector by remote control. At the same time, the floor manager gives the performer a roll-film cue by holding his left hand in front of his face and moving his right hand in a cranking motion *(see 9.36)*.

4.   The director gives the academy leader countdown aloud over the P.L. system: *Four—three—two—one—take* (or *dissolve to*) *F-one* (assuming that the film originates from film island No.1). If you have only one island, you may say: *Take film.*

5.   At count four, the floor manager gives a visual cue to the talent *(see 9.37)*.

6.   The performer is winding up his film introduction, synchronizing his introduction exactly with the countdown.

7.   The floor manager gives the *take film* cue and the T.D. switches the film on the air.

8.   The audio person kills the performer's mike and brings up the film's audio track. The performer must have finished talking, or the introduction will be upcut in favor of the film audio (assuming that the film introduced is a commercial; if it is an SOF news film, the newscaster's introduction usually overrides the sound track of the film).

Sometimes the performer will watch the countdown on a special preview monitor, or take his or her film cue from the camera tally light, which goes out as soon as the film is switched on the air. With the instantaneous start, the director rolls and puts the film on the air at the very end (last word) of the performer's introduction. The performer does not need a special film roll cue or any countdown. He simply reads the film introduction or whatever copy precedes the film roll and then hopes to find the film on the studio monitor when he is through.

End Cues and Timing The most accurate and most frequently used end cue for the exact spot where you should switch to another video source (usually the very end of the film) is a time cue. Each film must be accurately timed in minutes and seconds—or if necessary hours, minutes, and seconds—so that you can not only integrate it into the overall program time but also get the all-important *end cue.*

In order to *time* the film, you run it through either a film timer, which gives you a reading in hours, minutes, and seconds of elapsed film time, or a footage counter, which gives you the length of the film in feet. If you use a footage counter, you will need to use a conversion chart to convert the length of the film into running time. Make sure to time the film from the *first picture frame to the last* to be shown, not including the academy or opaque leaders.

If at all possible, don't time the film by running it through a regular 16mm projector that you might use for previewing the film. The projector speeds differ sufficiently to render such timing inaccurate, even for a relatively short piece of film.

When you roll a film, you start your stopwatch as soon as the first frame appears on the monitor. You then go by the *stopwatch* and call for a switch to the following video source as soon as your stopwatch indicates the end of the film. Let's assume your first news film (silent) timed out to exactly 58 seconds. There is narration over the silent film by the newscaster. Table 9.38 (page 248) shows how you, as a director, would get into and out of this film during a newscast.

Hopefully, you will have cut back to the newscaster before you hit the black leader or, worse,

9·37 Countdown.

get into the scratches and identification marks of the academy leader of the following film. As soon as you are back on the new video source, *reset* your stopwatch for the upcoming film. If the newscaster is early with his narration, you simply run the film silent to the end. If you have prescreened the film and know that the last few seconds of it are not essential to the story, you may want to cut out of the film and back to the newscaster on his narration. If you cut out of the film too early too often, however, your overall timing of the newscast may be off (you will run short) and you may have to stretch with filler material at the end of the newscast. On the other hand, if the newscaster runs long with his narration, you simply cut to him while he is finishing the narration on camera.

When running an SOF, you will have an additional end cue, the last few words that appear on the sound track of the film. Your out-cue is then not entirely the time (which nevertheless remains a valuable cue), but the *word end cue.* Your script might have the following information.

Video	Audio
FILM 1:20 *SOF* MAG (for 1:20 magnetic sound)	ENDS: ". . . looking forward to it."

Your roll and initial timing procedures are identical to those of the previous silent film. At the end of the SOF, however, after your 10-second cue, you now *listen* carefully to the end cue: ". . . looking forward to it." After "it" you cut to the next video source, even if your stopwatch may be a second or two over or under the end-time of 1:20 minutes. SOF commercials have *prominent audio end-cues.* A 10-second commercial spot may cost the client $10,000. For that much money, your client expects, and should get, his full 10 seconds' worth. Cutting a second off a commercial, simply because you missed the end

---

9·38   Director's Cues: Example.

Audio	Video	Your Actions
Newscaster finishes preceding story and intros film.	Newscaster	Watch for the word in the script you marked for a roll cue (assuming you use a 4-start).
Speaks cue word.	The telecine preview monitor shows the academy leader flash by.	*Roll film. Four—three—two—one—take F-one.*
Newscaster reads the copy over the silent film off camera.	The film appears on the line monitor.	Start your stopwatch. You read along with the newscaster in your script. Now *don't* take your film timing from the newscaster's narration. He may be off with his timing and finish his narration after the film has already ended. Look at your *stopwatch.* Give warning cues. *Thirty seconds to one* (assuming that camera 1 will be coming back on the newscaster).
The newscaster should have reached the end of the voice-over narration.	The newscaster is on the line monitor.	When your stopwatch* reads 45 (elapsed) seconds, you give the *ten seconds to one* cue. At 55 (elapsed) seconds you give your *ready one* cue. And an experienced director cuts to 1 at 57, or even 56 seconds, figuring in the delay from signal to switching execution by the T.D. *Take one.*

* Assuming that you use a standard stopwatch, or run your digital watch in the forward mode.

cue and don't want to be caught with a blank screen, can be a costly mistake.

The old, and foolproof, method of cue-marking a film with a special punch that puts tiny holes into the corner of a few film frames, is no longer used. The FCC declared any cuing devices that show up on the home screen illegal. Although the cue marks are supposed to appear as white dots in the extreme corner of the film frame so that they would not be seen on the home screen (because of the picture area loss through transmission), many of them were nevertheless visible. Since the risk of getting the cue marks on the air, and thereby violating FCC regulations, is fairly great, most stations have abandoned this type of film cuing.

As pointed out in the section on film projectors, you can use *automatic* start and end cues for self-cuing the projector to start and stop at a specified place. You simply put a small piece of conductive pressure-sensitive tape on the film, which is then read by the projector's self-cuing device. In computer-assisted operations, the film projectors are usually started and stopped and the film is put on the air at the appropriate time by computer.

If you are on camera, you will receive the roll cues for the start of the film and the necessary end cues from the floor manager. However, especially when reading narration over a silent film, you may want to use a stopwatch to time yourself to the length of the film.

Most film scripts written for local stations have no particular format. They consist of double-spaced typewritten commentary that matches the lengths of the individual film scenes and consequently the overall length of the film. You should obviously prescreen each film so that you can practice the voice-over narration and your timing, and, in case of a film breakdown, continue with a fairly accurate ad lib commentary.

Most news films from major news services

9·39 If you still use the cue-marking system, you should put two marks on the film, either in the upper or lower righthand corner. The first cue is a warning cue, and appears as a white dot anywhere from four to two seconds before the end of the film. The second cue mark appears as close to the end of the film as possible.

For cue marking you must use a special cue marker. There are several types available, some of which look like a train conductor's ticket puncher. Most cue markers perforate four frames of the film with round or triangular holes. It is best to start by placing the last cue mark about four inches from the end of the film. The first cue mark is then placed ahead of the second, at a distance depending entirely on the time span desired between cues (usually four seconds).

9·40 Film Script.

Color

<u>AUTOMOBILE SPEED AND CONTROL WITH DAN WHITE</u>

(Running Time   :60 sec.)

VIDEO	TIME	AUDIO
DAN WHITE IN DRAGSTER	:06	MY NAME IS <u>DAN</u> <u>WHITE</u> AND I USE SPEED AND CONTROL TO MAKE MY LIVING, LIKE THIS.....
BURN OUT	:04	(WILD SOUNDS OF DRAG RACING)
DAN WHITE'S TROPHY ROOM	:09	WITHOUT GOING FAST, ALL THESE TROPHIES WOULDN'T BE HERE. WITHOUT CONTROL, I WOULDN'T BE HERE. YOU <u>KNOW</u> WHAT COMES FIRST.
D.O.T. REPORT	:12	AN INDIANA UNIVERSITY STUDY FOR THE DE-PARTMENT OF TRANSPORTATION REPORTS THAT FOUR OUT OF FIVE ACCIDENTS ARE CAUSED BY DRIVERS WHO DON'T HAVE THEIR HEAD OR THEIR VEHICLE UNDER CONTROL.
RACE	:03	SPEED IS IMPORTANT ON A DRAGSTRIP.
TRUCK AND TRAILER	:02	BUT WHEN I'M DRIVING ON THE ROAD TO A RACE....
FAMILY CAR	:06	OR JUST DRIVING MY FAMILY TO THE STORE I TRAVEL AT SAFE REASONABLE SPEEDS.
DRAG ACTION	:08	DON'T TAKE CHANCES AT INTERSECTIONS. WHEN RACING, IF I JUMP THE YELLOW LIGHT I'M A LOSER.
NEAR ACCIDENT	:04	IF YOU JUMP THE YELLOW LIGHT, CHANCES ARE YOU'LL BE A LOSER.
DAN WHITE'S TROPHY ROOM	:06	YOU MAY NOT HAVE TO WIN TO MAKE A LIVING, BUT YOU SURE HAVE TO LIVE TO BE A WINNER.

:60

come supplied with scripts of standard format, indicating the picture sequence, the running film footage, and the running film time *(see 9.40)*. Even if you did not have time to prescreen and are forced to read the copy "cold" (without rehearsing) or "blind" (without even seeing the film in a monitor), you can still match your narration to the film pretty well simply by watching the elapsed time on your stopwatch.

Summary

Almost all television programs derive from either videotape or film.

Videotape is used principally for (1) time delay, (2) building of a whole show by assembling parts that have been recorded at different times and/or locations, (3) duplication and distribution of programs, and (4) records for reference and study.

There are two basic systems of videotape recording: (1) the transverse scanning process, or the quadruplex video recording system, and (2) the helical, or slant-track, recording system. The quadruplex videotape recorder (VTR) normally puts four different tracks on the 2-inch wide videotape: (1) the video track, (2) the audio track, (3) the cue or address track, and (4) the control track. Most small-format (1-inch or less tape width) helical videotape recorders put three tracks on the videotape: (1) the video track, (2) the audio track, and (3) the control track. With the exception of the 2-inch helical scan videotape recorders, the quadruplex recorders produce higher quality videotapes than the helical scan recorders.

There are three basic types of video recording devices: (1) reel-to-reel videotape recorders, (2) video cassette and cartridge machines, and (3) video discs.

When a program or program segment is videotaped, the program and each segment are preceded by a video leader, which gives program identification and technical references for video and audio.

Film is used principally as (1) motion picture features, (2) television film features, (3) news films, (4) local features, and (5) commercials.

Major film specifications include the width of the film and whether or not it includes sound. Film is generally labeled according to its width: 8mm and Super-8mm, 16mm, and 35mm. It can be silent, with no accompanying sound printed on it, or it can be SOF (sound on film) whereby the film carries an audio track alongside the pictures. SOF can be optical or magnetic.

The basic film chain, or island, consists of at least one film projector (usually 16mm for small stations), a slide projector, a multiplexer, and a telecine, or television film, camera.

These are the major operational factors for film use: (1) film quality check and storage, (2) film projection, and (3) film cuing and timing.

Like the videotape leader, the SMPTE, or academy, leader, aids in accurate cuing and picture alignment before the film is actually projected. For film projectors with automatic start- and end-cue devices, the academy leader is generally omitted.

Picturization, or Editing

In the last chapter, we talked about some of the machinery available for the recording and editing of television programs, and the technical processes of the recording and editing with videotape and film.

In this chapter we will attempt to give a brief introduction to the processes of editing, which we call picturization, and how the machines can be used. Picturization means the control and structuring of a sequence of shots. Specifically, these points are especially pertinent in the context of television production: (1) transition devices and their functions, including the cut, dissolve, fade, and wipe; (2) switching, or instantaneous editing, with a multicamera setup, and the switcher and its operation in continuity and complexity editing; and (3) postproduction work with emphasis on splicing silent and sound film, and electronic videotape editing with both simple machines and complex, computer-assisted systems.

In Chapter 4 we dealt with picture composition, the framing of a single shot, which is often referred to as *visualization*. Now we will turn our attention to the process of *picturization*, the control or the structuring of a *shot sequence*. Sometimes the whole process of picturization is called editing.

But while picturization includes all aspects of controlling a shot sequence so that it becomes a structural whole—such as its rhythmic continuity, and the various phases of its composition and how they relate, or even lead, from shot to shot—editing more accurately describes the process of selecting the shots and putting them together. Since a detailed discussion of picturization is beyond the scope of this book, we will limit our discussion to three basic factors: (1) transition devices, (2) switching, or instantaneous editing, and (3) postproduction editing.[1]

---

[1] For more information on picturization, see Herbert Zettl, *Sight-Sound-Motion* (Belmont, Calif.: Wadsworth Publishing Co., 1973), pp. 292–324.

Transition Devices

Whenever you put two shots together, you need a transition between them, a device that leads us to perceive the two shots as relating to each other in some specific way. There are four basic transition devices: (1) the cut, (2) the dissolve, (3) the fade, and (4) the wipe. All four have the same basic purpose: to provide an acceptable link from shot to shot. However, each one differs somewhat from the others in its function; that is, how we are to perceive the transition in a shot sequence.

The Cut

The cut is an instantaneous change from one image (shot) to another. It is the most common and least obtrusive transition device. The cut itself is not visible; all you see are the preceding and following shots. It resembles most closely the changing field of the human eye. Try to look from one object to another, one located some distance from the other. Notice that you don't look at things in

---

A-B Rolling Preparation of a film for printing. All odd-numbered shots are put on one reel (A-roll), with black leader replacing the even shots. The even-numbered shots, with black leader replacing the odd shots, make up the B-roll. Both rolls are then printed together onto one film, thus eliminating splices.

Address Also called birthmark. A specific location in a television recording, as specified by the time code.

Assemble Mode The adding of shots on videotape in a consecutive order.

Bus, or Buss A row of buttons on the switcher. Sometimes called bank.

Complexity Editing The juxtaposition of shots that primarily, though not exclusively, help to intensify the screen event.

Continuity Editing The preserving of visual continuity from shot to shot.

Cut The instantaneous change from one shot (image) to another.

Cutaway Shot A shot of an object or event that is peripherally connected with the overall event and that is neutral as to screen direction (usually straight-on shots). Used to intercut between two shots in which the screen direction is reversed.

Cut Bar A button or small metal bar that activates the mix buses alternately. The effect is cutting between the two mix buses.

Dissolve A gradual transition from shot to shot, whereby the two images temporarily overlap. Also called lap-dissolve, or lap.

between (as you would in a pan) but that your eyes jump from one place to the other, as in a cut.

The cut (like all other transition devices) is basically used for the clarification and intensification of an event. *Clarification* means that you show the viewer the event as clearly as possible. For example, in an interview show, the guest holds up the book she has written. In order to help the viewer see better, to identify the title of the book, you cut to a closeup.

Intensification means that you sharpen the impact of the screen event. In an extreme long shot, for example, a football tackle might look quite tame; when seen as a tight closeup, however, the action reveals its brute force. Through cutting to the closeup, the action has been intensified.

The main reasons for using a cut are: (1) To continue action. If the camera can no longer follow the action, you cut to another shot that *continues* the action. (2) To reveal detail. As indicated above, if you want to see *more event detail* than the present shot reveals, you cut to a closer shot. (3)

10·1 A shot is the smallest convenient visual unit in film and television. It is generally the interval between two distinct video transitions, such as cuts, dissolves, or fades.

Double Re-entry   A complex switcher through which an effect can be fed back into the mix bus section, or the mix output into the effects section, for further effects manipulation.

Editing   The selection and assembly of shots within the picturization concept.

Effects Bus   Rows of buttons that can generate a number of electronic effects, such as keys, wipes, and mattes.

Electronic A-B Rolling
1. The editing of a master tape from two playback machines, one containing the A-roll and the other the B-roll. By routing the A and B playback machines through a switcher, a variety of transition effects can be achieved for the final master tape.
2. The projection of an SOF film on one film chain (A-roll), with the silent film projected from the other island (B-roll). The films can be mixed through the switcher.

Electronic Editing   The joining of two shots on videotape without cutting the tape.

Fade   The gradual appearance of a picture from black (fade-in) or disappearance to black (fade-out).

Fader Bars   Two levers on the switcher that can produce dissolves, fades, and wipes of different speeds, and superimpositions.

To change place and time. A cut from an interior to the street indicates that the *locale* has now *shifted* to the street. In live television, a cut cannot reveal a change in time. But as soon as the event has been recorded on film or videotape, a cut can mean a jump *forward or backward in the event time,* or to another event that takes place in a different place at the same time (the "meanwhile back-at-the-ranch" cut). (4) To change impact. A cut to a tighter shot generally *intensifies* the screen event; a cut to a longer shot reduces the event impact. (5) To establish an event rhythm. Through cutting, you can establish an *event rhythm.* Fast cutting generally gives the impression of excitement; slow cutting that of calm and tranquility (assuming that the content of the screen material expresses the same feeling).

The Dissolve

The dissolve, or lap-dissolve, or simply "lap," is a gradual transition from shot to shot, whereby the two images temporarily overlap. While the cut itself cannot be seen on the screen, the dissolve is a clearly visible transition. As such, it constitutes not merely a method of joining two shots together as unobtrusively as possible, but *represents a visual element* in its own right. You should, therefore, use the dissolve with greater discretion than the cut.

Basically, you use a dissolve (1) as a smooth bridge for action, (2) to indicate a change of locale or time, and (3) to indicate a strong relationship between two images.

For an interesting and *smooth transition* from a wide shot of a dancer to a closeup, for instance, simply dissolve from one camera to the other. The movements will temporarily blend into each other and indicate the strong association between the two shots. The action is not interrupted at all.

Where the mood or tempo of the presentation does not allow hard cuts, you can use dissolves to get from a long shot to a closeup or from a closeup to a long shot. A closeup of a soloist, for

---

Film Base   The shiny side of the film.

Film Emulsion   The dull side of the film.

Film Splicer   The piece of equipment with which two lengths of film can be joined.

Frame   1. The smallest picture unit in film, a single picture. 2. A complete scanning cycle of the electron beam, which occurs every 1/30 second. It represents the smallest complete television picture unit.

Generation   The number of dubs away from the master tape. A first-generation dub is struck directly from the master tape; a second-generation tape is a dub of the first-generation dub (two steps away from the master tape), and so forth. The greater the number of generations, the greater the quality loss.

Hard Copy   A computer printout showing in typewritten form all editing decisions of the completed helical scan workprint or the quadruplex master tape. (Soft-copy information appears only on the computer screen.)

Insert Mode   The inserting of shots in an already existing recording, without affecting the shots on either side.

Instantaneous Editing   Same as switching.

instance, can be dissolved into a long shot of the whole choir, which may be more appropriate than an instantaneous cut.

You can use a dissolve during continuous music. This is at least one way to change cameras in the middle of musical phrases when it would be awkward to cut.

You may prefer to indicate a *change of locale* by dissolving rather than cutting to the new set area. A *change of time* can also be suggested by a slow dissolve (long time lapse, slow dissolve; short time lapse, fast dissolve).

Matched dissolves are used for decorative effects or to indicate an especially *strong relationship* between two objects. For instance, a decorative use would be a sequence of two fashion models hiding behind sun umbrellas. Model one closes her sequence by hiding behind an umbrella; model two starts her sequence the same way. You can now match-dissolve from camera 1 to camera 2. Both cameras must frame the umbrellas approximately the same way before the dissolve. An

example of an associative use is a closeup of a door in a very expensive dwelling match-dissolved to a closeup of a door in an old shack.

Depending on the overall rhythm of the event, you can use slow or fast dissolves. A very fast one functions almost like a cut and is, therefore, called a "soft cut."

Since dissolves are so readily available to you in television, you may be tempted to use them more often than necessary or even desirable. Don't overuse them; they create no rhythmic beat. Your presentation will lack precision and accent, and bore the viewer.

The Fade

In a fade, the picture either goes gradually to black (fade-out) or appears gradually on the screen from black (fade-in).

You use the fade to signal a definite beginning (fade-in) or end (fade-out) of a scene. Like the curtain in the theater, it defines the beginning and

---

Jump Cut Cutting between shots that are identical in subject yet slightly different in screen location. Through the cut, the subject seems to jump from one screen location to another for no apparent reason.

Mix Bus Rows of buttons that permit the "mixing" of video sources, as in a dissolve and super. Major buses for on-the-air switching.

Montage The juxtaposition of two (often seemingly unrelated) shots in order to generate a third, overall idea, which may not be contained in either of the two.

Off-Line Helical scan editing system for producing computer-assisted videotape workprints. The workprint information is then fed into the on-line system for (automated) production of the release master tape.

On-Line A computer-assisted master editing system, using quadruplex videotape recorders for high-band release master tapes.

Picturization The control and structuring of a shot sequence.

end of a portion of a screen event. As such, it is technically not a true transition.

Some experts use the term *cross-fade* for a quick fade to black followed immediately by a fade-in to the next image. Here the fade acts as a transition device, decisively separating the preceding and following images from each other. The cross-fade is also called a "dip to black."

If you fade one of the two pictures of a superimposition to black, you have a *split fade.*

In general, start each program by fading in the camera picture from black. The fade *from* black always indicates a beginning.

The fade *to* black suggests a complete separation of program elements. It usually indicates that one program element has come to an end. You should end every program by taking it to black. If you have to insert a commercial message in your program, you may want to go to black before the commercial, not so much to warn the viewer of the upcoming distraction as to tell him that this

is a segment not directly connected with the material of the show.

You can also use a fade to black in an emergency. Rather than showing the viewer all the details of a collapsing set, take the picture to black until the emergency has passed or until you have put up a "one moment, please" stand-by sign.

Be careful not to go to black too often; your program continuity will be interrupted too many times by fades that all suggest final endings. The other extreme is the "never-go-to-black" craze. Some directors won't dare go to black for fear of giving the viewer a chance to switch to another channel. If a constant dribble of program material is the only way to keep a viewer glued to the set, the program content, rather than the presentation techniques, should be examined.

The Wipe

In a wipe, one picture seems to push the other off the screen. This is such an unabashed transition

---

Postproduction Any production activity that occurs after (post) the production. Usually refers either to editing of film or videotape or to postscoring and mixing sound for later addition to the picture portion.

Postproduction Editing The assembly of recorded material after the actual production.

Preview Bus Rows of buttons that can direct an input to the preview monitor at the same time another video source is on the air.

Program Bus The bus on a switcher whose inputs are directly switched to the line-out.

Roll-Through Keeping the film (or tape) rolling while temporarily cutting back to another video source (usually a live camera).

Splice The spot where two shots are actually joined, or the act of joining two shots. Generally used only when the material (such as film or audiotape) is physically cut and glued (spliced) together again.

device that it must be classified as a special effect. There is a great variety of wipe configurations available (*see 11.13,* page 304). Like the fade, the wipe generally signals the end of one scene and the beginning of another. Unlike the fade, it does not put a permanent stop to the show; it simply pushes on the next video sequence. As a special effect, it seems rather obvious to treat the wipe with the utmost care. Use it sparingly, and only after you are convinced that no other transition could do the job better.

In television, all these transition devices are easily accomplished through the switcher. In film, a cut can be accomplished by simply cutting the film at one point and gluing (splicing) it onto another piece. All other devices must be done in the film laboratory during the printing process.

Therefore, special transition devices in film are not only much harder to accomplish technically, but they also prove much more expensive than in television.

Switching, or Instantaneous Editing

Whether you do a live television show, or record your show or show sections on videotape, you usually work with two or more video sources, such as two studio cameras and a film chain. The switching from one video source to another—such as cutting from one camera to the viewpoint of another, or from the live camera picture to a slide—while the show or a show segment is in progress represents *instantaneous editing.* Contrary to film or videotape editing, where you have ample time to deliberate exactly where and with what transition device to combine two shots, switching in a live situation demands instantaneous decisions. The decision for a cut and the execution of the cut are virtually simultaneous.

The technical device that makes such instantaneous editing possible is the *video switcher.* We will

Stock Shot A shot of a common occurrence—clouds, storm, traffic, crowds—that can be repeated in a variety of contexts since its qualities are typical. There are stock-shot libraries from which any number of such shots can be obtained.

Super Short for superimposition, the simultaneous showing of two full pictures on the same screen.

Switching A change from one video source to another during a show, or show segment, with the aid of a switcher.

Time Code Also called the SMPTE Time Code, or address code. An electronic signal recorded on the cue track of the videotape through a time code generator, providing a time "address" (birthmark) for each frame in hours, minutes, seconds, and frame numbers of elapsed tape.

Vector Line A dominant direction established between two people facing each other or through a prominent movement in a specific direction.

Wipe Electronic effect where one picture seems to push the other off the screen. (In film, an optical wipe can be accomplished in the special effects printer.)

now briefly describe (1) its basic layout and functions and (2) its basic operation.

Layout and Functions

Video switchers can be relatively simple or extremely complex in their production function and electronic design. However, even the most complex, all digital-controlled video switching system performs the same basic functions as a simple production switcher. The complex ones can perform more visual tricks than the simple ones, and with greater reliability and stability.

These are the *basic functions* of a production switcher: (1) to provide the fundamental transition methods between video sources: cut, dissolve, fade, wipe; (2) to create special effects: wipe patterns, key and matte inserts; and (3) to permit previewing of any video source or special effect before it is switched on the air.

Some of the more complex switchers perform an additional function: the automatic switching of program audio with the video (called "audio-follow-video"). The audio-follow-video switchers are especially important for master control switching, where you must switch from a live studio show to a commercial on videotape to network. When you switch from studio to VTR to network, you simply press the respective buttons for "studio," "VTR," and "network." The audio from these sources is automatically switched with the video. No special audio board operator is therefore necessary.

Let's look at a simple switcher that will perform the most basic production functions: a cut or dissolve from one video source to another (studio camera to studio camera, or studio camera to film, or studio camera to VTR); a fade from black and to black; a superimposition (one image overlaps the other, like stopping a dissolve in the middle); and a preview of the video source before it is actually put on the air. *(See 10.2.)*

As you can see in figure 10.2, there are four rows of buttons, or buses, as they are called. There is a *program bus,* two *mix buses* (mix bus A and mix bus B), and a *preview bus.* Their arrangement varies greatly with different types of switchers. The preview bus, for example, may be right above the program bus *(see 10.7).* Each bus has buttons for cameras 1 and 2, film (representing the film island with any one of two film projectors or a slide projector), VTR for videotape, and remote, which is an auxiliary input for any additional video source needed, such as a second VTR or film island, or an actual remote feed. Then there is a black button, which puts the screen to black. The preview and program buses have an additional mix button. Let's find out what the individual buses and their buttons can do. We will work from the bottom up, starting with the program bus.

Program Bus   The program bus represents in effect a selector switch for the line-out. It is a direct input-output link. Whatever button you press will send its designated video input (such as camera 1 or VTR) to the line-out.

The mix button represents the input from whatever comes down from the mix buses. If, for example, you press the mix button on the program bus, but no button is pressed on either mix bus, no video source will go to the line-out. If you press the camera 1 button on mix bus A (assuming that the fader bars are in the bus A position as in figure 10.2), with the mix button already pressed on the program bus, camera 1 will be on the air. Disregarding the mix button for a moment, you could accomplish simple cuts among cameras 1 and 2, film, and VTR, and black with the program bus only. For example, if you press the camera 1 button on the program bus, camera 1 will be on the air. If you now press the camera 2 button, camera 2's picture will instantly replace camera 1's image on the screen. In effect you have

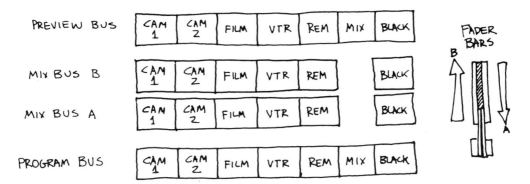

10·2 Basic Switcher: This simple switcher has four buses: a program bus, two mix buses, and a preview bus. Also, it has a pair of fader bars that can be pushed either individually or together into the mix bus A or B position. The program bus switches the inputs (cameras 1 and 2, film, VTR, remote) directly to the line-out. The mix buses go to the line-out, if the mix button on the program bus is punched up. The mix buses make possible the mixing of two inputs, as in a dissolve or super. Through the preview bus, any input can be previewed on a special monitor before being punched up on the air. The fader bars accomplish the mixing of two sources (dissolves, supers) and fades.

cut from camera 1 to camera 2. If you now press the black button, the screen will go to black instantly. In order to provide you with more transition possibilities than just simple cuts, such as dissolves and fades, and even such simple effects as a superimposition, we need, however, two additional buses, the mix buses (at least in our switcher design).

Mix Buses The mix A and mix B buses allow you to mix the images from two sources, such as the temporary mixing (overlapping) of camera 1 and camera 2 in a dissolve, or the total overlapping of the two cameras in a super. The *fader bars* gradually activate either bus A or bus B, depending on how far you move them toward the bus A position or the bus B position. The fader bars function as a pot (or fader) does on the audio

10·3 *Production switcher* refers to the switcher that is located in the control room of a studio or remote van. There are other switchers that simply assign videotape machines or film island to specific studios or monitors. These *assignment switchers* are distinct from the production switcher and will not be discussed here.

10·4 As in the audio control board, the line-out in video means that the selected (picture) material is sent to master control and distributed from there to the desired destination, such as the transmitter or a VTR machine. For the sake of convenience, we say that whatever is sent to the line-out is put "on the air."

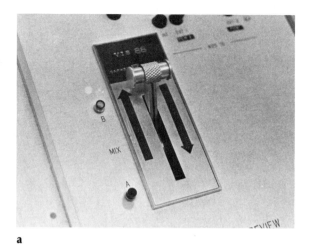

a

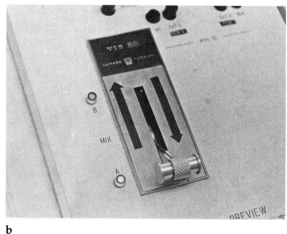

b

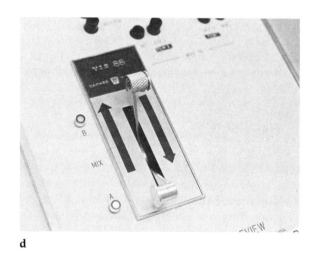

c

d

10·5 (a) With both fader bars in the up position, B bus is activated. (b) With both fader bars in the down position, A bus is activated. (c) With the fader bars split, with fader bar B in the B bus position and fader bar A in the A bus position, both buses are activated. If a video source is punched up on either bus, we will have a superimposition. (d) With the fader bars split against their direction (the B bar in the A bus position, and the A bar in the B bus position) neither of the mix buses will be activated. The screen remains in black. A warning: this method works only if the signal entering the switcher is noncomposite, which means that the video signal is without the sync signal. If your video signal is composite (with the sync signal), the overload may cause severe damage to the switcher.

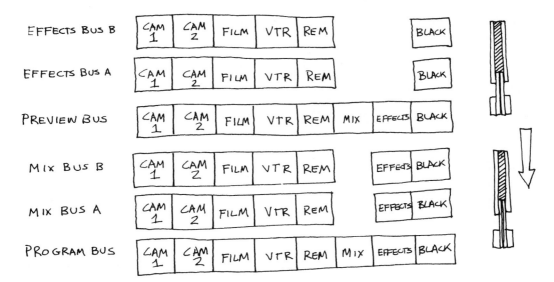

10·6 Switcher with Special Effects: In this case, the program bus, mix, and preview buses have an additional effects button, which assigns the effects buses to preview or the line-out.

board, except, of course, that the fader bars control the fading in or out of the picture, while the audio pot regulates the fading in and out, or mixing, of sound.

As you can see in figure 10.5, there are left and right fader bars, which can be moved independently, or both together. Since in most mixing tasks they are moved in unison, they have a locking device that keeps them together. In our simple switcher, the left bar activates mix bus B, the right bar mix bus A. When you move both levers in unison up to mix bus B, the left fader activates the B bus, while the A bus is deactivated (the A fader is away from the A bus in the B position) *(10.5a).* When you bring both faders down to the A bus position, the right A fader activates the A bus, while the left B fader, which is away from the B bus, has deactivated the B bus *(10.5b).* If you split the levers and move the left fader into the

B bus position and the right fader into the A bus position, you have activated both buses. In effect, you are sending whatever button is pressed on the B bus and on the A bus to the line-out simultaneously. On the line monitor the two video sources would appear as a superimposition *(10.5c).* If you move the left fader down to the A bus position, and the right fader up to the B position, you would deactivate both buses; the result would be a black screen *(10.5d).* How a dissolve, a fade-in or fade-out, and superimpositions are accomplished on our simple switcher will be discussed in the section on switcher operations.

Preview Bus The preview bus functions almost the same as the program bus, except that its line-out does not go on the air or to a recording device, but simply to a preview monitor. If, for example, you press the camera 1 button on your preview

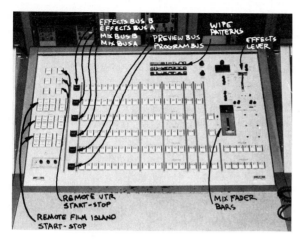

10·7 Large Production Switcher (Studio 1, San Francisco State University).

bus, that camera's image will appear on the preview monitor, regardless of what the line monitor shows. If you press film, you can, for example, preview the academy leader countdown before you switch the actual film on the air on your mix or program bus. When you press the mix button, you can preview whatever you have punched up on the mix bus or buses, including a superimposition.

Additional Buses More complex switchers have additional buses for effects, such as key and wipe effects. (We will discuss the electronic effects in Chapter 11.)

As you can see, the number of buttons and buses increases drastically the more complex a switcher gets. In order to reduce the number of buses so that one person can operate it without totally losing his or her sanity, many of the more complex production switchers combine the mix and effects buses. You can then assign to the bus either a mixing or special effects function (or mode). *(See 10.8.)*

With the expanded special effects on a large production switcher, you can insert the picture from one camera, such as lettering for a title, into a base picture (the picture from another camera), a process called *keying.* Then, if you like, you can fill the cut-out letters (usually white) with any one of a variety of background colors or shades of gray, or even with parts of an image from a third camera through a process called *matting.* You can also accomplish a variety of wipes, depending on the number and configurations of wipe patterns provided by your switcher. (See Chapter 11 for more detail on such special effects.)

Large production switchers also have at least one additional pair of fader bars for the control of special effects. Also, with a complex switcher (such as a "double re-entry" switcher, into which the effects are fed back twice for further manipulation) you can dissolve out of, or into, a split-screen or a keyed title, for example. With a less complex switcher, you can only take—that is, cut to—such effects.

Most switchers contain, or have close to them, remote start and stop buttons for VTR's and telecine equipment *(see 10.7).*

Some switchers contain a *cut bar.* This is a large button that will cut back and forth between two video sources as preset on the mix buses each time you press it. You could, of course, accomplish the same thing by pressing the buttons representing these video sources on the activated mix or program bus. In very fast cutting, the cut bar is a little easier to operate than the mix bus.

Operation

Using our simple switcher in figure 10.2, how could you achieve a cut, a dissolve, a super, a fade? Let's do some basic switching exercises.

Cut If you were to cut exclusively between two sources, without fading or dissolving, you could

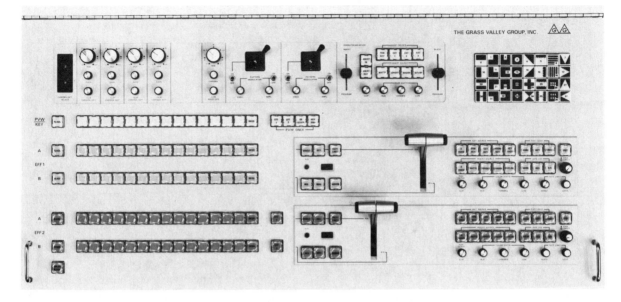

10·8 Large Grass Valley Production Switcher: On large production switchers, the various switching modes can be assigned to the buses, such as preview and key (top bus) and effects and mix (effects 1 and 2 buses).

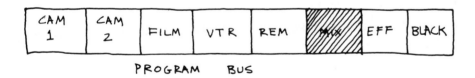

10·9 The mix button on the program bus activates the mix buses.

do the entire switching on the program bus. But as you know, the program starts and ends usually with a fade, and most programs contain one or more dissolves. Usually, we transfer our switching to the mix section, regardless of the types of transition devices contained in the show.

To connect the mix buses to the line-out, you first press the mix button on your program bus *(10.9)*. If nothing has been pressed on the mix bus,

or if both black buttons are punched up on the mix buses, the line monitor will remain in black.

Now you are operating in the mix bus section. You need to pay close attention to the location of the fader bars. If they are in the down position, mix bus A is activated (on our switcher) and you must do your simple cutting on mix bus A. If the fader bars are up in the mix bus B position, you must do your cutting on mix bus B *(10.10)*.

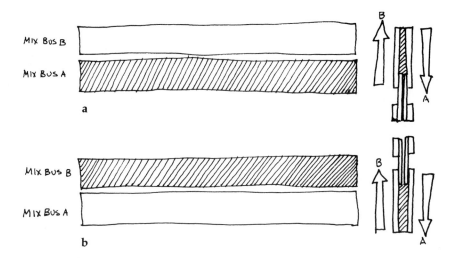

10·10 (a) Fader bars in the down position activate mix bus A *(see 10.5b)*. (b) Fader bars in the up position activate mix bus B *(see 10.5a)*.

Let's work with the fader bars in the down, bus A, position. The director says, *Ready one.* This means that a cut to camera 1 is coming up, in this case a take from black to camera 1. You should be ready to press the camera 1 button on mix bus A. *Take one.* You simply press the camera 1 button, bus A, and camera 1's picture will appear on the line monitor. If camera 1 doesn't show up on the line monitor, you may have missed one or both of these important preceding switching steps: (1) to press the mix button on the program bus, and (2) to have the faders in the bus A (down) position.

If you now want to cut to camera 2, simply press the camera 2 button on the same (mix A) bus. If you want to cut from camera 1 to film, simply press the film button instead of the camera 2 button. *(See 10.11.)*

In order to cut back to camera 1, simply press the camera 1 button again. If you want to see what camera 2 has to offer you before you take it (assuming now that camera 1 is on the air), simply press the camera 2 button on your preview bus. Camera 2 will now appear on your preview monitor. If you like what you see (especially in relation

to camera 1's image), you can take camera 2 by pressing the camera 2 button on mix bus A. In case the mix buses fail you completely because of a technical problem, you can simply press the camera 2 button on your program bus and thus put the camera back on the air. Remember to press the mix button again on your program bus before you resume switching in the mix bus section.

Dissolve   For a dissolve from camera 1 to camera 2, press the camera 2 button on bus B while camera 1 is already punched up on bus A (and on the air, since the fader bars are still in the down position, activating bus A) *(see 10.12a, b)*. Now move both fader bars up to the B position *(see 10.12c, d)*. Depending on how fast you move the levers to the bus B position, your dissolve will be either slow or fast. In any case, while you are moving the bars from A to B, you will gradually fade out camera 1's picture on bus A, while simultaneously fading in camera 2's picture on bus B. Once your fader bars are in the B position, only camera 2's picture will be on the air. The dissolve is finished.

If you stop the dissolve halfway between the A and B buses, you have a superimposition. If you

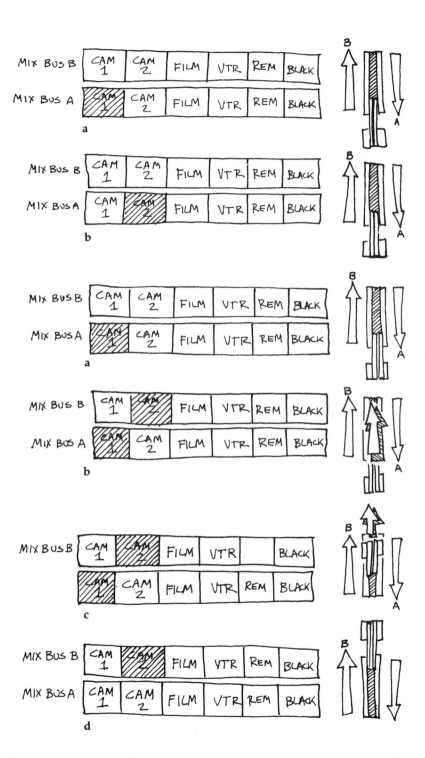

10·11 (a) With the A bus activated (both fader bars are down), the camera 1 button will put camera 1 on the air. (b) By pressing the camera 2 button, you accomplish a cut from camera 1 to camera 2.

10·12 (a) Camera 1 is on the air on bus A. (b) For a dissolve, you now punch up camera 2 on bus B. Nothing will happen as yet, since bus B is not activated (the fader bars are in the A bus position). (c) By bringing up the fader bars into the bus B position, you will cause camera 1 gradually to fade out, as camera 2 fades in. In the middle position of the fader bars, both buses are activated; at this stage, the dissolve is identical to a superimposition. (d) With the fader bars all the way in the B bus position, bus A is deactivated (with camera 1 no longer visible on the screen) with only camera 2 remaining on the B bus. The dissolve has been completed.

10·13 Split Fader Bars for Super: With the fader bars split in the direction of their assigned buses (fader A to bus A and fader B to bus B) a super can be achieved with more than half the signal strength for each image. This technique will give you more control over the signal strength for each of the images, especially if one or both of the two pictures are less than full signal strength to begin with.

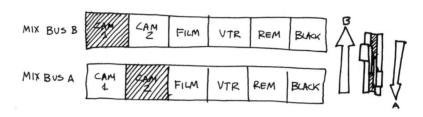

10·14 Fade: Camera 2 on bus B is faded in (from black). In effect, you "dissolve" from black (bus A) to camera 2 on bus B. If the fader bars are moved from bus B to bus A, you fade to black.

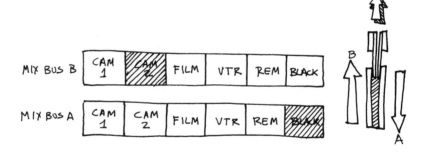

want to preview the super, simply press the mix button on your preview bus.

Super As we have just indicated, you can accomplish a superimposition by stopping a dissolve halfway between buses A and B *(see 10.12c)*. Both buses will be activated, each delivering a picture with exactly one-half video (signal strength). Most supers are accomplished this way. Another method, which provides for a little more control of picture strength for each individual video source (camera picture) is the splitting of

the levers and moving up the B fader bar, with the A fader bar remaining in the bus A position. If the full-strength bus A picture (camera 1) is too strong, you can move the A fader bar up toward the B bus a little, thus reducing its intensity somewhat *(10.13)*.

Fade You can fade in a picture on either bus by moving the fader bars from one mix bus, on which the black button has been punched up, to the other bus with the desired source punched up. Try to fade up on camera 2 from black. Assume that the fader bars are both in the bus A position. How would you do it? You can check your switching on figure 10.14. Bus A is activated by both fader bars in the A position. The line monitor shows black, since the bus A black button is punched up. On the B bus, you punch up the camera 2 button. Now move both fader bars up to the B bus. Camera 2 will gradually fade in from black. Going to black works in reverse. If you want to go from a video source to black, simply punch up the black button on the nonactivated bus and literally "dissolve" to black.

Special effects switching is similar to switching in the mix bus section. Special buttons control the *special effects mode* (wipe, key), the pattern of the wipe, and the matte configurations. For this kind of switching you either move to the special effects buses or assign the mix buses the special effects function. A special effects button on your preview bus shows the desired effect on the preview monitor, similar to the mix button that shows the specific mix (such as a super). We will discuss some of the special effects in Chapter 11.

Switching Principles

In switching, or instantaneous editing, we are, as in postproduction editing, basically concerned with two types of construction (1) continuity and (2) complexity. *Continuity editing* means the preserving of visual coherence from one shot to the next; it is basically concerned with the clarification of an event. *Complexity editing* means the selection and assembly of shots that primarily, though not exclusively, help to intensify the screen event.

For example, if you cannot follow a skier any longer with your on-the-air television camera, you must switch to another camera that has the skier in view. This type of cutting is indicative of continuity editing. You simply continue the ac-

tion from one shot to the next. If, however, you cut from a medium shot of the skier to a closeup of his legs in order to show the extreme strain he is undergoing while racing over rough terrain, you have begun with complexity editing.

In the following discussion, we will mention some of the major principles and conventions of continuity and complexity editing. Please realize that these principles are not absolutes. They work well under most circumstances, and are a basic part of the visual literacy of most television viewers and (hopefully) of television production personnel. However, depending on the event context or communication aim, some of the dos may easily become the don'ts and the don'ts the dos of editing.

Continuity Editing

In continuity cutting, you should try to preserve continuity in the *appearance* of the subject (sometimes called identification cutting), its *location* on the screen, and its screen *motion*.

Appearance   When cutting from camera to camera, try to keep the subject recognizable in each shot, avoiding any *extreme changes in distance or angles* that may prevent the viewer from readily identifying it or him. *(See 10.15 and 10.16.)* Cutting from an extreme long shot to an extreme closeup, or from extreme angles, makes for poor subject continuity. However, *don't cut* to nearly *identical shots* unless you want to repeat a certain picture sequence for effect. When you cut from one camera to another, the second camera shot should reveal the subject from a slightly different point of view. Why cut, if you show the viewer exactly the same thing? Two succeeding shots varying only slightly in viewpoint may produce a *jump cut,* in which the image merely shifts its position within the screen—for no apparent reason. If you cannot vary the shot, don't change it. Don't be

10·15 When you cut from an extreme long shot to a closeup, we may not be able to recognize exactly whose closeup it is. You should zoom in somewhat, or cut to a medium shot, before cutting to the closeup.

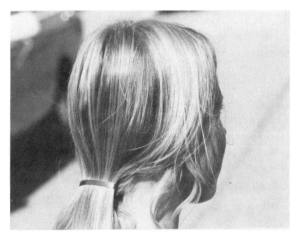

10·16 A similar problem arises if you cut from extreme angles. It is difficult for the viewer to tell exactly whether or not the reverse angle shot is of the same person.

afraid to stay on one camera, even for a relatively long period of time.

Location In order to make sense out of a series of shots, we try to locate—organize and stabilize in our mind—the picture field as much as possible. We tend to preserve continuity by remembering the relative screen positions of objects from one shot to the next. If, for example, you have two people talking to each other in an over-

10·17   When shooting closeups of two people conversing, bear in mind that the viewer expects them to remain in their relative screen positions. An abrupt position change would disturb the shot continuity.

the-shoulder two-shot, the viewer expects the people to remain in their relative screen positions even during closeups or reverse-angle shooting *(see 10.17 and 10.18).* By establishing a *vector line* —or, as it is also called, "line of conversation" —and keeping the cameras on one or the other side of it, you will avoid many confusing picturization mistakes. *(See 10.18.)*

But even if you establish and observe a main vector line, you can still violate the screen positions through improper placement of objects or subjects. In an interview in which a host talks with two or more guests, put the host, not in the middle, but to one side of the guests. Otherwise you will not be able to maintain proper screen positions. *(See 10.19 and 10.20.)*

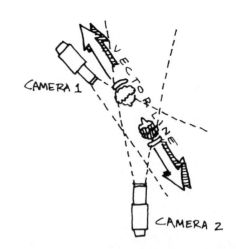

10·18 When two people face each other, you can draw an imaginary line, a vector line, connecting them. For closeups as well as over-the-shoulder shooting, keep both cameras on the same side of the vector line. Don't have one camera look at the scene from one side of it and the other camera from the other side.

Motion   When cutting on action and movement, you should try to continue the action as much as possible through the cut. Here are some of the major points to remember:

1.   When cutting on action, cut *during* the motion of the object or subject, not before or after it. For example, if you have a closeup of a person who is just preparing to rise from a chair, cut to a wider shot just after she has started to rise but before she stands. Or you let her almost finish the action on the closeup and then cut to a wider shot. A cut during action looks smooth and, if properly done, goes unnoticed.

2.   If you follow a moving object with a panning camera, don't cut to a stationary camera. Have the second camera panning too before you cut to it. Equally jarring is a cut from a stationary camera to a moving one. Remember that we are now speaking of *continuity editing.* In complexity editing, you may well use these don'ts in order to intensify the motion through a motion–no motion counterpoint.

10·19 If the host sits in the middle, you will not be able to maintain screen positions on subsequent two-shots. A cut from a three-shot to a two-shot with the guest on screen-left puts the host on the right side of the screen. A subsequent two-shot with the guest at screen-right will switch the host to screen-left.

3. A motion with a specific direction also forms a vector line. Therefore, don't cross this vector line with your cameras, or you will reverse the action on the screen when cutting. Hence, don't cut on lateral action from opposite sides, if you want to preserve continuity in screen direction *(10.21)*.

4. Sometimes the sound rhythm dictates certain cutting procedures. In an interview, the cut occurs generally at the end of a question or answer, since cutting at the end of a sentence or phrase produces a cleaner rhythm than in the middle. However, *reaction shots* are often smoother when they occur during, rather than at the end of, phrases or sentences. In any case, if someone moves while in the middle of delivering a speech, *cut on the action.* Don't wait until the performer has come to an appropriate point in his or her delivery. Action is usually the stronger motivation for a cut than dialogue.

In music, try to *cut with the beat.* Cuts are like visualized bars; they determine the beat of the visual sequence and keep the action rhythmically tight. Cutting against the beat in music generally does not produce increased

10·20 By isolating the host at one side of the guests, you will have no trouble maintaining screen positions. Keep the closeup of the host on the left side of the screen, since we remember his screen-left position from the previous shot.

tension through syncopation; rather it appears as sloppy switching. If the general rhythm of the music is casual or flowing, use dissolves instead of cuts.

Complexity Editing

Editing that is associated with the intensification of the screen event is generally more the province of postproduction editing, where you literally build up an intensified screen event from re-corded bits and pieces from one or several events. Nevertheless, there are possibilities for instantaneous complexity editing (switching a live event, even if the line-out leads to a videotape recorder rather than the transmitter) that include the use of (1) the closeup and extreme closeup, (2) zooms, (3) supers and keys, and other special effects, and (4) fast cutting.

Closeup Cutting to a closeup, or even extreme closeup, cannot fail to direct the viewer's atten-

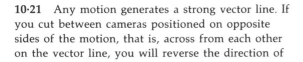

10·21 Any motion generates a strong vector line. If you cut between cameras positioned on opposite sides of the motion, that is, across from each other on the vector line, you will reverse the direction of the motion on the screen at each cut. Since such a reversal can become very confusing, you should keep all your cameras either on one or the other side of the vector line.

tion forcefully to event detail. Thus, the event is perceived more intensely than if shown in a medium or long shot. The closeup is an especially effective intensifier if the action remains largely internal, such as in a quandary of indecision, moments of extreme fear, or the supreme ecstasy of love.

Zoom   A fairly fast zoom-in on an event detail can be even more compelling than a simple cut to a closeup. In a zoom-in, the event is literally pushed into the viewer's lap. Be careful with such intensification devices: when overdone, the sensitive viewer will lose interest, simply as a defense against perceptual overkill.

Superimposition You can make a scene more complex by supering or keying two events or event details. If the actual event is highly complex, and not only justifies but demands a complex screen treatment, the portrayal of such complexity on the screen through multi-images can become a powerful intensification device. But don't super two images just because the original event is dull. In instantaneous editing you usually try to *reflect* the action and feeling of the actual event rather than constructing a new one, as in postproduction editing. For other special effects, see Chapter 11.

Cutting Fast cutting that reflects the fast pace of the event is also a powerful intensifier. Unfortunately, it is very difficult to do in switching. Unless you have twenty cameras in the field, your cutting will have to slow down after you have cut among the three or four available cameras, unless you are content to return to the same shots.

Of course the audio track, especially music, adds considerably to the intensification of a screen event.[2]

As pointed out before, complexity editing usually needs a careful and deliberate weighing of the available choices and their potential impact on the viewer. Yet switching a multicamera show rarely permits the time and overview necessary for the optimal choice. If, therefore, you intend to engage in intricate complexity editing, you should resort to postproduction editing.

Postproduction Editing

Postproduction editing means assembling shots and scenes that have been previously recorded on film or videotape into a meaningful whole. It is

so called because the editing takes place *after* (post) the production and not during it, as in switching. Editing this way offers some immediate advantages over instantaneous editing: (1) Once the material is recorded, you have more time to examine it and to ponder carefully over which of the shots should be included in the final edited show, and which should not. In switching, such deliberations are obviously extremely difficult, if possible at all. (2) You can reshoot some of the material if necessary, or draw on other sources to fill in missing shots, such as the *film stock library,* where you can obtain stock footage of airplane arrivals and takeoffs, clouds, crowd scenes, and others. (3) You have the opportunity—especially if you are engaged in complexity editing—of mixing a special sound track independently of the recorded video images for the final show.

Depending on the magnitude of the show project, the postproduction activity can take many times longer than the actual production. Some feature-film editors may spend a whole year, or more, on editing material that may have been shot in a few months.

In television production, especially in small station operation, you will not come across such ambitious postproduction jobs. Most often you are called upon to edit film or videotape material that has been shot for local news stories, documentaries, commercials, or an occasional ambitious entertainment show that proved too complex for one uninterrupted taping session. Film editing usually involves news films, locally produced documentaries, an occasional film commercial, and the cutting down of feature films to a reasonable length or inserting commercial spots in feature films.

Videotape editing spans a greater variety of show material. Generally, the videotaped scenes have been produced with a multicamera setup and have often been shot in the actual sequence, the first scene first, the second scene second, and

---

[2] Zettl, *Sight-Sound-Motion,* pp. 336–343, 358–373.

so on, with the closing shot last. In this case, videotape editing is merely a hooking together of shorter scenes onto a large reel.

However, many videotaped shows are produced in *film-style,* which means that only one television camera is used for all "takes" (shots), and that the shots are recorded not in their actual story sequence but according to production convenience. For example, if the opening and the closing scenes of the show occur in the same location, they are shot first, and the middle scenes later. We will talk more about film-style videotape later in this chapter.

Let us now briefly consider the areas of (1) editing principles (2) film editing, and (3) videotape editing. Before we go into any detail, you should realize that the art of editing cannot be mastered overnight. Indeed, editing—the building of screen space through a careful juxtaposition of visual and aural images—is as creative and challenging a task as directing. What we intend here is not to give an exhaustive treatment of the principles of editing but, rather, enough of an overview so that you can communicate intelligently with the editor, or perform simple editing jobs yourself without having to search elsewhere for basic references. But major editing should be left to the editing specialist.

Editing Principles

The principles of continuity and complexity editing, which we have discussed under switching, or instantaneous editing, apply of course also to the postproduction editing process. The basic aim of any editing process is to tell a story with clarity and impact.

Although there is a very basic aesthetic difference between film and the television image (film as a series of frozen pictures versus the evanescence of television scanning), we can discuss the postproduction principles for film and

10·22 Most feature films come already edited for television viewing before they reach the local station. Also, the places for the commercial inserts are usually labeled with a strip of film that says: "Place commercial here." If you don't want to "place your commercial there," you must clip out these commercial indicators before showing the film on the air.

10·23 Occasionally, in struggling with a show concept that calls for inventive, atypical complexity editing, you may find that you not only can, but must, violate many or all of the customary editing principles, such as continuity of action and screen direction. A jump cut, generally regarded as an editing mistake, may be just the right technique for portraying and intensifying a highly volatile situation, or a feeling of extreme anxiety and restlessness. But such exceptions do not render the common editing principles invalid. All this means is that even principles are *contextual;* their validity depends on the context, the specific circumstances, and communication purpose for which they are used.

television together; after all, both media are edited for the same small screen and the intimate atmosphere of most television viewing.[3] In the following list, we assume that in most television postproduction work you will be concerned primarily with continuity rather than complexity editing.

1.   Whenever approaching an editing job, have a clear idea of the *overall story,* its basic theme (what the story is all about), its plot (how the story develops from beginning to end), and its communication purpose (what you want the viewer to perceive and experience). Always edit (select what is important and what is unimportant) within the *context* of all story elements and the communication purpose. What is the show's central message? If you can't answer this question, you are not yet ready to edit. Don't be led astray by beautiful footage that has nothing to contribute to the central theme.

2.   The important prerequisites for story *continuity* are the continuity of pictures and sound. The viewer should be able to combine the various shots, scenes, and sequences into a complete whole, smoothly assimilating the jumps in time and space induced through editing. Maintaining visual continuity (maintaining proper location within the frame and screen directions) is more difficult in postproduction editing than in instantaneous editing, since the event has generally been shot in bits and pieces, with large portions of the actual event missing. A good camera operator will provide you with shots that "cut together" well, which means that the two shots provide for the necessary visual continuity. For example, if you end one shot with a medium closeup of a car, start your next shot from either closer or farther away, and from a distinctly different angle. A change of angles helps to prevent jump cuts.

If you work with a single camera, such as a film camera or a portable television camera, make sure that you don't cover a dominant action, such as somebody running in a specific direction, from one side of the action first and then the other. As with the multicamera setup, you must keep your single camera *on one side of*

the *vector line only,* unless you intend to reverse the screen direction on purpose. The same goes for getting over-the-shoulder shots with the single camera. Shoot from *only one or the other side of the vector line* (see page 275).

Since in news photography such careful camera positions are not always possible, get some cutaway shots that fit the overall event context. *Cutaway shots* are made of neutral event details, which do not indicate any specific screen direction, such as a straight-on shot of an emergency vehicle or another news photographer, a street sign, spectators. When two shots do not cut together directly (since, for example, they would change the screen direction without motivation), you can put a cutaway shot between them, thereby enticing the viewer to accept the change. What you have done with the cutaway shot is pretend to the viewer that there was a lapse of event time (a looking away) in which the shift of viewpoint could have taken place.

It goes without saying that the *audio track* must have continuity, too. In fact, good continuity of sound can at times help provide continuity to the video portion.

3.   In film, transitions other than cuts (dissolves, fades) are expensive unless they are done within the camera. Besides being cheaper, cuts keep the action rhythmically tighter than dissolves or fades. If you have a television system that allows you to edit videotape from two machines to the master recorder, you can probably route the various show segments to be edited through the studio switcher. Hence, you can add any number and kinds of transitions or effects to the show material during the editing process. The two playback VTR's that contain the unedited prerecorded material, with the unflattering designation of "slaves," simply act as video sources, very much like two studio cameras, and the "master" recorder as the VTR upon which the video material is assembled in an orderly fashion. Highly sophisticated editing facilities can be programmed to perform such editing tasks automatically (see pages 289–290). Again, use special effects and special transitions only if they indeed help to clarify and intensify the screen event.

4.   Since editing means the manipulation of prerecorded material for a specific communication purpose, you are ultimately responsible to the viewers for your

---

[3] See Zettl, *Sight-Sound-Motion,* for a detailed account on the aesthetic differences between television and film.

choices. Don't violate the trust they put in you. There is a fine line between intensifying an event through careful editing and willfully distorting an event so as to serve your aims rather than the viewers' needs. Except for the principles of communication that help you to avoid gross violations, there is no clear-cut guidebook to help you in this task. An essential prerequisite for the editor, as for any serious mass communicator, is respect and love for his fellow human beings.

Here are some examples of editing practices that range from the permissible to the unethical:

Event: A speech by a candidate running for political office.

Communication Aim: To give a condensed, yet balanced, overview of what the candidate said to the audience for the local evening news.

Your camera operator shot the speaker from opposite sides of the main vector line (running from speaker to audience) without any cutaway shots. You need a cutaway to splice between the two shots that were taken from opposite sides.

You pick some stock footage, showing a closeup of a news photographer taking a picture—permissible.

You pick a stock shot of somebody obviously bored with the whole thing—unacceptable. The cutaway might be misleading and grossly unfair to the generally high-energy event.

Manipulations with the audio track are even more dangerous. For example, to add applause, simply because the speaker said something that you happen to support, is a blatant case of lying. So, of course, is editing out all the statements that happen to go against your convictions, and leaving in only those with which you agree.

The use of the *montage* is an especially powerful, but potentially dangerous, device. It consists of a *juxtaposition* of two images that creates by *implication a third idea* not contained in either of the two shots. A montage might, for example, show a shot of soldiers taking aim at some unknown target, followed by a butcher, brutally slicing open the bellies of cattle. Idea implied: cruelty and brutality of war. A shot of crowded people followed by a shot of a herd of cattle might imply that people are living in subhuman conditions, or that people have the herd instinct of animals. A shot of somebody slightly drunk getting into a car, followed by a speeding ambulance with the lights flashing, might imply that this person had caused, or suffered, an accident.

Especially, if you edit a news story or a documentary (which means that you are not creating, but *documenting,* an event) stay away as much as possible from video and audio material that is not directly related to the event.

Film Editing

When you edit a film, you literally cut the film apart, pick out the sections that contribute to telling the story with optimal effectiveness, and glue the pieces back together again so that they form a continuous whole. The actual operation of gluing the film pieces together is called *splicing.* As with all skills, splicing can be learned only by doing it. Nevertheless, we will try to cover some aspects of sound film splicing and the basic points of electronic A-B rolling.

Splicing Sound Film Splicing double-system sound film is quite involved and generally left to the professional film editor. Most local news film is shot single-system, however, and you may occasionally have to edit single-system sound film. Even this simple kind of splicing can become quite tricky, since the sound does not run exactly parallel with the pictures but ahead of them.

In 16mm film, the sound precedes the corresponding picture by *26 frames* for *optical tracks,* and *28 frames* for *magnetic tracks.* In Super-8mm film, which usually has magnetic tracks, the sound is advanced by *18 frames.* (In 35mm, sound has a 20-frame advance.)

Editing Bench.

10·24   The minimum film equipment you need for simple 16mm film editing includes: (1) A film splicer. It will help you cut the film straight at the right place and press the tape over the splice (tape splicer), or hold the film in place while scraping the emulsion, and overlap it for the gluing (cement splicer). (2) A pair of rewinds and different-sized reels. With the rewind, you can wind the film backward and forward with ease and speed. (3) An action viewer. This is like a little projector. When you move the film through it with the aid of the rewinds, the film pictures appear on the small screen of the viewer. The faster you turn the rewinds, the faster the action appears on the viewer; the slower you turn the rewinds, the slower the action appears. You can stop the film and examine a single frame in the action viewer. (4) An optical and magnetic sound reader. Usually placed next to the splicer between the rewinds, the sound reader translates the optical or magnetic sound track into actual sounds. (5) A program timer, and (6) a four-gang synchronizer. The program timer, or the more cumbersome footage counter, gives you an accurate running time of the individual film sections, or the completed film. The four-gang synchronizer is needed only for double-system film editing (sound and pictures are edited separately and "married" later) or if you A-B roll your negative (see page 282 for an explanation of A-B rolling). And (7) miscellaneous material, such as film cement (a strong glue that dissolves the film base somewhat and literally cements the two pieces of film together), gloves to avoid fingerprints on the film, a trim barrel that catches in its cloth bag the temporarily discarded pieces of film, marking pencils, and film cleaner.

Film Tape Splicer: Contrary to the cement splicer, which welds the base sides of two pieces of film together with film cement, the tape splicer uses a piece of transparent tape for joining two pieces of film. The advantage of the tape splicer over the cement splicer is operational speed. No scraping is necessary, and there is no drying time for the cement. The film is cut and taped in one quick operation.

So, if you start your picture editing with somebody just opening his mouth for a statement, you have already lost part of the statement itself, because the sound precedes the picture by 26 frames (assuming a 16mm film with optical track). A good rule of thumb is to splice the film on *audio* for the beginning of a statement, and on *video* for the end of a statement. Operationally, you run the film through the action viewer and sound reader. If, for example, the statement you want is, "Your request for more up-to-date television equipment has been granted," you *mark the film* at the audio track directly at the sound head of the *sound reader* as soon as you hear the "Your." Then you look in your *viewer* until you see the person who is making the announcement has *closed his mouth* after the word "granted."

If he continues talking right after this statement, but you do not want the beginning of the second statement to be heard over the shot that follows, you must *bloop* (render inaudible) the audio track. If you have an optical track, you simply run a small piece of tape (blooping tape) along the 26 frames ahead of the last splice. With a magnetic track, you use a small magnet that degausses (erases) the 28 frames to the last splice. Sometimes you may want to cut the film on audio, which means that when you *hear* the speaker say the last word on the sound reader you cut the film. Your picture will, however, still show him mouthing a word. The next shot should, therefore, show a reaction that makes some sense, such as a shot of delighted production people hearing the good news.

If you have to splice together two statements by the same speaker, you need to cut the first statement on both ends (beginning and end of the statement) *on audio.* The beginning of the second statement needs to be cut on audio and end on *video.* The problem is that at the splice you see the speaker's lips obviously mouthing different words from what you actually hear. Fortunately,

10·25 As pointed out before, *single-system* sound means that the sound is recorded simultaneously with the pictures on the same film. The single-system sound track can be optical or magnetic. In *double-system* sound film, the pictures are recorded on one film (system one) while the sound is recorded at the same time or later on magnetic tape (system two). Pictures and sound are edited separately (with the aid of a four-gang synchronizer) and then printed together on one film, the *composite print.* ·

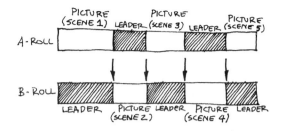

10·26 A-B Rolling: In A-B rolling, roll A is composed of all odd-numbered shots, separated by leaders that correspond exactly to the even-numbered shots; roll B is composed of all even-numbered shots, separated by leaders that correspond exactly to the odd-numbered shots.

this "lip flap" lasts for a relatively short while, and is generally ignored by the viewer (at least, let us hope so).

If your "lip flap" splicing is too distracting, you may want to cut back live to the newscaster, or insert a cutaway shot with voice-over from the newscaster. In either case, the film is kept rolling, which explains why such an editing method is often called a "roll-through" or "roll-thru." If you want to go back to the newscaster between two SOF statements, you splice either a black or an academy leader between the two SOF films, just long enough to cover the roll-through period (usually five seconds). If you use a cutaway shot (silent film), it must be long enough to cover the voice-over announcement of the newscaster. You can, of course, have roll-throughs between two silent films, in which case you simply cut back to the newscaster for the roll-thru voice bridge, with the academy leader or black leader rolling through off-air.

Electronic A-B Rolling In order to make the single-system SOF more flexible, a system of

electronic A-B rolling has been developed. "A-B rolling" is a term for film editing in which you splice the first, third, and all subsequent odd-numbered shots together on one reel, constituting the A-roll; and all even-numbered shots on another reel, the B-roll. All shots are separated by black leader, which is spliced opposite the shots on the other reel. Both rolls are then printed together for the final composite print. Through A-B rolling, all splices are eliminated in the printing process, and optical effects, such as dissolves and fades, can be accomplished. *(See 10.26.)*

Electronic A-B rolling uses a similar principle. Let us assume that you have to cover the construction of a music center in your city. With your single-system sound camera, you cover the interview with the director of the center in one continuous take at one location. In the interview, however, the director of the center makes many references to particular sections of the partially constructed building. After the interview, you film these sections of the building with a regular 16mm silent film camera. You then prepare a B-roll with the silent footage, making the pictures of the various building parts correspond exactly to the sound track of your SOF footage. The A-roll, containing the interview, is put on a film projector of one film island, let's say film island 1. The B-roll, containing the individual construction scenes, is put on a projector of another film island, in our case film island 2. Both films are started at the same time. The A-roll with the interview is put on the air first. But whenever the director of the music center is referring on the A-roll to one of the construction sites, you simply switch the video over to the B-roll on film island 2, with the explanatory audio still coming from the A-roll on film island 1. In other words, both films remain running throughout the interview. Thus, you have a running commentary from the music director, with the appropriate B-roll illustrations continuously paralleling it. In fact, you

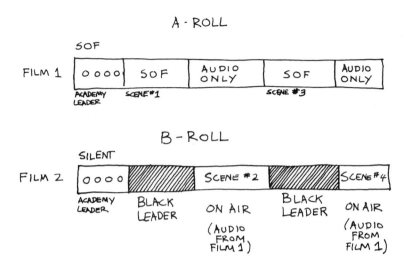

A - ROLL

FILM 1

SOF

| 0 0 0 0 | SOF | AUDIO ONLY | SOF | AUDIO ONLY |

ACADEMY LEADER   SCENE #1   SCENE #3

B - ROLL

FILM 2

SILENT

ACADEMY LEADER   BLACK LEADER   ON AIR (AUDIO FROM FILM 1)   BLACK LEADER   ON AIR (AUDIO FROM FILM 1)

10·27 Electronic A-B Rolling: In electronic A-B rolling, the complete SOF interview is played on one film island (constituting the A roll). The silent shots, which are carefully matched to the narration and separated from each other by black leader whenever necessary (when the A-roll is on the air with video and audio), are played simultaneously on the other film island (constituting the B roll). You can switch to the B-roll video while resuming the A-roll audio.

are "editing" your film on the air, using the original sound track as your editing guide. *(See 10.27.)*

Videotape Editing

Videotape editing ranges all the way from a simple hooking together of several long scenes that have been recorded in their natural sequence (the opening first, then the scenes as they occur, and the closing credits last) in a multicamera studio production, to the complex building of a show from many out-of-sequence shots obtained with a single camera, from other video sources, such as slides and film, and several independent audio tracks.

In the early days of videotape editing, the videotape had to be *cut physically* and fastened to the other piece of tape with a special splicing tape. In order to avoid picture roll at the splice, you had to cut both tape ends at exactly the right spot, one of the control track spikes (made visible through an iron-particle solution). Even with the help of a special splicing block and a magnifying glass, or even a low-powered microscope, the splices did not always turn out satisfactorily; not to speak of the necessity of cutting an expensive tape apart every time a splice was required.

Today, mechanical splicing is used only occasionally, mostly to repair tape needed for archival purposes. It is especially difficult to do with helical videotape recordings. Virtually all videotape editing is done, therefore, by means of *electronic editing*. In that way, you can insert new video and audio information into an existing videotape recording, or add various pieces of video and audio information in a desired sequence, all without cutting the tape. An "electronic editor" seeks out the sync pulses on the control track at the exact point you have selected for editing and puts the new material on the tape without any picture or

10·28   Ampex AVR-2
Editec Electronic Editor.

10·29   Ampex AVR-1
Editec Electronic Editor.

sound deterioration, however momentary, at the points of transition. The electronic editor permits the simultaneous editing of video and audio, or of either track (video or audio) separately, without affecting the other. *(See 10.28 and 10.29.)*

As mentioned before, the basic principles of editing—the principles of continuity and complexity—apply also to videotape editing. Operationally, however, electronic videotape editing differs considerably from switching (instantaneous editing) and film editing. We will, therefore, briefly discuss these five areas: (1) edit modes, (2) simple editing methods, (3) advanced methods, (4) SMPTE time code, and (5) editing production procedures.

Edit Modes   There are two basic edit modes, (1) the *assemble mode* and (2) the *insert mode.*

In the *assemble mode* you can add onto a blank master tape shot after shot selected from another videotape, or tapes. If, for example, you recorded a short play by "stopping down" (stopping the videotape machine) between scenes, and now want to hook them together into a unified whole, you can put the tape recording on the playback machine (sometimes called "slave") and add the scenes in consecutive order on the "master" videotape recorder. As you can see, you need at least two videotape machines for electronic editing: the *playback* machine, which supplies the various scenes, and the *recorder,* which edits them together.

In the assemble mode, you can add scene B to A, C to B, and so on, regardless of what video sources they may originate from. For example, scene A may be on one tape reel, scene B on another. But once the tape is assembled, you cannot go back and substitute a new scene B for the old scene B, without having to edit on all the subsequent scenes anew *(10.30).*

If you now want to substitute the new scene B for the old one, without affecting the previous or following scenes in any way, you must use the *insert mode (10.31.)* This allows you to insert any amount of material at any number of places in an existing tape, without having to re-record the adjacent material.

In the insert mode you can insert material into an existing recording, as well as *add shots* consecutively, as in the assemble mode. However, before you can *add* a series of shots or scenes in the insert mode, you must first "lay a control track"—that is, run the blank master tape through the videotape recorder and record the sync pulses of the control track for as long as you expect the finished, completely edited program to be. This control track will guarantee a synchronous match of the segments as they are added at the edit point, which means roll- or tear-free transitions. In the assemble mode, you do not have to prerecord a control track on the master tape. Whenever you record a new segment next to the old one, the tape will be totally erased for the new segment (from the previous segment on), and the new segment supplied with its own control track. The electronic editor then tries to match the two control tracks, the one from the previous shot and the one from the following, as best it can. Unfortunately, this matching does not always work out exactly right, and the transitions in assemble mode editing are highly susceptible to picture roll or tear. Most high-quality editing is, therefore, done in the *insert mode.*

Simple Methods Editing methods vary greatly, depending on how sophisticated your electronic editing equipment is.

In its most *elementary form,* you simply depress an *edit button* at the exact spot where you want the next shot to adjoin the preceding one. Holding

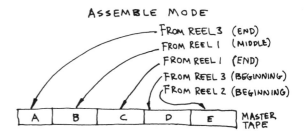

ASSEMBLE MODE

10·30 Assemble Mode Editing: In the assemble mode, any number of scenes can be assembled consecutively onto the master tape. But no inserts can be made without affecting the material that follows the desired insert.

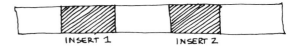

INSERT 1   INSERT 2

10·31 Insert Mode Editing: In the insert mode, material can be introduced into an existing recording without affecting the material preceding and following it. Also, if a control track has been laid before the insert-mode editing, any number of scenes can be assembled very much as in the assemble mode, except with higher electronic stability.

10·32 While all electronic editors can perform assemble mode editing, not all have an insert mode, especially on small helical scan videotape recorders.

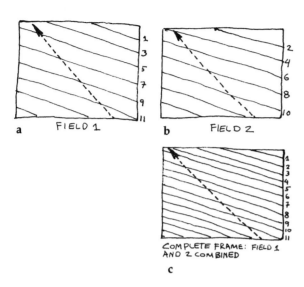

10·33 An *electronic frame* consists of one complete scanning process. The electron beam that scans the camera pickup tube and the surface of the kinescope tube moves from left to right, and from top to bottom, very much the way we read the lines in a book. Unlike reading, however, the beam skips every other line during its first scan (reading only odd-numbered lines [*see a*]) and then jumps back and scans all the even-numbered lines *(see b)*. This process is called *interlaced scanning*. The scanning of either the odd- or even-numbered lines constitutes a *field;* the scanning of two consecutive fields, that is, the one complete reading of both odd- and even-numbered lines, makes up a *frame (see c)*. The frame, then, constitutes the smallest complete picture unit. The broadcast television system works with 60 fields, or 30 frames per second. Note, however, that the frame is never visible on the videotape itself. The television frame consists merely of a *completed scanning cycle;* it is therefore visible only on the television screen. A film frame, on the other hand, is clearly visible on the film itself, and does not need to be projected to be seen.

this button down changes the machine from a playback mode to a record mode (thereby erasing everything on the master tape and replacing it with the new video material, which is being fed from the second, playback, machine). When the scene is finished, release the edit button, which returns the machine to the playback mode. It's a good idea to let the machine run for an additional 10 or 15 seconds before pressing the stop button, just in case the return to the playback mode does not happen immediately. Wind the machine back and check the edit. If it is good, you can advance to the next one. If you don't check each edit, you may later discover a bad "splice" right in the middle of your edited tape. Unless your machine has an insert mode, you will have to go all the way back to the error and start again.

Advanced Methods More advanced editing systems *cut in and out of the edit mode automatically.* What you do is place an "in" or "entrance" cue on the cue track of the videotape (done electronically through pressing a cue button), back up both tapes (the one on the playback machine with the scene to be transferred and the master tape) to the normal roll time (anywhere from six to ten seconds), and start both machines at the same time. As soon as the master recorder reads the edit signal on the cue track, it automatically shifts from a playback to an edit (record) mode and records the material from the other machine. You can also place an "out" or "exit" cue on the cue track, through which the master recorder is switched back from the edit (record) mode to the playback mode. Thus, insert edits can be precisely placed without any button pushing during the edit itself.

The trouble with this method lies in achieving precise synchronization of both machines and continuous identification of tape "addresses," locations on the tape that can be pinpointed quickly and repeatedly.

10·34 Time Code Reader.

SMPTE Time Code The development of the SMPTE Time Code has not only solved the address problem but also paved the way for extremely precise, computer-controlled editing. Through this invention, videotape became in every respect as flexible as film in building a show from prerecorded segments.

The SMPTE Time and Control Code is an electronic signal that, when recorded on the cue track of a videotape through a time code generator, provides an *address,* or a "birthmark" for each electronic frame. The address is given in elapsed time for each frame. The *time code reader* displays, like a digital clock, hours, minutes, seconds, and frames *(10.34).*

The numbers in the frame column run from 0 to 29, after which the seconds column is advanced by one digit (since we have 30 television frames per second). The readout works at any tape speed, whether you turn the reels by hand or run the recorder in fast forward or reverse.

Since each television frame can be located with ease and precision, the editing process itself can now be partially or fully automated. There are numerous computer-assisted systems in operation that can perform an astonishing array of editing tasks. Although in small station operations you may not need a highly sophisticated computer-controlled editing system very often, you should at least have an idea of what such a system could do for you. By simply pressing a few buttons of the command-display console, which might be located in your office, the computer-assisted editor performs, among others, these miracles:

Tells you what machines are available for editing, what the preroll requirements are for each machine, the types of tapes used on each of the playback machines, the length of the scenes on the playback tapes, and other such information.

Advances or rewinds the tape to the exact address stipulated. If you give an erroneous address that lies beyond the tape being previewed, the tape will automatically stop before it runs off the reel.

Calculates the entrance or exit addresses (in and out edits) from a given duration time of a scene, and displays continuously the time remaining until the end of an edit. Once the exit cue has been reached, the computer remembers it and changes it into an entrance cue for the next segment.

Lets you rehearse any number of edits before you actually record them on the master tape. Audio and video can be rehearsed together or separately. If you don't like the exact spot of the edit during rehearsal, you can shift the edit points somewhat without having to refigure new entrance or exit times. If the change is drastic, the computer will automatically shift the following edit points accordingly.

Activates in A-B rolling (using two playback machines so that the scenes can be assembled alternately onto the master tape) all machines at their proper time (even if they have different preroll requirements), keeps the machines synchronized, and overlaps the A-B rolls for dissolves or wipes.

Prints out a hard copy of every editing decision you have made for later reference.

Produces a punched paper tape that represents the final editing positions. When fed into the system, it activates the quadruplex machines for fully automated editing of the master tape.

But don't worry. You are still the most important element in the system. After all, it is responsible human beings that put the event on the tape in the first place, and it is your sensitivity, experience, knowledge of the overall context and communication aim, artistry, and technical skill that help to decide just which shot goes where, and what image should be juxtaposed with what other for maximum effectiveness. Even in these decisions, however, the machine can help.

Let's assume that you have been shooting on a documentary for several weeks, using a *single television camera* and a portable *quadruplex videotape recorder.* You now have a great number of small single 2-inch reels and are preparing for editing. Viewing and reviewing all the tapes on a quadru-

plex machine would be very costly. Also, the frequent plays of these master tapes may reduce their quality. What you can do, therefore, is to *transfer the 2-inch tapes to a 1-inch (or ¾-inch) helical tape* for initial viewing, decision making, and even precise edit preparation. All you need to do is put a time code on the 2-inch tapes. When dubbed down to the 1-inch tape, the time code readout can be keyed into, or supered over, the actual scenes. When you view the 1-inch tape, you can view the scene with its corresponding code address. Since the helical machines permit you to play back in slow motion or arrest the playback for a freeze frame, you can leisurely look for the best edit spot. Reading the time code addresses off the monitor screen, you can prepare an accurate *shot list.* Once you know exactly which shot goes where, you simply transfer this *off-line* time code information via a punched paper tape to the *on-line* electronic editing system of the quadruplex recorders and have lunch while the computer takes over *(10.35).*[4]

Production Procedures   As was just pointed out, technical sophistication in editing does not guarantee an effective end product. Your sensitive choices are still the major prerequisite for quality editing. Like any other production technique, efficient videotape editing requires you to pay close attention to certain basic procedural steps. Here they are:

1.   Hopefully, you have kept accurate records of each good or bad take during the actual videotaping. The search for the required segments is thus made relatively easy. Nevertheless, in a complicated editing job you will have to review the various tape segments a great number of times. Therefore, dub your original material down to a 1-inch or ¾-inch helical format (if you

[4] Central Dynamics, *PFC-102, The Computer Evolution in VTR Editing* (Montreal: Central Dynamics, 1973), p. 11.

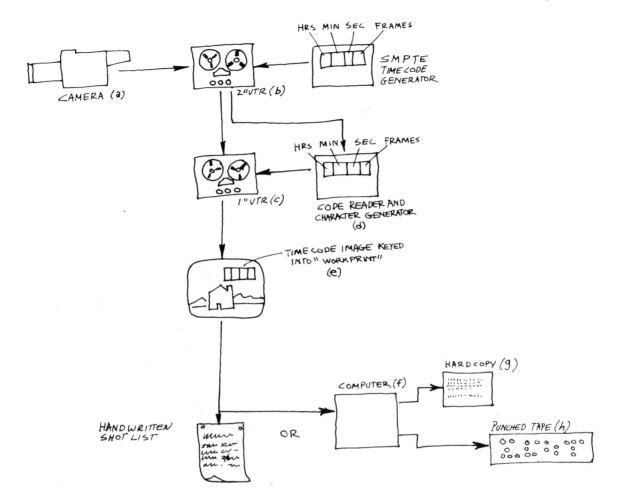

10·35 Off-Line Editing System: The scene is captured by the camera (a) and re-corded on the quadruplex master recorder (b). A time code is then added to the master tape (c). The master tape is then transferred onto helical tape with the time code reader (d) providing a visible time code key insert over the helical scan recording (e). From this information, you can then make your choices and tell the computer of your decisions (f). The computer remembers your choices, and makes a hard copy of your choices (a shot list, just in case yours isn't too accurate) (g), and at the same time produces a punched paper tape with the decision list (h). Your off-line editing is terminated at this point. You can now tape the paper tape and feed it into the computer for the actual on-line editing (which is done fully automatically).

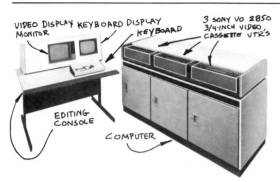

CMX System/50 Off-Line Videotape Editing.

10·36   The leading systems are the CMX systems by the Orrox Company, the Central Dynamics Systems, and the ¾-inch cassette systems by Sony.

10·37   A complex computerized system is, of course, very expensive to purchase. If you do not have access to one, however, you may think of renting the facility for a certain period. Its advantage is the speed and efficiency with which edits can be performed. An hour with one of these sophisticated editing systems gives you more, and more precise, edits than a whole day or two would produce with the machine-to-machine method.

recorded on 2-inch), or make a simple dub of all material recorded (if your original material was recorded on the 1-inch format) for a workprint.

2.   If you haven't done so during the shooting, write down some basic information about the various recorded segments, such as the cut number, scene number, take number, duration of the shot, the subject (what is the scene all about?), the time code addresses of the beginning and end of each recorded segment (if available), and whether or not the shot is good or bad (acceptable or unacceptable). *(See 10.38.)*

3.   When selecting the edit points (entrances and exits) for each shot, watch for visual and aural continuity. Write down briefly how each of the selected shots begins and ends with video and audio. For example, your video column in your shot sheet may read: "CU (closeup) of ¾ profile to screen left of Steve"; and your audio column, "Begins speech: 'In this crisis . . .,' ends with 'suggest these ten points.'" You should also write down any "wild" sounds that accompanied the speech, such as audience noise, or other prominent background sounds. These background sounds must continue through the subsequent shots, until the scene changes to another time and/or location *(see 10.39).* Sometimes you may find that you have to record the "sounds of silence"—the hisses or hums in an empty room—and dub them over the electronic edit points in order to maintain continuous noise. Otherwise your edits, though visually perfect, may be easily recognizable by short, yet distinct, drops in the hum present even during silent periods.

4.   If you edit with the SMPTE Time Code, list all the reel numbers, the entrance and exit addresses (as displayed by the time code), the duration of each shot, and the desired transitions in consecutive order. You might protect yourself by briefly indicating also the content of the shot, in case the numbers do not check out. Now you are ready to edit, that is, to press the buttons yourself or give it to the videotape editor or to the computer.

5.   Review the finished product carefully. Realize that the more *tape generations* you produce (number of dubs) during your editing process, the more the final product suffers in technical quality. Even a simple edit from the raw material to the master tape produces a second gen-

10·38   Basic Shot Information.

SCENE	SHOT	TAKE	LENGTH	TIME CODE ADDRESS		SUBJECT	OK	NO GOOD
				IN	OUT			

eration. If you then have to fix up the master tape by editing portions of it to a second master, you work already with a third generation. Only the very best high-band quadruplex recorders can perform such a feat without noticeable picture deterioration.

One final comment on videotape editing. The technical capability of frame-by-frame videotape editing does not necessarily mean good television. In fact, indiscriminate editing can often destroy television's great aesthetic potential of "aliveness," the immediate communication of the ever-changing moments of life. If the director or vid-

eotape editor does not recognize the specific requirements of the television medium—for example, editing rhythm—the various tempi of the individual segments and the overall pacing of the show may look artificial to the sensitive viewer. In a dramatic show it is often better to record as long a segment at a time as possible than to rely on many short takes, which must later be spliced together. The sustained action of the longer takes will often help to preserve a live, organic television quality in the performance and in the final rhythm of the play.

10·39   Editing Shot Sheet.

SHOT		VIDEO	AUDIO	WILD SOUNDS
	IN			
	OUT			
	IN			
	OUT			
	IN			
	OUT			

Summary

Picturization, the process of structuring a shot sequence, consists of three elements: (1) transition devices, (2) switching, or instantaneous editing, and (3) postproduction editing.

The four *basic transition devices* include (1) the cut, the instantaneous change from one image (shot) to another; (2) the dissolve, or lap-dissolve, the gradual transition from shot to shot whereby the

two images temporarily overlap; (3) the fade, whereby the picture goes gradually to black (fade-out) or appears gradually on the screen (fade-in); and (4) the wipe, in which one picture is partially or fully replaced by another.

Instantaneous editing is made possible by means of a *video switcher,* an electronic machine equipped with rows of buttons and fader bars. The switcher can bring about the basic transitions between any two video sources (such as two studio cameras, or camera to VTR, or studio camera and telecine camera) while the production is in progress. The switcher can also (1) create special effects, such as wipe patterns, key and matte inserts, and (2) permit previewing of any video source or special effect before it is switched on the air. Switchers that carry the corresponding audio portion of the program, together with the video portion are called *audio-follow-video switchers.*

The buttons on the switcher are usually arranged in rows, called *buses,* including a program bus, two mix and effects buses, and a preview bus. The mix and effects buses are usually switchable to either mode. Fader bars allow dissolves from one bus to the other, or the gradual appearance or disappearance of effects. In switching, as in postproduction editing, we are concerned with (1) *continuity editing,* the preserving of visual continuity from shot to shot, and (2) *complexity editing,* the juxtaposition of shots in order to intensify the screen event.

Postproduction editing means that shots and scenes that have been previously recorded on film or videotape are assembled after (post) the production into a meaningful program. The principles of continuity and complexity editing apply in postproduction editing the same way as they apply in instantaneous editing.

In *film editing,* we cut the film apart and splice the various pieces (shots) back together again in the desired order. A special film editing procedure is electronic A-B rolling, whereby one film carries the sound and one type of pictures (A-roll), while the other roll (B-roll) carries another set of pictures, but no sound. When televised, the sound of the A-roll is played throughout the film program, but the pictures fluctuate between A and B rolls.

In *videotape editing,* the shots are assembled on the videotape electronically. There are two types of edit modes: (1) the assemble mode and (2) the insert mode. Advanced videotape editing uses a *time code,* which permits frame-by-frame editing, and a computer for search of shots or shot sequences, execution of a variety of transitions, and the recording of the editing decisions made. Most computer-assisted editing has an *off-line* and an *on-line* system.

11   *Special Effects*

In this chapter, we are concerned with the three major types of special effects: (1) electronic, (2) optical, and (3) mechanical.

The electronic effects are generated electronically, within the circuitry of the television system. They consist of image combination effects, where two or more images are combined, and of image manipulation effects, where the picture is distorted in a predetermined way. An image combination effect is, for example, the adding of a show title to a background scene. An image manipulation effect is one in which the image takes on a prominent color, or where the image seems to disintegrate into an array of geometric patterns.

Optical effects are produced either by scenic devices, such as a slide projection in the studio that provides the background for a specific scene, or by actual optical distortions through mirrors or lens attachments. As simple a device as racking in and out of focus is an optical effect.

Mechanical effects include the simulation of rain, smoke, wind, and other such natural events that usually occur outside the studio.

As the term special effects indicates, the effects should remain "special." If overused, the special will soon lose its unusualness and effectiveness. With modern switching and electronic effects generating equipment, a great number of startling effects are so readily available that they may tempt the inexperienced television director to substitute effects for content. On the other hand, when judiciously used, special effects can enhance production to a considerable degree, and help greatly in the task of clarifying and intensifying the message.

Whenever you intend to use a special effect, you should ask yourself: (1) Is the effect really necessary? (2) Does it help in the clarification and intensification of my message? (3) Can the effect be easily produced? (4) Is it reliable? If you can give a "yes" answer to all these questions, the effect is in. If there is a "no" or even a "maybe" to any one or several of them, the effect is out.

There are two further factors you might con-sider before setting up complicated effects. One is the relative *mobility* of modern television equipment. Now that the television camera and VTR are no longer studio-bound, certain effects that need complex machinery for simulation in the studio, like snow or fog, can be obtained simply by taking the camera outdoors during a snowstorm or on a foggy day. The other is the enormous communication power of television *audio*. In many instances, you can curtail or eliminate complicated video effects by combining good sound effects with a simple video presentation. The sound effect of pouring rain, for example, combined with a closeup of an actor dripping wet may very well preclude the use of a rain machine, which produces rainlike streaks on the screen. To show a group of people sitting on the ocean beach, you don't need to set up a rear-screen projection of the ocean; a good sound effect of the surf over the closeup of the people basking in the sun will do the same job more easily. Or, better

---

Chroma Key A color matte; the color blue is generally used for the chroma key area that is to become transparent for the matte.

Clipper A knob on the switcher that selects the whitest portion of the video source, clipping out the darker shades. The clipper produces high-contrasting blacks and whites for keying or matting.

Colorizing The creation of color patterns or color areas through a color generator (without a color camera).

Debeaming The gradual reduction of the scanning beam intensity. The picture becomes a high-contrast picture, with the detail in the white and black areas no longer visible, gradually deteriorating into a nondistinct, light-gray screen.

Edge Key A keyed (electronically cut-in) title whose letters have distinctive edges, such as dark outlines or a drop shadow.

External Key A key signal that shapes the cut-in figure (into the background image). It is generated by a camera used exclusively for keying and fed into an external key input.

Gobo A scenic foreground piece through which the camera can shoot, thus integrating the decorative foreground with the background action. In film, a gobo is an opaque shield that is used for partial blocking of a light.

Internal Key A key signal that shapes the cut-in (into the background picture). It is supplied by any one of the studio cameras fed into the mix/effects bus.

Key An electronic effect. Keying means the cutting in of an image (usually lettering) into a background image.

yet, take your camera and VTR to the beach, if you happen to have one available. On television, reaction is often more effective than action. For example, you can suggest an atomic bomb explosion by showing a closeup of an actor's face combined with the familiar sound of such an explosion. A matting in of the mushroom cloud becomes superfluous.

Nevertheless, a judicious use of special effects presupposes that you know what effects are available to you.

We can divide special effects (referring to video only) into three large groups: (1) electronic effects, (2) optical effects, and (3) mechanical effects.

Electronic Effects

Most of the special effects used in television are produced electronically. There are basically *image combination* effects, where two or more images are combined, such as a superimposition, or the adding of a title over a background picture, and *image manipulation* effects, in which the whole picture is affected through certain color, brightness, or contrast manipulations.

The image combination effects include (1) superimposition, (2) key, (3) matte, (4) chroma key, and (5) wipe. The image manipulation effects include (1) sweep reversal, (2) polarity reversal, (3) debeaming, (4) video feedback, and (5) colorizing.

Image Combination: Superimposition

A superimposition, or "super," for short, is a form of double exposure. The picture from one camera is electronically superimposed over the picture from another. In effect, both pictures are simultaneously projected on the monitor screen.

Supers are used for adding specific information

Lens Prism   A prism that, when attached to the camera lens, will produce special effects, such as the tilting of the horizon line, or the creation of multiple images.

Matte   The keying of two scenes; the electronic laying in of a background image behind a foreground scene, such as the picture of a town meeting behind the newscaster reporting on this meeting.

Matte Key   Keyed (electronically cut-in) title whose letters are filled with shades of gray or a specific color.

Polarity Reversal   The reversal of the grayscale; the white areas in the picture become black and the black areas white, as the film negative is to the print.

Rear Screen   Translucent screen onto which images are projected from the rear and photographed from the front.

R.P.   Rear screen projection; also abbreviated as B.P. (back projection).

Special Effects Generator   An electronic image generator that produces a variety of special effects wipe patterns, such as circle wipes, diamond wipes, and key and matte effects, usually called S.E.G.

Sweep Reversal   Electronic scanning reversal; results in a mirror image (horizontal sweep reversal) or in an upside-down image (vertical sweep reversal).

Video Feedback   The picture on the television set is photographed by a television camera and fed back into the same monitor, producing multiple images.

11·1 If you have no key facility on your switcher, you can use a superimposition for some of the more common special effects.

For a ghost effect, have your performer dress in the traditional white bedsheet and move slowly in place in front of a black threefold. Make sure that he remains in one spot so that the camera does not overshoot the black backing. The ghost image is then superimposed over the picture from another camera, which may be slowly panning through the set of the haunted house. Although the figure actually remains in one spot, the panning of the second camera will create the illusion of a ghost floating weightlessly through the room. If you cannot find anyone with the strong desire to play a ghost, you can make one out of a handkerchief. Tie the handkerchief phantom to a string and move it violently in front of a black easel card.

Mystical writing that suddenly appears on a blackboard while the surprised professor looks on is no problem in television production. One camera frames up on the blackboard and the professor. Another camera is focused on a black easel card on which you can write (with white chalk) the mystical letters. You must wear a long black glove so that your hand and arm become completely invisible when supered over the blackboard. If you want the lettering to appear on the camera-left side of the blackboard, the easel card writing must be framed on the left side of the viewfinder. If your writing is to appear on the right blackboard area, the card must be framed on the right half.

11·2 Superimposition.

and for creating the effects of inner events—thoughts, dreams, processes of imagination—rather than outer, everyday events.

The most common information super is the adding of titles over a background picture or event. If your switching system does not allow keying, you must resort to supering titles. One camera takes the background picture (any kind of live event, say, a long shot of a football stadium), and the other camera is focused on the super card, which has white letters on a black background. Since the black card does not reflect any light, or only an insignificant amount, it will remain invisible during the super. Only the white letters will appear over the background picture from the other camera. The same principle applies to supering an isolated object over a background picture. Whatever it is, it must be placed in front of a plain black background (or any unlit area) so that only the lighted object will appear in the super. For example, if you want to have a burning candle appear in the midst of a mystical meeting, you simply put the candle in front of a black card or drape and super it over the shot of the set. In an information super, you should try to keep the super as clean as possible, which means that the viewer should be able to read the new information easily.

Regardless of background, however, you can super any two images as long as the video sources appear on different mix buses. In fact, when you are trying to express some inner event, such as a dream sequence, the superimposition may be quite complex. The traditional super of a dream sequence shows a closeup of a sleeping person, with his dream images supered over his face. Here, we are no longer trying to convey specific information but rather suggesting a general impression of the sleeping person's subconscious. As we know, the subconscious does not tend to reveal itself in an orderly, logical manner anyway.

Or let's take a dance. If you want to show the intensity and intricacy of the dance's rhythm rather than its sequence of steps, a complex super of the dancer's body as seen from two different points of view (shift in angle and distance, for example) might prove highly effective. It no longer matters whether we clearly see the various steps of the dancer; instead, we are given a new screen event that lets us perceive the dance in a novel, intensified way. We no longer photograph a dance; we help to create it. *(See 11.2.)*

But never super simply because the original event is dull. A super will intensify only when the event itself possesses enough energy and complexity to warrant such involved video treatment.

Key

The basic purpose for using a key is much the same as for a super: supplying additional specific information, such as a show title, to an existing background scene. Contrary to the super, there are several types of key effects: (1) normal, (2) edge, and (3) matte.

11·3 The normal key simply cuts the letters into the base picture as they appear on the title card or slide.

Normal Key In a normal key one picture is cut into the other electronically. The key looks similar to a super, except that the background picture does not bleed through the keyed-in picture. The most frequent use of a normal key effect is the insertion of letters, for example program titles or credits, over a base (background) picture.

A key card looks exactly like a supercard; it is usually a black card with white lettering on it (see Chapter 12). The letters for key inserts can also be produced electronically by a machine called *character generator,* about which we will talk more in Chapter 12.

In order to achieve a clean key, in which the white letters are cut into the base picture without any breakup or detriment to it, the card must be evenly lighted and the contrast increased by means of the *clipper.* A clipper is a knob on the switcher that selects the whitest portion of a video source, clipping out the darker shades (the blacks of the studio card). What remains of the key signal are the white letters, and these are then cut into the base picture. *(See 11.3.)*

Edge Key Most larger switchers allow you to select among various *edge modes.* This means that you can present the letters as they are on the key card or slide, or give each letter a distinctive outline electronically. The more visible types of outlines, or edges, are used to key letters over a busy (containing much detail) background. For exam-

11·4 The edge key puts a black border around the letters in order to make them more readable than with the normal key.

11·5 The drop-shadow key adds a prominent shadow to the letter (attached shadow) as though three-dimensional letters were illuminated by a strong key light.

11·6 The outline key makes the letters appear in outline form. It shows the contour of the letter only.

11·7 Of course, all electronic special effects, such as the various key and wipe configurations, are not simply an addition to the switcher functions; they need special electronic equipment. Appropriately enough, this equipment is called *special effects generator.* The complexity of these generators depends upon their functions; there are the borderline generator, the pattern generator, the pattern positioner, and a color matte generator that can fill the keyed images with different colors. Chroma key effects need, again, their own chroma key generator.

ple, in the *edge key* (or symmetrical outline) mode, each white letter (or any other keyed symbol or form) will have a thin black-edge outline around it *(11.4).* In the *drop shadow,* or simply shadow, mode, the letters will obtain a shadow contour, appearing three-dimensional *(11.5).* In the *outline* mode, the letters themselves will appear in outline form, only their contour remaining visible *(11.6).*

Matte Key In a matte key, the letters that are cut into the base picture can be filled with various shades of gray or a variety of colors.

Matte

Because matting is an electronic process very similar to keying, the terms keying and matting are often used interchangeably. Sometimes, matting refers to the "laying in" electronically of a *background* image, such as a scene of a fire, behind a foreground image, such as the newscaster. At other times, matting means the *filling in* of a *keyed-out* shape, such as letters, with other picture information, such as colors or textures. In any case, matting is an electronic image combination whereby the background scene does not bleed through the foreground scene, except where intended. How does a matte work?

In a *monochrome matte,* any black or very dark shadow area of a foreground picture becomes transparent and lets the background image show through. Any bright picture area, however, remains opaque, and appears therefore as overlapping the background scene.

Here is an example. Let us assume that you would like to show a dancer perform on a rooftop with the city skyline as the background. One camera will focus on a photograph of the city skyline; the other on the dancer, who performs in front of a black, or unlit, background. Through matting, you can now continually cut the dancer's

a

b

c

11·8 Electronic Matting: (a) In this black-and-white matting example, camera 1 focuses on a studio card showing a photo of a city skyline. (b) Camera 2 focuses on the dancer in front of a black background. The floor must also be rendered black, either by painting it or by putting a black cloth on it. (c) When camera 2 is keyed over camera 1, the matte is completed; the dancer seems to be dancing in front of the city skyline.

shape out of the photograph and fill the matted-out shape with the image of the dancer. As a result, the dancer appears to be dancing on the rooftop with the city skyline in the back. *(11.8.)*

If the video switcher is equipped for "double re-entry"—which means that the matting effect can be routed again through the mix bus, or any mix bus effect through the effects bus (you can achieve a double effect)—and if a third camera is used (which may be the television film camera),

further matting effects can be achieved. One camera takes the background, another provides the signal that cuts the foreground shapes out of the background picture, and the third supplies the material to fill in the cutout holes, which may be anything that has textural interest, such as rough cloth. With this technique you can create a number of surrealistic effects, as, for example, a number of heavy concrete blocks in the shape of a lithe female dancer moving on top of the ocean surf.

11·9   If you use one camera (1) to supply the key signal (the shape of the cut-in) and feed this signal directly into a special keying signal input, we speak of *external key.* The other cameras (2 and 3), which are fed into the mix buses, can then be used to "fill" the shape of the external key cut-in.

In *internal keying,* both cameras go through the mix/effects bus, with one supplying the background image and the other the cut-in keying signal.

Such visual adventures are, of course, definitely special effects, and should be reserved for special occasions.

Chroma Key

Chroma key is actually nothing more than a matte in color television. However, it has become such an important special effects technique that it deserves a slightly more detailed explanation.

Basically, the chroma key process uses a specific color, usually blue, instead of black for the background over which the matting occurs. Like the black, the blue becomes totally transparent during the matting and lets the picture of the second camera show through, without interfering with the foreground image. *(See 11.10.)* Blue is used since it is most opposite to the skin colors, thus reproducing them during chroma key matting relatively undistorted. Actually any other color could be used for chroma key matting, although no other background hue makes skin tones appear as natural as blue does.

As pointed out in Chapter 6, the chroma key area must be evenly painted (even saturation throughout the area) and especially evenly lighted. Any unevenness in lighting can interfere with the matting process.

Since anything in the foreground scene that approaches the blue chroma key background color becomes transparent during the matting, a newscaster, for example, should stay away from wearing blue in front of the chroma key set. A tie containing the same blue as the background will let the matted scene show through. Even some blue eyes become a problem during a closeup in chroma key matting, although, fortunately, most blue eyes reflect or contain enough other colors to keep them from becoming transparent. However, the shadow areas on the outline of very dark-haired or dark-skinned performers may occasionally turn blue (or reflect the blue back-

a

b

c

11·10   Chroma Key: (a) Studio camera 1 takes a picture of the woman standing in front of an evenly lighted blue background. (b) The background for the key effect is supplied by the film chain: a simple color slide of a mountain landscape. (c) The completed chroma key effect transports the woman into the landscape.

ground), causing the contour to become indistinct, to "tear," or to assume its own color. Again, as mentioned in Chapter 6, you can counteract this nuisance to some extent by using yellow or light orange gels in the back lights. Because the yellow back light neutralizes the blue shadows, it sets off, and separates the performer quite distinctly from, the blue background during the chroma key matting.

You can quite easily matte pictures behind the newscaster from any video source. The source can be the film chain, a VTR, or a live studio camera shooting a studio card. Frequently, the slides or cards that contain the background scene (such as a visual symbol representing the theme of the news story) have their own color. If the studio card is red, the newscaster will appear to sit in front of a red background during the chroma key matting. When you are not matting, the scene will show the chroma key blue background.

11·11 Vertical Wipe: In a vertical wipe, one picture is gradually replaced from the bottom up or from the top down.

11·12 Horizontal Wipe: In a horizontal wipe, one picture is gradually replaced from the side.

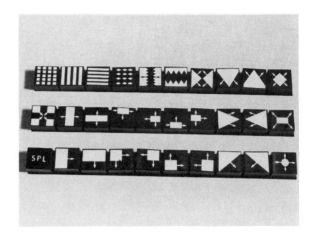

11·13 The more complicated wipes come in a variety of configurations. A group of push buttons on the switcher show the various patterns available to you.

Chroma key matting is far superior to the monochrome (black-and-white) process, since it provides for exceptionally sharp contours and stable, jitter-free effects.

Wipe

In a wipe, a portion or all of one television picture is gradually replaced by another. The second image literally wipes the first one partially or fully off the screen.

The two simplest wipes are the vertical and the horizontal. A *vertical wipe* gives the same effect as pulling a window shade down over the screen. Just as the window shade "wipes out" the picture you see through the window, the image from one camera gradually pushes the image from the other camera off the screen, either from top to bottom or from bottom to top. The *horizontal wipe* works the same way, except that the picture is pushed out sideways by the wipe image. *(See 11.11 and 11.12.)*

Wipe Patterns The more complicated wipes can take on many different shapes. In a diamond wipe, one picture starts in the middle of the other picture and wipes it off the screen in the shape of a diamond. Or the wipe can start from the corner of one picture and shrink the other off the screen (diagonal or corner wipe). Box wipes and circle wipes are also frequently used. *(See 11.13.)*

Operationally, you can select the appropriate wipe configuration either by pressing a wipe button or by turning a rotor selector to the respective wipe position. The speed of the wipe is determined by how fast you move the *special effects levers,* which are like a second pair of fader levers, wired for a different function. On some switchers, a mode-selector switch will assign to the regular fader bars the function of special effects levers.

11·14 Soft Wipe: The soft wipe reduces the demarcation line between the two images, without making the images transparent as in a super.

11·15 Linear Chroma Key: The linear chroma key permits the keying of transparent objects, such as a wine glass, over a base picture. While the edges key solidly over the scene, the glass itself remains transparent.

You can further influence the wipe pattern by feeding into it an additional signal from another source, such as the audio signal of the accompanying sound. If, for example, you modulate a circle wipe with an audio signal, the volume of the audio signal will influence the size of the wipe (the circle will shrink and expand with the volume fluctuations of the sound). The frequency (the high and low pitch) of the audio signal will influence the contour of the wipe. In our case, pitch fluctuations will alternately make the outline of the circle smooth or uneven.

Most complex switchers permit wipes with a *hard* or *soft edge.* A soft-edge wipe, for example, will reduce the demarcation line to a minimum and allow the images to blend into each other, similar to a super. *(See 11.14.)*

Wipe Positions Any of the wipes can be stopped any place during the process and can be adjusted to the horizontal and vertical size by splitting the special effects levers (one of which controls the vertical size, the other the horizontal size of the wipe pattern). Some switchers come equipped with *wipe reversal modes* and a *wipe positioner.* In the wipe reversal mode, you can have a vertical wipe, which normally moves from top to bottom, reverse its direction so that it moves from bottom to top. Or you can put it in a mode where it reverses itself automatically every time you move the levers. The wipe positioner, often called "joy stick," can move a wipe, such as an arrested circle wipe, anywhere on your screen. For example, if you want to move the circle, which originated in screen center, to the upper lefthand corner of the screen, simply move the joy stick to your upper left until the circle is in the desired position.

Split Screen If you stop a vertical, horizontal, or diagonal wipe in screen center, you have a

a

b

c

11·16 To set up for a horizontal split-screen effect, camera 1 frames the object designated to become the left half of the split screen in the left part of its viewfinder (a). Camera 2 frames the object designated for the right half in the right part of its viewfinder (b). In the completed split-screen image, the locations of subjects (a) and (b) are properly distributed (c).

split-screen effect, or, simply, a split screen. Each half of the screen will show a different picture. To set up for an effective split screen with a horizontal wipe, one camera must put its image (designated for the left half of the split screen) in the left side of its viewfinder, the other in the right side for the right part of the split screen. The unnecessary part of each picture is then wiped out by the other (split-screen) image. Always check such effects on the preview monitor. *(See 11.16.)*

A split-screen effect is frequently used to show an event from two *different viewpoints* on one screen.

It is commonly done in a baseball game, where you show the batter and pitcher on one side of the split screen and a man leading off first base on the other. Or, you can show widely *separated events simultaneously,* such as two people located in different cities talking to each other almost face-to-face. A quad-split is a screen split four ways. *(See 11.17.)*

So far, we have talked about the special effects that combine two or more images (video sources) electronically. Now we will take a look at *image*

11·18 When the horizontal scanning, or sweep, is reversed, you will get a mirror image of the original picture. Right and left are reversed.

11·19 In a vertical sweep reversal, the picture is put upside down. If used judiciously, such effects can be extremely powerful.

11·17 Some switchers permit a quad, or four-way, split. You can then fill each of the four screen areas with a different picture.

manipulation, in which a single image can be presented electronically so as to achieve various effects. As indicated before, the major image manipulation effects include (1) sweep reversal, (2) polarity reversal, (3) debeaming, (4) video feedback, and (5) colorizing.

Image Manipulation: Sweep Reversal

Most monochrome cameras are equipped for reversing the horizontal and vertical sweeps, or scanning. By changing the horizontal sweep (through a switch in the camera or at the CCU), you will get the effect of a mirror image; right and left will be reversed *(11.18)*. You could use this sweep reversal to correct an image taken off a mirror, for example.

The vertical sweep reversal projects a picture upside down. You can make a performer stand on his head or show a whole set upside down merely by flicking the vertical sweep reversal switch. Such reversals, sometimes used for comedy

scenes, have produced startling effects in modern dance, where the dancers all of a sudden seem to defy gravity, logic, and convention. *(See 11.19.)*

You can reverse horizontal and vertical sweeps simultaneously, if needed. Standard studio color cameras have no provisions for sweep reversals, however.

Polarity Reversal

Polarity reversal is a turnabout of the grayscale: all dark areas turn light, and all light areas turn dark. In the monochrome television film camera, for instance, a polarity reversal switch permits the projection of negative film (from which no positive print has been struck, and which looks like a negative of a still photo). But more importantly, in monochrome television polarity reversal can produce powerful aesthetic effects. By this technique, you achieve more than a change in appear-

11·20 Polarity Reversal: When you reverse the polarity of the television image, the event takes on a completely different appearance and feeling. The structure of the event has changed.

11·21 Debeaming: Through debeaming, the graphic expressiveness of this woman's face is greatly intensified.

ance. A structural change seems to occur. The screen event all of a sudden feels different. *(See 11.20.)*

Polarity reversal in color television is not possible with standard studio equipment. It requires specially constructed equipment or time-consuming adjustments of the color camera.

Debeaming

Debeaming is the gradual reducing of the intensity of the scanning beam. The more debeaming you do, the less brightness variation you have,

and the more the image will be reduced to stark black and white contrasts. The image seems first to glow, as if it would emit its own light, and then to burn itself up until nothing is left but a nondistinct, light-gray screen. Like the polarity reversal, debeaming has a powerful effect that seems to change the very structure of the event *(11.21)*.

Debeaming effects in color television can, of course, be even more dramatic. Some of the subtle colors that have blended harmoniously with the rest of the scene all of a sudden take on their own expressive life. They begin to dominate the scene first, and then consume it like a high-energy force. However, any indiscriminate use of such a powerful effect can just as easily and forcefully render the scene unbelievable, and thereby destroy, rather than intensify, your communication intent.

Video Feedback

When you photograph with a television camera an image off a studio monitor, and feed the photographed image back into the same monitor,

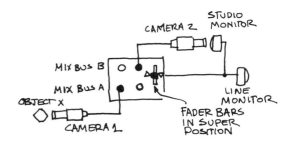

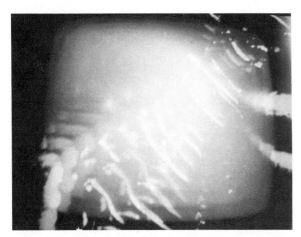

11·22 Video Feedback: By pointing the camera at the monitor that shows the camera's picture, and by feeding this monitor image back into the same monitor, you will achieve a video feedback effect that looks very much like the image created by two opposing mirrors.

11·23 The setup of video feedback is relatively simple. Camera 1 photographs object X and feeds it into the switcher on mix bus A. This picture is fed into the studio monitor. Camera 2 photographs the studio monitor, which now displays an image of object X. Camera 2 is fed into mix bus B. Cameras 1 and 2 are now superimposed and fed as a super into the line monitor, which now shows the multiple images of object X as multiplied by the closed feedback loop between cameras 1 and 2.

the resulting image is multiplied very much as with two opposing mirrors. If you move the feedback camera slowly about the face of the monitor, you can get highly intense, glowing images that weave back and forth.

By canting (holding somewhat sideways) a portable monochrome camera, for example, and by including part of the feedback monitor frame (to have a video reference), you can get unpredictable and highly interesting patterns. If you now move the camera ever so slowly in front of the feedback monitor, you will get an exciting variety of round, mandala-like feedback patterns. (See Chapter 17.)

Video feedback is the visual equivalent of sound reverberation (echo) effects.

Colorizing

With the aid of a special colorizing generator you can create any number of color patterns and sup-

ply a black-and-white image with a specific hue (color) or, in some cases, with two or three hues. Some colorizers shade all dark picture areas with one hue and all light ones with another. Needless to say, you can achieve highly unique color effects that would be difficult to get with a normal color camera. Some video artists prefer, therefore, to shoot their images in black and white for later colorizing. A more utilitarian application of the colorizer is to supply charts and graphs with various functional colors.

11·24 Some of these colorizers are custom built. They are often called *color video synthesizers* since they can produce color images on a monitor without the use of a color camera.

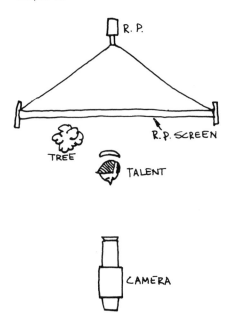

11·25   Rear Screen Projection:The rear screen projector throws a bright image onto the back of a translucent screen. The image is then picked up by the camera from the front, usually in combination with other scenic pieces and/or performers.

Optical Effects

Optical effects include scenic devices prepared for the television camera, and attachments to, or manipulations of, the lens. Since the development of sophisticated electronic effects, the optical effects have lost their prominence in television production. Electronic effects are much easier to produce and far more reliable. Yet, in the absence of such generators, you may have to produce some special effects through optical image manipulation.

There are eight major optical effects: (1) rear projection, (2) front projection, (3) gobos, (4) mir-

rors, (5) lens prisms, (6) star filter, (7) matte box, and (8) defocus effects.

Rear Projection

Contrary to a regular slide projector, which projects a slide onto the front side of a screen, the rear screen projector throws a slide image, or a moving crawl, onto the *back (11.25)*. The translucent screen, however, allows the camera to pick up the projection from the front. This way, scenic objects and performers can be integrated with the R.P (rear projection) without interfering with the light throw of the projector.

The *rear screen* is a large (usually 10 x 12 feet, or roughly 3.20m x 4.00m) sheet of translucent, frosted plastic stretched by rubber bands into a sturdy wooden or metal frame. The frame rides on four free-wheeling casters for easy positioning.

The rear screen projector is a large, high-powered projector for large (4 x 5-inch) glass slides. Preferably it has a short, undistorted wide-angle throw of a brilliant, high-contrast image. Through a simple crawl attachment, the projector can transmit a moving image, such as a landscape or a street scene whizzing by, as seen out of a moving car, for example. Such moving background projections are often used in motion picture work where, when photographed with an actual scene in the foreground, they are called "process shots."

If you don't have a large rear screen projector, you can try to use an ordinary 2 x 2 home slide projector. However, most of these lack the intensity necessary to overcome the inevitable spill light in front of the screen (see pages 139–140).

But even without a projector, the rear screen lends itself to several interesting studio effects. If you place a cardboard cutout or a three-dimensional object between the screen and a strong light source, such as an ellipsoidal spot or a bare

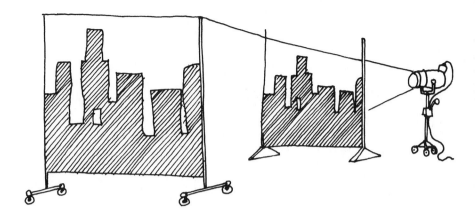

11·26 By placing a cardboard cutout, a sheet of plexiglass or plastic painted with translucent paints, or even a three-dimensional object between a strong light source and the rear screen, you can achieve many interesting effects.

projection bulb, you can produce a great variety of shadow patterns on the screen. This technique is especially effective when integrated with a stylized set. *(See 11.26.)*

Rear screen projection is often integrated with other parts of the studio set. A few simple foreground pieces that match parts of the projected scene will produce more realistic pictures than the R.P. will alone.

The use of a rear screen is, unfortunately, not without serious problems: (1) the setup takes up considerable studio space and time; (2) the lighting is difficult to do; (3) the number of performers (normally no more than two) and their action radius in front of the R.P. are severely limited; (4) the fairly noisy blower motors of the projector may be picked up by the studio microphone; and (5) the R.P. has fast falloff—meaning that the brightness of the projected image falls off as soon as the camera moves away from its central position and assumes an oblique angle.

11·27 Most R.P. slides can be rented from rear screen manufacturers. Their libraries usually contain important landmarks of the world, such as the Eiffel Tower or Big Ben, as well as a variety of such other useful settings as snow scenes, trees, mountains, and streets. You can make R.P. slides by painting directly onto 4 x 5 glass plates or by blackening the entire slide with India ink and then scratching designs on it. The extreme enlargement of the slide drawing produces interesting effects.

Most rear screen projectors reverse the slide horizontally and vertically. In order to insert it correctly, hold the slide right side up, flip it upside down, and then flip it sideways.

Front Projection

Elaborate front projection, as used in the theater, is not often attempted in small station operation since it is so easy for the performers to get be-

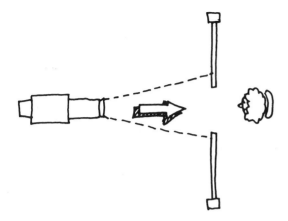

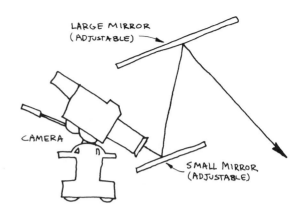

11·28 A television gobo is a cardboard cutout that acts as a special frame for a scene. Gobos are used as decorative effects; they are not meant to be perceived as an integral part of a highly realistic scene.

11·29 Periscope: The mirror periscope, consisting of two adjustable mirrors hung in a movable frame, permits a variety of overhead shots of fairly static scenes. When using it, you don't need to reverse the horizontal sweep in your camera, since the image will be corrected by the second mirror.

tween the projection source and the background. However, when the performers remain fairly stationary, it can be employed. Interesting background effects can be front-projected with special front projectors, or two or more standard overhead projectors, such as are used in nearly every school and college. Of course, projection of this kind demands as precise a studio lighting setup as rear screen projection. Very little if any light should spill onto the projection surface, which is often the cyclorama.

The most common type of front projection is the cucalorus projection, often called cookie (see page 135).

Television Gobos

In the motion picture industry, a gobo is an opaque shield that is put in front of a light source (similar to a movable barn door) to keep undesira-

ble spill light from hitting specific set areas. A *television gobo,* however, is a cutout that acts as a decorative foreground frame for background action *(11.28).*

If you have chroma key equipment, such gobo effects are generally matted into the scene electronically. The traditional gobos consist of picture frames for a nostalgic scene, or cartoon settings (oversized keyholes, windows, doors, old model cars) through which we can observe the live action.

Mirrors

Mirrors are sometimes used to create unusual camera viewpoints. But they are a hazard in the studio, even if you are not superstitious, because they can reflect the lens of the camera that is shooting the scene. Any shots off a mirror reverse the image, and you cannot correct it unless you

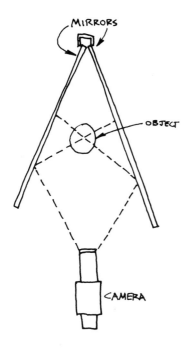

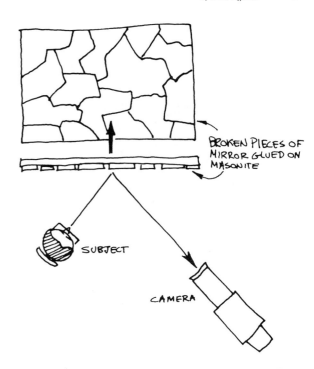

11·30 A multi-image, rosetta-like effect is achieved by mirrors reflecting each other's images, like barbershop mirrors that hang on opposite walls. Toy kaleidoscopes are based on this principle. You can duplicate the kaleidoscope effect by taping two small mirrors or ferrotype plates along one edge, so that the reflecting surfaces face each other. When the camera looks at the object that is placed in the resulting v, you will get a rosetta-like pattern of the object.

11·31 A cubistlike effect can be obtained by reflecting a scene or an object off a mirror mosaic. Simply break a mirror into several large pieces and glue them onto a sheet of plywood or masonite. When the camera shoots into this mirror mosaic at an angle (so that the camera will not be seen in the reflection), the reflected scene takes on a startling, cubistic effect.

have horizontal sweep reversals in your camera system. Also, now that portable cameras have become so flexible, use of mirrors for unusual angle shots has become unnecessary.

In the absence of a portable camera or special lens attachments, however, you may find the mirror-periscope and multi-image mirrors helpful in achieving certain effects. *(See 11.29, 11.30, and 11.31.)*

Lens Prisms

There are special rotating lens prisms that can be attached to the camera lens. The most common are the *image inverter prism* and the *multiple image prism.*

The image inverter prism rotates an image into any of several positions. The studio floor can become a wall or the ceiling, depending on the

11·32 With a prism inverter, you can cant a shot. This effect can contribute to the intensification of a scene, making it dynamic and dramatic.

angle camera, or the glitter on the singer's dress as seen by the closeup camera, are all transferred into prominent starlike light rays crossing over the entire scene on the television screen. (*See 2.13*, page 26.)

Matte Box

While in film a matte box has a variety of functions—shielding the lens from undesirable light, holding a filter or a matte slide, such as the well-known cutouts of a view through binoculars—the television matte box is simply a device to block the view partially of a wide-angle lens, or zoom lens position. The matte box physically reduces the field of view without changing the apparent distance from camera to object. If, for example, you want to matte (via chroma key) a tiny Alice-in-Wonderland figure into a large, oversized room, you can have one camera focus on the room interior, the other on the chroma key set. This set consists of a large roll of (usually) blue cloth or seamless paper (see Chapter 12) that can be pulled down like a window shade from a batten near the lighting grid so that it even covers part of the floor. Have Alice stand on the blue chroma key material, and photograph this scene from an extreme long-shot zoom position. The matte box prevents this camera from overshooting the chroma key set on this extreme long shot *(11.33)*.

rotation degree of the prism. While in black-and-white television you can very easily put an image upside down electronically, most standard color equipment does not permit a vertical sweep reversal. An image inverter prism can, however, produce the same effect. Furthermore, with a slight prism rotation, you can achieve a slight tilt, or *canting effect.* Such a disturbance of the horizon line can make a scene highly dynamic. *(See 11.32.)*

The multiple image prism produces strictly decorative effects very similar to the mirror kaleidoscope effects.

Star Filter

The star filter is a lens attachment that changes high-intensity light sources or reflections into starlike light beams. This method is often used to intensify the background for a singer, or a musical group. The studio lights as caught by the wide-

Defocus Effects

The defocus effect is one of the simplest, yet most highly effective, optical effects. The camera operator simply racks out of focus and, on cue, back into focus again. This effect is used as a transitional device, or to indicate strong psychological disturbances or physiological imbalance.

Since going out of focus will conceal the image almost as completely as going to black, it is possible to change your field of view or the objects in

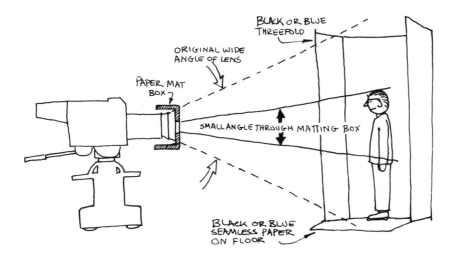

ORIGINAL WIDE
ANGLE OF LENS

BLACK OR BLUE
THREEFOLD

PAPER MAT
BOX

SMALL ANGLE THROUGH MATTING BOX

BLACK OR BLUE
SEAMLESS PAPER
ON FLOOR

11·33 Matte Box: With the aid of a matte box, you can isolate an object in an extreme long shot without overshooting the set. This technique is especially important if you want to reduce the size of an object or performer for chroma key matting.

front of the camera during complete defocusing. For instance, you can go out of focus on a young girl seated at a table, change actors quickly, and rack back into focus on an old woman sitting in the same chair.

A slight defocusing can make the camera subjective; for instance, it may assume the function of the actor's eye to indicate progressively worsening eyesight. Also, you can suggest psychological disturbances by going out of focus on a closeup of the actor's face.

If you want only partial defocusing, with part of the picture remaining in focus, you can use what is known in the motion picture industry as "Vaseline lens." This is a regular camera lens whose edges have been "fogged" with petroleum ointment. However, you should construct a device that allows for this effect without smearing or damaging the lens itself. Simply take a piece of clear glass and tape it in front of the camera lens. Grease the edges of the glass with Vaseline, leaving a clear area in the middle. The outer edges of the picture will now appear out of focus (the degree of the "fogging" depending entirely on the

11·34 Although there is a great variety of more or less complex matte boxes on the market, you can make an inexpensive but useful one yourself. Simply make a cardboard box that fits over the zoom lens (or a cylinder, if your zoom lens is round), cut a small opening (either rectangular or round) into the front part and paint the inside black. Then tape the matte box over your lens. If you use a monochrome turret camera, you can make the matte box out of a small paper cup that fits over the lens.

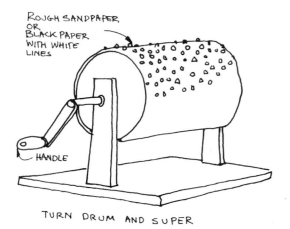

ROUGH SANDPAPER
OR
BLACK PAPER
WITH WHITE
LINES

HANDLE

TURN DRUM AND SUPER

11·35   Rain: A rain drum consists of a small drum (about ten inches [25 cm] in diameter), covered with rough black sandpaper or black paper with white "glitches" painted on it. Turn the drum fairly fast (depending on how hard you want it to rain), take a slightly out-of-focus closeup of the rotating paper, and super the glitches over the scene. Make sure that you turn the drum so that the rain is coming down instead of going up.

thickness of the grease), with the center remaining in sharp focus.

Mechanical Effects

Most mechanical effects are needed only in the presentation of television plays. Although small commercial stations may have little opportunity to do drama, colleges and universities are frequently involved in the production of plays.

The techniques for producing mechanical effects are not universally agreed upon. They offer an excellent opportunity for experimentation. Your main objectives must be (1) simplicity in construction and operation and (2) maximum reliability.

Remember that you can *suggest* many situations by showing an effect only partially and relying on the *audio track* to supply the rest of the information. Also, through chroma key matting, you can matte in many an effect from a prerecorded source, such as film or videotape.

Nevertheless, there are some special effects that are relatively easy to achieve mechanically, especially if the effect itself remains peripheral and authenticity is not a primary concern.

Rain

Soak the actors' clothes with water. Super the rain from a film loop or a rain drum *(11.35)*. Try to avoid real water in the studio, since even a small amount can become a hazard to performers and equipment. Best yet, cover a portable camera with a plastic bag, wait for real rain, and shoot outside.

Snow

Spray snow out of commercial snow spray cans in front of the lens. Have the actors covered with plastic snow or soap flakes.

Fog

Fog is always a problem. The widely used method of putting dry ice into hot water unfortunately works only in silent scenes, since the bubbling noise it makes may become so loud as to drown out the dialogue. If you have to shoot fog indoors, rent one of the large, commercially available fog machines.

Wind

Use two large electric fans. Drown out the fan noises with wind sound effects.

Smoke

Pour mineral oil on a hotplate. If the smell bothers the actors too much, super a stock shot of smoke over the scene.

Fire

Don't use fire inside the studio. The risk is simply too great for the effect. Use sound effects of burning, and have flickering light effects in the background. A film loop with fire matted over the scene can also be very effective. For the fire reflections, staple some silk strips on a small batten and project the shadows with an ellipsoidal spot on the set *(11.36)*, or reflect a strong spotlight off a vibrating plastic sheet.

Lightning

Combine four or six photofloods or two photo flash units to a single switch. Lightning should always come from *behind* the set. Don't forget the audio effect of thunder. Obviously, the quicker the thunder succeeds the light flash, the closer we perceive the thunderstorm to be.

Explosions

As with fire, stay away from explosive devices, even if you have "experts" guarantee that nothing will happen. But you can *suggest* explosions. Take a closeup of a frightened face, increase the light intensity to such a degree that the features begin to wash out, and come in strongly with the explosion audio. Or, better yet, debeam the face (or the whole scene) while the audio explosion rumbles on.

It should be pointed out again that one effect is rarely used in isolation. Effects, like any other production techniques, are contextual. They de-

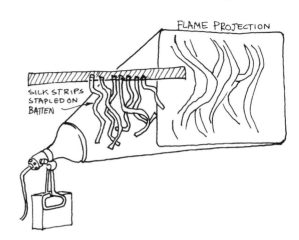

11·36 Fire: To project flickering fire onto the set, move a batten with silk strips stapled on it in front of a strong spotlight.

pend on the right blending of several visual and auditory elements, all within the context of the overall scene. The dialogue of the performers or actors is, of course, one of the prime means of reinforcing an effect, or making it believable in the first place.

Summary

Special effects can be grouped into three large categories: (1) electronic effects, (2) optical effects, and (3) mechanical effects.

Electronic effects consist of image combination and image manipulation. The *image combination* effects include (1) superimposition, (2) key, (3) matte, (4) chroma key, and (5) wipe. The *image manipulation* effects include (1) sweep reversal, (2) polarity reversal, (3) debeaming, (4) video feedback, and (5) colorizing.

There are eight major *optical effects:* (1) rear projection, (2) front projection, (3) gobos, (4) mirrors,

(5) lens prisms, (6) star filter, (7) matte box, and (8) defocus effects.

The *mechanical effects* include (1) rain, (2) snow, (3) fog, (4) wind, (5) smoke, (6) fire, (7) lightning, and (8) explosions.

All special effects should be used with great care; otherwise they will lose their uniqueness and effectiveness. Electronic effects, the most reliable and most easily produced, are used most frequently in television production.

12   *Design*

This chapter embraces the two major aspects of television design: (1) television graphics and (2) scenic design. Graphics include all two-dimensional visuals that are prepared for the television screen, such as title cards, maps, and charts. Scenery includes all three-dimensional items that are used in the studio, such as flats, furniture, and hand properties. The most prevalent dimensions and preparation methods of television graphics, and the most common types of scenery and properties, are briefly mentioned. The important idea behind design is that it should reflect continuity of style in every item seen on the screen. Thus, the viewer will learn to identify readily the "look" of your operation, and eventually form an image of your station as a whole.

Design is an overall concept that includes not only the lettering and layout on a studio card, or the plan for a set, but the logo of the station, its stationary, the office furniture, and the pictures in the hallways. Design, or the lack of it, permeates everything the station shows on the air and off. It sets the style for a broadcast operation. The logo for CBS, for example, induces us to expect the same high quality from the network's programming.

But a handsome logo will not automatically carry its design qualities over to the programming or to the on-the-air graphics or scenery. What is important here is developing a design consciousness for *everything* you do; a well-executed logo is merely the symbol for such awareness, not its sole cause.

In this chapter we will stress two of the most obvious aspects of design: graphics and scenery.

12·1   The logo of a station or network reflects its design consciousness; it often sets its overall design style. (Courtesy CBS.)

Graphics

Television graphics include all *two-dimensional* visuals especially prepared for the television screen, such as title cards, special illustrations,

Aspect Ratio   The proportions of the television screen, and therefore of all television pictures: three units high and four units wide.

Brightness   Attribute of color that indicates the grayscale value, whether the color photographs in black-and-white as a light gray or a dark gray. Sometimes called value.

Character Generator   A special effects generator that electronically produces a series of letters and numbers directly on the television screen, or keyed into a background picture.

Chroma Key Drop   A well-saturated blue canvas drop that can be pulled down from the lighting grid to the studio floor, or even over part of it, as a background for chroma key matting.

Compatible Color   Color signals that can be received as black-and-white pictures on monochrome television sets. Generally used to mean that the color scheme has enough brightness contrast for monochrome reproduction with a good grayscale contrast.

maps, or charts. There are three major factors to be considered: (1) overall specifications, (2) types of graphics, and (3) preparation and actual operation.

Specifications

Whenever you are preparing graphics for the television screen, you should pay close attention to (1) aspect ratio, (2) scanning and essential areas, (3) readability and balance, (4) color and color compatibility, (5) grayscale, and (6) style.

Aspect Ratio   The proportions of the television screen are 3:4; that is, anything that appears there is horizontally oriented within an area three units high and four units wide. All graphic information must, therefore, be contained within this aspect ratio. *(See 12.2.)*

Most artwork—studio cards or slides—is prepared in aspect ratio. You will find that a major problem with artwork prepared outside the television station is the total disregard for this essential proportion. Although our eyes can very readily adjust to some other aspect ratio, the television camera cannot. If you pull back far enough with your camera to include the entire out-of-aspect-ratio studio card, the information on it is likely to become so small that it is unreadable. Or, you can crop the card so that it fits the aspect ratio. But then you will lose important information.

Slides can be used only if they are horizontally oriented. Vertical slides not only lose a major portion of the information but also look bad on the screen. *(See 12.5.)*

You will find that blackboards can present a special aspect-ratio problem. If, for example, the

---

Crawl   Graphics (usually credit copy) that move slowly up the screen; often mounted on a drum, or crawl. More exactly, an up-and-down movement of credits is called a roll, and a horizontal movement is called a crawl.

Cursor   A dot produced on the screen by a special effects generator (usually a character generator), indicating the location of the first word or line.

Essential Area   The section of the television picture, centered within the scanning area, that is seen by the home viewer, regardless of masking of the set or slight misalignment of the receiver. Sometimes called critical area.

Flat   A piece of standing scenery used as background or to simulate the walls of a room.

Floor Plan   A plan of the studio floor, showing the walls, the main doors, and the location of the control room, with the lighting grid or batten pattern superimposed over the floor area. More commonly, a diagram of scenery and properties in relation to the studio floor area.

Graphic Mass   Any picture element that is perceived as occupying an area within the frame and as relatively heavy or light.

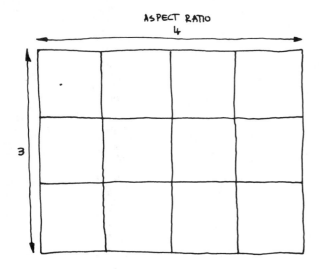

ASPECT RATIO
4
3

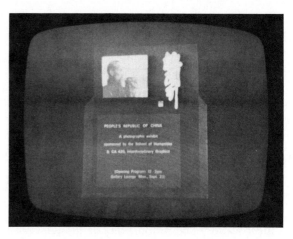

12·3   When showing an out-of-aspect-ratio studio card in its entirety, the information usually becomes so small that it is no longer readable.

12·2   The television aspect ratio is three units high and four units wide.

Graphics   All two-dimensional visuals prepared for the television screen, such as title cards, charts, and graphs.

Hue   The color itself, such as red, green, or blue.

Logo   A visual symbol that identifies a specific organization, such as a television station or network.

Moiré Effect   Color vibrations that occur when narrow, contrasting stripes of a design interfere with the scanning lines of the television system.

Open Set   A set constructed of noncontinuous scenery, with large open spaces between the main groupings.

Props   Properties: furniture and other objects used for set decorations and by actors or performers.

Roll   Graphics (usually credit copy) that move slowly up the screen; often called crawl.

Saturation   Attribute of color that indicates strength, as measured by a deep red or a washed-out pink. Sometimes called chroma.

12·4 By moving the camera in closer so that the graphic fits the aspect ratio of the television screen, important information is lost in the cropping process.

12·5 Vertically oriented slides should not be used on television, since they lose their top and bottom information. Also, there will be black spaces on the sides of the screen, since the vertical slide will not fill the entire screen width.

Scanning Area Picture area that is scanned by the camera pickup tube; more generally, the picture area actually reproduced by the camera and relayed to the studio monitors, which is further reduced by the masking of the home screen and general transmission loss.

Set Module Pieces of scenery of standard dimensions that allow a great variety of interchange and configuration.

Super Card A studio card with white lettering on a black background, used for superimposition of a title, or for keying of a title over a background scene.

Threefold Three flats hinged together.

Twofold Two flats hinged together. Also called a book.

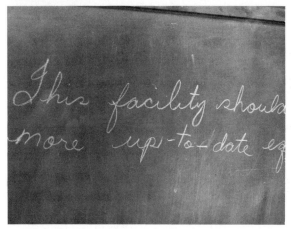

12·6 Normal writing on the blackboard can present a serious aspect-ratio problem. The camera cannot show a closeup of a sentence that stretches over the width of the blackboard.

television teacher writes on the blackboard in her usual way, starting on the left side and moving across to the right side, you will not be able to fit the whole sentence into the shot unless you take a long shot of the entire board and reduce the legibility of the information *(see 12.6)*. One work-

able solution is to have the blackboard divided into several aspect-ratio fields. If the teacher stays within the borders, you can show the entire information in a closeup shot *(see 12.7)*.

There are instances in graphics, however, where out-of-aspect ratio is not only usable but desirable. Take a chart with a steeply rising curve *(12.8)*. A slow, tight tilt up the curve reveals the information more vividly than a long shot of the whole chart, or a shot of a chart drawn within the aspect ratio. The same is true, of course, for a horizontally oriented, out-of-aspect-ratio chart whose information gains in impact by a gradual revelation through a pan.

If you need to use graphic material that must be shown in its entirety, yet which is out of aspect ratio, mount it neatly on a large card that is in aspect ratio. You simply frame up on the large card, keeping the out-of-aspect-ratio information as nearly screen-center as possible.

Scanning and Essential Areas But even when the graphic material is in aspect ratio, part of it still may not reach the home screen. Within the aspect ratio, there is a peripheral loss of picture area caused by the various electronic manipulations between camera and home reception and the masking of the television screen. The picture you see in the camera viewfinder usually shows more picture area than the control-room monitor, and a good deal more than the home receiver. Each time you record a picture and play it back, you lose some of it. The amount lost depends on the transmission factors, the number of tape generations, and especially on the masking and alignment (or rather misalignment) of the home receiver. The picture height and width may be simultaneously misadjusted on the receivers. In order to make sure that all the information on a card, for example, shows up on the home receiver, the camera must include in its shot the *scanning and essential areas* of the graphic.

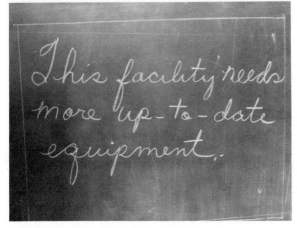

12·7 If the blackboard is divided into aspect-ratio fields, you can get a closeup of an entire sentence.

12·8 Tilting up on a chart that reveals its information step by step vertically is often more dramatic than showing the information all at once.

The *scanning area* is framed by the camera and shown by the preview monitors in the station. It is the area actually scanned by the camera pickup tube *(12.9a)*.

The *essential area,* sometimes called critical area, is centered within the scanning area. It is the portion seen by the home viewer, regardless of mask-ing of the set, transmission loss, or slight misalignment of the receiver. Obviously, all essential information should be contained within the essential area.

However, if you use illustrations in addition to written information, try to extend them to the scanning area so that, if your picture area loss is less than expected, your illustration does not break off suddenly, leaving empty screen space.

The preparation for a *slide* is the same as for a studio card. Since the scanning area for a slide is the area as approximately outlined by the standard mask, make sure that when photographing artwork, you line up your still camera near the outside edges of the studio card. This way you will be assured that the essential area of the slide

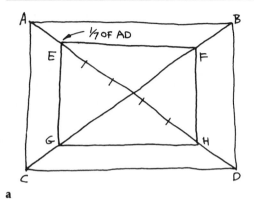

a

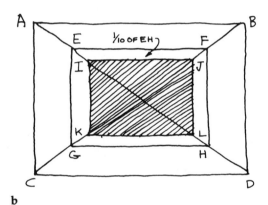

b

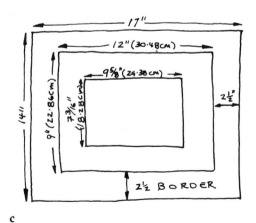

c

12·9   How large should the scanning and essential areas be in relation to the overall size of the studio card? Rather than quoting area percentages, which you may find difficult to translate into workable dimensions, let us consider a simple procedure. Assuming that your studio card is cut in a three-by-four ratio, draw a diagonal from corner to corner. Measure its length. Divide this figure (length of the diagonal) by seven. Take this new figure (¹⁄₇ of the diagonal) and mark it off on the diagonal, starting at one of the corners *(see a)*. This gives you the corner point for the scanning area.

Scanning Area: Draw diagonals *AD* and *BC* from the corners of the card. Measure one of the diagonals *(AD)*. Divide this figure by seven. Mark off this distance (¹⁄₇ of the diagonal) on the *AD* diagonal, starting at point *A*. This will give you point *E*. From *E*, draw lines parallel with the outside borders of the card. The points where the lines intersect with the diagonals *(E, F, G, H)* define the scanning area.

To arrive at the essential area, repeat a similar process, taking the *scanning* area as your new outside borders. Again, measure the diagonal from one corner to the next. Divide this figure (length of the diagonal of the scanning area) by ten. Take this new distance (¹⁄₁₀ of the diagonal) and mark it off on the diagonal of the scanning area, starting at one of the corners *(see b)*. This point gives you the corner for the essential area.

Essential Area: Measure the diagonal of the scanning area *(EH)*. Divide this figure by ten. Mark off this distance (¹⁄₁₀ of the diagonal of the scanning area) on the *EH* diagonal, starting at point *E*. This will give you point *I*. From *I*, draw lines parallel with the borders of the scanning area. The points where the lines intersect with the diagonals *(I, J, K, L)* define the essential area.

You will find that, by using the metric system, you will be able not only to measure the diagonals more accurately than with inches but also to divide the distances more easily into the ⅐ and ⅒ fractions.

The most popular studio card sizes are 14 × 17 inches (35.56cm × 43.18cm) and 11 × 14 inches (27.94cm × 35.56cm). You may want to simplify the metric measures to a 36cm × 43cm or a 27cm × 36cm format.

The advantage of the 14 × 17 format is that it has an equal 2½-inch border on all sides, defining easily the 9 × 12-inch scanning area. The essential area is easily defined from the 9 × 12 dimensions of the scanning area. The diagonal of the 9 × 12-inch scanning area measures 15 inches. One-tenth of 15 inches is 1½ inches. Since the 1½ inches are marked off from both ends of the diagonal, you are left with the diagonal of the essential area measuring 12 inches. When you now draw lines parallel to the borders of the scanning area, you arrive at an essential area within the scanning area of 7 3/16 inches by 9⅝ inches, or 18.28cm by 24.38cm *(see c)*.

A 14 × 17-inch studio card has a 2½-inch border on all four sides, defining the 9 × 12-inch scanning area (22.86cm × 30.48cm). The essential area is 7 3/16 × 9⅝ inches (18.28cm × 24.38cm).

An 11 × 14-inch studio card has a scanning area of 7.5 × 10 inches (19.05cm × 25.4cm), centered within the card. The essential area, centered within the scanning area, measures 6 × 8 inches (15.24cm × 20.32cm).

If you have already switched over to the metric system, or are willing to try now, you will want to work with a 31cm × 38cm studio card, which provides a 5cm border on all sides for the 21cm × 28cm scanning area. The essential area of the 31cm × 38cm card is 16.5cm × 22cm. The smaller 27cm × 36cm overall size is similar to the 11 × 14-inch card and has the same 19.05cm × 25.4cm scanning area, and the 15.24cm × 20.32cm essential area.

Once you have settled on a standard size for your studio cards, you may want to make a simple framing guide that immediately shows the scanning and

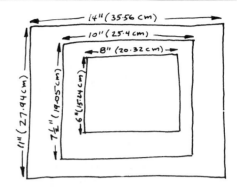

d

e

essential areas. Take a standard studio card (with the standard outside dimensions) and cut out four small slots to indicate the scanning area. Then cut the essential area from the center of the card *(see e)*. By placing this guide on top of a studio card, you can mark the respective areas quickly and accurately. Also, you can easily check whether or not the lettering of a card already prepared will fall within the essential area.

Through the slots you can mark the scanning area as a guide for camera framing. The cutout in the center will reveal the essential area. Only what shows through this window will appear on the television screen.

12·10 Keeping information within the essential area is especially important when using slides, since the television film camera cannot compensate for anything that lies outside this space.

will not be too close to the slide mask *(12.10)*. Observing the essential area is even more important for slides than for studio cards, since the television film camera cannot move on the slide to compensate for minor extensions. If the lettering goes beyond the essential area, the slide is unusable *(see 12.11.)*

Readability and Balance The amount of information that can be simultaneously projected onto the television screen is limited. As we have seen, the area that conveys essential information is severely contained. As you will remember from previous chapters, the limited resolution power of television will not reproduce artwork of small print satisfactorily. These restrictions are especially noticeable when motion picture credits roll by on the television screen. The smaller credit lines are usually impossible to read. But your main purpose in using television graphics is to communicate specific information to the viewer,

and to do so with style. If there is any single advice about this endeavor, it is this: *the simpler the graphic, the better the communication will be.*

Readability in the context of television graphics means the ability to read the words that appear on the television screen. As obvious as this statement is, it seems to have eluded many a graphic artist. The letters should be fairly large, and should have a bold, clean contour. The less information you cram into the essential area, the better. It is often more sensible to prepare a series of slides, each one displaying a small amount of information, than one slide with an overabundance.

Readability depends also on the relationship between foreground and background. A busy (highly detailed) background makes even the boldest foreground information hard to read. If you need to add lettering to a detailed background—such as a super or key of scores over the live picture of a football stadium—make sure that the printing is simple and bold. If the background is plain, you may get away with somewhat fancier lettering *(see 12.12, 12.13, and 12.14).*

Like any other type of graphic art, television graphics in order to be effective must exhibit both stability and tension. According to the subject matter, the relative tension might be either low (calm feeling) or high (excitement). The interrelationship of stability and tension is called *balance.* Balance depends on many different visual factors, a discussion of which would go far beyond the scope of this handbook.[1]

However, two factors are especially pertinent to television graphics. One is the angle of the *horizon line* relative to the screen, and the other is the distribution of *graphic mass.*

While the lettering is generally kept parallel with the bottom or top edge of the screen, the

---

[1] Herbert Zettl, *Sight-Sound-Motion* (Belmont, Calif.: Wadsworth Publishing Co., 1973), Chs. 6 and 7.

a

b

c

12·11 (a) Although we can see quite readily all the written information on this slide, the lettering goes beyond the limits of the essential area. (b) When used on the film chain, the letters just fit on the screen of the control-room monitor, which shows not only the essential area but also part of the scanning area. (c) But on the home screen, which reproduces the essential area only, some of the letters have been lost. This slide is, therefore, unusable for on-the-air transmission.

background may be tilted in various degrees so that its horizon line is out of whack. A tilted horizon expresses excitement, dynamism, increased energy, tension. We are no longer standing on level ground *(12.15)*.

A level horizon line, one that is parallel to the bottom or top screen edge, on the other hand, suggests normalcy, stability *(12.16)*.

You can also achieve the various degrees of balance—stable, neutral, and unstable—through a careful distribution of *graphic mass.* Graphic mass is any picture element that is perceived as occupying an area within the frame and as having relative weight.

A person standing in the middle of the frame is a graphic mass, as is a red dot in the screen

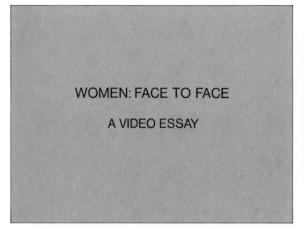

12·12 A modest amount of information written in simple, bold letters provides for maximum communication. When designing television graphics, keep in mind that the essential area and the resolution power of the television system are quite limited, and that the information displayed on the screen cannot be recalled by the viewer for closer examination.

12·13   This card reads well. The illustration and text are contrasting enough to show up well even under less than ideal reception conditions.

a

b

12·14   (a) This title does not read well. The brightness of the lettering and the background are much too similar for easy reading. (b) With more contrast between the lettering and the background, the title becomes more readable.

12·15 With a tilted horizonline, we assume a view different from everyday experience, thus increasing the visual energy of the scene and make it look and feel more dynamic.

12·16 A horizon that is level, in this case parallel to the bottom and top edges of the screen, with the verticals perpendicular to the horizon, suggests normalcy; it makes us feel as though we were standing upright on level ground.

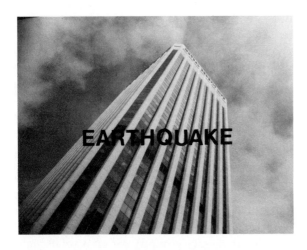

12·17 Though the lettering is usually kept parallel with the horizontal screen edges, and is therefore graphically stable, it does not render the background dynamism ineffective. On the contrary, the combination between foreground stability and background lability accentuates the general graphic energy of the title.

12·18 In a stable balance, the degree of stability is high, relative to pictorial dynamism. In a neutral balance, stability and dynamic factors are about even. In an unstable (or labile) balance, the dynamic pictorial factors outweigh the stable ones.*

* Zettl, *Sight-Sound-Motion,* p. 169.

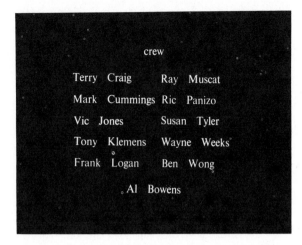

crew

Terry   Craig   Ray   Muscat

Mark   Cummings Ric   Panizo

Vic   Jones   Susan   Tyler

Tony   Klemens   Wayne   Weeks

Frank   Logan   Ben   Wong

Al   Bowens

12·19 If the written material is not organized into distinct areas of graphic mass, the screen area looks unbalanced and the information is hard to grasp.

corner, or a block of titles. In balancing a title card, you simply consider all pictorial elements *and* the lettering as various forms of graphic mass. As a matter of fact, most graphic artists balance a title card by trying to combine the written message into lettering *blocks.* Information is much easier to grasp when it is presented in blocks rather than randomly scattered all over the screen area *(see 12.19 and 12.20).*

Color and Color Compatibility   Since color is an important design element, you need to know something about its components and attributes, and how the television system reacts to them. This includes color compatibility, or the reproduction of color as shades of gray on the monochrome system.

Color is determined by three factors: (1) hue, (2) saturation, and (3) brightness. *Hue* refers to the color itself—that is, whether it is blue, green, red, or yellow. *Saturation* (sometimes called *chroma*) indicates the color strength—a strong red or a pale

blue, a washed-out green or a rich purple. *Brightness* (sometimes called *value*) indicates whether the color is dark or light.

If we had color production and color reception exclusively, hue and saturation would be our primary concern. In other words, you would be concerned primarily with the aesthetics of color—whether, for example, subtle greens and reds would harmonize (concern with hue), or whether you would like to have a stronger, more intense color instead of a pastel tone (concern with saturation). The lightness or darkness of the color (brightness) would, in this case, be relatively incidental.

The recognition and application of color harmony cannot be explained in a short paragraph. They need experience, practice, sensitivity, and taste. But there is one very general way of dealing with *color harmony* and *color balance* that may be of help to you. Rather than trying to say which colors go with what other colors, let us simply classify them in two main groups: (1) *high-energy* colors and (2) *low-energy* colors. The high-energy group includes basic, bright, highly saturated hues, such as red, yellow, orange, green, and a warm blue. The low-energy colors are more subtle hues with a low degree of saturation, such as the pastel colors, or the browns, dark greens, purples, and bluish grays.

To achieve balance, you can set a high-energy color against another high-energy color, so that they achieve equal graphic weight (such as yellow and red stripes), surround a high-energy color with a larger low-energy color area (such as a red dot on a dark gray ground), set off a small high-energy color area with a large low-energy color area (such as a subdued green area extending over most of the screen and a narrow red area filling the rest of it), or two low-energy colors of similar graphic weight (such as a wide horizontal stripe of brown covering the bottom third of the screen, with a subdued blue covering the top two-thirds).

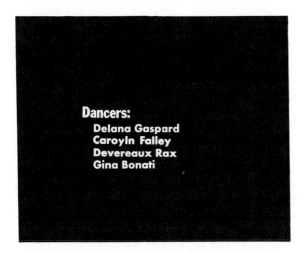

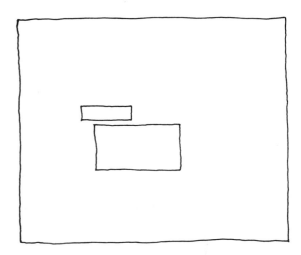

12·20 By arranging the titles in blocks of graphic mass, you achieve a degree of balance appropriate for the information, and help the viewer comprehend related facts at one glance.

One of the easiest ways to achieve balance is to use a low-energy color background, with the foreground design in high-energy colors.[2]

Although constant improvements are made in the image pickup devices (extended red Plumbicon tube, or separate mesh tubes), there are some things with which even the best color cameras have trouble. One is the color *red.* A highly saturated warm red or orange is not handled very well by the Plumbicon pickup tube. Even if it manages to reproduce the hue fairly accurately, the whole electronic system may rebel and produce excessive noise or, more frequently, color banding (clearly discernible bands of color that stretch horizontally over the whole screen). Another problem is any design containing narrow, contrasting color *stripes.* When the striped pattern coincides in a certain way with the lines of the scanning pattern, a *moiré effect* occurs, which shows up as color vibrations. As exciting as such vibrations may be as a special effect in a dance number, they are disturbing in a title card for a straight news show, or on the dress of a performer.

The monochrome television camera, and especially the monochrome receiver, is insensitive to hue and largely to saturation. All it shows you of a variety of colors is their relative *brightness.* Monochrome cameras and receivers are color-blind; they translate every color they see into shades of gray. When you design graphics in color, don't just be concerned with the combination of hue and the degree of saturation, but pay special heed to whether or not the colors differ enough in brightness so that they show up as different grays on the monochrome receiver. This translation of color into grays is called color compatibility.

As long as there are monochrome receivers in use, you must consider the problem of *color compatibility.* To achieve a color design that has enough brightness contrast for good compatibility is not always an easy job. Even if you select colors that have various degrees of brightness, intense light

---

[2] Zettl, *Sight-Sound-Motion,* pp. 94–96.

levels may wash out all but the most extreme brightness contrasts. If a dark color (low degree of brightness) is illuminated by a large amount of light, it may show up a lighter gray on the monochrome receiver than a light color that is in a shadow area.

12·21 The surest way to determine whether you have enough brightness contrast in your color scene—that is, whether your color scheme is compatible—is to watch the scene on your monochrome monitor. If the picture looks sharp, if it has "snap," your colors are all right. If it looks washed out, lacking proper contrasts, your colors are not compatible. Often it is enough just to put a few color swatches in front of the camera under normal lighting conditions to see how they register on the grayscale. In fact, with a little experience you will find that just by squinting your eyes you can determine fairly well whether two colors have enough brightness contrast to assure compatibility.

Experienced scenic and graphic artists often devise highly compatible color schemes without ever consciously checking relative brightness. A good painter usually juxtaposes colors that differ not only in hue but in brightness. You might want to look up some high-quality monochrome reproductions of famous paintings to see how "compatible" the color schemes are. *(See color plates V—IX, between pages 22 and 23.)*

Grayscale The brightness of a color is usually measured by how much light it reflects. We have already talked about reflectance percentages in our discussion on lighting (Chapter 6). The television system is not capable of reproducing pure white (100 percent reflectance) or pure black (zero percent reflectance); at best, it can reproduce an off-white (about 70 percent for monochrome television, and only about 60 percent for color), and an off-black (about 3 percent reflectance). We call these brightness extremes "TV white" and "TV black." If you now divide the brightness range between TV white and TV black into distinct steps, you have the television *grayscale.*

The most common number of brightness steps in a grayscale is ten *(12.22).* However, the system can reproduce all ten steps only under the most ideal conditions. A grayscale of seven steps is more realistic for monochrome television *(12.23),* and you may find that many color shows translate into only five *(12.24).* Just think if you had only five tubes of different grays to paint every conceivable scene on the television screen. This is the brightness limitation of most monochrome television.

In color television, it is often the hue that distinguishes one area from another. But if the hues have the same brightness—that is, if they reproduce on the monochrome receiver as the identical step on the grayscale—the viewer will not be able to distinguish between them *(see color plate V).* Make sure, therefore, that your background color is different from the foreground color not only in hue but also in brightness. A 2-step brightness difference between the foreground and

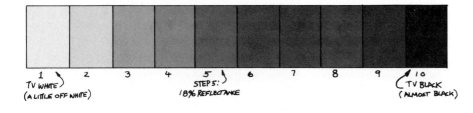

12·22 10-Step Grayscale: In the 10-step grayscale, the brightness range from the brightest point (TV white) to the darkest point (TV black) is divided into ten steps.

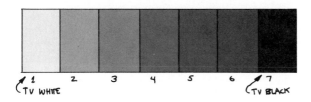

12·23 7-Step Grayscale: You will find that most good television systems reproduce only seven distinct steps of gray between TV white and TV black. The 7-step grayscale is, therefore, often preferred as the more realistic guide to color compatibility than the 10-step grayscale.

12·24 5-Step Grayscale: Many production people work on the assumption that most television receivers reproduce only five steps of gray, especially when reproducing a color show in black and white. They use the 5-step grayscale as a standard for graphic art.

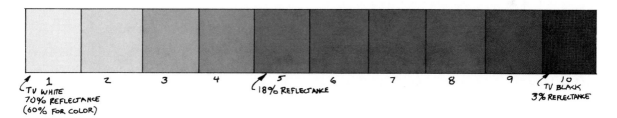

12·25 Since it takes relatively little reflected light to produce a dark gray or even a medium gray on the television monitor (approximately the middle of the grayscale), step five on a 10-step grayscale, or step four on a 7-step grayscale, does not coincide with the middle of the light reflectance range (50 percent). In fact, a color with a reflectance of 50 percent is in the upper ranges of the grayscale, and actually regis- ters as step two on the 10-step grayscale. A color that reproduces under normal circumstances in the middle ranges of a grayscale usually measures only about 18 percent reflectance. Since on the color receiver, white is actually a combination of red, green, and blue (additive mixing), TV white has only a 60 percent reflectance *(see illustration)*.

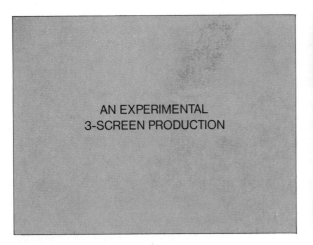

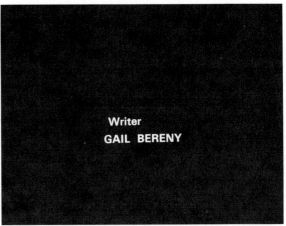

12·26 The plain title card is prepared for the studio camera. It is shown as is and is not mixed with any other video source.

12·27 A super, or key, card generally has white lettering on a black background. During the super or key operation the black background drops out and lets the second video source show through.

background colors is considered a minimum spread.

Style Style, like language, is a living thing. It changes according to the specific aesthetic demands of the people at a given location and time. To ignore it means to communicate less effectively. You learn style not from a book but primarily through being sensitive to your environment, by experiencing life with open eyes and ears, and especially an open heart. Some people not only sense the general style that prevails at a given time, but manage to enhance it with a personal, distinctive mark.

But whether you are a style setter or not, the style of the art work should match the style of your entire show. Even the opening titles should give some indication of its type and character. In a comedy show, for instance, cartoon lettering or an amusingly animated film opening helps to get the viewers' attention and prepare them for the show content. A dramatic show, on the other

hand, may be identified by supering simple and unobtrusive titles over live action. But don't go overboard on style and identify your guest performer from China with Chinese lettering, or your newsreel of the downtown fire with flame letters. Don't abandon good taste for effect.

Types of Television Graphics

The major types of television graphics include (1) the plain title card, (2) the super, or key, card, (3) the chroma key card, (4) the slide, (5) the crawl, (6) the character generator, and (7) maps and charts.

The Plain Title Card The plain title card has simple information, such as the title of the show, the names of performers, writers, producer, director, printed on a plain colored (or gray) background. The plain title card is shot by the camera and displayed on the screen. It is generally not combined with any other video source (such as

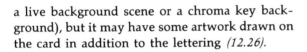

a

b

12·28 If you super a name over a medium shot of a person, keep the lettering as close to the bottom edge of the essential area as possible (a). During the super, the name will then cut across the person's chest rather than his face (b).

a live background scene or a chroma key background), but it may have some artwork drawn on the card in addition to the lettering *(12.26)*.

The Super, or Key, Card The super, or key, card is usually a black card containing white lettering. During a super or key, the black background drops out, revealing the background scene over which the white letters appear *(12.28)*. Since this title is combined with another video source, the background scene, the information given on the super card should be as terse as possible. Use simple, bold letters only, and try to restrict the amount of information. If your special effects on your switcher allows a reverse key, you can use a white background card with black lettering on it.

If you want to identify a guest by supering or keying his name over his picture on the screen, make sure that the super does not cut across his face. The viewer is interested in getting to know the guest on the screen as well as possible. Besides

defeating this goal, covering someone's face with writing seems rather impolite. To avoid this problem, put the name of the guest, or any other super identification, as close to the lower edge of the essential area as possible. The camera operator will be able to frame the super in the lower part (lower third) of the viewfinder, thus landing on the guest's chest rather than his face (assuming you are on a medium shot) *(12.28)*.

The Chroma Key Card The chroma key card is much like the regular super card, except that the background for the white lettering is blue instead of black. Instead of supering the card over the background scene, you key the lettering into the background scene through the chroma key process. Since blue drops out during the keying, only the letters remain. But chroma key cards also consist of various colored backgrounds with one or two words and a simple design placed in the upper right- or lefthand corner of the essential area. If slides are not available, such cards are used

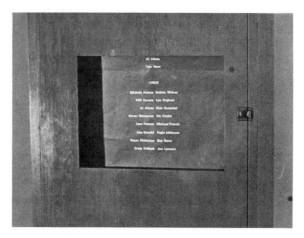

12·29   The crawl is a strip of paper on which the long list of credits is lettered. As you rotate the drum in a direction away from the camera, the credit lines seem to move up the screen. The faster the drum rotates, the faster the lines appear.

as background for news stories; matted into the news set, they provide an immediate visual identification of the story underway. More often, they are photographed and used as slides so that the change from one chroma key background to the next can be accomplished smoothly, without tying up a camera on the floor.

The Slide   Slides are often more advantageous than studio cards since they do not tie up a studio camera and are not difficult to change on the air. As pointed out before, all pertinent information must be kept within the essential area, since the telecine camera cannot adjust for wider copy.

Since the lamps in television slide projectors are usually quite hot, and the alignment of the slides relative to the multiplexer is quite critical, all slides should be mounted between thin *glass* plates. Thus, they cannot buckle in the heat and go out of focus.

The Crawl   If you have a good deal of information to display on the screen, such as the closing credits for a large production, you should use a crawl instead of a large number of slides. By this method the written information seems to roll up the screen in one continuous motion. Since the dimensions of a crawl differ widely, there are no standard specifications. Its length depends on the amount of information, and its width must be sufficient to accommodate the *longest line within the essential area*. The lines are usually lettered on a strip of black paper that is then mounted onto the crawl *(12.29)*.

The drum is rotated either by hand, or, more commonly, by motor. Since the letters generally move from screen-bottom to screen-top, the drum should rotate away from the camera, not toward it.

The Character Generator   For the majority of written graphics, most professional television operations use the character generator. This is a special effects device that creates letters and numbers in a variety of sizes and fonts (letter designs). Some of the more sophisticated character genera-

12·30 Character Generator: A character generator produces a variety of letters electronically. They can be stored and recalled at any time for a key or matte key. The lines can be moved right or left on the screen, rolled up or down, or crawled sideways.

tors can even produce simple graphic displays such as sales curves and bars that show percentages. Through a colorizer, the letters can be programmed in various colors *(12.30)*.

To prepare the material, you type the needed titles on a computer-type keyboard. The information is then stored on a disc and can be recalled from the switcher and keyed like any other special effect. Since the letters are electronically generated, they can be placed anywhere on the screen. A *cursor* (location indicator) shows you the exact location where the first word will appear. By moving the cursor into various positions, with the words or lines following, you can center the information, or put it off-center, roll it up and down or sideways on the screen.

Although you have just learned that a crawl is a series of lines moving up the screen by means of a rotating drum, you must modify this terminology somewhat when using a character gen-

a

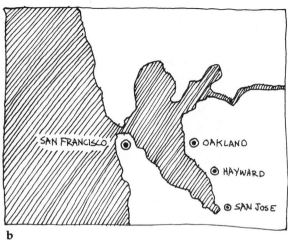

b

12·31   (a) When the water areas are lighter than the land areas, the water seems to be above the land. Therefore, the viewer may see the water and the land as exactly opposite to what they really are.

(b) In order to make the land areas appear higher than the water, simply make them lighter in color (or brightness).

erator. A *crawl* by this method means moving the lines *sideways* on the screen; an *up or down* movement is called a *roll.*

Maps and Charts   Maps are an important visual aid for many television programs, especially newscasts. Usually, they are extremely simplified, showing only the detail that is most essential for the specific communication. For example, if you make a weather map of your area, you don't need to draw in the freeways. On the other hand, if you use the map to show the traffic patterns in your city, you need to show the major streets but not necessarily the location of parks and public buildings.

Commercially available maps are much too detailed to be of much use in television. If you have to use an existing map, emphasize the major areas through bold outlines and distinctive colors. Make sure that all colors have enough brightness contrast for good black-and-white reception.

If large water areas are to be set off against land, as in a map of the San Francisco Bay Area, you will have to decide whether to make the water darker or lighter than the land. The difficulty is that the viewer may see the map in reversed polarity, which will make water areas look like land and land areas look like water. In general, making the land areas lighter assures the correct orientation *(see 12.31).*

If you work in color, a fairly dark, saturated blue for the water and a light beige or green for the land will make the water lie under, rather than above the land. Also, in monochrome reception, the water will appear dark and the land light.

We have already indicated that certain *charts* may be presented out of aspect ratio, if you intend to reveal the information gradually through a tilt or pan. In all other cases, try to contain the data in aspect ratio, so that the camera can take close-ups without losing important information.

Make sure that the charts are easy to read. Matter that gets lost in the transmission process is of no use to the home viewer. Maximum clarity—together with adherence to scanning and essential areas—should be your chief objective in preparing charts for television.

Preparation and Operation

Basic graphic arts techniques apply also to the preparation of television graphics. For graphics to come through as an intrinsic part of the television presentation, their assembling and manipulation before the cameras require skill, practice, and planning.

Preparation If you have an electronic character generator, the need for mechanical lettering is drastically reduced. If, however, you do not enjoy such luxury, you may still have to rely on manual methods, such as rub-on or glue-on letters. The *hotpress* has been the mainstay of the television art department for many years, and is likely to remain the chief lettering tool for some time to come. The reasons for its popularity are simplicity of operation, versatility, and quality results. Standard lead type is heated by the press (to about 250°) and pressed upon a plastic film. The film is literally melted onto illustration board, clear acetate cells, or any other material you may want to use as a background *(12.32)*.

There is a variety of colored *illustration board* available, which you can cut up into the studio card size of your choice. Make sure that it has a mat surface to prevent glares.

As mentioned before, *slides* are prepared exactly as studio cards and then photographed and mounted. A quick and simple system is to photograph the artwork with a Polaroid camera equipped with special 2 × 2 slide accessories.

If you prepare artwork for a normal super, or key, slide, print *black letters* on a *white card.* The photographic process reverses the polarity of the

artwork, and you can use the film negative with the black background and the white letters directly for your super slide.

If you want to use a photograph, or a picture from a book, as a slide background, you can print your text on an acetate cell (clear plastic), put the cell on top of the background picture, and photograph both together.

In preparing a *crawl,* you may want to print the various names on strips of black paper and mount them on the crawl paper. This way you will not have to redo the whole crawl if you discover a misspelling. Also, you can rearrange the strips quite easily in order to accommodate another credit line.

Operation Studio cards are put on studio easels for easy camera pickup. You will need at least two easels per studio so that you can cut from card to card. You can also change the cards on a single easel, either by flipping or pulling one after the other. Such "hot" flips or pulls, however, need practice so that they look smooth on the air. Although you should flip the cards as fast as you can, you should realize that a neat, slow flip looks better than a fast, sloppy one.

Always *bring the easel to the camera,* not the reverse. When placing the easel, make sure that it is square with the camera. Otherwise, the title will look as if it is running uphill or downhill on the screen. If the lettering runs uphill (high on the right), rotate the easel clockwise *(12.33)*. If the lettering runs downhill (high on the left), rotate the easel counterclockwise *(12.34)*.

Special effects wipes have all but eliminated *animated graphics.* There are, however, two methods that are simple and reliable enough to be used on a live camera. One is the *pulloff card,* the other the *pulloff strip.*

A pulloff card is simply a black card that is put over the title card. If you pull the cover card from camera-left to camera-right, the lettering on the

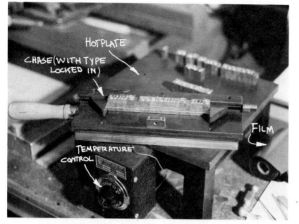

HOTPLATE

CHASE (WITH TYPE LOCKED IN)

FILM

TEMPERATURE CONTROL

a

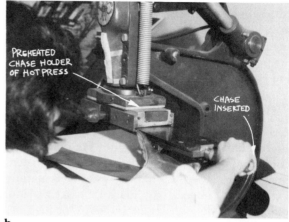

PREHEATED CHASE HOLDER OF HOT PRESS

CHASE INSERTED

b

FILM (WITH SHINY SIDE UP)

c

LEVER (BROUGHT DOWN; HOT TYPE MELTING FILM ONTO CARD)

d

12·32 (a) First, lock the type in mirror image into the chase and preheat the whole thing on a special hotplate to approximately 250°. (b) Then insert the chase into the hotpress, whose head has also been preheated to the same temperature. (c) Line up the card underneath the chase and place the plastic film (which comes in a variety of colors) on it with the shiny side up. (d) Bring the lever down quickly and hold the hot type on the card very briefly. If you keep the lever down too long, the heated plastic will seep into the material and make the letters fuzzy-edged.

card underneath will be revealed gradually. The faster you pull, the faster the letters will appear.

The pulloff strip is used to animate simple charts. To demonstrate the flight path of a com-munication satellite, for example, cut a small slot into the card for the flight path and back-light the whole graphic. Then place opaque masking tape over the slot to prevent the back light from shin-

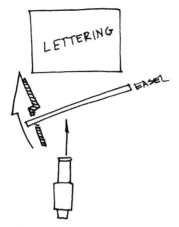

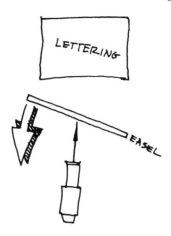

12·33 If the lettering is high on the right, rotate the easel clockwise.

12·34 If the lettering is high on the left, rotate the easel counterclockwise.

ing through. As you pull off the tape, the flight path will gradually come into view *(12.35)*.

One final word, about *copyright*. Whenever you present printed material, including reproductions of famous paintings, professional photographs, illustrated books, and similar matter, you must obtain permission from the copyright holders.

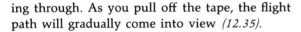

Scenery

Television scenery consists of the *three-dimensional* elements of design that are used in the studio. Its principal function is to create a specific environment—a faithful recreation of a Victorian living room for a dramatic scene, a somewhat stylized workroom for a news show, a simple definition of space through pillars and sculptures for a modern dance number. In any case, television scenery should allow for optimum camera movement and camera angles, microphone placement and boom movement, appropriate lighting, and maximum action by the performers and actors.

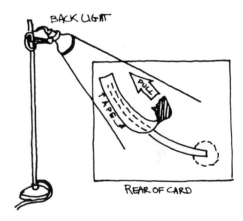

12·35 By pulling a masking tape off a back-lighted slot, directional movement is applied to a graphic.

Since the television camera looks at a set both at close range and at a distance, scenery must be detailed enough to appear realistic yet plain enough to prevent cluttered, busy pictures. And, since it is the camera and not the studio spectator that looks at the set, the scenery does not have to be continuous. One part of the set—for example, the main entrance of a house—may be in one corner of the studio, and another part—say the hallway—in another corner. The location of these portions depends entirely on the shooting sequence and on the director's camera placement.

Fortunately, the relative mobility of the television (or film) camera has made the building of elaborate sets largely unnecessary, at least in small station operation. If you need to shoot inside an elaborate Victorian parlor or a motel bedroom, go there. Take the cameras to the location; don't try to bring the location into the studio.

Contrary to film, where the environment is an important dramatic agent, television's primary dramatic material and focus of attention is the human being. In general, the scenic environment, though important, remains secondary.

Nevertheless, all human actions take place in some sort of environment. The empty studio is rarely the most appropriate, or the most pleasing, one for human interaction. Even if you are seldom, if ever, called upon to design or construct elaborate scenery, you should nevertheless know the elements of this calling. The knowledge will aid you in managing the studio space, as well as screen space in general. The basic elements are (1) scene design, (2) the floor plan, (3) types of scenery and construction, and (4) properties and set dressings.

Scene Design

Before you design a set, you must know what the show is all about. Talk to the director about his concept of the show, even if it is a simple interview. Arrive at a set by defining the necessary spatial environment for optimal communication rather than by inquiring what other stations are doing. For example, you may feel that the best way to let your viewers in on what's new is not by having an authoritative newscaster read stories from a pulpitlike contraption, but instead by

moving the cameras into the newsroom itself, or, better yet, out into the street where it's happening. If you have an interviewer probing tactfully, yet persistently, into the guest's attitudes and feelings, you don't need a whole living room as a set. Two comfortable chairs in front of a plain background may make the scene complete. In any case, before deciding on a set, try to see the entire show in *screen images.* Try to imagine those you would like the viewers to see and work backwards from there.

For example: "If in an interview I would like the viewer to see intimate closeups throughout the show, what set do I need?"

"Two chairs."

Designing scenery is a highly specialized profession, and should therefore be left to the specialist. Elaborate sets are designed by the art department, or in small station operations often by a free-lance designer. In college operations, the theater arts department usually takes care of the more ambitious set design and construction jobs. However, you need to know at least the basic components of scene design.

Set Background   The set background is an important scenic element. It not only helps to *unify* a sequence of shots and place the action in a single environment, but also provides necessary *variety.*

Unification of shots can be achieved through keeping the background in a *uniform color,* or by decorating it in such a way that the viewer can easily relate one portion of the set to another. Since in television we see mostly *environmental detail,* you must give the viewer clues so that he can apply closure to the shot details and achieve, at least in his mind, a continuous environment. A uniform background color or design, or properties that point to a single environment, such as the typical furnishings of a kitchen—all help the viewer relate the various shots to a specific location. The *variety* is achieved by breaking up large

12·36 This set designer provided proper background variety for the long shot only. The picture between the two people breaks up the center of the picture reasonably well and provides some visual interest for an otherwise dull shot.

12·37 But on a closeup of the guest—the most frequent shot in the show—we have no background variety. The same is true in a closeup shot of the host.

12·38 Now the picture is properly hung for background variety, although you would ordinarily not hang a picture in this position.

background areas into smaller, yet related, areas providing the cameras with elements necessary for inducing a certain amount of graphic tension. Hanging pictures on a plain wall is as simple a method for background variety as it is effective.

However, make sure that such design elements are indeed in the view of most camera shots *(see 12.36, 12.37, and 12.38)*. As so often happens, pictures are hung the way we expect them to appear in a living room, for example, rather than in range

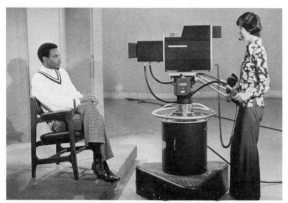

12·39 To avoid looking down at persons who are seated, place the chairs on a platform. The cameras can operate at a comfortable working height and yet shoot the scene from eye level.

of the camera shot. But what the camera does not see, the viewer will not see, and therefore it remains utterly useless *(12.37).*

Eye Level Camera operators have the undesirable habit of adjusting their cameras to the most comfortable working height, and not necessarily to the most effective aesthetic point of view. Therefore, if you place persons in normal chairs on the studio floor, they are positioned lower than the average camera working height; the camera looks down on them. This point of view carries subtle psychological implications of inferiority and also creates an unpleasant composition. You might do well, therefore, for any event where the performers are sitting most of the time, to place the chairs on a platform (anywhere from

12·40 The open set is discontinuous. It does not have connecting walls as in an actual room or a closed set, which duplicates an actual room. Rather, the space is defined by a few major pieces of scenery and furniture. (See shots—opposite—of set from different points of view.)

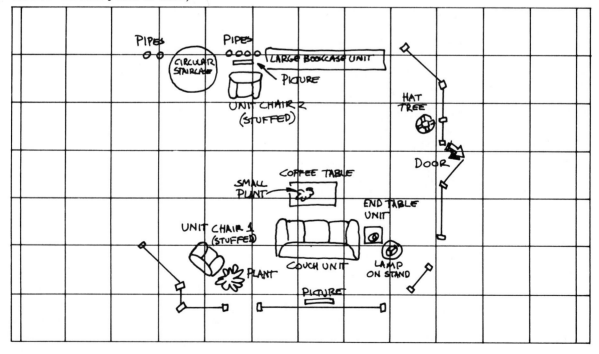

6 to 12 inches high). Thus, the camera can remain at a comfortable operating height, shooting at the scene at eye level.

The Open Set   Contrary to the closed set, where the scenery is continuous, very much like the walls in an actual room, the open set is discontinuous. This means that you use only the most important parts of a room—perhaps the door, a sofa, a table with a lamp as a foreground piece, a few freestanding walls with pictures on them, and so forth *(12.40)*. Since the camera rarely sees the whole room anyway, but only significant details, the viewer mentally fills in the missing parts of the room. This is called psychological closure.

There are many advantages of the open-set method: (1) The camera can look at the set and the action from many points of view without being restricted by closed walls. (2) The performers or actors have great freedom of movement. (3) The set is relatively easy to set up and strike (take down). (4) The set is easy to light. (5) The microphone boom can operate rather freely. And (6) the set is economical; it needs only a few flats and set pieces.

The open set can look extremely real, provided that its individual portions are realistically treated (furniture, flats, pictures, lamps) and that the director knows how to shoot *inductively*, to suggest a continuous environment by showing only significant details. The uniform background for the open set may be the unlighted cyclorama, which appears not piecemeal, as holes in the set, but as a solid dark unit.

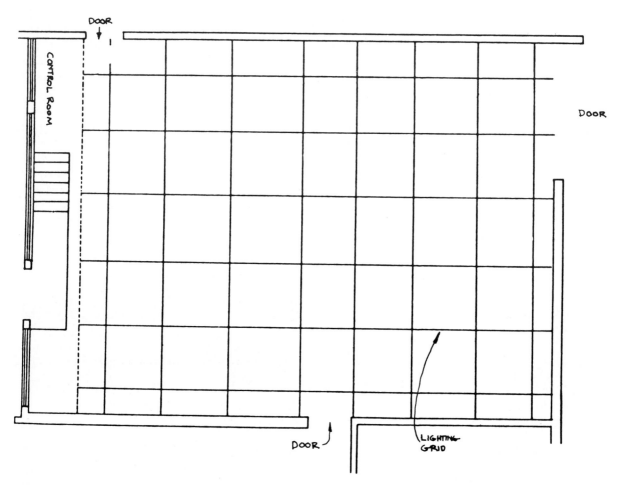

12·41 The floor plan shows the studio floor area, which is further defined by the lighting grid or the pattern of the lighting battens.

Studio Floor Treatment   One of the headaches of the scenic designer is the treatment of the studio floor. In long shots, it usually looks unattractive, as though the designer got tired of his idea before he reached the bottom of the picture.

The problem with decorating the studio floor is that the adornment must not interfere with camera travel. *Rugs,* for instance, make sense only in areas that are not used by cameras. Fortunately, the zoom lens can substitute for camera travel to some extent, thereby allowing floor coverings in certain scenes or sets.

A flexible *rubber tile,* which you can get in large (3 × 3 foot or roughly 1 × 1m) squares, makes excellent floor patterns. You simply lay it tightly on the studio floor in the desired pattern, and natural adhesion will keep the tiles in place.

For some sets, you can *paint* a design on a portion of the studio floor, or on a platform that supports part of the action. In an interview set, for example, you can decorate the platform with multicolored rug stripes or paint it in some appropriate pattern, without having to worry about the rest of the studio floor.

The Floor Plan

All set design is drawn on the floor plan, which is literally a plan of the studio floor. It shows the floor area, the main studio doors, the location of the control room, and the studio walls. To have a specific orientation pattern according to which the sets can be placed, the lighting grid, or batten locations, are drawn on the floor area *(12.41).* In effect, the grid resembles the orientation squares of a city map. *(See 12.44.)*

The scale of the floor plan varies, but it is normally ¼ inch = 1 foot. All scenery and set properties (furniture, lamps, and so forth) are then drawn to scale in the proper position relative to the studio walls and the lighting grid *(see 12.44).*

The floor plan is an important aid for all

12·42   You may want to consider using the metric scale for your floor plan. You will find that this is a much easier way to figure out proportions and fractions than the English system of measurement. One scale may be 1cm = 1m.

12·43   Although you may not want to become a set designer, you should nevertheless learn how to draw a basic floor plan and translate it into an actual set, into movement of performers and cameras and, finally, into television screen images.

When drawing a floor plan, watch for these potential problem areas: (1) Most often, a floor plan shows scenery backing that is insufficient for the foreground piece, for example, a single 10-foot-wide flat as backing for a whole set of living room furniture. The tendency is to draw furniture and other set pieces too small in proportion to the covering background flats. For indicating the prop furniture in your floor plan, it may help you to use the templates architects use. You can then place the furniture first and draw the necessary background later. (2) During the setup, you may notice that the available studio floor is always less than your floor plan indicates. Make sure, therefore, to limit your set design to the actual *available* floor space. (3) Always place your active furniture (used by the performers) at least six feet (roughly two meters) from the set wall, so that the back lights can be directed at the performance areas at not too steep an angle. Also, the director can use the space between wall and furniture for camera placement.

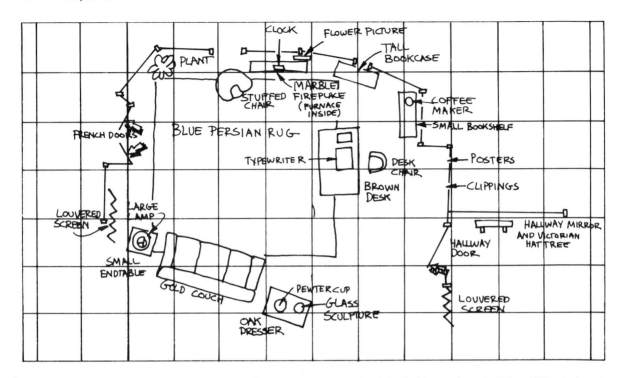

The floor plan shows labels: CLOCK, FLOWER PICTURE, TALL BOOKCASE, PLANT, MARBLE FIREPLACE (FURNACE INSIDE), STUFFED CHAIR, COFFEE MAKER, FRENCH DOORS, BLUE PERSIAN RUG, SMALL BOOKSHELF, TYPEWRITER, DESK CHAIR, POSTERS, BROWN DESK, CLIPPINGS, LOUVERED SCREEN, LARGE AMP, HALLWAY MIRROR AND VICTORIAN HAT TREE, SMALL ENDTABLE, HALLWAY DOOR, GOLD COUCH, PEWTER CUP, GLASS SCULPTURE, LOUVERED SCREEN, OAK DRESSER

12·44 The completed floor plan shows the exact location of the scenery and set properties, relative to the lighting grid or pattern of battens. The floor personnel use this plan as a guide for setting up the scenery and placing the major properties.

production and engineering personnel. It is essential for the floor crew, who must set up the scenery and place the major set properties. The lighting technician needs it to plot the general lighting layout. The director uses it to visualize the show and block the major actions of performers, cameras, and microphone boom. The audio engineer can familiarize himself with specific microphone placement and other possible audio requirements. The performers will be able to anticipate their movements and spot potential blocking problems.

If you use the floor plan for your lighting plot, simply add a transparent overlay to draw in your major light sources. If you design a set, or if you have to arrange a simple one without the aid of a floor plan, try to put it *where the lights are.* This means that you should place it in such a way that the back lights, key lights, and fill lights hang approximately in the right position. Sometimes a set is placed in a corner of the studio where most of the lighting instruments have to be rehung to get proper illumination, when in another part of the studio the same set could have been lighted without moving a single instrument. As you can see once again, you cannot afford specializing in one television production activity by disregarding the other production aspects. Everything interrelates, and the more you know about the other production techniques and functions, the better your coordination of the various elements will be.

Types of Scenery and Construction

If you are a member of the floor crew, or if you want to communicate intelligently with the scene designer, you should know the basic types of scenery and some major methods of scene construction. We can divide scenery into three major groups: (1) standard set units, (2) hanging units, and (3) set pieces.

Standard Set Units   Standard set units have a uniform height, yet various widths. The height is usually ten feet (3.05m); the widths range from one to five feet (30.5cm to 1.52m). Single units are called *flats.* When two or three flats are hinged together, they are called *twofolds* or *threefolds.* If you have a low-ceiling studio, you may find the 8-foot height (2.44m) more convenient.

For small station operation, where you do not have the luxury of building new sets for every show, you might consider the use of set modules that can be used in a variety of configurations. A *set module* consists of flats that can be used either right-side up or on their side, and whose widths are such that, when several flats are stacked sideways, they are equal to the height of the flats, or when connected sideways, they are equal to the width of a twofold, for example. Many architects work with such modules, especially in large structures, where prefabrication is an essential building factor *(see 12.45).*

Hanging Units   While the flats stand on the studio floor, hanging set units are supported from the lighting grid or battens. The most versatile hanging background unit is the *cyclorama* or *cyc,* a continuous piece of muslin or canvas stretched along two, or all four, studio walls. Some cycs have a scrim (loosely woven material) stretched in front of them in order to break the light before it hits the cyc, thus producing a very soft, uniform background. *(See 12.46.)*

The *drop* is a wide roll of canvas with some sort of background scene painted on it. It commonly serves stylized settings, where the viewer is very much aware that the action is taking place in front of a canvas drop. Some drops consist of large photomurals for very realistic background effects.

The *chroma key drop* is a wide roll of chroma key blue canvas that can be pulled down and even stretched over part of the studio floor for chroma key matting.

A variety of normal *drapes* for interior sets also belong in the category of hanging units.

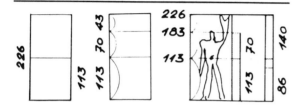

a

b

12·45   One of the by now famous modules has been designed by the Swiss-French architect Le Corbusier. His *Modulor* consists of a set of proportions that are modeled after the basic proportions of the human figure (a).

You may want to try to use these dimensions for your scenery modules (b).

Set Pieces   Standing pieces of scenery that are neither flats nor furniture are described as set pieces. They include pillars, pylons (which look like three-sided pillars), periaktoi (a periaktos is a three-sided standing unit, very much like a large pylon, that swivels on casters for quick scene changes), sweeps (a curved piece of scenery, similar to half a very large pillar), steps, blocks and pedestals, platforms and wagons (a wagon is a platform on casters), and a variety of folding screens.

Set pieces are an important scenic element. They can define the large studio space for a dance number, for example, without blocking the movement of the camera and dancers, or as foreground pieces. Or, they can be used at the outer edges of a set, to signal to the cameras not to shoot beyond. *(See 12.47.)*

The platforms and wagons serve as elevation devices. You might want to mount a whole set on wagons so that it can be rolled in and out of the studio quickly. Blocks and pedestals are generally used for simple displays. Screens serve as backgrounds for simple displays, as set end pieces, or to simulate windows or doors.

The *construction* of scenery is usually done by a professional stage carpenter or similarly qualified personnel. The materials and techniques used are extremely varied and depend entirely on the purpose of the show. Sometimes the scenery must represent as real a setting as possible; at other times, the set is purposely stylized, serving more of a decorative function. The availability of a great variety of plastic panels and the ability to mold existing plastic sheets into any number of relief patterns have made it possible to construct amazingly realistic scenery at a rather low cost. Also, the use of slotted steel instead of wood frames, and hardwall material instead of canvas, has led to the creation of highly flexible, durable, and realistic pieces of scenery *(12.48)*.

When setting up scenery, make absolutely

12·46 The cyclorama provides an ideal background for a great number of productions, especially for open-set designs.

12·47 Set pieces are freestanding elements of scenery that define studio space without blocking large areas, serve as foreground pieces, or signal the outer limits of a set.

certain that all pieces are safely anchored so that they will not tip over when bumped against by performers or cameras. As in all other aspects of television production, do not forsake safety for convenience or speed.

Properties and Set Dressings

Properties and set dressings are essential scenic elements. In television, they often do more to signify a particular environment than the background does.

There are three basic types of properties: (1) stage properties, or props, (2) set dressings, and (3) hand props.

Stage Props Stage props include the common type of furniture and items constructed for a specific purpose, such as news desks, lecterns, or panel tables.

For the normal complement of shows, you will need enough furniture to create settings for a modern living room, a study, an office, or a com-

12·48 The use of slotted steel has made television scenery extremely flexible.

fortable interview area. You can use real furniture. For the interview area, small simple chairs are more useful than large, elaborate ones. It is often difficult to bring oversized chairs close enough together for intimate spacing of the two-shot. The edges of the screen seem to attract items within the frame, making them appear farther apart than they really are. Small chairs can be placed close enough together so that they do not look too far apart on the screen, without making the persons sitting on them too awkward or fidgety. Try to get chairs and couches that are not too low; otherwise sitting and rising gracefully may become a problem.

Stage props for special shows, such as news desks and panel tables, are specially built to fit the overall design. But make sure that these props look stylish and that they work well. Since most sets of this kind are seen in their entirety only in the opening or closing shots, it is very important that the properties used in them be functional and look appropriate on the screen in a *closeup* as well as a long shot.

Set Dressings Set dressings are a major factor in determining the *style* and character of the set. While the flats may remain the same from one type of show to another, the dressing will give each set its distinguishing characteristic.

Set dressings include draperies, pictures, lamps and chandeliers, fireplaces, flower pots, indoor plants, candleholders, sculptures. Secondhand stores provide an unlimited fund for these things. In case of emergency, you can always raid your own living quarters.

Hand Properties Hand properties consist of all items that are actually *handled* by the performer or actor during the show. They include dishes, silverware, ashtrays, telephones, typewriters. If you have to use food, make sure that it is fresh, and the dishes and silverware are meticulously clean. Liquor is generally replaced by water (for clear spirits), tea (for whiskey), or soda pop (for red wine). With all due respect for realism, such substitutions are perfectly legitimate.

The most important thing about hand props is to have them actually on the set for the performer to use. They represent a major production item and are anything but incidental.

One last word about design. In a successful design, all items interrelate and harmonize with one another, from the largest, such as the background scenery, to the smallest, such as the ashtray on the end table, or the title card. Good design displays a *continuity of style*.

Summary

Design sets the style for a television station and its operation. The two major design factors are (1) graphics and (2) scenery.

Television graphics include all two-dimensional visuals that are especially prepared for the television screen, such as title cards and credit crawls, special illustrations, maps, and charts. These are the major factors of television graphics: (1) overall specifications, (2) types, and (3) preparation and actual operation.

The *specifications* include (1) aspect ratio, (2) scanning and essential areas, (3) readability and balance, (4) color and color compatibility, (5) grayscale, and (6) style.

The major *types of television graphics* are (1) the plain title card, (2) the super, or key, card, (3) the chroma key card, (4) the slide, (5) the crawl, (6) the character generator, and (7) maps and charts.

There are many methods of graphics *preparation*. In the absence of an electronic character generator, most title cards are hotpressed onto gray, black, or colored illustration board. All graphics must meet the electronic requirements of the camera and the operational requirements in the studio.

Scenery consists of the three-dimensional elements of design that are used in the studio. The elements of television scenery are (1) scene design, (2) floor plan, (3) types of scenery and construction, and (4) properties and set dressings.

The *floor plan* shows what scenery is used and where it is used relative to studio space.

The major types of scenery are (1) standard set units, (2) hanging units, and (3) set pieces.

Properties and set dressings include (1) stage properties, such as furniture, desks, and lecterns; (2) set dressings, such as draperies, pictures, lamps; and (3) hand properties, such as dishes, ashtrays, telephones, and other items that are handled by the talent.

13　*Television Talent*

In this chapter, we are concerned with television talent and the major ways of behaving in front of the camera, doing makeup, and selecting what to wear. The material is divided into four sections:

1. Performing techniques, including the performer's relationship to the camera, to audio, and to timing, and the ways he or she receives cues and prompting.

2. Acting techniques, which differ markedly from stage and motion picture acting methods.

3. Makeup, in respect to improving the talent's appearance. Corrective and character makeup are not discussed because they are seldom required in small station operation.

4. Clothing and costuming, containing some of the basic principles of how dress should be adjusted to the requirements of the camera. No attempt has been made to include aesthetic criteria for what to wear, since they—like color harmony, for example—are discussed extensively in related literature.

The people who appear on the television screen have varied communication objectives: some seek to entertain, educate, inform; others, to persuade, convince, sell. Nevertheless, the main goal of each of them is to communicate with the television audience as effectively as possible.

We can arbitrarily divide all television talent (which stands, not always too accurately, for all people performing in front of the television camera) into two large groups: (1) performers and (2) actors. The difference between them is fairly clear-cut. The *television performer* is engaged basically in nondramatic activities. Performers play themselves and do not assume roles of other characters; they sell their own personalities to the audience. The *television actor or actress,* on the other hand, always portrays someone else; he or she projects a character's personality rather than his or her own.

Performing Techniques

The television performer speaks directly to the camera or communicates with other performers or the studio audience, fully aware of the presence of the television audience. His or her audience is not a mass audience but only a small, intimate group that has gathered in front of a television set. If you think of yourself as a performer, it may help you to imagine your audience as being a family of three, seated in their favorite room, about ten feet away from you.

The definition of the television audience as usually expressed by modern sociologists is thus drastically changed for the television performer. The large, anonymous, and heterogeneous mass becomes a small group of people, a family seated in a favorite room, watching television. With this picture in mind, there is no reason for the per-

---

Actor, or Actress A person who appears on camera in dramatic roles. The actor or actress always portrays someone else.

Blocking Carefully worked out movement and actions by the talent, and movement of all mobile television equipment.

Clothing Regular clothes worn on camera, in contrast to a costume.

Costume Special clothes worn by an actor or actress to depict a certain character or period; in contrast to clothing, the regular clothes worn by a performer.

Cue Card Also called idiot sheet. A hand-lettered card that contains copy, usually held next to the camera lens by floor personnel.

Pancake A makeup base, or foundation makeup, usually water-soluble and applied with a small sponge.

Pan Stick A foundation makeup with a grease base. Used to cover a beard shadow or prominent skin blemish.

former to scream at the "millions of people out there in video land"; rather, the more successful approach is to talk quietly and intimately to the family who were kind enough to let you come into their home.

When you assume the role of a television performer, the camera becomes your audience. You must adapt your performance techniques to its characteristics and to other important production elements, such as audio and timing. In this section we will, therefore, discuss (1) the performer and the camera, (2) the performer and audio, (3) the performer and timing, (4) the floor manager's cues, and (5) prompting devices.

Performer and Camera

The camera is not a piece of dead machinery; it sees everything you do or do not do. It sees how you look, move, sit, and stand—in short, how you behave in a variety of situations. At times it will look at you much more closely and with greater scrutiny than a polite person would ever dare to do. It will reveal the nervous twitch of your mouth when you are ill at ease and the expression of mild panic when you have forgotten a line. The camera will not look politely away because you are scratching your ear. It will faithfully reflect your behavior in all pleasant and unpleasant details. As a television performer, therefore, you must carefully control your actions without ever letting the audience know that you are conscious of doing so.

Camera Lens   Since the camera represents your audience, you must look directly into the lens whenever you intend to establish eye contact with your viewer. As a matter of fact, you will

---

Performer   A person who appears on camera in non-dramatic shows. The performer plays himself or herself, and does not assume someone else's character.

Speed Up   A cue to the talent to speed up whatever he or she is doing.

Stretch   A cue to the talent to slow down whatever he or she is doing.

Taking Lens   Also called on-the-air lens. Refers to the lens on turret cameras that is actually relaying the scene to the camera pickup tube.

Talent   Collective name for all performers and actors who appear regularly on television.

Teleprompter   A mechanical prompting device that projects the moving copy over the lens, so that it can be read by the talent without losing eye contact with the viewer.

Wind Up   A cue to the talent to finish up whatever he or she is doing.

discover that you must stare into the lens and keep eye contact much more than you would with an actual person. The reason for this seemingly unnatural way of looking is that, when you appear on a closeup shot, the concentrated light and space of the television screen highly intensifies your actions. Even if you glance away from the lens ever so slightly, you break the intensity of the communication between you and the viewer; you break, though temporarily, television's magic. Try to look into the lens as much as you can, but in as casual and relaxed a way as possible. If you work with a turret camera, make sure that you look into the "taking," or on-the-air, lens, whose location differs with almost every turret camera. Ask the floor manager or the camera operator which lens you should look at.

Camera Switching   If two or more cameras are used, you must know which one is on the air so that you can remain in direct contact with the audience. When the director changes cameras, you must follow the floor manager's cue (or the change of tally lights) quickly but smoothly. Don't jerk your head from one camera to the other. If you suddenly discover that you have been talking to the wrong one, look down as if to collect your thoughts and then casually glance into the "hot" camera and continue talking in that direction until you are again cued to the other camera. This method works especially well if you work from notes. You can always pretend to be looking at your notes, while, in reality, you are changing your view from the "wrong" to the "right" camera.

In general, it is useful to ask your director or floor manager if there will be many camera changes during the program, and approximately when the changes are going to happen. If the show is scripted, mark all camera changes in your script.

If the director has one camera on you in a medium shot (MS) or a long shot (LS), and the other camera in a closeup (CU) of the object you are demonstrating, it is best to keep looking at the long-shot camera during the whole demonstration, even when the director switches to the closeup camera. This way you will never be caught looking the wrong way, since only the long shot camera is focused on you.

Closeup Techniques   The tighter the shot, the harder it is for the camera to follow fast movement. If a camera is on a closeup, you should restrict your motions severely and move with great care. Ask the director whether he plans closeups and approximately when. In a song, for example, he may want to shoot very closely to intensify an especially tender and intimate passage. Try to stand as still as possible; don't wiggle your head. The closeup itself is intensification enough. All you have to do is sing well.

When demonstrating small objects on a closeup, hold them steady. If they are arranged on a table, don't pick them up. You can either point to them or tilt them up a little to give the camera a better view. There is nothing more frustrating for camera operator and director than a performer who snatches the product off the table just when the camera has a good closeup of it. A quick look in the studio monitor will usually tell you how you should hold the object for maximum visibility on the screen. If two cameras are used, "cheat" (orient) the object somewhat toward the closeup camera. But don't turn it so much that it looks unnaturally distorted on the wide-shot camera.

Warning Cues   In most nondramatic shows—lectures, demonstrations, interviews—there is generally not enough time to work out a detailed blocking scheme. The director will usually just walk you through some of the most important crossovers from one performing area to the other, and through a few major actions, such as especially complicated demonstrations. During the on-the-air performance, therefore, you must give the director and the studio crew visual and audible warning of your unrehearsed actions. When you want to get up, for instance, shift your weight first, and get your legs and arms into the right position before you actually stand up. This will give the camera operator as well as the microphone boom operator enough time to prepare for your move. If you pop up unexpectedly, however, the camera may stay in one position, focusing on the middle part of your body, and your head may hit the microphone, which the boom operator, not anticipating your sudden move, has solidly locked into position.

If you intend to move from one set area to another, you may use audio cues. For instance, you can warn the production crew by saying: "Let's go over to the children and ask them . . . ." or, "If you will follow me over to the lab area, you can actually see . . . ." Such cues will sound quite natural to the home viewer, who is generally unaware of the number of fast reactions these seemingly unimportant remarks may trigger inside the television studio. You must be specific when you cue unrehearsed visual material. For example, you can alert the director of the upcoming slides by saying: "The first picture (or even slide) shows. . . ." This cuing device should not be used too often, however. If you can alert the director more subtly yet equally directly, do so.

Don't try to convey the obvious. It is the director who runs the show, and the talent is not the director. An alert director does not have to be told by the performer to bring the cameras a little closer to get a better view of the small object. This is especially annoying if he or she has already obtained a good closeup through a zoom-in. Also, avoid walking toward the camera to demonstrate an object. Through the zoom lens, the camera can get to you much faster than you to the camera.

Also you may walk so close to the camera that the zoom lens can no longer keep focus.

Performer and Audio

As a television performer, you must not only look natural and relaxed but you must also be able to speak clearly and effectively; it rarely comes as a natural gift. Don't be misled into believing that a super bass and affected pronunciation are the two prime requisites for a good announcer. On the contrary: first, you need to have something important to say; second, you need to say it with conviction and sincerity; third, you must speak clearly so that everybody can understand you. Nevertheless, a thorough training in television announcing is an important prerequisite for any performer.[1]

Microphone Techniques In Chapter 7 we have already discussed the most basic microphone techniques. Here is just a short summary of the main points about the performer's handling of microphones or assisting the microphone operator.

Most often you will work with a *lavaliere microphone.* Once it is properly fastened, you don't have to worry about it anymore. If you have to move from one set area to another on camera, make sure that the mike cord does not get tangled up in the set or set props. Gently pull the cable behind you to keep the tension off the mike itself.

When using a *hand microphone,* make sure that you have enough cable for your planned actions. Treat it gently. Speak across it, not into it. If you are interviewing somebody in noisy surroundings, such as in a downtown street, hold the microphone near you when you are doing the talk-

---

[1] Stuart W. Hyde, *Television and Radio Announcing,* 2nd ed. (Boston: Houghton Mifflin Co., 1971).

ing, and then point it toward the person as he responds to your questions.

When working with a *boom microphone,* be aware of the boom movements without letting the audience know. Give the boom operator enough warning so that he or she can anticipate your movements. Slow down somewhat, so that the boom can follow. Especially don't make fast turns, for they involve a great amount of boom movement. If you have to turn fast, try not to speak. Don't walk too close toward the boom; the operator may not be able to retract it enough to keep you "on mike" (within good microphone pickup range).

Try not to move a *desk mike* once it has been placed by the audio engineer. Sometimes the microphone may be pointing away from you toward another performer, but this may have been done purposely to achieve better audio balance.

Audio Level   A good audio engineer will take your audio level before you go on the air. Many performers have the bad habit of mumbling or speaking softly while the level is being taken, and then, when they go on the air, blasting their opening remarks. If a level is taken, speak as loudly as though you are actually going into your opening remarks. Thus the audio engineer will know where to turn the pot for an optimum level.

Opening Cue   At the beginning of a show, all microphones are dead until the director gives the cue for studio audio. You must, therefore, wait until you receive the opening cue from the floor manager. If you speak beforehand, you will not be heard. Don't take your opening cue from the red tally lights on the cameras unless you are instructed to.

Performer and Timing

Television operates on split-second timing. Although the director is ultimately responsible for getting the show on and off on time, the performer has a great deal to do with successful timing.

Aside from careful pacing throughout the show, you must learn how much program material you can cover after you have received a three-minute, a two-minute, a one-minute, and a thirty-second cue. You must, for example, still look comfortable and relaxed although you may have to cram a great amount of important program material into the last minute. On the other hand, you must be prepared to fill an extra thirty seconds without appearing to be grasping for words and things to do. This kind of presence of mind, of course, needs practice and cannot be learned solely from a television handbook.

Floor Manager's Cues

The floor manager, who is the link between the director and you, the performer, can communicate with you nonverbally even while you are on the air. He can tell you whether you are too slow or too fast in your delivery, how much time you have left, whether or not you speak loudly enough or hold an object correctly for the closeup camera. We can group these visual cues into three types: (1) time cues, (2) directional cues, and (3) audio cues. Although stations use slightly different cuing signals and procedures, they still will fall into one of the above categories. If you are working with an unfamiliar production crew, ask the floor manager to go over his cues before you go on the air.

React to all cues immediately, even if you think one of them is not appropriate at that particular time. Your director would not give the cue if it were not absolutely necessary. A truly professional performer is not one who never needs any cues and can run the show all by himself; he is the one who can react to all signals quickly and smoothly.

Don't look nervously for the floor manager if

13·1   Floor Manager's Cues.

Time Cues

Cue		Meaning	Hand Signal
Stand By		Show about to start.	Extends arm above his head and points with other hand to camera that will go on the air.
Cue		Show goes on the air.	Points to performer or live camera.
On Time		Go ahead as planned. (On the nose.)	Touches nose with forefinger.
Speed Up		Accelerate what you are doing. You are going too slowly.	Rotates hand clockwise with extended forefinger. Urgency of speedup is indicated by fast or slow rotation.
Stretch		Slow down. Too much time left. Fill until emergency is over.	Stretches imaginary rubber band between his hands.
Wind Up		Finish up what you are doing. Come to an end.	Similar motion as speed up, but usually with extended arm above head. Sometimes expressed with raised fist, or with a good-bye wave, or by hands rolling over each other as if wrapping an imaginary package.
Cut		Stop speech or action immediately.	Pulls index finger in knifelike motion across throat.

13·1 Floor Manager's Cues (cont.).

Time Cues

Cue		Meaning	Hand Signal
5 (4, 3, 2, 1) Minute(s)		5 (4, 3, 2, 1) minute(s) left until end of show.	Holds up five (four, three, two, one) finger(s) or small card with number painted on it.
½ Minute		30 seconds left in show.	Forms a cross with two index fingers or extended hands. Or holds card with number.
15 Seconds		15 seconds left in show.	Shows fist (which can also mean wind up). Or holds card with number.
Roll Film (and Countdown)		Projector is rolling. Film is coming up.	Holds extended left hand in front of face, moves right hand in cranking motion.
4–3–2–1 Take Film or VTR		Academy numbers as they flash by on the preview monitor, or VTR beeper countdown.	Extends four, three, two, one fingers; clenches fist or gives cut signal.

Directional Cues

Cue		Meaning	Hand Signal
Closer		Performer must come closer or bring object closer to camera.	Moves both hands toward himself, palms in.
Back		Performer must step back or move object away from camera.	Uses both hands in pushing motion, palms out.

Directional Cues (cont.)

Cue		Meaning	Hand Signal
Walk		Performer must move to next performing area.	Makes a walking motion with index and middle fingers in direction of movement.
Stop		Stop right here. Do not move any more.	Extends both hands in front of him, palms out.
O.K.		Very well done. Stay right there. Do what you are doing.	Forms an "O" with thumb and forefinger, other fingers extended, motioning toward talent.

Audio Cues

Cue		Meaning	Hand Signal
Speak Up		Performer is talking too softly for present conditions.	Cups both hands behind his ears, or moves right hand upwards, palm up.
Tone Down		Performer is too loud or too enthusiastic for the occasion.	Moves both hands toward studio floor, palms down, or puts extended forefinger over mouth in shhh-like motion.
Closer to Mike		Performer is too far away from mike for good audio pickup.	Moves right hand toward his face.
Keep Talking		Keep on talking until further cues.	Extends thumb and forefinger horizontally, moving them like the beak of a bird.

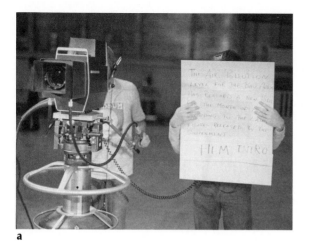

a

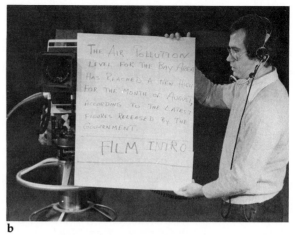

b

13·2 (a) This is the wrong way to hold a cue card. First, the card is too far away from the lens, forcing the talent to lose eye contact with the viewer (the lens). Second, his hands cover up important parts of the copy. Third, he cannot follow the lines as read by the talent. He will not be able to change cards for smooth reading. (b) This is the correct way of holding a cue card. The card is as close to the lens as possible, the hands do not cover the copy, and the floor manager reads along with the talent, thereby facilitating smooth card changes.

you think you should have received a cue; he will find you and draw your attention to his signal. When you receive a cue, don't acknowledge it in any way. The floor manager will know whether you have noticed it or not.

The table of cues *(13.1)* indicates the standard time cues, directional cues, and audio cues that are used by most television stations with only minor, if any, variations.

Prompting Devices

In addition to direct cues, television prompting devices are of great help to the performer who fears suddenly forgetting his lines or who has had no time to memorize a difficult copy that may have been handed to him just before the performance. The sensitive studio microphones make most audible prompting impossible. Since earphones and hearing-aid methods have not proved very successful, most television line prompters depend upon sight.

The visual prompting device must be designed so that the television viewer is not aware of it, and the performer must be able to read the prompting sheet without appearing to lose eye contact with the viewer. The equipment must be reliable, so that the performer can deliver his lines uninterrupted by mechanical failure. Two major prompting devices have proved highly successful: (1) cue cards, or idiot sheets, and (2) the teleprompter.[2]

Cue Cards Cue cards or, as they are often called, idiot sheets are generally held by a member of the production crew as close to the lens of the on-the-air camera as possible *(see 13.2).* There are many types, and the choice depends largely on what the performer is used to and what

---

[2] As a trademark, it is spelled TelePrompTer.

he likes to work with. Usually they consist of large cardboard sheets on which the copy is hand-lettered with a large felt pen. The size of the cards and the lettering depends on how well the individual can see and how far the camera is away from him.

In using the cue cards, you must learn to glance at the copy without losing eye contact with the lens for more than a moment. Make sure the floor manager has the cards in the right order. If the cue sheet operator forgets to change them, snap your fingers to attract his or her attention; in an emergency you may have to ad-lib until the system is functioning again. Hopefully, you will have studied the copy sufficiently so that your ad-lib makes sense.

Teleprompter The most advanced and frequently used prompting device is the teleprompter, a device that pulls a long sheet of paper with the copy on it from one roller to another at a speed adjustable to your reading pace. The lettering is magnified and projected onto a glass plate placed directly in front of the camera lens. Thus you can read the copy, which appears in front of the lens, and maintain eye contact with the viewer at the same time. The projected letters are invisible to the camera, since they are too close to the lens to come into focus. The roll of paper, on which copy is typed with an oversized typewriter, can hold continuous information for a full hour's newscast, for example. Most newscasters read their copy off the teleprompter, with the script serving as backup in case the mechanism should fail. *(See 13.3.)*

There are some disadvantages to this otherwise highly useful prompting device: (1) The rental fee for the teleprompter is relatively high. (2) The camera with the teleprompter attachment is no longer flexible, since it must stay with the performer at all times. (3) If frequent cutting from camera to camera is intended (as happens in a

newscast), teleprompters that run in sync or monitor must be placed either on all active cameras or on floorstands.

Acting Techniques

Contrary to the television performer, the television actor or actress always assumes someone else's character and personality.

To become a good television actor or actress, you must first of all learn the art of acting, a subject beyond the objective of this chapter. This discussion will merely point out how you must adapt your acting to the peculiarities of the television medium.

Many excellent actors consider television the most difficult medium in which to work. The actor always works within a studio full of confusing and impersonal technical gear; and yet he must appear on the screen as natural and lifelike as possible.

Many times the "television" actor also works in motion pictures. The production techniques and the equipment used in film for television are identical to those of film for motion picture theaters, but film making for television is considerably faster. Film shot for the television screen, in contrast to the large motion picture screen, requires acting techniques more closely related to live or videotaped television.

It is difficult to establish rigid principles of television acting techniques that are applicable in every situation. The particular role and even the director may require quite different forms of expression and technique from the actor or actress. The television medium, however, dictates some basic behavior patterns that the actor must accept if he wants to make it work for him instead of against him. Let's look briefly at some of these requirements, among them (1) audience, (2) actions, (3) blocking, (4) speech, (5) memorizing

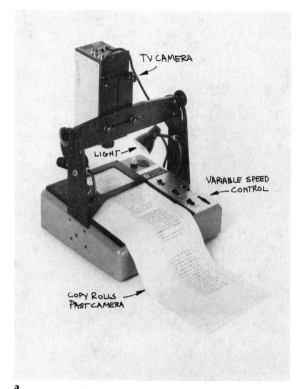

a

13·3 Television Prompting Device: (a) The copy, typed on a news typewriter with oversized letters, is placed in a special variable-speed crawl. A simple vidicon camera picks up the copy and relays it to a

b

monitor, or monitors, mounted on one or all the active cameras. (b) The monitor that displays the copy is mounted on the camera. A mirror projects the copy as it appears on the monitor screen onto a glass

lines, (6) timing, and (7) director-actor relationship.

Audience

When you act on television, you have no rapport with the audience—people you can see, or at least feel, and who applaud and elevate you to your best possible performance. In television, you are acting before constantly moving cameras that represent your assumed audience. Like the television performer, you must be camera-conscious,

but you should never reveal your knowledge of the cameras' presence. The viewer (now the camera) does not remain in one position, as he would in the theater; he moves around you, looks at you at close range and from a distance, from below and from above; he may look at your eyes, your feet, your hands, your back, whatever the director selects for him to see. And at all times you must look completely convincing and natural; the character you are portraying must appear on the screen as a real, living, breathing human being.

MIRROR PROJECTING MONITOR IMAGE TO GLASS PLATE

MONITOR DISPLAYING COPY

COPY AS IT APPEARS TO TALENT

c

plate directly over the lens. (c) You can then read the copy without losing eye contact with the lens (the viewer). The advantage of this system is that a single copy can be displayed on two or more cameras.

Keep in mind that you are playing to a camera lens and not to an audience; you need not (and should not) project your motions and emotions as you would when acting on stage. The television camera does the projecting—the communicating—for you. *Internalization,* as opposed to externalization, of your role is a key factor of your performance. You must attempt to *become* as much as possible the person you are portraying, rather than to *act him out.* Thus, your reactions are equally as effective on television as your actions.

Actions

The television camera is restrictive in many ways. It looks at the set and at you mostly in closeups. This means that your physical actions must be confined to the particular area the camera chooses to select, often unnaturally close to the other actors.

The television closeup also limits the extent of your gestures, concentrating on more intimate ways of emotional expression. A closeup of a clenched fist or a raised eyebrow may reflect your inner feelings and emotions more vividly than the broad movements necessary for the theater.

Blocking

You must be extremely exact in following rehearsed blocking. Sometimes mere inches become important, especially if the cameras are set up for special effects. The director may, for instance, want to use your arm as a frame for the background scene or position you for a complicated over-the-shoulder shot. The precise television lighting and the limited microphone radius (especially in small station production) are also factors that force you to adhere strictly to the initial blocking.

Once the show is on the air, you have an obligation to follow the rehearsed action carefully. This is not the time to innovate just because you have a sudden inspiration. If the director has not been warned of your change, the new blocking will always be worse than the previously rehearsed one. The camera has a limited field of view; if you want to be seen, you must stay within it.

Sometimes the director will place you in a position that looks entirely wrong to you, especially if you consider it in relation to the other actors. Don't try to correct this position on your own by arbitrarily moving away from the designated spot. A certain camera position and a special lens position may very well warrant unusual blocking to achieve a special effect.

The television cameras quite frequently photograph your stage business in a closeup. This means that you must remember all the rehearsed business details and execute them in exactly the same spot in which they were initially staged.

Speech

Compared to radio, the television boom microphone is generally a good distance away from you. You must, therefore, speak clearly. But speak naturally; projecting your voice in the theater tradition sounds very artificial on television.

Memorizing Lines

As a television actor or actress, you must be able to learn your lines quickly and accurately. If, as is the case in the soap operas, you have only one evening to learn a half-hour's role for the next day, you must indeed be a "quick study." And don't be misled into thinking that you can ad-lib during such performances, since you have "lived" the role for so long. Most of your lines are important not only from a dramatic point of view but also because they serve as video and audio cues for the whole production crew.

Even for a highly demanding role, you may have only a few weeks to prepare. As a television actor, you should not rely on prompting devices; after all, you should live, not read, your role.

Timing

Just like the performer, the actor in television must have an acute sense of timing. Timing matters for pacing your performance, for building to a climax, for delivering a punch line, and also for staying within a tightly prescribed clock time.

Even if you are videotaping a play scene by scene, you still need to observe carefully the stipulated running times for each take. You may have to stretch out a fast scene without making the scene appear to drag, or you may have to gain ten seconds by speeding up a slow scene without destroying its solemn character. You must be flexible without stepping out of character.

Always respond immediately to the floor manager's cues. Don't stop in the middle of a scene simply because you disagreed with one. Play the scene to the end and then complain. Minor timing errors can often be corrected later during the editing process.

Director-Actor Relationship

As a television actor, you cannot afford to be temperamental. There are too many people who have to be coordinated by the director. Although the actor is important to the television show, so are other people—the floor crew, the engineer at the transmitter, the boom operator, and the video engineer.

Even though you may find little opportunity for acting in small station operation, make an effort to learn as much about it as possible. An able actor is generally an effective television performer; a television director with acting training will find himself in good stead in most of his directing assignments.

Makeup

All makeup is used for three basic reasons: (1) to *improve* appearance, (2) to *correct* appearance, and (3) to *change* appearance.

Standard street makeup is used daily by many women to accentuate and improve their features. Minor skin blemishes are covered up, and the eyes and lips are emphasized.

Makeup can also be used to correct closely or widely spaced eyes, sagging flesh under the chin, a short or long nose, a slightly too prominent forehead, and many similar minor faults.

If a person is to portray a specific character in a play, a complete change of appearance may be necessary. Drastic changes of age, race, and character can be accomplished through the creative use of makeup techniques.

The different purposes for applying cosmetics require, of course, different techniques. Improving someone's appearance calls for the least complicated procedure; to correct someone's appearance is slightly more complicated; and changing an actor's appearance may require involved and complex methods.

Most shows in small station operation require only makeup that improves the appearance of a performer. More complicated makeup work, such as making a young actress look eighty years old, is left to the professional makeup artist. Therefore, there is no need for you to burden yourself with learning all about corrective and character makeup techniques. All we will do is to give you some idea about television makeup in respect to its basic (1) technical requirements, (2) materials, and (3) techniques.

Technical Requirements

Like so many other production elements, makeup, too, must yield to some of the demands of the television camera. These are (1) color distortion, (2) color balance, and (3) closeups.

Color Distortion   As we pointed out repeatedly through the preceding chapters, the skin tones are the only color references the viewer has for the correct adjustment of colors on his home receiver. Their accurate rendering is, therefore, of the utmost importance. Makeup plays a major role in this endeavor.

Generally, cool colors (hues with a blue tint) have a tendency to overemphasize their bluishness, especially in high color-temperature lighting. Also, cool reds turn dark on the monochrome set. Warm colors (warm reds, oranges, browns, and tans) are therefore preferred for television makeup. They usually provide more sparkle, especially when used on a dark-skinned face.

The basic foundation color should match the natural skin tones as closely as possible, regardless of whether the face is light (Caucasian or Oriental) or dark (Chicano or Black). However, since the camera might emphasize dense shadow areas with a bluish or purple tint, especially on dark skin, warm rather than cool foundation colors are preferred. Be careful, however, that the skin color does not turn pink. As much as you should guard against too much blue in a dark face, you must watch for too much pink in a light face.

The natural reflectance of a dark face (especially of very dark-skinned Blacks) often produces unflattering highlights. These should be toned down by a proper pancake or a translucent powder; otherwise, the video engineer will have to compensate for the highlights through shading, rendering the dark picture areas unnaturally dense.

Color Balance   Generally, it is a good plan for the art director, scene designer, makeup artist, and costume designer to coordinate all the colors in production meetings. In small station operations, there should be little problem with such coordination since these functions may all be combined in one or two persons. At least you should be aware of this coordination principle and apply it whenever possible. Although the colors can be adjusted by the video control operator, the adjustment of one hue often influences the others. A certain balancing of the colors beforehand will make the technical "painting" job considerably easier.

In color television, the surrounding colors are sometimes reflected in the face and greatly exaggerated by the camera. Frequently, such reflections are inevitable, but you can keep them to a minimum by carefully watching the overall reflectance of the skin. It should have a normal sheen, neither too oily (high reflectance) nor too dull (low reflectance but no brilliance—the skin looks lifeless).

Closeups   Television makeup must be smooth and subtle enough so that the performer's or actor's face looks natural even in an extreme closeup. This is directly opposed to theater makeup, where features and colors are greatly exaggerated for the benefit of the spectator in the last row. A good television makeup remains largely invisible, even on a closeup. Therefore, a closeup of a person's face under *actual production lighting* conditions is the best criterion for the necessity for and quality of makeup. If the performer or actor looks good on camera without makeup, none is needed. If the performer needs makeup and the closeup of his or her finished face looks normal, your makeup is acceptable. If it looks artificial, the makeup must be redone.

Materials

Various manufacturers produce a great variety of excellent television makeup materials. Most makeup artists in the theater arts departments of a college or university have up-to-date lists readily available. In fact, most large drug stores can supply you with the basic materials for the average makeup for improving the performer's appearance.

While women performers are generally quite experienced in cosmetic materials and techniques, men performers may, at least initially, need some advice.

The most basic makeup item is a *foundation* that covers minor skin blemishes and cuts down light reflections from an overly oily skin. The water-base cake makeup foundations are preferred over the more cumbersome grease-base foundations. The Max Factor CTV-1W through CTV-12W pancake series is probably all you need for most makeup jobs. It ranges from a warm light ivory color to a very dark tone for Blacks and other dark-skinned performers.

Women can use their own *lipsticks* or lip rouge, as long as the reds do not contain too much blue. For Black performers and actresses especially, a warm red, such as coral, is more effective than a darker red that contains a great amount of blue.

Other materials, such as eyebrow pencil, mascara, and eye shadow, are generally part of every woman performer's makeup kit. Special materials, such as hair pieces or even latex masks, are part of the professional makeup artist's inventory. They are of little use in the everyday small station operation.

Techniques

It is not always easy to persuade performers, especially men, to put on necessary makeup. You may do well to look at your guests on camera before deciding whether they need any. If they do, you must be tactful in suggesting its application. Try to appeal not to the performer's vanity but, rather, to his desire to contribute to a good performance. Explain the necessity for makeup in technical terms, such as color and light balance.

If you have a mirror available, seat the performer in front of it so that he or she can watch the entire makeup procedure. Adequate, even illumination is very important. If you have to work in the studio, have a small hand mirror ready.

Most women performers will be glad to apply the more complicated makeup themselves—lipstick and mascara, for instance. Also, most regular television talent will prefer to apply makeup themselves; they usually know what kind they need for a specific television show.

When using *pancake base,* simply apply it with a wet sponge evenly over the face and adjacent exposed skin areas. Make sure to get the base right up into the hairline, and have a towel ready to wipe off the excess. If closeups of hands are shown, you must also apply pancake base to them and the arms. This is especially important for men performers who demonstrate small objects on camera. If an uneven suntan is exposed (especially when women performers wear bareback dresses or different kinds of bathing suits) all bare skin areas must be covered with base makeup. Baldheaded men need a generous amount of pancake foundation to tone down obvious light reflections and to cover up perspiration.

Be careful not to give your male performers a baby-face complexion. It is sometimes even desirable to have a little beard area show. Frequently, a slight covering up of the beard with a beardstick is all that is needed. If additional makeup foundation is necessary, a pan stick foundation around the beard area should be applied first and set with some powder. For color shows, a very light application of a yellow or orange greasepaint counteracts the blue of a heavy beard quite satisfactorily.

Clothing and Costuming

In small station operation you will be concerned mainly with clothing the performer rather than costuming the actor. The clothes of the performer should be attractive and stylish but not too conspicuous or showy. The television viewer expects the person to be well dressed but not to overwhelm him with flashy outfits. After all, he or she is a guest in the viewer's home, not a night club performer.

Clothing

Naturally, the type of clothing worn by the performer depends largely on his or her personal taste. It also depends on the type of program or occasion and the particular setting.

There are, however, some types of clothing that look better on television than others. Since the television camera may look at you from a distance and at close range, the lines and overall color scheme of your clothes are just as important as their texture and details.

Line Television has a tendency to put a few extra pounds on the performer. Clothing cut to a slim silhouette helps to combat this problem. Slim dresses and rather tight-fitting suits look more attractive than heavy, horizontally striped material, and baggy dresses and suits. The overall silhouette of your clothing should look pleasing from a variety of angles, and slim but comfortable on you.

Color The most important thing to remember about the colors you wear is that they harmonize with the set. If your set is lemon yellow, don't wear a lemon-yellow dress. Also, avoid wearing a chroma key blue, unless you want to become translucent during the chroma key matting; then even a blue tie may give you trouble.

Although you can wear black or a very dark color, or white or a very light color, as long as the material is not glossy and highly reflective, try to avoid wearing a combination of the two. Or, if the set is very dark, try not to appear in a starched white shirt in front of it. If the set is kept in extremely light colors, don't wear black. As desirable as a pleasant color contrast is, especially when considering compatibility with monochrome reception, extreme brightness variations offer difficulties. Stark-white, glossy clothes can turn exposed skin areas dark on the television screen, or distort the more subtle colors. Black performers should try not to wear highly reflecting white or light yellow clothes. If you wear a dark suit, reduce the brightness contrast by wearing a pastel-colored shirt. Pink, light green, tan, or gray all photograph well on color and monochrome television.

As always, if you are in doubt as to how well a certain color combination photographs, check it on camera under actual lighting conditions and in the set you are going to use.

Texture and Detail   While line and color are especially important on long shots; texture and detail become important at close range. Textured material often looks better than plain, but don't use patterns that are too contrasting or too busy. We have already talked about the moiré effect that is caused by closely spaced geometric patterns such as herringbone weaves. Also, stripes in your clothing may extend beyond the fabric and bleed through surrounding sets and objects, an effect similar to color banding. Extremely fine detail in a pattern will either look too busy or appear smudgy.

The way to make your clothing more interesting on camera is not by choosing a detailed cloth texture, but by adding decorative accessories, such as scarves and, especially, jewelry. Although the style of the jewelry depends, of course, on the taste of the performer, in general, she should limit herself to one or two distinctive pieces. The sparkle of rhinestones, which used to cause annoying glares on monochrome television, turns into an exciting visual accent on color television.

When wearing a tie, again try to avoid tight, highly contrasting patterns. And, elegant as a tie pin may look on camera, it often interferes with the lavaliere microphone.

If a man and a woman, who are scheduled to appear on a panel show or an interview, were to ask you now what to wear for the occasion, what would you tell them?

Here is a possible answer. Both of them should wear something in which they feel comfortable, without looking wide and baggy. Both should stay away from blue, especially if chroma key matting is to be used behind them during the interview. The woman might wear a slim suit, pantsuit, or dress, all with plain colors. Avoid black-and-white combinations, such as a black skirt and a highly reflecting white blouse or shirt. Also, avoid highly contrasting narrow stripes or checkered patterns. Wear as little jewelry as possible, unless you want to appear flashy. If possible, find out the color of the set background and try to avoid similar colors in your outfit.

The man might wear a slim suit, or slacks and plain coat. Wear a plain tie or one with a very subtle pattern. Don't wear a white shirt under a black or dark blue suit or coat. Avoid checkered or herringbone patterns.

Costumes

For small station operation, you don't need costumes. If you do a play or a commercial that involves actors, you can always borrow the necessary articles from a local costume rental firm or from the theater arts department of your local high school, college, or university. The theater arts departments usually have a well-stocked costume room from which you can draw most standard period costumes and uniforms.

If you use stock costumes on television, make sure that they look convincing even in a tight closeup. Sometimes the general construction and, especially, the detail of theater accessories are too coarse for the television camera. The color and pattern restrictions for clothing also apply for costumes. The total color design, the overall balance of colors among scenery, costumes, and makeup, is important in some television plays, particularly in musicals and variety shows where long shots often reveal the total scene, including actors, dancers, scenery, and props.

Summary

Television talent stands for all persons who perform in front of the television camera. They are classified in two large groups: (1) television performers and (2) television actors and actresses.

Television *performers* are basically engaged in nondramatic shows, such as newscasts, interviews, music shows. They always portray themselves. Television *actors and actresses* always play someone else; they project someone else's character.

Because their communication purposes are different, the two kinds of talent use somewhat different techniques. Specific *production factors* for the *performer* include (1) the performer and the camera, (2) the performer and audio, (3) the performer and timing, (4) the floor manager's cues, and (5) prompting devices. The specific *production factors* for the *actor or actress* include (1) audience, (2) actions, (3) blocking, (4) speech, (5) memorizing lines, (6) timing, and (7) director-actor relationship.

\Makeup, clothing, and costuming are important aspects of the talent's preparation for on-camera work.

All *makeup* is used for three basic reasons: (1) to improve appearance, (2) to correct appearance, and (3) to change appearance. The technical requirements of makeup demand consideration of (1) color distortion, (2) color balance, and (3) closeups.

Clothing is worn by the performer, *costumes* by the actor or actress. When clothing is selected for on-camera use, attention must be paid to its general line, color, texture, and detail. When costumes are used, they must be chosen with the same discernment. In addition, for the costumed show, it is important to achieve an overall color balance among the various pieces of costume and the scenery.

14　Producing

This chapter describes the major aspects of producing. Since the range of activities a producer may encounter will vary with the particular task, the emphasis here will be on the principles of the production process. These areas include:

1. Systems design for production, with four principal factors: need assessment, viewer involvement, medium requirements, and feedback and evaluation. Special emphasis is put on the process message objective, derived from the interaction between the audiovisual stimuli of the program and the involvement of the viewer, the percipient.

2. Above-the-line production, which includes the functions of such personnel as producers, writers, and talent.

3. Below-the-line production, which covers the technical facilities and the engineers and production people responsible for their operation and coordination, such as studio, camera, audio, and lighting personnel.

4. Special production aspects having to do with program types, copyrights and other clearances, union affiliation, and legal matters.

5. Steps in the production process, which demonstrate a reasonable flow of activities, from the need assessment to the feedback and evaluation.

Producing means to see to it that a worthwhile idea gets to be a worthwhile television show. As a producer, you are in charge of this process. You are involved in managing a great number of people and in coordinating an even greater number of activities and other production details. As an originator of a mass communication process, you must bear responsibility toward the perceivers of the television program, the viewers, and toward the originating institution, the station for which you are working.

You will find that it is not always easy to serve both masters. In trying to fulfill your obligation to the public, you may propose a program series that is counter to the economic interests of your station. The program manager may tell you that he or she, the sales manager, and the general manager of the station are in agreement on the worth of your program idea of how a university campus operates and what college learning is all about; however, they all feel that such a series would probably attract only a highly specific audience, produce low ratings, and therefore hardly be an attractive package for time buyers who want to reach as large an audience as possible with their commercials. How about carrying such a series as *sustaining* (noncommercial) programs, as part of the station's public service? The program manager asks you to check with the public service director and to prepare a budget for the first three shows.

As you can see, you are already in the middle of rather delicate negotiations, the selling of your idea to people who look at the program series from highly divergent points of view and who apply different criteria for the relative success of the show. And all this work, before you have even had a chance to think much about the creative aspects of the production! Such is the lot of a producer.

Some people may get dismayed at the thought of having a show turned down because it does not

---

Above-the-Line A budgetary division of production elements. It concerns mainly nontechnical personnel.

AFTRA American Federation of Television and Radio Artists. A broadcasting talent union.

Below-the-Line A budgetary division of production elements. It concerns technical personnel and facilities.

Canon 35 Deals with the question of allowing television equipment in a courtroom.

Demographic Data Audience research data that are concerned with such items as age, sex, marital status, and income.

Ecological Data Audience research data that are concerned with where the members of the audience live, such as city, suburb, country, and so forth.

Effect-to-Cause Approach A production approach, or a system, that starts with the definition of viewer experience and works backwards to the production elements the medium requires in order to produce such a viewer experience.

IBEW International Brotherhood of Electrical Workers. Union for studio and master control engineers; may include floor personnel.

seem financially feasible. But a skillful producer will anticipate such problems, and approach a show idea from a business as well as a creative point of view. There is nothing intrinsically wrong with combining art and money. The fact that novelists and painters get paid for their art does not cheapen their products. But if you sell an idea that has little or no aesthetic or social value, for the sole purpose of improving the ratings and beating the competition, you are abusing the public and you are acting irresponsibly, even though you make money in the process.

Realizing that as a producer you must operate within the public's "interest, convenience, and necessity," how, then, can you develop an idea into an on-the-air television show? What are the techniques of television production?

Although each show idea has certain peculiar production requirements, there are nevertheless techniques, or at least approaches, that apply to television production in general. We will, there-fore, attempt to acquaint you with a *systems design* that covers the major points of production. You should keep in mind, however, that some productions may require procedures that differ considerably from the standard. The systems approach as mentioned here should serve as a *guide* to problem solving; don't take it as a recipe.

Specifically, we will discuss (1) systems design for production, or the "effect-to-cause approach," (2) above-the-line production, (3) below-the-line production, (4) special production aspects, and (5) the steps in the production process.

Production Systems Design

Since production involves a great number of processes, each one interacting with the others, at least to some degree, we learn its function most profitably by considering it as a *system*. In the produc-

---

Libel Written defamation.

NABET National Association of Broadcast Employees and Technicians. Union for studio and master control engineers; may include floor personnel.

Percipient The television viewer in the act of perceiving television audio and video stimuli (a television program). It implies more than mere watching of a program; it requires a certain degree of involvement.

Process Message The interaction between the percipient and the audiovisual stimuli of the television program.

Section 315 Section of the Communications Act that affords candidates for public office equal opportunity to appear on television. All candidates must, for example, be charged equal fees.

Slander Oral defamation during a television program.

Sustaining Program Program that is not commercially supported.

System The interrelationship of various elements and processes.

Systems Design A plan that shows the interrelation of two or more systems. In television production, it shows the interrelation of all major production elements, as well as the flow (direction) of the production processes.

14·1 Basic Television
Communication System.

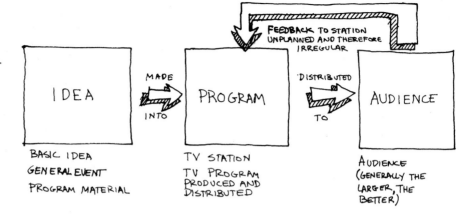

IDEA →(MADE / INTO)→ PROGRAM →(DISTRIBUTED / TO)→ AUDIENCE

FEEDBACK TO STATION UNPLANNED AND THEREFORE IRREGULAR

BASIC IDEA
GENERAL EVENT
PROGRAM MATERIAL

TV STATION
TV PROGRAM
PRODUCED AND
DISTRIBUTED

AUDIENCE
(GENERALLY THE
LARGER, THE
BETTER)

tion system, as in any other, various elements and processes are linked together and interact with one another so as to achieve the desired product —in this case, the television audience experiencing the televised material in a specific way.

The system helps you to identify quickly, and fairly accurately and reliably, the major production elements each program requires, and the necessary interaction among them. Simply, the system assists you in determining which people you require, what they should do, and what equipment is necessary at what time in order to televise a show that fulfills a specific need of the audience, or that entices the audience to a specific reaction.

Content Approach

Traditionally, such a system begins with content, material for a program that is produced into a television show and transmitted to an audience.[1] Many productions for instructional television op-

erate within such a system. The content expert (the professor who knows history of twentieth-century painting, for example) gets together with the medium expert (the teacher of television production or the student producer), who then takes the material from the content expert and prepares it so that it will appear more or less intelligible on the television screen. The students, under the threat of a grade, try to gain as much information from the show as possible so that they will do reasonably well in the next test. *(14.1 and 14.2.)*

As widespread as this system may be, it has some serious flaws. (1) The content (program material) is selected by someone who has little or no knowledge of how television works. Thus, the "content expert" selects his or her material simply by *what* should be communicated, and not by *how* it may *appear* on the television screen, or how it will be *received* by a television audience. (2) The so-called medium expert is handed the task of distributing the already selected material via television. In this way, the final criteria as to the television program's worthwhileness are generally stipulated by the content expert, and not by the medium expert, or even the eventual receiver

---

[1] Wilbur Schramm and Janet Alexander, "Broadcasting," *Handbook of Communication,* ed. by Ithiel de Sola Pool *et al.* (Chicago: Rand McNally Publishing Co., 1973), p. 584.

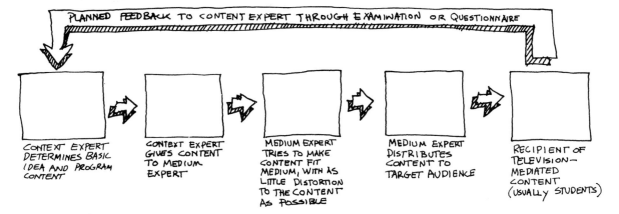

PLANNED FEEDBACK TO CONTENT EXPERT THROUGH EXAMINATION OR QUESTIONNAIRE

CONTEXT EXPERT DETERMINES BASIC IDEA AND PROGRAM CONTENT

CONTEXT EXPERT GIVES CONTENT TO MEDIUM EXPERT

MEDIUM EXPERT TRIES TO MAKE CONTENT FIT MEDIUM, WITH AS LITTLE DISTORTION TO THE CONTENT AS POSSIBLE

MEDIUM EXPERT DISTRIBUTES CONTENT TO TARGET AUDIENCE

RECIPIENT OF TELEVISION— MEDIATED CONTENT (USUALLY STUDENTS)

14·2   Content-to-Medium-to-Audience Process.

of the message. Thus, the medium expert has little influence on the content, which may or may not be suited to the television medium or the television audience. (3) The separation of content expert and medium expert only fosters the development of mutual mistrust. (4) Most seriously, the medium is considered a mere distribution device rather than a production element that has a great influence on the content as well as its reception by the television audience. (5) The effect of the program is presupposed because of the content alone, not by how and how much the television viewer is affected.

A more viable systems design seems to be the one that focuses more on *viewer need* and, ultimately, on what he *experiences* during the program and his *response* afterward, rather than on content and how it can be molded into a television show. In effect, once you have ascertained a specific viewer need or desire, you work backwards from viewer experience to what the medium requires in order to produce such an experience. Because the system starts with the viewer experience and works backwards, we call it the *effect-to-cause approach* to production. *(See 14.3.)*

Effect-to-Cause Approach

The effect-to-cause approach to production, or the effect-to-cause systems design, stresses (1) need assessment, (2) viewer involvement, (3) medium requirements, and (4) feedback and evaluation.

Need Assessment   Common sense and the FCC tell us that we should ascertain the basic needs and desires of the television audience for specific programming, rather than superimposing programs upon an unsuspecting public. Indeed, the FCC stresses need assessment as an important factor in granting license renewals.[2] The FCC requires the broadcaster (1) to make meaningful efforts to determine the tastes, needs, and desires of those within its service area, and (2) to provide programs in response to those needs. According to the FCC, the need assessment must include consultation with (1) the general viewing public,

---

[2] FCC Report and Order 66–904, Docket 13961, Section IV-A. October 10, 1966.

14·3   Effect-to-Cause
System.

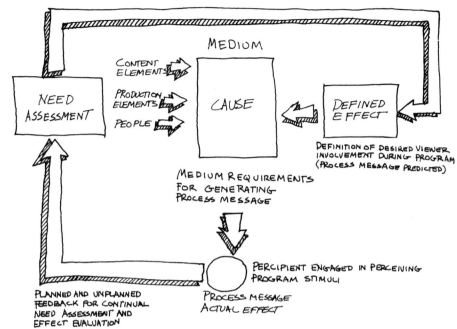

MEDIUM

CONTENT ELEMENTS

PRODUCTION ELEMENTS

PEOPLE

NEED ASSESSMENT

CAUSE

DEFINED EFFECT

DEFINITION OF DESIRED VIEWER INVOLVEMENT DURING PROGRAM (PROCESS MESSAGE PREDICTED)

MEDIUM REQUIREMENTS FOR GENERATING PROCESS MESSAGE

PERCIPIENT ENGAGED IN PERCEIVING PROGRAM STIMULI

PROCESS MESSAGE ACTUAL EFFECT

PLANNED AND UNPLANNED FEEDBACK FOR CONTINUAL NEED ASSESSMENT AND EFFECT EVALUATION

14·4   Indeed, every station should institute a need assessment department, whose members could use scientific methods not only for assessment projects but also for the evaluation of need satisfaction through programming.

(2) leaders in the community, and (3) professional and eleemosynary (charitable) organizations.[3]

Such surveys will tell you something about the overt needs of a community, but how about the viewer's covert needs—needs of which the viewer himself is not aware? For many centuries, the arts have catered to and even fulfilled covert emotional and social needs of the public. But the way we have gone about assessing and fulfilling these needs has been more than haphazard. In order to promote emotional and social stability, we must become more discerning. But how can you do all this as a producer?

If your station does not have a need assessment expert, you may consider employing an independent research firm, or, better yet, seeking the help of the mass communication, sociology, and psychology departments of the nearby uni-

[3] Editors of BM/E Magazine, *Interpreting FCC Broadcast Rules and Regulations,* Vol. 2 (Blue Ridge Summit, Pa.: Tab Books, 1968).

versity. After all, these departments know of the latest developments in their field and usually have a number of expert faculty and students available to undertake such projects.

Viewer Involvement Involvement describes the state of the viewer while watching a television program, and his response to the program afterward. Usually, the experience of the viewer relative to the program (the audiovisual stimuli) is extremely complex. Although we cannot make this perception process any less complex through programming, we can, to a certain degree, channel the viewer's experience and response. In its most obvious forms, a comedian can make us laugh with a funny joke; the closeup of a tender kiss of the reunited couple can make us experience human warmth and compassion, even love; a police officer approaching the gunman's trap can increase our anxiety; and an especially tragic news event or play can make us cry.

If the program is indeed geared to the viewer's overt and/or covert needs, the process of viewing the program is no longer a simple watching and listening but an involvement and, in its most ideal state, a *participation* in the audiovisual event. The viewer thus becomes a *percipient,* and we can define the perception process as an event (X) that—for the convenience of assigning it a place in the system—we put between the screen and the percipient *(14.5).* In other words, the real message of the communication lies in the interaction between the percipient and the audiovisual stimuli and not in an arbitrarily predetermined content that is distributed by television. This message we call the *process message.* It cannot exist independently of the viewer, or even before the actual process of perception.

Now, in order to arrive at this process message, we must give some direction to the viewer experience—or, more precisely, the percipient involvement. Taking a cue from instructional systems

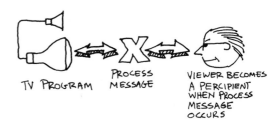

14·5   Process Message.

and programmed learning, we simply state a desired process message, an experience objective. Here are some examples:

1.   *The process message* (perceived during the program) *should help the percipient to learn, and later apply, five simple steps of energy conservation.* In this objective we simply want the viewer (percipient) to *learn* five ways of energy conservation, which he might not have known before, and learn them well enough so that he can not only recount them but use them in his daily activities. (Obviously, they do not contain the recommendation for shutting off the television set; otherwise all subsequent process messages would not occur.) The process message contains action cues for overt activities, not unlike much advertising, which persuades the viewer to go and buy a specific product.

2.   *The process message should make the percipient vicariously experience the beauty as well as the immense physical power inherent in a football game.* Here the objective is not to entertain the viewer with selected delayed football action but to give him a certain experience while he is perceiving the program. The ordinary televising of football games often fails to communicate the immense physical power of the sport, especially if the viewer has never actually played football. At the same time, the movements of the players, their reactions to one another in a play, and the structure of teamwork have an inherent beauty that, too, is often not clarified and intensified enough for the average viewer. But such a process mes-

sage, which stresses the aesthetic values of football, could certainly contribute to emotional literacy, especially of those viewers who do not seek aesthetic stimuli in other programs, such as dance, drama, or music, or in other experiences, such as going to a concert or a dance recital.

3. *The process message should help the percipient to relax and escape for a while from the reality of the daily routine, laugh with the talent on the screen, and, hopefully, about himself.*

With the value of the objective for the process message clearly established, we will now move to the medium requirements—probably one of the most important points for the producer.

Medium Requirements   Since, as you have seen in previous chapters, the medium demands certain production equipment and procedures, such as shot composition and sequence, lighting, and audio, you should now ask what it needs in order to meet the stated objective as fully as possible. When we talk about *medium,* we do not mean just the different pieces of production equipment, such as cameras, lights, and microphones, but also the people and agencies that work in television or are somehow connected with its operation. Let's take objective 2 (power and aesthetics of a football game) and see what the medium might require so that the process message can be accomplished. We will simply jot down some of the major points that come to mind, without worrying at this time how they should be organized or how they may fit the systems design.

We will state the objective again: *The process message should make the percipient vicariously experience the beauty as well as the immense physical power inherent in a football game.*

1.   Who should be the percipients? Where and how should they perceive the program, and when? We are now approaching a precise audience definition. Housewives usually have a viewing pattern quite different from working women. Teenagers watch at different times from adults. Viewing customs on weekends are different from the rest of the week. Usually the program manager will have a great deal to say about when the program will be aired, but you should have some idea of the preferred broadcast time. The type of audience will generally dictate the ideal broadcast time.

2.   There are some key phrases in the objective: vicarious experience, physical power, and beauty. To give the percipient vicarious experience, you must *involve* her (or him) in the action, not just show her something to look at. Involvement and power immediately suggest an extremely tight camera throughout the program. Closeups and extreme closeups will not only intensify the physical force of the game but also bring the viewer into the fray. You may even want to try some subjective camera techniques, whereby the camera participates in the action.[4] In this case, your equipment must be highly mobile—portable cameras and videotape units, for instance. Do you have them available? How many? If not, can you rent some? You may even try to shoot black-and-white with ½-inch videotape format recorders (such as portapaks), for later dubbing up (with the aid of a time base corrector), colorizing, and other possible electronic manipulations. Or you may want to use some videotape slow motion or freeze frames. Again, when talking to the production manager, or engineering supervisor, you should have a pretty good idea of what you need and why. Perhaps you may have to, or want to, resort to film. Since this football experience is a staged event, almost like a play, you may justify the lack of immediacy through added production control and ease that film can afford you. Film is mobile, yields readily to slow motion, editing, and other production manipulations. Perhaps you may want to combine videotape and film. In any case, postproduction activities will play an important part in this project.

3.   Since you are building an event through several takes, with the action shot from various viewpoints, angles, and sometimes in slow motion (power and beauty elements), you will have to repeat a specific

---

[4] Herbert Zettl, *Sight-Sound-Motion* (Belmont, Calif.: Wadsworth Publishing Co., 1973), pp. 230–233.

action over and over again. The shooting requirements make the coverage of a single game impractical, if not impossible. What you probably need is a football team that is willing to participate in this project. A high school or college team will probably be more willing than a professional team. In any case, they will be less expensive.

4. The power factor suggests a heavy use of audio. Because you are filming (or videotaping with mobile gear with some slow-motion film inserts), you may want to do double-system sound. Since the production demands heavy editing, the independent audio will make the cutting easier than with single-system sound. Also, you can get close with your portable audiotape recorders to get the full impact sounds (thumps, groans, crashes). Since the production is not a mere *look at* a football game, but a *look into* a creative conception of the game, you can liberally add music or other related sounds for the intensification of the action.

5. Unless the background music is especially written for the show and played by friends, you need clearance for the recording used. By the way, you need written clearances from all the football players, the coach, and the school official (such as the athletic director or the dean). Don't ever rely on a verbal agreement. If you can't get it in writing, look for another show.

6. Beauty again. Oh, yes. Color is a must. Perhaps you can intensify the event by manipulating the colors. Check with the film lab or, if done in videotape, with the video engineer. Perhaps you want to shoot it in black-and-white and colorize it later.

7. The heavy postproduction activities involved in this project need careful scheduling of editing equipment and time. You need an expert editor; and, of course, an extremely sensitive director, whose major qualifications may not be an expert knowledge of football (though this would help) but should include a great sense of motion, composition, dynamic picturization. The camera operators must have similar qualifications.

This coordination calls for preproduction meetings: with the director, camera operators, audio engineers, editor, floor manager, and production assistants. In fact, you may need to spend a great deal of time in such meetings. A thorough understanding of the process

14·6 Audiences are usually identified and categorized by the traditional sociological, demographic, and ecological classification system. Demographic data include age, sex, income, profession, and so forth. Ecological data include where people live, such as city, small town, suburb, country. If you have a need assessment study at your disposal, the socio-psychological data will permit an even more precise audience classification. Don't forget that your audience is a great number of *individual* percipients, not a collective.

message by all members of the production team will greatly facilitate the actual production later on. A second meeting should involve the players. The director should clue them in about the purpose of the show, and the process message.

8.   When can you get the players to meet? Where? Is the field reserved? What if it rains that day?—perhaps the rain will add to the power idea, and to beauty. You will need several shooting days. How many? How many production people do you need?

9.   What is it going to cost? Do you have a budget large enough to pay for the participants, the equipment used, and the materials needed (film, audiotape, and so forth)?

10.   The station wants to give the program wide publicity; it has already interested several local sports shops in buying program time. That brings up another thought. How many commercial inserts should you expect during the half-hour program time assigned to you by the programming department? Check with the sales department.

11.   The show requires special graphics. The art director should sit in during the first two briefing sessions.

12.   Will you need narration in certain places? Perhaps some rather poetic statements that express the power and beauty of the game? Or will the natural sounds and the music be enough to clarify and intensify the event? If you decide on narration, you need a writer, unless you tackle the writing yourself. Also, the announcer will have to be included in the postproduction schedule and the budget.

As you can see, the list goes on and on. The better your knowledge of the medium, the more you know about the specific requirements, the more detailed your list will be and, most of all, the more prepared you will be for the actual production. A good producer is the one who works out the problems *before* they arise. *Thorough preparation* is the key to an efficient and successful production.

What happened to content? It has become simply part of the medium requirements. If you go back over the previous list, you will discover that "content" appears in several of the points listed. Thus, what is finally seen and heard and, hopefully, perceived by the viewer is not just subject matter that has been predetermined independently of the medium and simply distributed thereby, but images that have been created as part of the medium requirement within the context of the basic process message.

Figure 14.7 will show the basic medium requirements as they occur in the average production.

Feedback and Evaluation   How will you know whether or not a show has been successful; whether or not your process message has indeed been perceived? This aspect of production is probably one of the most difficult to ascertain. When, as sometimes happens, viewers respond by telephone calls, postcards, and letters, try to make provisions so that their comments are recorded as to positive and negative responses. Try not to dismiss the negative response. Analyze it and see what you can learn from it. Certain program formats include some stimulus for feedback; the talent may ask for the viewer's response, or the viewer may be obligated to respond—as when he is enrolled in a tele-course, for example. Ratings, of course, test viewer contact with the show, but not necessarily *impact.* Generally, however, a very popular show with a high rating must fulfill some kind of viewer need; otherwise the viewers wouldn't watch it.

Press reviews are sometimes biased and therefore not always reliable. Perhaps as a producer you may want to ask faculty and students of broadcasting to help in designing and administering a significant program evaluation test. In fact, you may want to evaluate the various steps of your system prior to the actual telecast so that you can *predict the process message* with some reliability.

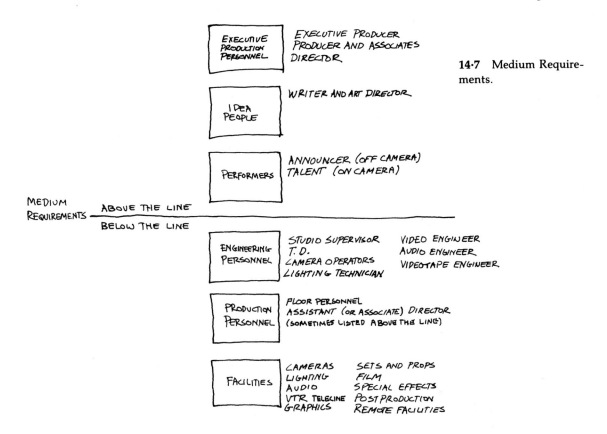

14·7   Medium Requirements.

Above-the-Line Production

As you can see from figure 14.7, medium requirements that deal with nontechnical elements— writers, producers, directors, talent, art directors, and others—are diagramed "above the line," while technical facilities—studio, cameras, scenery, graphic arts, and engineering personnel—are listed "below the line." This division comes from the custom of preparing two separate budgets, an above-the-line budget and a below-the-line budget. We will adopt this convenient grouping in our discussion of specific production elements.

The *above-the-line production* is accomplished mainly by nontechnical personnel. Figure 14.8

shows the major above-the-line production workers with their principal functions, and the major facilities of a typical medium-sized television operation.

In large productions, the above-the-line personnel may also include script or dialogue editors (who edit the script for the specific show requirement), composers (for the original score), conductor and musicians (if there is live music during the production, or for postproduction dubbing), designers and art directors, a unit manager (in charge of day-to-day schedules and budgets), and production assistants. Of course, most small or medium-sized stations use their regular employees, who are on the station's payroll anyway,

14·8   Above-the-Line Personnel.

Personnel	Function
Executive Producer	In charge of one or several program series, has overall responsibility of complete series. Takes care of entire budget and handles station management, advertising agencies, financial supporters, salaries for principal actors.
Producer	In charge of individual production. Is responsible for all supervisory personnel working on it. Responsible for coordinating technical and nontechnical production elements. Often serves as writer in small station operation, and sometimes as director of the show as well.
Assistant or Associate Producer	Assists the producer in all production matters. Often does the actual coordinating job, such as telephoning talent, confirming schedules, worrying about deadlines, picking up the slides from the art department. Unfortunately, many secretaries are made to function as assistant or even full-fledged producers without the benefit of the authority and financial reward that ordinarily go with this responsibility.
Director	In charge of directing talent and technical facilities. Is responsible for transforming a script into video and audio images, for creating the medium's part of the process message (the other part being the involvement of the percipient). A *residue director* or *duty director* coordinates the program sequence of prerecorded materials. Often, this function is taken over by master control personnel or by computer. Small stations combine the producing and directing functions in a *producer-director.*
Art Director	In charge of creative design aspects of show (set, display, graphics).
Talent	Performers and actors who appear on television, either live, on videotape, or on film. Large productions include dancers, singers, or extras in a play.
Writer	Writes television scripts. In small station operations, the writer's function is often assumed by the producer or the director.
Announcer	Performer who does not appear on camera. If on camera, the announcer moves up into the talent category.

except for occasional outside talent. Only large networks, or independent production companies, usually hire freelance above-the-line personnel.

Below-the-Line Production

The *below-the-line production* has to do with coordinating the engineering and production personnel who operate equipment during the production, as well as the necessary production equipment and facilities. Most often, the director of the show, the production manager, and the engineering supervisor (either studio supervisor or assistant chief engineer) will determine exactly which technical facilities will be necessary. However, as a producer, you cannot afford to leave all the below-the-line decisions to the director or the engineering personnel. Otherwise you may find yourself losing control not only of the production but especially of the below-the-line budget, for which, after all, you are responsible. A producer who is knowledgeable of all aspects of television production techniques (including the potentials and limitations of the major equipment, such as cameras, lights, and audio equipment) can save considerable time, effort, and money without limiting the concept or production scope of the proposed show.

Figure 14.10 shows some of the major below-the-line production personnel and facilities.

Again, the below-the-line personnel are usually employed by the station. When you rent your facilities to an outside agency, however, the engineering and production personnel need to be included in the below-the-line budget.

The above- and below-the-line production categories make it mandatory for you to organize the medium requirements into a specific *production sequence.* Sometimes, the process message requires that you start with the above-the-line items and then move to the below-the-line items. At other times, you must involve them both simultaneously. A careful analysis of the objective of the process message, however, will generally suggest a production sequence to you. Obviously, you cannot order title slides if the writer has not yet finished the script and given you the title of the show. Nor can you argue with the director over the number of cameras before the sets have been designed and the action tentatively blocked by the director.

Besides helping you to determine the production sequence, the systems design will aid you greatly in the production of a *program series.* You can, for example, state the objective of the process message and identify the medium requirements for each of the shows. You will then be able to see which of the production activities overlap for the whole series. For example, you may find that the same set will do for the whole series, or that you can use certain graphics for more than one show. Or you may even be able to videotape two shows on the same day, one right after the other.

14·9   News operations usually have their own above-the-line personnel, which includes a news producer, assignment editor, writers, and reporters. But since most of them are regularly employed by a station, their salaries need not be considered in an above-the-line budget.

14·10   Below-the-Line Personnel and Facilities.

Division	Function
Personnel: Engineering	
Studio or Remote Supervisor	Oversees all technical operations.
T.D.	Technical director; usually acts as crew chief and does the switching.
Camera Operators	Operate the cameras; often take care of the lighting.
Lighting Technician	In charge of lighting; usually in large production centers, or for large productions only.
Video Engineer	Shades cameras; often serves also as videotape operator on remotes.
Audio Engineer	In charge of all audio operations. Works the audio board during the show.
Videotape Engineer	Runs the videotape machines, and takes care of the videotape editing.
Personnel: Production	(Some of these functions may be performed by engineering personnel. In small station operations, and especially in college and university operations, the engineering and production personnel functions often overlap considerably. For example, the simplified operation of the television camera certainly makes it possible for nonengineering personnel to function as camera operators. Certain labor union restrictions, however, may delimit the personnel functions quite explicitly.)
Floor Manager	In charge of all floor activities. Directs talent on the floor, relays director's cues to studio talent, and supervises floor personnel.
Floorpersons (also called grips, stagehands, facilities persons)	Set up scenery and dress sets. Operate easel cards and graphics. Sometimes operate microphone booms and camera dollies. Assist camera operators in pulling cables. Usually act as properties, wardrobe, and makeup people, especially in small stations.
Associate or Assistant Director	Classified as below-the-line personnel in most television operations. Assists the director in all his duties. Often supervises rehearsals and does the timing during the actual production. In difficult shows, gives the appropriate "ready" cues to cameras, audio, lighting, VTR, and so forth.
Graphic Artists	Prepare studio cards, slides, and other graphic material.
Facilities	**Producer's Involvement** *(Although most of these facilities are stipulated by the director of the specific show, you, as a producer, are nevertheless ultimately responsible for their use and cost):*
Studio Use	Requests studio use and confirms studio schedules with production manager. Studio needs to be scheduled for rehearsal, setup, lighting, and actual production time.

Facilities (cont.)	**Producer's Involvement** (cont.)
Cameras	Checks with director on the agreed number of cameras. Establishes whether all the requested cameras are, indeed, needed.
Lighting	Checks with the T.D. or lighting person whether he or she has the proper information about the lighting needed. (Floor plan and lighting plot should be in the hands of the lighting person.)
Audio	Confirms with audio engineer special audio requests, such as guest to play a guitar number, or the exact instrumentation of a rock group.
VTR	Confirms with the videotape engineer the approximate length of the show, or various takes, and any special requests. This is simply a double-check on the director's request.
Telecine	Checks on availability and scheduling of film islands.
Graphics	Often requests the necessary graphics, and sees to it that they are promptly delivered to master control (slides) or the studio (charts, easel cards). This is an especially important job for the producer. A missing slide can seriously impair the whole production. Watches for unity in style.
Sets and Properties	Follows through on special set construction, and the purchase of special properties. Since some art directors may get carried away when sent on a shopping trip for properties, the producer should keep close watch over all purchases.
Film	Checks with the film editor about special film inserts, or film footage. Some producers are actively supervising the entire editing, especially in a documentary film production.
Special Production Effects	Checks with engineering (studio supervisor) on all special effects that involve additional equipment and manpower, or unusual equipment use.
Postproduction	Checks on all postproduction schedules and facilities (VTR's editing facilities, video and audio dubbings, as well as personnel.)
Remote Facilities	Checks on all aspects of remote productions (see Chapter 16).

Note: In large productions, you may also have to include special makeup and wardrobe services in the below-the-line production activities and budget.

You may find that you can combine on-location work and shoot several sequences with the same crew.

Such a system is particularly beneficial if you produce a series of commercials, all treating the same product, or if you have to produce an instructional television series covering the same topic. *(See 14.11.)*

Special Production Aspects

Besides the above- and below-the-line production processes, there are other important production aspects that you must consider. These are (1) definition of program types, (2) copyright and clearances, (3) union affiliation, and (4) code and legal aspects.

Program Types

All program types have been standardized by the FCC into eight categories: (1) Agricultural (A), (2) Entertainment (E), (3) News (N), (4) Public Affairs (PA), (5) Religious (R), (6) Instructional (I), (7) Sports (S), and (8) Other (O). The last (O) includes all programs not falling within the first seven. These program types are not to overlap one another.

Furthermore, there are subcategories, which may overlap with any of the above types. They are (1) Editorials (EDIT), (2) Political (POL), and Educational Institution (ED); the last (ED) includes any program prepared by, on behalf of, or in cooperation with educational institutions.[5]

---

[5] For more information concerning program type definitions, see Editors of BM/E Magazine, *Interpreting FCC Broadcast Rules,* Vol. 3 (Blue Ridge Summit, Pa.: Tab Books, 1972); and Sydney W. Head, *Broadcasting in America,* 3rd ed. (Boston: Houghton Mifflin Co., 1976).

Copyright and Clearances

If you use copyrighted material on your show, you must procure proper clearances. Usually, the name of the copyright holder and the year of the copyright are printed right after the © copyright symbol. Some photographs, reproductions of famous paintings, and prints are often copyrighted, as are, of course, books, periodicals, short stories, plays, and musical scores. Check with the station's attorney about special copyright clauses and public domain.

You will need clearances for the use of recorded music, as well as the performance of written music, on the air. All published music is subject to performance royalties, with three major organizations holding most of the music copyrights: (1) ASCAP—the American Society of Composers, Authors and Publishers; (2) BMI—Broadcast Music, Incorporated; and (3) SESAC—The Society of European Stage Authors and Composers. If the licensing society is not indicated on the label of the recording, for example, check the large music catalogs of any one of these societies. Larger stations have standing contracts with these societies; all you have to do then is to report the music used on the air.

Union Affiliation

Most directors, writers, and talent belong to a guild or union, as do almost all below-the-line personnel. As a producer, you must be alert to the various union regulations in your production area, the minimum fees and specific work jurisdictions such as overtime, turnaround time (stipulated hours of rest between workdays), rest periods, who can legally run a camera and who cannot, and so forth. If you use nonunion personnel, check with the respective union for proper clearance.

These are the most important television unions:

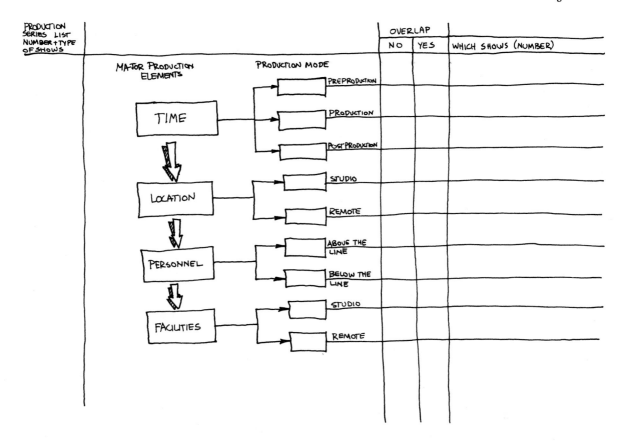

14·11 Multiple Production System.

American Federation of Television and Radio Artists (AFTRA). Most television talent.

American Guild of Musical Artists (AGMA).

American Guild of Variety Artists (AGVA).

Directors Guild of America, Inc.

Writers' Guild of America, Inc.

Screen Actors Guild (SAG); Screen Extras Guild (SEG). Important only when film commercials are produced.

International Brotherhood of Electrical Workers (IBEW). Studio and master control engineers; may include floor personnel.

National Association of Broadcast Employees and Technicians (NABET). Studio and control room engineers; may include floor personnel.

International Alliance of Theatrical Stage Employees and Motion Picture Machine Operators (IATSE).

In small station operation, some members of the production crew may belong to engineering unions also. Directors sometimes belong to AFTRA, especially when they double as announcers.

Always be careful when you ask a studio guest

to do anything but answer questions during an interview. As soon as he (or she) gives a short demonstration of his talents, he may be classified as a performer and automatically become subject to AFTRA fees. Also, don't request the floor crew to do anything that is not directly connected with their regular line of duty, or they, too, may collect talent fees. Camera operators usually have a contract clause that assures them a substantial penalty fee if they are willfully shown by another camera on the television screen.

Code and Legal Aspects

Before you accept a script or go into rehearsal, make sure that the material is well suited for television presentation. Sometimes a script that reads well may become quite objectionable when presented in a certain manner. Be guided by good taste and respect for the viewing public, not just by laws. There is a fine line between using an expletive simply to "liven up an otherwise dull interview" and using it as an essential part of characterization by one of the actors.

The NAB (National Association of Broadcasters) periodically issues a Television Code that suggests guidelines for responsible broadcasting. As a producer, you should certainly keep abreast of such information.[6]

Check with the station attorney or legal counsel about up-to-date rulings on libel (written defamation), slander (oral defamation), the right of privacy (not the same in all states), Canon 35 (courtroom television), obscenity laws, Section 315 of the Communications Act (affording candidates for public office equal opportunities), and similar matters.

---

[6] The Television Code is subject to change. Up-to-date information is available from the Director, Code Authority, National Association of Broadcasters, 1771 N Street, N.W., Washington, D.C. 20036.

Production Process

Because each television production is unique, it has very specific production requirements. Therefore, the clearest way to give you an idea of the entire production process is to list a series of steps and add some of the major factors and questions you ought to consider along with them. The steps you will follow in a real situation may not always match the ones outlined here, either in number or sequence, but the basic patterns of activity will remain. The factors indicated here follow the effect-to-cause systems design, as mentioned previously.

1. *Need Assessment:* Is the program idea truly in the public interest? If the idea were developed into a television show, what, if anything, would the viewer gain by it? Don't forget that relaxation and entertainment, just plain fun, are indeed important program objectives. Check with the assessment person, the program director, the public service director, or anyone else whose judgment you trust, about defined needs. Most of all, stay attuned to life around you. Keep up with the news; observe how people live, what they say, how they feel. Talk to community leaders. Exchange ideas with communication experts, such as mass communication educators, sociologists, philosophers, and artists. Sensitive artists are usually very much aware of the prevailing social climate and of future needs.

2. *Formulation of Program Idea and Research:* Before stating a program objective, try to arrive at a general program idea. Narrow it down to manageable proportions. Don't try to solve all the world's problems in 27:30 minutes. If you have decided on a worthwhile issue, do some research on it. Try to get all the information you can so that you can present a balanced point of view. Local high school and college libraries are a great resource for information, as are newspaper offices and public libraries.

3. *Stating Objective for Process Message:* What would you like the viewer to get out of your program? What do you want him to experience, to feel, to think, during

the show? After the show? What specifically will the percipient gain by your program?

4. *Audience:* What specific type of audience would you like to reach? Teenagers? Senior citizens? Families? Housewives? Working women and men? General works on mass communication research, and sociological studies, as well as rating services, usually have a fairly good definition of audience types and their demographic and ecological parameters. If the issue is important enough, fight for the right of minority audiences (audiences that have special interests, in contrast to mass audience; not an audience defined by ethnic criteria) to receive the information, despite the likelihood that the ratings will be low. Although in a commercial station one of your major objectives is to make money, you also have a responsibility as a public servant.

5. *Time:* In general, the type of audience determines a specific telecasting time, such as morning, noon, late afternoon, early evening, late evening, weekend. What time would be ideal for your purposes? What are your extreme time limits? What compromises are you prepared to make? For example, if your target audience is working women, and you get a Tuesday morning from ten to eleven program time, you will most likely not reach your intended audience.

6. *Tentative Budget:* Work out a tentative budget, although you do not as yet know all the above-the-line and below-the-line requirements. If the show is produced in your station, the above-the-line cost will probably be absorbed by the station (directors, announcers, art director, and so forth are all employed by the station on a regular salary). The estimate for the below-the-line budget must be based on the *approximate* facilities you think you need. Check with the engineering supervisor on the current rates. Again, it may be that your station requires a budget only for moneys that are *actually paid out,* such as the construction of a new set by an outside agency, union scale for freelance talent, copyright release fees, and others. Larger stations, however, require a budget for both above-the-line and below-the-line expenditures, regardless of whether the cost is, at least partially, absorbed by the salaries of regularly employed personnel.

7. *Show Approval:* You should now write up the proposal, mentioning the items above. Include the tentative budget (see page 398). Present the proposal to the program manager, or the public service director if the program falls into the public service category. The program manager will present your proposal to higher management; in small stations, to the general manager and the comptroller or business manager. Be realistic in your initial budget, but don't make it too small. It is psychologically, as well as financially, more appropriate to agree to a budget cut than to have to ask for more money later on.

If your show is to be sponsored (either by a single client or through participating spots), the sales manager will, of course, participate in the initial decision-making process. Often the presumed "salability" of your program idea is a decisive factor in the preliminary negotiations. The sales manager would like to know how the show is going to turn out before you have even started producing it. The networks usually pretest pilot programs as to public appeal.

If a single client becomes the sponsor of your show, you will have to include his representative in at least the preliminary production meetings. The client is usually very much interested in your budget.

8. *Above-the-Line Considerations:* As soon as you have the go-ahead for your project, select your above-the-line personnel, unless these functions are assigned to you.

Select a *director* in whom you have confidence and who is sufficiently sensitive to the program topic that he or she can work toward the process message. In small stations, you probably will have to direct as well as write the script for the show.

In larger production centers, you may have the luxury of hiring a *writer,* who must know the medium and also show some interest in the project. Make sure that this specialist understands the program objective and, especially, the proposed process message. If he or she disagrees with the process message or the whole idea of the program and does not come up with a better one, don't use him or her. The script such a writer will produce may be technically quite efficient but will probably lack inspiration and enthusiasm. Agree on a fee before delivery of the script; some writers charge amounts that can swallow up your whole budget.

You still may need to hire *talent.* For most simple shows—interviews, panel discussions, documentaries, or in-depth reports—you will have the talent in mind when you conceive the program format. However, if you have to cast the talent, consult the director of the show. It should be the director, not you, who makes the final talent selection, assuming that the talent falls within the allocated budget. Your budget should remain flexible as to categories. Try to establish some money reserves in a contingency fund.

The assistant producer, if you have one, is most likely assigned to you permanently and needs no special consideration. The art director, too, works within the station and is readily available for consultation.

9. *Initial Production Conference:* Before the below-the-line considerations, ask the writer to come up with a show treatment (a rough outline of what he thinks should be in the script). Then call the initial production conference, which, ideally, should be attended by the producer, assistant producer, director, writer, art director, talent (if already specified), production manager, and engineering supervisor. Sometimes, in small operations, the program manager sits in on the initial meeting. In any case, you may want to invite him. In this meeting you present the process message objective and let the writer discuss the basic show treatment (the basic video and audio images that the writer thinks are essential for achieving the process message). Listen carefully to all suggestions, but don't let the conference deteriorate into an anecdote session. Have your assistant write down all major suggestions. If the program is relatively simple, many below-the-line items will be discussed in this initial meeting. These are the specific assignments that should be made there: (1) To writer: complete script with deadline. (2) To art director: tentative floor plan (set design) with deadline. (3) To director: list of complete technical facilities with deadline, and list of talent (if not decided already). (4) To production manager: schedule rehearsal and air times, as well as studio facilities and floor crews. (5) To engineering supervisor: assignment of T.D. and crew. (6) To all: precise budget figures for all necessary expenditures. From now on, the various key production people will establish their own lines of communication and contact one another in order to fulfill the assignment within the specified time. Obviously, the art director must get together with the writer and the director in order to work out a suitable set, and the director must consult the production manager about specific technical requirements, such as number of cameras, type of audio equipment, preproduction work (pretaping or filming of certain show elements) or postproduction (editing, dubbing).

Many of the production activities occur from now on simultaneously, or in an order most convenient to the parties involved. However, you must keep track of all such activities. Since deadlines are essential for efficient teamwork, make sure that they are adhered to. List the telephone numbers (home and work) and address of each key production member.

10. *Script Conference:* As soon as the writer has finished the script, call another production conference. Ideally, it should include the same people who attended the first one. But now you are involved primarily in below-the-line matters. These persons are especially important to this meeting: writer with *completed* script (the script still being open for minor changes), art director with tentative floor plan, T.D. with a good idea of technical facilities needed, production manager, floor manager, and talent. Previous to this conference you should have received the completed script and talked over the medium requirements with the director.

In case the process message requires an unusually precise and thorough understanding of all production members (as in the football show mentioned earlier in this chapter), you should schedule subsequent meetings with the entire production personnel (camera operators, audio engineers, videotape editors, floor personnel) so that the director can communicate the specific production concepts and medium requirements. Such meetings are not a waste of time. The more the entire production staff understands the total concept of the show, the less work you will have during actual production (see Chapter 15).

In this script conference, or shortly thereafter, you should work out two important production details: scheduling and facilities request.

11. *Scheduling:* Check with the production manager (who, in turn will be in touch with the engineering supervisor) about studio availability for rehearsal and

taping sessions (or live on-the-air presentation). Check with the director about rehearsal schedules. Make sure that time schedules are distributed to all production and engineering personnel. If a schedule change becomes necessary, let everybody connected with your production know immediately, including any production people who work outside your station. Double-check all schedule items. Have your assistant call the people about the schedule and send them a reminder by mail. Then call again.

12. *Facilities Request:* The person who fills out the final facilities request form varies from station to station. In small station operations, it is often the producer. The facilities request usually contains information as to date and time of rehearsal or taping sessions, or on-the-air performances; title of production, names of producer and director (and sometimes talent); and all technical facilities, such as cameras, microphones, lights, sets, graphics, costumes, makeup, VTR's, and special production needs. It also lists the studio and control room needed and, if you work closed-circuit, the distribution facility *(14.12).* The facilities request, like the script, is an essential communications device. Be as accurate as you possibly can when preparing it. Later changes only invite costly errors.

The facilities request should generally have the floor plan and lighting plot attached. Make sure that the graphics (slides, crawl) are ordered well in advance (unless you use a character generator). The art department has many other things to do, and generally adheres strictly to deadlines.

Since several key departments must receive the same information, carbon copies are necessary. Usually, they are different colors, each of which is assigned permanently to a specific department; for example, the yellow copy may go to engineering, the blue to the art department, the pink to the originator of the facilities request, and so on. The departments that generally get copies of the facilities request are (1) production, (2) engineering, (3) film editing, (4) traffic, and (5) art.

If you have a computer facility, the facilities request could become part of the computer program.

13. *Budget:* The facilities request will give you the exact data you need for the below-the-line budget. You

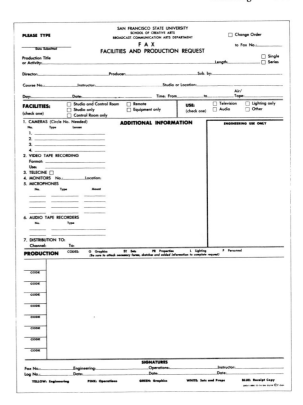

14·12 Facilities Request Form.

are now ready to prepare the final budget for the show. The sample includes above-the-line production expenses although, as pointed out before, they are automatically absorbed by salaries to station personnel. In order to prevent any misunderstanding on how much a specific service or item costs, no actual figures are supplied here *(14.13).* Check with the union headquarters about their minimum fees (most services in larger cities are above the stated minimum rates). A performer who works for scale (minimum union rate) is sometimes hard to find. Every station has a rate card for its below-the-line production costs, such as studio rentals for a minimum number of hours, daily rates (which then are somewhat less than the hourly rate), and the equipment and production personnel supplied.

SHOW:				
VTR DATES:				
AIR DATES:				
TECHNICAL EQUIPMENT AND SERVICES--PRODUCTION	Rate per hour	Hours	Estimate	Actual Cost
Cameras				
Audio				
Lighting				
VTR				
Slo-mo				
Telecine				
Telco (Telephone Co. for remotes only)				
Electronic Support				
Videotape Stock				
SUBTOTAL:				
TECHNICAL EQUIPMENT AND SERVICES--POSTPRODUCTION				
VTR Edition				
Dubbing				
Electronic Support				
Videotape Stock				
SUBTOTAL:				
NON-TECHNICAL EQUIPMENT AND SERVICES				
Sets and Properties				
Graphics				
Make-up				
Wardrobe				
SUBTOTAL:				
PERSONNEL				
Technical Supervisor				
Technical Director				
Engineers (Audio, video, cameras, boom, VTR, maintenance)				
Floor Manager				
Floor Crew				
VTR Editor				
SUBTOTAL:				

		Estimate	Actual Cost
Technical Equipment and Services--Production SUBTOTAL:			
Technical Equipment and Services--Postproduction SUBTOTAL:			
Non-technical Equipment and Services SUBTOTAL:			
Personnel SUBTOTAL:			
TOTAL:			

SHOW:		
VTR DATES:		
AIR DATES:		
SERVICE	ESTIMATE	ACTUAL COST
Producer		
Director		
Associate Director		
Associate Producer		
Writer		
Production Assistant		
Secretary		
Casting Director		
Costume Designer		
Art Director/Scenic Designer		
Music (Orchestra Leader)		
SUBTOTAL:		
Cast		
Contingency		
TOTAL:		
DATE:	AUTHORIZED BY:	

14·13 Sample Budget: Note that in small and medium-sized stations the producer, director, associate producer and director, writer, secretary, and art director are part of the regularly employed production staff. As salaried personnel, they do not require special above-the-line budget considerations. The services of casting director, costume designer, and orchestra leader are required for large-scale productions only. (Budget adapted from ABC program estimates. Courtesy of ABC Television.)

14. *Log Information:* As a producer, it is your responsibility to give the traffic department, which prepares the log, all the necessary information, such as rehearsal dates and times (if they involve equipment), commercial inserts, if any, and major facilities used. Generally, a copy of the facilities request goes directly to traffic. But double-check, nevertheless, on whether they have all the vital information. If the log is made up by computer, you can easily check at any one of the keyboard terminals as to whether the complete information has reached traffic, and, ultimately, the computer.

15. *Publicity and Promotion:* The best show is worthless if nobody knows about it. While the preproduction activities are in full swing, meet with the publicity and promotions departments (usually combined in one department, especially in smaller stations).

The function of these departments is to minimize the gap between the potential and the actual television audience. In other words, it is the job of publicity and promotion to inform all set owners of upcoming shows and to stimulate them to tune to those programs. The higher the number of actual television viewers in relation to set owners, the higher the rating figure will be. Although the quality and success of your show are not necessarily expressed by high ratings, it is still desirable to reach as many viewers in your desired audience as possible. Be sure, therefore, to inform your publicity and promotion people of exact data concerning your show.

16. *Rehearsals and Performance:* From now on, the director of the show takes over. She, or he, will conduct the necessary rehearsals and direct the final videotape or on-the-air performance. Try to stay out of her way as much as possible. If you have suggestions concerning the show, take notes during the rehearsal and then discuss them with the director during the break. During the actual performance, don't interfere at all, unless something totally unexpected happens that needs your immediate decision.

Make a special effort to receive all your guests properly. It doesn't benefit the image of your station if VIP's are left wandering around the hallways, trying to find the right studio.

17. *Feedback and Evaluation:* The rehearsals (if any) will give you the opportunity to evaluate the initial show concept and make changes when necessary. Also, listen to the suggestions of other people, without becoming dependent upon them. If the show solicits feedback ("please call such-and-such a number"), see to it that the feedback facilities are indeed working. There is nothing more annoying to the viewer than to find that his well-intentioned efforts to communicate with the station are ignored. Keep accurate records of all feedback received. Don't forget to write thank-you notes to the people who have made special contributions to the program.

Complete all required reports (such as music clearances and AFTRA forms) unless the director takes care of such matters. Pay all bills promptly.

As we said in the beginning, producing means coordinating many people, activities, and things. Triple-check everything. Don't leave anything to chance. Yet, even the most skillful producer will not be able to come up with a successful program if he does not have an important idea to start with. If you really care about helping people to live better and happier lives, if you are indeed sensitive to your surroundings, then you will find significant program ideas in abundance.

Summary

Producing means to see to it that a worthwhile idea gets to be a worthwhile television show. Significant aspects of production are (1) systems design for production, (2) above-the-line production, (3) below-the-line production, (4) special production aspects, and (5) a sample production process.

The *systems approach to production* stresses the effect-to-cause approach, including (1) need assessment, (2) viewer involvement, (3) medium requirements, and (4) feedback and evaluation. The clear statement of the *process message* is one of the most important aspects of the effect-to-cause approach.

The *above-the-line production* involves nontechnical personnel, such as producer, director, talent, and writer, and the expenditures connected with their work.

The *below-the-line production* consists of coordinating and financing of the engineering and production personnel who are actually operating equipment during the production, as well as the necessary production equipment and facilities. The engineering personnel includes T.D., camera operators, lighting technicians, video and audio engineers; the production personnel includes, among others, floor manager, floor personnel, graphic artists. The facilities include all standard studio and remote equipment, such as camera, lighting, audio, telecine, and VTR.

Special production aspects include (1) definitions of program types, (2) copyright and clearances, (3) union affiliations, and (4) code and legal aspects.

The *production process* shows major steps of decision making and a possible flow of activities, including need assessment, formulation of program idea and research, stating objectives for process message, audience definition, time slot, tentative budget, show approval, production conference, scheduling, facilities request, budget, log information, publicity and promotion, rehearsal and performance, and feedback and evaluation.

15 *Directing*

This chapter covers the major aspects of television directing, which means controlling the complex production machinery. Important aspects are the director's language, the interpretation of a production plan or script into video and audio images, and the coordination of production personnel and talent during rehearsals and on-the-air performance. The discussion falls into these subdivisions:

1. Terminology, the means of coordinating a great many production elements and persons with a maximum of communication effectiveness.

2. Timing—its dual aspects in television and some techniques of time control.

3. Visualization and picturization, the processes by which the director perceives a scene in screen images and maps the sequence of actions.

4. Different types of script formats.

5. Script preparation, including analysis and script marking.

6. Rehearsals for both technical crews and talent.

7. On-the-air directing, together with stand-by procedures and postshow duties.

8. Postproduction activities from the director's point of view.

As a television director, you are involved in coordinating a great number of production elements and people within a rigid time limit. You will find that in the beginning the coordination of the various production elements—cameras, audio, film, slides, videotape, remote feeds, and the clock—seems to provide the greatest challenge. Managing this complex production machinery is, indeed, no easy job. During a simple two-camera show, for example, you find yourself (1) talking and listening to studio engineers and production crew: camera operators, microphone boom operator, floor manager, floorpersons; (2) conversing with the people in the control room, telecine, and VTR room: T.D., audio engineer, light board operator, telecine operator, videotape operator, and master control engineers; (3) watching at least six monitors all the time: two camera preview, telecine, VTR, general preview, and line; (4) watching the time: the control-room clock for the schedule times, and the stopwatch for the running times of the individual show segments and inserts; (5) listening to the program audio (usually one of the most difficult tasks for the beginning director); and (6) following the script.

But once you have mastered the control of the machine to some extent, you will notice that your most difficult job is, after all, the translation of a show idea or script into medium requirements, and the dealing with people, those in front of the camera (talent) and those behind it (production crew and engineers).

We will, therefore, cover in this chapter some aspects of controlling the complex production machinery, with special emphasis on the director's language, the major points of interpreting a production plan or script into video and audio images, and the coordination of production people and talent during rehearsals and on-the-air performances. Specifically, we will stress these

---

Back-Timing The process of figuring additional clock times by subtracting running times from the clock time at which the program ends.

Camera Rehearsal A full rehearsal with cameras and other pieces of production equipment. Similar to the dress rehearsal in theater.

Character The person who appears in a play. Usually defined by clarifying and intensifying specific physiological traits (the way the person looks, moves, runs, behaves, dresses) and psychological traits (the way the person thinks, feels, plots, schemes, loves).

Climax The high point in the plot, usually expressed as the major conflict—as distinguished from a crisis, which is relatively less intense.

Clock Time Also called schedule time. The time at which a program starts or ends.

eight points: (1) terminology, (2) timing, (3) visualization and picturization, (4) script formats, (5) script preparation, (6) rehearsal, (7) on-the-air performance, and (8) postproduction activities.

Terminology

Like any other human activity where many people work together for a common task, television directing demands a precise and specific language. This jargon, which must be understood by all members of the team, is generally called the director's *terminology*. By the time you get to learning television directing, you will probably have mastered most of the production jargon in general and perhaps even the greater part of the director's specific language. But since the latter is such an essential factor for the successful functioning of the production team, you may want to review some of the most common director's signals to its various members *(see 15.1 through 15.6)*. If you use this section as a general review, simply cover up the column that shows the director's signal and try to call out the necessary commands by looking at the picture or the action.

Like any other living language, the director's terminology is subject to habit and change. You may find that in some stations the directors use a term that differs somewhat from yours or one listed here, although the list shown here is fairly standard throughout the industry. Whatever language you use, it must be understood by everyone concerned. It also should be precise and clear. There is little time during a show to do much explaining; the shorter and less ambiguous the signals are, the better the communication will be. In the tables *(15.3 through 15.6)*, we list the director's terminology in these groups: (1) visualization, (2) picturization, (3) special effects, (4) audio, (5) film chain and VTR cues, and (6) floor directions.

Density The number of events happening within a certain time unit. Visual density can be expressed as a multiple superimposition or key, or successively as a series of quick, montage-like cuts. Audio density may be a chord consisting of many notes, or a rapid series of many notes, or the simultaneous playing of several audio tracks. Or: the degree of complexity in the vertical (depth) development of an event.

Dry Run A rehearsal without equipment during which the basic actions of the talent are worked out. Also called blocking rehearsal.

Fact Sheet Also called rundown sheet. Lists the items to be shown on camera and the key ideas that should be expressed verbally by the performer. Serves often as a guide to a show format.

Front-Timing The process of figuring out clock times by adding given running times to the clock time at which the program starts.

Fully Scripted Used to describe a show for which the dialogue is completely written out, as well as detailed video and audio instructions.

Horizontal Development The way the story moves forward from one event to another; similar to plot.

Timing

Correct, split-second timing is essential in all television operations. Every second of a day's telecast is preplanned and logged. All television stations work on similarly tight program schedules. For them time is money, and they hire salespersons to sell time. Your Standard Rate and Data Book will tell you how much your station's time is worth in dollars and cents.

Timing is important to television in another sense as well. It produces the pace of a show. In a well-paced show, the viewer perceives the progression, the speed, to be appropriate with the theme and the mood of the content or the story.

We will first take up the control of the clock time, the *physical* or *objective* time as listed in the log. Then we will briefly discuss the time we feel, *psychological* or *subjective* time, and how we relate it to program matter.

Objective Time

When you look at the log (see page 206), you will see that it lists two types of time: (1) the time when a program, or program segment, such as a commercial, begins and ends, and (2) how long a program, or program segment, runs.

The start-stop time is called *clock time* or *schedule time*. The time specifying how long a program runs is called *running time* or *length.* Except for the very beginning and end of the broadcast day, the end-time of one program always marks the beginning time for the next. The running time may be as short as 10 seconds for a commercial announcement, or as long as two or three hours for a television special or a film.

All clocks in all television stations are synchronized with one another, as far as the minute and second hands are concerned. Only the hour hands show local time. *Clock time,* therefore, is the single

---

Objective Time Also called clock time. The time we measure by the clock.

Pace Perceived duration of the show or show segment. Part of subjective time.

Plot How the story develops from one event to the next.

Running Time The duration of a show or show segment. Also called program length.

Schedule Time See Clock Time.

Semiscripted Used to describe a show for which the dialogue is indicated but not completely written out. The opening and closing of the show are usually fully scripted, with the middle only semiscripted.

Shot Sheet Lists every shot a particular camera has to get. Is attached to the camera as an aid to the camera operator for remembering a shot sequence.

Show Format Lists the order of the various show segments according to appearance.

Show Rhythm Indicates how well the parts of the show relate to each other sequentially, how well the show flows.

most important element of synchronizing programs within a station and among stations. If, for example, your log shows that the network news program comes in at 6:30:00 P.M., your local programming must end exactly at 6:30:00 P.M. Master control will then switch from your local news program, which may have started at 6:00:00 P.M., to network at 6:30:00 P.M. The network will come in on this time, regardless of whether you are ready for it or not, that is, whether you have ended your local news program a little earlier or whether your local newscaster is still in the process of saying good-bye to the audience.

Obviously, you must control the *running time* of your newscast (30:00 min.) so that your program finishes at the exact time the network comes in. Or you may have several commercial inserts within a feature film. If you take too long with getting in and out of the commercials at the scheduled breaks, you will run long with the last part of the film and miss the start-time of the next program. Or, if you don't control the running time of a commercial, you may cut it short by two or three seconds. Considering that each second of a commercial can cost the sponsor as much as $1,000, this seemingly slight timing error can become quite costly.

In order to control objective time (the clock, or schedule, time, and the running time, or length), you must keep an eye on at least two instruments: the *control-room clock* and your *stopwatch.*

The *control-room clock* will help you meet the schedule times—the end times of programs, which represent the beginning times of other programs. In a computer-controlled operation, these schedule times are fed into the computer. The computer than prerolls films and VTR's so that they come on the air exactly at the specified clock time, or switches from one program source to another at the exact clock time as shown in the log.

Storyboard A series of sketches of the key visualization points of an event, accompanied by corresponding audio information.

Subjective Time The duration we feel. Also called psychological time.

Theme What the story is all about; its essential idea.

Time Cues Cues to the talent in regard to the time remaining in the show. Usually consist of a 3-minute cue, a 2-minute cue, a 1-minute cue, a 30-second cue, and a 15-second cue.

Vertical Development The way a situation takes on complexity and depth.

Walk-Through An orientation session with the production crew (technical walk-through) and talent (talent walk-through), by actually walking through the set and explaining the key actions to both parties.

Walk-Through Camera Rehearsal A combination of walk-through and camera rehearsal in order to save time. Usually conducted by the director from the studio floor, with all technical production positions manned and operational.

Z-Axis The imaginary line that extends in the direction the lens points from the camera to the horizon. Z-axis motion is the movement toward or away from the camera.

15·1   Visualization Cues.

Action		**Director's Cue**
From:	**To:**	

Headroom.

Center it, or pan left.

Pan left.

Pan right.

Tilt up.

Action		Director's Cue
From:	**To:**	

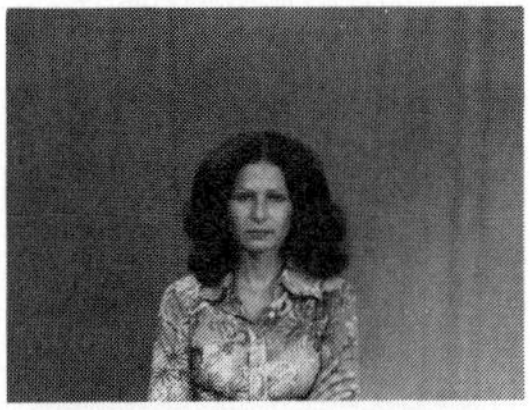

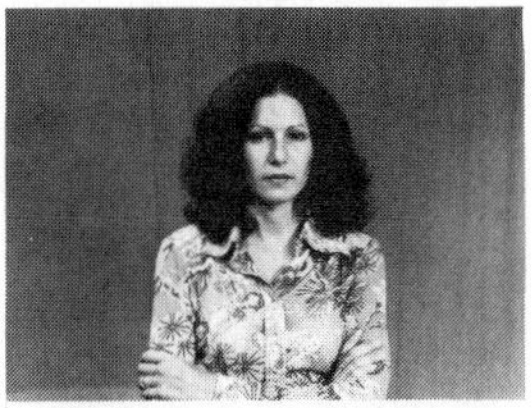

Tilt down.

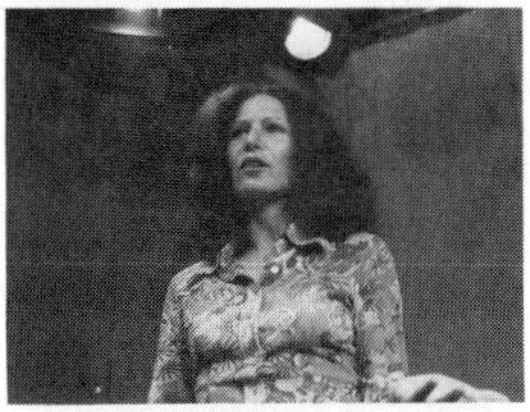

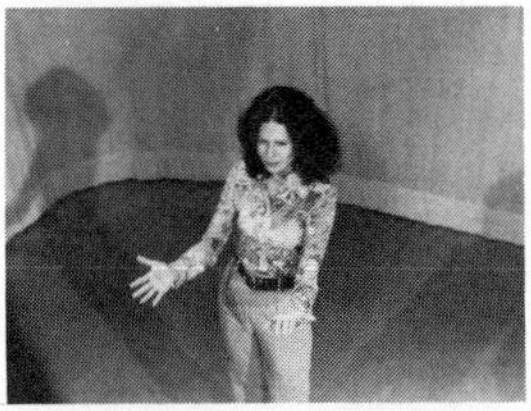

Pedestal up, or crane up.

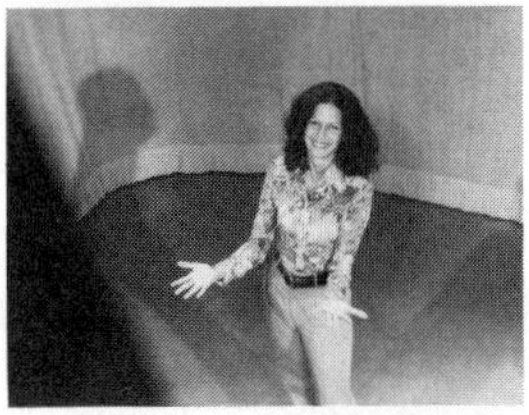

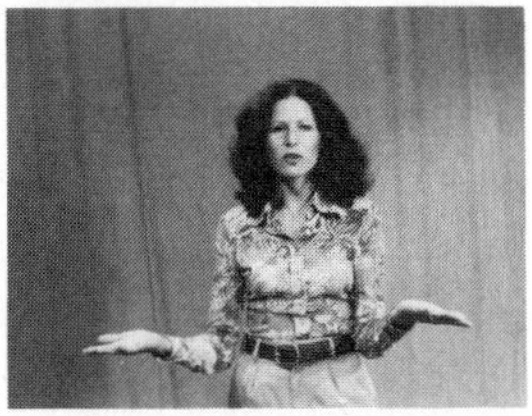

Pedestal down, or crane down.

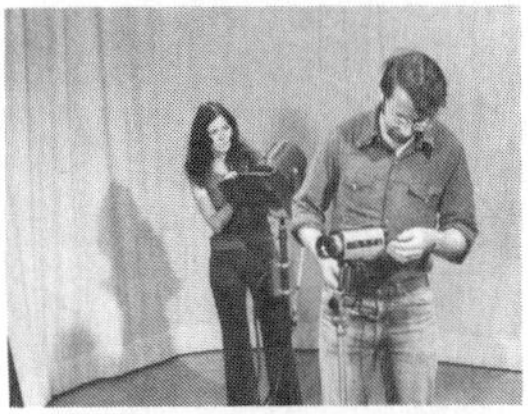

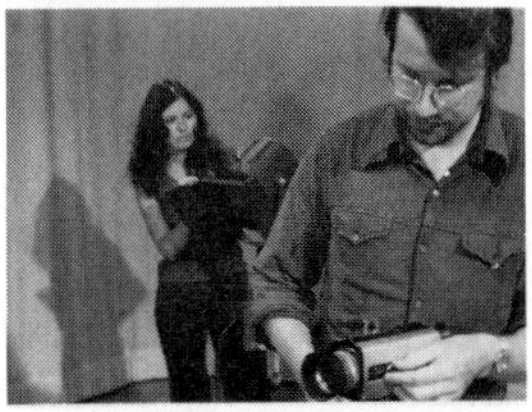

Dolly in.

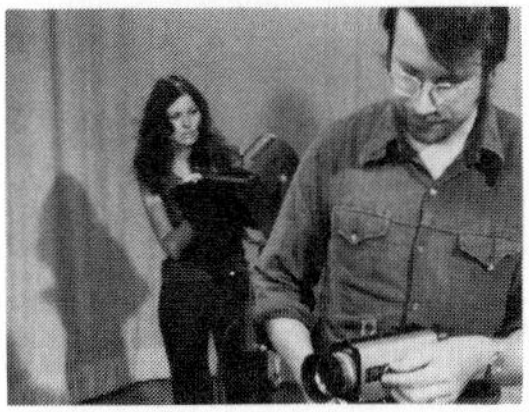

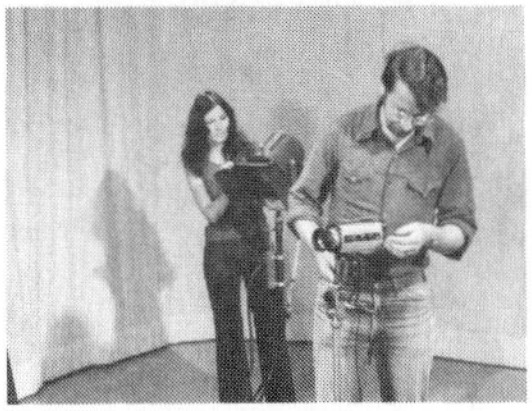

Dolly out.

15·1   Visualization Cues (cont.).

Action

From: **To:**   **Director's Cue**

Zoom in, or tighter.

Zoom out, or looser.

Truck right.

Arc left.

15·2 Picturization Cues.

Action	Director's Cue
Cut from camera 1 to camera 2.	*Ready two—take two.*
Dissolve from camera 3 to camera 1.	*Ready one for dissolve—dissolve.*
Horizontal wipe from camera 1 to camera 3.	*Ready three for horizontal wipe* (over 1)—*wipe.*
Fade in camera 1 from black.	*Ready fade in one—fade in one.* Or: *Ready up on one—up on one.*
Fade out camera 2 to black.	*Ready black—go to black.*
Short fade to black between cameras 1 and 2.	*Ready cross-fade to two—cross-fade.*
Cut between camera 1 and film on F-2.	*Ready F-two* (assuming that the film is coming from film chain 2)—*take F-two.* (Sometimes you simply call the camera number as it appears on the switcher. If, for example, the telecine camera of film island No. 1 is labeled 6, you will say: *Ready six—take six.*)
Cut between film and slide.	*Ready slide—take slide.* Or: *ready slide on F-two—take F-two* (assuming that the film is on F-1 and the slide on F-2).
Cut between slide and slide.	*Ready to change slide—change slide.*
Going to black or taking out super before new slide comes up.	*Ready slide out—slide out, change slide, up on slide.*
Dissolve between camera 3 and VTR (assuming that VTR is already rolling and locked in).	*Ready VTR two for dissolve—dissolve.*

15·3   Special Effects.

Action	**Director's Cue**
Super camera 1 over 2.	*Ready super one over two—super.*
To return to camera 2.	*Ready to lose super—lose super.* Or: *Ready to take out one—take out one.*
To go to camera 1 from the super.	*Ready to go through to one—through to one.*
Super slide over base picture on camera 1.	*Ready super slide* (over 1)—*super.* Or: *Ready super F-two* (assuming that the slide appears on F-2)—*super.*
Key studio card title on camera 1 over base picture on camera 2.	*Ready key one over two—key.*
Fill keyed-out title from studio card on camera 1 with yellow hue over base picture on camera 2.	*Ready matte-key one, yellow, over two—matte-key.*
To have title from character generator appear in drop-shadow outline over base picture on camera 1.	*Ready C.G.* (for character generator) *drop shadow over one—key C.G.* (Sometimes, the director may use the name of the character generator manufacturer, such as Chiron. Thus, you would say: *Ready Chiron over one—key Chiron.* Since the character generator information is almost always keyed, the "key" is usually omitted in the ready cue.) Or: *Ready effects, drop shadow—take effects.*
To have background scene from slide (F-1) appear behind newscaster on camera 2.	*Ready matte* (or *chroma,* or *chroma matte*) *one over two—matte.* Or: *Ready F-one effects over two—effects.*
To have a wipe pattern appear over a picture, such as a scene on camera 2 replace a scene on camera 1 through a circle wipe.	*Ready circle wipe two over one—wipe.*
	(Any other wipe is called for in the same way, except that the specific wipe pattern is substituted for the circle wipe.)
	(If you need a soft wipe, whereby the edges of the wipe pattern are purposely soft and indistinct, simply call for *Ready soft-wipe* instead of *Ready wipe.*)
To have the picture become high-contrast and lose detail (attain a solarizing effect) of camera 1 picture.	*Ready debeam one—debeam.*
To have one part of the picture defocus while another part is getting into focus (selective focus).	*Ready to rack focus on foreground—rack focus.* Or: *Ready to rack focus on background—rack focus.*

15·4 Audio Cues.

Action	Director's Cue
To activate microphone in the studio.	*Ready to cue talent* (or something more specific, like "Mary")—*cue her.* (The audio engineer will automatically open her mike.) Or: *Ready to cue Mary—open mike, cue her.*
To start music.	*Ready music—music.*
To bring music under for announcer.	*Ready to fade music under—music under, cue announcer.*
To take music out.	*Ready music out—music out.* Or: *Fade music out.*
To close the microphone in the studio (announcer's mike) and to switch over to the sound on film or videotape.	*Ready SOF* (or SOT, sound on tape; close mike) *track up.* Or: *Ready SOF* (SOT)—*SOF* (SOT).
To roll audio tape.	*Ready audio tape—roll audio tape.* (Don't just say: Roll tape, since the T.D. may start the VTR.)
To fade one sound source under and out while simultaneously fading another in (similar to a dissolve).	*Ready cross-fade from* (source) *to* (other source)—*cross-fade.*
To fade one sound source out and then fade another one in.	*Ready segue from* (source) *to* (other source)—*segue.*
To increase the volume of the program speaker for the director.	*Monitor up, please.*
To play sound effect from cartridge machine.	*Ready sound effect No. X on audio cart.* Or: *Ready cart No. X—sound effect.*
To start videotape beeper.	*Ready beeper—beeper.*
To put slate information on videotape (either open floor manager's mike or talkback patched to VTR).	*Ready to read slate—read slate.*

15·5 Film Chain and VTR Cues.

Action	**Director's Cue**
To cut from camera 1 to film (SOF) on F-2.	*Ready to roll film, F-two, SOF—roll film, four—three—two —one, take F-two, SOF.* (Assuming that you still work with a countdown. Otherwise: *Ready film, SOF, F-two —take F-two.* The T.D. rolls and takes the film at the same time.) Don't forget to start your stopwatch as soon as the film appears in the F-2 monitor.
To start black-and-white videotape for recording of a program.	*Ready to roll VTR one—roll VTR one.* (Now you have to wait for the "in-record" confirmation by the VTR operator.)
To "slate" the program after the VTR is in the record mode. The slate is on camera 2, the opening scene on camera 1. We are assuming that you are not using the optional 35-sec. alignment signal and reference level audio tone, but that you use the customary 10-sec. beeper countdown.	*Ready two, ready to read slate—take two, read slate.*
Putting the opening beeper on the audio track and fading in on camera 1. (Don't forget to start your stopwatch as soon as camera 1 fades in.)	*Ready black. Ready beeper—black, beeper. Ten—nine—eight— seven—six—five—four—three—two—one—up on one.*
To start a color videotape for recording a program.	*Ready to roll VTR two—roll VTR two.* (Again, you have to wait for the "in-record" confirmation by the VTR operator.)
To put on the color bars and the reference audio tone.	*Ready bars—take bars. Tone.* (Start your stopwatch and record the bars for 60 seconds.)
To "slate the program" after the color bars.	As above in black-and-white recording. But leave slate on for 15 seconds minimum.
To beep the program.	As above in black-and-white recording.

Action

To roll a VTR as a program insert, while you are on camera 2; sound is on tape. Assuming a 6-sec. roll.

To return from film or VTR to camera and live announcer on camera 2. (Don't forget to stop your watch and reset it for the next insert.)

To A-B roll, with SOF on F-1 and silent footage on F-2. SOF scene comes up first, then you switch to B-roll with SOF continuing from A-roll, then back to A-roll with SOF.

We are now back in the SOF on F-1.

If you shift to VO (voice over) on the B-roll while discontinuing the SOF from the A-roll, you will have to give audio cues; otherwise, the audio engineer simply lets the A-roll SOF continue.

To cut to VTR commercial (SOT) from a tape cassette or cartridge. (Usually, the switchers are labeled CART, regardless of whether the VTR is from a cassette machine or a cartridge.)

Director's Cue

Ready to roll VTR three, SOT—roll VTR three, six—five—four—three—two—one, take VTR three, SOT.

If you don't use a countdown because of instant start, simply say, *Ready VTR three, take VTR three.* (Start your stopwatch for timing the VTR insert.)

Ten seconds to two, five seconds to two. Ready two, ready cue announcer—cue announcer, take two.

Ready A-B roll on F-one and two. A-roll SOF on F-one. (This is merely a confirmation. In case the films have been switched, the telecine operator would call over the intercom and inform you, the T.D., and the audio engineer of the switch.)—*Roll them, four—three—two—one, up on F-one, SOF.* (Start your stopwatch and keep track of the time and the word cue for the switchover.) *Five seconds to B-roll.* Or, more accurately: *Five seconds to F-two. Ready F-two—take F-two. Ready F-one on a dissolve—dissolve to F-one.*

Ready F-two (or B-roll), *ready VO, studio* (or "Bob" or whoever supplies the VO)—*take F-two, cue Bob.*

Ready to take cart—take cart. (Usually the VTR carts have instant start, so no prerolls are necessary. Some directors call them "video carts" to distinguish them from audio carts.)

15·6 Floor Directions.

Action		**Director's Cue**
From:	**To:**	

Move talent to camera left.

Move talent to camera right.

Have talent turn toward camera, face camera, or turn in.

	Action		**Director's Cue**
From:		**To:**	

Have the woman turn to her left.

Turn the object clockwise (counterclockwise).

To floor manager to flip from one studio card to another.

Ready change card—change card. Or simply: *Card.*

To microphone boom operator to raise boom so that microphone will no longer appear in the camera shot.

Boom up, or mike up.

To stop the entire action.

Cut.

4:24:30 — 5
4:26:30 — 3
4:27:30 — 2
4:28:30 — 1
4:29:00 — ½
4:29:15 — 15 SEC.
4:29:30 — BLACK → START HERE

BACK TIME TO HERE ↑

15·7 Back-Timing Cues.

If a schedule change becomes necessary, traffic (or anyone responsible for the change) will feed the new information to the computer, which then will automatically adjust the schedule times of all programs ahead of the change. If you don't end a locally produced program on time, the computer will override you and switch to the network according to the schedule time as logged. So, you had better be ready.

The *stopwatch* will help you measure the length of show segments, the running time of film or videotape inserts, such as a piece of news film or a VTR commercial. Don't use your stopwatch to time entire shows, unless they are videotaped for later playback. Except for the highly accurate digital ones, stopwatches may be off as much as two seconds in a 30-minute program. Worse yet, if you go by the running time as shown on your stopwatch for timing a local program, you may not be able to meet the next program source at the scheduled time.

In videotaping a show, you can use the stopwatch for the overall timing since the tape timer on the VTR machine, or the time code, will give you a highly accurate timing of the overall show anyway. If you have VTR inserts within the show you are videotaping, you will need to use two stopwatches: one for measuring the overall time of the show, the other for the running times of the inserts.

Don't forget to start your stopwatch at the beginning of each program insert and to stop it and reset it at the end. Inexperienced directors are apt

to have difficulty in remembering to start their watches at the beginning of a film or VTR insert.

In order to meet the times as scheduled in the log, you are greatly aided by (1) back-timing and (2) front-timing.

Back-Timing   One of the most common time controls involves cues to the talent, so that he or she can end the program, such as a newscast, on the scheduled time. In a 30-minute program, the talent normally expects a 5-minute cue, and subsequent cues with three minutes, two minutes, one minute, thirty seconds, and fifteen seconds remaining in the show. In order to figure out such time cues quickly, you simply *back-time* from the scheduled end-time, or (which is the same thing) the start-time of the new program segment. For example, if your log shows that your live "What's Your Opinion?" panel discussion show is followed by a Salvation Army PSA (Public Service Announcement) at 4:29:30, at what clock times do you have to give the talent the standard time cues? You simply start with the end-time, 4:29:30, and *subtract* the various time segments. For example, your 15-second cue should come at 4:29:30 − 0:00:15 = 4:29:15. Figure 15.7 shows you the cues as determined through back-timing.

If you tape a show and time the VTR with your stopwatch, you simply back-time from the *running time* as shown on your stopwatch. Let's assume that your show has a running time of 28:30 minutes. Your time cues would have to come at the following stopwatch times:

23:30—5-min. cue

25:30—3-min. cue

26:30—2-min. cue

27:30—1-min. cue

28:00—30-sec. cue

28:15—15-sec. cue

28:30—BLACK

Digital stopwatches can be made to run forward or in reverse. When you are videotaping a program, you will probably want the watch to run backwards, showing you at any point in the show the *remaining* running time. Since the watch in the reverse shows the time left till the end of the program anyway, no back-timing is necessary.

Although your log usually shows both schedule times and running times, your script or program format may, for example, give you only start– and end–clock times for each program segment. In order to figure running times from clock times, you must, once again, back-time. As an example, we will take a feature film that is interrupted by commercials and PSA's. Since the end cues for the films are determined by running time (stopwatch times) only (in that end cue marks are no longer used), you must figure out the running time for each program segment from the clock times as indicated on your program format *(15.9)*.

What is the running time for each segment? Again, you start at the last clock time given and work backward. How long is the last feature film segment as shown on the format? 5:23:51 — 5:11:33 = 12:18 min. Try now to figure out all the remaining running times, before checking your results *(see 15.10)*.

Front-Timing If you are given the running times for each program segment and only the schedule times for the opening and closing of the total program (such as the entire film feature), you will need to figure out the remaining clock times. The running times alone are not enough. You need to know the actual clock times for each break so that you can tell whether your show segment is exactly on schedule. Since the running times of each show segment are timed with the stopwatch and not with the clock, your running somewhat late or early at various breaks will not show up until the very end of the program, when it is too late to do anything about it. With the clock times available at each break, you can then

$$
\begin{array}{rcl}
5:15:22 & \rightarrow & 5:14:82 \\
-\quad 14:27 & \rightarrow & -\quad 14:27 \\
\hline
& & 5:00:55
\end{array}
$$

$$
\begin{array}{rcl}
5:02:43 & \rightarrow & 4:62:43 \\
-\quad 55:30 & \rightarrow & -\quad 55:30 \\
\hline
& & 4:07:13
\end{array}
$$

15·8 In subtracting time, you may find it convenient to take one minute from the minute column and convert it into seconds, especially when you have to subtract a high number of seconds from a small number. The same way, you can take an hour from the hour column and convert it into minutes.

15·9   Timing: Example.

SCHEDULE (or CLOCK) TIME	SEGMENT TITLE	RUNNING TIME (or LENGTH)
5:00:20	OPENING	
5:00:35	FEATURE FILM	
5:11:03	TRAFFIC SAFETY PSA	
5:11:13	SOAP COMMERCIAL	
5:11:33	FEATURE FILM	
5:23:51	SALVATION ARMY PSA	
etc.		

15·10   Timing: Example with running times.

SCHEDULE TIME	SEGMENT TITLE	RUNNING TIME
5:00:20	OPENING	00:15
5:00:35	FEATURE FILM	10:28
5:11:03	TRAFFIC SAFETY PSA	00:10
5:11:13	SOAP COMMERCIAL	00:20
5:11:33	FEATURE FILM	12:18
5:23:51	SALVATION ARMY PSA	

dry-run the feature film (rolling the film but not putting it on the air right away) for two or three seconds during a break to make up for lost time, or put up an I.D. slide in order to stretch the break a little, if you run somewhat short.

In order to figure out the additional clock times for each break, simply *add* the running times to the initial clock time as shown in the log or the program format. Try to figure out the additional clock times for the program rundown *(see 15.11)*. At what clock time, for example, does the PSA come up? Look at 15.12 to see how your schedule (clock) times should appear on your log, or pro-

gram rundown sheet. If you figured correctly, you will have to hit the PSA slide at exactly 6:34:40.

Subjective Time

The control of subjective, or psychological, time, the time we feel, is much more subtle and difficult than the control of objective time. Unfortunately, there is no mechanical timing device that will tell you whether an actor races through his lines too fast, or whether a whole scene is paced too slowly, and therefore drags for the viewer. In determining subjective time, you must rely on your subjective judgment and on your sensitivity to

SCHEDULE TIME	SEGMENT TITLE	RUNNING TIME
6:29:30	NEWS PROMO	0:10
	OIL CO. COMMERCIAL	0:20
	NEWS LV	2:17
	NEWS FILM SOF	1:05
	NEWS LV	0:20
	NEWS FILM SILENT	0:58
	SAFETY PSA SLIDE	0:10

15·11 Log Segment: Example.

SCHEDULE TIME	SEGMENT TITLE	RUNNING TIME
6:29:30	NEWS PROMO	0:10
6:29:40	OIL CO. COMMERCIAL	0:20
6:30:00	NEWS LV	2:17
6:32:17	NEWS FILM SOF	1:05
6:33:22	NEWS LV	0:20
6:33:42	NEWS FILM SILENT	0:58
6:34:40	SAFETY PSA SLIDE	0:10

15·12 Log Segment: Example with schedule times.

the relation of one movement to another or one rhythm to another. Although two persons move with the same speed, one may seem to move much more slowly than the other. What makes the movements of the one person appear faster or slower? *(See 15.15.)*

Watch how rush-hour traffic reflects nervous energy and impatience while actually the vehicles move considerably more slowly than when traveling on an open freeway. Good comedians and musicians are said to have a "good sense of timing." This means that they have excellent control of their subjective time.

When dealing with subjective time, we have many ways of expressing its relative duration. You hear of speed, tempo, pace, hurrying, dragging, and other similar expressions. In order to simplify the subjective time control, you may want to use only two basic concepts: *pace* and *rhythm.* The *pace* of a show or a show segment is how fast or how slow the segment or the entire show feels. Show *rhythm* has to do with the pacing of each show segment in relation to the next, and to the whole show.

There are many ways of increasing or decreasing the pace of a scene, a segment, or an overall

15·13   In front-timing, as in back-timing, remember to compute time on a sixty scale rather than a hundred scale.

$$\begin{array}{r} 6:33:42 \\ +\quad 0:58 \\ \hline 6:33:100 \end{array} \rightarrow \ 6:34:40$$

Simply compute the seconds, minutes, and hours individually, and then convert them to the sixty scale.

$$\begin{array}{r} 4:39:47 \\ 45:29 \\ +\quad 18:30 \\ \hline 4:102:106 \end{array} \rightarrow \ 4:103:46 \ \rightarrow \ 5:43:46$$

15·14   Try to pick three or four recordings of the same piece of music, such as Beethoven's Fifth Symphony, as interpreted by different conductors. Most likely, you will find that some play the same piece of music much faster than others, depending on their overall concept of the piece and, of course, their personal temperament and style. Which tempo, or pacing, do you like best? Why?

15·15   As a director, you are concerned primarily with a four-part division of a program: (1) the overall *show*, which is constructed of several segments, (2) the show *segment*, which consists of two or more scenes, (3) the *scene*, which consists of a series of shots, and (4) the *shot*, which is the smallest workable program unit.

In controlling subjective time, you will have to consider show pace and rhythm, segment pace and rhythm, and scene pace and rhythm. The shot, as the smallest program unit, has a duration but not a pace.*

* Herbert Zettl, *Sight-Sound-Motion* (Belmont, Calif.: Wadsworth Publishing Co., 1973), pp. 275–276.

show. One is to *speed up* the action or the delivery of the dialogue, very much like picking up the tempo of a musical number. Another is to *increase* the *intensity,* the relative excitement, of a scene. Usually, this is done by introducing or sharpening some *conflict,* such as raising the voices of people arguing, having one car almost go out of control while being pursued by another, or having the lead mountain climber slip at an especially tricky point. A third possibility is to *increase* the *density* of the event, by simply having more things happening within a specific section of running time. For slowing down a scene, you do just the opposite. Whatever you change, you must always perceive your pacing in relation to the other parts of the show and to the whole show itself. Fast, after all, is fast only if we are able to relate the movement to something slower.

Visualization and Picturization

As a director, you should be able to convert a scene mentally into television images—video and audio images that appear on the screen and from the loudspeaker. Directing starts with *visualizing* the *key images* and deciding on where the people and things should be placed relative to the camera, and the camera relative to the event (people and things). Then, you must consider the *sequence* of the events, the *picturization.* By this process you will determine how and where the people will have to move, and how many cameras you will need in order to achieve the event sequence with all the necessary transitions.

As indicated in the previous chapter, the director, as well as the producer, should start with the process message, the experience the percipient is supposed to undergo during or after the program, and work *backward* to what the medium needs in

```
INTERVIEW

DATE:     March 9, 1979

PLACE:    Studio 2

TIME:     4:00-5:00 p.m.

MODE:     VTR (quad) record

LENGTH:   10:00 min.



        VIDEO

CU of host.                    HOST--INTRODUCES SHOW.
Host faces camera.

2-shot of host and guest.      HOST--INTRODUCES GUEST.

Host turns to guest.           HOST--ASKS FIRST QUESTION.
CU guest.
                               GUEST-ANSWERS.
_____

INTERVIEW:                     INTERVIEW WITH GREAT EMPHASIS ON
Favor guest with CU's          WHAT GUEST HAS TO SAY.
and XCU's.

_____

CLOSING:

2-shot of host and guest.      HOST--MAKES CLOSING REMARKS.
Host faces camera and
closes show.
```

15·16 Two-Person Interview: Sample script.

order to precipitate such an experience (see Chapter 14).

What and how much equipment do you need? How should it function? These questions can be answered quickly and accurately only after a great deal of experience. In general, try to get by with as *little* equipment as possible. If you can do a show with two cameras, don't request three. Otherwise, you might feel obliged to use the third camera, not because you need it but because it is there. Such redundancy is not only costly but often an obstacle to the picturization process of the beginning director. You might, for example,

be enticed to cut frequently among the three cameras instead of staying on the one camera that delivers the most expressive picture.

Here is an example. Assuming that you have to videotape a two-person interview (host and guest), with the process message objective stating that the percipient should gain a deeper insight into the thinking and feeling and general behavior of the guest. The script only indicates the opening and the closing by the host, and leaves the visualization and picturization basically up to you, the director *(see 15.16)*. What would you do?

How do you preconceive this interview? How

15·17   One Approach to Interview Scene with One Camera.

Video	Staging	Visualization and Picturization	Audio
Opening CU of host. Host faces camera.			Introduces show.
Zoom back to 2-shot.			Introduces guest.

do you see it and hear it? The process message and the admittedly vague script suggest that the *key visualization* should be a closeup of the guest's face. The viewer should not only see the guest but be able, at least to some extent, to look into his personality.

With all due respect to the host, he simply is not important in this interview. Therefore, you don't need to show him at all, except for the opening and closing of the show.

In figuring out the medium requirements, we can decide on two obvious production items right away. Since the participants don't move about, we can use lavaliere mikes for the audio pickup. The lighting should be normal; that is, we should have enough light on the guest's face so that his features are clearly visible and the colors as undistorted as possible. How about cameras? Three or two? You really don't need three, and if you picturize the show within the context of the process message, you may not even need two. Your jus-

tification for one camera is that you will stay on the guest's face throughout the interview, sometimes viewing it at very close range, and sometimes from a little farther back. Figure 15.17 shows a possible visualization and picturization approach to this interview with only one camera.

As you can see in this exercise, the director first reveals the basic relationship of host and guest. They are obviously sitting next to each other. Then the director concentrates on the guest, the object of the process message.

The way the interview is staged (set up for the camera), the camera does not have to move at all. The host will turn into the camera for the opening and closing, but he will face the guest for the rest of the interview. The camera zooms in on the guest and stays there.

If you want the host to play a more active role visually, you can maintain the same setup but have the camera zoom back to a two-shot from time to time, or even arc right, in order to get more

Video	Staging	Visualization and Picturization	Audio
Host turns to guest. Zoom in to CU of guest.			Asks first question.
During interview stay on guest. Vary between MS and XCU.			
Closing Zoom back to 2-shot. Host faces camera.			Closes show.

of a full-face shot of the host than is possible from the original camera position.

In this exercise it is assumed that the titles are supplied by telecine and not by a studio camera.

Three of the most important aids for the visualization and picturization processes are (1) the storyboard, (2) the floor plan, and (3) the script.

The *storyboard* shows the key visualization points, the major shots of an event, and gives some idea as to the major picturization *(see 15.18 and 15.19)*.

The *floor plan* shows you the physical environ-

15·18 Through thoughtful staging for the single camera, even a rather complex scene can be handled well. As you can see in this illustration, the people move and converse along the *z-axis,* the illusionary axis that extends from the camera to the horizon.* If you have placed the entrance camera-left and the bar camera-right, you cannot, of course, cover the whole action with only one camera. In planning your shots, stage your action for the camera, and not for an audience as you would in the theater.

Video	Staging	Visualization and Picturization (Storyboard)	Audio
Two people (A and B) enter room. Go to the house bar, get a drink.	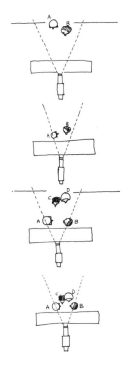		
			They start arguing with each other.
Two more people (C and D) enter room and participate in the conversation.			
			C and D try to make A and B see reason.

* Zettl, *Sight-Sound-Motion,* Chapters 8 and 9.

ment of the whole setting, the major positions of the performers or actors, and where they can move, if any movement is required (pages 346 and 350). You should learn to interpret a floor plan into *camera shots,* into key visualizations from the point of view of the camera. The floor plan will give you an essential clue as to where your cam-

eras should be in order to achieve certain key images. By thinking the camera positions through carefully relative to the setting as shown on the floor plan, you can often anticipate, and therefore correct, production problems. *(See 15.20.)*

A good *script* will give you some of the most accurate cues for visualization, picturization, au-

15·19   Storyboard: Keep America Beautiful, Inc.,
The Advertising Council, Inc., and Marsteller Inc.

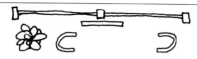

SET: 2 HARDWALL PANELS (PLAIN, OFF-WHITE)
SET PROPS: 2 CHAIRS (LARGE UPHOLSTERED)
         1 RUBBER PLANT
         1 MONET PAINTING (NOTRE DAME)
HAND PROPS: NONE
a   CAMERAS: 2 RCA TK44Bs
MICROPHONES: 2 LAVALIERES
LIGHTING : NORMAL

15·20 Let us go through some visualization and picturization activities and see how we can spot potential problems, if any, simply by studying the floor plan carefully. Above are the floor plan, as given to you by the new art director, and the basic props and equipment list for the show *(a)*.

From your script, you learn that this set is designed for a simple 7-minute interview. Take a look at the floor plan and try to visualize some of your key shots, such as a CU of the guest, an opening two-shot, with the host introducing the guest, an occasional reaction shot of the host.

The way the chairs are placed, a two-shot would be difficult to achieve *(a, b, c)*.

If the camera shoots from straight on, the chairs are much too far apart. At best, the two people would seem glued to the edges of the screen, putting undue emphasis on the painting in the middle. Also, you would overshoot the set on both ends. *(b)*

If you shoot from the extreme left, you will get an over-the-shoulder shot from the host to the guest. Assuming that you pull your camera way back in order to get a narrow-angle zoom lens position (reducing the space between the two people), you will again overshoot the set and not see the host straight on. *(c)*

If you cross-shoot with the other camera, you can get a reverse-angle shot of the host, but again you will overshoot. Also, you will have the rubber plant growing out of the host's head. *(d)*

b

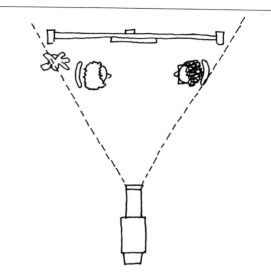

What other problems do we have with the setup as indicated on the floor plan? Let's go down the prop list. Two *plain, off-white* hardwall panels are hardly the most interesting background for this color telecast (see make of cameras). The surface will be too plain, and its off-white color will be too bright for the foreground scene, rendering the skin tones of the two persons unusually dark. If a performer happens to be Black, the contrast problem with the white background is even more extreme. And you can't correct the problem by selective lighting. See how close the chairs are to the background flats? Any key light and fill light will inevitably strike the background too. Also there is not enough room between the chairs and the flats for adequate back-lighting, unless you want to tolerate a top light shining straight down on the people. The acoustics may also prove to be less than desirable, since the microphones are very close to the hardwall flats.

The *large upholstered chairs* are definitely not the right chairs for an interview. They look too pompous and would engulf their occupants in upholstery. Moreover, the chairs cannot be placed close enough to each other for adequate camera shots.

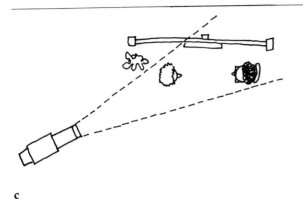

c

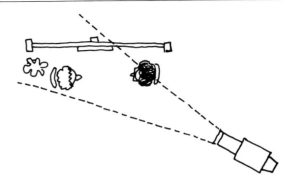

d

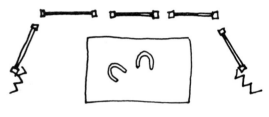

e

The *rubber plant* will be in the way, from whatever angle you might shoot; at least it will not make much sense if part of it is seen behind the host only.

Since most of the shooting must be done from extreme angles (assuming that you have to go ahead with this setup), the *painting* is utterly useless. If you want to break up some of the plain background with a picture, it must hang in such a way that you will have it in the *actual shot* of one of the cameras (which means that it would have to hang in a spot where there are presently no flats to support it). You may even wonder about the compatibility of Monet's subtle impressionistic colors when viewed in black-and-white television. As pleasant as this painting may look in color, in black-and-white the viewer may see nothing but a few indistinct gray blobs.

Lastly, because the chairs are not on a platform, the cameras will have to look *down* on the performers, unless the camera operators pedestal all the way down and work the whole interview from a very awkward position.

Now, let's suggest to the new art director some possible solutions to these problems: (1) Enlarge the background. Use flats of a different color and texture (such as medium-dark wood panel pattern). Perhaps break up the background with a few narrow flats or large pylons. (2) If you hang pictures on the flats to break up plain surfaces, hang them in places where they will be seen in the most frequent camera shots. (3) Put the whole set on a platform. (4) Use smaller and simpler chairs and place them closer together. (5) Get rid of the rubber plant. Although rubber plants in a set look great to the naked eye, they become a compositional obstacle when the camera is on. And (6) move the chairs out, away from the background flats. Figure *e* shows how the suggested corrections might be integrated in a new floor plan.

What other ways could you suggest to solve these problems? As you can see, even a cursory study of the floor plan can tell you a great deal about potential production methods. The more complicated the show becomes, the more time and effort you should give to the basic preproduction analysis of the floor plan.

```
VIDEO

Fade in LS of rock group.

Key slide 1 (name group).

Key slide 2 (members).

Key slide 3 (produced and directed by).

Cut to MC (Master of Ceremonies) intro-
    ducing group.

Cut to group MS, playing first number.

Cut to CU's of solos.

Chroma-key psychedelic figures from VTR
    insert.

Dissolve to MC at end of number.
```

15·21 Partial Video Column.

dio elements, and other production factors *(15.25).* This is one of the reasons why a nondramatic script is usually divided into a *video column,* concerned with what the viewer should *see,* and an *audio column,* concerned with what the viewer should *hear.* As a director, you must translate these video and audio instructions into production equipment and its operation. Since the video instructions are generally more indicative of the overall production requirements, many directors begin their analysis of medium requirements by reading that column in a script. Looking at the partial video column in 15.21, what facilities would you need, assuming that the whole show is to be videotaped without postproduction editing?

The "cut to" instructions from rock group to CU's, and the cutting to the MC, suggest a minimum of two cameras. The keying of slides means a film chain. The chroma key VTR insert means that you need a second VTR in addition to the master VTR on which you are recording the whole program. It also presupposes that the rock group plays in front of a chroma key background, and that you do have chroma key special effects available.

The number of players in the group and the list of what instruments they play will give you, or at least the audio engineer, a clue to what and how many microphones are needed.

Before we go into a very brief discussion on how the director should prepare a script for production, you should acquaint yourself with the major script formats.

Script Formats

There are four basic types of script formats: (1) the fully scripted show, (2) the semiscripted show, (3) the show format, and (4) the fact or rundown sheet.

The Fully Scripted Show

A complete script includes every word that is to be spoken during a show, as well as detailed audio and video instructions. Dramatic shows, comedy skits, news shows, and most major commercials are fully scripted. There are advantages and disadvantages in directing this sort of show. The advantages are that you can visualize and picturize the complete show before going into rehearsal. You have definite cue lines, and you know where the camera goes at what time and what shot it gets. The disadvantages are that you are tied down to following the script very carefully, and this is an additional burden to the many things you already have to do during a performance. Also, if the actor or performer forgets to give you the exact text, your shooting procedure may be seriously affected.

Newscasts are usually fully scripted. Figure 15.22 shows an excerpt from a typical one. The large

15·22 Fully Scripted Newscast (Excerpts). Courtesy of KNXT, Los Angeles.

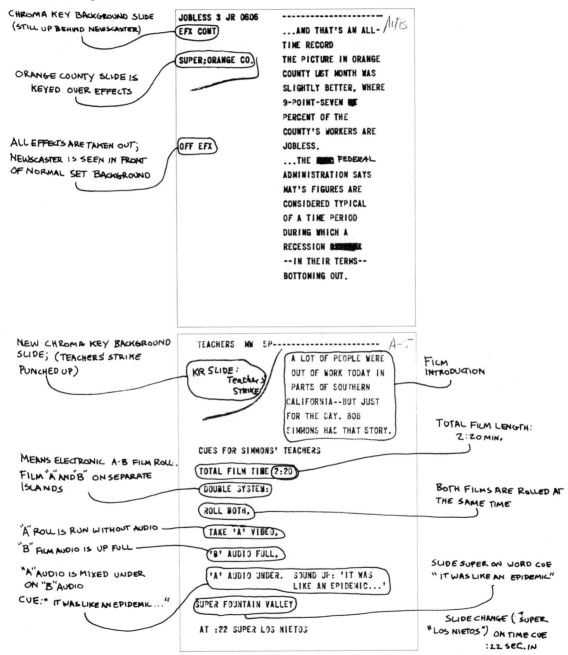

CHROMA KEY BACKGROUND SLIDE
(STILL UP BEHIND NEWSCASTER)

JOBLESS 3 JR 06:06

EFX CONT

SUPER; ORANGE CO.

ORANGE COUNTY SLIDE IS
KEYED OVER EFFECTS

ALL EFFECTS ARE TAKEN OUT;
NEWSCASTER IS SEEN IN FRONT
OF NORMAL SET BACKGROUND

OFF EFX

...AND THAT'S AN ALL-
TIME RECORD
THE PICTURE IN ORANGE
COUNTY LAST MONTH WAS
SLIGHTLY BETTER, WHERE
9-POINT-SEVEN
PERCENT OF THE
COUNTY'S WORKERS ARE
JOBLESS.
...THE FEDERAL
ADMINISTRATION SAYS
MAY'S FIGURES ARE
CONSIDERED TYPICAL
OF A TIME PERIOD
DURING WHICH A
RECESSION
--IN THEIR TERMS--
BOTTOMING OUT.

NEW CHROMA KEY BACKGROUND
SLIDE; (TEACHERS' STRIKE
PUNCHED UP)

TEACHERS MW 5P----------------------- A-5

KR SLIDE:
Teachers'
Strike

A LOT OF PEOPLE WERE
OUT OF WORK TODAY IN
PARTS OF SOUTHERN
CALIFORNIA--BUT JUST
FOR THE DAY. BOB
SIMMONS HAS THAT STORY.

FILM
INTRODUCTION

CUES FOR SIMMONS' TEACHERS

TOTAL FILM LENGTH:
2:20 MIN.

MEANS ELECTRONIC A·B FILM ROLL.
FILM "A" AND "B" ON SEPARATE
ISLANDS

TOTAL FILM TIME (2:20)

DOUBLE SYSTEM:

ROLL BOTH,

BOTH FILMS ARE ROLLED AT
THE SAME TIME

"A" ROLL IS RUN WITHOUT AUDIO

TAKE 'A' VIDEO,

"B" FILM AUDIO IS UP FULL

'B' AUDIO FULL,

"A" AUDIO IS MIXED UNDER
ON "B" AUDIO
CUE: " IT WAS LIKE AN EPIDEMIC..."

'A' AUDIO UNDER. SOUND UP: 'IT WAS
LIKE AN EPIDEMIC...'

SLIDE SUPER ON WORD CUE
"IT WAS LIKE AN EPIDEMIC"

SUPER FOUNTAIN VALLEY

AT :22 SUPER LOS NIETOS

SLIDE CHANGE (SUPER
"LOS NIETOS") ON TIME CUE
:22 SEC. IN

typeface is quite popular—the talent and the director can read the large type more easily than the normal pica typeface.

Some news scripts use white paper for all straight on-camera news copy, and yellow (or any other agreed-upon color) paper for all film and tape insert copy. This way the newscasters and you, the director, will know by the color of the paper whether straight copy or a film or VTR is coming up. This type of color coding is especially helpful when you have to pull some copy in order to keep the show on time.

Documentaries or *documentary-type* shows, too, are frequently fully scripted. The major camera shots and the major actions of the performers are listed in the video column, and every spoken word and sound effect is listed in the audio column. Figure 15.23 shows an example of a fully scripted documentary-type show.

As you can see in this script sample, the video and audio instructions are separated. This script format is widely used for nondramatic shows. The video column is generally on the left side of the page, and the audio column on the right. Note that in the audio column all instructions for audio control are usually written in upper case letters, while the spoken lines are upper and lower case.

Dramatic shows have a script format all their own *(see 15.24)*. The exact camera shots are generally left to the director. But the actor's internal and external actions are generally spelled out, as are the dialogue (upper and lower case) and additional audio material (upper case only).

The Semiscripted Show

A show is semiscripted when the dialogue is indicated but not completely written out. In general, the opening and closing remarks are fully scripted, while the bulk of the dialogue or commentary is only alluded to, such as: DR. HYDE TALKS ABOUT NEW EDUCATIONAL IDEAS; DR. WOLFRAM REPLIES.

This type of script is almost always used for interviews, for programs of an educational nature, for variety programs, and for other types in which a great amount of ad-lib commentary or discussion occurs.

The important part in semiscripting a show is to indicate specific cue lines that tell the director when to roll a film or when to break the cameras to another set area. *(See 15.25.)*

The Show Format

The show format lists only the order of particular show segments, such as "interview from Washington," "commercial No. 1," "book review," and so forth. It also lists the major set areas in which the action takes place, or other points of origination, and major clock and running times for the segments. *(See 15.26a,b.)*

A show format is frequently used in shows that have established performance routines, such as a daily morning show, or a variety show. Most panel discussion shows, or daily interview shows with one established host and several guests, are directed from a show format.

The Fact, or Rundown, Sheet

A fact or rundown sheet lists the items that are to be shown on camera and indicates roughly what should be said. No special video and audio instructions are given. The fact sheet is usually supplied by the advertising agency that likes to have a particular performer ad-lib its commercials *(see 15.27)*.

Generally the director rewrites the fact sheet into a show format so that he and the talent know what they are supposed to do. Directing solely from a fact sheet is not recommended. Ad-libbing by both director and talent rarely works out satisfactorily. Their efforts will necessarily remain uncoordinated.

```
                          (THIRD SEGMENT)

Up on full color slide    IN CUE:  "HIGH BLOOD PRESSURE IS MAINLY A DISEASE
  Wipe to:
FILM                      OF THE CARDIO-VASCULAR SYSTEM OF THE BODY...."
  (showing animated
  cardio-vascular system
  of body)
                          OUT CUE:  "...MILDER ONES ARE HEADACHES,

                          ESPECIALLY AT THE BACK OF THE NECK...

                          DIZZINESS...AND DROWSINESS."

Glenda on Cam                 Of course, having these symptoms doesn't

                          necessarily mean you have high blood pressure.

                          But, if you haven't seen a doctor in a long time,

                          you might check.

                              By the time you get mild symptoms, the disease

                          may be fairly well advanced.

Zoom out and                  And, further down the road there are more
  Super "Strokes...7,000"
                          severe complications, such as stroke, from which
Also super:  "GENERAL
  POPULATION - 1 in 1,000"  over seven-thousand people died in Los Angeles
  "BLACK POPULATION -
  2 TO 3 IN 1,000"        County in 1970.

                              The rate of death for black people from strokes

                          is up to three times as high as that of the general

                          population, which adds another kind of meaning to

                          that old phrase:  "different strokes for different

                          folks."

FILM                      IN CUE:  "OTHER COMPLICATIONS ARE THE INCREASED

                          PROBABILITY OF ATHEROSCLEROSIS..."

                          OUT CUE:  "...THROUGH THE NARROWED BLOOD VESSELS

                          TO THE HEART AND/OR LUNGS."
```

15·23 Documentary. Courtesy KNXT, Los Angeles. (Excerpt from "Hypertension: The Silent Killer.")

15·24   Drama.

MARY-ALICE SHOWS UP, FINALLY. WE SEE HER FROM LYNDA'S PERSPECTIVE
MAKING HER WAY THROUGH THE CROWDED COCKTAIL ROOM OF THE CHARLIE
BROWN BAR. SHE FINALLY REACHES LYNDA'S TABLE AND DROPS INTO THE
EMPTY CHAIR LIKE SOMEONE WHO HAS MANAGED TO GRAB THE ONLY REMAINING
SEAT ON THE SUBWAY DURING RUSH HOUR.

                        MARY-ALICE:
Sorry, I'm late. But I couldn't get off work any sooner.

                          LYNDA:
Work? I thought the teachers' strike is still on. (BREAKS OUT IN
A SHORT LAUGH, FULL-BODIED AND COMING FROM THE BELLY, AS ONE WOULD
EXPECT FROM A PROFESSIONAL SINGER.)
By God, what are you all dressed up for? Sit down, relax.

                        MARY-ALICE:
Yes, it is still on. But I have another--well, how are you?

                          LYNDA:
Another job? What job? What would you like to drink? Still on
daiquiris? (TRIES TO GET THE ATTENTION OF THE COCKTAIL WAITRESS
WHO IS BUSY WITH THE ADJOINING TABLE. BOTH LYNDA AND MARY-ALICE
WATCH THE GIRL IN ANTICIPATION. LYNDA FINALLY SUCCEEDS IN GETTING
THE WAITRESS'S ATTENTION.)

                          LYNDA:
Miss!

                        WAITRESS:
Yes. Can I help you?

MARY-ALICE:

(NOT WAITING FOR LYNDA TO ORDER THE DRINK FOR HER)

Bring me a good daiquiri.

(THE WAITRESS TURNS TO LYNDA.)

LYNDA:

And another Dubonnet on the rocks for me.

(THE WAITRESS LEAVES. LYNDA TURNS TO ALICE.)

Well, now tell me about the new job.

MARY-ALICE:

Well, the teachers' strike is not all that good. We don't get any

money from the union. This is OK for the teachers whose husbands

have good jobs. But for the ones who live alone...

LYNDA:

Isn't Robert helping out?

MARY-ALICE:

Bob? No. On the contrary. He is still expecting gourmet food,

exclusive French wines, you know.

LYNDA:

You call him "Bob" now? He didn't like that.

MARY-ALICE:

I don't know how to tell him that I don't have any money and that

we have to change our life style. At least as long as the strike

is on. Well, a change would be good anyhow. I don't know.

LYNDA:

Do you still love him?

15·25 Semiscripted Show. Courtesy of KNXT, Los Angeles. (Adapted from "It's a Matter of Fat," a KNXT community special.)

<u>VIDEO</u>	<u>AUDIO</u>
	GLENDA:
Two-shot of Glenda and Mario	But more important are the reasons that involve health. Medical science has linked obesity to a number of harmful diseases, including diabetes, strokes, heart attacks, hardening of the arteries, cancer of the uterus, and high blood pressure.
	MARIO:
	Because of this high rate of health hazards the insurance companies put a different kind of pressure on fat people: high insurance rates. Isn't that true, Dr. Ryan?
	DR. RYAN:
Cut to CU of Dr. Ryan	(SAYS THAT THIS IS QUITE TRUE AND THAT INSURANCE COMPANIES DO NOT GENERALLY INSURE MARKEDLY OVERWEIGHT PEOPLE AT NORMAL INSURANCE RATES.)

-2-

MARIO:

Cut to CU   And what about employers? How do they feel
of Mario   about fat people? Here are four people who
              can tell us about their experiences.

LYNN:

Cut to CU   (SAYS THAT SHE FOUND MANY MEDIUM SIZED OR
of Lynn   SMALL COMPANIES HAVE A WEIGHT LIMIT FOR
              EMPLOYEES AND CAN THEREFORE NOT HIRE HER.)

JUDY:

Cut to CU   (AGREES WITH LYNN AND SAYS THAT THERE IS
of Judy   NO QUESTION THAT THERE IS A GREAT AMOUNT
              OF DISCRIMINATION IN JOBS FOR FAT PEOPLE.
              ELABORATES.)

              Etc.

15·26 Show Format.
(a) Courtesy of KTVU,
Oakland–San Francisco.

VIDEO	AUDIO
	Studio - Betty Ann Bruno:
	FOR THE NEXT 2½ HOURS WE WILL EXAMINE COMMUNITY DEVELOPMENT IN OAKLAND. WE HAVE KEY CITY, COUNTY AND FEDERAL OFFICIALS HERE IN OUR STUDIO AS WELL AS MANY LEADERS FROM THE COMMUNITY TO DISCUSS THIS VITAL ISSUE. YOU CAN PARTICIPATE, TOO, ON OUR OPEN TELEPHONE DURING THE BROADCAST.
OPENING FILM :30 SUPER SLIDE: "CDA: WHAT'S IT ALL ABOUT?" DISSOLVE TO FULL SCREEN COLOR SLIDE: "CDA: WHAT'S IT ALL ABOUT" WITH MAP B.G.	SILENT FILM - THEME MUSIC
	STUDIO - LIVE
INTERVIEW #1 - 8:00 AREA #2	INTERVIEW #1 - ZELLICK & PRICE INTRO OF GUEST DISCUSSION

```
              VIDEO                        AUDIO


SUPER SLIDE:
"JIM PRICE"
   HUD

   (PRICE MAY BRING IN
   SOME SLIDES TO BE
   USED IN THIS SECTION)

                                    STUDIO - LIVE

INTERVIEW #2 - 8:00         INTERVIEW #2 - BRUNO & READING
AREA #1
                            INTRO OF GUEST
                            DISCUSSION

SUPER SLIDE:
"JOHN READING"
MAYOR OF OAKLAND


INTERVIEW #3 - 8:00         INTERVIEW #3 - ZELLICK & WILLIAMS
AREA #2
                            INTRO OF GUEST
                            DISCUSSION

SUPER SLIDE:
"JOHN WILLIAMS"


GRAPHICS:  MAP, CHARTS
2 EASELS




BREAK--------------------
1:10
```

15·26 Show Format (cont.) (b) Courtesy of KNXT, Los Angeles.

CLAREMONT COLLOQUIUM: A CONTEMPORARY VIEW

(CLCO-74-   )   SHOW FORMAT

INDIVIDUAL SCRIPT ATTACHED

VTR DATE: FAX:
AIR DATE: VTR:
DIRECTOR: TOTAL TIME: 28:35

O P E N

VIDEO	AUDIO
OPENING TEASER/16mm COLOR	THEME MUSIC UP - S.O.F. - MAG TRACK
TITLE SLIDE	ANNOUNCER: KNXT AND THE CLAREMONT COLLEGES PRESENT CLAREMONT COLLOQUIUM: A CONTEMPORARY VIEW.......A SERIES OF SELECTED TOPICS IN LIBERAL STUDIES.
SUPER FULL SLIDE OF TOPIC TITLE	TODAY'S TOPIC IS:

C L O S E

ADDRESS SLIDE	ANNOUNCER: TO OBTAIN A READING LIST FOR THESE INSTRUCTIONAL PROGRAMS, WRITE TO: CLAREMONT COLLEGES P. O. Box 400 CLAREMONT, CALIFORNIA 91711 PLEASE ENCLOSE A SELF-ADDRESSED ENVELOPE.

CLAREMONT COLLOQUIUM: A CONTEMPORARY VIEW

FILM AND SLIDE RUNDOWN   VTR DATE:_____

FILM	SLIDES
	O P E N (FULL SLIDES)
	1. KNXT AND THE CLAREMONT COLLEGES
	2. CLAREMONT COLLOQUIUM: A CONTEMPORARY VIEW
	3.
	4.
	W I T H I N S H O W (SUPER LOWER THIRDS)
	C L O S E (FULL SUPER SLIDES)
SUPER OVER 16mm FILM	1. KNXT
WITH GATES THEME	2. THE CLAREMONT COLLEGES
	3. PRODUCED BY VICTOR M. WEBB
	4. DIRECTED BY: _____
	5. CREATED BY CENTER FOR CONTINUING EDUCATION & SPECIAL ACADEMIC PROGRAMS, THE CLAREMONT COLLEGES
	6. IN CONJUNCTION WITH THE PUBLIC AFFAIRS OFFICE, CLAREMONT UNIVERSITY CENTER
	7. PRODUCER FOR THE CLAREMONT COLLEGES GANELL S. BAKER
	8. ART DIRECTOR - BOB OLSON GRAPHIC ARTIST - GEORGE GARDNER STUDENT PROD. INTERN - NATALIE HIGGINS
	9. TECHNICAL DIRECTOR:_____ AUDIO MIXER: _____
	10. CLAREMONT COLLOQUIUM (BUG)

15·27   Fact Sheet.

```
JENNER ALBUM COMMERCIAL           DATE:      TIME:

PROPS:  Jenner Album

        Jenner Poster with Band Background

        Jenner Album Display

NOTE:   Play  Cut 1, Side 2, of Jenner Album

        as background during commercial.

1.  New Choban recording of songs by Jenner.

2.  Best yet.  Great variety.

3.  New arrangements.  Excellent band backing her up.

4.  Songs that touch everybody.  Sung with passion.

5.  Excellent recording.  Technically perfect, true

    Choban quality.  Wide frequency range does full

    justice to her voice.  Available in stereo or

    four-channel.

6.  Special introductory offer.  Expires Oct. 20.

    Hurry.  Ask for the new Choban recording of Jenner.

    At Tower Records.
```

Script Preparation

To explain all the intricacies of analyzing and interpreting nondramatic and dramatic scripts would go far beyond the scope of this handbook. We have already pointed out the importance of translating a script into medium requirements, through proper visualization and picturization processes.

Script Analysis

Let us emphasize some of the major points once more: (1) Read the video and audio columns to get an overall idea of what the show is all about and how complex the production will be. (2) Try to "lock in" on a key shot, key action, or some key technical maneuver. For example, you may lock in on the part in a script where lead guitar player has a particularly beautiful solo. How do you see him? How do you want this passage to appear on the screen? Then you can work backward from the selected shot to the actions that precede it and forward to the ones that follow it. In a dramatic script, this locking in may occur at the very opening scene, at the closing scene, or at any particularly striking scene somewhere in the middle. And (3) in the context of the process message objective, translate the script into specific video and audio images, and, of course, the necessary production equipment and procedures.

After analyzing the script, you should mark it accordingly for on-the-air presentation.

Script Marking

Since the many monitors in the control room command your close attention, you should free yourself from the script as much as possible. One way is to mark the major cues on it in your own way. Although there are standard marking sym-

15·28 Analyzing a dramatic script is, of course, quite a bit more complicated than translating the video and audio instructions of a nondramatic script into the director's production requirements. A good dramatic script operates on many conscious and unconscious levels, all of which need to be interpreted and made explicit. Above all, you should be able to define the *theme* of the play (the basic idea; what the story is all about), the *plot* (how the story moves forward and develops), the *characters* (how one person differs from the others), and the *environment* (where the action takes place). In general, television drama emphasizes theme and character rather than plot, inner rather than outer environment.

bols, you will probably develop some special ones that work best for you. Whatever symbols you may use, keep these points in mind: (1) Your marking symbols should be clear and unambiguous. (2) Once you have arrived at a workable system, stick to it. Standardize your symbols as much as possible. (3) Don't overmark your script. Too many confusing symbols are worse than none at all. (4) Place your cue markings before the desired action. And (5) if the shots or camera actions are clearly written in the video column, or the audio cues in the audio column, simply underline or circle the printed information. This will keep the script looking clean. But if the printed instructions are hard to read, don't hesitate to repeat them with your own symbols *(15.31)*.

Before you mark a script, you should have the process message, the key visualization points, and the major picturization processes in your head. In most cases this means that you will need a floor plan prior to your script marking, unless the show occurs in a standard set, such as for the daily newscast. If the show requires rehearsals, do your preliminary script marking *in pencil* so that you will be able to make quick changes without creating a messy or illegible script. Once you are ready for the dress rehearsal, however, you should have marked the script in bold letters so that you can read your markings even in the relatively dim light of the control room. Have the A.D. and the floor manager copy your markings for their own scripts.

Figures 15.29 to 15.32 are examples of marking a variety of script formats.

Rehearsal

Ideally, you should be able to rehearse everything that goes on videotape or on the air. Unfortunately, in practice this is hardly the case. Since the scheduled rehearsal times always seem insuffi-

cient, the prerehearsal preparations, just discussed, become extremely important. To make optimal use of the available time during the scheduled rehearsals, there are several methods that may help: (1) script reading, (2) dry run, or blocking rehearsal, (3) walk-through, (4) camera rehearsal, and (5) walk-through camera rehearsal combination.

Script Reading

Under ideal conditions each major production would begin with a script-reading session. Even for a relatively simple show, you should meet at least once with the talent, the producer, and the key production personnel (associate director, T.D., floor manager) to discuss and read the script. Bring your floor plan along. In this session, which normally doubles as a production meeting, explain these points: (1) process message objective, including the purpose of the show and its intended audience; (2) major actions of the performers, the number and use of special hand props, major crossovers; (3) the performer's relationship to guests. In an interview, for example, clue in the host to the key questions, what you know about the guest, and the general tone expected. Usually such talent preparation is done by the producer. Try to get a rough timing on the show, by clocking the major scenes and show segments as they are read.

Dry Run or Blocking Rehearsal

Dry runs or blocking rehearsals are required only for complex shows, such as dramas or scenes from variety shows. After the script-reading session, you will call for the *dry run,* during which the basic actions of the talent are worked out. By that time, you must have a very good idea of where the cameras should be in relation to the set, and the actors in relation to the cameras. The dry run

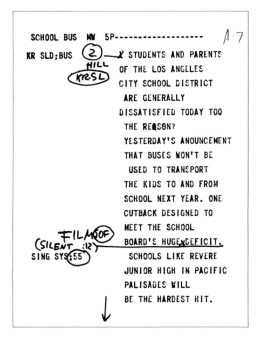

15·29 Marking Fully
Scripted Newscast.
Courtesy of KNXT, Los
Angeles.

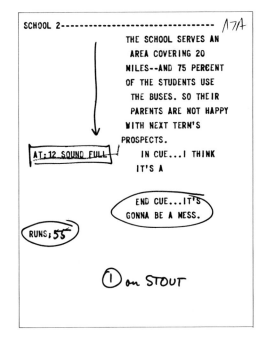

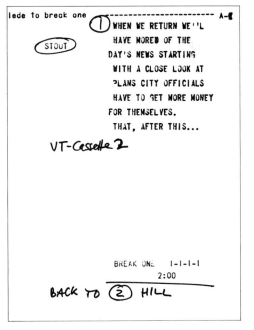

15·30 Marking Semi-scripted Show. Courtesy of KNXT, Los Angeles.

PRODUCER: VICTOR M. WEBB

LEARNING CAN BE FUN/QUIEN
LF-73-3
VTR: 2/25/
AIR: TBA

LEARNING CAN BE FUN: "QUIEN SOY YO?"

VIDEO	Roll Film AUDIO
(:00) STANDARD FILM OPENING (SPANISH VERSION)	SOF (:35)
(:35) DISSOLVE TO SET ACTIVITY W/ TITLE SLIDES ② SS-1 SS-2	(Theme under booth announcer) ANNCR: "LEARNING CAN BE FUN" -- A PROGRAM OF BILINGUAL-BICULTURAL EDUCATION. PRESENTED IN COOPERA- TION WITH THE LOS ANGELES CITY SCHOOLS. YOUR TELEVISION TEACHER: CARMEN SALAZAR. (:12)
① LS (:47) CARMEN W/ GROUP ZOOM IN CARMEN	CARMEN PREPARES GROUP FOR FILM (a) INTRODUCTION TO THE TOPIC (b) BRIEF DISCUSSION (c) INTRODUCTION TO FIRST FILM SHOWING (1:00)
ROLL Film (1:47) FILM: "QUIEN SOY YO?"	SOF (5:39)
CARMEN W/ group ① LS	POST-FILM ACTIVITIES
(6:56)	(a) BRIEF DISCUSSION OF FILM (3:00)
(9:56) .... ② CU'S	(b) COMPARISON CHART (IN SPANISH) CHILDREN TELL WHO ARE THE MEMBERS OF THEIR OWN FAMILIES; CARMEN MARKS ON CHART (2:30)

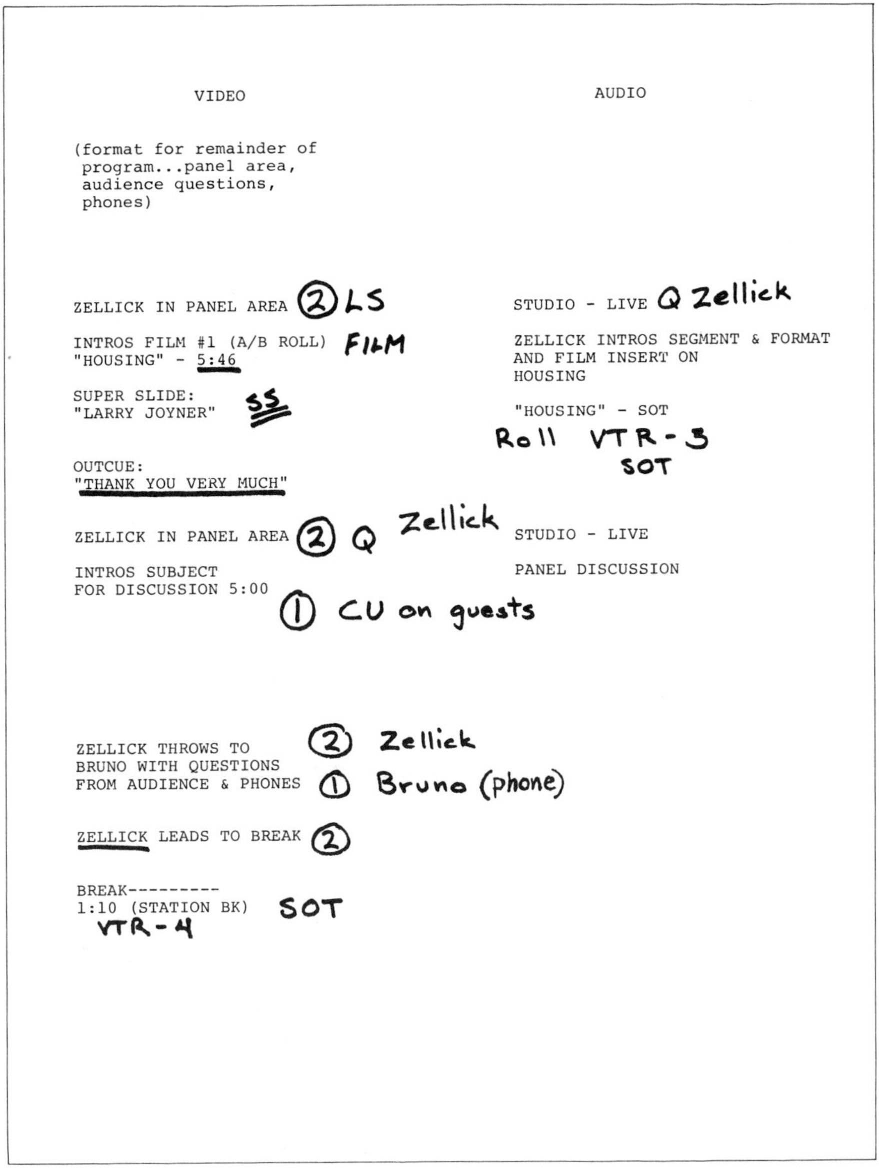

VIDEO

AUDIO

(format for remainder of
program...panel area,
audience questions,
phones)

ZELLICK IN PANEL AREA   ② LS

INTROS FILM #1 (A/B ROLL)   F ILM
"HOUSING" - <u>5:46</u>

SUPER SLIDE:
"LARRY JOYNER"   <u>SS</u>

OUTCUE:
"<u>THANK YOU VERY MUCH</u>"

ZELLICK IN PANEL AREA   ② Q   Zellick

INTROS SUBJECT
FOR DISCUSSION 5:00
                    ① CU on guests

ZELLICK THROWS TO   ② Zellick
BRUNO WITH QUESTIONS
FROM AUDIENCE & PHONES   ① Bruno (phone)

<u>ZELLICK</u> LEADS TO BREAK   ②

BREAK---------
1:10 (STATION BK)   SOT
     VTR - 4

STUDIO - LIVE   Q Zellick

ZELLICK INTROS SEGMENT & FORMAT
AND FILM INSERT ON
HOUSING

"HOUSING" - SOT

Roll VTR - 3
        SOT

STUDIO - LIVE

PANEL DISCUSSION

15·31 Marking Semi-scripted Show: Sometimes, when no specific video and audio instructions are given, you must write them in. Courtesy KTVU, Oakland–San Francisco.

15·32 Marking Dramatic Scripts: Dramatic scripts generally have no audio or video instructions written in. This way the writer does not dictate the director's specific visualization and picturization processes. You should, therefore, write the key video instructions into the script yourself. Sometimes it is quite helpful to use small thumbnail sketches to indicate key visualization or blocking maneuvers.

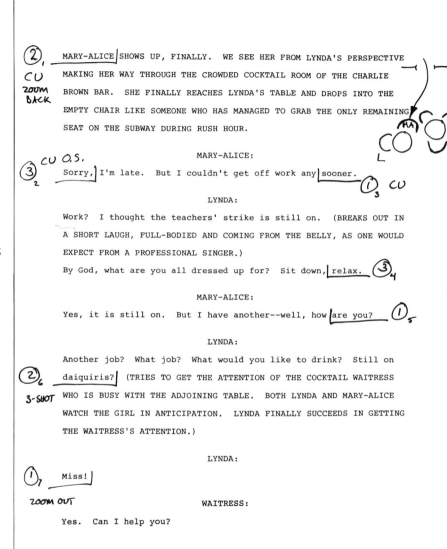

②₁ CU ZOOM BACK   MARY-ALICE| SHOWS UP, FINALLY. WE SEE HER FROM LYNDA'S PERSPECTIVE MAKING HER WAY THROUGH THE CROWDED COCKTAIL ROOM OF THE CHARLIE BROWN BAR. SHE FINALLY REACHES LYNDA'S TABLE AND DROPS INTO THE EMPTY CHAIR LIKE SOMEONE WHO HAS MANAGED TO GRAB THE ONLY REMAINING SEAT ON THE SUBWAY DURING RUSH HOUR.

                    MARY-ALICE:

③₂ CU O.S.   Sorry,| I'm late. But I couldn't get off work any| sooner. ①₃ CU

                    LYNDA:

Work? I thought the teachers' strike is still on. (BREAKS OUT IN A SHORT LAUGH, FULL-BODIED AND COMING FROM THE BELLY, AS ONE WOULD EXPECT FROM A PROFESSIONAL SINGER.)
By God, what are you all dressed up for? Sit down,| relax. ③₄

                    MARY-ALICE:

Yes, it is still on. But I have another--well, how |are you? ①₅

                    LYNDA:

Another job? What job? What would you like to drink? Still on
②₆ 3-SHOT   daiquiris?| (TRIES TO GET THE ATTENTION OF THE COCKTAIL WAITRESS WHO IS BUSY WITH THE ADJOINING TABLE. BOTH LYNDA AND MARY-ALICE WATCH THE GIRL IN ANTICIPATION. LYNDA FINALLY SUCCEEDS IN GETTING THE WAITRESS'S ATTENTION.)

                    LYNDA:

①₇ Miss!|

ZOOM OUT   WAITRESS:

Yes. Can I help you?

MARY-ALICE:

(NOT WAITING FOR LYNDA TO ORDER THE DRINK FOR HER)

③₈ Bring me a good daiquiri.

MS   (THE WAITRESS TURNS TO LYNDA.)

LYNDA:

②₉ And another Dubonnet on the rocks for me.

2-SHOT (THE WAITRESS LEAVES. LYNDA TURNS TO ALICE.)

Well, now tell me about the new job. ③₁₀

CU M.A.

MARY-ALICE:

Well, the teachers' strike is not all that good. We don't get any

money from the union. This is OK for the teachers whose husbands

have good jobs. But for the ones who live alone...

LYNDA:

Isn't Robert helping out?

MARY-ALICE:

Bob? No. On the contrary. He is still expecting gourmet food,

exclusive French wines, you know. ①₁₁ CU LYNDA

LYNDA:

You call him "Bob" now? He didn't like that. ③₁₂

MARY-ALICE:

I don't know how to tell him that I don't have any money and that

we have to change our life style. At least as long as the strike

is on. Well, a change would be good anyhow. I don't know. ①₁₃ XCU

LYNDA:

Do you still love him? ③₁₄ MCU

ZOOM IN M.A.

15·33 The script-reading sessions are, of course, particularly important if you are rehearsing a television drama. Indeed, the more thorough the script reading is, the easier the subsequent rehearsals will be. In such sessions, you should discuss at length, besides the obvious process message objective, the structure of the play (theme, plot, environment) and the substance of each character. An extremely detailed analysis of the characters is probably the most important aspect of the dramatic script reading session. The actor or actress who really understands his or her character, role, and relation to the whole event will have mastered the major part of his or her screen performance. More than any other, the television actor or actress must understand a character so well that he or she is no longer "acting out" the role but living it. Such internalization can be facilitated through extensive script reading sessions.

You will find that after this kind of session, the actors will tend to block themselves (under the director's careful guidance, of course) and to move and "act" naturally. There is no need for you to explain each move. Once the actors understand their roles with head and heart, their actions will be motivated most of the time.

presupposes a detailed floor plan and a thorough preparation by the director. It also presupposes that the actors have internalized (understood with head and heart) their characters and roles. Tell them approximately where the action is supposed to take place (the approximate location in the imagined set area; the actual set is rarely available at this point), and let them block themselves. Follow their actions with the director's viewfinder. Watch their actions as *screen images,* not from the point of view of a live audience. Adjust their blocking and your imagined camera positions so that you have a reasonable assurance that you will achieve the visualized screen image in the actual camera rehearsal. Be ready to give *precise directions* to the actor who is asking what to do next. A good actor, rather than always knowing what to do without the director's help, asks what he or she should do, and then does it with precision and conviction.

Generally, try to observe these points in your dry run: (1) Hold the dry run in the studio or a rehearsal hall. In an emergency, any room will do. Use tables, chairs, chalk marks on the floor for sets and furniture. (2) Work on the blocking problems. Use your viewfinder. Have your assistant make notes of the major blocking maneuvers. (3) Keep the camera and microphone movements in mind when blocking the actors. Some directors walk right into the spot where the active camera will be and watch the proceedings from the camera's point of view. (4) Call out all major cues, if it will help. (5) Go through the scenes in the order in which they are to be taped. If you do your show live, or videotape it in one uninterrupted session (sometimes called "live-tape"), try to go through the whole script at least once. (6) Time each segment and the overall show. Allow time for long camera movements, music bridges, announcer's intro and close, the closing credits, and so forth. And (7) reconfirm the dates for the upcoming rehearsals.

Walk-Through

The walk-through is an orientation session that will help the production crew and performers understand the necessary medium and performance requirements quickly and easily. You can have both a *technical* and a *talent walk-through* or, if you are pressed for time, a combination of the two. The walk-throughs as well as camera rehearsals occur shortly before the actual on-the-air performance or taping session.

Technical Walk-Through   Once the set is in place, gather the production crew (A.D., floor manager, floor personnel, T.D., lighting director, camera operators, audio engineer, boom operator), explain to them the process message objective and your basic concept of the show. Then walk with them through the set and explain these key factors: (1) basic blocking and actions of talent, (2) camera locations and traffic, (3) special shots and framings, (4) mike placements and boom location, (5) basic cuing, (6) scene changes and prop changes, if any, (7) major lighting effects, and (8) easel positions.

The technical walk-through is especially important on *remote telecasts* where the crew must often work during the setup under the guidance of the floor manager rather than the director, who is isolated in the remote truck.

Talent Walk-Through   While the production people go about their tasks, take the performers or actors on a short excursion through the set and explain once again their major actions, positions, and crossings. Always try to block talent in such a way that the talent rather than your cameras will do most of the moving. Tell them where the cameras will be in relation to their actions. Here are some of the more important aspects of the talent walk-through: (1) Point out to each performer or actor his or her major positions and walks. (2) Explain briefly where and how they should work with specific props. For example, tell the actress that the coffee urn will be here, and how she should walk with the coffee cup to the couch: in front of the table, not behind it. Explain your blocking to the talent from a camera point of view. (3) Once again explain the major visualization and picturization aspects. (4) Have each performer or actor go through his opening lines and then have him skip to the individual cue lines. And (5) give everyone enough time for makeup and dressing before the camera rehearsal.

During this talent walk-through, try to stay out of the production people's way as much as possible. Finish your walk-through rehearsal early enough so that everybody can take a break before camera rehearsal.

Camera Rehearsal

In small station operation, camera rehearsal and final dress rehearsal are almost always the same. Frequently, your camera rehearsal time is cut short by technical problems, such as minor or major lighting adjustments and camera adjustments. One attribute you must have as a television director is patience. You may get nervous when you see most of the technical crew working frantically on your key camera five minutes before air time. There is nothing you can do, however, except realize that you are working with (1) a highly skilled group of technicians who know just as well as you do how much depends on a successful performance, and (2) a highly complicated machine which, like all other machines, sometimes works and sometimes doesn't.

There are three basic methods of conducting a camera rehearsal: (1) the stop-start method, (2) the uninterrupted run-through, and (3) the film-style rehearsal. The first two are usually conducted from the control room, the film-style rehearsal from the floor.

15·34 In complicated, fully scripted shows, your task as a director will be considerably aided if you supply the camera operator with a *shot sheet*. This lists every shot a particular camera has to get *(see a)*. As soon as her camera is free (momentarily off the air), the camera operator, seeing that the tally light is off, can look at the shot sheet and frame up the next shot without specific instructions from the director or the associate director. Some cameras come equipped with a shot-sheet holder directly below the viewfinder. Such sheets may be quite detailed,

telling the camera what to get, how to frame it, and what position the zoom lens should be in; others simply indicate the basic framing, in the hope that the camera operator remembers the rehearsed shot. Since the director labels all his shots in consecutive order, regardless of the camera used, the numbers of the shots for an individual camera are not in consecutive order. Figure b shows an example of a portion of the director's script with the shots numbered in consecutive order.

```
SHOT SHEET        CAMERA 2

SHOT              VISUALIZATION
NUMBER

  1               MS of Mary-Alice entering bar.  Follow her through crowded
                  tables.

  6               3-shot of Mary-Alice, Lynda, and waitress.  Favor waitress
                  serving at other table.

  9               2-shot.  Lynda and waitress.
```

a

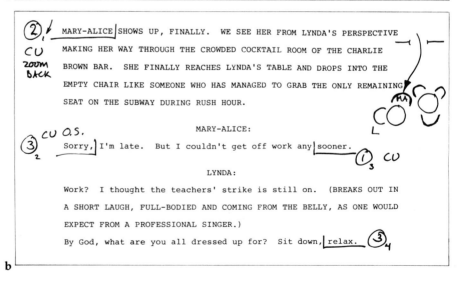

b

MARY-ALICE:

Yes, it is still on. But I have another--well, how are you? ①₅

LYNDA:

Another job? What job? What would you like to drink? Still on

②₆ daiquiris? (TRIES TO GET THE ATTENTION OF THE COCKTAIL WAITRESS

3-SHOT WHO IS BUSY WITH THE ADJOINING TABLE. BOTH LYNDA AND MARY-ALICE

WATCH THE GIRL IN ANTICIPATION. LYNDA FINALLY SUCCEEDS IN GETTING

THE WAITRESS'S ATTENTION.)

LYNDA:

①₇ Miss!

ZOOM OUT   WAITRESS:

Yes. Can I help you?

MARY-ALICE:

(NOT WAITING FOR LYNDA TO ORDER THE DRINK FOR HER)

③₈ Bring me a good daiquiri.

MS (THE WAITRESS TURNS TO LYNDA.)

LYNDA:

②₉ And another Dubonnet on the rocks for me.

2-SHOT (THE WAITRESS LEAVES. LYNDA TURNS TO ALICE.)

Well, now tell me about the new job. ③₁₀

CU M.A.

MARY-ALICE:

Well, the teachers' strike is not all that good. We don't get any

money from the union. This is OK for the teachers whose husbands

have good jobs. But for the ones who live alone...

LYNDA:

Isn't Robert helping out?

MARY-ALICE:

Bob? No. On the contrary. He is still expecting gourmet food,

exclusive French wines, you know. ①₁₁ CU LYNDA

LYNDA:

You call him "Bob" now? He didn't like that. ③₁₂

The Stop-Start Method   With the stop-start method you interrupt the camera rehearsal whenever you find something wrong; then you go back to a logical spot in the script and start again, hoping that the mistake is not repeated. This is a thorough, but time-consuming, method.

The Uninterrupted Run-Through   The uninterrupted run-through rarely remains uninterrupted. However, you should call for a "cut" (stop all action) only when a grave mistake has been made, one that cannot be corrected at a later time. All minor mistakes and fumbles are corrected *after* the run-through. Since most plays are videotaped, your uninterrupted run-through will be interrupted at each scene or segment as marked in the script. Since camera rehearsals are generally videotaped for protection and for additional material in the postproduction editing process, you will need the scene breaks to stop and start the videotape and to slate each scene. If you plan to do the entire show live, or videotape the show in one uninterrupted take, you should go through as long a segment as possible in the uninterrupted run-through. A long stretch without any interruptions will not only give you an overview of the general development and build of the play, but will also help the performers or actors enormously in their pacing. The uninterrupted run-through is one of the few opportunities for you to get a feeling of the overall rhythm of the show.

The Film-Style Rehearsal   Closely related to the stop-start method is the film-style rehearsal. You rehearse each take (shot) immediately prior to videotaping it. Then you stop, reset the technical facilities—such as lighting, changing of set and properties—rehearse the next shot, and videotape it immediately thereafter. Thus, you end up with a great number of bits and pieces of videotape that will be put together into a (hopefully) coherent story in the postproduction proc-

ess. Since the film-style rehearsal is used only when you videotape with a single camera in film style, you conduct the rehearsal and the actual videotaping from the studio floor. All you need is a monitor so that you can see what the camera operator sees in the viewfinder.

You will find that even after the most careful script preparation you will be forced to change certain camera shots and blocking procedures. Try to be as quick and firm in your decisions as possible. Be open-minded to suggestions from the production and engineering crews, as well as talent, but don't be indecisive. Once you have made a change, and it seems to work, stick to it. If some blocking or camera movement gives you special problems, solve them right then and there. Don't think that you "can take care of it" in the postproduction activities. Even the most skillful editor can't perform miracles. The better the raw material the editor gets, the easier it will be for him to shape it into a good show.

In the final camera rehearsal (if you have the luxury of going through the show more than once), you should rehearse the complete show, including all video and audio elements—film, tape, sound effects, slides, studio cards, lighting changes. Be sure to finish the rehearsal early enough to allow time to reset the rehearsed production elements and *to give crew and talent a short rest* before the actual on-the-air performance or taping session. Don't rehearse right up to air time.

Walk-Through Camera Rehearsal Combination

Necessary as the above-mentioned rehearsal procedures seem, they are rarely possible in small station operations. First of all, most of your directing chores in a small station will be of a nondramatic nature, demanding less rehearsal effort than for dramatic shows. Second, because of time and space limitations, you are lucky to get rehearsal time equal to or slightly more than the running time of the entire show. Forty minutes rehearsal time for a half-hour show is not uncommon. Most often, you will have to jump from a cursory script reading to a camera rehearsal immediately preceding the on-the-air performance or taping session.

In these situations, you will have to resort to a walk-through camera rehearsal combination. Since you can't rehearse the entire show, you simply pick the most important parts and rehearse them as well as possible. Usually these are the *transitions* rather than the parts between the transitions.

Here are some of the major points for conducting a walk-through camera rehearsal: (1) Do this type of rehearsal from the *studio floor*. If you try to conduct it from the control room, you will waste valuable time in explaining your shots and blocking through the intercommunication system, even if you happen to have a first-rate floor manager. (2) Get all production people into their respective positions—all camera operators at their cameras (with the cameras uncapped and ready to go), the microphone boom ready to follow the sound source, the floor manager ready for cuing, the T.D. and audio engineer ready for action in the control room. (3) Walk the talent through all the major parts of the show. Rehearse only the critical transitions and shots. For example, if the performer has to demonstrate a small object, show her how to hold the object and the camera operator how to frame it. (4) Call your shots over the "hot" boom (or any other) microphone into the control room and have the T.D. switch the particular camera on line, so that everybody can see the image on the line monitor from the studio floor. (5) As soon as the talent knows how to go on from there, skip to the end of his segment and have her introduce the following segment. (6) Rehearse all major walks and crossovers on camera. Look through the camera's viewfinder to check the framing (especially of the camera that is getting ready for the next shot; the on-the-air camera is punched up already on the studio monitor). (7) Give all cues for music, sound effects, lighting, film clips, tape inserts, videotape rolls, slating procedures, and so forth to the T.D. via the open studio mike, but don't have them executed (except for the music, which can be reset rather easily). (8) Have the floor manager cue the talent and mark the crucial spots with chalk or masking tape on the studio floor.

If everything goes fairly well, you are ready to go to the control room. Don't get hung up on some minor detail while on the floor. Always view the problems in the context of the overall show. For example, don't fret over a picture that seems to hang slightly high while neglecting to rehearse the most important crossovers with the talent. In the control room, contact each camera by number and find out whether he can communicate with you. Then from the control room rehearse once more the most important parts of the show—the opening, the closing, major talent actions, and camera movements. *(See 15.35.)*

It is always a good idea for the director to have rehearsed the opening and closing of a show from the script for himself, prior to camera rehearsal. Simply take the script, sit in a quiet corner, take your stopwatch (for practice) and start calling out the opening shots: *Ready to roll VTR two, roll it,* and so on, or *Fade in two, ready to key F-one,* and so on. By the time you enter the control room, you will practically have memorized the opening and closing of the show and will be able, therefore, to pay full attention to the monitors and audio.

As much as you may be pressed for time, try to remain cool and courteous to everybody. Also, this is not the time to make drastic changes. Yes, there are probably some other ways in which the show might be directed, and even improved, but the camera rehearsal is not the time to try them out. Give crew and talent enough time before the

15·35 Once you are in the control room, the only way you can see the action on the floor is through the camera preview monitors. Most control-room windows are either blocked with monitors or scenery or, as in most modern control rooms, nonexist-

ent. You should, therefore, develop the ability to determine camera positions and zoom lens positions from how the pictures appear on the monitors. Figures a and b show two obvious examples.

a

Since the normal camera setup is from left to right —with camera 1 on the farthest left side of the action and the highest-number camera on the farthest right side—camera 1 should give you a view from

slightly left, and camera 3 from slightly right. In this illustration, the cameras are obviously crossed. It will simplify your directing chores if you keep them in the basic left-to-right position.

b

The relative size of objects can sometimes give you a clue as to the focal length of the zoom lens setting. Camera 1 is zoomed in quite tightly while camera 2

is on a wide-angle zoom position. Camera 2 can, therefore, be moved while on the air; camera 1 cannot.

actual taping or on-the-air performance to take care of last-minute details.

Some disadvantages of the walk-through camera rehearsal combination make this method less than perfect: (1) No one, including you as the director, ever has a chance to go through the whole show continuously. (2) You don't have the opportunity to see and call all the shots from the control room and to see complete studio traffic develop. And (3), you cannot time the whole show.

On-the-Air Performance

Directing the on-the-air performance, or the final taping session, is, of course, the most important part of your job as a director, as important as all the preparations put together. After all, the viewer does not sit in on your script conferences or your rehearsals; all he sees and hears is what you finally put on the air. From now on, we will call this phase the on-the-air directing, since, even if you are videotaping the show, you should always act as though it were going on the air at the same time. If you relax too much during videotaping (since "you can always redo a scene if it goes wrong"), you will find that your whole crew and the talent too will assume a dangerous "I-don't-really-care" attitude.

Stand-by Procedures

Here are some of the most important stand-by procedures immediately preceding the on-the-air telecast: (1) Call on the intercom every member of the production team that needs to react to your cues—camera operators, boom operator, floor manager and other floor personnel, videotape operator, lightboard operator, audio engineer. (2) Check with the floor manager and make sure that everyone is in the studio and ready for action. (3) Announce the time remaining until the on-the-air telecast (or taping) and ask whether the floor

manager is ready with the slate (for videotape identification). Much precious time has been lost in television studios simply because the slate wasn't ready or properly labeled. Indicate which camera will take the slate, choosing one that is not involved in the opening shot. (4) Alert everyone to the first cues. (5) Tell the floor manager who gets the first cue. (6) Check with the videotape engineer as to whether he is ready to roll the tape, and with the camera operators and audio engineer about their opening actions. (7) Line up the slate on one camera and the opening shot on the other. (8) Check on the opening slide, film, VTR insert, or character generator display.

The Show

Assuming that you videotape your show, you must first go through the videotape rolling procedures *(see 15.5)*. Once your videotape is rolling and properly slated, you can begin with the actual recording. You are now *on the air*. Let's repeat the fading in of the opening shot on camera 1:

Up on (or *fade in*) *one. Music. Fade music, cue announcer. Ready to key F-two over one* (slide over opening shot). *Key F-two. Change slide. Change slide. Change slide. Key out* (or *F-two out*, or *lose key*). *Music out. Slowly. Ready two on Lynn* (the performer). *Ready to cue Lynn. Cue Lynn, take two. One, get a closeup of the book* (Lynn is holding). *Ready one, take one. Two, stay on Lynn. Ready two on Lynn. One on the easel. Zoom out a little. Good. Ready one, take one. Two on the easel. Good. Ready two for a dissolve. Dissolve to two. Ready to roll SOF on F-one. Roll film. Four—three—two—one, take F-one. SOF* (assuming that you still use a 4-second film start; otherwise you simply call for *Ready F-one, Roll F-one;* or simply, *Take F-one).*

By now you are well into the show. Don't forget to watch the time carefully. After the 5-minute cue (if any), you must prepare for the closing. Are the closing slides or the closing crawl ready? Again, watch the time.

Thirty seconds. Wind her up. Wind her up. Fifteen (seconds). *One on the crawl. Two zoom out. Ready music. Cut her. Music. Good. Music under, cue announcer. Two, keep zooming. Ready to roll crawl. Roll it. Ready to key one over two. Key. Speed up the crawl. Key out. Fade to black. Music out. Hold. Stop VTR. OK, all clear.*

Good job, everyone.

Unfortunately, not every show goes as smoothly as that. You can contribute to a smooth performance, however, by paying attention to these important on-the-air directing procedures:

1.   Give all your signals clearly and precisely. Appear relaxed but alert.

2.   Cue your talent before you come up on him with the camera. By the time he starts to speak, you will have faded in the picture.

3.   Indicate talent by name. Don't tell the floor manager to cue just "him" or "her," especially when there are several anticipating "hims" or "hers" in the studio.

4.   Don't give a ready cue too far in advance, or the person may have forgotten it by the time your take cue finally arrives.

5.   Don't pause between the "take" and the number of the camera. do not say: *Take*——(pause)——*two.* Some T.D.'s will punch up the camera before you say the number.

6.   Keep in mind the number of the camera already on the air, and don't call for a take or dissolve to that camera.

7.   Don't ready one camera and then call for a take of another. In other words, don't say: *Ready one, take two.* If you change your mind, nullify the ready cue and then give another.

8.   Talk to the cameras by number and not by the name of the camera operator. What would you do if both your camera operators were named Mary?

9.   Call the camera first before you give instructions. For example: *Camera 2, give me a closeup of the display. Camera 3, cover shot. Camera 1, dolly in.*

10.   After you have put one camera on the air, *immediately* tell the other camera what to do next. Don't wait till the last second; for example, say *Take two. One, stay on this medium shot. Three, on the easel.* If you reposition a camera, give the operator time to reset his zoom lens; otherwise the camera will not stay in focus during subsequent zooming.

11.   If you make a mistake, correct it as well as you can and go on with the show. Don't meditate on how you could have avoided it while you are neglecting the rest of the show. Pay full attention to what is going on. If videotaping, stop the tape only when absolutely necessary. Too many false starts can take the energy out of even the most seasoned performer and production crew.

12.   Spot check the videotape after each take to make sure that the take is technically acceptable. Then go on to the next one. It is always easier to repeat a take, one right after the other, than to go back at the end of a strenuous taping session.

13.   If you use the stop-start method or, especially, the film-style approach to videotaping, you may want to play back each take before going on to the next one. If you don't like the take, you can always do another one immediately.

14.   If there is a technical problem that you have to solve from the control room, tell the floor manager about it on the intercom, or use the S.A. system to inform the whole floor about the slight delay. This way the talent will know that there is a technical delay and, what's more, that the delay wasn't caused by them.

15.   If you rely heavily on postproduction editing, get some cutaways.

16.   During the show, speak only when necessary. If you talk too much, people will stop listening and may miss important instructions.

Postshow Duties

After the show, give thanks to crew and talent. If something went wrong, don't storm into the studio blaming everyone but yourself. Wait until you can think objectively about the situation. Then don't just criticize but, instead, make suggestions on how to avoid similar mistakes in the future.

Don't forget the necessary production reports, music lists, and union contracts (if you act as producer-director). File your marked script for future reference.

Postproduction Activities

If a show is assembled in the postproduction editing process, the director is generally still in charge of the editing decisions. In practice, however, relatively simple editing tasks are generally handled by the videotape editor, with a minimum of supervision (or, as editors like to call it, "interference") by the director. Nevertheless, it is a good idea for you as a director to work with the editor until the completion of the postproduction. Actually, there is little difference from a directing point of view whether you tell the T.D. to take 2, or tell the editor to splice this shot to that. In any case, try to work *with* him, and not against him. If he is experienced, he can help you greatly in the picturization process. But don't be afraid to assert yourself, especially if you feel strong about a certain editing decision, especially if you are the *producer*-director.

Off-line editing systems have made the postproduction editing process extremely simple. Assuming that you are lucky enough to have such a system available to you, you can sit in front of the editing console (see pages 289–290) and make all the editing decisions yourself before giving the small-format copy or the punched paper tape to the on-line editor for the 2-inch master copy. While editing, try to apply the major principles of continuity and complexity editing (see pages 269–276), unless you intend to produce special effects in the picturization.

When finished, check the entire tape for serious technical and aesthetic discrepancies. If every-

thing looks all right, time the entire videotape recording and have a protection copy made immediately.

General Comments

As a television director, you have to bear responsibility toward your *audience,* the great many individuals whose lives you will inevitably touch, however temporarily; to your *station,* whose members have put their trust in you to use their efforts for a successful communication of their ideas and messages; toward your *production team,* whose performance is directly dependent upon your skill; and finally toward *yourself.* Like any other artist, you must always try to do your best possible job, no matter how trivial it may seem at the time. After all, the mark of the professional is *consistency,* to come up consistently with a quality product, regardless of the scope of the task.

Directing, finally, means to guide with sureness, understanding, and compassion; to guide and coordinate a great number of people and events into a coherent whole, into video and audio images that ultimately affect the percipient in a positive way.

Summary

Television directing, which calls for coordinating a great number of production elements and people within a rigid time limit, requires understanding and mastery of (1) terminology, (2) timing, (3) visualization and picturization, (4) script formats, (5) script preparation, (6) rehearsal technique, (7) on-the-air performance, and (8) postproduction activities.

Terminology is the language the director uses in order to achieve optimally efficient communication with all persons involved in the production.

A large part of this terminology consists of cues to engineering and production personnel, and to talent.

Timing relates to the control of physical, or objective, time, and psychological, or subjective, time. The *control of objective time* includes (1) differentiating between clock time, or schedule time, and running time, or length, (2) back-timing, and (3) front-timing. The *control of subjective time* has to do with the balance of pace and rhythm.

Visualization means seeing single visual images of an object or event. *Picturization* means controlling and structuring these images into a shot sequence. Both processes are essential to television directing. Good television scripts usually indicate the major visualization and picturization factors.

There are four basic types of *script formats:* (1) the fully scripted show, (2) the semiscripted show, (3)

the show format, and (4) the fact, or rundown, sheet.

The two major points of *script preparation* are (1) script analysis and (2) script marking.

The major *rehearsal* methods consist of (1) script reading, (2) dry run, or blocking rehearsal, (3) walk-through, (4) camera rehearsal, and (5) walk-through camera rehearsal combination.

On-the-air performance by the director includes specific, standardized stand-by procedures, specific cues during the show, and certain customary postshow duties.

The *postproduction activities* may involve the director in the editing process, whereby he or she, in conjunction with the film or videotape editor, makes the final picturization decisions. Usually, the director and editor work together on the final editing.

16 *Remote Operations*

Remote operations cover television production activities that take place away from the studio. We will discuss them in the context of preproduction, production, and postproduction activities.

The preproduction activities include the production and engineering remote surveys and the preplanning by the director as to camera locations, microphone setup, and other production requirements.

In the production section, we will consider the function of the remote truck, instant replay, and major production procedures from the point of view of the director, the floor manager, and the talent.

Camera setups for the remote pickup of some major sports are briefly mentioned.

When a television show is done outside the studio, we speak of it as a *remote telecast* or, simply, a remote. During a remote, the program material can be either telecast live or videotaped for broadcasting at a later time. A remote involves the use of electronic cameras. Filming outside the studio is not considered a remote.

A remote is usually done to "pick up" a special event that has not been staged specifically for television. The event—most often a sports or news happening—is merely reported by the cameras, not created for them.

Large, single events, such as football games, are normally covered with a multiple camera set up and coordinated from a mobile control center, the remote truck. Some unforeseen news incidents, or events that are staged outdoors for postproduction editing, are often covered with a single camera (called mini-camera) and sent through microwave relays to the station or transmitter for immediate (live) broadcast or recorded on a portable videotape recorder.

As a director of remote telecasts, you have a rather difficult assignment: you should show the event as realistically as possible, and yet, since you can't show everything at once, you nevertheless must pick out sections that are characteristic of the whole. At the same time, you have to clarify and intensify the occasion while it is unfolding. Even though you have never seen the event before (and, therefore, could not really rehearse the telecast), you should try to report it as faithfully as possible. For example, if the happening is dull, don't try to energize it through fancy closeups and fast cutting. A director who constantly cuts to cute shots of spectators during lull periods of a baseball game does not understand that the viewer at home is not really interested in what the spectators look like; what he wants to do is experience the game with its fast *and* slow

---

Isolated Camera   A camera used for instant-replay action only. It is not used for the general pickup of the event.

Microwave Relay   A transmission method involving the use of several microwave units from the remote location to the transmitter.

Multiplexing   A method of transmitting the video and audio signals on the same carrier wave. Also, the transmitting of separate color signals on the same channel without mixing.

Remote   A television production done outside the studio.

Remote Survey   An inspection of the remote location by key production and engineering persons so that they can plan for the setup and use of production equipment.

Remote Truck   The vehicle that carries the program control equipment, such as CCU's, switcher, monitors, audio control console, and intercom systems. The director and the T.D. work out of the remote truck.

Spotter   A person who helps the director or the announcer to identify significant parts of an event, such as prominent players in a football game, or the nature of a play formation.

Video Disc Recorder   A recording device whereby the video signals are recorded on and played back from a disc, which looks like a phonograph record.

periods. On the other hand, if the event bursts with high-energy action, try to reflect this energy. Don't have your cameras just sit there and look at it coolly from a distance. Get closeups. Let the percipient see a high-energy football game, for example, and *feel* it too.

Since the telecast happens away from the studio, some of the *medium requirements* and therefore *production procedures* are different from the usual studio productions. We will, therefore, discuss these production aspects: (1) preproduction: remote survey, (2) production: equipment setup and operation, (3) postproduction: some editing considerations and postshow duties.

Preproduction

If you have to cover a scheduled event, such as a parade, a political gathering, or a sports event, thorough preparation is essential to the success of the remote. The major part of this preparation involves the *remote survey.*

Remote Survey

As the name implies, this is an investigation of the premises and the circumstances carried out in advance of the telecast. It should provide you with answers to some key questions as to the *nature of the event* and the *technical facilities* necessary to televise it. Your first concern is, therefore, to talk to somebody who knows about the event. This person, called the *contact person,* or simply *contact,* may be the public relations officer of an institution, or some other person in a supervisory capacity. On the phone, find out how much the contact person knows about the event to be covered, and whether or not he or she can refer you to other people who might answer some of your questions. In any case, get the full name, position, address, business phone, and home

phone of the contact. Then make an appointment for the actual remote survey. Ideally, the time of day of the survey should be the same as the scheduled remote telecast, since the location of the sun is extremely important for outdoor remotes.

The survey itself is concerned with production and technical problems. The *remote survey party* includes, therefore, people from production and engineering. The minimum party usually consists of the producer, the director, and the T.D. of the remote. Additional supervisory personnel from production and engineering, such as the production manager and the engineering supervisor, may join the survey party, especially if the remote is to cover an important event.

In general, the production part is determined first; engineering then tries to make the planned production procedures technically possible. Depending on the complexity of the telecast, extensive compromises must often be made by production people as well as engineers.

As a director, you can make such compromises only if you know what the particular technical setup and pickup problems are and what changes in your production procedures will help to overcome them. You should, therefore, familiarize yourself with the production problems as well as the engineering problems of television remotes. Although many of the production and engineering survey questions overlap, we will, for better clarification, consider them separately.

The table *(16.1)* shows some of the key questions for the *production* survey.

In the *engineering* survey *(see table 16.2),* only such points with a direct influence on production procedures and, ultimately, on your portion of the remote survey will be listed. Technical points that have already been mentioned in the production survey, such as cameras and microphones, will not be indicated again. Although most of the points below concern the engineering department, as producer-director you should be thor-

16·1   Remote Survey Production

Survey Item	Key Question	Survey Item	Key Question
Contact	Who is your principal contact? Title, address, business phone, home phone. Who is your alternate contact? Title, address, business phone, home phone.		ally located in the shadow side of the stadium.
Place	Where is the exact location of the telecast? Street address, telephone number.		Always survey the remote location during the exact time of the scheduled telecast—from 2:00 to 4:00 P.M., for instance—so that you can observe the exact location of the sun and the prevailing lighting conditions. If it is not a sunny day, try to determine the position of the sun as closely as possible.
Time	When is your remote telecast? Date, time.		
Nature of Event	What is the exact nature of the event? Where does the action take place? What type of action do you expect? Your contact person should be able to supply the necessary information.		Are there any large objects blocking the camera view, such as trees, telephone poles, or billboards? Will you have the same field of view during the actual time of the telecast? A stadium crowd, for instance, may block the camera's field of view, although at the time of the survey the view was unobstructed.
Cameras (stationary)	How many cameras do you need? Try to use as few as possible.		
	Where do you need the cameras? Never place your cameras on opposite sides of the action. In general, the closer together they are, the easier and less confusing the cutting will be. Shoot with the sun, never against it. Keep it behind or to the side of the cameras for the entire telecast. The press boxes of larger stadiums are gener-		Can you avoid large billboards in the background of your shots, especially when the advertising competes with your sponsor's product?
			Do you need special camera platforms? How high? Where? Can the platforms be erected at this particular point? Can you use the

Survey Item	Key Question	Survey Item	Key Question
	remote truck as a platform? If competing stations are also covering the event, have you obtained exclusive rights for your camera positions?	Lighting	For the remote originating indoors, you will almost always need additional lighting.
Cameras (mobile)	Do you need to move certain cameras? What kind of floor do you have? Can the camera be moved on a field dolly, or do you need remote dollies (usually with rubber tires)? Can you use portable cameras (usually much more flexible than the studio cameras)? If you have to use studio cameras, make sure that the camera and the dolly can pass through hallways, doors, if necessary. How far does the cable permit the camera to go?		If you need additional lighting, what kind and where? Again, the particular event may make certain lighting procedures difficult, if not impossible. If you put your cameras in an orchestra hall, you will find that the musicians almost always complain about "too much glare and heat" from the additional lighting required. Or, if you cover a committee hearing, the members are usually less than delighted to be in this kind of spotlight. They like to look good but are often hesitant to accept the technical requirements of good television.
	For some events, the camera should be as unobtrusive as possible. Indeed, there is some concern that it and other television gear might act as a catalyst in touchy situations, such as riots and demonstrations. An unobtrusive camera location somewhat removed from the center of action might be preferred to a portable camera that is moved up close to the event.		Can the lighting instruments be hung conveniently, or do you need light stands?
			Do you need to make special arrangements for back lights? Will the lights be high enough so that they are out of camera range?
			Do you have to shoot against windows? If so, can they be covered or filtered to block out undesirable daylight that may turn

16·1 (cont.)

Survey Item	Key Question	Survey Item	Key Question

| | everything in the foreground into silhouette? | | special audio arrangements, such as program sound at the scene? For example, if you have a singer walk through the park, singing her favorite song, she needs to hear the program audio (her recording of the song) so that she can synchronize her "mouthing" to the recording. |

Audio

Proper sound pickup is usually a major problem on remotes. Either your microphones are too far away from the sound source, or the ambient noise is too great. What type of audio pickup do you need? Where do you need it?

What is the exact action radius as far as audio is concerned?

Can the microphones be seen? Can they be used by the sound source? Generally, remote telecasts tolerate the microphone to be seen in the shot.

What type of microphone do you need? Can you get by with lavalieres? Try to use them as much as possible, even outdoors. Besides assuring good audio pickup, the lavaliere usually allows the person wearing it to feel less conscious of having to speak "for the microphone" than if he or she is confronted with a hand mike close to the face. Where do the microphones have to be? How many do you need?

Do you need wireless microphones? Otherwise, how long must the mike cables be? Do you need

Do you need long-distance mikes for special sound pickups over great distances?

Intercommunications

The importance of a reliable intercommunication system for remotes cannot be stressed enough. It is not uncommon for the members of the production team to be widely scattered over the whole production area and physically isolated. The only contact they have with one another and the director is the intercom system. What type of intercom system do you need? Do you have to string special lines or can the floor crew plug their earphones into the cameras?

If you need separate lines, where do they have to go? Don't forget intercom lines for the talent (usually an announcer).

The P.I. (Program Interrupt) system is very important during

Survey Item	Key Question	Survey Item	Key Question

remotes. If the director has to coordinate different people at the production site from the remote truck, he needs a P.A. (Public Address) talkback system. Since the floor manager can't be in several locations at once, the talkback system permits the director immediate contact with the people in the performance area.

Do you have an outside telephone available in the remote truck? (The engineers usually hook up a telephone so they can communicate with the station and the transmitter.)

Miscellaneous Production Items

Where do you need easels for title cards (or other title devices)?

Do you need a special clock? Where?

Do you need line monitors, especially for the announcer? How many? Where should they be located?

If your program is videotaped, the floor manager will need a VTR slate. Is one slate enough? Sometimes you may want several in order to be able to slate a program from any one of the cameras used. How much videotape do you need?

Permits and Clearances

Have you (or the producer, if you don't act as producer-director) secured clearances for the telecast from the police and fire departments? Do you have clearances from the originators of the event? In writing? Do you have parking permits for the remote truck and other station vehicles?

Do you have passes for all engineering and production personnel, especially when the event requires admittance fees or has some kind of admission restrictions?

Do you have proper liability insurance, if necessary? Check with the legal department of your station.

Special Production Aids

Does everybody involved in the telecast have a rundown sheet of the approximate order of the events? These sheets are essential for the director, floor manager, and announcer, and extremely helpful to the camera operators, audio engineer, and additional floor personnel. Does the director have a "spotter" assigned to him—somebody who knows the event intimately and who can spot and identify the major action and people involved? In sports, spotters are essential.

16·2   Remote Survey: Engineering

Survey Item	Key Question	Survey Item	Key Question
Power	Assuming that you don't work from a battery pack or your own generator, is enough electricity available at the remote site? Where? You will need at least 80–125 amperes for the average remote operation, depending on the equipment used (color generally needing more power than monochrome television). Has your contact person access to the power outlets? If not, who has? Make sure that he is available at the times of the remote setup and the actual production. Do you need special extensions for the power cable?		Do you need special CCU's for portable cameras? Do you need special receiving stations for wireless video and/or audio equipment? Where are they located?
Location of Remote Truck and Equipment	Where should the remote truck be located? Its proximity to the available power is the most important factor. Are you then close enough to the event location? Keep in mind that there is a maximum length for camera cables beyond which you will experience video loss (usually beyond 2,000 feet or roughly 700 meters). Does your truck block normal traffic? Does it interfere with the event itself? Make sure that parking is reserved for the truck.	VTR	If the program is recorded, do you have the necessary VTR equipment in the truck? If you have to feed the signal back to the station to be videotaped, are the remote signal transmission devices (microwave link and telephone wire if the audio is sent separately) working properly? Do you have enough tape to cover the full event? Have you made provisions for switching reels without losing part of the event (switching over to a second VTR)?
		Signal Transmission	If the event has to be fed back to the station for videotape recording or directly to the transmitter for live broadcasting, do you have a good microwave location? You can send the video signal (or the multiplexed video and audio signals) only if you have a clear, unobstructed line of sight from the point of origin to the transmitter.

Survey Item	Key Question	Survey Item	Key Question
	Otherwise you need microwave relays, a service generally supplied by the telephone company. Have you made arrangements about this with the telephone company? Or can you send the video signal via cable? Sometimes you can use existing cable systems for signal transmission. Watch for possible sources of video and audio signal interference, such as nearby X-ray machines, radar, or any other high-frequency electronic equipment.		of someone's tripping is at least minimized. Put a floor mat over the cables at the key traffic points. If you have to cover a great span with free-hanging cables, relieve the tension by tying them on a strong rope stretched over the same distance. Be careful not to run mike cables parallel to power cables.
Routing of Cables	How many camera cables do you need? Where do they have to go? How many audio cables do you need? Where do they have to go? How many intercom lines do you need? Where do they have to go? How many A.C. (power) lines do you need? Where do they have to go? Route your cables in the shortest possible distance from remote truck to pickup point, without, however, blocking important hallways, doors, walkways, and so on. Try to route cables above doorways and doors. Tape all loose cables to the floor so that the danger	Lighting	Are there enough A.C. outlets for all your lighting instruments? Are the outlets fused for your lamps? Don't overload ordinary household outlets. Do you have enough extension cords and distribution boxes (or simple multiple wall plugs) to accommodate all your lighting instruments? Don't forget the A.C. line for the announcer's monitor and the electric clock.
		Telephone Lines	Do you have access to telephone lines for communication to the station and transmitter? For the audio feeds? Make prior arrangements with the phone company.

16·3 Sketch of Remote
Location: Hearing
Room.

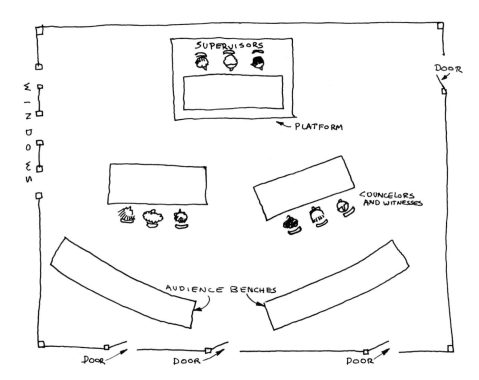

oughly familiar with them so that you can, if
necessary, gently remind the engineers of their
particular survey duties. The table *(16.2)* shows
the major survey items and key questions concerning the engineering part of the remote survey.

A good sketch of the location in which the
remote is to take place can, very much like a floor
plan, help you greatly in preparing for the production and in anticipating major production
problems. *(See 16.3, 16.4 and 16.8.)*

Problems: An Example

Assuming that you could not attend the preliminary survey yourself, your associate director
brought you a fairly accurate sketch (though not
in scale) of the remote site. The occasion is an
important public hearing in the city hall *(16.3)*.

What can you tell from this sketch? How much
preparation can you do? What key questions does
the sketch generate?

Limiting the questions to the setup within this
hearing room, what are your camera, lighting, audio, and intercom requirements? Let's take these
problems one by one.

Cameras   How many cameras do you need and
where should they be located? You should be able
to see all three supervisors on an LS and get CU's
of each one. You should be able to see the witnesses and counselors, in CU's and LS's. You
should also see some of the audience reaction and
the workings of the press. This means one camera
looking at the supervisors and one at the witnesses, the counselors, and the audience.

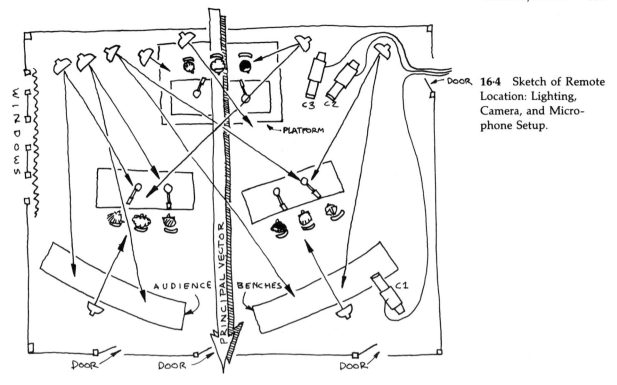

16·4 Sketch of Remote Location: Lighting, Camera, and Microphone Setup.

Actually, two cameras will do. Where should they be placed? Look again at figure 16.3. Since the supervisors will talk with the witnesses and counselors rather than with the audience and the press, they will look most frequently in the direction of the witness table. Similarly, the witnesses and the counselors will look at the supervisors' bench. This direction (from witness to supervisor) will represent the line of conversation, the *principal vector* that you should not cross with your cameras. If you placed cameras on both sides of it, your screen directions would be reversed when you switch from one camera to the other. The supervisors and the witnesses would no longer seem to talk to each other in subsequent closeups, but away from each other. To shoot the faces from as straight on as possible, the cameras should be placed on the right side rather than the left side of the vector. Fortunately, there is a side door through which the cameras can enter and all the cables can be routed without blocking the main access doors in the rear of the chamber. Also, fortunately, the supervisors' bench is high enough so that you can shoot with one of your cameras over the witnesses without the need for a special platform. The other camera (which covers the witnesses and the audience) has a clear view of the witness table *(see 16.4).* Through zooming in and out, you can get tight closeups, or cover the whole bench in a long shot. The normal 10 : 1 zoom range should do, without the necessity for range extenders (at least according to the sketch). If you want a third camera for additional shots and protection, it should be located next to camera 2, facing the witness table and the audience. Why there? In this location

(16.4), camera 3 can get reaction shots from the audience and the press, and relieve camera 2 for closeups or long shots of the witness table. In an emergency, if camera 1 should fail, camera 2 can still truck left and get a reasonably good shot of the supervisors' bench. Try, therefore, to get three cameras for this remote, although, as we said before, you could manage with two.

There is no indication about the surface of the chamber floor. But you can assume that it is fairly smooth, either wood, tile, or a short-hair carpet. In any case, the regular field dolly and tripod will do just fine; they allow you some camera movement if necessary.

Lighting   Your A.D. informs you that, in spite of the large window, the lighting was quite dim inside the chamber. The hearing is scheduled for 10:00 A.M. The large window presents a definite lighting problem. Although it does not provide sufficient light for the room, its glare certainly will tend to silhouette the persons who are sitting between the camera and the window. The sketch does not indicate any draperies. Try, therefore, to arrange to have the window covered with something before the telecast.

Now you need additional lighting. How high is the chamber ceiling? Quite high, as your A.D. assures you. You can, therefore, tell your T.D. or lighting director to get some back lights into the corners of the room behind the supervisors' bench, which may also serve as audience lights; some lights for the witnesses and some lights for the supervisors' bench. Exactly where the lights should be can be judged more accurately once the lighting director (or camera operator) sees the chamber. In any case, the lights should not blind the people, nor should the cables block access doors, or aisles. Try to get by with as few instruments (floodlights) as possible. Are the wall outlets sufficiently fused for your lighting instru-

ments? Make sure that the additional lighting is tolerated by the supervisors and that they and the witnesses are prepared for it. Usually, when people know what to expect, they accept the temporary inconvenience more readily *(see 16.4).*

Audio   Since the chamber is already equipped with a P.A. system, tie into the existing mikes. If the system is not operational, desk mikes are the most logical answer. Set up a dual redundancy system for extra protection. Make sure that the mike cables will not interfere with your camera movement. String the cables behind the cameras, not in front of them *(16.4).*

Intercommunications   Since there is no cuing involved (no cues are given to the supervisors, for example), the floor personnel (one person for each camera) can eliminate additional cables by plugging their earphones into the cameras. Don't forget the slate.

Special Considerations   The camera that needs most protection by the floor manager is camera 1, since it is closest to an access door. Perhaps you can have this area closed off with ropes that can be struck quickly in case of an emergency. Don't lock this right door unless you have checked with the fire marshal and received his OK. By the way, do you have *written* clearances from the Board of Supervisors and the counselors? Again, try to make the additional lighting as inconspicuous as possible. The counselors, the witnesses, or the audience may occasionally stand up. Can you still shoot around them? If the doors are kept closed during the hearing, you can always move camera 1 in front of the middle door for an unobstructed shot of the bench.

As you can see, at least at this point, the remote of the public hearing does not seem to present too many unusual problems. With the preparation as just demonstrated, you should have little trouble with the actual production, barring unforeseen technical problems.

More complicated remote productions need, of course, more intricate and thorough survey and preparation procedures than in the example above. But basically the *process* remains the same. As in any other production, the more time and effort you spend on preparation, the easier the actual production will be.

Production

There is no clear-cut formula of how to set up equipment for a remote telecast. As with a studio production, the number of cameras, the type and number of microphones, the lighting, and so forth depend entirely on the event to be covered or, rather, the process message as defined in the pre-production meetings.

Employing a great number of cameras and microphones, and other types of technical equipment, does not necessarily mean you will end up with a better telecast than when using less equipment. In fact, one or two portable cameras and backpack videotape recorders *(16.5)* are sometimes much more flexible and effective than a cumbersome remote truck with the fanciest of video, audio, recording, and switching gear. With the constant development of high-quality, small portable camera chains and videotape recorders or transmission equipment, the large remote truck is becoming more and more obsolete, especially for coverage that demands flexibility and speed of operation, such as an unplanned news event. However, for such standard remote operations as the coverage of major sports events, the comfort of the remote truck and its technical convenience will still be necessary. An elaborate control center

16·5 Portable Videotape Recorder: This Ampex 2-inch portable tape recorder can be carried as a backpack by the camera operator. Usually, however, the VTR is carried and operated by a second production person.

on wheels, it still permits productions of the highest technical quality. *(See 16.6.)*

While in general the setup in a remote does not differ significantly from the setup and use of the cameras in studio productions, the instant-replay procedures deserve special mention since they are used almost exclusively in remote operations.

Instant Replay

Instant replay means that a key play or other important event is repeated for the viewer, often

16·6 Remote Truck: The remote truck represents a complete control center. It contains preview monitors, line and off-the-air monitors, CCU's, a complex switcher, audio control equipment, and videotape facilities. The larger remote units also contain character generators for titles, and instant-replay equipment. For especially complex remotes, a second remote truck contains the equipment for instant-replay operations.

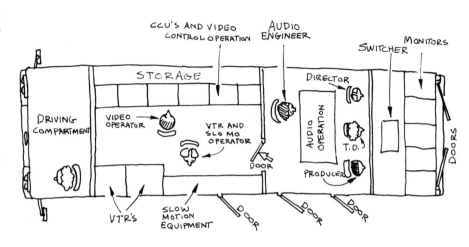

in slow motion or stop motion, immediately after it has happened. Instant-replay operations are quite complex and need several additional pieces of television equipment: (1) an isolated camera, or cameras, (2) an instant-replay switcher, and (3) an instant-replay video recorder.

Isolated Camera When watching an instant replay of a key action, you may notice that the replay either duplicates exactly the sequence you have just seen or, more frequently, shows the action from a slightly different angle. In the first case, the picture sequence of the regular game coverage—that is, the line output—has been recorded and played back; in the second case, the pickup of a separate camera, which was not involved in the general coverage, has been recorded and played back. This separate camera is called the "isolated camera." Its sole function is to follow key plays and other key action for instant replay. In large productions, two or more isolated

cameras are used and controlled from a separate instant-replay remote truck.

Instant-Replay Switcher Since the instant-replay operation is largely self-contained and independent of the general coverage, it frequently uses separate switching facilities. A small switcher is usually installed right next to the main switcher or in the special instant-replay remote unit, enabling the T.D. to feed the instant-replay recorder, or recorders, with either the isolated camera picture or the line-out picture of the regular coverage *(see 16.7)*.

Instant-Replay Video Disc Recorder In order to be maximally effective, the replay of the key action must, indeed, be almost instant—that is, it must follow the action as soon as possible. Also, the replay of the action should permit the viewer to analyze the action somewhat more critically than was possible during the normal coverage.

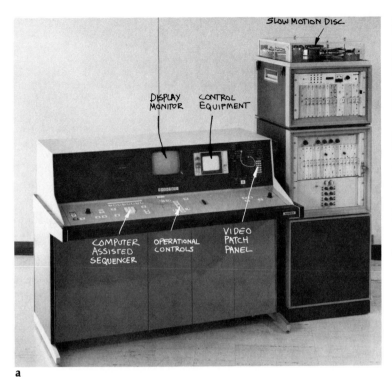
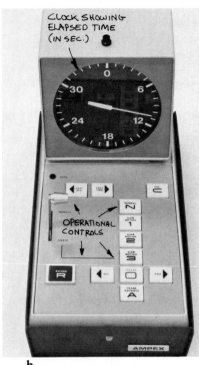

16·7   (a) Ampex Slow Motion Unit. (b) Simple Operator Controls.

The video recorder used for instant playbacks must therefore permit extremely fast recuing and also slow and stop motion. Special video recorders have been developed to fulfill these requirements to some degree, although not without sacrificing picture quality. Since the rewinding and cuing of videotape is relatively time-consuming, a disc recorder has been developed that operates somewhat like a disc dictaphone machine. No rewinding is necessary since the video pickup "arm" can be reset to the beginning of the recorded action very quickly. Special attachments to the recorder allow the action to be replayed either in a form of slow motion (which looks like a rather jerky series of several frames) or in stop motion (which

shows each frame individually). Depending on the instant-replay requirements, one or more video disc recorders are used. *(See 16.7.)*

The instant-replay operation is often guided by the producer or the associate director rather than the director because (1) the director is much too occupied with the regular coverage of the event to worry about which actions should be replayed; and (2) the producer, free to follow the game, can become adept at spotting key plays and deciding which ones to have replayed; hence he can pay full attention to the replay procedures.

Instant-replay operations are very expensive and complicated and are, therefore, rarely attempted by small stations.

As far as the *operation* is concerned for remote telecasts, let us briefly discuss some of the major production procedures for (1) the director, (2) the floor manager, and (3) the talent.

Director's Procedures

Here are some of the major production items you should consider during the remote setup, the on-the-air telecast, and directly after the telecast.

Setup   The setup includes all activities before the actual telecast of the remote event. Thorough set-up planning is especially important for sports remotes *(see 16.9)*.

1.   As soon as the remote truck is in position, conduct a *thorough* technical and talent walk-through. Tell the technical staff where you want the cameras located, where they should move, what lighting you want, where the major action is to take place, what audio you need, where the announcer is going to be, what intercom system you need where, and so forth. Explain the major visualization points to the camera operators. Explain to everybody the process message objective.

2.   Be as decisive and precise as possible. Don't change your mind a hundred times before deciding on what you really want. There is simply no time for such deliberations on a remote.

3.   Work through your floor manager and T.D. as much as possible. Don't try to direct everything yourself.

4.   Pay special attention to the intercom system. During the telecast, you will have no chance to run in and out of the remote truck to the actual site of the event; all your instructions will come via remote control from the truck. Make sure that your floor manager thoroughly understands the whole proceedings. He holds one of the most important production positions during a remote.

5.   Usually, you as a director have no control over the event itself; you merely try to observe it as faithfully as possible. If an announcer is involved for narration

and explanation of the event, walk through the event site with him and explain as best you can what is going to happen. Double-check on the announcer's rundown sheet and the specific information concerning the occasion.

6.   Check the telephone line to the transmitter or station.

7.   Check with the videotape operator on the length of the tape. Will it be sufficient to cover the whole event, or at least part of it, before a new tape is needed? If you have only one VTR in the truck, when is the best time for a reel change?

8.   Walk through the site again and try to visualize the event from the cameras' positions. Are they in the optimal shooting position? Do you have all of them on only one side of the principal vector so that you will not reverse the action on the screen when cutting from one camera to the other? If you are outdoors, is any one of the cameras shooting into the sun? Where will the sun be at the end of the telecast? Try to get your cameras as close to the action as possible in order to avoid overly narrow-angle zoom lens positions.

Realize that you are a *guest* while covering a remote event. Try to work as quickly and as unobtrusively as possible. Don't make a big spectacle out of your production.

On-the-Air Telecast   Once you are on the air and the event is unfolding, there is no way you can stop it because you may have missed a major point. Try to keep on top of the event as well as possible. If you have a good spotter, you will be able to anticipate certain happenings and therefore be ready for them with your cameras. Here are some general points you will want to remember:

1.   Speak loudly and clearly. Usually there is lots of noise at the site, and it is often hard for the camera operators and the floor crew to hear. Yell if you have to, but don't get frantic.

2.   Listen to the floor manager. He or she may be able

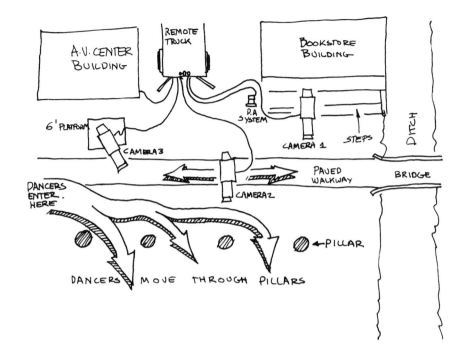

16·8 Sketch of Remote Location: Outdoor Dance.

to spot special events and report them to you as they occur.

3. Watch your monitors carefully. Often the off-cameras will show you especially interesting shots. But don't be tempted by cute, yet meaningless or even event-distorting, shots. If, for example, the great majority of an audience listens attentively to the speaker, don't single out the one who is sound asleep, as colorful a shot as this may be. Report the event as truthfully as you possibly can. If the event is dull, show it. If it is exciting, show it. Don't use production tricks to distort it to fit your previous expectations.

4. Listen to the audio. Often, this will give you clues as to the development of the event.

5. If things go wrong, keep calm. If a spectator blocks the camera, cut to another camera, but don't scream at the camera operator.

6. Exercise propriety and good taste in what you

show to the audience. Don't capitalize on accidents (especially during sports events), or situations that are potentially embarrassing to the person in front of the camera, even if such situations might appear hilarious to you.

After the Show   The remote is not finished until all equipment is struck and the remote site restored to its original state. Here are some points that are especially important for the director:

1. If something went wrong, don't storm out of the remote truck accusing everybody of making mistakes except yourself. Cool off first.

2. Thank everyone for his or her efforts. Nobody ever *wants* a remote to look bad. Thank especially the contact person and others responsible for making the event and the remote telecast possible. Leave as good an impression of you and your team as possible with the persons

16·9   Many remote telecasts are devoted to the coverage of sports events. The number of cameras used and their function depend almost entirely on who is doing the remote pickup of the event. Networks use a great amount of equipment and personnel for the average sports remote. As mentioned before, dual remote units are often used, with one truck taking care of the regular pickup, and the other entirely devoted to instant replay. Local stations, if engaged in a sports pickup at all, must get by with far less equipment. In order to obtain a general idea of how many cameras you would need and where to put them for minimum pickup requirements, refer to our list of the setup methods for some major sports events.

Sport	Number of Cameras
Baseball	3 or 4

Location

Camera 1: behind home plate. Should be able to move to either side to accommodate right-or lefthanded batters.

Camera 2: middle of first-base line.

Camera 3: near first base.

Camera 4 (optional): opposite camera 1 (watch action reversal) or high behind home plate.

Football	4

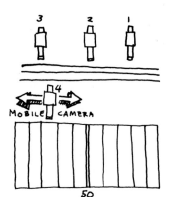

Cameras 1, 2, 3: high in the stands, near the 20–50–20–yard lines. Opposite sun (press box, shadow side).

Camera 4: portable or on special dolly in field. (No isolated cameras considered.)

Basketball   3

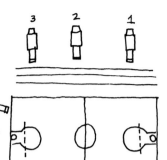

Camera 1: high in stands, left field.

Camera 2: high in stands, center field.

Camera 3: high in stands, right field.

Camera 4 (optional: at one end of court, low, behind, and to one side of basket.)

Tennis   3

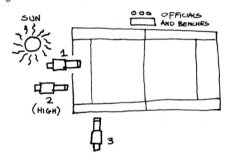

Camera 1: at end of court, high enough so it can cover total court, shooting with sun.

Camera 2: next to camera 1, but higher.

Camera 3: at side of the court, opposite officials or place where players rest between sets.

Boxing or
Wrestling   2

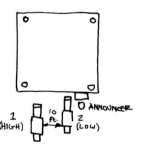

Camera 1: high enough so that it can overlook the entire ring.

Camera 2: about 10 feet to the side of camera 1, low, slightly above the ropes.

responsible. Remember that you are representing your station and, in a way, the whole of the "media" when you are on remote location.

3. If you don't have a producer, complete all the necessary production forms.

4. Thank the police for their cooperation in reserving parking spaces for your remote vehicles, controlling the spectators, and so forth. Don't forget that you will need them again for your next remote telecast.

5. See to it that the floor manager returns all the production equipment to the station.

Floor Manager's Procedures

As a floor manager (also called stage manager), you have, next to the director, the major responsibility for the success of a remote telecast. Since you are close to the scene, you have often more overview of the event than the director, who is isolated in the remote truck. Here are some of the major points you should consider:

1. Familiarize yourself with the event ahead of time. Find out where it is taking place, what its major development is, where the cameras and microphones are relative to the remote truck. Make a sketch of the major event developments and the equipment setup *(16.8)*.

2. Triple-check the intercom system. Find out whether you can hear the instructions from the remote truck, and whether you can be heard there. Check whether the intercom is working properly for the other floor personnel.

3. Try to control the traffic of onlookers around the major equipment and action areas. Be polite, but firm. Try to work around the crews from other stations. Be especially aware of reporters from other media. It wouldn't be the first time that a news photographer just happened to stand right in front of the key camera while snapping his pictures. Try to appeal to their sense of responsibility. Tell them that you, too, have a job to do in trying to inform the public.

4. Have your slate ready if the telecast is to be video-taped.

5. Check on all cables and make sure they are properly secured so that potential hazards are minimized.

6. Try to contact a member of the police assigned to the remote. Clue him or her in on its major aspects. You will find the police quite cooperative and especially helpful in controlling spectator traffic.

7. Help the camera operators in spotting key event detail and in moving their cameras.

8. Give all your cues immediately and precisely. Make sure that the talent sees your cues. (Most of the time, announcers are hooked up to the program interrupt system via small earphones, so that the director can cue them directly without the floor manager as an intermediary.)

9. Have the necessary title cards ready and in order. You will need a large clip to fasten the cards to the easel during a windy day. While doing hot flips of title cards, hold the cards behind the one you are pulling so that they don't all come flying off the easel.

10. After the telecast, pick up all the production equipment for which you are directly responsible—easels, platforms, sandbags, slates, earphones. Double-check whether you have forgotten anything before you leave the remote site.

Talent Procedures   The general talent procedures, as discussed in Chapter 13, also apply for remote operations. However, here are some points that are especially pertinent for remote telecasts:

1. Familiarize yourself thoroughly with the event and your specific assignment. Know the process message objective and try to do your part to effect it.

2. Check out your microphone and your communication system. If you work with a program interrupt system, check it out with the director or the T.D.

3. Check whether your monitor is working. Have the T.D. punch up a camera on the line-out.

4. Check with the director on your show format and fact sheet.

5.   If you have the help of a contact person or a spotter, discuss with him or her the major aspects of the event and the communication system between the spotter and yourself, once you are on the air. How is the spotter going to tell you what is going on while the microphone is hot?

6.   While on the air, tell the audience what they cannot see for themselves. Don't tell them the obvious. For example, if you see the celebrity stepping out of the airplane and shaking hands with the people who came to meet him, don't say, "The celebrity is shaking hands with some people," but tell who is shaking hands with whom. If a football player lies on the field and can't seem to get up, don't tell the audience that apparently the player got hurt; they can see that for themselves. But tell them who the player is and what might have caused what type of injury. Also, follow up this announcement with more detailed information on the injury and how the player is doing.

7.   Don't get so involved in the event that you lose your objectivity. On the other hand, don't remain so detached that you appear to have no feelings whatsoever.

8.   If you make a mistake in identifying someone or something, admit it and correct it as soon as possible.

9.   Don't identify parts of the event solely by color. There are still many viewers who watch the telecast in black-and-white. Don't refer just to the boxer in the red trunks, but also to the one on the left side of your screen.

10.   As much as possible, let the event itself do the talking.

Postproduction

If you have done a remote pickup for postproduction editing, try to match in the final edited tape version the relative energy and general feeling of the original event. This is true especially when the process message objective implies a *reflection* of the event rather than a reconstruction of it. Don't try to energize the screen event by fast cuts and mon-

tage effects. Simply edit for continuity. Try to avoid jump cuts and reversals of screen directions. Hopefully, you will have provided the editor with enough cutaways so that he can bridge a reversal of screen directions without too much effort or loss of continuity (see Chapter 10). Usually the audio will provide the necessary continuity, even if your visuals may not always cut together as smoothly as you might desire.

As a producer or a director, or a combination thereof, your major postshow duty is to write thank-you letters. Don't neglect this task, as anticlimactic as it may seem after a successful production. If you had little cooperation, try to find the source of the trouble and gently suggest ways of improving cooperation. Don't get angry. It is more likely than not that you will have to work with the same people in future telecasts.

Again, check on the release forms and file them for future reference. If you have time, hold a postproduction meeting with the production people and the talent, and talk about the good points and the not-so-good points of the remote. Listen to the suggestions of the crew and try to apply them during your next remote.

Summary

A television show done outside the studio is called a remote telecast, or a *remote.*

Remote production falls into three major parts: (1) preproduction: remote survey, (2) production: equipment setup and operation, and (3) postproduction: editing considerations and postshow duties.

The *remote survey* is the major preproduction activity. It concerns ascertaining what the event is all about and how it can best be televised. This study is usually done by a survey party, normally consisting of the producer, the director, the technical director, and an engineering supervisor.

The *production* remote survey is concerned principally with (1) place, time, and nature of the remote event, (2) cameras, (3) lighting, (4) audio, (5) intercommunications, (6) miscellaneous production items, (7) permits and clearances, and (8) special production aids.

The *engineering* remote survey is concerned principally with (1) electrical power, (2) location of remote truck and equipment, (3) VTR possibilities, (4) signal transmission, (5) routing of cables, (6) lighting, and (7) telephone lines.

The *production* of a remote includes (1) equipment setup, (2) instant replay, and (3) production procedures for the director, the floor manager, and the talent.

While a great number of remotes are telecast, or videotaped uninterrupted for later playback, some are done for *postproduction editing.*

17   *Small-Format Television*

In this chapter we examine a production activity and its major types of equipment, called (misleadingly) "video." Video refers to a variety of nonbroadcast television production activities by individuals or small groups outside the broadcast industry. Whatever the production purpose may be, the video functions are one of these three, or a combination of them: (1) the camera (representing the whole video gear) looks at, fulfilling primarily an observational function; (2) the camera looks into, providing an insight into an event; and (3) the camera creates, producing a screen event that has no live counterpart anywhere. The event is the electronic screen and speaker image.

The equipment (cameras and videotape recorders) is called small-format in contrast to large-format broadcasting equipment. Most video productions are done with small, highly portable cameras and videotape recorders. Though lacking broadcast quality, this equipment produces amazingly good pictures and sound, especially when used for closed-circuit distribution. We will describe, therefore, the most common small-format equipment and its principal operations.

When we speak of television production, we tend to think immediately of broadcast operations. But a major portion of television production is done for nonbroadcast, or closed-circuit, communication.[1]

There is a wide array of nonbroadcast television. Closed-circuit television can be used to watch parking lots or hospital beds, and it can be used to distribute full-fledged productions to large audiences in theaters. Television programs are produced to instruct art or chemistry students, or to show a new bank teller how to cash a check. Except when it serves a merely observational function (such as watching a parking lot), the production techniques for closed-circuit television are usually not drastically different from the ones

used in broadcasting stations. The equipment may differ—you may have small monochrome cameras and a simple switcher rather than the latest color equipment, and you may work out of a converted classroom rather than an elaborate studio—still, the basic steps are quite similar to the ones we have described in the preceding chapters. In many cases, the mode of transmission (open- or closed-circuit) influences the production method not at all, or perhaps only to a slight degree. But there is one use of television that is sufficiently different from the broadcast-type production to warrant special attention. This is what is ordinarily, and somewhat misleadingly, called *video*.

Video generally refers to the use of small-format television equipment by individuals or very small groups to satisfy their creative urge, or to record their immediate experiences for an equally immediate audience—friends, family, close community.

[1] Robert K. Avery, "Telecommunication Education at the University Level: A General Status Report" (University of Utah, 1974).

AGC Automatic gain control. Regulates the volume of the audio or video automatically, without the use of pots.

Closed-Circuit Distribution of audio and video signals other than broadcasting. Includes direct video and audio feeds from the camera and the audio board, from the videotape recorder into a monitor, or the RF (radio frequency) distribution via cable.

Deck Or videotape deck. Short form of videotape recorder.

EIAJ Abbreviation for Electronic Industries Association of Japan. Established the EIAJ Type No. 1 Standard for ½-inch helical scan videotape recorders. In general, the standard assures that any monochrome tape recorded on one such recorder can be played back on any other monochrome or color recorder, and any color tape can be played back on any other color VTR, provided that they meet the EIAJ Type 1 Standard.

Impedance A type of resistance to the signal flow. Important especially in matching high- or low-impedance microphones with high- or low-impedance recorders. Also, a high-impedance mike works properly only with a relatively short cable (a longer cable has too much resistance), while a low-impedance mike can take up to several hundred feet of cable. Impedance is also expressed in high-Z or low-Z.

With small-format television equipment, you can now produce, shoot, play back, and even edit your own television program. The small-format video cassette or cartridge makes it possible for you to watch a program anywhere, at any time, and as often as you wish; the option is no longer with the sender (the television station), but with the percipient. The introduction of relatively inexpensive, easy-to-operate equipment has, indeed, caused a quiet but significant communication revolution. Television, or rather video, has become the province of the individual. The various manifestos of the early video artists and communicators are ample proof that these pioneers were very much aware of this revolution.[2]

Video is providing, or at least has the potential for providing, programming that is a true alternative to that of the broadcasting stations. Video can serve small, immediate community or even individual needs. Video can be used to explore the graphic potential of the television screen, to let a patient see himself or herself as part of a therapy session, or to inform us via cable of the giant sale at a corner supermarket. Video can furnish the community access to television way beyond what the open-circuit broadcasting station has to offer—not because the broadcaster is unwilling, but because his machinery is not geared to service the uninitiated amateur.

The users of video are so diversified in approach and goal that it is hard to find a common thread. And this is exactly its strength—to be free from tradition. Nevertheless, two types of users can be identified rather easily: (1) the video artists, who see in the machine a new tool for aesthetic expression, and (2) community communicators, who want to reflect (often rather naively) the various life styles of their commu-

---

[2] See early issues of *Radical Software*.

Monitor/Receiver A television receiver that can reproduce direct video and audio feeds (from the VTR, for example) as well as signals that are broadcast on a channel.

Portapak Formerly a trade name of the Sony Corporation, for a highly portable camera and videotape unit, which could be easily carried and operated by one person. It now refers to all such equipment, regardless of manufacturer or model.

RF Abbreviation for Radio Frequency, necessary for all broadcast signals, as well as some closed-circuit distribution.

Small Format Refers to the small size of the camera pickup tube (usually ⅔-inch) or, more frequently, to the narrow width of the videotape: ¼-inch, ½-inch, ¾-inch, and even 1-inch (although 1-inch is often regarded as large-format tape). Small-format equipment (cameras and videotape recorders) is actually very small in size and highly portable.

Stripe Filter Extremely narrow, vertical stripes of red, green, and blue filters that, repeating themselves many times, are attached to the front surface of the camera pickup tube. They divide the incoming white light into the three light primaries without the aid of dichroic mirrors.

Video Nonbroadcast production activities and the use of small-format equipment for a variety of purposes. Usually the equipment includes a portable camera, a microphone, a videotape recorder or video cassette recorder, and a monitor.

17·1   Small-format television equipment refers to the small-image format of the camera pickup tube in small portable cameras, and the narrow width of the videotape (from ¼-inch to 1-inch).

nity. While the former group produces abstract images through video feedback or other planned manipulation of the scanning pattern, the latter videotape anything that happens around them, from people preparing breakfast to the local school board meeting. Since communication, especially video communication, becomes the more effective and formative the more everyday experiences are *clarified* and *intensified* into precise messages, the two groups would profit from pooling their experiences (and sometimes they do).

Small-format equipment, like all television equipment, must be used with skill, understanding, and empathy. You need to know the potentials and limitations of your equipment in order to make it work for you instead of against you. And there we have arrived at exactly the point that was made in the beginning of this book: in order to be an effective, creative communicator, you must know the communication tool; you must know how to work the machine so that it becomes a true extension of yourself, rather than a message-distorting intermediary.

As soon as you begin to clarify and intensify the experiences around you with a specific medium, such as small-format television, and convey them to your friends or fellow community members, you are acting as a communicator, as an artist, as a molder of opinion. Hence, you cannot help but realize that you are burdened with the ultimate responsibility of every serious artist and communicator: to contribute to positive social change, to help people become aware of themselves, to live full, happy, free, and responsible lives.

In general, the basic production approaches that we discussed previously, such as the statement of the process message objective and the fulfilling of identified medium requirements, are still valid in respect to small-format television. However, there are three points that merit discussion, without infringing on your creative use of video. These are (1) basic video functions, (2) basic small-format equipment, and (3) basic operation.

Video Functions

The camera (representing the whole video and audio gear) can *look at, look into,* and *create.* Let's take these three functions, which can guide the process message objective, one at a time.

Camera Looks At

When the camera *looks at* the event, it strictly *observes* as objectively as possible. The video (and, of course, audio) acts basically as a recording device for a specific event. Since the camera is nevertheless innately selective (it cannot see everything at once), you still have to make certain decisions about what to include and what to leave out in your recording. You should, therefore, try to select the essential parts of the event for your video experience. When recording an athlete so that he can see himself after the performance, you use video to *look at.* Video is often more effective than film in this function, since you can play back the event immediately after it occurred. For example, by videotaping your girl friend running over the hurdles, you can show her immediately after each run how she did, what she did right and what she did wrong. She then can go back and correct the mistakes as shown on the videotape. With film, she would have to wait at least one day before she could see what she did wrong, with no chance for immediate feedback. Video, thus, can contribute to a *learning process* which otherwise would be difficult to achieve.

The recording of events for archival purposes or easy distribution is another important *looking at* function.

17·2   When *looking at* an event, the camera merely reports it as faithfully as possible. The camera takes on an objective point of view.

Camera Looks Into

When the camera *looks into* the event, it scrutinizes from an extremely close point of view. Consequently, it reveals aspects of the event we ordinarily would not, or could not, see. Let's take modern dance, for example. If you *look at* the event through the camera, you simply record the dancers' movements as well as possible. The camera observes the dance as someone who is watching it in the theater *(see 17.2).* But if you use the camera to *look into* the dance, you select and intensify only some of its essential parts *(see 17.3).* Perhaps we will never see the dance exactly the way we see it in the rehearsal hall or on stage. But we will see portions of arms, bodies, hands, feet, revealing the basic movements, the basic structure of the dance, and intensifyng the essential rhythm. In sports we would no longer watch how somebody takes the high hurdles, for the purpose of studying the athlete's technique, but we would instead fasten on the skill, the grace, and the beauty of the motion. Or, perhaps, you could use

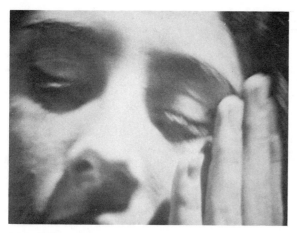

17·3   When *looking into* an event, the camera scrutinizes it from a variety of points of view. The camera looks at the event at close range. The camera's viewpoint becomes *introspective.*

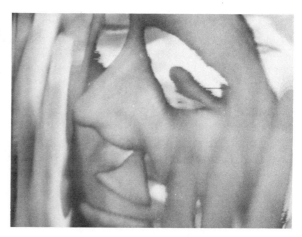

17·4   When the camera creates, it takes the outer event simply as raw material for the electronic manipulation. The actual event can exist only as a screen event.

your camera in such a way that the screen event reveals the incredible physical and psychological strain of such a race.

Note, however, that we are still using the event as the prime material for the video experience. We do not go beyond the event but simply into it. We are probing its essence.

Camera Creates

When we create a video event, we use the external event, such as the dance or the hurdler, simply as raw material for our electronic manipulations. The event as *created* by the camera exists nowhere except on the screen. The *screen* event is the *primary* experience. For example, in the modern dance you would use the dancers as space manipulators, to define screen space, or simply as energy sources for your electronic manipulations. Through keying or matting, a dancer moving by may become an abstract pattern in motion, which,

nevertheless, is caused by the energy of the dancer herself. *(See 17.4.)*

Since you are now concerned mainly with the electronic manipulation of the screen image, you can do away with the camera altogether and manipulate the scanning pattern in the monitor directly by feeding in any number of external energy sources, such as the audio signal from the accompanying music, or the energy generated by a video synthesizer, similar to the Arp or Moog synthesizers in the audio field.

In reality, these distinctions are not always as clear-cut as they might appear in this discussion. The three medium functions frequently overlap to some extent. However, a clear understanding of each function will certainly help you in your basic approach to the subject matter, in the formulation of the process message objective. If you want just to report an event, such as the planting of new trees along the neighborhood street, you look at it from a rather detached point of view. If you want to show the importance of these trees for beautifying the neighborhood and for helping to make people happier by their presence, then you should move your camera into the event, and capture the reactions of the people looking at the trees, touching the trees, putting their hands into the soil while planting the trees. If you want to demonstrate the symbolic importance of the trees as bearers of new life and hope, as elements that counteract decay, then you may want to create an appropriate experience with the camera based on the energy of the tree-planting event, such as leaf patterns, the movement of groping hands keyed into the fresh branches, and so on.

It is quite likely that your process message objective allows any one of the three camera approaches within a single program. Your coverage of the original event should, therefore, be handled in such a way that you have all three options open in the postproduction process.

As with producing a program for on-the-air presentation, the translation of a program objective into the video and audio images requires that you know what the equipment can do and how to make it work. We will, therefore, briefly describe some of the major small-format equipment and its operation.

Small-Format Equipment

Small-format television equipment comes in a dazzling variety of names, sizes, sophistication, and quality. Every year, new stuff is produced that is supposed to outperform the old. Any attempt to describe small-format cameras and video recorders in detail would be not only futile but not really helpful for you in learning how to manage small-format video production. Let us, therefore, concentrate on a few major equipment

17·5 When working in video, you will generally have no one close by that can undertake minor or major equipment repairs. Consequently, you will either have to learn how to do some of the maintenance and even minor repair jobs yourself, or take the defective equipment to a factory service center or a manufacturer-authorized service center. It is a good idea to buy the equipment from a store that has an authorized service center, since you can always bring it back to the same place for repairs.

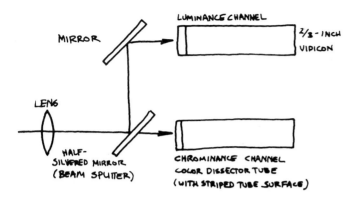

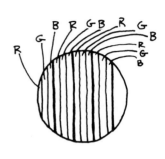

a

b

17·6 Schematic of Two-Tube Color Camera: In the two-tube color camera, one of the tubes takes care of the black-and-white picture information (luminance); the other with the color information (chrominance). As in the larger, three-tube color cameras, the incoming light is split and directed into the two tubes. The luminance tube consists of a ⅔-inch vidicon and acts like a black-and-white camera. The chrominance tube (or color dissector tube, as it is sometimes called) has on its target area extremely narrow stripes of red, green, and blue color filters, which split the incoming light into three additive primaries. This filter is called the stripe filter. The two signals are then combined with each other (matrixed) exactly as in the bigger studio cameras.

items. These are (1) the small-format camera, (2) the portapak, (3) audio equipment, (4) videotape recorders, (5) playback monitors, and (6) lighting.

The Small-Format Camera

As with any other television camera, the small-format camera consists of a pickup tube, or pickup tubes, electronic accessories (with a built-in CCU or a small, portable CCU unit), a lens, and a viewfinder. As mentioned before, the camera is called "small format" because of its small-sized pickup tube.

The *monochrome camera* has as its *pickup tube* a

⅔-inch vidicon. Depending on the sophistication of the electronic circuits, the camera can range in size from an average-sized book to a shoebox.

The *color camera* works with either one or two color pickup tubes.

Since the pickup tubes are small format, even the color cameras are not much larger than their black-and-white equivalents. Unfortunately, the quality of the color in the two- or one-tube cameras is still far below that of the three-tube studio cameras. However, for nonbroadcast purposes and especially for experimentation, the portability and relatively low cost of the small-format camera by far outweigh the quality hand-

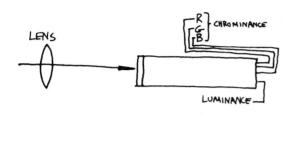

a

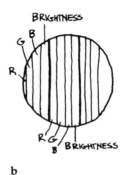

b

17·7 Schematic of One-Tube Color Camera: In the one-tube color camera, the target area of the tube is striped with a four-way filter, which takes care of the chrominance and luminance information. The filter consists of sequential red, green, and blue stripes, plus a fourth stripe that controls brightness.

icap. You should realize that quality becomes a major concern primarily when you broadcast the camera's signal. If you distribute it closed-circuit (from camera to cassette recorder and back to a monitor), the picture information loss is minimal and the color pictures produced by the small-format camera look amazingly good.

Most small-format cameras have a *zoom lens* with a 4 : 1 or 5 : 1 zoom range, and a maximum aperture anywhere from $f/1.2$ to $f/2.0$, with $f/1.9$ being the most common.

The zooming is done right at the lens, with no other zoom controls (such as cables or rods) necessary. The zoom lens has a C-mount and is, therefore, interchangeable with fixed-focal-length C-mount lenses. You may find that for some shooting assignments the zoom lens is not the most convenient to use. Zooming in to a TCU while handholding the camera rarely works out well. Even before you have arrived at the TCU, your picture will wiggle and jump because of the narrowing angle position (longer) of your zoom lens. A wide-angle *fixed-focal-length lens* (such as a 10mm for the ⅔-inch tube format) may some-

times prove much more satisfactory for portable work than a zoom lens. The wide-angle lens permits you to walk right into the scene (you will remember that it has a large depth of field) without undue focus problems. Furthermore, it minimizes rather than emphasizes camera wiggles, unless you get extremely close to the object.

Most small-format cameras have a small *electronic viewfinder,* which, in some cases, is magnified optically for comfortable viewing. On some cameras (such as the portapak), the viewfinder also acts as a playback monitor when you are checking a videotape recording.

Some small-format cameras have a *pistol grip* for easier "shooting." You may, however, find that this is not an ideal camera handling device. Although the camera is generally light, holding it by the pistol grip for any length of time will quickly tire your hand and arm. Many experienced camera operators prefer to rest the camera directly on their hand without the aid of the pistol grip, or to construct a shoulder harness, similar to the harnesses for film cameras. Most pistol grips are easily removable from the camera base.

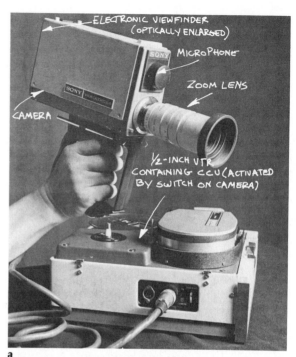

a

17·8   (a) Sony Video Rover. (b) Akai VT-120 System. (c) Akai VTS-150 Color System.

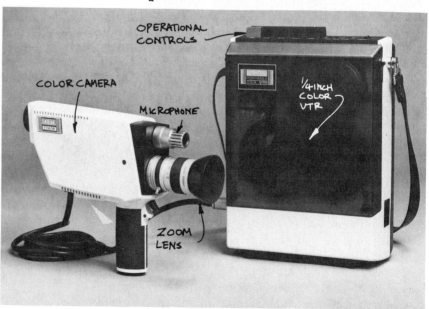

c

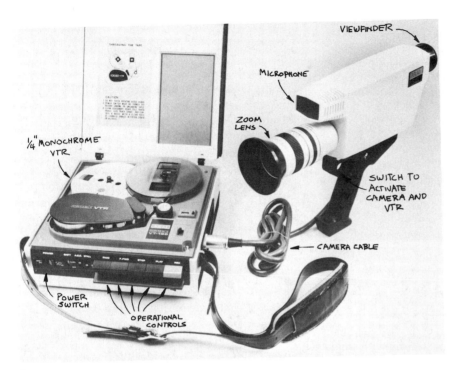

b

A sturdy *tripod* is still as important a camera mount for the small-format camera as it is for the heavier studio cameras.

The Portapak

The portapak unit[3] consists of a small portable vidicon camera usually connected to a small portable ½-inch reel-to-reel videotape recorder. This camera-recorder unit has probably contributed more to the video revolution than any other single piece of television equipment. The portapak is an immensely useful instrument and, if used properly, can produce videotapes of excellent quality. Its chief virtues are complete mobility and independence of any other piece of equipment. The portapak unit can run off a battery pack (which is part of the VTR machine) or off regular 110-volt house current (which is changed to DC—direct current—in the battery charger unit). The portapak camera has a built-in microphone (some of the older models have a small mike attached to the top of the camera), with

[3] The first small-format camera-recorder units were called Portapak by the Sony Corporation. Later, Sony changed the name to Video Rover (registered trademark). However, video people still like the name "portapak" and use it almost exclusively to denote any portable small-format camera-VTR combination.

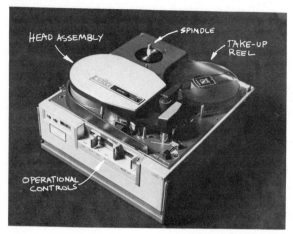

HEAD ASSEMBLY   SPINDLE   TAKE-UP REEL

OPERATIONAL CONTROLS

17·9 ½-inch Videotape Recorder of the Portapak Unit (Sony).

additional facilities for an external mike input at the recorder unit.

The Portapak Camera   The portapak camera can be monochrome or color. Since the color camera uses the one-tube system, it is not very much bigger than the monochrome camera. If you work in color, you will also need a tape deck that will record the color signal from the camera in color.

Most portapak cameras come equipped with a 4 : 1 (12.5mm to 50mm), $f/1.9$ zoom lens with a C-mount. As with all other small-format cameras, you may want to replace the zoom lens with a wide-angle lens for especially mobile camera pickups.

As has been discovered by many a portapak user, the cable that leads from camera to VTR deck is usually too long when you carry the camera and the VTR unit, and too short if you want to move away from the VTR unit for some interesting camera angles.[4] You may want to have the

[4] Richard Robinson, *The Video Primer* (New York: Links Books, 1974), p. 13.

camera cable shortened, and then use some additional cable for the "independent" camera operation.

The Portapak Videotape Recorder   The videotape recorder, usually referred to as *portapak deck,* is a small ½-inch reel-to-reel model, which holds a 1,200-foot roll of videotape. With a reel this long you can record up to thirty minutes' worth of programming. This tiny portapak VTR not only records video and audio signals but also provides the electronics necessary for the camera to operate properly. The camera cannot function without the VTR unit. Figure 17.9 shows the major parts of the portapak deck.

Power Supply   You can "drive" the portapak unit with rechargeable batteries that fit into the tape deck unit, or external battery packs that are adapted to the portapak power requirements (usually 12 volts DC). Or, you can use regular AC power from the household outlet, which is then changed into the low-voltage DC power through a converter located in the battery charger *(17.10)*.

Make sure that the batteries are always fully charged before using the portapak with battery power. You should recharge them as soon as you get back from a "remote," or, better yet, every day, so that you will have full power whenever you need it. A second battery unit is almost a must if you use the portapak frequently. Not only can you recharge one unit while using the second one, but you will also extend the rechargeability of each battery unit. Don't let a battery become completely discharged or it will not hold a recharge.

Audio Equipment

Good audio is as difficult to achieve in small-format television production as it is when using studio-type equipment. Again, the quality de-

17·10 Sony AC-3400 Battery Charger and AC Adapter.

17·11 Most portapak cameras have an omnidirectional microphone attached or built in, pointing into the direction of the lens.

pends almost more on how the microphone is used than on its relative sophistication. A high-quality microphone badly used will give you worse sound than a lower-quality mike used properly.

If you work with a portapak, you can use either (1) the microphone that is attached to the camera or built into it, or (2) a microphone that is independent of the camera and can be used close to the sound source, very much like the kind used for studio-type productions.

The Built-in Microphone   This omnidirectional mike points into the direction of the lens *(see 17.11)*. As desirable as such a sound pickup device is from an operational point of view (you don't have to worry about handling a separate microphone), it is difficult to get good sound with it. Here are some of the problems: (1) Unless you work the camera very close to the sound source, thereby sticking the camera into the face of the speaker, the omnidirectional microphone will pick up

many extraneous noises. (2) The *automatic gain control,* or AGC, which is necessary because you don't have anyone to "ride gain" (control the volume) for the built-in mike, will tend to emphasize the loud sounds, regardless of whether they are the desired sounds or just background noises. Additionally, the mike, controlled by the AGC, is subject to distortion as a result of input overload (see page 149). (3) The microphone, which is attached to the camera, is sensitive to the inevitable rubbing noises and shocks connected with the handling of the camera.

When the desired sounds are general, such as music from a marching band or the screams of an excited crowd during a football game, the built-in microphone will work just fine. Whenever you need to emphasize one particular source over another, however, you will need to use a microphone that is independent of the camera, or several microphones and a mixer, very much as you would use a microphone setup in a studio production.

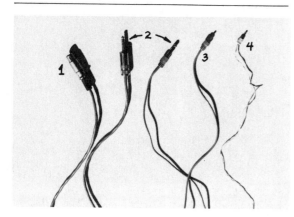

17·12 There are generally four major types of audio cable connectors: (1) the Cannon connectors, (2) the phone plug, (3) the RCA plug, or phono plug, and (4) the mini plug.

17·13 Impedance is also expressed by the letter Z. High-Z means high impedance (high resistance and therefore short cable); low-Z means low impedance (low resistance and therefore long cables).

Independent Microphone When using a microphone that is separate from the camera, you simply select the appropriate type (such as a lavaliere, hand mike, or highly directional microphone) and plug it into the appropriate receptacle at the recorder unit. When using an independent mike, you must watch out for two things: (1) that the microphone plug matches the receptacle at the recorder unit, and (2) that the *impedance* of the microphone matches the impedance of the recorder.

For all practical purposes, impedance means resistance to the flow of an electronic signal, such as an audio signal. There are high and low impedance mikes. *High impedance mikes* have a slightly *higher output signal* than low, but there is also a *high resistance* in the cable from mike to input (recorder); at least there is a *high loss* of certain frequencies. *Low impedance mikes* have a *lower output*, but also *low resistance,* or *low loss,* in the cable. While the high impedance mikes can tolerate only about a 15-foot (approx. 5m) cable, low impedance mikes can use very long (up to several hundred feet) cables with a minimum of signal loss. High-quality mikes are usually low-impedance, while home-recording mikes are often high-impedance.

The portapak microphone input is low impedance. You must, therefore, use a low-impedance mike for your independent (away from the camera) audio pickup. A high-Z mike will not work, even if its plug matches the receptacle of your recorder unit.

If you use more than one microphone for your audio setup, you need a mixer, as described in Chapter 7.

Small-Format Videotape Recorders

In the small-format field, there are almost as many types of videotape recorders on the market as there are cameras. As already pointed out in

a

b

17·14 (a) Sony AV-8650 ½-inch Color Videotape Recorder has insert and assemble editing modes, as well as slow-frame and still-frame capabilities.

(b) Editing Bench, using Sony AV-3650 ½-inch Monochrome Videotape Recorders.

Chapter 9, small-format videotape recorders allow you to record a television signal from a television camera, a television set, or another videotape recorder. Some recorders have electronic editing capabilities, and slow and stop motion *(17.14)*.

There are basically two types of small-format videotape recorders: (1) reel-to-reel and (2) cassette.

Reel-to-Reel Recorders   These come in a variety of videotape formats, with tape widths of ¼-inch, ½-inch, ¾-inch, and 1-inch. All are *helical scan* models. The more sophisticated ones have electronic editing and playback facilities for slow motion and stop motion. Some recorders record and play back in black-and-white only, while others can record and play back in either black-and-white or color.

Unfortunately, not all small-format recorders are compatible. You may find that a ½-inch videotape you recorded on one machine cannot play back at all on another type of ½-inch recorder. Some standardization has been achieved through the Electronic Industries Association of Japan (EIAJ) for ½-inch black-and-white and color machines, although 1-inch and ¾-inch machines have not yet been standardized. When using EIAJ (Type No. 1) ½-inch VTR's, you can play a tape recorded on one machine on any other machine, with no, or only minor, playback adjustments (such as tracking). For example, you can play back a monochrome tape (recorded on a monochrome EIAJ machine) on another EIAJ monochrome videotape recorder, or on an EIAJ color recorder (on which the tape will, of course, appear in black-and-white). Or you can play back an EIAJ color tape on a monochrome VTR, on which it will appear in black-and-white. Or you can play back an EIAJ color tape on any other EIAJ color VTR in color.

The typical reel-to-reel recorder is small enough so that one person can carry it from place to place. But only the portapak model can be carried rather easily while the camera is in operation.

17·15 The EIAJ Type No. 1 standard embodies some operational and electronic standards. For example, the tape must be ½-inch wide; the tape speed is always 7½ ips; the recorder must hold 2,400 feet of videotape, which is good for recording or playing back one hour's worth of programming; the audio track is always on the top edge of the tape, the slant-track video signal in the middle, and the control track on the bottom edge.

Video Cassettes Like the reel-to-reel recorders, the cassettes come in a variety of formats, using either ½-inch or ¾-inch videotape. Most of them record and play back color and monochrome. The big advantage of the cassette recorder over the reel-to-reel is the ease of operation. All you do is plug the completely self-contained cassette into the machine and press the play button. The cassette recorder will do the rest. When recording, you simply push the record button. When the tape is finished, the machine will stop itself and eject the cassette *(Fig. 17.17)*. Some models even change up to twelve cassettes automatically.

A further advantage is that you can mail the cassette easily, just like a small package.

Whether to use the ½-inch or the ¾-inch tape format depends on the quality of the machine or your particular need. Generally, the video cassette machines use ¾-inch tape.

While most cassette recorders are designed for straight recording and playback of program material, some of the more sophisticated models have electronic editing and slow- and stop-motion facilities for postproduction work.

Some cassette recorders, which are completely portable and can be used like the portapak, can hold cassettes with a maximum of twenty minutes' running time.

17·16 A close cousin to the cassette recorder is the video player, which uses 8mm film instead of videotape for playback through a television monitor. In effect, the video player is a small 8mm film chain, all neatly packaged in an easy-to-operate cassette-like machine.

Most cassette recorders back themselves up about 12 seconds whenever you push the stop button during a playback. This way, when you resume the playback, the tape has time to stabilize electronically without any loss of program mate-

a   b

17·17   (a) Video Cassette Recorder. (b) Video Cassette (¾-inch).

rial. It is especially important for you to be aware of this automatic backup system if you do editing on the cassette recorder.

Playback Monitors

Unless you don't mind viewing your production achievements through the 1-inch viewfinder of your portapak camera, you will need a monitor for your playback.

A *monitor* is a television set that cannot receive broadcast programs but only direct video and audio from the videotape, or camera and microphone. Since the signals come directly from the recording and not as a radio frequency from the antenna (RF), the picture and sound are usually of higher quality than if they were received off-air. If you want to record off-air certain television programs, you should get a *monitor/receiver.* This instrument can act as a monitor (playing straight video and audio that has not been broadcast) or as a regular television set that can be tuned to a broadcast channel. The monitor/receiver usually

has a variety of inputs and outputs on the back panel, besides a switch to designate the monitor or receiver mode *(17.18).*

With an RF adapter (radio frequency adapter), you can play the signal from the small-format videotape recorder through an ordinary home television set. The output of the RF adapter is then connected to the VHF (very high frequency) antenna terminal of the set.

Lighting

Although the small-format camera performs remarkably well in all types of available lighting, you will not get professional pictures without sufficient baselight. Three small quartz instruments (with 600–1,000-watt lamps, focus adjustment mechanism, and barn doors), three lightweight collapsible stands, and an adequate AC extension cord will suffice for most additional lighting jobs. As pointed out in Chapters 5 and 6, backlighting the scene is one of the most important additional lighting effects.

a

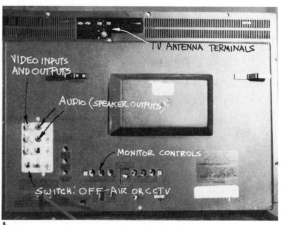

b

17·18   TV Monitor/Receiver.

Of all the wide array of available equipment, which one should you use? This is a question you should not answer until you know exactly what type of production you want to do.

Again, you should define the video functions, as mentioned in the beginning of this chapter, as carefully as possible. If you are going to use video mostly for *looking at,* such as observing children in a classroom, then you probably can get by with a simple camera mounted on a tripod, a simple cassette recorder, and a monitor. But if you are going to be mostly *looking into* or even *creating* events, then you will need more sophisticated equipment. If you do much in-the-field recording, you are probably better off with a portapak system than with a larger camera-recorder unit. But if you do video experimentation in your studio, then you may want some more flexible, or better quality, camera and recorder units.

Operation

The basic production techniques for small-format video are not much different from those em-

ployed for large studio-type equipment. Basic camera handling for proper visualization, the lighting principles, audio pickup techniques, picturization principles—are all the same. However, the portability of the equipment and its relative ease of operation might seduce you into using techniques that are not becoming either to the program or the equipment. We will, therefore, stress only those that are rather special to the small-format equipment. The area of concern is mostly in camera handling.

Here are some points you should keep in mind when operating a small-format camera:

1.   Before using the camera, make sure that you have enough cable for your action radius. If you use a portapak with battery power, check the battery and all the connections from videotape recorder to camera. Make sure that the switch on the recorder unit is on "camera" and not on "TV."

2.   Do a short test recording to see whether the whole system operates properly.

3.   When playing back the test recording, put the switch to "TV." Don't forget to return the switch to the "camera" position before the actual recording.

4. If you use the recorder unit on a backpack, it is more comfortable to carry around; but you can't operate it while running the camera. You will find that the unit is easier to handle when it is hanging from your shoulder than when it is tucked away behind your back. Preferably you will have a two-person team. One of you can then run the camera, the other the videotape deck and the audio.

5. Although the vidicon tube can tolerate a great amount of light, never point the camera directly into a light source, and *never,* really never, into the sun, or into popping flash units from still cameras. Your tube will simply burn out.

6. Since the mechanism that holds the camera pickup tube is rather delicate, *don't* point the camera *straight down.* You will damage the camera. If you need a straight-down shot, use a mirror.

7. As with the big cameras, it is a good idea to let the camera warm up a little before using it.

8. Once it is warm, treat the camera very gently. Lay it down gently; don't just drop it on the table or the floor. Get a firm grip on it when you start shooting. Remember that the tripod is still one of the most useful camera supports available.

9. Don't move the camera around widely without a reason. Let the objects in front do most of the moving. There is nothing more revealing of a novice operator than excessive camera movement. Some amateurs move the camera about as though they were using a firehose on a burning building.

10. If you walk with your camera, hold it tightly so that it becomes an extension of yourself. Walk smoothly. Have your zoom lens in the extreme wide-angle position, or use a wide-angle lens.

11. Unless your camera is supported on a tripod, try to avoid much zooming—in any case, zooming in to tight CU's. If you have to zoom, zoom out. That way, you will end up in a wide-angle lens position, which minimizes the camera wiggles.[5]

---

[5] For more information on the operation of small-format cameras, see Robinson, *The Video Primer.*

12. Keep looking through your viewfinder. Everything the camera sees is there.

13. Avoid shooting objects against the lights or a light window. The objects will inevitably turn into silhouettes.

14. Don't forget to check your videotape from time to time. Make a reel change *before* you run out of tape; this way you won't lose the material close to the end of the tape.

15. The closer the microphone is to the sound source, the better your sound will be. Most remote operations permit the microphone to be in the picture. If you have to keep it out of the picture, you need a good directional mike. Remember that the built-in mike on the portapak unit is for general background sounds only. It will not do a good job for specific sound pickups.

16. If you use a mixer, you can use several microphones. If the sound does not have to be synchronous with the action, you can record it separately and then dub it onto the videotape in postproduction.

17. Look at the lighting. When shooting indoors, you most likely need additional light. When shooting in color, see whether the lighting is excessively warm (way below 3,200 K) or cool (way above 3,200 K). If so, use the appropriate color temperature filter on your camera (if your camera happens to have such a device). Again, avoid shooting into the sun.

18. If you intend to edit the program in postproduction, get enough cutaways so that your work will be simplified later on.

19. Double-check the threading of the videotape. An improperly threaded tape can do great harm to the recorder as well as to the tape.

20. Keep all equipment clean, and please treat it gently. Because of the need to keep things small, a large amount of electronic components are wedged into a small space, making the small-format equipment quite a bit more vulnerable to shock than its large-format counterpart.

Finally, here are a few production hints. (1) Even if you don't intend to use the videotaped program on the air, get the proper releases from the people in your show, especially if it is a non-public event (someone at his home or in her office, for example). (2) Label your videotapes immediately after each recording. Indicate the machine on which the program was recorded, the subject and running time of the program, and the date of the recording. And (3) try to *say something* with each program you produce. There is enough visual pollution surrounding us as it is. If you want to communicate your experiences, clarify and intensify them so that they help us become more aware of ourselves and the world we live in than we would ordinarily be.

Summary

Video, in contrast to broadcast television, refers to the use of small-format equipment by individuals or small groups. Video is providing an alternative to the programming of broadcasting stations. Like any other form of television production, it can perform three principal *functions:* (1) to look at, (2) to look into, and (3) to create. *Looking at* means to observe an event as objectively as possible, the television equipment being used principally as a recording device. *Looking into* means to scrutinize an event from an extremely close point of view, the television equipment being used to intensify the event. *Creating* means to generate an event that exists nowhere in this particular form except on the television screen.

Small-format equipment includes (1) the small-format camera, (2) the portapak, (3) audio equipment, (4) small-format videotape recorders, (5) playback monitors, and (6) lighting.

Small-format *cameras* can be monochrome or color, and can be carried and operated easily by one person. The portapak consists of a small camera and a small-format videotape recorder, both of which one person can manage. The *audio* equipment ranges in size and sophistication from a microphone built into the camera to normal low-impedance microphones and mixers.

Small-format *videotape recorders* include (1) reel-to-reel machines, using tape ranging from ¼ inch to 1 inch in width, and (2) video cassettes (self-contained tape cassettes), most commonly using ¾-inch videotape. Many ½-inch videotape recorders, as well as many video cassettes, conform to the EIAJ (Electronic Industries Association of Japan) standard, which permits interchangeability of tapes that are recorded and played back on different machines.

The *monitors* used for playback are fed either directly by the camera or by the videotape recorder. An RF (radio frequency) signal can be reproduced by an ordinary television set. Most video operations use a monitor/receiver combination that can reproduce either direct video or an RF signal.

Most small-format equipment is built so that it can operate under normal lighting conditions. However, additional lighting will help to produce higher quality pictures.

In respect to the actual operation of this highly mobile equipment, as well as the aesthetic production principles, video production is not drastically different from that of normal television.

Additional Reading

The following list represents sources that, for the most part, are more specialized or more technical than the treatment in *Television Production Handbook*. Following each annotated listing, there is an indication (in parentheses) of the chapter, or chapters, in *Television Production Handbook* to which the given book is particularly applicable.

Banathy, Bela H. *Instructional Systems.* Belmont, Calif.: Fearon Publishers, 1968. Clear introduction to basic instructional systems. Useful as a guide for systems design in television production. (Chapter: 14)

Bay, Howard. *Stage Design.* New York: Drama Book Specialists, 1974. Good reference for all types of stage design. Useful for large-scale television productions. (Chapter: 12)

Bermingham, Alan, and others. *The Small TV Studio: Equipment and Facilities.* New York: Hastings House, 1975. As stated in the title, the book deals with basic small television studio equipment and production facilities. Useful reference. (Chapters: 2, 6, 8, 17)

Bliss, Edward, Jr., and John M. Peterson. *Writing News for Broadcast.* New York: Columbia University Press, 1971. Points up the special writing requirements of broadcast news. Gives good examples. (Chapters: 15, 16)

Blumenberg, Richard M. *Critical Focus: An Introduction to Film.* Belmont, Calif.: Wadsworth Publishing Co., 1975. A comprehensive coverage of grammar, history, theory, and criticism of narrative, documentary, and experimental film. Also includes a brief section on filmmaking activities. (Chapter: 9)

Bobker, Lee R. *Making Movies: From Script to Screen.* New York: Harcourt Brace Jovanovich, 1973. A good, solid text on how a motion picture evolves, from idea to screen experience. Many parts are equally valid for television production. (Chapters: 9, 10, 14, 15)

Burder, John. *16mm Film Cutting.* New York: Hastings House, 1976. A useful, though rather basic, how-to-do approach to film cutting. (Chapter: 10)

Burder, John. *The Technique of Editing 16mm Films,* rev. ed. New York: Hastings House, 1971. A rather comprehensive text on 16mm film editing and cutting. (Chapter: 10)

Burroughs, Lou. *Microphones: Design and Application.* Plainview, N.Y.: Sagamore Publishing Co., 1973. A good, though rather technical treatment of how the different types of microphones function, and how they can be optimally used. (Chapter: 7)

Chester, Giraud, Garnet R. Garrison, and Edgar E. Willis. *Television and Radio,* 4th ed. New York: Appleton-Century-Crofts, 1971. Presents a good overview of television production, usually from a network point-of-view. (Chapters: 1, 2, 8, 12, 14, 15)

Churchill, Hugh B. *Film Editing Handbook: Technique of 16mm Film Editing.* Belmont, Calif.: Wadsworth Publishing Co., 1972. A very practical, concise text on how to make editing decisions and how to go about cutting 16 mm film. Especially suited to editing 16mm news footage. (Chapter: 10)

Costa, Sylvia Allen. *How to Prepare a Production Budget for Film and Video Tape.* Blue Ridge Summit, Pa.: Tab Books, 1973. A useful guide for producers who have to prepare budgets. (Chapter: 14)

Davis, Desmond. *The Grammar of Television Production.* London: Barrie and Rockliff, 1960. Although quite old, this little book contains a wealth of valid information on how to stage a variety of events for the television screen. (Chapters: 4, 15)

Dean, Alexander, and Lawrence Carra. *Fundamentals of Play Directing,* 3rd ed. New York: Holt, Rinehart and Winston, 1974. An extremely useful guide on play directing for the stage. Many of the principles also apply to the television screen. (Chapter: 15)

Editors of *BM/E Magazine. Interpreting FCC Broadcast Rules and Regulations,* Vols. 1–3. Blue Ridge Summit, Pa.: Tab Books, 1968–1972. Extremely useful summaries of the most important FCC rulings, with hints on how these rulings apply in actual station operation. (Chapters: 14, 15)

Editors of Time-Life Books. *The Camera.* New York: Time-Life Books [Life Library of Photography], 1970. Excellent discussion on the basic principles of the camera and photography in general. Must reading for anyone engaged in television production. (Chapters: 2, 3, 15)

Fang, Irving W. *Television News,* 2nd ed. New York: Hastings House, 1972. A comprehensive treatment of most aspects of modern electronic journalism. Many illustrations and examples. (Chapters: 10, 14, 15, 16)

Fell, John. *Film: An Introduction.* New York: Praeger Publishers, 1975. Treatment of basic points of understanding motion pictures, such as film elements, how films are made, film theory, and film criticism. (Chapter: 9)

Green, Maury. *Television News: Anatomy and Process.* Belmont, Calif.: Wadsworth Publishing Co., 1969. Although some of the information is now out of date, the basic principles for covering news on television are still very valuable and still very much in use. (Chapters 10, 14, 15, 16)

Grey, David L. *The Writing Process.* Belmont, Calif.: Wadsworth Publishing Co., 1972. A brief book on how to approach writing and, hopefully, how to become a better writer. The book stresses process, not too dissimilar from that of television production. (Chapters: 14, 15)

Head, Sydney W. *Broadcasting in America,* 3rd ed. Boston: Houghton Mifflin Co., 1976. An excellent survey of all major aspects of American television and radio operations. Covers the basic technical, programming, and legal aspects of broadcasting. (Chapters: 1, 14)

Heighton, Elizabeth J., and Don R. Cunningham. *Advertising in the Broadcast Media.* Belmont, Calif.: Wadsworth Publishing Co., 1976. Comprehensive coverage of theoretical, practical, and social aspects of broadcast advertising. (Chapters: 12, 13, 14, 15)

Hilliard, Robert L. *Writing for Television and Radio,* 3rd ed. New York: Hastings House, 1976. A helpful guide to television writing. Many script samples and hints on writing precise broadcast language. (Chapters: 14, 15)

Hurrell, Ron. *Van Nostrand Reinhold Manual of Television Graphics.* New York: Van Nostrand Reinhold, 1974. One of the few useful books on television graphics. (Chapter: 12)

Hyde, Stuart W. *Television and Radio Announcing,* 2nd ed. Boston: Houghton Mifflin Co., 1971. An excellent, comprehensive book on television announcing and performing. Stresses correct pronunciation and the notation of foreign language pronunciation. Many useful exercises. (Chapters: 7, 13, 15)

Jones, Gary William. *Electronic Film/Tape Post-Production Handbook.* Edmonton, Alberta, Canada: Jones Family Reunion, 1974. An excellent little booklet, containing all major aspects of videotape editing, such as computer-assisted on- and off-line systems. Contains useful addresses of major postproduction companies in the United States. (Chapters: 9, 10)

Jones, Peter. *The Technique of the Television Cameraman,* rev. ed. London: Focal Press, 1968. A somewhat outdated book on basic camera operation, but still useful in some respects. (Chapters: 2, 3, 4, 15)

Kehoe, Vincent J.-R. *The Technique of Film and Television Make-Up,* rev. ed. New York: Hastings House, 1969. Fairly thorough treatment of film and television makeup materials and procedures. Deals with corrective and character makeup for film and television. Many diagrams, several in color. (Chapter: 13)

Klein, Maxine. *Time, Space, and Designs for Actors.* Boston: Houghton Mifflin Co., 1975. Some of the newer concepts of acting put together in a stimulating book. Deals with such aspects as the body commanding space, the body acting centers, and transformation to character. Especially valuable to the television actor whose job it is to live the character rather than to act it out. (Chapters: 13, 15)

Levitan, Eli L. *An Alphabetical Guide to Motion Picture, Television and Videotape Production.* New York: McGraw-Hill Book Co., 1970. A very useful dictionary with clear explanations of the major production equipment and procedures. Motion picture oriented. Many useful diagrams. (Chapters: 2, 3, 4, 5, 6, 7, 9, 11, 12)

Lewis, Colby. *The TV Director/Interpreter.* New York: Hastings House, 1968. Though slightly out-of-date, most of the basic principles discussed are still valid in modern television production. Many useful diagrams. (Chapter: 15)

Mager, Robert F. *Preparing Instructional Objectives*. Belmont, Calif.: Fearon Publishers, 1962. Although this little book deals with educational principles, the process of preparing instructional objectives is very useful to the television producer who would like to reach the television audience with optimal effectiveness. (Chapter: 14)

Marsh, Ken. *Independent Video*. San Francisco: Straight Arrow Books, 1974. A useful guide to how the major small-format television equipment operates. Though fairly technical, the explanations are usually simple. Many diagrams. (Chapters: 2, 3, 10, 11, 17)

Mascelli, Joseph V. *The Five C's of Cinematography*. Hollywood: Cine/Grafic Publications, 1965. A richly illustrated book, in which the five "C's" of cinematography are discussed: camera angles, continuity, cutting, closeups, and composition. Many principles are adaptable for television. (Chapters: 12, 15)

Mattingly, Grayson, and Welby Smith. *Introducing the Single-Camera VTR System*. New York: Charles Scribner's Sons, 1973. A rather simple, yet useful introductory text to small-format television operation. Does not include small-format color. (Chapter: 17)

Millerson, Gerald. *Basic TV Staging*. New York: Hastings House, 1974. A simplified text, including some of the principles of television staging, as elaborated upon in Millerson's *Technique of Television Production*. (Chapter: 12)

Millerson, Gerald. *The Technique of Lighting for Television and Motion Pictures*. New York: Hastings House, 1974. A comprehensive treatment of film and television lighting. Many diagrams and photographs. (Chapters: 5, 6)

Millerson, Gerald. *The Technique of Television Production*, 9th ed. New York: Hastings House, 1972. A comprehensive treatment of all aspects of television production. The discussion of equipment and some of the production techniques is somewhat outdated. (Chapters: 2, 3, 4, 5, 6, 7, 10, 11, 12)

Millerson, Gerald. *TV Camera Operation*. New York: Hastings House, 1974. A small, simple, yet useful guide to the beginner of television production. Contains many diagrams. (Chapters: 2, 3, 4)

Millerson, Gerald. *TV Lighting Methods*. New York: Hastings House, 1975. A simple version of Millerson's TV and film lighting book for the beginner. Contains many diagrams. (Chapter: 6)

Nisbett, Alec. *The Technique of the Sound Studio*, 3rd ed. New York: Hastings House, 1972. A comprehensive treatment of equipment and basic operations of the sound studio. Many diagrams. (Chapter: 7)

Nisbett, Alec. *The Use of Microphones*. New York: Hastings House, 1974. A very useful guide to the various types of microphones and how they are best used in the recording and television studios. Many diagrams. (Chapter: 7)

Quaal, Ward L., and James A. Brown. *Broadcast Management*, 2nd. ed. New York: Hastings House, 1976. Discusses the major aspects of managing a station. Especially useful to the producer who would like to learn the management's point of view. (Chapters: 14, 15)

Robinson, Richard. *The Video Primer*. New York: Links Books, 1974. An excellent, comprehensive discussion of small-format television equipment and its operation. Also includes basic production concepts. Many useful diagrams and a useful glossary. (Chapters: 2, 3, 7, 9, 17)

Rondthaler, Edward, and Photo-Lettering Inc. staff (eds.). *Alphabet Thesaurus: A Treasury of Letter Design*. New York: Reinhold Publishing Corp., 1971. Comprehensive collection of letters and styles of printing from every culture for every use. Good illustrations. (Chapter: 12)

Spottiswood, Raymond (ed.). *The Focal Encyclopedia of Film and Television: Techniques*. New York: Hastings House, 1968. Defines and describes major equipment and production techniques in dictionary form. Many diagrams. (Chapters: 2, 3, 5, 6, 7, 9, 10, 11)

Stanislavski, Constantin. *An Actor Prepares*. New York: Theatre Arts Books, 1956. A classic on acting. Many principles are especially useful to the television actor. (Chapters: 13, 15)

Toohey, Daniel W., Richard D. Marks, and Arnold P. Lutzker. *Legal Problems in Broadcasting*. Lincoln, Neb.: Great Plains Instructional Television Library, 1974. Contains major aspects of legal problems in television broadcasting. (Chapters: 14, 15)

Trapnell, Coles. *An Introduction to Television Writing*, rev. ed. New York: Hawthorn Books, 1974. A useful book with many good hints on writing for television. Most of the examples are limited to the writing for television film. (Chapters: 14, 15)

Videofreex. *The Spaghetti City Video Manual.* New York: Praeger Publishers, 1973. Despite the far-out title, the book contains conventional, useful information on small-format television equipment and operation techniques. (Chapter: 17)

Zakia, Richard D., and Hollis N. Todd. *Color Primer I and II.* New York: Morgan & Morgan, 1974. A basic color theory book, arranged for programmed learning. Good introductory material. Color plates and diagrams. (Chapters: 6, 12)

Zettl, Herbert. *Sight-Sound-Motion: Applied Media Aesthetics.* Belmont, Calif.: Wadsworth Publishing Co., 1973. A comprehensive treatment of the basic image elements of television and film: light, space, time-motion, and sound, and their use in television and film production. Many diagrams and photos. (Chapters: 6, 7, 10, 12, 15)

For the latest information on television equipment, you should consult the current catalogs of the equipment manufacturers.

Generally, the following magazines and journals carry useful and fairly up-to-date information on all aspects of television equipment and occasionally on specific production problems:

American Cinematographer

BM/E Magazine

Broadcasting

Broadcast Engineering

db

Educational Broadcasting

Educational and Industrial Television

Journal of Broadcasting

Journal of the Society of Motion Picture and Television Engineers (often called the SMPTE Journal)

Public Telecommunications Review (PTR)

VideoPlayer

Glossary

A-B Rolling 1. Preparation of a film for printing. All odd-numbered shots are put on one reel (A-roll), with black leader replacing the even shots. The even-numbered shots, with black leader replacing the odd shots, make up the B-roll. Both rolls are then printed together onto one film, thus eliminating splices. 2. Electronic A-B rolling means that on one film chain an SOF film is projected, while on the second film chain a silent film is projected. The films can be intermixed (A-B rolled) through the television switcher.

Above-the-Line A budgetary division of production elements. It concerns mainly nontechnical personnel.

AC Alternating Current; electrical energy as supplied by normal wall outlets.

Academy Leader Also called the SMPTE Universal Leader. A piece of film marked with numbers ranging from 8 to 3, each one second apart. It is attached to the head of a film for the purposes of cuing up and aligning the film.

Acetate 1. Cellulose acetate, usually called cell: a transparent plastic sheet used in preparation of graphic material. 2. Film base.

Acoustic Treatment Application of sound-deadening material to the walls of a television (or sound) studio to create an environment for optimal sound pickup (usually by rendering the studio less "live").

Actor or Actress A person who appears on camera in dramatic roles. The actor or actress always portrays someone else.

A.D. Assistant or Associate Director.

Additive Primary Colors Red, blue, and green. Ordinary white light (sunlight) can be separated into the three primary light colors, red, green, and blue. When these three colored lights are combined in various proportions, all other colors can be reproduced.

Address Also called birthmark. A specific spot in a television recording, as specified by the time code.

Ad Lib Speech or action that has not been scripted or specially rehearsed.

AFTRA American Federation of Radio and Television Artists. A broadcasting talent union.

AGC Automatic Gain Control. Regulates the volume of the audio or video automatically, without the use of pots.

Alpha Wrap An indication of how the videotape is wound around the head drum of a helical scan VTR. In this case, the tape is wound completely around the head in an alphalike configuration.

Animation Process of filming a number of slightly different cartoon drawings to create the illusion of movement.

Ann. or Anncr Abbreviation for Announcer.

Aperture Diaphragm opening of a lens; usually measured in *f*-stops.

Arc To move the camera in a slightly curved dolly or truck.

Aspect Ratio The proportions of the television screen, and therefore of all television pictures: three units high and four units wide.

Assemble Mode The adding of shots on videotape in a consecutive order.

Audio The sound portion of television and its production. Technically, the electronic reproduction of audible sound.

Audio-Follows-Video   A switcher that automatically changes the accompanying audio along with the video source.

Audio Track   The area of the videotape that is used for recording audio information.

Audition   Testing of a talent's abilities; the talent usually performs in front of a television camera, and the performance is judged by station and agency personnel.

Back Focus   The distance between zoom lens and camera pickup tube at which the picture is in focus at the extreme wide-angle zoom position. In monochrome cameras, the back focus can be adjusted by moving the pickup tube through the camera focus control.

Background Light   Also called set light. Illumination of the set and set pieces such as backdrops.

Back Light   Illumination from behind the subject and opposite the camera.

Back-Timing   The process of figuring additional clock times by subtracting running times from the clock time at which the program ends. Back-timing helps the director and talent to pace the show properly and finish it at the scheduled time.

Balance   1. Video: relative structural stability of picture elements (objects or events). Balance can be stable (little pictorial tension), neutral (some tension), or unstable (high pictorial tension). Refers to the interrelationship between stability and tension in a picture. 2. Audio: a proper mixing of various sounds.

Barn Doors   Metal flaps in front of lighting instruments that control the spread of the light beam.

Base   1. See Baselight. 2. Film base: the material of which motion picture film is made; the light-sensitive emulsion is then superimposed onto it.

Baselight   Even, nondirectional (diffused) level of studio lighting. Customary baselight levels: for standard three-tube Plumbicon color cameras, 200 ft-c (footcandles)–400 ft-c; for image-orthicon monochrome cameras, 75 ft-c–100 ft-c; for portable monochrome vidicon cameras, 100 ft-c–300 ft-c, with 200 ft-c–250 ft-c the norm.

Beeper   A series of eight low-frequency audio beeps, exactly one second apart, put at the beginning of each take for videotape cuing.

Below-the-Line   A budgetary division of production elements. It concerns technical personnel and facilities.

B.G.   Background; an audio term. "Music to B.G." means to fade the music and hold under as a background effect.

Bias Lighting   An electronic boosting of low light levels that enter the camera so that the pickup tubes can operate relatively noise-free.

Black   Darkest part of the grayscale, with a reflectance of approximately 3 percent; called TV black. "To black" means to fade the television picture to black.

Blast Filter   A bulblike attachment (either permanent or detachable) to the front of the microphone that filters out sudden air blasts, such as plosive consonants (*p*'s, *t*'s, *k*'s) delivered directly into the mike. Also called pop filter.

Blocking   Carefully worked out movement and actions by the talent, and movement of all mobile television equipment.

Blocking Rehearsal   See Dry Run.

Book   1. TV scenery term: a twofold flat. 2. To decrease the angle of an open twofold.

Boom Up or Down   Raising or lowering the microphone boom or camera boom.

Brightness   Attribute of color that indicates the grayscale value, whether the color photographs in black-and-white as a light gray or a dark gray. Sometimes called value.

Broad   A floodlight with a broadside, panlike reflector.

Burn-in   Image retention by the camera pickup tube. If the camera is focused too long on an object with strong contrast, the picture tube may retain a negative image of the contrasting scene, although another object is being photographed. Occurs especially in I-O (image-orthicon) tubes, or occasionally in vidicons, that have been in use for a relatively long time. Also called sticking.

Bus, or Buss   1. Video: a row of buttons on the switcher. Sometimes called bank. 2. Audio: a common central circuit that receives from several sources or feeds to several separate destinations; a "mix bus" collects the output signals from several mixing controls (pots) and feeds them into one master volume control.

Bust Shot   Framing of a person from the upper torso to the top of the head.

Busy Picture   The picture, as it appears on the television screen, is too cluttered.

Cameo Lighting Foreground figures are lighted with highly directional light, with the background remaining dark.

Camera The general name for the camera head, which consists of the lens (or lenses), the main camera with the pickup tube or tubes and the internal optical system, electronic accessories, and the viewfinder.

Camera Chain The television camera (head) and associated electronic equipment, consisting of the CCU (the camera control unit), the power supply, the sync generator, and the encoder (for color cameras only).

Camera Control Unit Equipment, separate from the camera head, that contains various video controls, including color balance and contrast and brightness. It is operated by the video engineer before camera operation (camera setup) and during camera operation (camera shading).

Camera Head The actual television camera, which is at the head of a chain of essential electronic accessories. In small-format cameras, the camera head may contain all the elements of a camera chain.

Camera Left and Right Directions given from the camera's point of view; opposite of "stage left" and "stage right," which are directions given from the actor's point of view (facing the audience or camera).

Camera Light Small spotlight, called inky-dinky, mounted on the front of the camera; used as additional fill light. (Frequently confused with Tally Light.)

Camera Rehearsal A full rehearsal with cameras and other pieces of production equipment. Similar to the dress rehearsal in theater.

Cam Head A special camera mounting head that permits extremely smooth tilts and pans.

Canon 35 Deals with the question of allowing television equipment in a courtroom.

Cans Earphones.

Cap 1. Lens cap; a rubber or metal cap placed in front of the lens to protect it from light or dust. 2. Electronic device that eliminates the picture from the camera pickup tube.

Cardioid The heart-shaped (cardioid) pickup pattern of a unidirectional microphone.

Cart See Cartridge.

Cartridge Also called "cart" for short. A video- or audiotape recording or playback device that uses tape cartridges. A cartridge is a plastic case containing an endless tape loop that rewinds as it is played back, and cues itself automatically.

Cassette A video- or audiotape recording or playback device that uses tape cassettes. A cassette is a plastic case containing two reels, a supply reel and a takeup reel. Many cassettes cue and rewind themselves automatically.

Cathode Ray Tube Also called CRT. The main picture tube of a television receiver, or a computer display tube.

CATV Community Antenna Television; also called cable television. A system in which home receivers get their signal from a coaxial cable connected to a master antenna. The CATV companies charge a monthly fee for this service.

C-Clamp A metal clamp with which lighting instruments are attached to the lighting battens.

CCU See Camera Control Unit.

Cell See Acetate.

Character The person who appears in a play. Usually defined by clarifying and intensifying specific physiological traits (the way the person looks, moves, runs, behaves, dresses) and psychological traits (the way the person thinks, feels, plots, schemes, loves).

Character Generator A special effects generator that electronically produces a series of letters and numbers directly on the television screen, or keyed into a background picture.

Cheat To angle the performer or object toward a particular camera; not directly noticeable to the audience.

Chroma Key A color matte; the color blue is generally used for the chroma key area that is to become transparent for the matte.

Chroma Key Drop A well-saturated blue canvas drop that can be pulled down from the lighting grid to the studio floor, or even over part of it, as a background for chroma key matting.

Chrominance Channel The color (chroma) channels within the color camera. A separate chrominance channel is responsible for each primary color signal—that is, one for the red, one for the blue, and one for the green.

Chrominance Signal The color information in a video signal (containing hue and saturation, but not brightness).

Client Person or agency advertising on television.

Climax The high point in the plot, usually expressed as the major conflict—as distinguished from a crisis, which is relatively less intense.

Clip 1. Short piece of film or tape, generally used as a brief program insert. 2. To cut off abruptly the audio portion of a program. 3. To compress the white and/or black picture information, or prevent the video signal from interfering with the sync signals.

Clipper A knob on the switcher that selects the whitest portion of the video source, clipping out the darker shades. The clipper produces high-contrasting blacks and whites for keying or matting.

Clock Time Also called schedule time. The time at which a program starts or ends.

Closed-Circuit Distribution of audio and video signals other than broadcasting. Includes direct video and audio feeds from the camera and the audio board, from the videotape recorder into a monitor, or the RF (radio frequency) distribution via cable.

Closeup Object or any part of it seen at close range and framed tightly. The closeup can be extreme (extreme or big closeup) or rather loose (medium closeup).

Closure Short for psychological closure. Mentally filling in spaces of an incomplete picture.

Clothing Regular clothes worn on camera, in contrast to a costume.

Color 1. Atmosphere; "color shots" are intended to acquaint the television audience with the atmosphere of the happening. 2. Color television.

Color Bars A color standard used by the television industry for the alignment of cameras and videotape recordings.

Colorizing The creation of color patterns or color areas through a color generator (without a color camera).

Color Temperature Relative reddishness or bluishness of light, as measured in degrees of Kelvin; television lighting instruments have a range of 3,000° K–3,400° K, with 3,200° K the norm. Color temperature can be measured with a color-temperature meter.

Comet-Tailing See Image Retention.

Compatible Color Color signals that can be received as black-and-white pictures on monochrome television sets. Generally used to mean that the color scheme has enough brightness contrast for monochrome reproduction with a good grayscale contrast.

Complexity Editing The juxtaposition of shots that primarily, though not exclusively, help to intensify the screen event.

Composite Signal Complete video signal with the sync pulse.

Condenser Microphone A microphone whose diaphragm consists of a condenser plate that vibrates with the sound pressure against another condenser plate, called the backplate.

Continuity 1. Even, logical succession of events. 2. All material presented between shows. 3. Continuity department, in charge of commercial acceptance and continuity writing.

Continuity Editing The preserving of visual continuity from shot to shot.

Contrast Contrast between black and white; especially important for colors used on television, which may have strong color distinctions but little brightness contrast. See Contrast Ratio.

Contrast Ratio The difference between the brightest spot and the darkest spot in a scene (often measured by reflected light in foot-candles), expressed in a ratio, such as 20:1.

Control Room A room adjacent to the studio in which the director, the T.D. (technical director), the audio engineer, and sometimes the lighting technician perform their various production functions.

Control Track The area of the videotape that is used for recording the synchronization information (sync spikes), which is essential for videotape editing.

Cookie See Cucalorus.

Copy All material to be read on the air.

Costume Special clothes worn by an actor or actress to depict a certain character or period; in contrast to clothing, the regular clothes worn by a performer.

Cover Shot Wide-angle shot giving basic orientation of place and action; covers a great area.

Crab Sideways motion of the camera crane dolly base.

Cradle Head Cradle-shaped camera mounting head. Permits smooth up-and-down tilts and horizontal pans.

Crane 1. Camera dolly that resembles an actual crane in both appearance and operation. The crane can lift the camera from close to the studio floor to over ten feet above it. 2. To move the boom of the camera crane up or down. Also called boom.

Crawl Graphics (usually credit copy) that move slowly up the screen; often mounted on a drum, or crawl. More exactly, an up-and-down movement of credits is called a roll, and a horizontal movement a crawl. Both the roll and the crawl can be produced by the character generator.

Credits List of names of persons who participated in the creation and performance of a telecast; usually at end of program.

Cross-fade 1. Audio: a transition method whereby the preceding sound is faded out and the following sound faded in simultaneously. The sounds overlap temporarily. 2. Video: a transition method whereby the preceding picture is faded to black and the following picture is faded in from black.

CRT See Cathode Ray Tube.

Cucalorus Also called cookie, sometimes kookie. Shadow pattern projected on a scenic background by means of a special cutout placed in front of a strong spotlight.

Cue Signal to start, pace, or stop any type of production activity or talent action.

Cue Card Also called idiot sheet. A hand-lettered card that contains copy, usually held next to the camera lens by floor personnel.

Cue Track The area of the videotape that is used for such audio information as in-house identification or the SMPTE address code. Can also be used for a second audio track.

Cursor A dot produced on the screen by a special effects generator (usually a character generator), indicating the location of the first word or line.

Cut 1. The instantaneous change from one shot (image) to another. 2. Director's signal to interrupt action (used during rehearsal).

Cutaway Shot A shot of an object or event that is peripherally connected with the overall event and that is neutral as to screen direction (usually straight-on shots). Used to intercut between two shots in which the screen direction is reversed.

Cut Bar A button or small metal bar that activates the mix buses alternately. The effect is cutting between the two mix buses.

Cut-in Insert from another program source, such as network cut-in during a local show.

Cyc Cyclorama; a U-shaped continuous piece of canvas for backing of scenery and action.

DC Direct Current.

Dead Equipment not turned on or not functioning, such as a "dead mike" or a "dead camera."

Debeaming The gradual reduction of the scanning beam intensity. The picture becomes a high-contrast picture, with the detail in the white and black areas no longer visible, gradually deteriorating into a nondistinct, light-gray screen.

Deck 1. Videotape deck: short form of videotape recorder. 2. Audio recorder deck: usually the recording and playback device without the amplifier. 3. Videotape editing deck: a videotape recorder with editing facilities, used in conjunction with a second videotape recorder that supplies the program material.

Definition Degree of detail in television picture reproduction.

Demographic Data Audience research data that are concerned with such items as age, sex, marital status, and income.

Density 1. The number of events happening within a certain time unit. Visual density can be expressed as a multiple superimposition or key, or successively as a series of quick, montage-like cuts. Audio density may be a chord consisting of many notes, or a rapid series of many notes, or the simultaneous playing of several audio tracks. 2. The degree of complexity in the vertical (depth) development of an event.

Depth of Field The area in which all objects, located at different distances from the camera, appear in focus. Depth of field is dependent upon focal length of the lens, *f*-stop, and distance between object and camera.

Depth Staging Arrangement of objects on the television screen so that foreground, middleground, and background are clearly defined.

Diaphragm 1. Adjustable lens-opening mechanism that controls the amount of light passing through a lens. 2. The vibrating element inside a microphone that moves with the air pressure from the sound.

Dichroic Mirror   A mirrorlike color filter that singles out, of the white light, the red light (red dichroic filter) and the blue light (blue dichroic filter), with the green light left over.

Diffused Light   Light that illuminates a relatively large area with an indistinct light beam. Diffused light, created by floodlights, produces soft shadows.

Dimmer   A device that controls the intensity of the light by throttling the electric current flowing to the lamp.

Directional Light   Light that illuminates a relatively small area with a distinct light beam. Directional light, produced by spotlights, creates harsh, clearly defined shadows.

Dish   Parabolic reflector for microwave transmission; sometimes called dishpan.

Dissolve   A gradual transition from shot to shot, whereby the two images temporarily overlap. Also called lap-dissolve, or lap.

Distortion   1. Optical: near objects look large, far objects look comparatively small; achieved with wide-angle lenses. 2. Electronic: exaggeration of either height or width of the television picture. 3. Audio: unnatural alteration or deterioration of sound.

Dolly   1. Camera support that enables the camera to move in all directions. 2. To move the camera toward (dolly in) or away from (dolly out or back) the object.

Double Headset   A telephone headset (earphones) that carries program sound in one earphone and the P.L. information in the other. Also called split-intercom.

Double Re-entry   A complex switcher through which an effect can be fed back into the mix bus section, or the mix output into the effects section, for further effects manipulation.

Double-System   The simultaneous recording of pictures and sound on two separate recording devices: the pictures on film, and the sound on audiotape recorder, synchronized with the film camera.

Dress   1. What people wear on camera. 2. Dress rehearsal: final camera rehearsal. 3. Set dressing: set properties.

Drop   Large, painted piece of canvas used for scenery backing.

Dropout   Loss of part of the video signal, which shows up on the screen as white glitches. Caused by uneven videotape iron-oxide coating (bad tape quality or overuse) or dirt.

Dropout Compensator   An electronic device that detects dropout (partial loss of the video signal) and substitutes the missing information with the information from the preceding scanning line. Usually part of the more sophisticated videotape recorders.

Dry Run   A rehearsal without equipment during which the basic actions of the talent are worked out. Also called blocking rehearsal.

Dual Redundancy   The use of two identical microphones for the pickup of a sound source, whereby only one of them is turned on at any given time. A safety device that permits switching over to the second microphone in case the active one becomes defective.

Dub   The duplication of an electronic recording. Dubs can be made from tape to tape, or from record to tape. The dub is always one generation down (away) from the recording used for the dubbing, and is therefore of lower quality.

Dubbing Down   The dubbing (transfer) of picture and sound information from a larger videotape format to a smaller one.

Dubbing Up   The dubbing (transfer) of picture and sound information from a smaller videotape format to a larger one.

Dynamic Microphone   Microphone whose sound-pickup device consists of a diaphragm attached to a movable coil. As the diaphragm vibrates with the air pressure from the sound, the coil moves within a magnetic field, generating an electric current. The dynamic mike is sensitive but rugged, and therefore widely used in television operations.

Ecological Data   Audience research data that are concerned with where the members of the audience live, such as city, suburb, country, and so forth.

ECU   Extreme Close-Up. Same as XCU.

Edge Key   A keyed (electronically cut-in) title whose letters have distinctive edges, such as dark outlines or a drop shadow.

Editing   The selection and assembly of shots within the picturization concept.

Effects Bus   Rows of buttons that can generate a number of electronic effects, such as keys, wipes, and mattes.

Effect-to-Cause Approach A production approach, or a system, that starts with the definition of viewer experience and works backwards to the production elements the medium requires in order to produce the defined viewer experience (medium requirements).

EIAJ Abbreviation for Electronic Industries Association of Japan. Established the EIAJ Type No. 1 Standard for ½-inch helical scan videotape recorders. In general, the standard assures that any monochrome tape recorded on one such recorder can be played back on any other monochrome or color recorder, and any color tape can be played back on any other color VTR, provided that they meet the EIAJ Type 1 Standard.

Electron Gun Produces the electron (scanning) beam.

Electronic A-B Rolling 1. The editing of a master tape from two playback machines, one containing the A-roll and the other the B-roll. By routing the A and B playback machines through a switcher, a variety of transition effects can be achieved for the final master tape. 2. The projection of an SOF film on one film chain (A-roll), with the silent film projected from the other island (B-roll). The films can be mixed through the switcher.

Electronic Editing The joining of two shots on videotape without cutting the tape.

Electronic Film Transfer Kinescoping of a program from videotape to film by filming the images that appear on a very sharp television monitor.

Ellipsoidal Spotlight Spotlight producing a very defined beam, which can be shaped further by metal shutters.

Emulsion Light-sensitive layer put on the motion picture film base.

Equalization 1. Video: controlling the video signal by emphasizing certain frequencies and eliminating others. 2. Audio: controlling the audio signal by emphasizing certain frequencies and eliminating others. Equalization can be accomplished through an equalizer manually or automatically.

Essential Area The section of the television picture, centered within the scanning area, that is seen by the home viewer, regardless of masking of the set or slight misalignment of the receiver. Sometimes called critical area.

Establishing Shot Orientation shot, usually a long shot.

E.T. Electrical Transcriptions; a somewhat outdated designation for large phonograph records.

External Key A key signal that shapes the cut-in figure (into the background image). It is generated by a camera exclusively used for keying and fed into an external key input.

External Optical System The zoom lens, or the various lenses on a lens turret.

Fact Sheet Also called rundown sheet. Lists the items to be shown on camera and the key ideas that should be expressed verbally by the performer. Serves often as a guide to show format.

Fade 1. Video: the gradual appearance of a picture from black (fade-in) or disappearance to black (fade-out). 2. Audio: the gradual decrease of sound volume.

Fader A sound-volume control that works by means of a button sliding vertically or horizontally along a specific scale. Similar to pot.

Fader Bars Two levers on the switcher that can produce dissolves, fades, and wipes of different speeds, and superimpositions.

Fairness Doctrine Deals with the right of responsible spokesmen to reply to certain issues previously broadcast.

Falloff The "speed" (degree) with which a light picture portion turns into its shadow areas. Fast falloff means that the light areas turn abruptly into shadow areas. Slow falloff indicates a very gradual change from light to dark, or little contrast between light and shadow areas.

Fast Lens A lens that permits a relatively great amount of light to pass through (low *f*-stop number). Can be used in low lighting conditions.

Feed Signal transmission from one program source to another, such as a network feed or a remote feed.

Feedback 1. Video: wild streaks and flashes on the monitor screen caused by re-entry of a video signal into the switcher and subsequent overamplification. 2. Audio: piercing squeal from the loudspeaker, caused by the accidental re-entry of the loudspeaker sound into the microphone and subsequent overamplification of sound. 3. Communication: Reaction of the receiver of a communication back to the communication source.

Field One-half a complete scanning cycle, two fields being necessary for one television picture frame. There are 60 fields per second, or 30 frames per second.

Field of View   The extent of a scene that is visible through a particular lens; its vista.

Fill   Additional program material in case a show runs short.

Fill Light   Additional light, usually opposite the key light, to illuminate shadow areas and thereby reduce falloff. Usually accomplished by floodlights.

Film Base   The shiny side of the film.

Film Chain   Also called film island, or telecine. Consists of one or two film projectors, a slide projector, a multiplexer, and a television film, or telecine, camera.

Film Clip   Short piece of film used as a brief program insert.

Film Emulsion   The dull size of the film.

Film Loop   Piece of film with its ends spliced together; this loop runs through the projector continuously and can be used for special effects or for dubbing.

Film Splicer   The piece of equipment with which two lengths of film can be joined.

Fishpole   A suspension device for a microphone; the microphone is attached to a pole and held over the scene for brief periods.

Flare   Dark, or colored, flashes caused by signal overload through extreme light reflections off polished objects or very bright lights.

Flat   1. A piece of standing scenery used as background or to simulate the walls of a room. 2. Even, not contrasting; usually refers to lighting; flat lighting is highly diffused lighting with soft shadows.

Floodlight   Lighting instrument that produces diffused light.

Floor Plan   1. A plan of the studio floor, showing the walls, the main doors, and the location of the control room, with the lighting grid or batten pattern superimposed over the floor area. 2. A diagram of scenery and properties in relation to the studio floor area.

Fluorescent Light   Cold light produced by large, gas-filled glass tubes.

FM Microphone   A wireless microphone that contains not only the sound pickup and generating elements but also a tiny FM transmitter.

Focal Length   The distance from the optical center of the lens to the front surface of the camera pickup tube with the lens set at infinity. Focal lengths are measured in millimeters or inches. Short-focal-length lenses have a wide angle of view (wide vista); long-focal-length (telephoto) lenses have a narrow angle of view (close-up). In a variable-focal-length lens (zoom lens) the focal length can be changed continuously from wide angle to narrow angle or vice versa. A fixed-focal-length lens has a single designated focal length only.

Focus   A picture is in focus when it appears sharp and clear on the screen (technically, the point where the light rays refracted by the lens converge).

Follow Focus   Controlling the focus of the lens so that the image of an object is continuously kept sharp and clear, regardless of whether camera and/or object move.

Footage   Length or portion of a film; sometimes used qualitatively: good footage, bad footage.

Foot-Candle   The measure of light intensity, or unit of illumination. The amount of light produced by a single candle on a portion of a sphere one foot away; one foot-candle per square foot is called one lumen. (Foot-candles times the surface area in square feet = lumens.)

Format   Type of television script indicating the major programming steps; generally contains a fully scripted show opening and closing.

Frame   1. The smallest picture unit in film, a single picture. 2. A complete scanning cycle (consisting of two fields) of the electron beam, which occurs every 1/30 second. It represents the smallest complete television picture uint.

Freeze Frame   Arrested motion, which is perceived as a still shot.

Fresnel Spotlight   One of the most common spotlights, named after the inventor of its lens, has steplike concentric rings.

Friction Head   Camera mounting head that counterbalances the camera weight by a strong spring. Good for relatively light cameras only.

Front Focus   The proper relationship of the front elements of the zoom lens to ensure focus during the entire zoom range. Front focus is set at the extreme closeup position with the zoom focus control. Color cameras have a front-focus adjustment only because the pickup tubes cannot be moved.

Front-Timing   The process of figuring out clock times by adding given running times to the clock time at which the program starts.

f-**Stop** The calibration on the lens indicating the aperture, or diaphragm opening (and therefore the amount of light transmitted through the lens). The larger the *f*-stop number, the smaller the aperture; the smaller the *f*-stop number, the larger the aperture or diaphragm opening.

Full Track An audiotape recorder, or recording, that uses the full width of the tape for recording an audio signal.

Fully Scripted Used to describe a show for which the dialogue is completely written out, as well as detailed video and audio instructions.

Gaffer Grip A strong clamp used to attach small lighting instruments to pieces of scenery, furniture, doors, and other set pieces. Sometimes called gator clip.

Gain Level of signal amplification for video and audio signal. "Riding gain" is used in audio, meaning to keep the sound volume at a proper level.

Gator Clip Same as Gaffer Grip.

Gel Short form for gelatine, a colored material that acts as color filter for lighting instruments. A red gel in front of a spotlight will color its beam red. Since gels are sensitive to moisture and extreme heat, plastic gels, such as cinemoid, are generally used in television lighting.

Generating Element The major part of a microphone. It converts sound waves into electrical energy.

Generation The number of dubs away from the master tape. A first-generation dub is struck directly from the master tape, a second-generation tape is a dub of the first-generation dub (two steps away from the master tape), and so forth. The greater the number of generations, the greater the quality loss.

Genlock 1. Locking the synchronizing generators from two different origination sources, such as remote and studio. Allows switching from source to source without picture rolling. 2. Locking the house sync with the sync signal from another source (such as a videotape). The videotape can then be intermixed with live studio cameras, for example.

Ghost Undesirable double image on screen; caused by signal reflection in poor reception areas.

Giraffe A medium-sized microphone boom that can be operated by one person.

Gobo 1. A scenic foreground piece through which the camera can shoot, thus integrating the decorative foreground with the background action. 2. In film, a gobo is an opaque shield that is used for partial blocking of a light.

Graphic Mass Any picture element that is perceived as occupying an area within the frame and as relatively heavy or light.

Graphics All two-dimensional visuals prepared for the television screen, such as title cards, charts, and graphs.

Grayscale A scale indicating intermediate steps from TV black to TV white. Maximum range: 10 grayscale steps; good: seven steps; poor: five steps.

Half-Track An audiotape recorder, or recording, that uses half the width of the tape for an audio signal on the first pass, and the other half on the reverse pass.

Halo Dark or colored flare around a very bright light source or a highly reflecting object. Same as flare.

Hand Props Objects, called properties, that are handled by the performer.

Hard Copy A computer printout showing in typewritten form all editing decisions of the completed helical scan workprint or the quadruplex master tape. (Soft-copy information appears only on the computer screen.)

Head 1. Video head: a small electromagnet that puts electric signals on the videotape or reads (induces) the signals off the tape. Video heads are usually in motion. 2. Audio head: a small electromagnet that puts electric signals on the audiotape (recording head) or reads (induces) them off the tape (playback head) or erases the signal from the tape (erase head).

Headroom The space left between the top of the head and the upper screen edge.

Helical Scan, or Helical VTR A videotape recording of one- and two-head videotape recorders, whereby the video signal is put on the tape in a slanted, diagonal way (contrary to transverse scanning, which goes across the tape). Since the tape wraps around the head drum in a spiral-like configuration, it is called "helical" (from helix, spiral). Also called slant-track.

High-Band Refers to the frequency of the video information. High-band videotape recorders operate on a high-frequency range (10 megacycles), which provides operationally higher quality pictures with less video noise and better resolution than low-band recordings. Most high-quality color machines are high-band.

High Key High-intensity overall illumination. Background is generally light.

High-Z High impedance.

Holy Factor Additional illumination to fill in shadow "holes"; especially important in color lighting.

Horizontal Development The way the story moves forward from one event to another; similar to plot.

Horizontal Sweep The horizontal scanning.

Hot 1. A current or signal-carrying wire. 2. Instruments that are turned on, such as a hot camera or a hot microphone.

Hot Spot Undesirable concentration of light in one spot; especially noticeable in the middle of a rear screen projection.

House Number The in-house system of identification; each piece of recorded program must be identified by a certain code number. This is called the house number, since the numbers differ from station to station (house to house).

Hue The color itself, such as red, green, or blue.

IBEW International Brotherhood of Electrical Workers. Union for studio and master control engineers; may include floor personnel.

Iconoscope Old model camera pickup tube; no longer in use.

I.D. Station identification.

Idiot Sheet Prompting device for talent. The cue sheets are held close to the camera lens by a member of the floor crew.

Image-Orthicon, or I-O A specific type of pickup tube used in some monochrome cameras.

Image Retention A cometlike smear that seems to follow a moving object. Especially noticeable when vidicon tubes are used under low light level conditions. Also called smear, lag, follow-image, comet-tailing.

Impedance A type of resistance to the signal flow. Important especially in matching high- or low-impedance microphones with high- or low-impedance recorders. Also, a high-impedance mike works properly only with a relatively short cable (a longer cable has too much resistance), while a low-impedance mike can take up to several hundred feet of cable. Impedance is also expressed in high-Z or low-Z.

Incandescent Light The light produced by the hot filament of ordinary glass-globe lightbulbs. (In contrast to fluorescent or quartz light.)

Incident Light Light that strikes the object directly from its source. Incident light reading is the measure of light (in foot-candles) from the object to the light source. The foot-candle meter is pointed directly into the light source.

Input Overload Distortion A distortion caused by a microphone when subjected to an exceptionally high-volume incoming sound. Condenser microphones are especially prone to this kind of distortion.

Insert Mode The inserting of shots in an already existing recording, without affecting the shots on either side.

Instantaneous Editing Same as Switching.

Instant Replay The recording of short event sections (such as key plays in sports) and immediate playback, sometimes in slow motion. Usually done with a video disc-recording device.

Intercom Abbreviation for intercommunication system. The system uses telephone headsets to facilitate voice communication among all production and engineering personnel involved in the production of a show.

Internal Key A key signal that shapes the cut-in figure (into the background image). It is generated by any one of the cameras fed into the mix bus.

Internal Optical System The dichroic mirrors, reflecting mirrors, relay lenses, and color filters inside the color camera.

Interruptible Feedback Also called the I.F.B. system. Same as Program Interrupt.

In-the-Can Finished television recording, either on film or videotape; the show is now "preserved" and can be rebroadcast at any time.

I-O Image Orthicon camera pickup tube.

ips An abbreviation for inches-per-second, indicating tape speed.

Iris Same as lens diaphragm. Adjustable lens-opening mechanism.

Isolated Camera A camera used for instant replay action only. It is not used for the general pickup of the event.

Jack 1. Stage brace to hold up flat. 2. A socket or phone-plug receptacle (female).

Jump Cut Cutting between shots that are identical in subject yet slightly different in screen location. Through the cut, the subject seems to jump from one screen location to another for no apparent reason.

Key 1. An electronic effect. Keying means the cutting in of an image (usually lettering) into a background image. 2. Key light: principal source of illumination. 3. Lighting: high- or low-key lighting.

Key-in To switch to a sound source via an on-off (or channel) key.

Kicker Kicker light, usually directional light coming from the side and back of the object.

Kill To eliminate certain parts of the action or to turn off certain equipment. For example, kill the mike (turn off the microphone).

Kine Short for Kinescope Recording.

Kinescope Recording Television program filmed directly off a kinescope (television picture) tube.

Knee Shot Framing of a person from the knees up.

Lag, or Comet-Tailing Same as Image Retention.

Lavaliere An extremely small microphone that can be clipped onto the revers of a jacket, a tie, a blouse, or other piece of clothing. A larger variety is suspended from a neckcord and worn in front of the chest. Also called neck or chest mike.

Lens Optical lens, essential for projecting an optical (light) image of the scene onto the front surface of the camera pickup tube or tubes; lenses come in various fixed focal lengths or in a variable focal length (zoom lenses), and with various maximum apertures (lens openings).

Lens Format A somewhat loose term for the grouping of lenses that have focal lengths appropriate to a particular size of film or camera pickup tube. There is a lens format for 35mm film, another for 16mm film; one for 3-inch I-O pickup tubes, another for 1-inch Plumbicons.

Lens Prism A prism that, when attached to the camera lens, will produce special effects, such as the tilting of the horizon line, or the creation of multiple images.

Lens Speed Refers to the maximum aperture of a lens. Fast lenses have a large maximum lens opening (low f-stop number) letting a relatively large amount of light to pass; slow lenses have a relatively small maximum lens opening (higher f-stop number) letting less light to pass. Under low lighting conditions, fast lenses are better than slow lenses.

Lens Turret Round plate in front of a camera holding up to five lenses, each of which can be rotated into "shooting position."

Level 1. Audio: sound volume. 2. Video: signal strength (amplitude) measured in volts.

Libel Written defamation.

Light Angle The vertical angle of the suspended lighting instrument. A 45-degree angle is considered normal.

Lighting Triangle Same as Photographic Principle: the triangular arrangement of key, back, and fill lights.

Light Level Light intensity measured in foot-candles.

Light Plot A plan that shows the lighting instruments used. A plan, similar to a floor plan, that shows the type, size (wattage), and location of the lighting instruments relative to the scene to be illuminated and the general direction of their beams.

Light Ratio The relative intensities of key, back, and fill. A 1:1 ratio between key and back lights means that both light sources burn with equal intensities. A 1:½ ratio between key and fill lights means that the fill light burns with half the intensity of the key light. Because light ratios depend on many other production variables, they cannot be fixed. A key:back:fill ratio of 1:1:½ is often used for normal triangle lighting.

Limbo Any set area used for shooting small commercial displays, card easels, and the like, having a plain, light background.

Line Monitor Also called master monitor. The monitor that shows only the line-out pictures, the pictures that go on the air, or on videotape.

Lip Sync Synchronization of sound and lip movement.

Live 1. Direct transmission of a program at the time of origin. 2. Indicates that a camera or microphone is in active use.

Log The major operational document. Issued daily, the log carries such information as program source or origin, scheduled program time, program duration, video and audio information, code identification (house number, for example), the title of the program, the program type, and additional special information.

Logo A visual symbol that identifies a specific organization, such as a television station or network.

Long Shot Object seen from far away or framed very loosely. The extreme long shot shows the object from a great distance.

Loop See Film Loop.

Low-Band Refers to the frequency of the video information. Low-band recorders operate in a relatively low-frequency range, which suffices for monochrome pictures but introduces excessive video noise in color.

Low Key   Low-intensity overall, yet selective illumination. Background is generally dark.

Lumen   The basic quantity of light produced by one candle on one square foot.

Luminance Channel   A signal that is matrixed (combined) from the chrominance channels and provides the black-and-white signal. The luminance channel gives the color picture the necessary brightness contrast (with the chrominance channel supplying the hue and the saturation) and allows a color camera to produce a signal that is receivable on a black-and-white television set.

Macro Lens   A lens that can be focused at very close distances from the object. Used for closeups of small objects.

Magnetic Sound Film   Sound tape that looks like 35mm or 16mm double-perforated film. (16mm magnetic sound film also comes in single perforations.) Not to be confused with sound film that has a magnetic rather than an optical track.

Magnetic Sound Track   Also called mag track or recording stripe. Consists of a narrow magnetic tape that runs down one side of the film. It operates exactly like a normal audiotape. Sometimes a second stripe runs along the opposite side of the film in order to achieve the same thickness for both film edges.

Mag Track   See Magnetic Sound Track.

Makeup   1. Facial makeup: used to enhance, correct, and change facial features. 2. Film makeup: combining several films on one big reel.

Master Control   Nerve center for all telecasts. Controls the program input, storage, and retrieval for on-the-air telecasts. Also oversees technical quality of all program material.

Master Monitor   Same as Line Monitor. Shows only the line-out pictures, the pictures that go on the air or on videotape.

Matte   The keying of two scenes; the electronic laying in of a background image behind a foreground scene, such as the picture of a town meeting behind the newscaster reporting on this meeting.

Matte Key   Keyed (electronically cut-in) title whose letters are filled with shades of gray or a specific color.

M.C.   1. Master of Ceremonies. Performer who usually introduces people and acts of a variety show. 2. Master Control.

Medium Shot   Object seen from a medium distance. Covers any framing between long shot and closeup.

Microphone   Also called mike or mic. A small, portable assembly for the pickup and conversion of sound into electrical energy.

Microwave Relay   A transmission method involving the use of several microwave units from the remote location to the transmitter.

Mike   Microphone.

Mix Bus   Rows of buttons that permit the "mixing" of video sources, as in a dissolve and super. Major buses for on-the-air switching.

Mixing   1. Audio: the combining of two or more sounds in specific proportions (volume variations) as determined by the event (show) context. 2. Video: the combining of various shots via the switcher.

mm   Millimeter, a one-thousandth of a meter. 25.4 mm = 1 inch.

Modeling Light   Same as Key Light. Principal source of illumination.

Moiré Effect   Color vibrations that occur when narrow, contrasting stripes of a design interfere with the scanning lines of the television system.

Monitor   1. Audio: speaker that carries the program sound independent of the line-out. 2. Video: high-quality television receiver used in the television studio and control rooms. Cannot receive broadcast signals.

Monitor/Receiver   A television receiver that can reproduce direct video and audio feeds (from the VTR, for example) as well as signals that are broadcast on a channel.

Monochrome   Literally "one color." In television, it means black-and-white, in contrast to color.

Montage   The juxtaposition of two (often seemingly unrelated) shots in order to generate a third, overall idea, which may not be contained in either of the two.

Multiple-Microphone Interference   The canceling out of certain sound frequencies when two identical microphones in close proximity are used for the same sound source and amplifier.

Multiplexer   A system of mirrors or prisms that directs images from several projection sources (film, slides) into one stationary television film, or telecine, camera.

Multiplexing 1. A method of transmitting the video and audio signal on the same carrier wave. 2. The transmitting of two separate audio signals on the same carrier wave for stereo broadcasts. 3. The transmitting of separate color signals on the same channel without mixing.

NABET National Association of Broadcast Employees and Technicians. Union for studio and master control engineers; may include floor personnel.

Neutral Density Filter A filter that reduces the amount of the incoming light without distorting the color of the scene.

Noise 1. Audio: unwanted sounds that interfere with the intentional sounds; or unwanted sound signals. 2. Video: electronic interference that shows up as "snow." See Video Noise.

Normal Lens A lens with a focal length that will approximate the spatial relationships of normal vision when used with a particular film or pickup tube format.

Nose Room The space left in front of a person looking toward the edge of the screen.

Objective Time Also called clock time. The time we measure by the clock.

Off-Camera Performance or action that is not seen on camera, such as narration over film or a videotape recording.

Off-Line Helical scan editing system for producing computer-assisted videotape workprints. The workprint information is then fed into the on-line system for (automated) production of the release master tape.

Omega Wrap An indication of how the videotape is wound around the head drum of a helical scan VTR. In this case, the tape is wound halfway around the head drum, in an omegalike configuration.

Omnidirectional A type of pickup pattern in which the microphone can pick up sounds equally well from all (omni) directions.

On-Line A computer-assisted master editing system, using quadruplex videotape recorders for high-band release master tapes.

On-the-Nose 1. On time. 2. Correct action.

Open Set A set constructed of noncontinuous scenery, with large open spaces between the main groupings.

Optical Sound Track Variations of black and white patterns, photographed on the film and converted into electrical impulses by an exciter lamp and a photoelectric cell. There are two kinds of optical tracks: variable area and variable density.

Oscilloscope Electronic measuring device showing certain electronic patterns on a small screen.

Over-the-Shoulder Shot Camera looks over a person's shoulder (shoulder and back of head included in shot) at another person.

P.A. Public address loudspeaker system. Same as Studio Talkback.

Pace Perceived duration of the show or show segment. Part of subjective time.

Pan Horizontal turning of the camera.

Pancake A makeup base, or foundation makeup, usually water-soluble and applied with a small sponge.

Pan Stick A foundation makeup with a grease base. Used to cover up a beard shadow or prominent skin blemish.

Pantograph Expandable hanging device for lighting instruments.

Patchboard Also called patchbay. A device whereby audio, video, or light cables can be routed to specific audio, video, or light controls.

Patching Interconnecting audio, video, or light cables into a common circuit for each.

Pattern Projector An ellipsoidal spotlight with a cookie (cucalorus) insert, which projects the cookie's pattern as shadow.

Pedestal 1. Heavy camera dolly that permits a raising and lowering of the camera while on the air. 2. To move the camera up and down via studio pedestal. 3. The black level of a television picture. Can be adjusted against a standard on the oscilloscope.

Percipient The television viewer in the act of perceiving television audio and video stimuli (a television program). It implies more than mere watching of a program; it requires a certain degree of involvement.

Performer A person who appears on camera in nondramatic shows. The performer plays himself or herself, and does not assume someone else's character.

Periaktos A triangular piece of scenery that can be turned on a swivel base.

Perspective 1. All lines converging in one point. 2. Sound perspective: far sound must go with far picture, close sound with close picture.

Photographic Principle   The triangular arrangement of key, back, and fill lights, with the back light opposite the camera and directly behind the object, and the key and fill lights opposite each other to the front and side of the object. Also called triangle lighting.

Pickup   1. Sound reception by a microphone. 2. Origination of picture and sound by television cameras and microphones.

Pickup Pattern   The territory around the microphone within which the microphone can "hear well," that is, has optimal sound pickup.

Pickup Tube, or Camera Tube   The main camera tube that converts light energy into electrical energy, the video signal.

Picturization   The control and structuring of a shot sequence.

Pin   To sharpen (focus) the light beam of a spotlight, either by pulling the light-bulb reflector unit away from the lens or by moving the lens away from the light bulb. The opposite of spread.

P.L.   Abbreviation for Private Line, or Phone Line. same as Intercom.

Playback   The playing back on a monitor or television receiver of videotape-recorded material through a videotape recorder (in the playback mode).

Plot   How the story develops from one event to the next.

Plumbicon   A registered trademark of N. V. Philips for a vidicon-type pickup tube. Used almost exclusively in good- to high-quality color cameras. Because the Plumbicon has a lead-oxide-coated photoconductive (light-sensitive) front surface, variations of it are sometimes called lead-oxide tubes.

Polarity Reversal   The reversal of the grayscale; the white areas in the picture become black and the black areas white, as the film negative is to the print.

Polar Pattern   The two-dimensional representation of a microphone pickup pattern.

Pop Filter   Same as Blast Filter.

Portapak   Formerly a trade name of the Sony Corporation for a highly portable camera and videotape unit, which could be easily carried and operated by one person. It now refers to all such equipment, regardless of manufacturer or model.

Ports   1. Slots in the microphone that help to achieve a specific pickup pattern and frequency response. 2. Holes in a multiplexer for various video sources.

Post-Dubbing   The adding of a sound track to an already recorded (and usually fully edited) picture portion.

Postproduction   Any production activity that occurs after (post) the production. Usually refers either to editing of film or videotape or to postscoring and mixing sound for later addition to the picture portion.

Postproduction Editing   The assembly of recorded material after the actual production.

Pot   Abbreviation for potentiometer, a sound-volume control.

Pot-in   To fade in a sound source gradually with a pot or fader.

Pre-empt   Telecasting time made available for a special event, regardless of the regular scheduled program.

Preset Board   A program device into which several lighting setups (scenes) can be stored, and from which they can be retrieved, when needed.

Preview Bus   Rows of buttons that can direct an input to the preview monitor, at the same time another video source is on the air.

Preview Monitor   1. A monitor that shows the director the picture he intends to use as the next shot. 2. Any monitor that shows a video source, except for the line (master) and off-the-air monitors.

Primary Movement   Object or subject movement in front of the camera.

Prism Block   A compact internal optical system that combines the dichroic (color-separating) elements (filters) and light-diverting elements (prisms) all in one small blocklike unit.

Process Message   The interaction between the percipient and the audiovisual stimuli of the television program.

Process Shot   Photographing foreground objects against a background projection.

Producer   Creator and organizer of television shows; usually in charge of all financial matters.

Program Bus   The bus on a switcher whose inputs are directly switched to the line-out.

Program Interrupt   Also called the P.I. system. A system that feeds program sound to a tiny earphone worn by the performer. It can be interrupted with P.I. information at any time.

Program Monitor Speaker, or Program Speaker   A loudspeaker in the control room or studio that carries the program sound. Its volume can be controlled without affecting the actual line-out program feed.

Program Storage The physical storage of recorded program material (film or videotape).

Props Properties: furniture and other objects used for set decorations and by actors or performers.

Pylon Triangular set piece, similar to a pillar.

Quad Abbreviation for quadruplex videotape recorders.

Quadruplex A scanning system of videotape recorders that uses four rotating heads for recording and playing back of video information. All quadruplex, or quad, recorders use 2-inch-wide videotape.

Quarter-Track An audiotape recorder, or recording, that uses one-fourth of the width of the tape for recording an audio signal. Generally used by stereo recorders. The first and third tracks are taken up by the first pass of the tape through the recording heads; the second and fourth tracks by the second pass, when the tape has been "reversed" (that is, the full takeup reel becomes the supply reel for the second recording).

Quartz Light A high-intensity light whose lamp consists of a quartz or silica housing (instead of the customary glass) and a tungsten-halogen filament. Produces a very bright light of stable color temperature.

Quick-Study Actor or performer who can accurately memorize complicated lines and blocking within a very short time; especially important for television talent.

Racking 1. Rotating the lens turret in order to change lenses. 2. Moving the camera tube closer to or farther away from the stationary lens by means of the focus knob on the camera.

Rack-through Focus Moving the focus control on a camera from one extreme position to the other.

Radio Frequency Usually called RF; broadcast frequency, which is divided into various channels. In an RF distribution, the video and audio signals are superimposed on the radio frequency carrier wave.

Range Extender An optical attachment to the zoom lens that will extend its narrow-angle focal length.

Rear Screen Translucent screen onto which images are projected from the rear and photographed from the front.

Reel 1. Spool for tape or film. 2. Film on spool.

Reel-to-Reel A tape recorder that transports the tape past the heads from one reel, the supply reel, to the other reel, the takeup reel. Used in contrast to cassettes or cartridge recorders.

Reflected Light Light that is bounced off the illuminated object. Reflected-light reading is done with a light meter (most of them are calibrated for reflected light) that is held close to the illuminated object from the direction of the camera.

Registration Adjusting the scanning of the three color tubes so that their images overlap (register) perfectly.

Relay Lens Part of the internal optical system of a camera that helps to transport (relay) the separated colored light into a pickup tube.

Remote A television production done outside the studio.

Remote Survey An inspection of the remote location by key production and engineering persons so that they can plan for the setup and use of production equipment.

Remote Truck The vehicle that carries the program control equipment, such as CCU's, switcher, monitors, audio control console, and intercom systems. The director and the T.D. work out of the remote truck.

Resolution The fine picture detail as reproduced on the video monitor. A high-resolution picture is desirable.

Return Narrow flat lashed to a wider flat at approximately a 90-degree angle.

Reverberation Audio echo; adding echo to sound via an acoustical echo chamber or electronic sound delay; generally used to liven sounds recorded in an acoustically dull studio.

RF Abbreviation for Radio Frequency, necessary for all broadcast signals, as well as some closed-circuit distribution.

Ribbon Microphone A microphone whose sound pickup device consists of a ribbon that vibrates with the sound pressures within a magnetic field. Also called velocity mike. Rather sensitive to shock.

Riser 1. Small platform. 2. The vertical frame that supports the horizontal top of the platform.

Roll 1. Graphics (usually credit copy) that move slowly up the screen; often called crawl. 2. Command to roll tape or film.

Roll-through Keeping the film (or tape) rolling while temporarily cutting back to another video source (usually a live camera).

R.P.   Rear screen projection; also abbreviated as B.P. (back projection).

Rundown Sheet   Same as Fact Sheet.

Running Time   The duration of a show or show segment. Also called program length.

Runout Signal   The recording of a few seconds of black at the end of each videotape recording in order to keep the screen in black for the video changeover.

Run-through   Rehearsal.

Saturation   Attribute of color that indicates strength, as measured by a deep red, or a washed-out pink. Sometimes called chroma.

Scanning   The movement of the electron beam from left to right and from top to bottom on the television screen.

Scanning Area   Picture area that is scanned by the camera pickup tube; more generally, the picture area actually reproduced by the camera and relayed to the studio monitors.

Schedule Time   See Clock Time.

Scoop   A scooplike television floodlight.

Scrim   A spun-glass material that is put in front of a scoop as an additional light diffuser.

Secondary Motion   Movement of the camera (dolly, truck, arc, and zoom, although the camera does not move during a zoom).

Section 315   Section of the Communications Act that affords candidates for public office equal opportunity to appear on television.

SEG   See Special Effects Generator.

Segue   An audio transition method whereby the preceding sound is faded out and the following sound faded in immediately after.

Selective Focus   Emphasizing an object in a shallow depth of field through focus, while keeping its foreground and background out of focus.

Semiscripted   Used to describe a show for which the dialogue is indicated but not completely written out.

Separate Mesh   A screen in a vidicon or Plumbicon tube that helps to cut down comet-tailing.

Servo Controls   Zoom and focus controls that activate motor-driven mechanisms.

Set   Arrangement of scenery and properties to indicate the locale and/or mood of a show.

Set Light   See Background Light.

Set Module   Pieces of scenery of standard dimensions that allow a great variety of interchange and configuration.

Shading   Adjusting picture contrast; controlling color and black-and-white levels.

Shot Box   Box containing various controls for presetting zoom speed and field of view; usually mounted on the camera panning bar.

Shotgun Microphone   A highly directional microphone with a shotgun-like barrel for picking up sounds over a great distance. Also called machine-gun microphone.

Shot Sheet   Lists every shot a particular camera has to get. Is attached to the camera as an aid to the camera operator for remembering a shot sequence.

Show Format   Lists the order of the various show segments according to appearance.

Show Rhythm   Indicates how well the parts of the show relate to each other sequentially, how well the show flows.

S.I.   Station Identification (sometimes sponsor identification).

Signal-to-Noise Ratio   The relation of the strength of the desired video (picture) signal to the accompanying electronic interference, the noise. A high signal-to-noise ratio is desirable (strong video signal and weak noise).

Signature   A specific video and/or audio symbol characteristic of one particular show.

Silent Film   Film without a sound track, or film run silent.

Single-System   The simultaneous recording of pictures and sound on the same film.

Slander   Oral defamation.

Slant-Track   Same as Helical Scan.

Slate   A little blackboard, or whiteboard, upon which essential production information is written, such as title of the show, date, scene and take numbers. It is recorded at the beginning of each videotaped take.

Slave   1. A videotape recorder that records a program copy off the master recorder. 2. The videotape recorder that supplies the various program segments to be assembled on the master VTR.

Slow Lens A lens that permits a relatively small amount of light to pass through (high *f*-stop number). Can be used only in well-lighted areas.

Slow Motion A scene in which the objects appear to be moving more slowly than normal. In film, slow motion is achieved through high-speed photography (exposing many frames that differ only minutely from one another) and normal (24 frames per second, for example) playback. In television, slow motion is achieved by multiple scanning of each television frame.

Small Format Refers to the small size of the camera pickup tube (usually ⅔-inch) or, more frequently, to the narrow width of the videotape: ¼-inch, ½-inch, ¾-inch, and even 1-inch (although 1-inch is often regarded as large-format tape). Small-format equipment (cameras and videotape recorders) is actually very small in size and highly portable.

SMPTE Society of Motion Picture and Television Engineers.

SMPTE Universal Leader See Academy Leader.

Snow Electronic picture interference; looks like snow on the television screen.

SOF Sound on film.

Softlight A television floodlight that produces extremely diffused light. It has a panlike reflector and a light-diffusing material over its opening.

SOT Sound on tape. The videotape is played back with pictures and sound.

Sound Effects Special sounds—such as wind, thunder, car traffic, jet airplanes recorded in advance for multiple use in a variety of productions.

Space Staging Arrangement of scenery to indicate foreground, middleground, and background, with room for movement of talent and camera.

Special Effects Generator, or SEG An electronic image generator that produces a variety of special effects wipe patterns, such as circle wipes, diamond wipes, and key and matte effects.

Speed Up A cue to the talent to speed up whatever he or she is doing.

Splice The spot where two shots are actually joined, or the act of joining two shots. Generally used only when the material (such as film or audiotape) is physically cut and glued (spliced) together again.

Spotlight A light instrument that produces directional, relatively undiffused light.

Spotter A person who helps the director or the announcer to identify significant parts of an event, such as prominent players in a football game, or the nature of a play formation.

Spread To enlarge (diffuse) the light beam of a spotlight by pushing the light-bulb reflector unit toward the lens, or the lens closer to the light bulb. Also called flood. The opposite of pin.

Sprockets Small, evenly spaced perforations in the film. Single sprockets: holes are in only one side of the film; double sprockets: holes are on both sides of the film.

Stability The degree to which a camera (or camera chain) maintains its initial electronic setup.

Stand-by 1. A button on a videotape recorder that activates the rotation of the video heads or head drum independently of the actual tape motion. In the standby position, the video heads can come up to speed before the videotape is actually started. 2. A warning cue for any kind of action in television production.

Star Filter A filter-like lens attachment that changes high-intensity light sources into starlike light images.

Station Break Interruption of a show to give station identification (usually on the half-hour or hour).

Sticking See Burn-in.

Stock Shot A shot of a common occurrence—clouds, storm, traffic, crowds—that can be repeated in a variety of contexts since its qualities are typical. There are stock-shot libraries from which any number of such shots can be obtained.

Stop-Motion A slow-motion effect in which one frame jumps to the next, showing the object in a different position.

Storyboard A series of sketches of the key visualization points of an event, accompanied by corresponding audio information.

Stretch A cue to the talent to slow down whatever he or she is doing.

Strike To remove certain objects; to remove scenery and equipment from the studio floor after the show.

Stripe Filter Extremely narrow, vertical stripes of red, green, and blue filters that, repeating themselves many times, are attached to the front surface of the camera pickup tube. They divide the incoming white light into the three light primaries without the aid of dichroic mirrors.

Strip Light   Several low-wattage lightbulbs arranged in a strip; used for even lighting of the cyclorama.

Studio Monitor   A monitor located in the studio (television set carrying the video of the line monitor) showing the program in progress.

Studio Talkback   A public address loudspeaker system from the control room to the studio. Also called S.A. (studio address) or P.A. (public address) system.

Subjective Time   The duration we feel. Also called psychological time.

Subtractive Primary Colors   Magenta (bluish red), cyan (greenish blue), and yellow. When mixed, they act as filters, subtracting certain colors.

Super   Short for superimposition, the simultaneous showing of two full pictures on the same screen.

Super Card   A studio card with white lettering on a black background, used for superimposition of a title, or for keying of a title over a background scene. For chroma keying, the white letters are on a chroma-key blue background.

Supply Reel   Reel that holds film or tape, either of which it feeds to the takeup reel.

Sustaining Program   A program that is not commercially supported.

Sweep   1. Curved piece of scenery, similar to a large pillar cut in half. 2. Electronic scanning.

Sweep Reversal   Electronic scanning reversal; results in a mirror image (horizontal sweep reversal) or in an upside-down image (vertical sweep reversal).

Switcher   1. Engineer or production person who is doing the video switching (usually the T.D., the technical director). 2. A panel with rows of buttons that permits the selection of a specific video input and the change from one video source to another through a variety of transition devices, or the simultaneous presentation of two or more video sources.

Switching   A change from one video source to another during a show, or show segment, with the aid of a switcher.

Sync   Electronic pulses that synchronize the scanning in the origination source (live cameras, videotape) and the reproduction source (monitor or television receiver).

Sync Generator   Part of the camera chain; produces electronic synchronization pulses.

Sync Roll   Vertical rolling of a picture caused by switching from remote to studio, thereby momentarily losing synchronization; also noticeable on a bad videotape splice.

System   The interrelationship of various elements and processes.

Systems Design   A plan that shows the interrelation of two or more systems. In television production, it shows the interrelation of all major production elements, as well as the flow (direction) of the production processes.

Take   1. Signal for a cut from one video source to another. 2. Any one of similar repeated shots taken during filming. Sometimes take is used synonymously with shot. A "good take" is the successful completion of a shot, a show segment, or the videotaping of the whole show. A "bad take" means an unsuccessful recording; another "take" is required.

Takeup Reel   Reel that takes up film or tape from the supply reel. Must be the same size as the supply reel in order to maintain proper tension.

Taking Lens   Also called on-the-air lens. Refers to the lens on turret cameras that is actually relaying the scene to the camera pickup tube.

Talent   Collective name for all performers and actors who appear regularly on television.

Talkback   See Studio Talkback.

Tally Light   Red light on camera and inside the camera viewfinder, indicating when the camera is on the air.

Tape   Plastic ribbon, approximately 1/1000-inch thick, varying in width from ¼ inch to 2 inches and coated with iron oxide (dull side). It is used to record magnetic impulses from video or audio sources.

Tape Cartridge   See Cartridge.

Target   Light-sensitive front surface of the camera pickup tube, which is scanned by an electron beam.

T.D.   Technical Director; in charge of technical studio crew. Usually does the switching during a telecast.

Telecine   1. Same as Film Chain, or film island. 2. The place from which the film islands operate. The word comes from *tele*vision and *cine*matography. Occasionally, the telecine is used for film storage and some minor film-editing jobs.

Telephoto Lens Same as long-focal-length lens. Gives a closeup view of an event relatively far away from the camera.

Teleprompter A mechanical prompting device that projects the moving copy over the lens, so that it can be read by the talent without losing eye contact with the viewer.

Tertiary Motion Movement created by a sequence of shots.

Test Pattern Special graphic design of converging lines and alignment marks that aids camera picture alignment and registration.

Theme What the story is all about; its essential idea.

Threefold Three flats hinged together.

Tight Shot Same as Closeup.

Tilt To point the camera up and down.

Time Base Corrector An electronic accessory to a videotape recorder that helps to make playbacks or transfers electronically stable. A time base corrector helps to maintain picture quality even in dubbing-up operations.

Time Base Stability A stable scanning process. Can be maintained with a time base corrector.

Time Code Also called the SMPTE Time Code or address code. An electronic signal recorded on the cue track of the videotape through a time code generator, providing a time "address" (birthmark) for each frame in hours, minutes, seconds, and frame numbers of elapsed tape.

Time Cues Cues to the talent in regard to the time remaining in the show. Usually consist of a 3-minute cue, a 2-minute cue, a 1-minute cue, a 30-second cue, and a 15-second cue.

Title Any graphic material shown on camera; more specifically, studio title card or slide.

Title Drum Large drum on which title sheets can be fastened for credit supers and keys; same as Crawl.

Tongue To move the boom with the camera from left to right or from right to left.

Tracking 1. The angle at which the videotape passes the video heads. Refers commonly to the electronic adjustment of the video heads so that in the playback phase they match the recording phase of the tape. Prevents picture breakup and misalignment, especially in tapes that have been recorded on a machine other than the one used for playback. 2. Another name for truck (lateral camera movement).

Transverse Scanning The direction of the video signal scanning in quadruplex recorders. Transverse scanning puts the signal across (transverse) the videotape rather than in a helical (diagonal) or a lengthwise pattern.

Traveler A large curtain, similar to a theater curtain, which opens horizontally from the middle or from one side.

Triangle Lighting See Photographic Principle.

Tripod A three-legged camera mount, usually connected with a dolly for easy maneuverability.

Truck To move the camera laterally by means of mobile camera mount.

Tungsten-Halogen The kind of lamp filament used in quartz lights. The tungsten is the filament itself; the halogen is a gaslike substance surrounding the filament.

Turret Lens A lens that is mounted on the turret of a camera. Usually in contrast to a zoom lens.

Twofold Two flats hinged together. Also called a book.

Two-Shot Framing of two people.

UHF Ultra-High Frequency, television transmission channels above channel 13 (channels 14-83).

Unidirectional A type of pickup pattern in which the microphone can pick up sounds better from one direction (uni), the front, than from the sides or back.

Unit Set Standardized, interchangeable scenery.

Variable Area Track An optical sound track on film. It modulates the light of the exciter lamp through various shapes of translucent areas so that, when received by the photoelectric cell, the light variations produce identical variations in the electric current (audio signal).

Variable Density Track An optical sound track on film. It modulates the light of the exciter lamp from clear film to various shades of gray so that, when received by the photoelectric cell, the light variations produce identical variations in the electric current (audio signal).

Variable-Focal-Length Lens Zoom lens.

Vector Line A dominant direction established between two people facing each other or through a prominent movement in a specific direction.

Vectorscope An electronic display device, similar to the oscilloscope, through which the colors from a camera or videotape can be quantitatively defined.

Vertical Development The way a situation takes on complexity and depth.

Vertical Interval Switcher A switcher that produces extremely clean cuts, since it changes video sources during the vertical retrace of the scanning beam (when the beam jumps back to the top of the screen after it has traced the scanning lines from top to bottom).

Vertical Key Light Position The relative distance of the key light from the studio floor, specifically with respect to whether it is above or below the eye level of the performer. Not to be confused with high- and low-key lighting, which refers to the relative brightness and contrast of the overall scene.

Vertical Sweep The vertical scanning.

VHF Very High Frequency, television transmission channels 2 through 13.

Video 1. Picture portion of a telecast. 2. Nonbroadcast production activities and the use of small-format equipment for a variety of purposes. Usually the equipment includes a portable camera, a microphone, a videotape recorder or video cassette recorder, and a monitor.

Video Cartridge A plastic container with a single reel from which the videotape is fed into a special recorder for recording and playback of short program segments.

Video Cassette A plastic container in which a videotape moves from supply to takeup reel, recording and playing back short program segments through a video cassette recorder. Similar in construction and function to the audio cassette recorder.

Video Disc A phonograph record–like disc that can store video (picture) information of short event segments. Used for instant playbacks, slow motion, and freeze frames.

Video Disc Recorder A recording device whereby the video signals are recorded on and played back from a disc, which looks like a phonograph record.

Video Engineer Controls the camera pictures before they are sent on the air (or videotape recorded); also called shader.

Video Feedback The picture on the television set is photographed by a television camera and fed back into the same monitor, producing multiple images.

Video Leader Visual (and auditory) material that precedes any color videotape recording. The SMPTE prescribes for the standard video-portion blank tape for threading; 10 sec. of color bars; 15 sec. of slate information; 8 sec. of numbers or black; 2 sec. of black ahead of the program information.

Video Noise A spurious electronic signal that interferes with the desired video signal. Generated unavoidably within the system, it shows up as "snow," white (or colored) spots in the picture.

Video Signal Electrical impulses (voltage) generated by the camera pickup tube or the VTR. The amplified video signal provides the necessary information for generating a picture.

Videotape A plastic, iron-oxide-coated tape of various widths (from ¼-inch to 2-inch) for recording of video and audio signals, as well as additional technical code information.

Videotape Recorder Also called VTR. Electronic recording device that records and stores on videotape video and audio signals for later playback or postproduction editing.

Videotape Room The place where all large videotape recorders are kept. Often serves also as videotape storage and editing room.

Video Track The area of the videotape that is used for recording the video information.

Vidicon A type of pickup tube, used extensively in small, portable, monochrome cameras as well as in color cameras.

Viewfinder Generally meaning electronic viewfinder (in contrast to the optical viewfinder in a film or still camera); a small television set that displays the picture as generated by the camera.

Volume The relative intensity of the sound, its relative loudness.

VTR VideoTape Recorder or recording.

VU Meter A volume-unit meter; measures volume units, the relative loudness of amplified sound.

Walk-through An orientation session with the production crew (technical walk-through) and talent (talent walk-through), by actually walking through the set and explaining the key actions to both parties.

Walk-through Camera Rehearsal A combination of walk-through and camera rehearsal in order to save time. Usually conducted by the director from the studio floor, with all technical production positions manned and operational.

Warm-up 1. Keeping the cameras turned on for a time until all the electrons have properly stabilized. 2. Getting the studio audience in the proper spirit for the show.

Waveform Monitor Same as Oscilloscope.

Wind Screen Similar to or same as Pop Filter. A rubberlike material that is put over the front end of the microphone to cut down undesirable wind noises in outdoor use.

Wind Up A cue to the talent to finish up whatever he or she is doing.

Wipe Electronic effect where one picture seems to push the other off the screen. (In film, an optical wipe can be accomplished in the special effects printer.)

XCU Extreme Closeup. Same as ECU.

Z-Axis The imaginary line that extends in the direction the lens points from the camera to the horizon. Z-axis motion is the movement toward or away from the camera.

Zoom Lens Variable-focal-length lens. It can change from a wide shot to a closeup, or the reverse, in one continuous move.

Zoom Ratio The zoom range, from the widest angle position to the narrowest angle position, expressed in a ratio, such as 10:1 (wide angle 17mm to a narrow angle 170mm).

Index